Islamic Tombs in India

The Iconography and Genesis of Their Design

Contours of Indian Art & Architecture, no. 2

Islamic Tombs in India

The Iconography and Genesis of Their Design

Fredrick W. Bunce
Professor Emeritus of Art
Indiana State University

D.K. Printworld (P) Ltd.
New Delhi

Cataloging in Publication Data — DK

Bunce, Fredrick W. (Fredrick William), 1935 –
Islamic Tombs in India.
(Contours of Indian art & architecture, no. 2).
Includes bibliographical references (p.)
Includes index.

1. Tombs — India. 2. Architecture, Islamic — India. 3. Islamic art and symbolism — India. I. Title. II. Series: Contours of Indian art & architecture, no. 2

ISBN 81-246-0245-X
First Published in India in 2004

Published and printed by:
D.K. Printworld (P) Ltd.
Regd. office : '*Sri Kunj*', F-52, Bali Nagar
New Delhi - 110 015
Phones : (011) 2545-3975; 2546-6019; *Fax* : (011) 2546-5926
E-mail: dkprintworld@vsnl.net
Web: www.dkprint.com

Contents

Contents (Continued)

List of Plates

List of Plates (Continued)

Appendix B

List of Plates (Continued)

Appendix C

Proportional Comparison with *Deshiya Mandala*

Proportional Comparison (Elevations)

Ninefold Examples

Sections

Elevations & Elevatins with Podium

List of Plates (Continued)

List of Figures

List of Figures (Continued)

List of Figures (Continued)

List of Figures (Continued)

List of Figures (Continued)

List of Figures (Continued)

List of Figures (Continued)

Abbreviations

AH	A. B. M. Husain, *Fathepur-sikri and its Architecture*
AP	Amjad Bohumil Prochazka, *Architecture of the Islamic Cultural Sphere*
CA	Catherine B. Asher, *Architectureof Mughal India.*
CJ	C. G. Jung, *Mandala Symbolism*
CS	C.M. Villiers Stuart, *Gardens of the Great Mughals*
EG	Ernst Grube,et al, George Mitchell (ed.) *Architecture of the Islamic World: Its History and Social Meaning*
EH	E. B. Havell, *Encyclopaedia of Architecture in the Indian Subcontinent*
EK	Ebba Koch, *Mughal Architecture: An Outline of Its History and Development 1526-1858.*
FWB	Fredrick W. Bunce, *The Iconography of Plans: A Study of the Influence of Buddhism and Hinduism on Architectural Plans of South and Southeast Asia.*
GC	George Coedès, *The Indianized States of Southeast Asia.*
GG	Godfrey Goodwin, *A History of Ottoman Architecture*
GT	G.H.R. Tillotson, *Mughal India.*
HC	Henry Cousens, *Bijapur and Its Architectural Remains: With an Historical Outline of the Adil Shahi Dynasty;*
HS	Henri Stierlin (ed.), *Architecture of the World: Islamic India.*
HS 2	Henri Stierlin (ed.), *Architecture of the World: India.*
IS	Issam El-Said and Ayse Parman, *Geometric Concepts in Islamic Art*
JP	Jose Pereira, *Islamic Sacred Architecture: A Stylistic History*
KC	K.A.C. Creswell, *A Short Account of Early Muslim Architecture*
KR	K.V. Soundara Rajan, *Islam Builds in India*
MA	Mohammad al-Asad, et al. Martin Frishman and Hasan-Uddin Khan, eds. *The Mosque: History, Architectural Development & Regional Diversity.*
MC	Manekshah Sorabshah Commissariat, *A History of Gujarat: Including a Survey of its Chief Architectural Monuments and Inscriptions.*
MN	M.A. Nayeem, *The Splendour of Hyderabad : The Last Phase of an Oriental Culture (1591-1948 A.D.)*
MS	Margaret Sevcenko, ed., *Theories and Principles of Design in the Architecture of Islamic Societies*
MW	Mohammad Waliullah Khan, *Lahore and its Important Monuments*
PB	Percy Brown, *Indian Architecture* (*Islamic Period*).

Abbreviations (Continued)

RH	Robert Hillenbrand, *Islamic Art and Architecture.*
RH 2	Robert Hillenbrand, *Islamic Architecture: Form, Function & Meaning*
RM	Rustam Mehta, *Masterpieces of Indo-Islamic Architecture*
RN	R. Nath, *Fathepur Sikri and its Monuments.*
RN2	R. Nath, *History of Mughal Architecture.*
RN3	R. Nath, *History of Sultanate Architecture.*
RS	K. V. Soundara Rajan, *Ahmadabad.*
RS 2	K. V. Soundara Rajan, *Islam Builds in India*
SC	Stephen Carr, *Archaeology and Monumental Remains of Delhi.*
SG	Satish Grover, *Islamic Architecture in India*
SN	S. A. A. Naqoi, *Humanyn's Tomb and Adjacent Buildings*
SS	Shehbaz H. Safrani, *Golconda and Hyderabad*
TC	Thomas Crump, *The Anthropology of Numbers.*
VM	Vettam Mani, *Puranic Encyclopaedia*

Preface
&
Introduction

Preface

For years, while visiting and then living in Southeast Asia, I had avoided travel to India. My education had made me aware of some of the architectural glories which that country possessed, but my awareness of the poverty in which millions exixted colored my desire to travel to India.

Then, I was invited to New Delhi by my publisher. The graciousness with which I was treated was beyond what I had ever experienced before. At that time, I was taken around Delhi, New Delhi and then to Agra!

Somehow, the glories of Indian architecture, both Hindu and Islamic, neutralized my reactions to the desperate conditions in which so many people existed. I was not prepared for the incredible beauty of the "Red Fort" (*Shahjahanabad*) of Delhi or of the "Red Fort" (*Akharabad*) of Agra. Luckily, I viewed these two marvels before being taken to the famed *Taj Mahal*, the *Tomb of Hazrat Mumtaz-uz-Zamani*!

Upon entering through the main gate/pavilion into the *chahar-bagh* and being confronted with the magnificent mausoleum, I was totally unprepared for my reaction! Tears rolled down my cheeks as I cried at the sheer, unrivaled, transcendental beauty of that place. Nothing! **Nothing** which I had seen before had affected me in the way that the *Taj Mahal* had, with the exception of Java's famed *Borobudur*. The adjectives that are applied to this ensemble are puny in comparison to the actual sight!

I then began to immerse myself into the architecture of Hindu India. What was revealed was, in a word, incomparable! I had visited, studied and photographed the Gothic cathedrals in western Europe and reveled in their beauty. But, upon viewing the many Hindu temples of India, I was struck with what can only be described as "awe." There was also, for me, a kind of mystical aura that surrounded these structures.

Was it because they were new to my ken? Was it because they were vastly different from the architecture in which I had been so long immersed? Was it a composite reaction between the plight of so many Indian peoples and the magnificence of the structures? Or, was it something else? I do not know! I do know that many of the temples and tombs of India rival the best of Europe in their beauty. It is like comparing apples and oranges! Nonetheless, the architecture of this country, of these people is incomparable!

As I have stated, my first contact with Indian architecture was Indo-Islamic. Besides the three monuments noted above, I also viewed on that first fateful trip the *Quwwat-ul-Islam Masjid*. Fortuitous! Later I was able to see the *Tomb of Humayun* as well as the *Tomb of Safdar Jang*. In these two tombs are literally the "Alpha and Omega" of Mughal tombs.

For years these experiences had resided and nestled deep in my consciousness. It has only been recently that they have come to the fore and asserted themselves. I have spent the last two decades studying and considering first Buddhist and then Hindu iconography. My concentration on Indo-Islamic is, therefore, a natural progression.

Many works have been devoted to the architecture of India--Buddhist, Hindu and Islamic. These works, predominantly, are of a general nature, either treating the whole--i.e., Buddhist or Hindu or Islamic--or various dynasty and/or areas--e.g., Bijapur, Gujarat, Gupta, Hoysala, etc. To find examples of Indo-Islamic tombs, one is forced to consult numerous tomes in order to gain a clear and relatively comprehensive overview of the subject.

Therefore, this brief consideration was undertaken to treat thirty-six tombs from: the *Tomb No. 36*, Delhi, a. 1230 C.E., to the *Tomb of Safdar Jang*, Delhi, c. 1754 C.E.--i.e., a span of a little over five-hundred years. My interest is their apparent genesis as well as the iconography inherent in these monuments. Plans are central to this consideration. However, elevations are not to be discounted. In the presentation of the elevations in this study, they are " proportional"--i.e., they are the depiction of major architectural forms and masses--and are not purported to be precise in the presentation of their minor, architectural details. The computer was utilized in the construction of these elevations. The plans, on the other hand, are relatively precise.

Introduction

Historical overview

Some three-hundred-fifty odd years after the death of Nabi Muhammad (c. 570-632), Islam had made its way into the northern regions of India. The Turks, through military slaves, were to establish various reigns until the early Sixteenth Century. Sabuktigin of Ghazni (977-997) established his dynasty in Afganistan, invaded southward to the shore of the Indus River and established the Ghaznavid dynasty in northern India. While the western Ghaznavid succumbed to the Seljuks, the Indian-Afgani part of the kingdom remained. Sabuktigin was followed by his son Mahmud of Ghazni. In 1173 Muhammad of Ghur defeated the Ghaznavids and subdued the northwestern territories as far as Delhi. Qutb-ud-din, a former military slave, a general in Muhammad of Ghur's army occupied Benares and was later to achieve additional notoriety and power.

Muhammad of Ghur was assassinated in 1206 and Qutb-ud-din Aibak was elected as commander in chief and later assumed the title of Sultan of Delhi. He was succeeded by Sultan Iltutmish (c. 1206-1290) and lived through the early Mongol invasions of northern India. For a number of years one ruler succeeded another, usually through assassination--a bloody and all too frequently, a normal occurrence in India and other Islamic kingdoms where he law of primogeniture usually did not apply. In 1320 Ghiyas-ud-din Tughluq assumed power. He was followed by his son Muhammad bin Tughluq. The Tughluqs were supplanted by Firuz Shah and he, in turn, was followed by a number of weak sultans. Again the Mongols invaded under the leadership of Timur and the Turkish Sultanate was destroyed forever in India.

In quick succession, Northern India was ruled by various Sayyids and followed by the Lodis. Then, Zahir-al-Din Muhammad Babur, a Chagatai Turk, King of Ferghana (now in Uzbekistan), "the Great Mughal," a descendent of Timur through his father and Chingiz (Ghengis) Khan through his mother, captured Kabul and began to expand his Afghani empire southward. This was the beginning of the great Mughal Empire in India. Humayun succeeded his father, Babur, and was in turn succeeded by Akbar the Great, Akbar the builder, Akbar the conqueror, Akbar the seeker of the Divine, and the Mughal Empire was firmly established and lasted until the British incursions at which time it had weakened from within to the point of near collapse.

Burial Practices

The Mughals followed a practice long established in the Islamic world--i.e., the construction of tombs for the deceased. Within this potentially rich land--i.e., rich in manpower and natural resources--the Mughals elevated tomb building to a level unmatched aesthetically by any other civilization. Nonetheless, they did not deviate from traditional burial practices. The body of the deceased was ritually washed and wrapped in a white shroud without any adornment whatsoever. Every man, woman and child met his *Maker* as he entered the world on an equal basis. However, their equal status before Allah did not apply to the tomb in which they were laid.

The body was always laid parallel to the *qibla* or perpendicular to the direction of Mecca. Iconographically, this allowed the deceased to merely turn onto his or her side to face Mecca. In addition, the body was placed in a 'vault' so that he or she may sit up in order to reply to the Angels of the Grave when they appeared on the night after burial.[1]

Tomb Types

Six tomb types in the Islamic world may be noted by plan[2]--i.e., 1) the canopy tomb which is open on all sides and generally possesses four or eight supporting pillars or piers, 2) a modified canopy tomb in which a *qibla* wall is established, 3) an enclosed tomb generally square but may also be octagonal with a single entrance, 4) a tomb with a courtyard attached, 5) a tomb to which other tombs are attached creating a single roofed area, and 6) the *mashhad* or a domed, square area with an ambulatory on three sides.[3]

Five specific Indo-Islamic, general tomb types may be identified. They are derived, in part from the six tomb types noted by Hillenbrand. First, the canopy tomb (See: **Figure 1**) and hereafter referred to as **Type A**. This tomb type is characterized by an open plan in which the roof and dome, where applicable, is supported by a series of columns or piers. An example is seen in the *Sayyid Usman Rauza* (pp. 78-81).

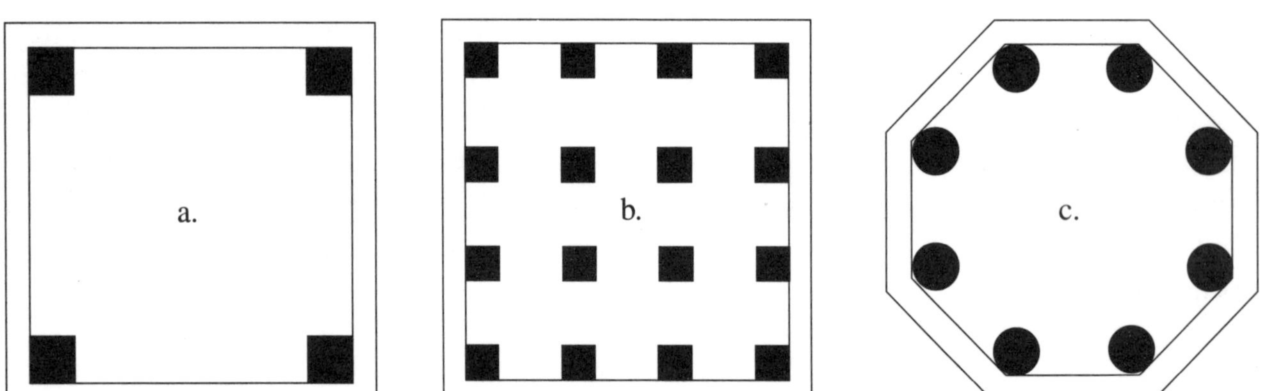

Figure 1: canopy tomb type-- a **Type A** basic plan

Second, is an enclosed square with one, three or four entrances and may be surrounded by a covered verandah of one or two aisles (a *qibla* wall being the feature of the one and three entranced square tomb) (See: **Figure 2**) and hereafter referred to as **Type B**. This type is characterized by solid masonry walls covered by a dome without a surrounding verandah. Generally, it consists of a single storey. An example is seen in the *Tomb of Sultan Iltutmish* (pp. 38-41).

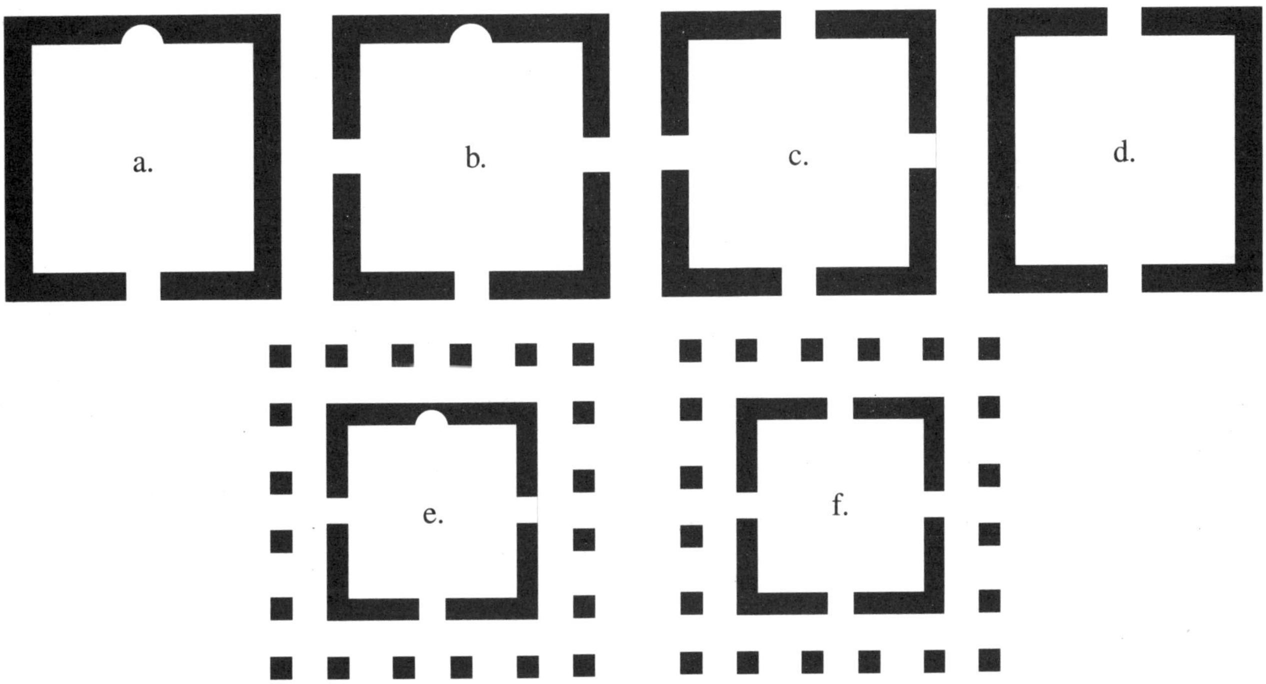

Figure 2: square tomb with one, three or four entrances-- a **Type B** basic plan

Third, is a square plan with four corner towers or minarets extending at 45^0 beyond the corners of the square, or incorporated as part of a square plan. Generally this type is shown with a *qibla* (See: **Figure 3**) and hereafter referred to as **Type C**; 4). As a rule, this type possesses multi-storeys, although there may be a single storey. Examples are seen in the *Tomb of Sultan Ghari* or *Tomb of Muhammad Ghaus* (pp. 34-37 and 126-129).

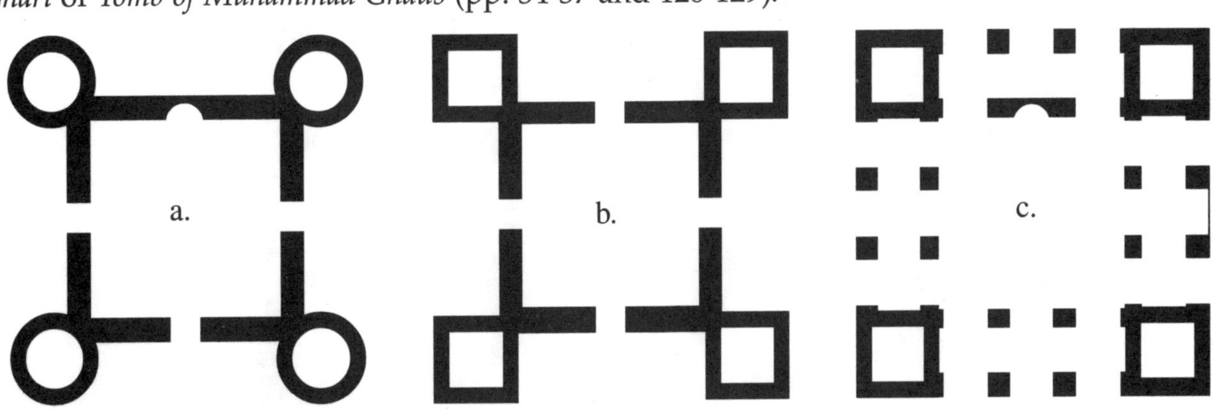

Figure 3: tomb with four towers or minarets-- a **Type C** basic plan

Introduction (Continued)

Fourth is an enclosed octagon or an enclosed octagon within an octagonal verandah, a type that enjoyed considerable use from the 14th through the 16th Centuries, C.E. This type may be found with one, three, four, seven or eight entrances to the central area (See: **Figure 4**) and hereafter referred to as **Type D**. The latter variation--i.e., the octagon with an octagonal verandah--generally is characterized by three open arches on each face of the verandah amounting to twenty four arches. Examples of this type are seen in the *Tomb of Shah Rukn-i 'Alam* or *Tomb of Sher Shah* (pp. 42-45 and 98-103).

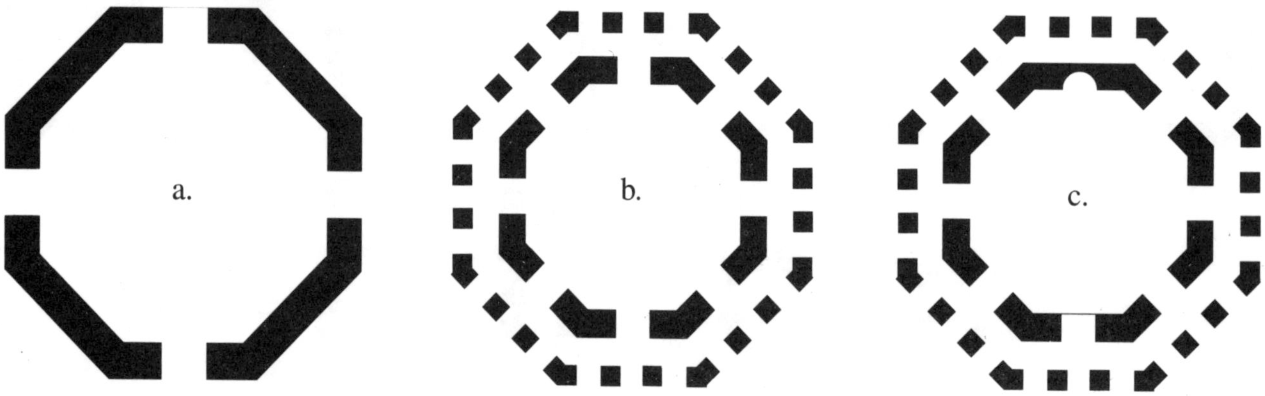

Figure 4: octagonal tomb-- a **Type D** basic plan

Fifth is a combination generally of square and octagon. Particularly, this type is characterized by the employment of a *muthamman baghadi*, and incorporates the ninefold plan--i.e., the plan in which a central chamber is surrounded by eight smaller chambers or areas, four at the cardinal points and four at the intercardinal points (See: **Figure 5**) and hereafter referred to as **Type E**. As a rule, this type possesses multi-storeys and are often set upon a podium and within a *chahar-bagh*, and is the most developed of the various tomb plans. Examples are seen in the *Tomb of Humayun* or the *Taj Mahal* (pp. 114-125 and 210-213).

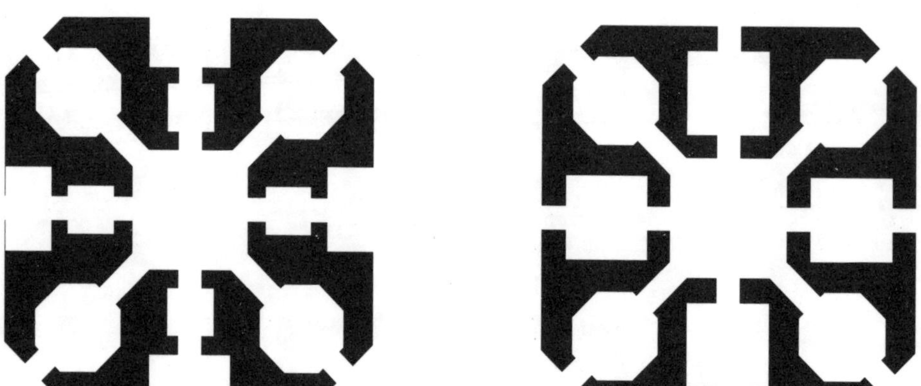

Figure 5: tomb with square and octagon combination (***muthamman baghdadi***)-- a **Type E** basic plan

Introduction (Continued)

The early Indo-Islamic tombs, particularly of the Slave or Mamluk Dynasties tended to be square--e.g., the *Tomb of Sultan Ghari*, the *Tomb of Sultan Iltutmish*, the *Tomb of Ghiyas-ud-din Tughluq I*, etc. However, the *Tomb of Khan-i Jihan Tilangani* ushered in the octagonal tomb with a verandah. Following this monument, a majority of the mausolea, particularly for rulers of the Sayyid Dynasty, tended to be octagonal. Later, this form was employed for lesser nobles during the Lodi Dynasty and the subsequent Mughal or Timurud Period. With the ascendancy of the Great Mughals--i.e., from Humayun (1530-1556 C.E.) through Shah Jahan (1628-1666), the Great Timuruds, tombs of monumental proportions appeared. Most of these tombs were based upon the square, or a variation with the square as the base--e.g., the *Tomb of Akbar*, the *Tomb of Jahangir*, the *Gol Gumbaz*, the *Tomb of Jahan Begum*, the *Tomb of Safdar Jang*, etc.

Scope

This study will, therefore, consider those Islamic tombs of India from the Slave or Mamluk Dynasty--i.e., the *Tomb of Sultan Ghari*--to the last of the important Mughal tombs--i.e., the *Tomb of Safdar Jang*--and the genesis of their design, or plan. Emphasis will be placed upon the use and type of internal space, the derivation of the plan(s), the application of design principles inherent in both Islamic and Hindu faiths in India, and a consideration of possible iconographic implications.

Plans

The plan is the starting point, therefore, each plan will be the axis of this consideration. The plans were constructed via computer and are relatively exact in their proportions and dimensions. Nonetheless, the elevations are not without their importance as they are outgrowths of the plan.

Elevations

The elevations herein supplied are proportional renderings of the various masses and salient details of each tomb. They are not 'scale drawings' in the strict sense. Nonetheless, they do follow the major masses accurately. In addition, it was observed that a number of the elevations' horizontal forms fell within the confines of a *Deshiya Mandala*. Therefore, this *mandala* was applied to all elevations as a standard elevation proportion. The twelve *pada* may have special numerological significance. It is known that both Buddhist and Hindu placed great faith in the belief and the science of numerology--so to does the Islamic world. Twelve is an auspicious, cosmic number which comprehends all numbers lower than itself. It is associated with the circle ($12 \times 30 = 360^0$), the number of daylight hours, number of signs in the Zodiac and the number of months in a year.

Mandalas

Although the tombs are Islamic, the ancient influence of Buddhist and Hindu preexistent forms and such treatises as the *Manasara* and *Mayamata* were ingrained in the *sthapati* who were often employed by the sultans and emperors. Two *mandala* were especially applicable in the history of Buddhist and Hindu structures, especially temples--i.e., the *Manduka Mandala* and the *Paramashayika Mandala*. The *Manduka Mandala* is constructed of sixty-four *pada* (eight ranks of eight) while the *Paramashayika Mandala* consists of eighty-one *pada* (nine ranks of nine). It is seen that either the *Manduka Mandala* or the *Paramashayika Mandala* are often applicable to the square plans of these Indo-Islamic tombs. Similarly, the circular *Manduka Mandala* is seen as applicable, especially to the octagonal mausolea. (See: **Figure 6**).

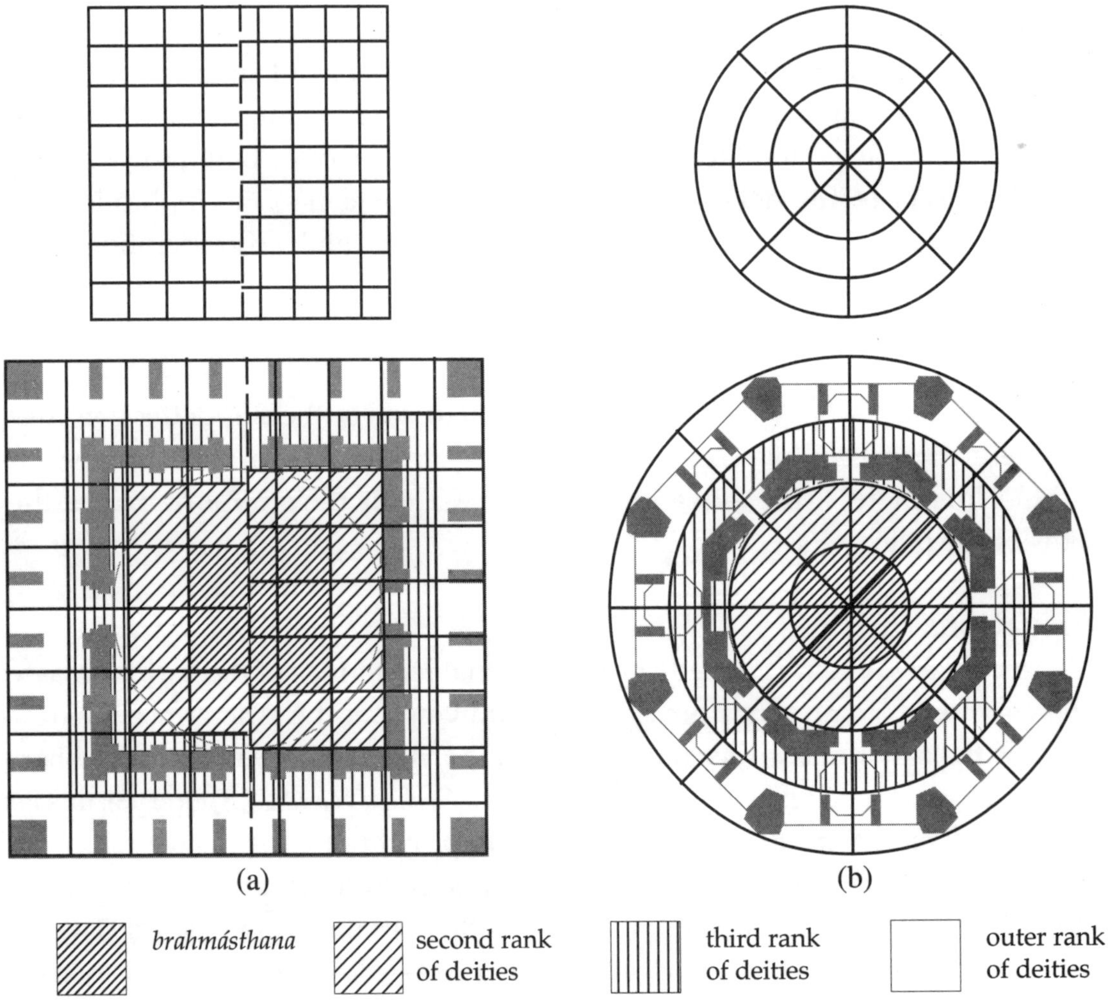

Figure 6: (a) -- *Manduka Mandala* (right) & *Paramashayika Mandala* (left) applied to *Tomb of Mohammed Quli Qutub Shah*. (b) -- Circular *Manduka Mandala* applied to *Tomb of Mubarak Shah*

Appendices

Following the body of this consideration appears a Bibliography and five appendices--i.e., Appendix A, a glossary of applicable terms; Appendix B, Ensembles and the Chahar-bagh, discusses the relevancy of this form to the tombs under consideration; Appendix C, Miscellaneous Comparisons and Plans, as they apply to the body of this consideration; Appendix D, Major Muslim Rulers of India; and, Appendix E, a Chronology of Muslim Monuments in India, as well as of the Islamic World at large and appropriate Western monuments as a comparison.

Introduction

The Genesis of Form

The Genesis of Form

"Islamic architecture serves several functions, but its main effect--an very likely its main purpose--appears to be the creation of non-tectonic values, the dissolution of all those values that in other architectural traditions emphasize the structure and the balance and counterbalance of loads and stress. . . . Islamic architecture at its best, and at its most 'Islamic,' is truly a negation of architecture as conceived in Europe, that is, of structure. . . ."[4]

Little, in the endeavors of man, springs from nothing! That master computer which we call the brain stores incalculable amounts of information and images which may be applied to various activities or drawn upon at any time. That is not to say that man, in his infinite need to stamp a personal imprimatur on his creations, doesn't innovate. Indeed, he does. But, that innovation is built upon a foundation of visual and experiential relicts from the past--both near and distant--on which he or she decants from that vast mental reservoir those things which are appropriate.

The Islamic tombs of India, as magnificent as many are, find their genesis not only in the Indian subcontinent--both Buddhist India and Hindu India--but also from other cultures of Asia, Africa and the Mediterranean.

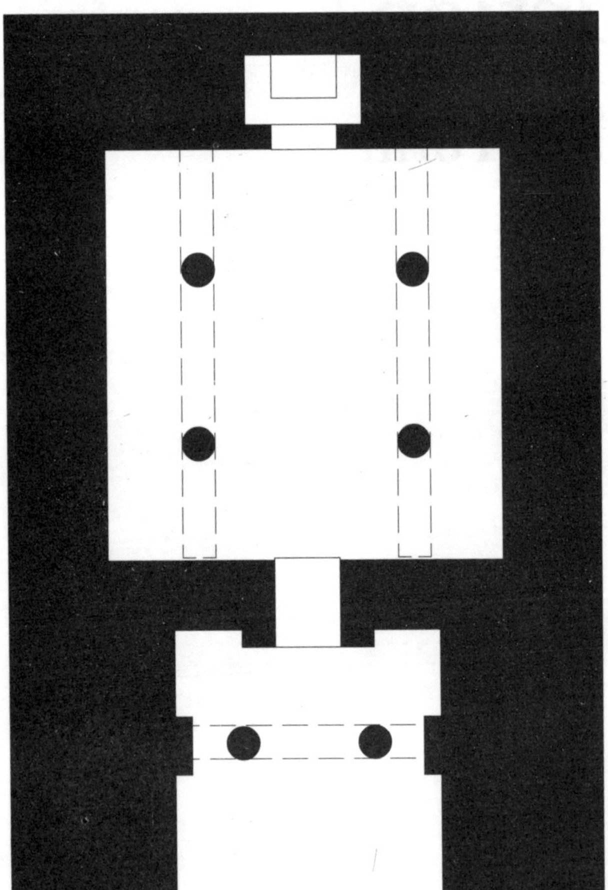

Figure 7: *Rock-cut Tomb* (plan, after Banister Fletcher), Beni Hasan, Egypt (c. 2000 BCE)

Figure 8: *Rock-cut Tomb* indication of internal space, Beni Hasan, Egypt (c. 2000 BCE)

Following Hebrew and Early Christian traditions, Muslims buried their dead. This was done in the sure belief that resurrection would one day occur. The elaborate preservation of the body as was practised by the Egyptians was not required by Islam.

In the Islamic tradition, the body is ritually cleansed, wrapped in a white shroud and placed in mother earth. There is no exception! Some groups bury their dead in a seated position so that they will be ready to answer for their life's work, but this is not a universal practice in Islam. The burial was and is simple. Simple, except for the wealthy and powerful who were constrained to construct shelters over their earthly remains. Mausolea which mirrored their power, wealth and importance were raised as a testament to their status. Yet, their bodies still rested in mother earth. Usually, the body of the deceased is placed on his/her side, facing Mecca. The sarcophagi that are seen in many Muslim tombs are but empty shells, the body, generally is placed in the ground in a lower crypt which also may have possess another non functional sarcophagus--a two tiered arrangement.

The raising of tombs for the great and glorious has been practised for millennia--e.g., the pyramids of Egypt--but it seems to have

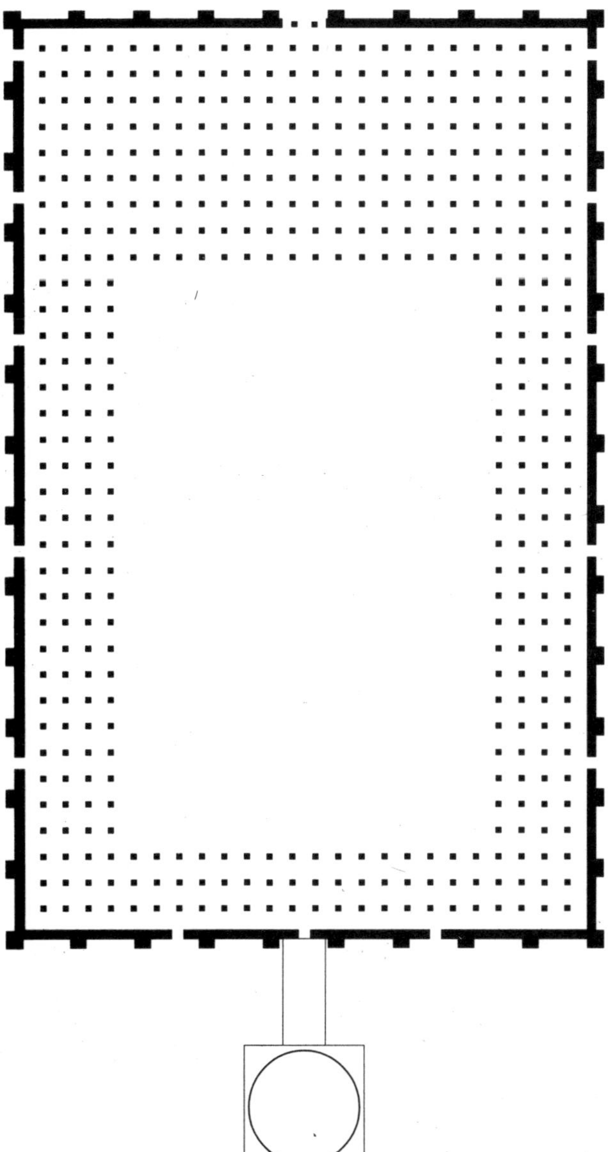

Figure 9: *Great Mosque* (plan), Samarra, Iraq (848-852 CE)

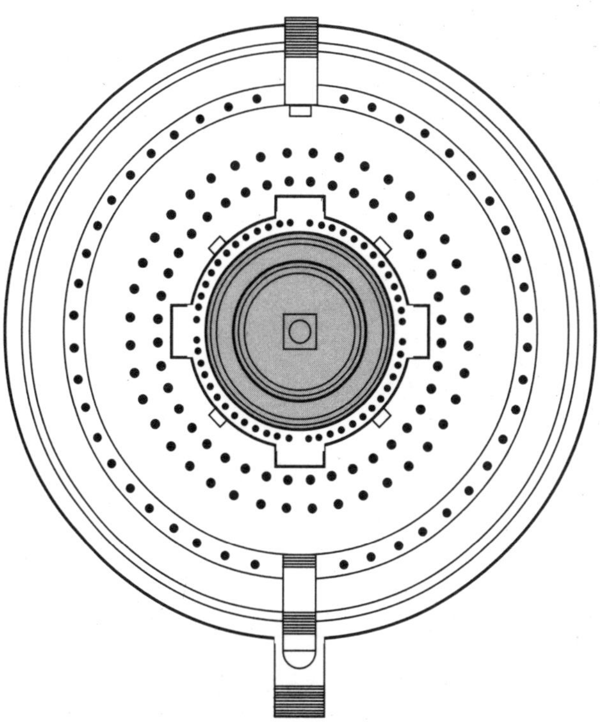

Figure 10: *Thuparama Dagoba* (plan), Anuradhapura, Sri Lanka (III C. BCE)

reached an apogee in Mughal India. For scale and its environs, what can rival the *Tomb of Humayun*? For sheer beauty, what can approach the *Tomb of Hazrat Mumtaz-uz-Zamani*--the *Taj Mahal*? For the delicacy and completeness, what can approximate the *Tomb of I'timad-ud-daula*?

The pyramids of King Zoser or those at Gizeh are indeed massive! They are technical and engineering wonders, marvels. However, in the ancient world only the *Mortuary Temple of Queen Hatshepsut* (c. 1450 BCE) presents a genuinely awesome vista; one that is not again seen 'til the tombs of great Mughal rulers of India. It is of interest to note that those religions which believed or believe in a resurrected after life--i.e., Pharaonic Egypt, Judaism, Christianity and Islam--only Egypt and Islam lavished so much time, effort and expense in the construction of great mausolea, especially for the rich and famous. The tombs of Charlemagne, Henry VII, Elizabeth I, Charles V (The Holy Roman Emperor), the Empress Maria Theresa, Peter the Great, Catherine the Great, etc., are all minuscule and of little interest in the flow of architecture. Not so with the tombs of the great rulers of Islam, and especially not so with the tombs of the great Mughals of India. Their lustre outshines the fabled *Koh-i-Noor* which also sprang from the soil of mother India! This is doubly interesting in that Nabi Mohammad spoke against lavish tombs with studied vehemence

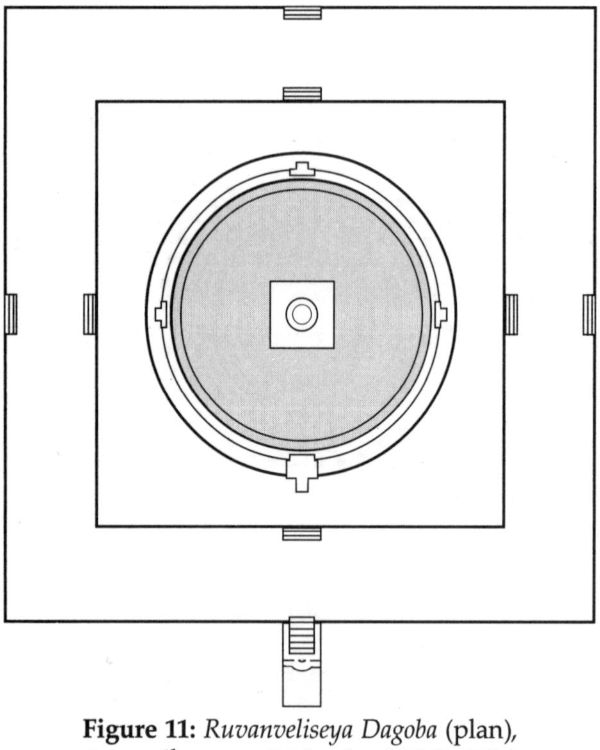

Figure 11: *Ruvanveliseya Dagoba* (plan), Anuradhapura, Sri Lanka (II-I C. BCE)

There is a thread that can be followed. From early mortuary temples or tombs of Egypt--e.g., the Rock-cut Tombs, *Beni Hasan* (c. 2000 BCE) (See: **Figure 7**)--a square form is seen to be utilized. In addition the internal space is relatively spacious in comparison to the inner chambers of the pyramids. Megalithic architecture allows for this expansion of space (See: **Figure 8**). This use of the square is to become one of the more preferred forms for Mughal mausolea in India. Although it must be admitted that in the construction of mosques (*masjid* or *cami*) the rectangle seemed to be the most popular form developed early in the Islamic world.

One of the early rectangular *masjid* of great size was the *Great Mosque at Samarra* (See: **Figure 9**). It indicates a symmetrical or axial plan consisting of two rectangles--i.e., the outer girdle wall of considerable height and an inner rectangle, offset towards the spiral minaret. The substantial girdle wall with its crenellated top punctuated by heavy buttress-like forms gave the appearance of a great fortress. In form, if not concept, the *Great Mosque at Samarra* is not unlike the Egyptian temples or even the temples of Greece before the Common Era. However, the amount of enclosed space, even with the plethora of columns is massive! It mirrors the Islamic need of space, great spaces for worship of the masses.

On the other hand, early Buddhist mortuary monuments took a circular form as exemplified in the stupa (*chaitya, chetiya* or *dagoba*). Whereas the square was a sacred form to the Brahmanic (Vedic and Hindu) faiths, the circle was considered to be a hallowed shape to the Buddhists. *Stupa I* of Sanchi is a prime example. It was copied by various other cultures of the region--e.g., the *Thuparama Dagoba*, Sri Lanka (See: **Figure 10**). Even though neither Buddhism nor Hinduism looked forward towards a resurrected form after death, and both tended to cremate the body and scatter the ashes; there were great sages (*arhats*) or holy men (*yogin*) whose ashes were placed within *stupa*--relics to be venerated. The form of the *stupa* is seen to be derived from burial tumuli--not an uncommon practice. The circle bounded by the square represents the celestial world--the circle-- and the terrestrial--the square. This is made even more evident in the *Ruvanveliseya Dagoba* (See: **Figure 11**), three dimensionally, in which the upper half of the sphere--the hemisphere--represents the cosmic domains while the lower half--the implied half--embodies earthly regions bounded by the square base.

The circle was not only a form utilized in mortuary monuments, it was also utilized in structures of worship--temples and later churches. Rome utilized the circular form in the temples of Vesta. Temples which possessed a small bathing tank for the purification rites which many architectural historians see as precursors to the Christian baptistery as seen in the *Campo Santo* or *Campo dei Miracoli*, of Pisa. However, the circle was also utilized in the conception of churches, places of worship--e.g. *Santa Costanza* of Rome (See: **Figure 12**). Here, as in the *Pantheon* of Rome, the linear movement implied by a rectangle is broken and a radial symmetry is established. Within early Christian thought, the circle was viewed as a form of perfection--having no beginning and no end. In addition, the plan of *Santa Costanza* indicates an interior space of considerable dimension (See: **Figure 13**). The

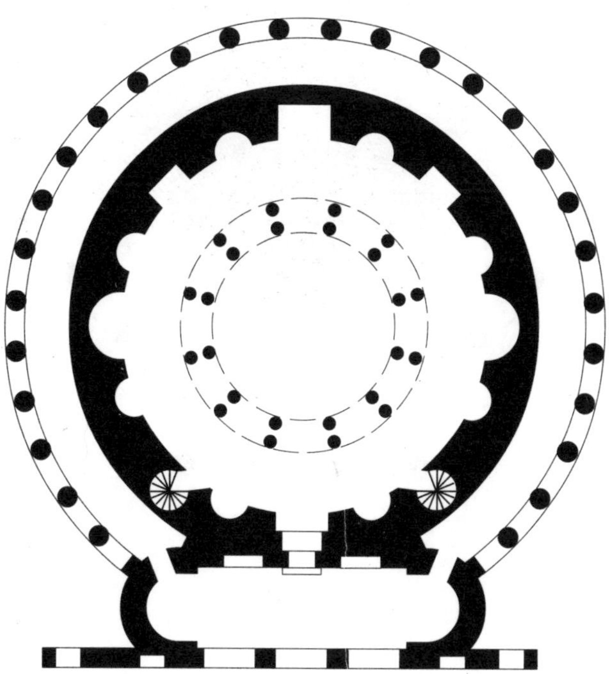

Figure 12: *Santa Costanza* (plan), Rome, (c. 350 CE)

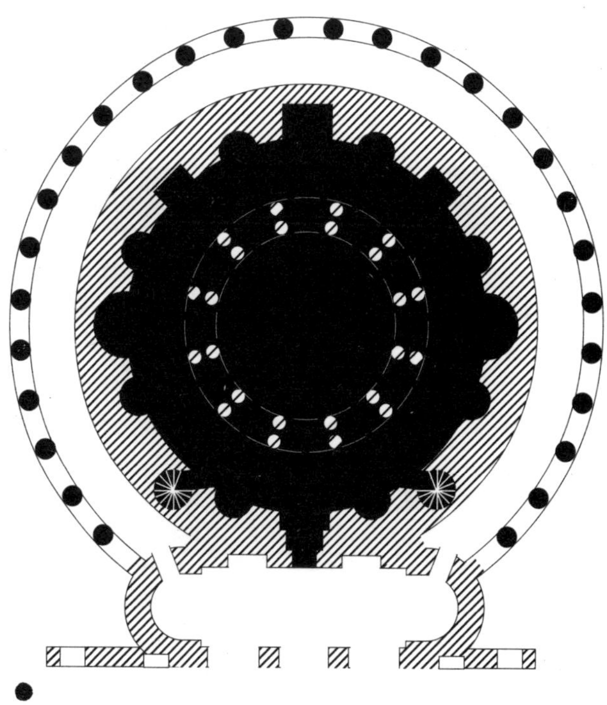

Figure 13: *Santa Costanza*, indication of internal space, Rome, (c. 350 CE)

central dome is supported by a double ring of columns and the sanctuary area is merely another niche placed in the east wall of this circular form. *Santa Costanza* mirrors one of the iconic devices of the pantheon, the reduction of importance of a/or *the* main altar. The thick walls were required to buttress the weight and stresses of the central dome, but they do not compare to the thickness of a number of the temples of Pagan or those Hindu temples of India.

The second form which assumes great important in Mughal mausolea is the octagon. The octagon has a special place in the eastern Mediterranean and south Asia. Throughout the Near East, South and Southeast Asia, the numeral eight is seen as particularly auspicious. It denotes perfection, good fortune, and on the divine plane: justice and balance between attraction and repulsion, positive and negative. This integer as even, is representative of motherhood. It is promising in its makeup being an evenly even number and the first cube number, 2^3. Within the Islamic world, eight is represented as a geometric form--the octagon--more than any other shape. It may be viewed as a transitional element between a circle and a square--e.g., a dome on squinches which was frequently employed by Islamic builders. As a form applied to a house of worship, the late Romans employed the octagonal form to the *Temple of the Palace of Diocletian* at Split (See: **Figure 14**). Internally, the space hearkens to the interior of the *Pantheon*

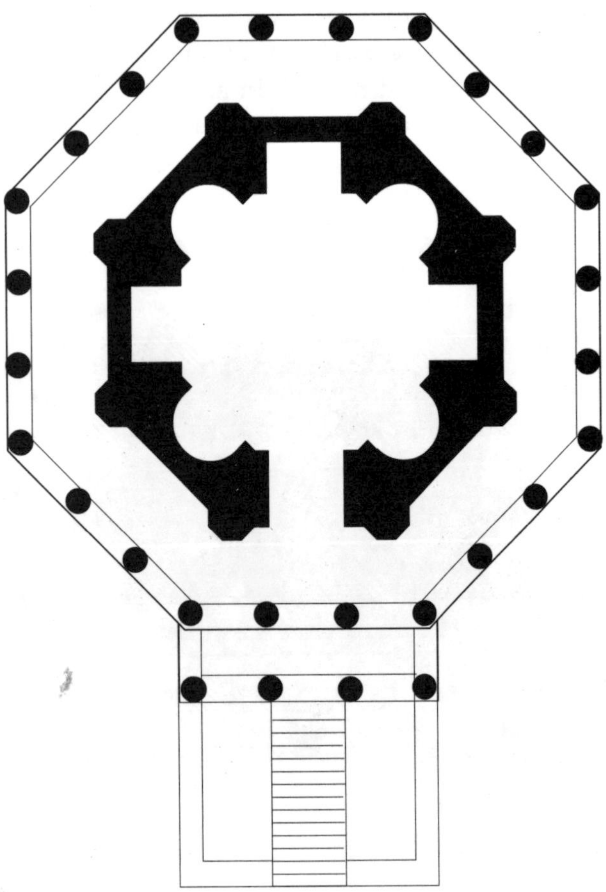

Figure 14: *Temple of the Palace of Diocletian* (plan), Split, Croatia (450 CE)

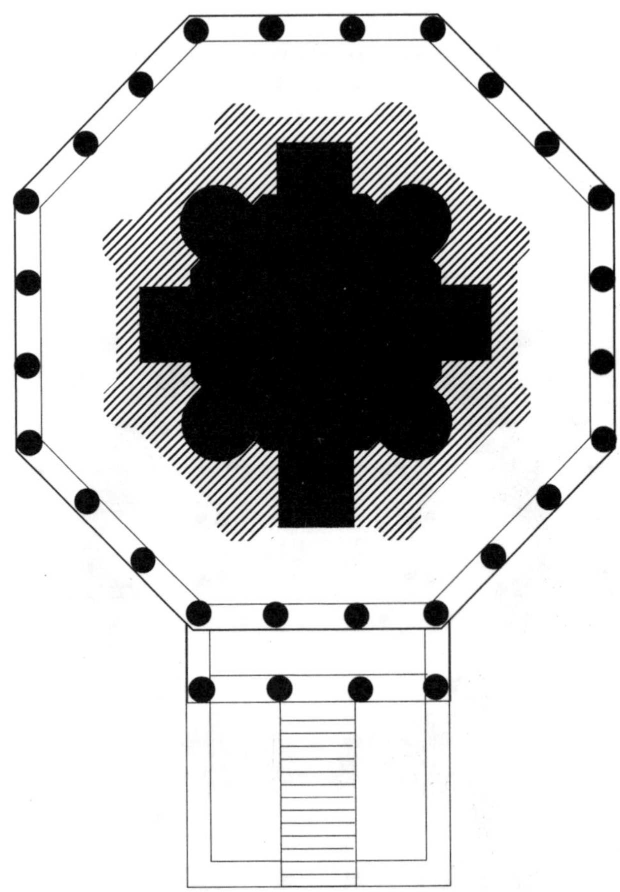

Figure 15: *Temple of the Palace of Diocletian*, indication of internal space, Split, Croatia (450 CE)

with the exception of the octagonal form of the exterior. However, another aspect is seen to be of some importance. The octagon encloses two shapes--i.e., a cross which is more reminiscent of a Greek cross and a square form with rounded corners. Certainly the internal variations--the circular niche and the rectangular--not only create visual/spatial interest, but the rectangle is seen as masculine and the circle as feminine. Perhaps, originally, the rounded niches held goddesses and the rectangular ones possessed gods. Again, the internal space for this rather modest temple is rather expansive (See: **Figure 15**).

During the same period that the construction of the *Palace of Diocletian* was taking place, the resurgence of Brahmanic beliefs in India was in full flower under the modern appellation: Hinduism. Whereas the Buddhists were seen to overthrow the preeminent Vedic form--the square--in favor of the circle as a manifestation of the Divine; the Hindu returned to the old form. The square is seen as the elemental form in the *Ladh Khan* at Aihole (See: **Figure 16**). The square is so intense in its employment that the original altar was in the center of the structure, rather than in the west end or side.

"The square with its four equal sides and four equal angles becomes the standard, the preferred form for Hindu/Indian architecture. It symbolizes order, unequivocal form, the male,

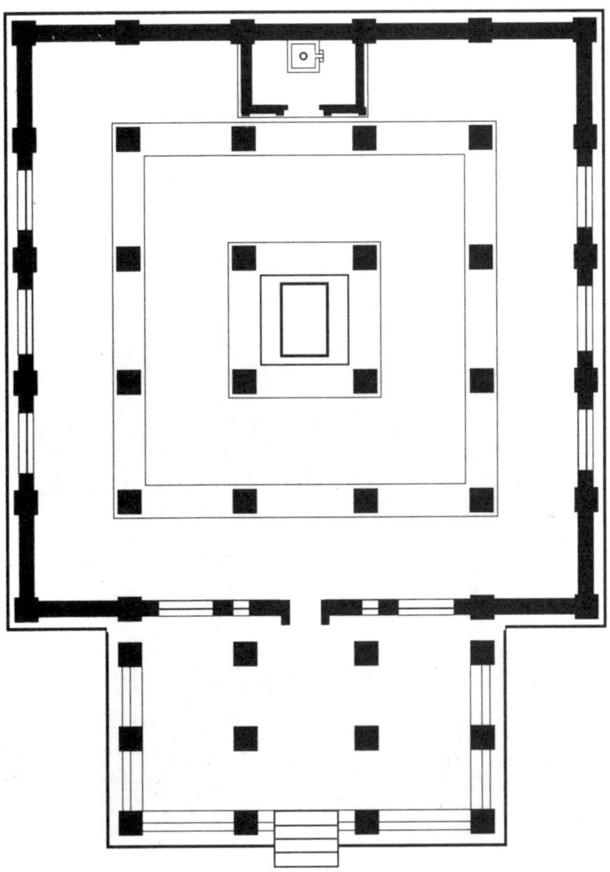

Figure 16: *Ladh Khan* (plan), Aihole, India (450 CE)

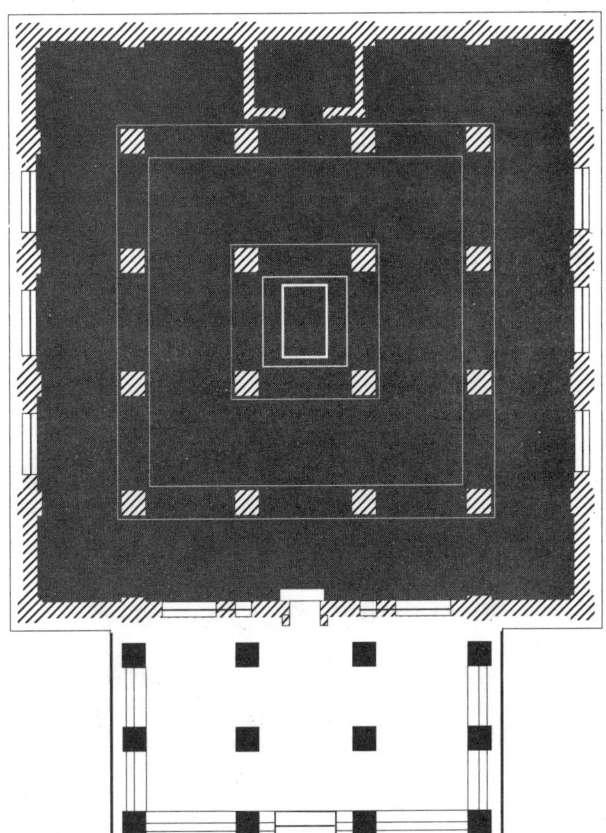

Figure 17: *Ladh Khan*, indication of internal space, Aihole, India (450 CE)

the celestial sphere and The Absolute. Shrines, particularly the sanctuary or *garbha-griha* . . . are generally square in shape or in the case of later developments--e.g., the *triratha* and *pancharatha* . . . . Even secular structures are often based on this shape--e.g., the *Garden Pavilion*, Kotilal Fort, Delhi . . . ; the *House of Raja Birbal*, Fathepur Sikri; and the *Feria Bagh*, near Ahamdnagar.

"The square is unequivocal, constant--a square is a square. Its shape is always the same though its dimensions may be large or small. It is unlike the rectangle whose shape may vary.

"It is of interest to note that the square with its four equal sides and four equal angles--four being a feminine number--is considered to be a masculine form to the Hindus. It is assigned to the celestial sphere (Indic: *loka*) and represents The Absolute."[5]

What is of further interest in the *Ladh Khan* is the enormous percentage of open space in comparison to the total. This temple is seen as an interesting manifestation of the resurgence of the Brahmanic faith in the guise of Hinduism, and is further seen to mimic the meeting hall form that was prevalent in India during this period. Nonetheless, the amount of internal space in proportion the whole is noteworthy (See: **Figure 17**).

A century had not passed from construction of the *Palace of Diocletian* before the Byzantine church of *San Vitale*, Ravenna, was built (See: **Figure 18**). The octagon was employed as the basic form and an apse was added, extending towards the northeast. This type of extension was not new in Early Christian and/or Byzantine rectangular churches, but it is a bit of an anomaly in circular or octagonal edifices. There will appear, from time to time, a similar

Figure 18: *San Vitale* (plan), Ravenna, Italy (526-547 CE)

Figure 19: *San Vitale,* indication of internal space, Ravenna, Italy (526-547 CE)

"extension" in Mughal mausolea a millennium later (See: *Gol Gumbaz*, **Plates 73 & 74**). The plan of *San Vitale* is somewhat deceiving. Internal walls and pillars appear to predominate. Indeed, they play a major role. However, the interior space is considerable as befits a congregational religious edifice (See: **Figure 19**). The proportion of internal space in relation to the whole is nearly equal to that found in *Ladh Khan*.

Within one-hundred-fifty years of the construction of *San Vitale* in Ravenna another sacred structure was erected in the area of the eastern Mediterranean, the *Qubbat as-Sakhra*, or the *Dome of the Rock*, in Jerusalem (See: **Figure 20**). It is one of the holiest places in the Islamic world, next to Mecca. The *Dome of the Rock* indicates a strong relationship to other Mediterranean architectural models--e.g., the *Temple of the Palace of Diocletian* at Split as well as *San Vitale* at Ravenna. The octagon had come to represent not only imperial preferences, but also ecclesiastical predilections as well. The octagonal plan of the *Dome of the Rock* is seen by some not to be a substantive geometric form in itself, but based upon the square which, once established, is rotated 45^0 forming the octagon.[6] This interpretation may well be an attempt to divorce the *Dome of the Rock* from its obvious preceding, pagan and Christian architectural models--i.e., the *Temple of the Palace of Diocletian* and *San Vitale*. Nonetheless, the plans begs . . . Nay! It demands comparison! Even the inclusion of an ambulatory mimics that of its Ravenna counterpart--*San Vitale*. Of course, the major difference is the raising of a dome over the central area. The dome soars over the squat octagonal mass with its low pitched roof, providing a none too satisfactory solution to the whole. The interior supports are arranged in a circle--i.e., four large piers, oriented towards the intercardinal points, are interspersed with three pillars, for a total of twelve. There was no attempt to modulate from the octagon (double squares) to the circular space of the dome as later Islamic architects did with such stunning variation. As unsatisfactory as the three

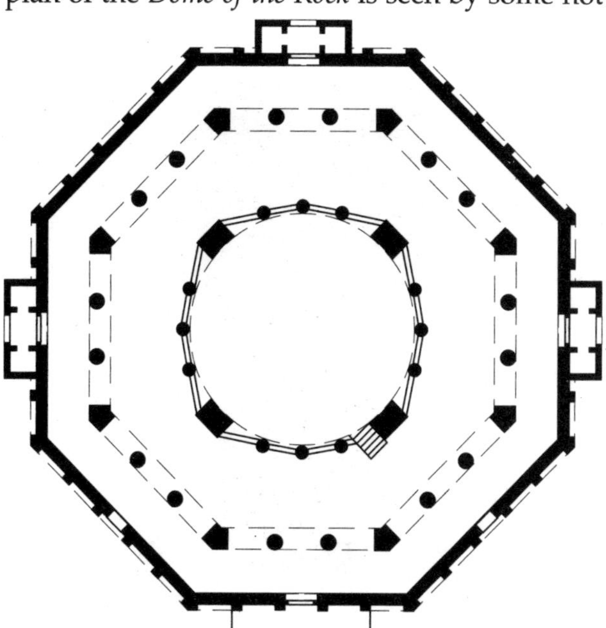

Figure 20: *Dome of the Rock* (*Qubbat as-Sakhra*) (plan), Jerusalem, Israel (690-692CE)

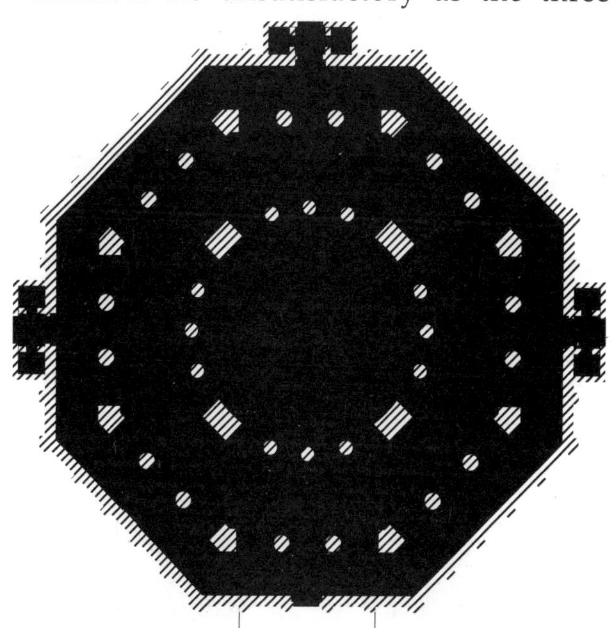

Figure 21: *Dome of the Rock* (*Qubbat as-Sakhra*), indication of internal space, Jerusalem, Israel (690-692CE)

dimensional form of the *Dome of the Rock* may be, the plan possesses interesting variations on a theme which goes back some two-hundred-forty odd years and reinterpreted one-hundred-fifty years prior.

However, as with *San Vitale*, the interior space of the *Dome of the Rock* predominates as befits a congregational faith (See: **Figure 21**). Its major variance with most of subsequent mosques is in its octagonal form. Prior to the Twentieth Century, subsequent mosque architecture is overwhelmingly rectangular in plan.

The square, the circle and the octagon--forms that had been employed in mortuary or ecclesiastical architecture since the 2nd Millennia BCE around the Mediterranean, the Near East and South Asia--found interesting variations within India, in particular. As has been stated, the circle was not viewed by the Hindu of India as a sacred form. Yet there are isolated examples of circular temples--e.g., the *Shiva Temple*, Masaon (c. 950 CE) or the *Round Temple of Trichur*, Kerala (c. 8th C. CE). The *Shiva Temple* at Indore provides an interesting adaptation or variation (See: **Figure 22**). The plan implies the circle, yet it is derived from a square component that is rotated 30^0, three times, giving the impression of a circle. The extensions provide a dodecagon, the form of which is subdued in importance. A strange compromise! But, what is truly Indian, and more precisely Brahmanic Indian is the internal space (See: **Figure 23**). It is minuscule in comparison to the anomalous *Ladh Khan*! Here the concept of the *garbha-griha* is stated and preserved. The internal space is less than a quarter of the whole mass and the narrow entrance would, naturally, restrict the amount of natural light to illuminate the inner space.

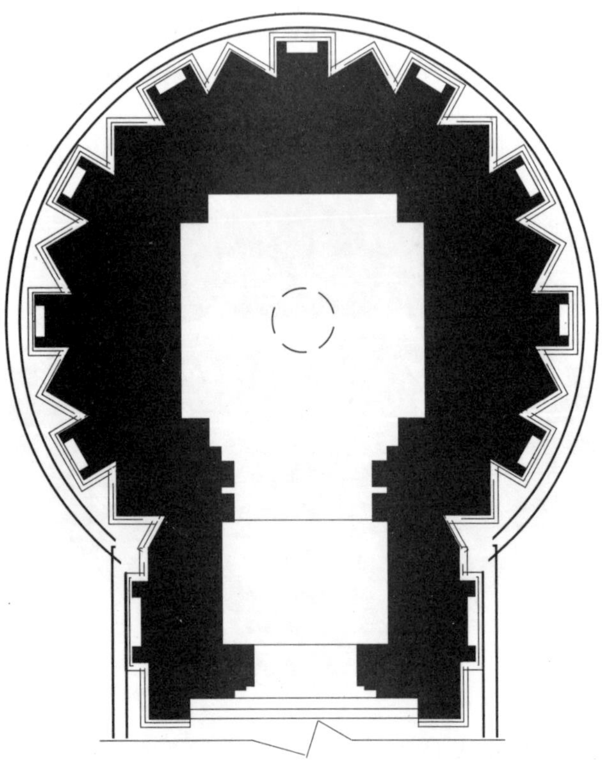

Figure 22: *Shiva Temple* (plan), Indore, India (c. 775 CE)

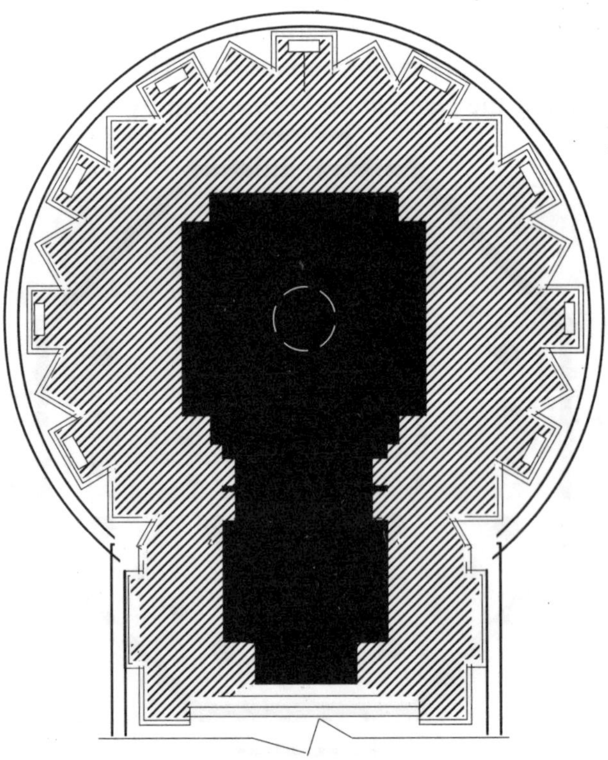

Figure 23: *Shiva Temple*, indication of internal space, Indore, India (c. 775 CE)

The Genesis of Form (Continued)

Built towards the end of the Ninth Century a tomb is found in Samarra which rivals in importance the *Great Mosque* of the same city. Called the *Qubbat as-Sulaybiyya* (892 CE), it is considered, by most, to be the oldest surviving example of Islamic tomb architecture (See: **Figure 24**).[7] An octagonal structure with an octagonal inner chamber and possibly a rudimentary dome, *Qubbat as-Sulaybiyya* can trace its lineage from the *Dome of the Rock*, through *San Vitale*, back to *Temple of the Palace of Diocletian*. Its internal space is not as vast as the *Dome of the Rock*, but appears to mirror *San Vitale* (See: **Figure 25**). The preference for the octagon over the square or the hexagon not only finds its roots in theses precedent structures, but possibly in the importance of the number eight. Not only is eight the first cubed number (2^3), it is deemed to be a perfect number, represents good fortune and is manifested in the ubiquitous eight-pointed star and the octagon. Further, Islam believes in eight paradises and in eight angels which bear the throne of *The Divine One*. The arrangement of the ten companions of the Nabi Mohammad within an octagon symbolizes paradise (See: **Figure 57**).

Yet, there are clearly areas in which the square is utilized as an eminently suitable form for Islamic tomb architecture. The *Tomb of the Samanids* found near Bukhara, Uzbekistan, is remarkably well preserved considering its age (See: **Figure 26**). Of further interest is the material of construction--i.e., brick. Although not large, it is monumental in its proportions. Basically square with engaged corner columns which act as a support for the taper of the cube--slight as it is. An architrave with a set in arcade, topped by a balustrade encircles the top of the cube. At the corners, over the engaged columns, are small finials in the form of elongated hemispheres. A hemispherical dome caps the whole and provides a dramatic interior as well as exterior. The internal space is deminished due to the thickness of the brick construction. Nonetheless it is relatively substantial (See: **Figure 27**). The square form harkens to the *Ladh Khan* (See: **Figure 16**) and the covering of the interior space finds its

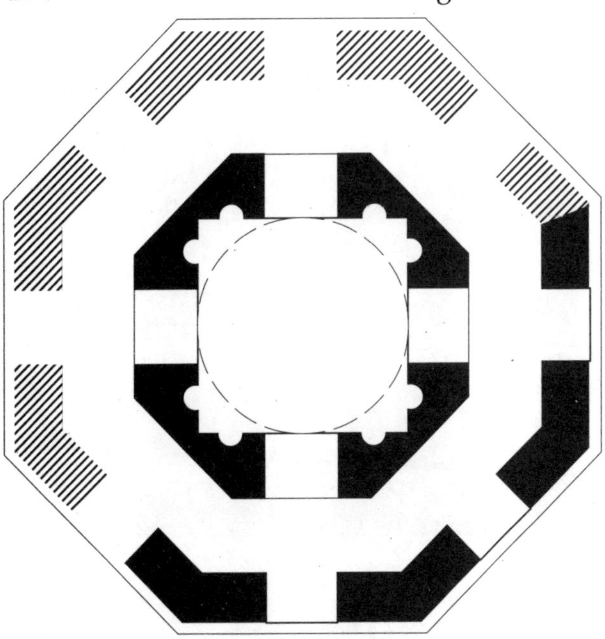

Figure 24: *Qubbat as-Sulaybiyya* (plan), Samarra, Iraq (c. 892 CE)

Figure 25: *Qubbat as-Sulaybiyya*, indication of internal space, Samarra, Iraq (c. 892 CE)

genesis in late classical Mediterranean architecture.

Clearly circular is the *Shiva Temple* at Chandrehe (See: **Figure 28**). Not only is the outer form circular, but it also possesses a circular *garbha-griha*--highly unusual! The narrow niches or indentations around the exterior, if followed around the whole divide the circle into sixteen segments. Sixteen is an important number to the Hindu. It is a feminine number, whose š is four. Sixteen signifies completeness and a balance between opposites--i.e., the Sun and Venus. In addition, it denotes divine destruction, which is applicable to the Lord Shiva as the Divine Destroyer. Actually, the circular form found in southern India is almost always dedicated to the Lord Shiva. This form, in Hindu India as applied to other temples throughout the land was not to survive beyond the southern part of the sub continent and beyond the 10th Century in any major form or number. It is also of interest to note that this form--i.e., the round plan--is not found in any major Mughal mausolea. What is of further interest is that the internal space in proportion to the whole is somewhat larger than that found at the *Shiva Temple* at Indore (See: **Figure 29**).

It is the square shaped plan that becomes not only the accepted norm in Hindu India for temple architecture, but is also a form that carries an unequivocal imprimatur for the Hindu. The *garbha-griha* is normally square and enclosed by thick masonry walls--partly to support soaring *shikhara* and partly to maintain a cool interior. Thick masonry walls do not shift their temperature easily. The *Brihadeshvara Temple* at Tanjore with its enclosed *garbha-griha*, and an internal *pradakshinapatha* underlines this point (See: **Figure 30**). Here the internal space is greatly reduced (See: **Figure 31**). Here thick walls predominate. Only the passageways leading to the *pradakshinapatha* are wider. In addition the transitional space between the *garbha-griha* and the *mandapa*, the *antarala*, is wide as befits a

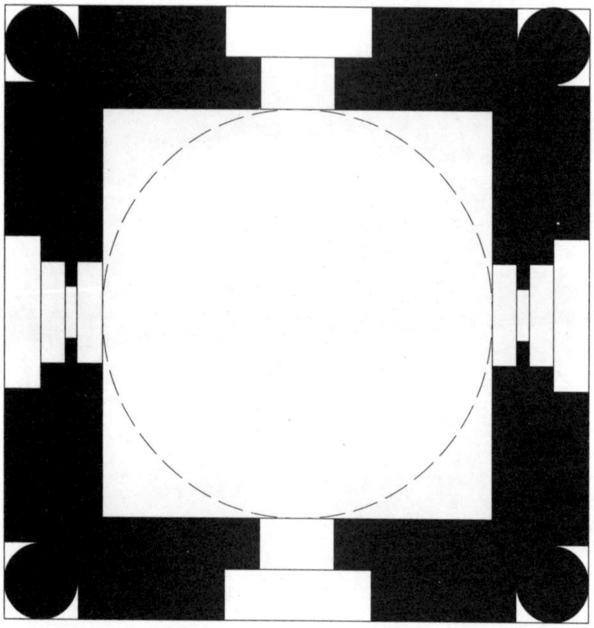

Figure 26: *Tomb of the Samanids* (plan), Bukhara, Uzbekistan (c. 920 CE)

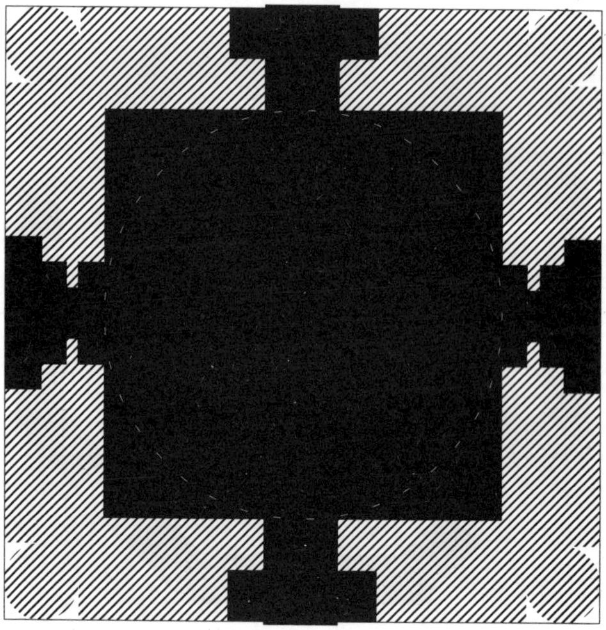

Figure 27: *Tomb of the Samanids* , indication of internal space, Bukhara, Uzbekistan (c. 920 CE)

congregating area which leads to that sacred place. The dimension of the sanctuary is barely twice the width of the outer wall.

In all Hindu temples orientation is an important factor. The preferred orientation is towards the East--i.e., the entrance is facing East. Orientation of temples, churches and/or mosques have generally been a prime consideration. Christian Churches--particularly major edifices--are oriented towards the West. The iconography being that one goes from darkness--the West--towards light and salvation--the East where the altar is situated. Mosques, on the other hand are not specifically oriented towards any compass point. Rather, the the *qibla* and the *mikhrab* (aka *mikhrab*), and, therefore the mosque is always oriented towards Mecca. Islamic tombs, particularly Mughal mausolea, are not necessarily oriented towards Mecca unless the mausolea is part of a mosque or has a surau attached. But the Mecca orientation is preferred.

The close association that the various cultures of the Mediterranean and Middle East enjoyed was not limited to trade alone. Not only was the exchange of goods beneficial, one with the other, much more was gained! The great buildings of preexisting cultures--e.g., Egypt, Greece, Rome, etc.--must have been sources of envy to those traders, merchants and envoys who came from areas which were less developed. As commerce expanded their coffers, they found numerous ways to enjoy their gains and to impress those around them. Great homes and palaces were erected and furnished with the riches of the area. Those of extreme wealth and the rulers, by way of advertising their greatness, may have seen that the construction of a mausolea to receive their august remains was relevant. Preexisting forms or models were adapted to their particular needs, cultures under their control.

Adaptations were made, compromises of

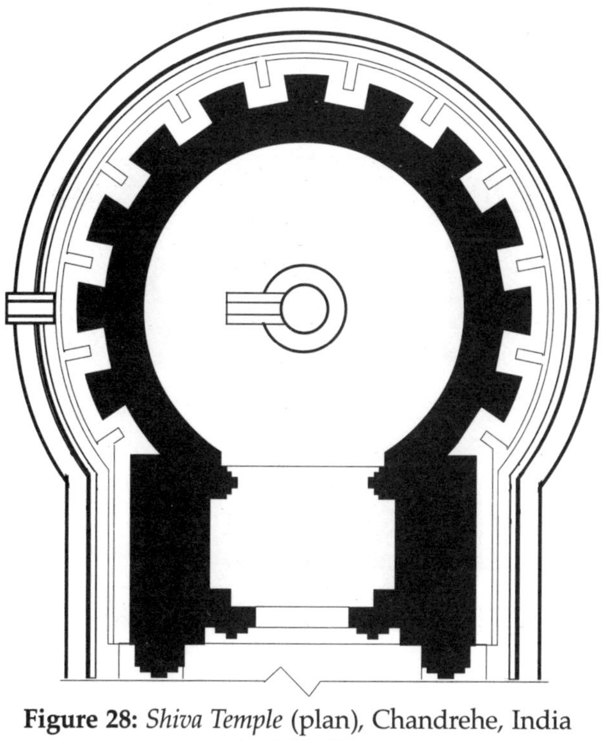

Figure 28: *Shiva Temple* (plan), Chandrehe, India (c. 950 CE)

Figure 29: *Shiva Temple,* indication of internal space, Chandrehe, India (c. 950 CE)

necessity, local materials were utilized and out of this emerged new forms genetically related to numerous regional predecessors in a family tree of architectural descent. One of the most interesting forms are the tomb towers that are to be found in northern Iran and western Afghanistan. Often their brick construction displayed the technical genius of the mason as well as the wealth of design and/or decorative possibilities that were developed within a faith where the depiction of animal or human was forbidden.

The octagonal *Tomb Tower* at Demavand, Iran (See: **Figure 32**) finds predecessors in the plan of the *Temple of the Palace of Diocletian*, Split, or *San Vitale*, Ravenna, with a parallel amount of internal space (See: **Figure 33**). Both Split and Ravenna would have been known, even renown, in the region--they were ports-of-call. Their repute would have washed over the Mediterranean region and influenced other forms. The *Gunbad-i-Kabus* at Gurgan indicates a variation on this plan (See: **Figure 34**). The tomb tower's construction is rather simple, being made up of an octagon with engaged, brick columns at the corners. These columns not only break up the surface vertically, they also add a small measure of support for the simple masonry roof. Three horizontal bands create a visual entablature at the top, but more importantly they create twenty-two, more-or-less square panels (See: **Figure 36**). Each of these panels possess unique and separate design motifs in brick. Because of the design of the *Tomb Tower* and the material employed, the internal space could be substantially increased (See: **Figures 33 & 35**).

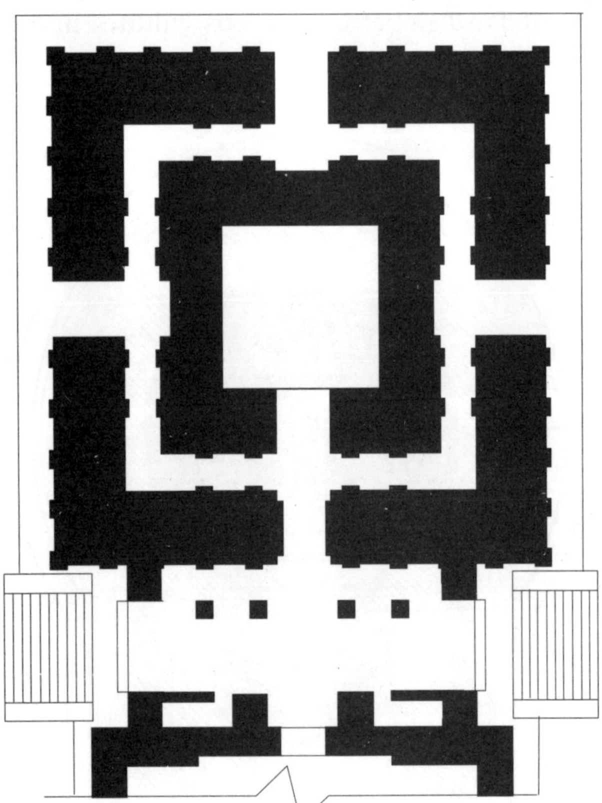

Figure 30: *Brihadeshvara Temple*, Garbha-griha (plan detail), Tanjore, India (1010 CE)

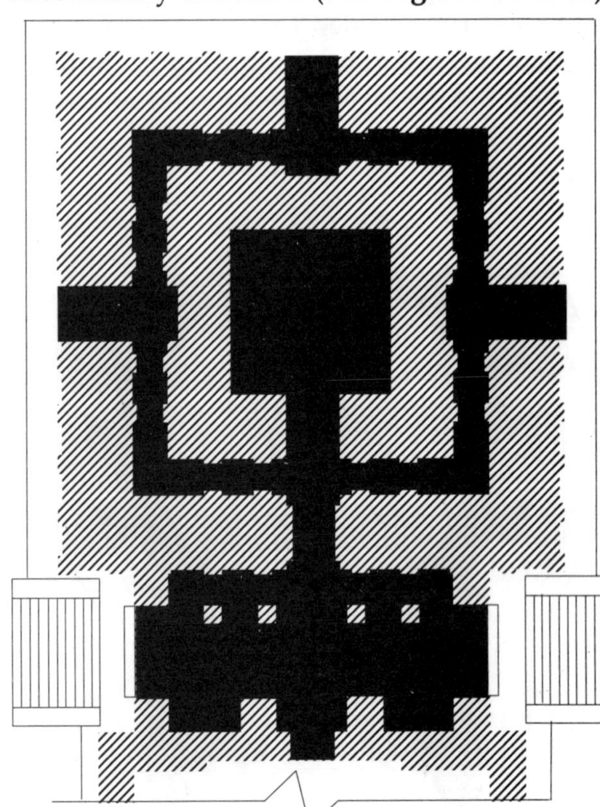

Figure 31: *Brihadeshvara Temple, Garbha-griha,* indication of internal space, Tanjore, India (1010 CE)

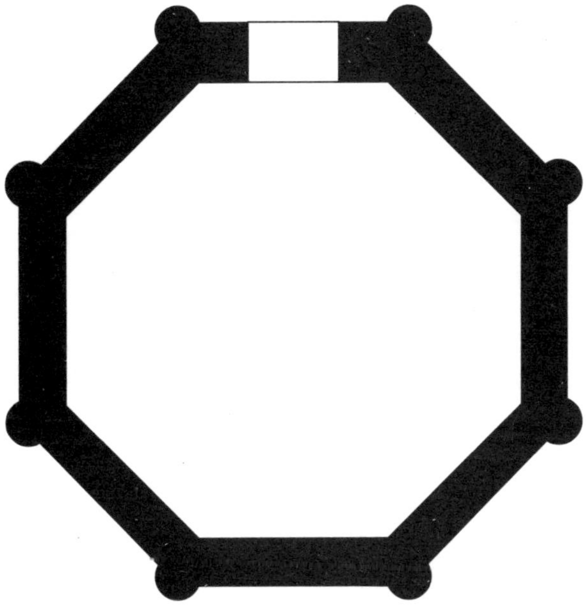

Figure 32: *Tomb Tower* (plan), Demavand, Iran (a. 1075)

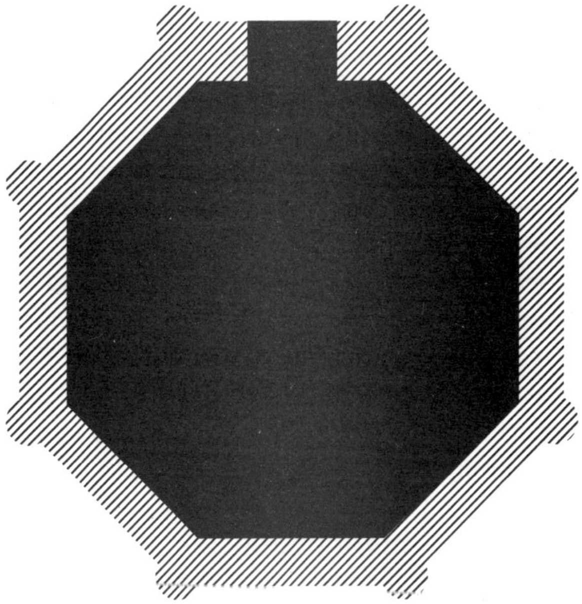

Figure 33: *Tomb Tower,* indication of internal space, Demavand, Iran (a. 1075)

This in part is due to the scale of the building and that the masonry roof was such as to be easily carried in this structure.

But, why a tower form? Certainly a tower is prominent! Some see them as decidedly phallic, which, of course, they are. They jut proudly upwards, asserting their presence and authority (See: **Figures 37**). However, high places or towers

Figure 34: *Gunbad-i-Kabus* (plan), Tomb of Kabus, Gurgan, Iran (1006-1107)

Figure 35: *Gunbad-i-Kabus,* indication of internal space, Tomb of Kabus, Gurgan, Iran (1006-1107)

had long been constructed in this area--e.g., the *ziggurats* of Sumeria, the high places of the Zoroastrians, and, later, the minaret of the *Great Mosque* at Samarra. Were they an attempt at scraping the celestial regions and thus gaining the attention of the Divine? Possibly. Were they attempts at gaining merit through the expenditure of funds and the employment of those less fortunate? Possibly. Were they an icon of wealth and status? Most certainly. Was there an iconic relationship to Islam in their plan? Also, most certainly in as much as the octagon and the number eight is seen as most auspicious to the Muslims.

A bit more impressive in scale and structurally interesting than the *Tomb Tower* at Demavand is the *Gunbad-i-Kabus, Tomb of Kabus,*

Figure 36: *Tomb Tower* (proportional elevation), Demavand, Iran

Figure 37: *Gunbad-i-Kabus,* Tomb of Kabus (proportional elevation), Gurgan, Iran

Gurgan, Iran. Whereas the bricks employed in the Demavand structure were low fired brick, those of the *Tomb of Kabus* are high fired. The conical roof upon its substantial shaft aggressively pierces, even invades the sky--an apt tomb form for the warrior Kabus. This tower would dwarf its modest Demavand counterpart in height. If it lacks the exquisite and varied design elements of the former it does so in favor of a simplified dodecagram with its sharp edges--most masculine! The star-like quality of the dodecagram serves two major purposes. First, the prism forms created are incredibly strong when bound together in this manner, allowing for the attainment of great height. Secondly, in an areas which is unremittingly hit during the long dry summers the angles allow for more shade and therefore less heat transmitted inside. Interestingly, however masculine the form may be, twelve is a feminine number. It is an auspicious cosmic numeral as well as a integer comprehending all numbers lower than itself. Its formation is also propitious (3 x 4 = 12, 5 + 7 = 12 and 6 + 6 = 12) and connotes the cosmic and is associated with the circle (12 x 30 = 360^0). Twelve denotes sacrifice and is related to immortality. Again, the internal space is impressive--far more than is required for a simple burial site. In diameter is over twice the size of its Demavand counterpart . The *Tomb of Kabus* is one of the rare few mausolea in which the circle is found as a major element.

The octagon was also utilized in other Islamic areas. The *Mausolea of Huand Hatun* at Kayseri, Turkey, makes use of this form (See: **Figure 38**). *En plan*, it is closely related to the *Tomb Tower* at Demavand, the later which preceded it by nearly two-hundred years. However, here small windows were place high up on seven of the eight walls, allowing light to filter in. In addition, the *Mausolea of Huand Hatun* was constructed of stone which allowed for a more daring utilization of space in comparison to the whole. Another interesting feature is the roof

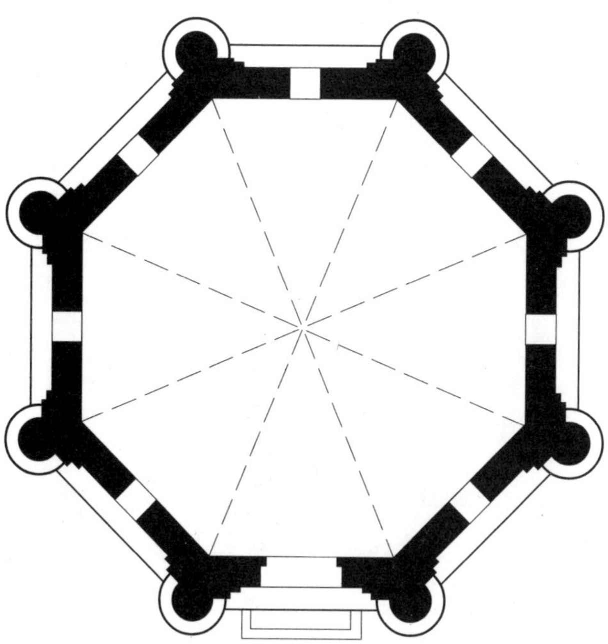

Figure 38: *Mausoleum of Huand Hatun* (plan), Kayseri, Turkey (1237-1238 CE)

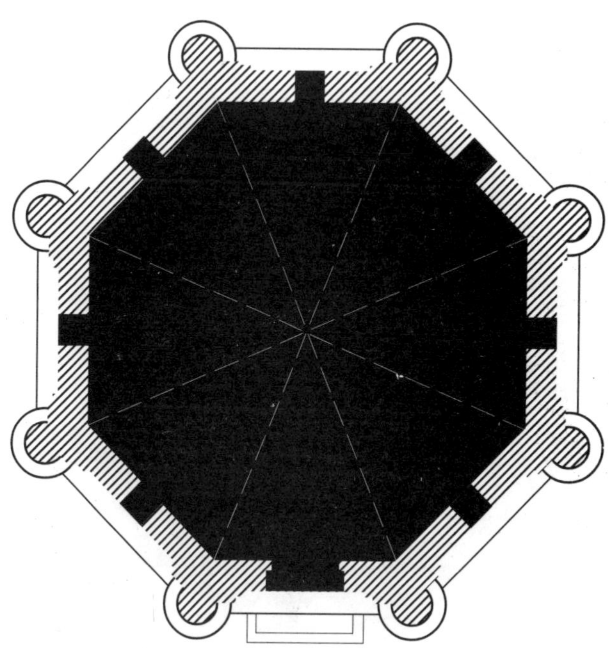

Figure 39: *Mausoleum of Huand Hatun*, indication of internal space, Kayseri, Turkey (1237-1238 CE)

form. It is not domed, but rather an eight sided conical form--a faceted variation, if you will, of the conical form seen at the *Gunbad-i-Kabus, Tomb of Kabus*. Here the engaged columns at the corners act as buttresses, supporting the roof structure. The engaged columns allow for a thinner wall and more internal space which would have been created to hold the sarcophagus of Huand Hatun (See: **Figure 39**). It is a mausolea of modest proportions, others, later tombs would dwarf the *Mausolea of Huand Hatun*.

The octagon was further the basis for the interesting *Doner Kumbet* of Kayseri. A massive square stone base rises from the earth, is transmuted by facets into an octagonal shape, from this base rises a form of sixteen sides and the inner space is circular--an architectural pantheon (See: **Figure 40**). Its internal space with its *mikhrab* is relative commodious (See: **Figure 41**). Are these numbers and their arithmetic progression of any significance--i.e., 4 + 8 (4 + 4) + 16 (4 + 4 + 4 + 4)? Eight, as the first cubed number (2^3), is deemed perfect, represents good fortune and is manifested in the ubiquitous eight-pointed star and the octagon. Sixteen, whose š is 4, is complete, propitious and signifies the balance of opposites. Unlike most Islamic tombs, the crypt, the burial chamber of the *Doner Kumbet* is not below ground level, but found within the massive, stone base. This merely indicates one of the many directions the Islamic tombs diverged. Finally, it relates closely to the *Tomb Tower* of Demavand as well as the *Gunbad-i-Kabus* of Gurgan in shape as it pierces the sky.

As seen in the enormous *Mausoleum of Oljeitu Hudabanda* at Sultaniya, the octagon was the preferred form employed as it was for other great tombs of West Central Asia, although here it takes on a decidedly aberrant form (See: **Figure 42**). There appears some confusion between the octagon and the square! Oljeitu (1294-1307), a descendent of the Great Khan, first conceived of this structure as a place of pilgrimage for the body of 'Ali, Nabi Mohammad's son-in-law, which he planned to move to Sultaniya. He was dissuaded and the nearly complete structure was then designated as his tomb.

Such a grand structure for a warrior king

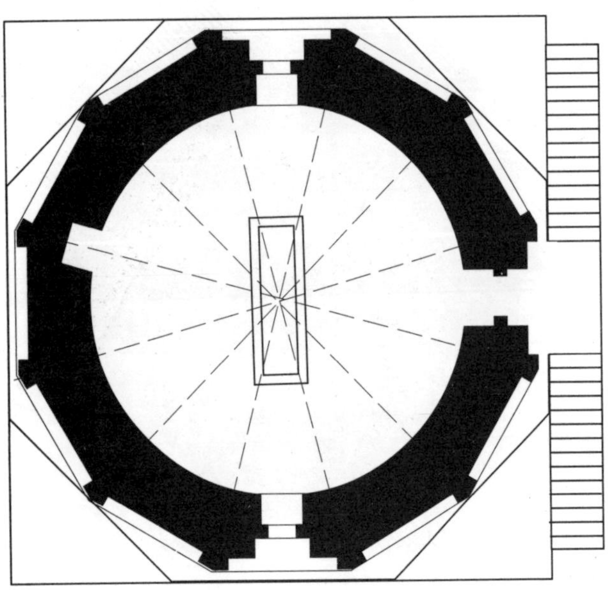

Figure 40: *Doner Kumbet* (*mausoleum*) (plan), Kayseri, Turkey (c. 1276 CE)

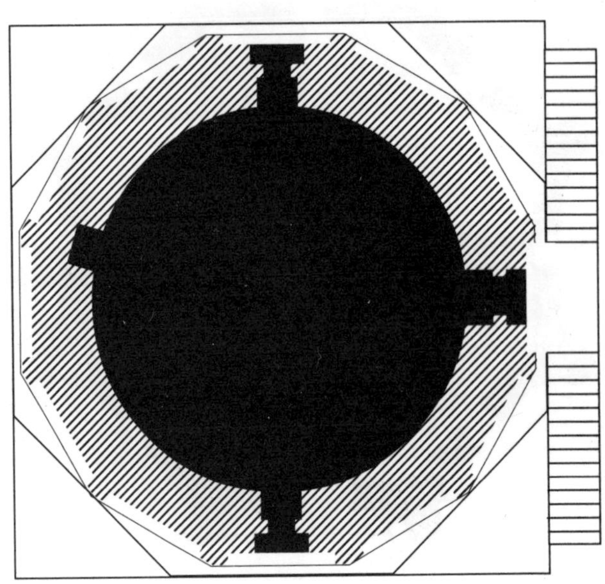

Figure 41: *Doner Kumbet* (*Mausoleum*), indication of internal space, Kayseri, Turkey (c. 1276 CE)

is not antithetical in Islam as it was not for Christian warrior kings. Whether Crusade or Jihad, the holy war and the holy warrior, the war of the conquest of the faith and the warrior who pursued that conquest possessed a laudatory position of some importance, but beneath that of a saint (Arab.: *awliya'*). A holy man, an *awliya'* possessed such spiritual power that it was believed that it transcended death and found its psychic center at the grave site of the saint. This idea of sacred power, this spiritual effervescence (Arab.: *baraka*) created numerous pilgrimages sites throughout the Islamic world. Is it little wonder, therefore, that tombs of warrior kings came to exhibit a grandeur heretofore unseen. In their attempt to effect not only their temporal position--i.e., their dynasty--but to attempt to materially affect their spiritual destiny they not so subtly assumed *baraka*.

Thick masonry walls enclose the lower regions and other areas of congregation (See: **Figure 43**). The massive dome is supported on equally massive pier-like forms created by negative spaces--i.e., the piercing of doorways and deep, equally proportioned niches. A rather anomalous extension is "added" forming a porch of dubious aesthetic worth. Nonetheless, it carries on the tradition of octagonal mausolea and a fit tomb for a descendent of the great Ghengis Khan. The soaring dome arches over a considerable space and is supported by massive

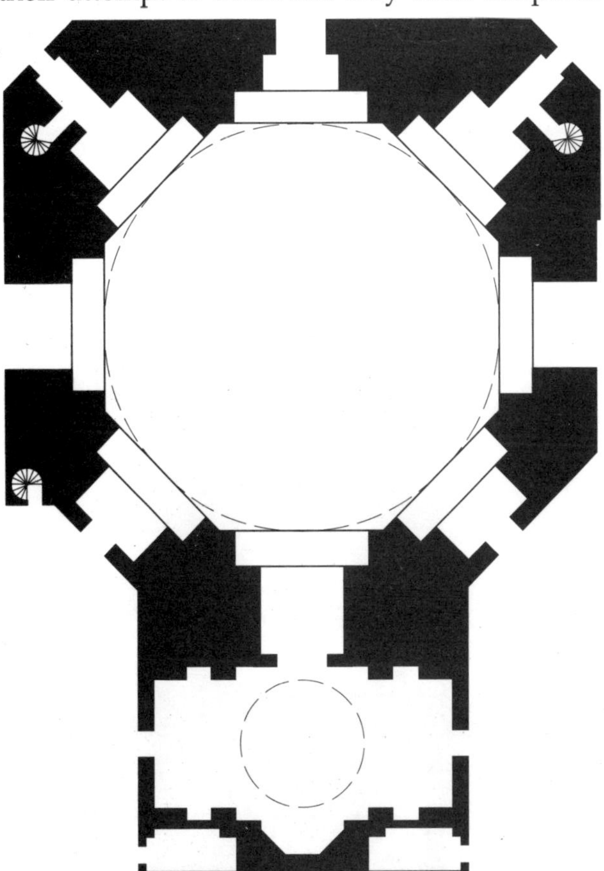

Figure 42: *Mausoleum of Oljeitu Hudabanda* (plan), Sultaniya, Iran (1304-1313 CE)

Figure 43: *Mausoleum of Oljeitu Hudabanda,* indication of internal space, Sultaniya, Iran (1304-1313 CE)

pier-like forms. The thickness of the masonry walls and the amount of enclosed space Not only refer to the greatness of Oljeitu Khan, but also because Sultaniya is an area that is relatively arid and very hot in the summer. These thick masonry walls would have offered respite from the heat to those who came to offer their respect to the deceased ruler.

Soon after the construction of the *Mausoleum of Oljeitu Hudabanda*, the *Tomb of Sultan Hasan* at Cairo was built. Rather than being based upon the octagon this mausoleum is square in shape and cubic in form (See: **Figure 44**). It shape, its internal space is reminiscent of the *Rock Tomb* at Beni Hasan (See: **Figure 7**) a far earlier tomb of this country and the *Tomb of the Samanids* (See: **Figure 26**). Mayhaps, Islamic tombs are more closely aligned with the predominant architectural forms of the particular area in which they are found than anything else. The *Tomb of Sultan Hasan* is attached to a *madrasah* of equal dimension. However, since the tomb is a square extension from an ostensibly flat, unadorned wall and due to its imposing dome, it dominates its surroundings--a fit tribute to a Sultan of no mean attainment. The walls are relatively thick, but the space is equally ample (See: **Figure 45**).

Cairo, during this time, was the premier city of Islam. Thousands came from all over the Islamic world to Cairo--it was second only to Mecca. The great buildings were awe inspiring and the pilgrims took back haunting memories of her obvious wealth and grandeur--a fit tribute to Islam. It is not, therefore, unseemly that the square plan would assume some importance. This square plan coupled with the predilection for the square in Hindu Indian architecture influenced greatly the plans of later mausolea in Muslim India.

One of the most interesting tombs, *en plan*, is the *Tughtabeg Khatun Tomb*, Urgench, Uzbekistan (See: **Figure 46**). Unlike any of the precedent mausolea heretofore considered the

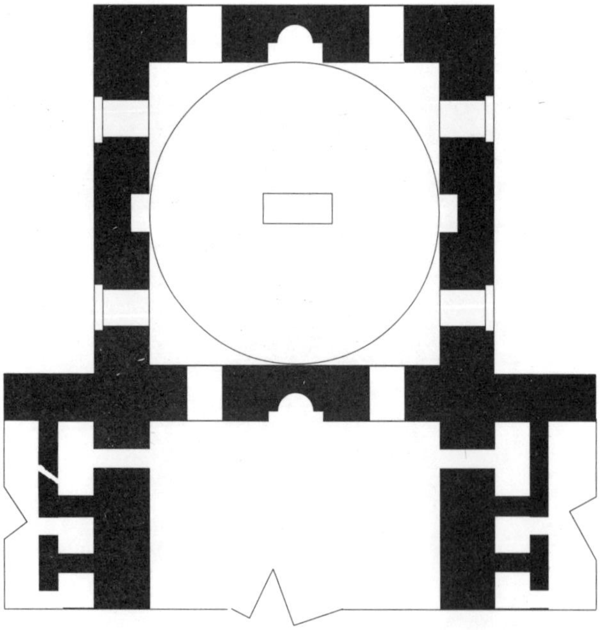

Figure 44: *Tomb of Sultan Hasan* (attached to Madrasah), Cairo, Egypt (1356-1363 CE)

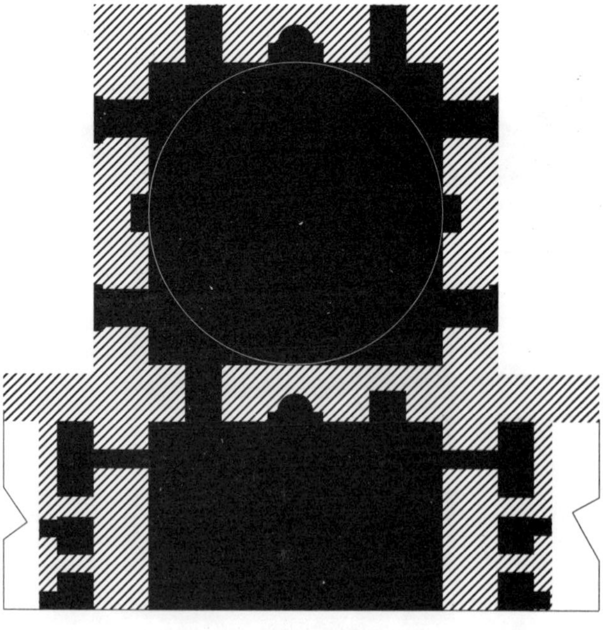

Figure 45: *Tomb of Sultan Hasan*, indication of internal space, Cairo, Egypt (1356-1363 CE)

Tughtabeg Khatun Tomb's interior is formed from a hexagon. On the other hand the exterior finds its geometric genesis in the dodecagon. Not only is this unusual combination employed, there are a series of indentions and piers set at the various angles correlated to both forms. Finally, the four exposed, exterior niches are formed from octagons. *En plan,* the effect is seen in a repeat of incredibly complex system of piers, more reminiscent of European Baroque or Rococo architecture than Fourteenth Century Islamic structures. A prominent vestibule extends to the front and faced with a tall, narrow *pishtaq* frequently encountered in other Central Asian Islamic buildings, thereby, extending the internal space (See: **Figure 47**). An apse-like extension at the rear is capped by a small dome mirroring the central dome which sits upon a tall drum. A final derivation that is to be seen in the *Tughtabeg Khatun Tomb* is in the fact that it is strictly and resolutely axial, rather than cross axial as most Islamic mausolea tend to be.

Again Turkey offers another example to follow the two previous from Kayseri. Referred to as: "The Green Tomb" or the *Tomb of Mehmet I,* it presents yet another variation. Closely related to *Mausoleum of Huand Hatun* in plan, it indicates an interesting variation (See: **Figure 48**). The

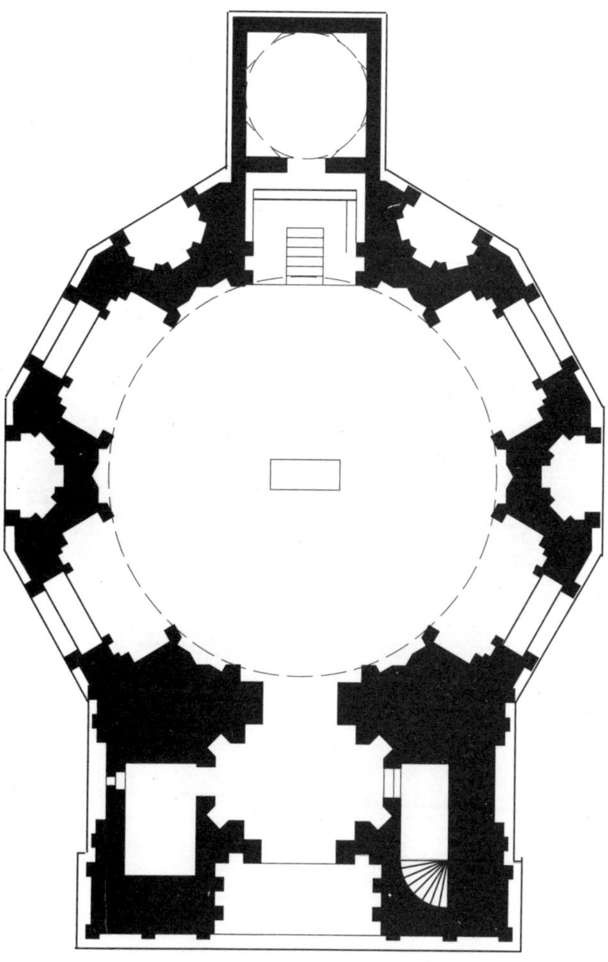

Figure 46: *Tughtabeg Khatun Tomb*, Urgench, Uzbekistan (c. 1370 CE)

Figure 47: *Tughtabeg Khatun Tomb*, indication of internal space, Urgench, Uzbekistan (c. 1370 CE)

elevation indicates an octagonal plinth rising from the larger octagon of the main form. From this plinth a dome appears, the majority of the hemisphere is hidden within this form. Nonetheless, it bears to the preference of the octagon as a form for mausolea within the Islamic world as well as the variations that are practised even on as modest a tomb in size and scale as the *Tomb of Mehmet I* with its ample interior (See: **Figure 49**).

After the Islamic armies from the north and west had invaded and assumed power in the northern part of India, there appeared an interesting tomb form referred to as the *Indo-Islamic Canopy Tomb* (See: **Figure 50**). It appears to be an adaptation of Hindu preference and Islamic necessity. Doubtless, the invaders recognized the engineering and architectural quality of the indigenous Hindu and employed them in the design and construction of these early Muslim tombs in and around Delhi. The conclusion to this fortuitous amalgamation was a tomb which was square, *en plan*, with an arcade of columns supporting an octagonal transition topped with a pseudo-dome. The square base bears obvious reference to the Hindu predilection. The octagonal transition with the pseudo-dome atop is obviously Islamic in influence. This compromise also allowed for the space that the Islamic Mughals required (See: **Figure 51**).

As the Mughals imposed themselves upon Northern India, one finds that the plans of the Islamic mausolea in India tended to be square. They possess an applied or implied octagon as well as circles and domes as secondary

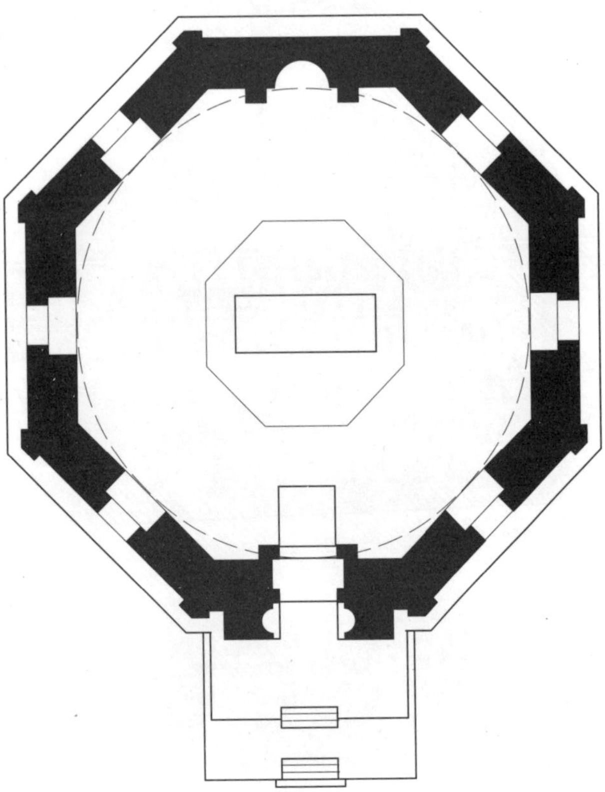

Figure 48: *Tomb of Mehmet I*, Bursa, Turkey (c. 1421 CE)

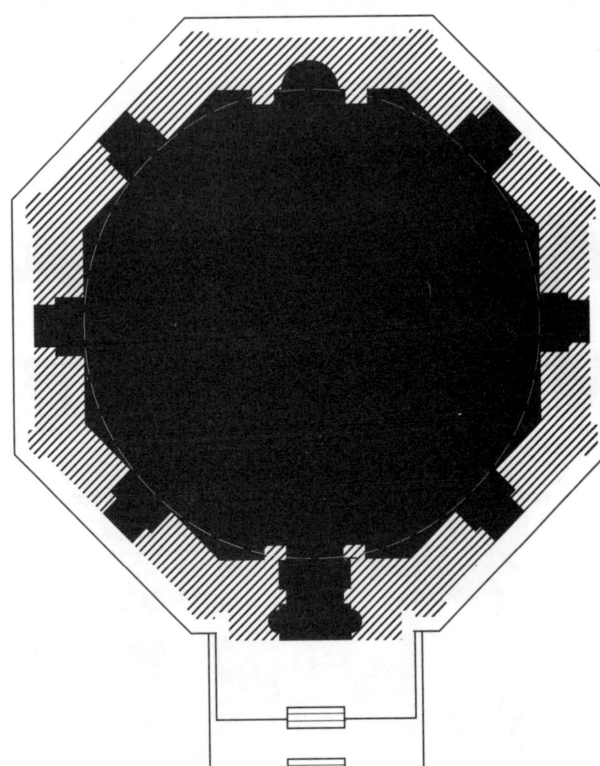

Figure 49: *Tomb of Mehmet I*, indication of internal space, Bursa, Turkey (c. 1421 CE)

or supporting elements. In elevation, the dome was most prominent. This can be seen again and again throughout the vast subcontinent that was ruled by Islamic sultans and emperors. To be a bit descriptive and subjective, it was as if the Mughals utilized the Hindu skin, muscles and bones, but dressed the structure in Muslim raiment.

The octagon and dome may have been important forms, *en plan* and elevation. However, more notable within the Indo-Islamic tombs and Mughal mausolea is the abundance of space. Architecture has been defined, in part, as the art of enclosing space. When the space--interior space--of the Hindu temples is considered, one thing becomes imminently clear to all--space is minimal at best. When comparing the proportion of interior space to the masonry mass, the interior space is much less, in proportion. An example is the *Brahmeshvara Temple* of Bhuvaneshvar in Orissa (See: **Figure 52**). Not only is the internal area subservient to the masonry mass, there is virtually no fenestration. The only light allowed into the interior filters in via the narrow door way.

The same is true when considering Buddhist temples as well, although to a somewhat lesser degree. The *Ananda Temple* of Pagan, Burma (Myanmar) (a. 1105 CE) is as apt an example as any (See: **Figure 53**). Here the interior consists of a number or encircling passageways (Indic: *pradakshinapatha*) with even narrower connecting passages. The only areas of greater volume, in proportion, are the four vestibules. Again, within the *Ananda Temple* as in the *Brahmeshvara Temple* internal illumination is minimal at best. The *Ananda Temple* does, however, possess a number of narrow windows along the outer ambulatory (*pradakshinapatha*), but the light that is allowed to filter into the four sanctuaries is only the smallest amount.

When one compares the internal space of the Indo-Islamic or Mughal mausolea, or, for that matter, any of the Islamic mosques of India, one thing becomes obvious and apparent--the greater

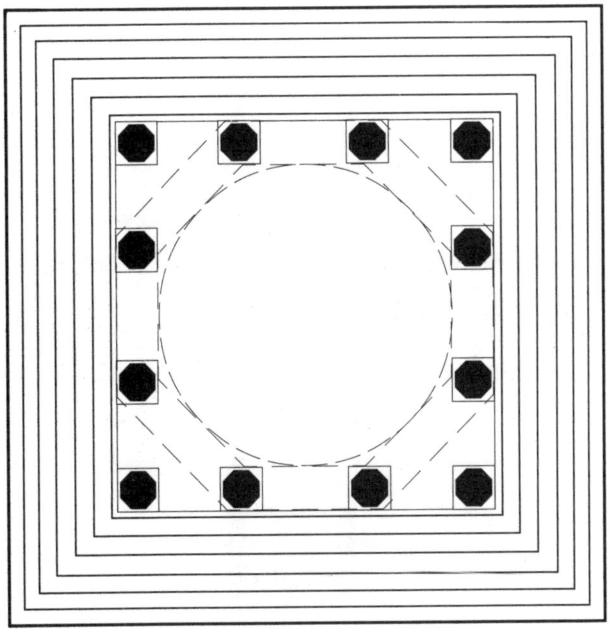

Figure 50: *Indo-Islamic Canopy Tomb* (plan) (13th C. CE)

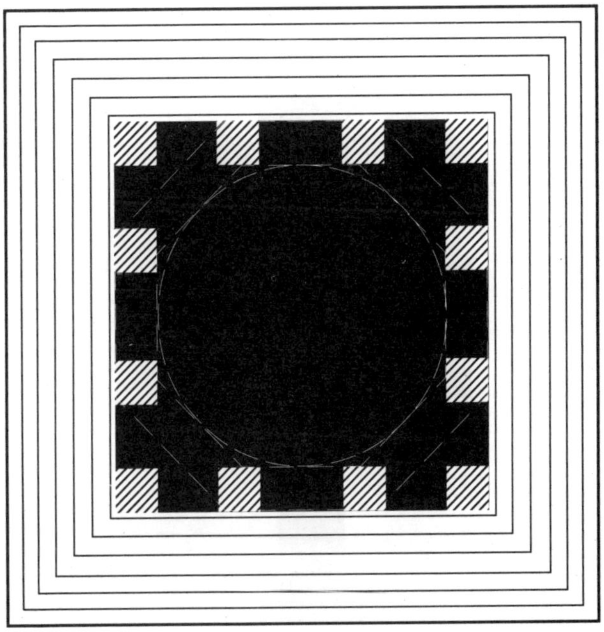

Figure 51: *Indo-Islamic Canopy Tomb,* indication of internal space(13th C. CE)

amount of internal space available. This is evident in the mosques (See: **Figure 54**) as well as in the mausolea (See: **Figure 55**) of the Great Mughals. The predilection, the need, the requirement for larger space, may, in part, be due to the congregational requirement of Islam as opposed to the more individual attendance of Buddhism and the Hindu faith.

Finally, a brief mention must ba made with regard to the role geometry played in the desigh of Islamic architecture, and specificaly tombs. Numerous scholars have commented on the apparent geometric basis for much of the architecture.[8] Geometry, in the Muslim world was viewed with respect and lauded. Architects, on the other hand, were not so honored. Yet architects and geometricians regularly consorted. Theoretical geometrical treatises were written dealing with their application to architecture. However, basic handbooks or design treatises--i.e., the Hindu *Mahamata* or *Mayamatam*--were not written, or if they were, none are known to be extant. Nonetheless, it seems apparent that certain geometric principles must have been employed in the design of certain structures (See: **Figure 56**).[9]

"Of the major world religions Hinduism and Buddhism are two which tend to be non-congregational. (The) . . . regular--i.e., daily or weekly--established or required gatherings of the devout, *en masse*, is not a prerequisite for belonging. The gathering together, the congregating of Christians on Sunday, or of the Muslims on Friday is not practised by these two

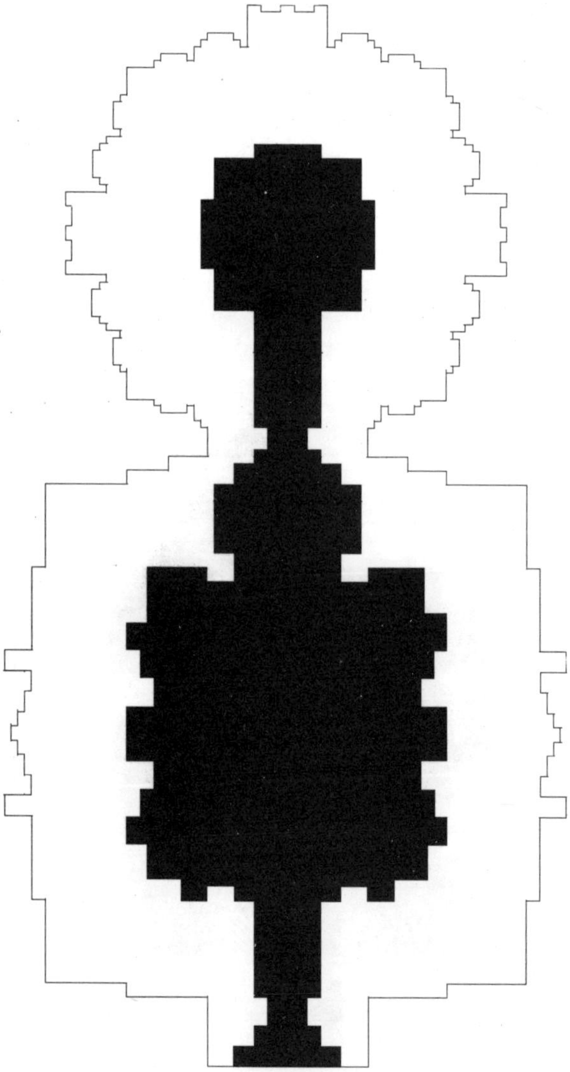

Figure 52: *Brahmeshvara Temple*, Bhuvaneshvar, Orissa (1075 CE), indication of internal space

Figure 53: *Ananda Temple*, Pagan, Burma (Myanmar)(a. 1105 CE), indication of internal space

faiths. Rather, it is the individual's worship, in what ever mode he or she sees fit, at regular intervals that are convenient which is the norm. When one visits a Hindu or Buddhist shrine, one becomes aware of the constant comings and goings of devotees, particularly during the daylight hours. There are exceptions: there are various festivals or holy days on which masses may gather at a particular locale to worship. However, for both of these faiths it is possible to worship any time, or any place--the emphasis is placed upon the individual."[10]

One cannot consider the possible indigenous Hindu influence upon the Islamic mausolea without considering one of the basic Hindu plan considerations--the *mandala*. "The place and role of the *mandala* in Buddhist and Hindu architecture is central and paramount. It is the conceptual and real foundation from which each and every ecclesiastical structure is based. Unlike Christianity which utilized the cruciform plan, with its numerous variations,[11] for its major liturgical structures--e.g., cathedrals, basilicas, abbeys, etc.--but not always in lesser churches. The Buddhists and Hindus invariably employed the *mandala*. To conceive of and/or to construct a temple or shrine without the prime consideration of a *mandala* was absolutely antithetical to their beliefs. . . .

"A magic circle/*mandala* . . . based on the cardinal and intercardinal points resembles closely the circular *Manduka Mandala* . . . .

"At the core of the architectural designed *mandala* is the *Vastu-purusha Mandala* . . . . The term *Vastu-purusha* is defined as existence.[12] Therefore, in its most simplified sense, the *Vastu-purusha Mandala* refers to the 'form of existence.' However, this existence does not refer to the material world, but the higher realms.

"It is manifested in the square. The square

Figure 54: *'Pearl Mosque,' Red Fort,* Delhi (a. 1658 CE)

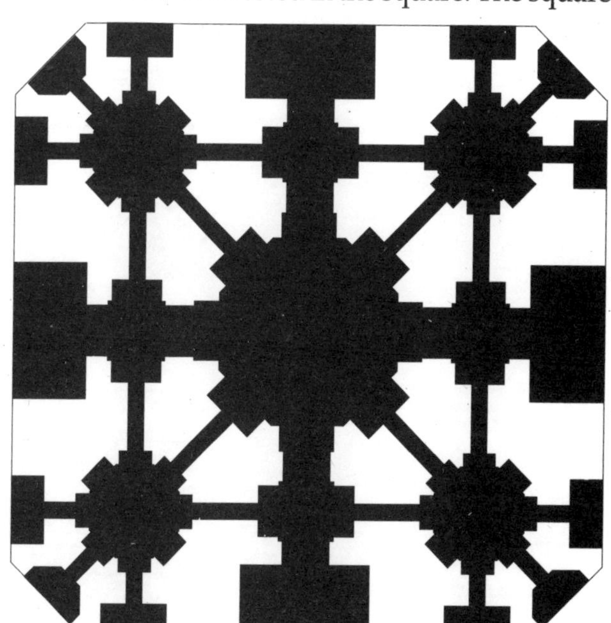

Figure 55: *Taj Mahal, Tomb of Hazrat Mumtaz-uz-Zamani,* indication of internal space

is considered by the Hindu to be a perfect, immutable form and a physical manifestation of the *mandala*. The square represents The Ultimate, The Absolute of a higher level. The earth in it physical form is represented as a circle, however, if it is a representation of *Brahma*, as opposed to *Brahmá* (or the Lord *Brahmá*), then it is represented by a square and oriented on the cardinal points of the compass. The term *purusha* specifically refers to male form. . . . [13]

"When a *mandala* is chosen and used to lay out a structure there are numerous other considerations. For example, the intersecting lines of the *mandala*, particularly those of the

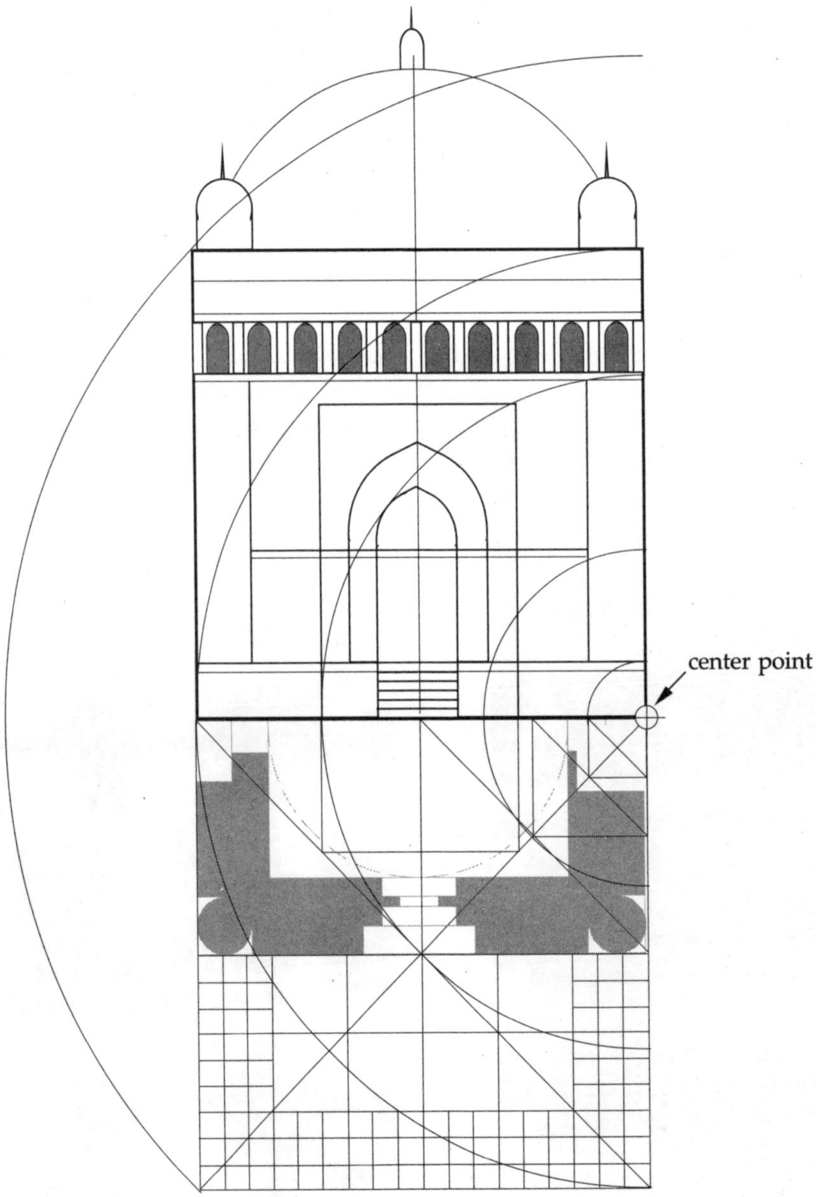

Figure 56: *Proportional Geometric System,* applied to, *Tomb of the Samanids,* Bukhara, Uzbekistan (c. 920 CE)

central area occupied by *Brahmá*, may not be crossed or interrupted by those of the structure . . . . . This is considered not only inauspicious but will result in poor design. Various geometric forms are employed in the design of a temple--i.e., circles, triangles. . . . ."[14]

The assurance of an afterlife, dwelling in Paradise was one of the tenets of the Islamic faith that found manifestation in the here and now. The raising of a mausoleum within a paradisal garden (*chahar bagh*) and accompanied by a *serai* or mosque acted as a transition point. A three part cosmological environment. The *serai* services the living and acknowledges the senses. The garden hints with its theological promise at Paradise. The mausoleum "protect(s) the grave and ensure(s) the perpetuation of the historical fact committed to its care."[15]

Within its adopted environment the Mughals constructed some of the most magnificent and varied mausolea the world has seen. Nowhere else have so many monuments, houses, palaces for the dead been raised which mirror, extol the occupants greatness for all to see and, therefore, to honor, than in Mughal India.

Figure 57: *The Ten Companions of Muhammad* (calligraphic design within an octagon), Egypt (c. 18th C. CE)

The Tombs

Tomb No. 36

Delhi, a. 1230 C.E.

Tomb No. 36[16] at Delhi exemplifies the earlier Indo-Islamic mausolea in as much as it embodird the requirements of established and preexistent Islamic tombs with the architectural milieu of Hindu India--a pre-Mughal adaptation. This tomb appears to be more closely identified with the Mediterranean area as it carries on the tradition seen as early as the *Temple of the Palace of Diocletian, San Vitale,* and the *Tomb Tower* at Demavand.

It is a simple, thick octagonal mass of masonry, thicker than the octagonal bulk of the *Tomb Tower* at Demavand, and possessing a square inner space with eight niches--i.e., a modified **Type D-c** basic plan. This interior harkens more to the Hindu predilection for the square than does the outlines of exterior plan--the octagon (See: **Figure 58**). Stierlin refers to this arrangement as: ". . . primarily a square with sloping corners or as octagonal with niches in the interior making it look square."[17] This seems like a superfluous observation. The transition from the square interior to the octagonal exterior seem like a clear transition. After all, the Renaissance was consumed with squaring the circle or circling the square--a far more difficult transition.

On all eight sides of the exterior are openings pierced into the face. Four serve as vestibules with passageways leading to the inner space, and four are deep porches, formed from octagons with niches in two of the surfaces. Within the square inner space a sixteen-sided form serves as a transition from the square to the surmounting dome.

The thickness of the masonry and the square interior space indicates the strong debt to the Hindu precursors--e.g., the *Shiva Temple,* Indore; the *Brihadeshvara Temple,* Tanjore; and the *Brahmeshvara Temple,* Bhuvaneshvar. When comparing the ratio of mass to space in the *Tomb No. 36* to later Indo-Islamic mausolea--e.g., the *Tomb of Sultan Iltutmish,* the *Tomb of Ghiyas-ud-din Tughluq I,* or the *Tomb of Sher Shah*--one is aware of the substantial employment of thick masonry. Certainly, this direction is not

Figure 58: *Tomb No. 36*: indication of internal space

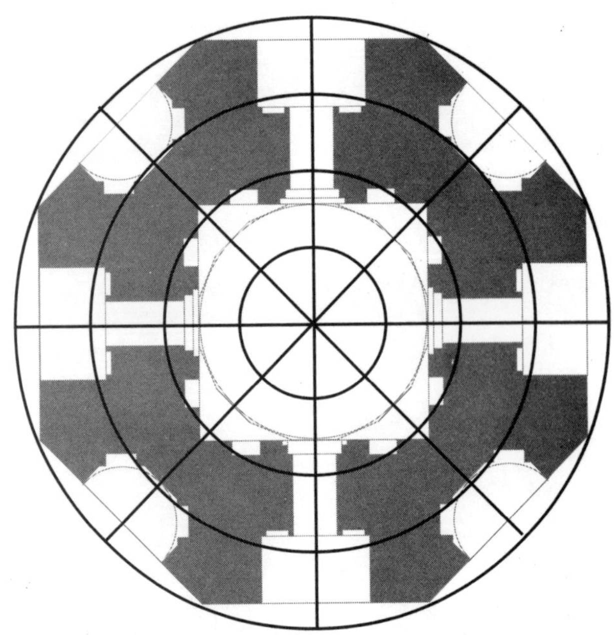

Figure 59: *Tomb No. 36*: application of a circular *Manduka Mandala*

Plate 1
Tomb No. 36 (Plan)

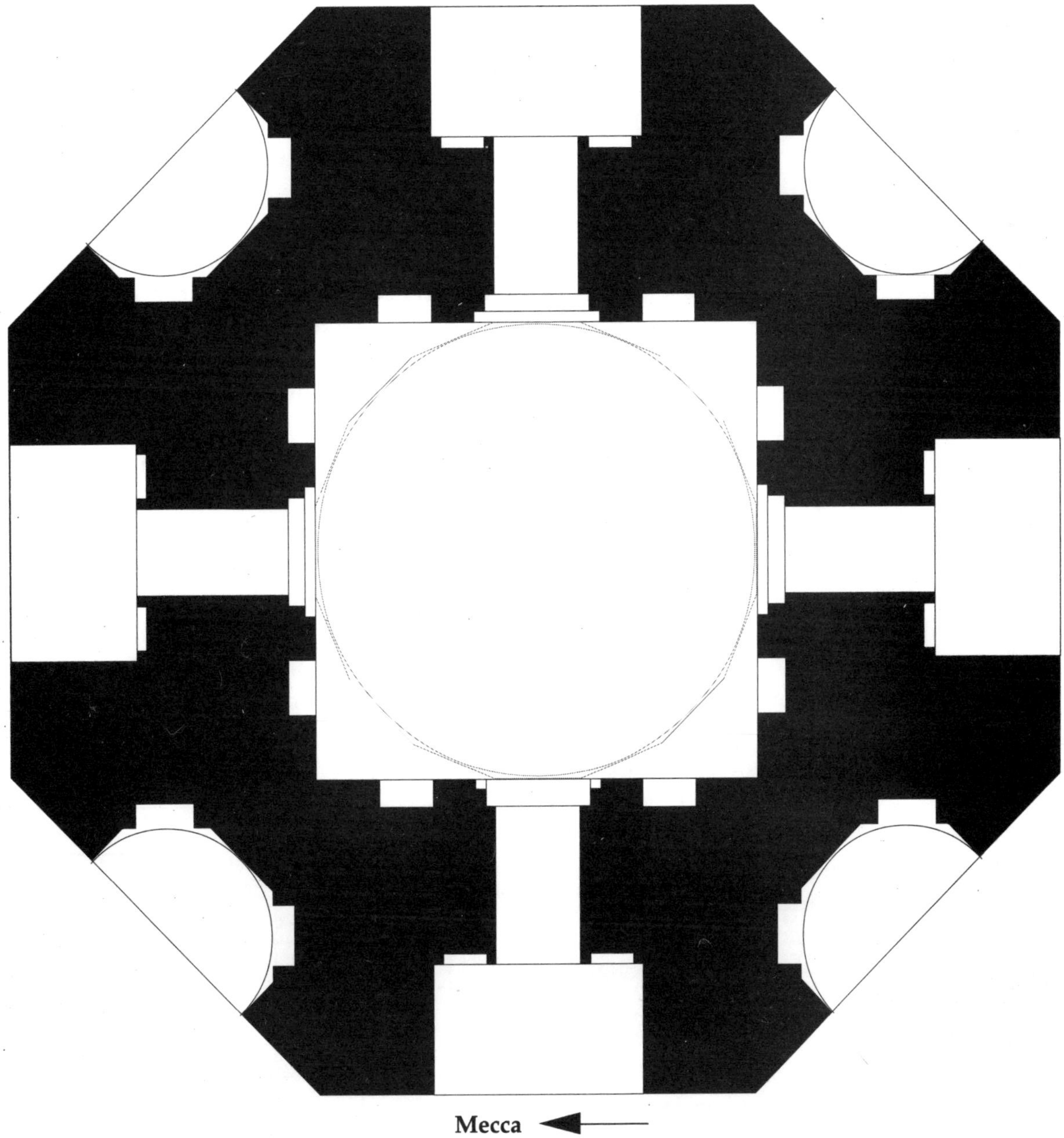

necessarily a structural demand. Rather, it appears to be employed more as a means of keeping the interior somewhat cooler--a typical Hindu consideration in the hot Indian subcontinent.

The thick walls coupled with the relatively narrow passageways restricts the amount of light that is allowed into the inner volume of space. Although the theological concept of the *garbha-griha*--the womb--is not part of the Islamic theology, the cave did play an important part as a space of renewal and protection. Certainly a tomb, a mausolea is womb-like in that it is the receptacle for the body of the deceased, but, Islamic tombs, as their mosques, were more apt to be flooded with light as a requirement of a congregational religion.

Although the imposition of a *mandala* upon a Muslim structure would appear diametrically opposed to the precepts of Islam, the fact that the construction of the tomb took place within a predominantly Hindu country is of importance. Doubtless, the ruling Muslim elite would have readily deferred to the indigenous and practiced builder/architects. Of course, Islamic requirements and precepts would have been strictly required and maintained--e.g., orientation towards Mecca and the eschewal of any form that might refer to other major religion as a cruciform might do. Nonetheless, the circular *Manduka Mandala* does offer some interesting parallels for consideration (See: **Figure 59**). The outer ring encloses the octagon comfortably, as one would expect. What begins to pique one's interest is that the second circle touches the inner surface of the four, radiating , outer porches. The third circle is closely associated with the inner square space and the eight rectangular niches which flank the passageways. The inner circle encloses the space where the body was laid in a crypt beneath the main floor--a pseudo sarcophagus appearing on the main floor establishing two tiered arrangement typical of Islamic tombs.

The elevation of this tomb (See: **Plate 2**) indicates a rather low, substantial form with a shallow dome. If a square, the width of the whole, is superimposed over the elevation, it is noted that the octagonal structure accounts for virtually half of the height of the square and with the dome the height accounts for a bit more than a three-quarters of the square. Not a monumental tomb, it, nonetheless, appears to be a standard that is followed during the early years of Islamic India.

It is to be noted that the block of the structure, minus the dome and its octagonal drum is within the lower half of the *Deshiya Mandala* (See: **Figure 60**). In addition, the second and third file enfolds the angled niches while the middle two bracket the portal form. Therefore, the proportion is 12:9.25.

The utilization of indigenous artisans in the design and construction of the tomb was a fortuitous cross fertilization. It presaged what was to come.

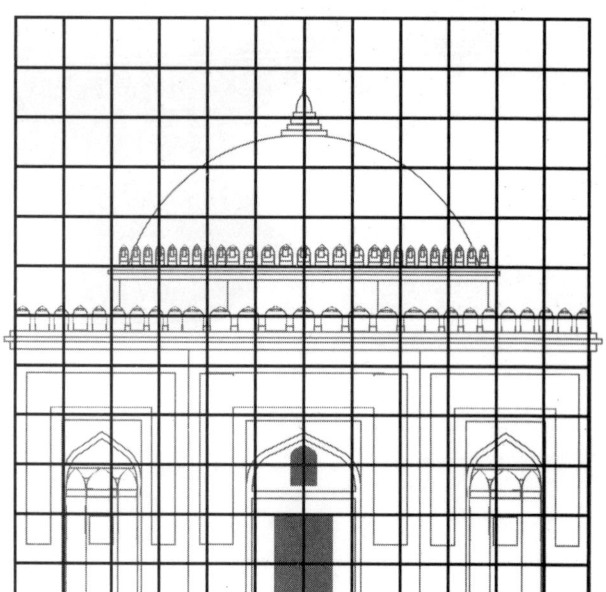

Figure 60: *Tomb No. 36* , application of a *Deshiya Mandala* over the elevation

Plate 2
Tomb No. 36, Delhi (Elevation & half plan)

Tomb of Sultan Ghari

Delhi, 1231 C.E.

Nasir-ud-Din Muhammad died in 1228 while his father, Sultan Shams-ud-din Iltutmish, still sat on the throne at Delhi. The *Tomb of Sultan Ghari* (Sultan of the Cave) is so named because the crypt, minus the covering *kiosk*, which has since disappeared, plus the enclosure is all that remains of the whole. The crypt, the cave, the *ghari* extends beneath the floor of the platform and only the raised outline of what may have been the pavilion--i.e.podium--remains. The total appears to be far more elaborate than the subsequent tomb of his father, the Sultan Iltutmish (See: following, *Tomb of Sultan Iltutmish*) and some say that it is the first Islamic tomb of the Delhi Sultanate. Certainly, it is the first tomb of monumental mien.

The *Tomb of Sultan Ghari*[18] is not a mere mausoleum as is *Tomb No. 36.* It, on the other hand, incorporates a prayer area complete with a *qibla* and a *mikhrab* within its own domed enclosure and is mimicked in its external aspect by the *Kalan Masjid* in Delhi of 1380.[19] The tomb of Nasir-ud-Din Muhammad adjacent to a mosque or within a prayer area paralleled the predilection of numerous rulers and men of high status to entrust their earthly remains to a monastery or church where constant prayers would somehow bring additional merit to the deceased. This is an honored practice amongst Christian Monarchs--e.g., the fabulous *El Escorial* outside Madrid, and *S. Denis* outside Paris, and *Westminster Abbey,* London. It is understandable that it would be the choice of Islamic rulers as well. It also appeared to be a reinterpretation of the Roman belief that immortality rested in ones greatness and the constant retelling of one's accomplishments and/or the construction of a suitable edifice to remind future generations of the deceased. There may also be an implication of a type of *baraka* that was not all together spiritual but a variety that merited association.

The enclosed area of the tomb is considerable as befits a tomb-cum-*masjid* or *surau*--i.e., a **Type C-a** basic plan. Even the crypt

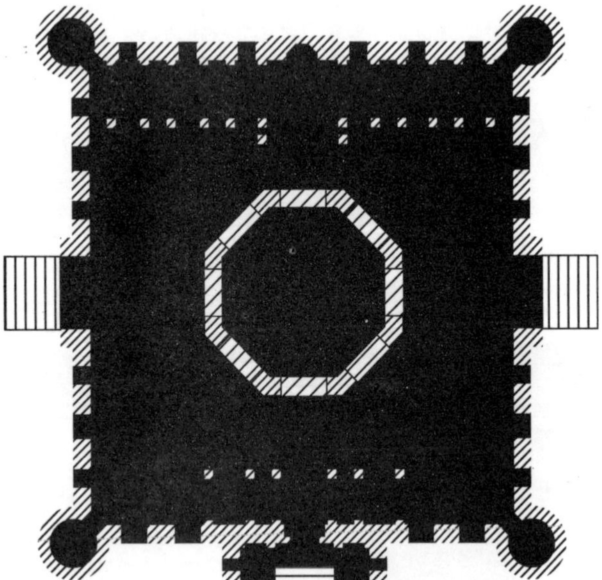

Figure 61: *Tomb of Sultan Ghari*: indication of internal space

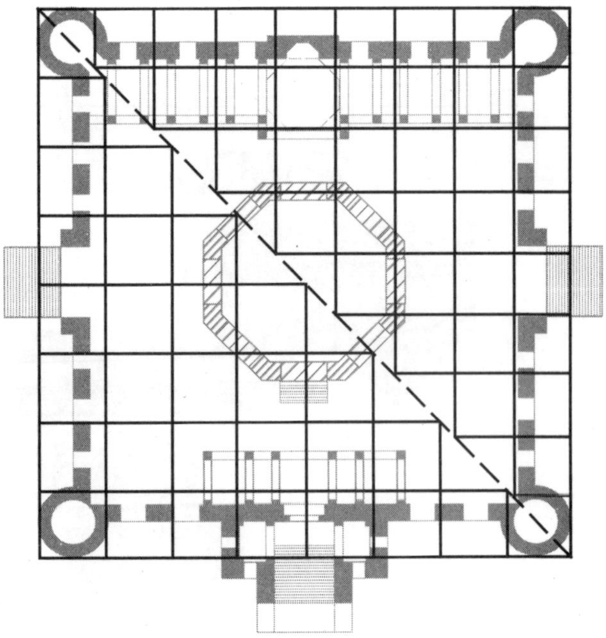

Figure 62: *Tomb of Sultan Ghari,* application of *Manduka* and *Paramashayika Mandala*

Plate 3
Tomb of Sultan Ghari (Plan)

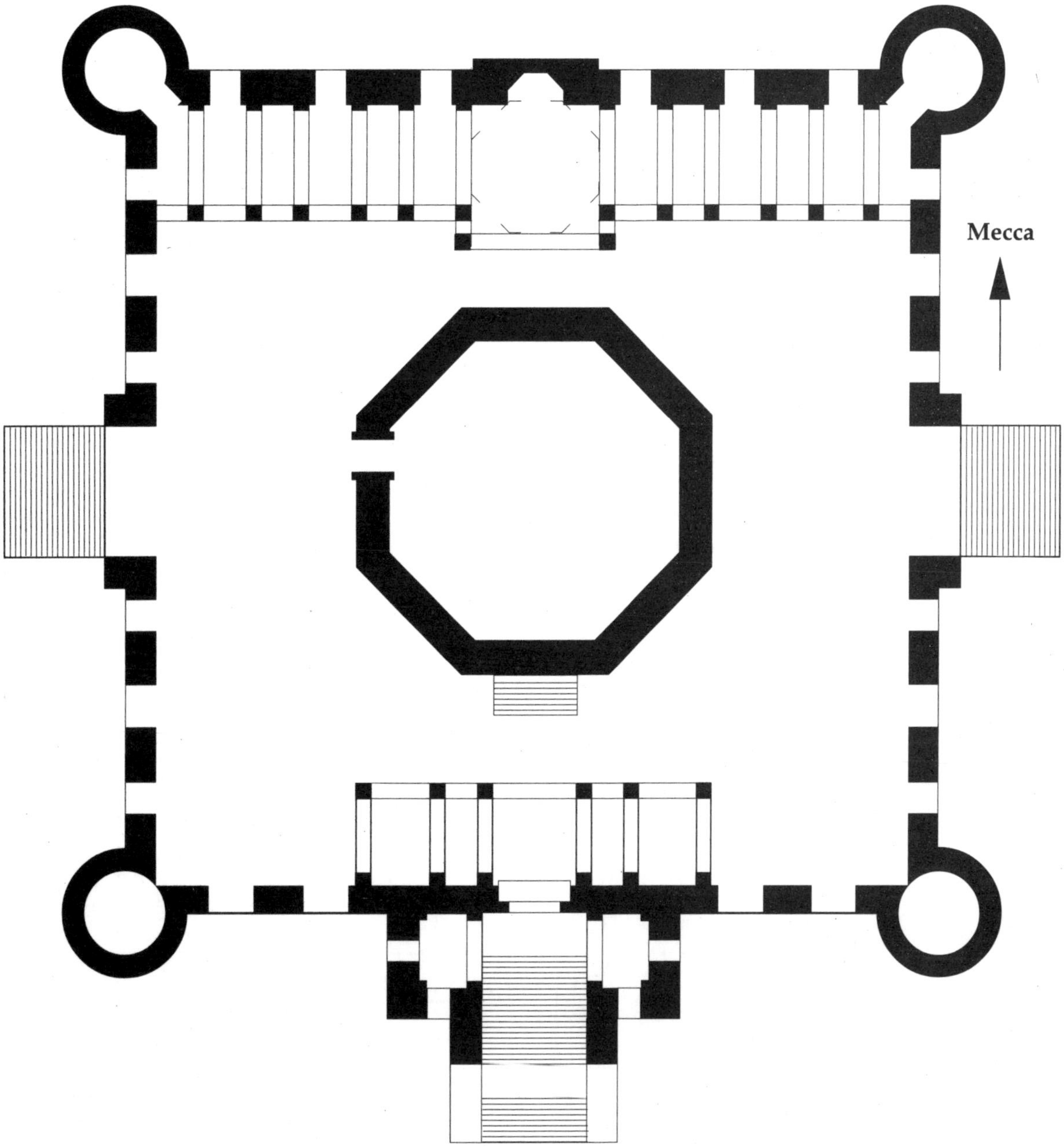

Tomb of Sultan Ghari (Continued)

area, enclosed as it is in the mass of the tomb, is commodious (See: **Figure 61**).

The crypt, set below the floor of the enclosed structure, doubtlessly covered by a kiosk or pavilion, is octagonal in form--i.e., a **Type D** basic plan. The walled, fenestrated area, raised on a high platform possessed a monumental entry opposite the *qibla* and two additional entrances in the side walls. The whole had the look of a fortification--an approach that was followed by a number of the rulers of the Slave Dynasty.

The *Tomb of Sultan Ghari* unlike many later tombs does not possess a developed form over the vault. This, in itself, is of some interest. However, the missing *kiosk,* based upon the remaining platform and the crypt was octagonal. Therefore the application of either a *Manduka Mandala* or a *Paramashayika Mandala,* based on the square presents some problems when placed over the whole (See: **Figure 62**). The imposition of a circular *Manduka Mandala* is far more satisfactory. In this case the crypt is encircled by the *brahmásthana* (See: **Figure 63**).

The lower half of a *Deshiya Mandala* is applied to the elevation with significant results (See: **Figure 64**). The first rank of *pada* brackets the plinth on which the whole rests. The second and third rank enfold the encircling walls and the towers' mass, while the fourth identifies the limit of the entrance pavilion and the base of the dome. Therefore, it can be stated that the proportions are 12:4

This form--i.e., the square (in this case a 'near' square) with towers at the corners--will appear again and again in later Islamic tombs in India. It presents the impression of a fortified palace, an apt receptacle for the deceased.

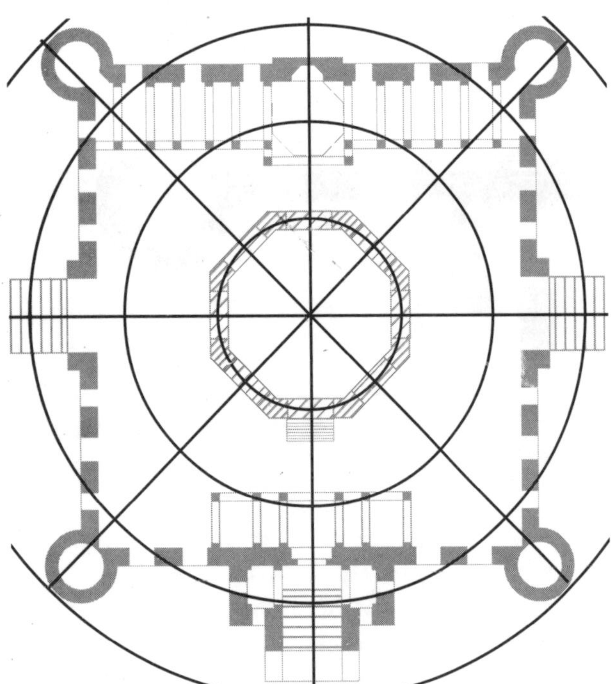

Figure 63: *Tomb of Sultan Ghari*: application of a circular *Manduka Mandala*

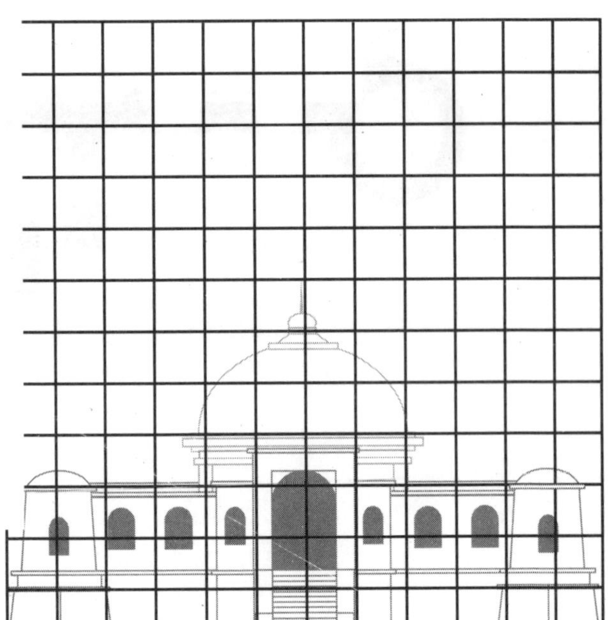

Figure 64: *Tomb of Sultan Ghari*, application of a *Deshiya Mandala* over the elevation

Plate 4
Tomb of Sultan Ghari (Elevation with proposed kiosk)

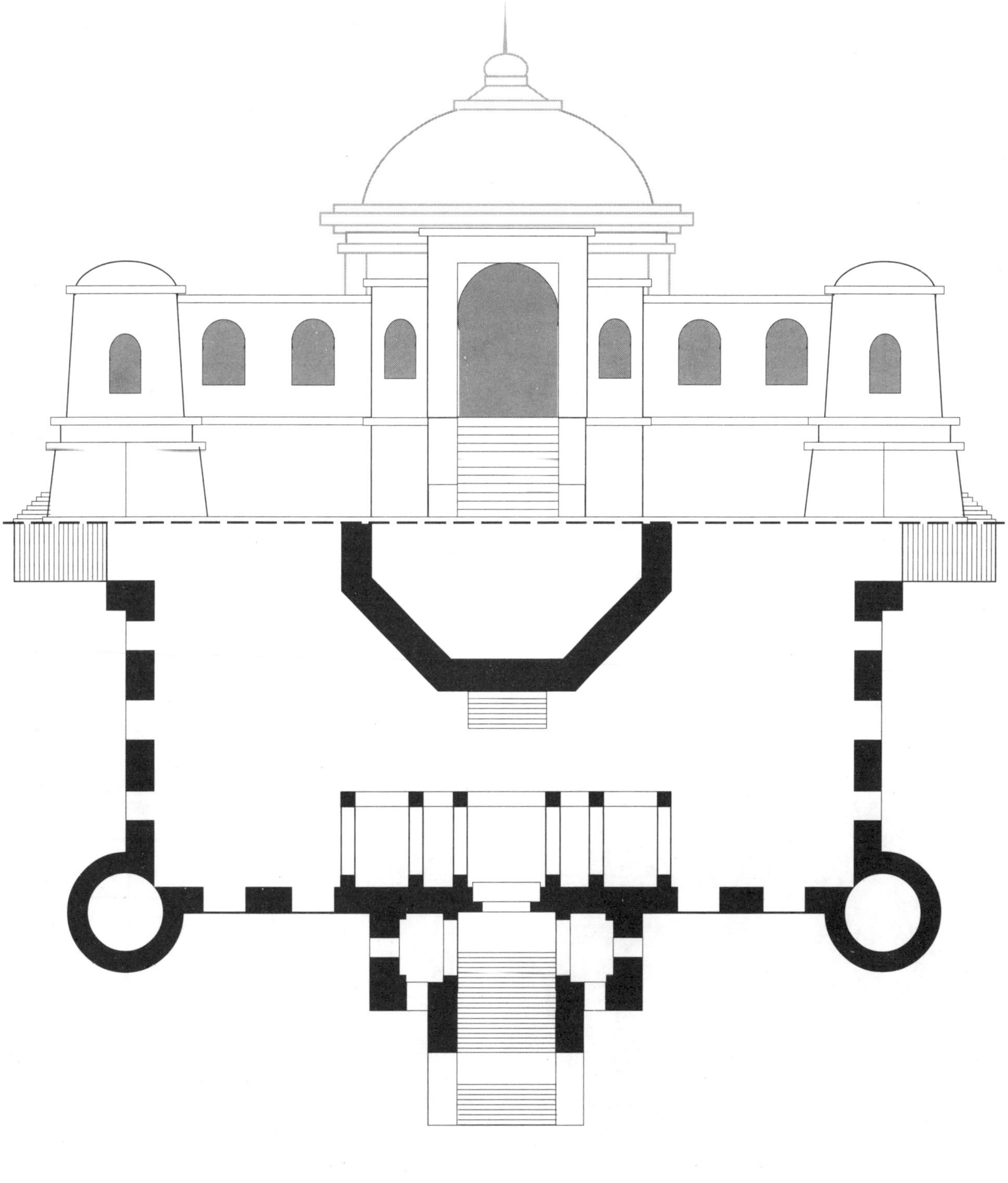

Tomb of Sultan Iltutmish

Delhi, 1235 C.E.

Often times referred to as the first monumental Islamic tomb in India, the tomb of the Sultan Shams-ud-din Iltutmish--aka:Abdul Muzaffar Altamsh--is small when compare to the later tombs and even insignificant in size when compared to the Mughal tombs. It is certainly less elaborate than the one he constructed for his son, Nasr al-Din Muhammad, called the *Tomb of Sultan Ghari*. The *Tomb of Sultan Iltutmish*[20] was constructed outside the west wall of the *Quwwat-ul-Islam*, it is dwarfed by the size of this mosque. It is said that the tomb was constructed by his daughter, Sultan Raziyah Begam after the first enlargement of the *Quwwat-ul-Islam* and was then placed at the northwest corner.[21] Again, the association of a mausoleum with a place of worship has been noted.

Unlike the octagonal *Tomb No. 36*, Iltutmish's tomb is square in shape with a square chamber--i.e., a **Type B** basic plan. This chamber is approximately two-thirds the size of the whole with three large doorways offering ingress to the interior. The ample portals allow a fair amount of light into the interior, unlike the narrow passage ways that are seen in *Tomb No. 36*. In addition, the walls, in proportion are not as thick as found in earlier tombs or in contemporary Hindu temples.

By way of transition from the square sepulchral chamber to the pointed dome are squinches, an early Sassanian solution to this problem. This was a technique that heretofore had not been in the repertoire of Indian/Hindu builders and they are seen as not altogether satisfactory. Nonetheless, this tomb may be seen as an adaptive transition of Hindu builders employed by Muslim masters. The dome is a true dome, not the corbelled "false dome" that had been employed earlier.

The comparative size of the sepulchral chamber is, likewise, a Hindu to Muslim transition. The interior space is ample in comparison to the whole (See: **Figure 65**).

In the west wall of the chamber, the *qibla*, are three niches. The central one is considerably larger an developed--a *mikhrab*. It does present

Figure 65: *Tomb of Sultan Iltutmish*, indication of internal space

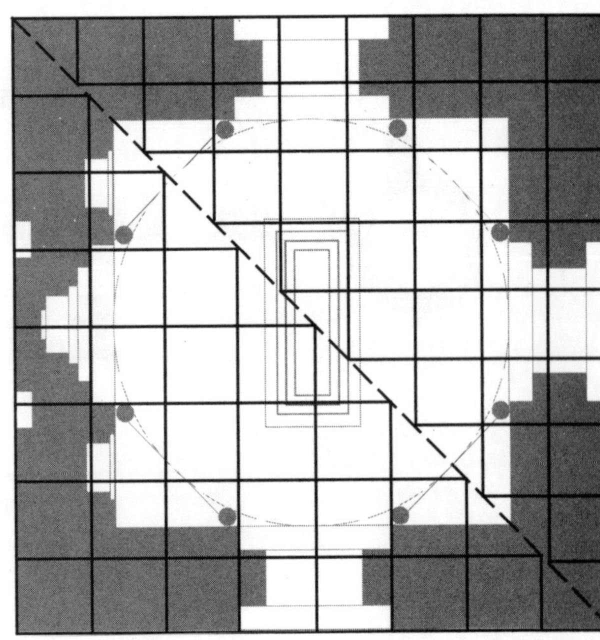

Figure 66: *Tomb of Sultan Iltutmish*, application of *Manduka* and *Paramashayika Mandala*

Plate 5
Tomb of Sultan Iltutmish (Plan)

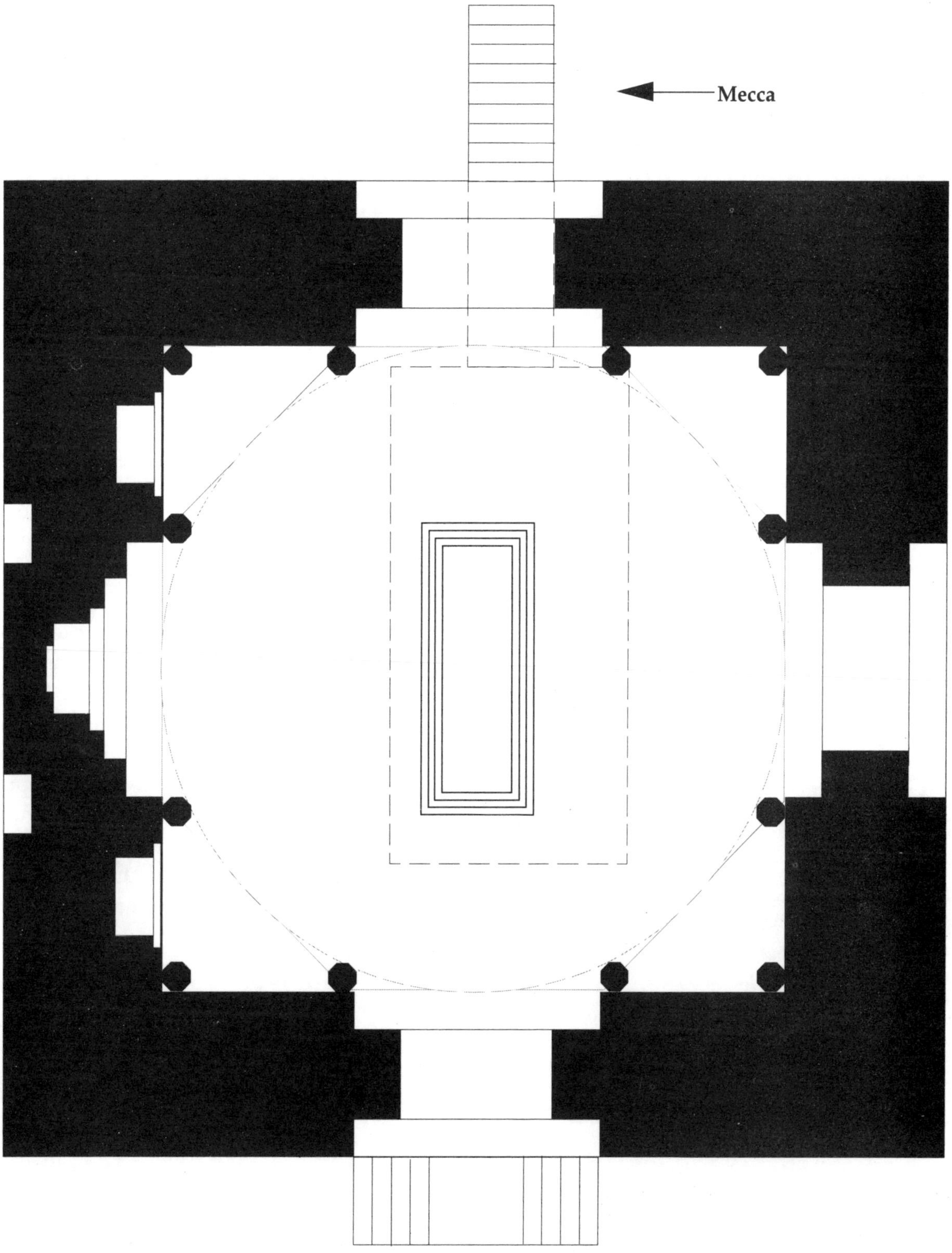

an interesting theological/philosophical problem. As stated, *Nabi Mohammed* railed against ostentatious tombs and sanctuaries, but did allude to the benefits gained from visiting the tombs of holy men. If there are going to be great numbers assembling, then, certainly there ought to be such structures as are big enough to house the pilgrims. Mayhaps, Sultan Iltutmish saw himself as one of illustrious enough character as to draw people to his tomb! Therefore, a chamber must be large enough to hold a number of people and one in which prayers may be offered to *Allah*.

Hindu builders employed the *mandala* in the design of all their structures. It is not untoward that they would have done the same in this case as well. But, when comparing either a *Manduka Mandala* or the *Paramashayika Mandala*, the two preferred *mandalas* for Hindu temples, neither seems to be adequate in this tomb (See: **Figure 66**). However, it must be noted that in neither of these two *mandalas* are the *marmas* violated when placed over the plan! This is of prime importance.

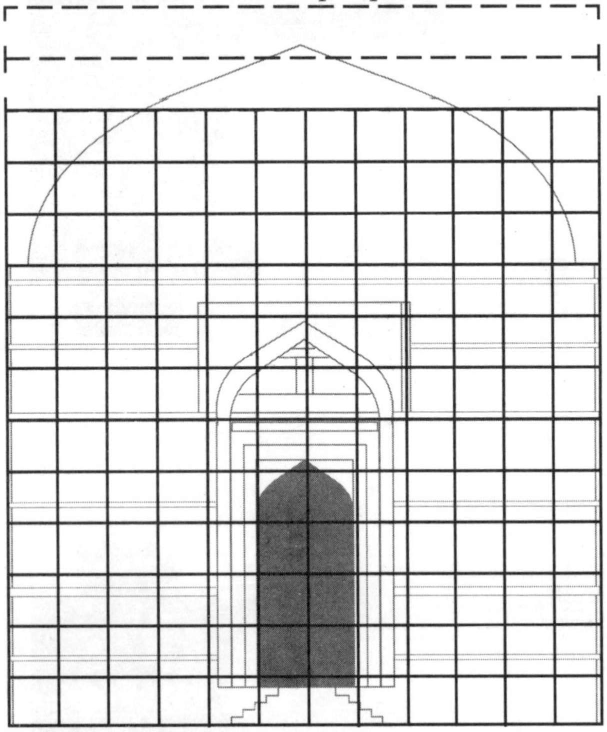

Figure 67: *Tomb of Sultan Iltutmish* , application of a *Deshiya Mandala* over the elevation

The application of a *Deshiya Mandala* over the elevation offers some conjunctions of interest (See: **Figure 67**). It is to be noted that the height of the tomb is in excess of the width by a little over one *pada*. However, the main block is nine *pada* high, the portal reaches within the eighth rank of *pada*, and the portal is bracketed by the four central files of *pada*. Therefore, the proportions of the tomb are seen to be 12:13.2.

A comparison between the *Tomb of Sultan Iltutmish* and Tomb *No. 36* indicates that the former is less squat than the earlier sepulchre. The height of the square block is fully two-thirds its width. When the dome is includes, the whole is a bit taller than the width. The elevation of the tomb surely imparts a monumental quality (See: **Plate 6**).

Plate 6

Tomb of Sultan Iltutmish (Elevation & half plan)

Tomb of Sheikh Rukn-i 'Alam

Multan, c. 1320 C.E.

The *Tomb of Sheikh Rukn-i 'Alam*[22] was purportedly started by Ghiyas-ud-din Tughluq I as his own mausoleum. Upon his ascending the throne in 1320 and subsequently moving his court to Delhi, he assigned this tomb to his spiritual advisor and philosopher, a Pakistani: one Sheikh Rukn-ud-Din Abdul Fath, called Shah Rukn-i 'Alam.

Although the *Tomb of Khan-i Jihan Tilangani,* Delhi, is said to be the first mausoleum with an octagonal plan in India, the *Tomb of Sheikh Rukn-i 'Alam* is certainly 'based' on the octagon--a **Type D-b** basic plan.[23] The prominent circular, battered bastions on each corner may mitigate this assignment. Certainly this tomb is more in keeping with the fortress-like tombs of the Tughluqs than the octagon of the *Tomb of Khan-i Jihan Tilangani.*

The militaristic, defensive quality of the outer section would appear to correlate with the General Ghiyas-ud-din Tughluq's desires.[24] However, the octagonal podium upon which the dome rests is more in keeping with later developments. The walls of the octagon slope inward slightly as they rise to their uppermost limits, creating an interior space that appears less voluminous than other tombs of the same period (See: **Figure 68**). The eight circular, corner bastions, on the other hand, are not only battered, but tilt inward towards the axis of the octagon. Three doorways offer entrance to this interior as well as a certain amount of light. Opposite the main portal is the *qibla* with its *mikhrab*. As with most Islamic tombs in India there is a false sarcophagus within the chamber, while the true burial vault is below floor level--a traditional two tiered design.

The layout of the plan of the *Tomb of Sheikh Rukn-i 'Alam* is eminently suited to the application of a circular *Manduka Mandala* (See: **Figure 69**). Although the Delhi Sultanate had been in existence for nearly one-hundred years when the construction of this tomb commenced, its relatively brief and turbulent existence did not

Figure 68: *Tomb of Sheikh Rukn-i 'Alam* , indication of internal space

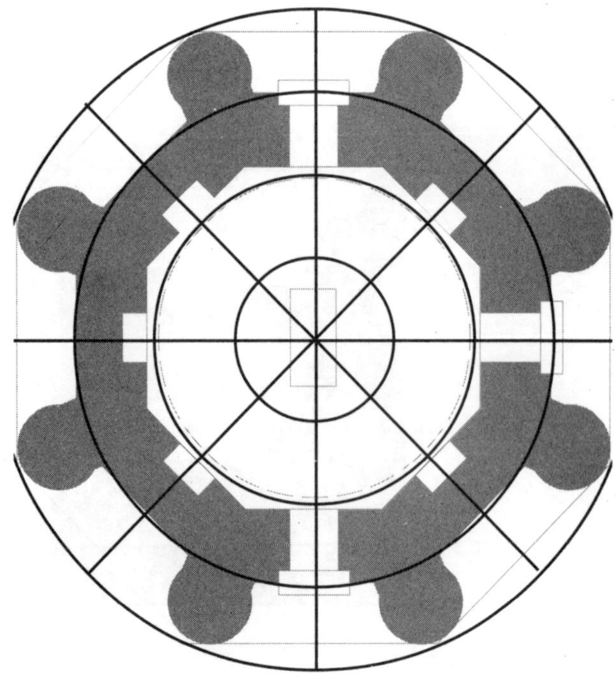

Figure 69: *Tomb of Sheikh Rukn-i 'Alam* , application of circular *Manduka Mandala*

Plate 7
Tomb of Sheikh Rukn-i 'Alam (Plan)

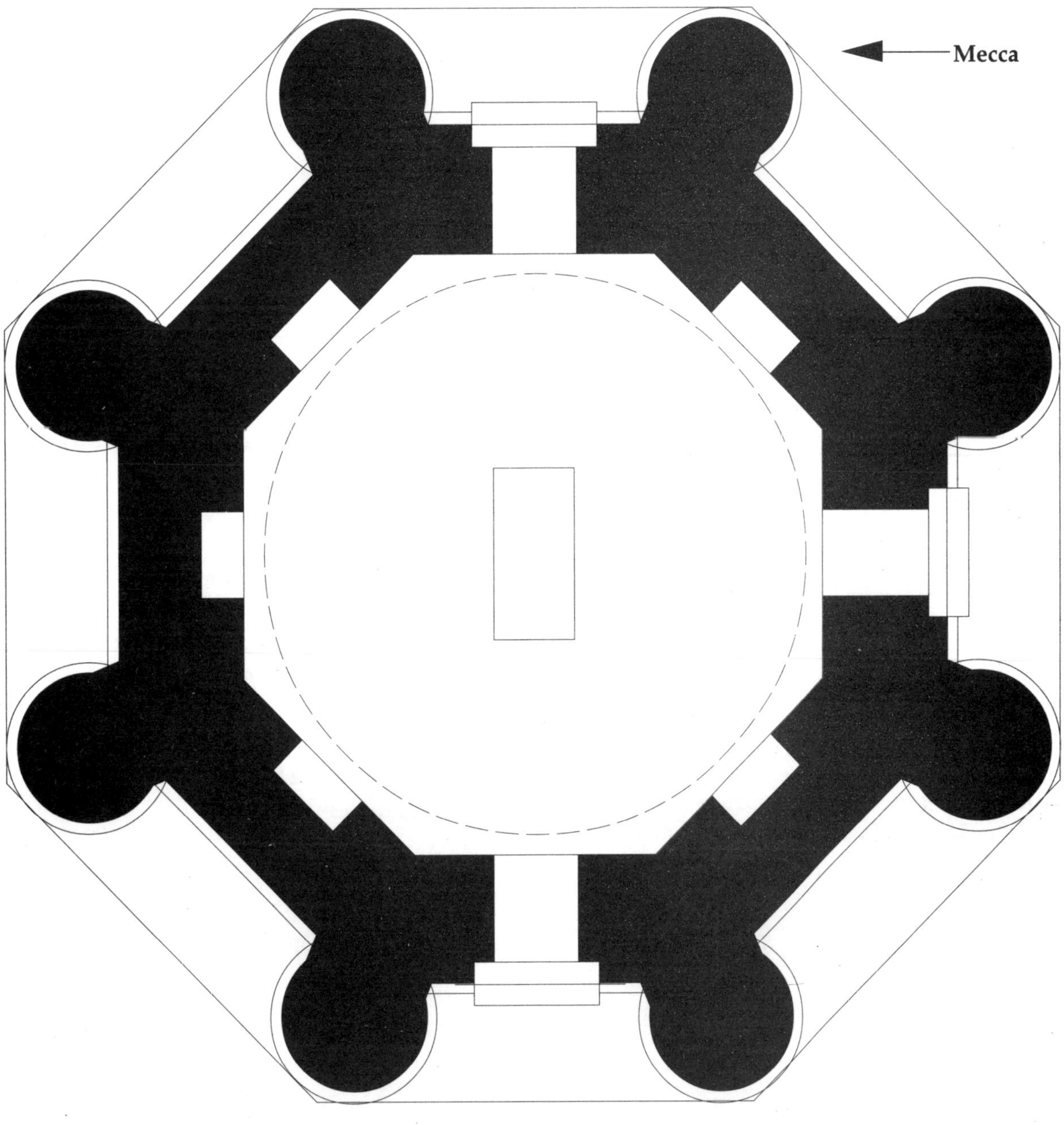

allow for a vital and, more importantly, a relaxed form of commerce and interaction with political entities beyond its borders. The wide and varied influence that was to flow into India during the Mughal period was somewhat restricted during this time. Hence, it does not seem strange that the indigenous *sthapati* (builder-cum-architects) would have been able to wielded such influence as to have the tomb based on an ancient Buddhist-Hindu *mandala* plan pattern. The application of the sacred Hindu square *mandala* would have to wait for the *Tomb of Akbar* and the *Tomb of Jahangir* for full realization.

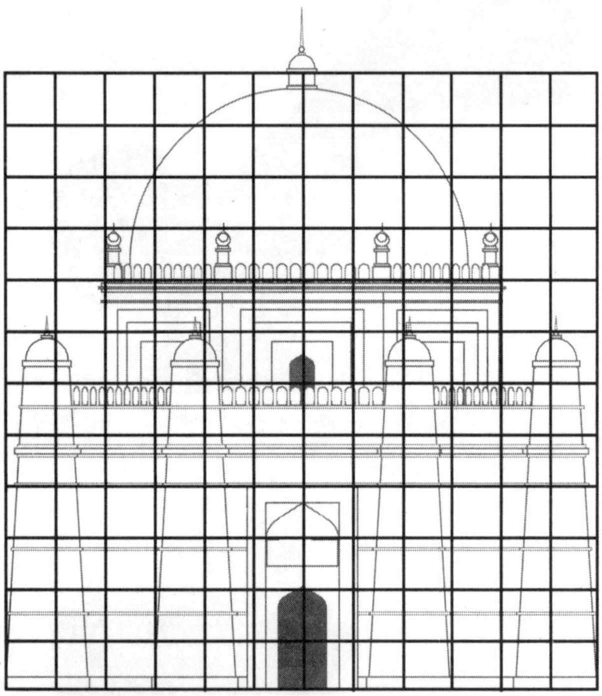

Figure 70: *Tomb of Sheikh Rukn-i 'Alam*, application of a *Deshiya Mandala* over the elevation

In placing a *Deshiya Mandala* over the elevation of the *Tomb of Sheikh Rukn-i 'Alam* certain conjunctions occur (See: **Figure 70**). The main block falls within the first seven ranks of *pada*. The octagonal podium rises an additional two ranks to the ninth rank. In additional the octagonal podium falls within the central eight *pada* files. The height of the dome reaches well into the twelfth rank. Therefore, the proportions of the *Tomb of Sheikh Rukn-i 'Alam* are 12:12.

In addition, mention must be made of the fact that the *Tomb of Sheikh Rukn-i 'Alam* is far more monumental in form than the *Tomb Ghiyas-ud-din Tughluq I*. The dome of the *Tomb of Sheikh Rukn-i 'Alam* is the second largest in India--*Gol Gumbaz* being larger. However, the ensemble of the latter is more impressive in its erratic and fortified form than the former. Nonetheless, Ghiyas-ud-din Tughluq's devotion to his spiritual leader by providing him with such a resting place is to be commended.

Plate 8
Tomb of Sheikh Rukn-i 'Alam (Elevation & half plan)

Tomb of Ghiyas-ud-din Tughluq I

Delhi (Tughluqabad), a. 1325 C.E.

Ghiyas-ud-din Tughluq (aka Ghiyath-ud-Din), a general of Sultan 'Ala-ud-din, assumed control of the throne in 1320. Partly because of his eminently successful life in the army and partly because of the excesses of the later rulers of the Slave Dynasty, Ghiyas-ud-din Tughluq, the first of the Tughluq Dynasty, was a reactionary with a decided puritanical streak. He was more at home on the back of his war horse than in the sumptuous halls of the court at Delhi. Not so his rapacious son and successor, Muhammad Shah Tughluq (1325-1351), who is said was responsible for Ghiyas-ud-din Tughluq's death. He was crushed by a pillar in a reception pavilion that was knocked down by an elephant. Therefore, as befitting his Spartan and military life style, Muhammad Shah Tughluq finished the construction of a small fortress-tomb in an equally small artificial lake at Tughluqabad, the royal town near Delhi as his final abode. This, the murderous son completed wihin a year of his father's demise.

The style of the *Tomb of Ghiyas-ud-din Tughluq I*,[25] called "Daru'l-Aman" (Abode of Peace), is not without precedence in its iconographic concept. Whereas, holy men emit a spiritual power from their grave (Arab.: *baraka*), it was felt that great men, especially great warrior kings in the service of Islam also exuded a power-based *baraka*. The tomb, therefore, became a manifestation of the warrior *baraka* in this case. The tomb was a real manifestation of the power base of the inhabitant. "Islam is a religion for poets, it is no less a faith for warriors, with an . . . emphasis on holy war and martyrdom."[26] The *Tomb Ghiyas-ud-din Tughluq I* extols, by its very form, the sanctification of *jihad*, and emphasizes the power and might of the family by association.

Additionally, the vault is perpendicular to the direction of Mecca, a normal practice as noted above. However, like a number of other tombs, this mausoleum does not possess a *qibla* and its corresponding *mikhrab* as does the *Tomb of Shah Rukn-i 'Alam.*

Notwithstanding the fact that the dynasty had certain connections with kingdoms outside

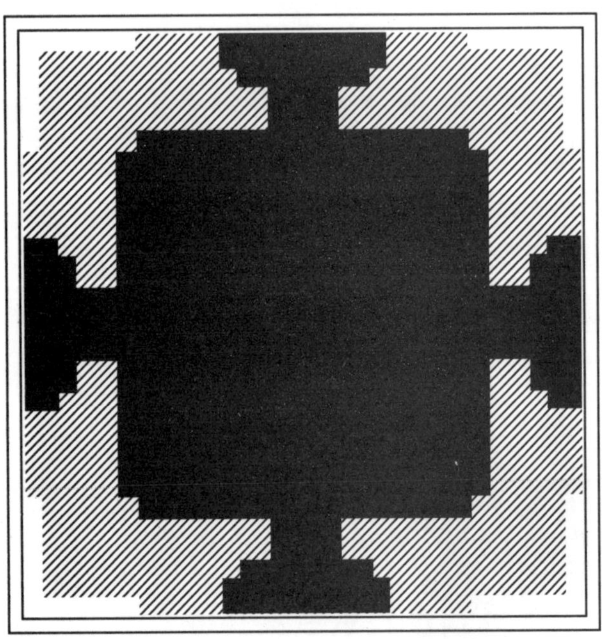

Figure 71: ***Tomb of Ghiyas-ud-din Tughluq I,*** indication of internal space

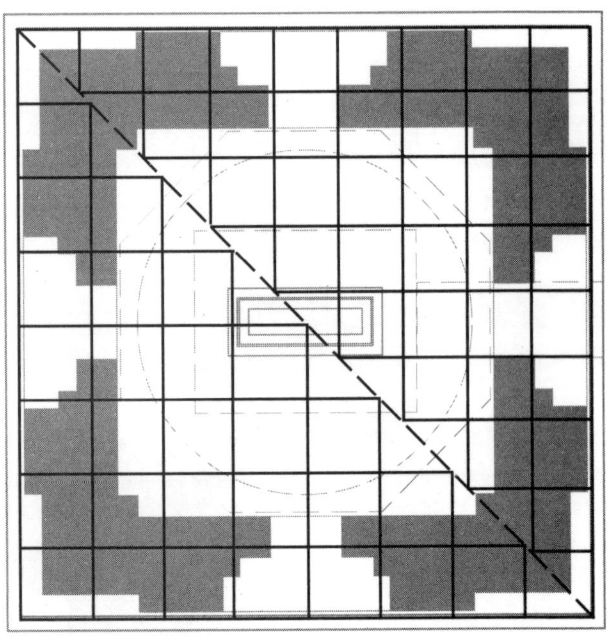

Figure 72: ***Tomb of Ghiyas-ud-din Tughluq I,*** application of *Manduka* and *Paramashayika Mandala*

Plate 9
Tomb of Ghiyas-ud-din Tughluq I (Plan)

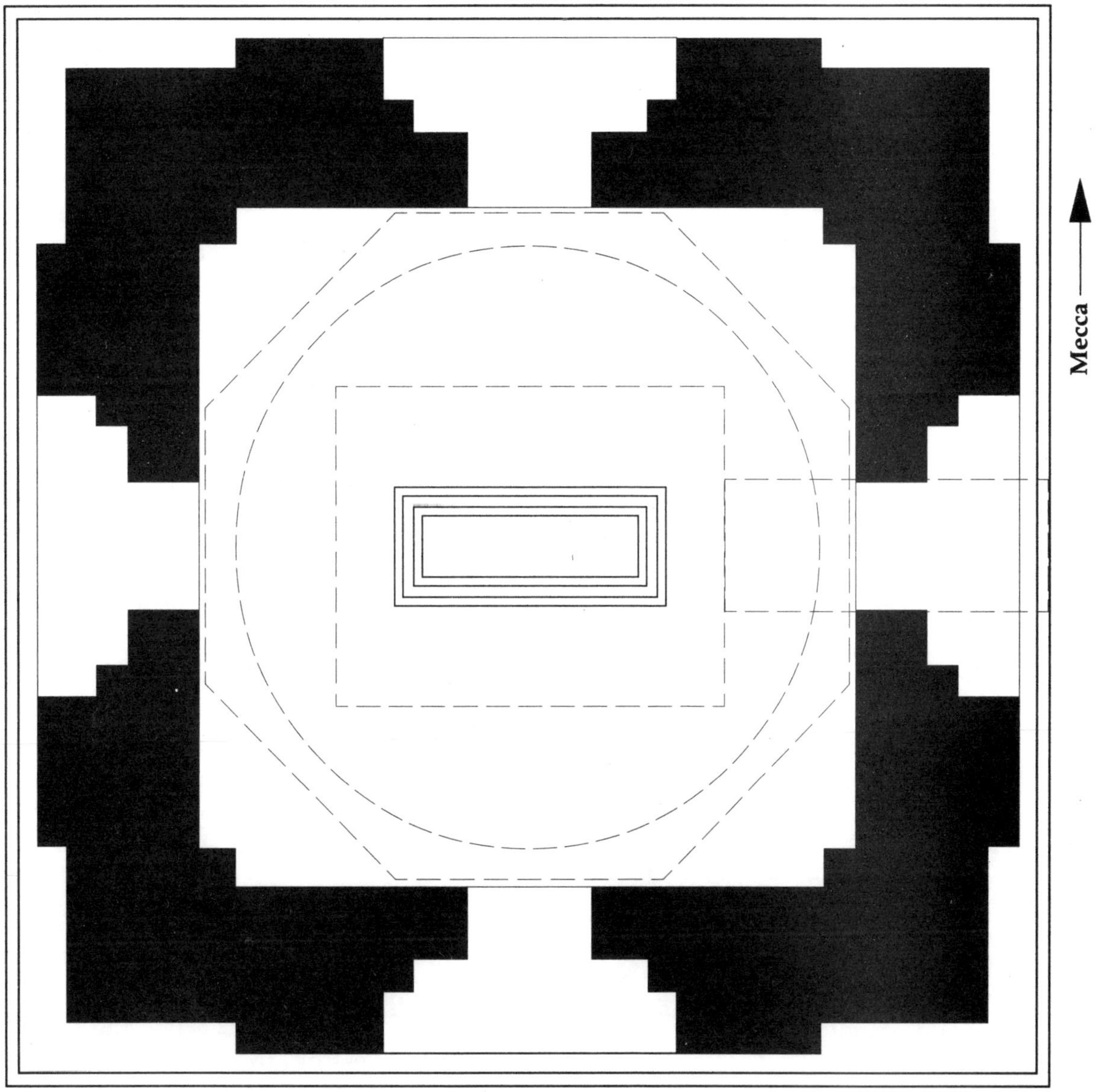

Tomb of Ghiyas-ud-din Tughluq I (Continued)

India, notably Persia, the tomb was constructed not within a garden, but the confines of a fortress-like enclosure. The plan of the "fortress" is erratic in its irregularity with five unequal sides and five bastions of equally irregular shape and size. It is truly eclectic and finds precious few, if any, parallels within India except for true fortresses. The floor plan of the mausoleum is not unique. It is basically square with a shallow extension in the center of each of the four walls, recalling the *triratha* design of earlier Hindu temples--i.e., a **Type B-c** basic plan. The sepulchral chamber is, likewise, square with doorways in the four façades and containing a false sarcophagus. A dome, the single Indo-Islamic manifestation, is a hemisphere which sits upon an octagonal plinth which, in turn, is supported by squinches on the interior.

The interior space is ample in comparison to the whole and relates to the *Tomb of Sultan Iltutmish* in its internal space proportion (See: **Figure 71**). The entrances, although not wide, do allow for sufficient ambient lighting into the interior as to make easy visualization of the chamber's inner aspects. In addition, there are small windows high on each of the four walls which also add to the relative brightness of the chamber. In the one-hundred years since the construction of the *Tomb of Sultan Iltutmish* the proportion of the inner chamber to the whole had become somewhat standardized in Islamic mausolea of India.

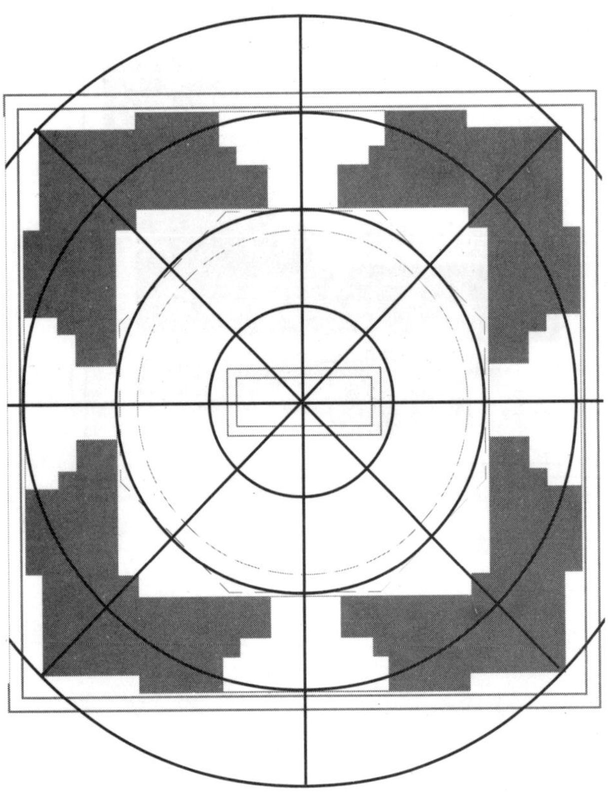

Figure 73: *Tomb of Ghiyas-ud-din Tughluq I,* application of circular *Manduka Mandala*

As with the previous tomb, the application of the *Manduka Mandala* and *Paramashayika Mandala* to the plan is less than completely satisfactory even though we are dealing with a plan that is essentially square. Still the *marmas* are not intersected and the false sarcophagus rests within what would be considered as the *brahmásthana* of both *mandalas* (See: **Figure 72**). On the other hand, the circular *Manduka Mandala* offers a better solution with a number of auspicious conjunctions. The second ring touches the outer edges of the extension (Ind.: *ratha*). The third circle touches the outer edge of the inner chamber and encloses the dome. Finally, the inner ring encircles the false sarcophagus as well as the one in the crypt below (See: **Figure 73**).

The elevation is what makes this tomb most interesting and carries on the eclectic, asymmetric nature of this tomb's ensemble; although, the plan indicates a strict cross-axial design. The walls are battered. A battered wall is a form that is not usually seen in Hindu architecture. However, its form is apparent in the massive *gopura* of southern Indian temples, and, one may add, the *ziggurats* of ancient Mesopotamia which would not be widely known to the builders of India. On the other hand, battered walls were widely employed in the

Plate 10

Tomb of Ghiyas-ud-din Tughluq I (Elevation & galf plan)

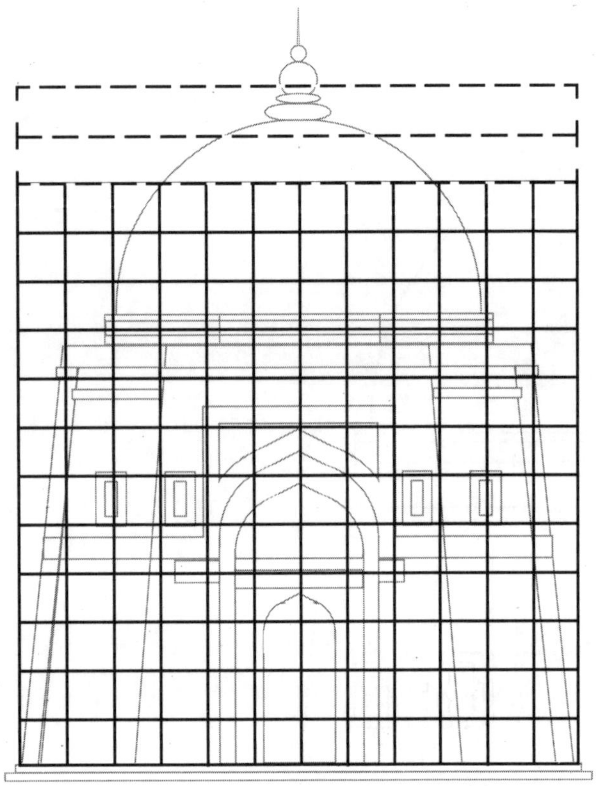

Figure 74: *Tomb Ghiyas-ud-din Tughluq I,* application of a *Deshiya Mandala* over the elevation

construction of fortified walls throughout India.

When a *Deshiya Mandala* is placed over the elevation it is seen that the central portal falls within the central four files of *pada* (See: **Figure 74**). The dome falls within the central eight files of *pada* and other conjunctions may be observed. The total proportion, it is to be noted, indicates a tomb that is higher than it wide. Therefore, the proportions of *Ghiyas-ud-din Tughluq I* are seen to be 12:13.5.

The *Tomb Ghiyas-ud-din Tughluq I* is certainly representative of the man and his profession. It must, also, stand as a testament to his usurping son Muhammad Shah Tughluq. Nonetheless, not monumental in the same way that the *Gol Gumbaz* or the *Tomb of Akbar*, the *Tomb Ghiyas-ud-din Tughluq I* is unique in its whole--i.e., the tomb and its ensemble--and is an apt representative of early Islamic tomb architecture in India.

Plate 11
Tomb of Ghiyas-ud-din Tughluq I (Ensemble)

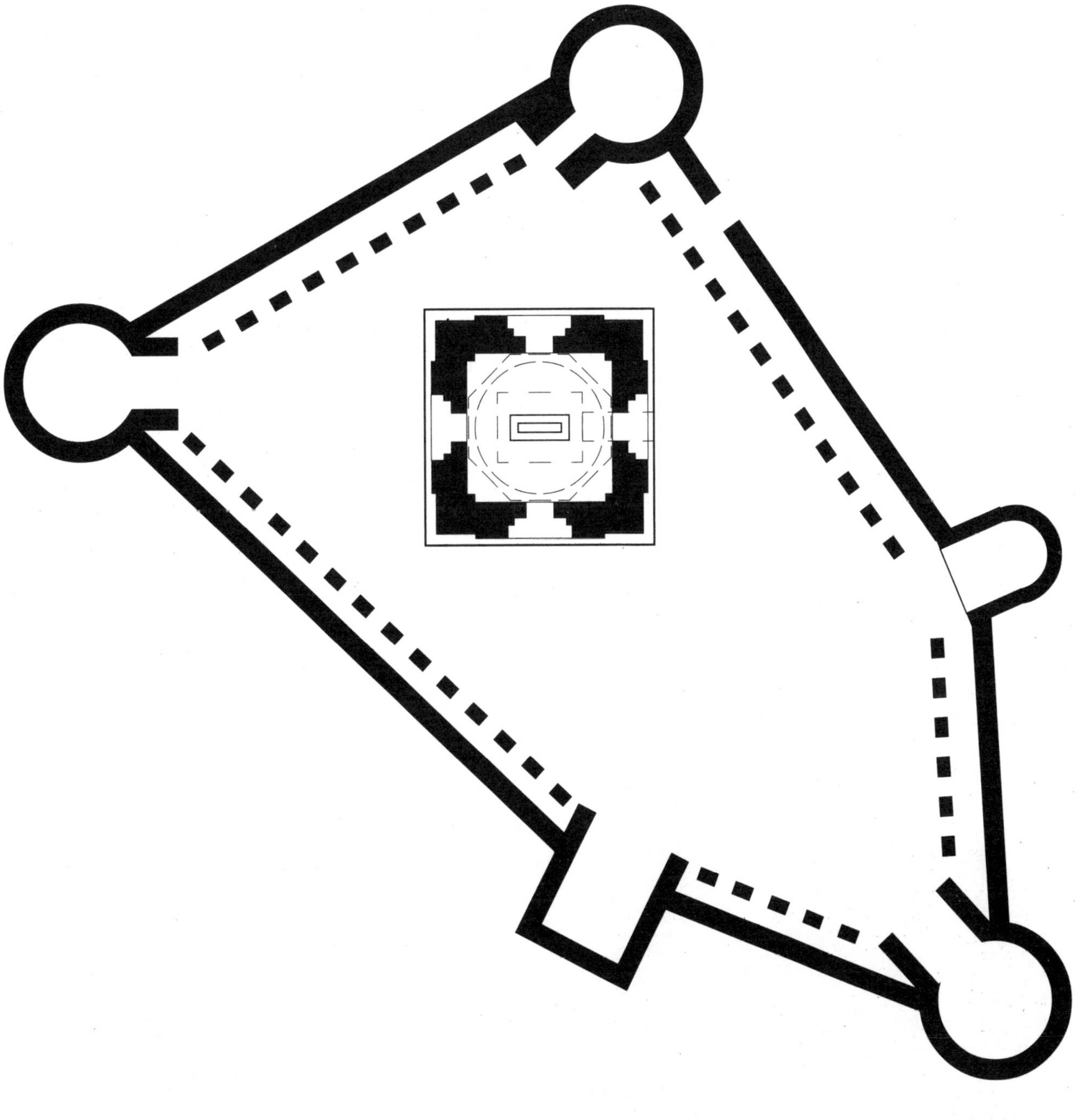

Tomb of Khan-i Jihan Tilangani

Delhi, 1388 C.E.

The *Tomb of Khan-i Jihan Tilangani,* the Prime Minister of Firuz Shah Tughluq, is viewed by some as being the first mausoleum in India with an octagonal plan.[28] Yet, as noted, the *Tomb of Shah Rukn-i 'Alam* (1320-1324 CE) at Multan, appears to predate this tomb (See: pp. 42-45). However, what can be stated is that the *Tomb of Khan-i Jihan Tilangani* does appear to set a pattern of what is often referred to as the Indo-Islamic canopy tomb--i.e., a **Type D-e** basic plan which possesses an octagonal interior, octagonal ambulatory, triple arch on each of its eight façades, cupolas over each of the central arches and a larger dome rising over the central chamber. This type, this archetype, if you will, can be seen in numerous later mausolea--e.g., *Tomb of Mubarak Shah Sayyid* (1434), *Tomb of Hasan Khan Sur* (c. 1535), *Tomb of Sher Shah* (1540), *Tomb of Isa Khan* (1547), and as late as the *Tomb of Adham Khan* (a. 1561), among others.

The central octagonal chamber possesses walls of considerable thickness. This may be due to the fact that here, in this mausoleum, the walls are of ruble construction faced with a relatively thin veneer of dressed stone. This may allow for considerable reduction in cost. However, it is at the expense of a reduction in wall thickness, an inherent strength in solid stone construction. In addition, the thick walls enclosing the central chamber may be viewed as another influence of preexistent Hindu architectural practices in their employment of unusually thick walls--i.e., both for temperature control[29] and as a manifestation of the sacred cave. However, in this type of tomb, thick inner walls are superfluous as a thermal barrier--i.e., since the plan with its ambulatory and high inner space achieves the ame desired effect. Nonetheless, this plan does allow for adequate internal space (See: **Figure 75**). In addition, the seven entrances do allow for a certain amount of ambient light to filter into and illuminate the interior, and to a lesser extent bathe the dome's interior.

Opposite what must be considered as the main entrance is the *qibla* with a stepped recessed *mikhrab*. More than a mere tomb the *Tomb of Khan-*

Figure 75: *Tomb of Khan-i Jihan Tilangani* , indication of internal space

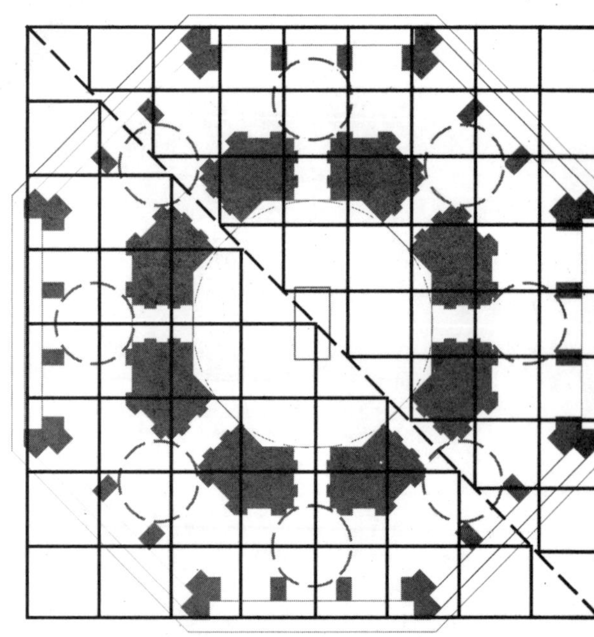

Figure 76: *Tomb of Khan-i Jihan Tilangani* , application of a *Manduka & Paramashayika Mandala*

Plate 12
Tomb of Khan-i Jihan Tilangani (Plan)

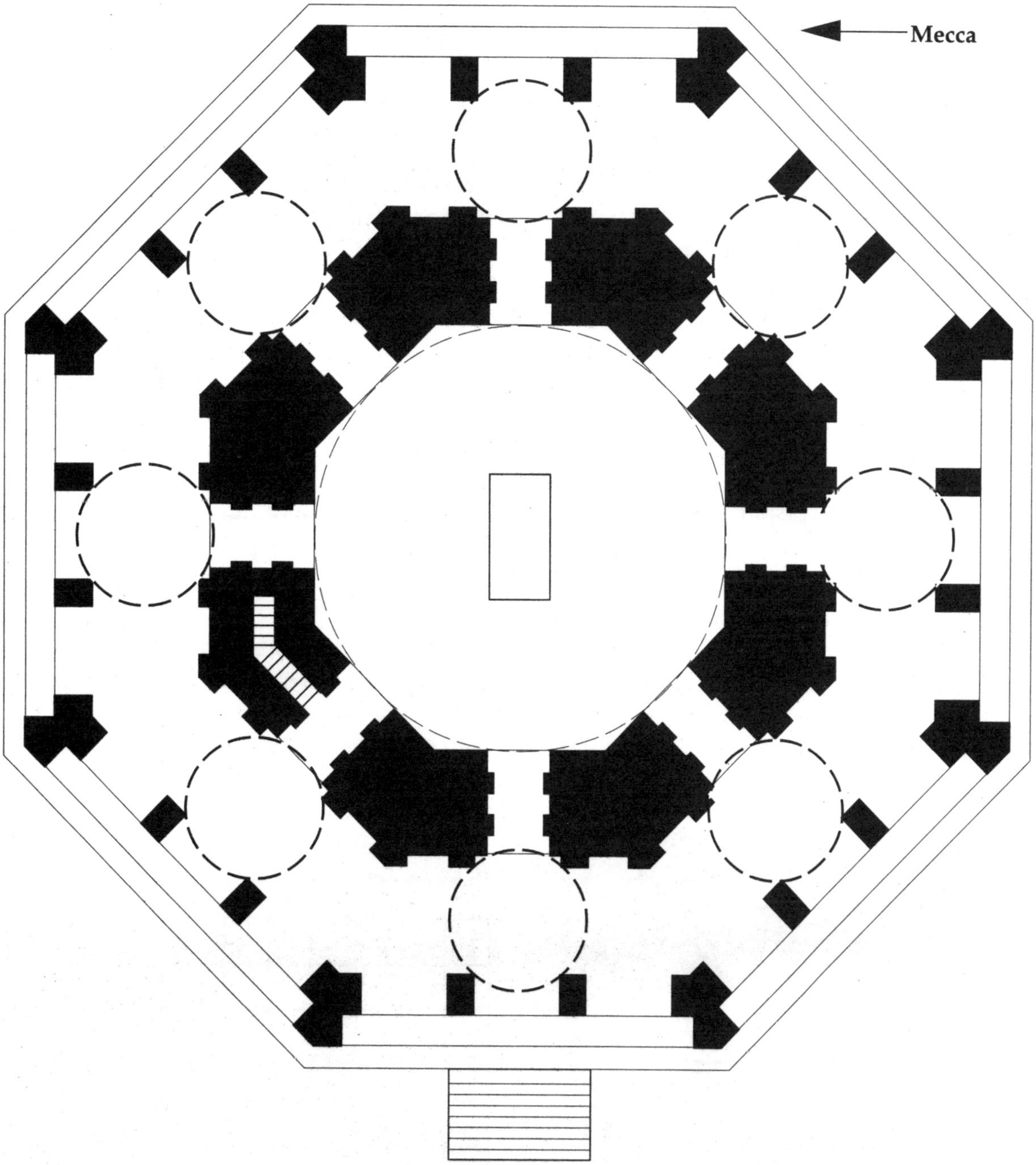

Tomb of Khan-i Jihan Tilangani (Continued)

i Jihan Tilangani indicates that this employment is rather egalitarian in those who possess the funds to construct a tomb and not just for the highest ranked members of the society. A false sarcophagus sits centered beneath the dome and over the crypt beneath the floor level--again the two tiered arrangement.

A verandah or ambulatory surrounds the central chamber giving the tomb the term "canopy." The term ambulatory is used. In the Islamic world circumambulation, especially around the *Ka'ba,* the Islamic *axis mundi,* is seen as a marked and required religious activity. Not only is the *Ka'ba* circumambulated, but also tombs of important Islamic saints as well. It is not required, but is considered a mark of respect for saints andor holy men.

An octagon does not lend itself to a thoroughly acceptable application of a square *mandala*--i.e., either a *Manduka Mandala* or a *Paramashayika Mandala* (See: **Figure 76**)--although none of the *marmas* are disturbed. A circular *Manduka Mandala* is more acceptable albeit with certain minor problems--i.e., the middle two rings run through the center of the inner wall and within the area of the verandah, respectively (See: **Figure 77**).

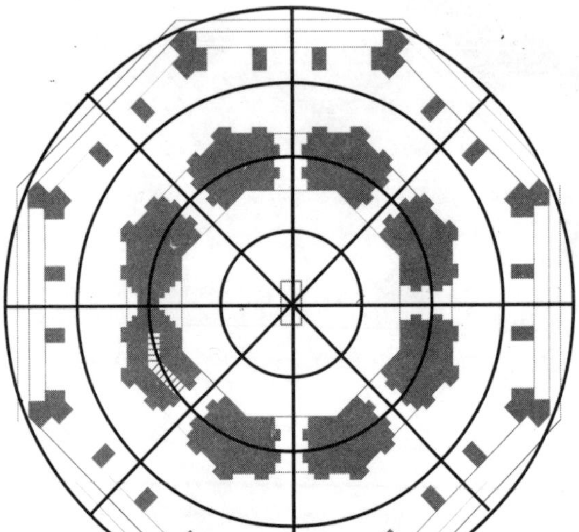

Figure 77: *Tomb of Khan-i Jihan Tilangani* , application of a circular *Manduka Mandala*

The proportion of the elevation of this mausoleum is decidedly 'squat.'[30] The application of the *Deshiya Mandala* over the elevation of the *Tomb of Khan-i Jihan Tilangani* produces a number of interesting conjunctions, particularly within the horizontal lines (See: **Figure 74**). The exposed dome rests almost exclusively within the ranks of the two central *pada*--i.e., ranks six and seven. Within the bottom two ranks are the portals and the *chajja* falls within the bottom three ranks. The proportions of the *Tomb of Khan-i Jihan Tilangani* are: 7:12 if the top of the dome is the measuring point, or 8:12 if the finial is included (See: **Appendix C, Plates 103-120** for other comparisons).

This plan and the proportions mentioned above are relatively standard in other similar mausolea, particularly the ones under consideration in this study--e.g., the *Tomb of Mubarak Shah Sayyid, Tomb of Sher Shah,* and the *Tomb of Isa Khan*. Therefore, the designation of "the first" is certainly applicable to type rather than an octagonal plan.

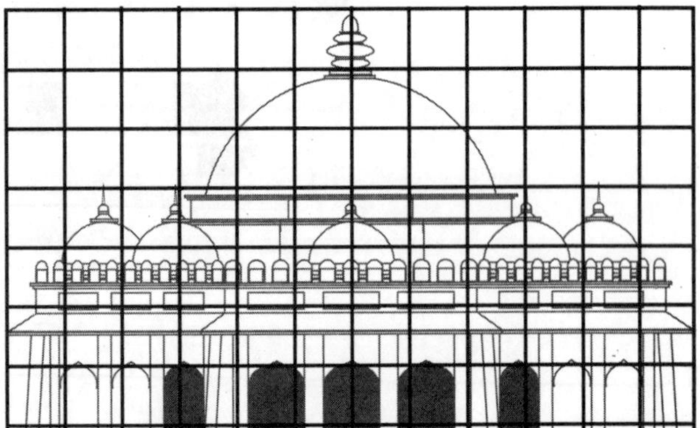

Figure 78: *Tomb of Khan-i Jihan Tilangani,* application of a *Deshiya Mandala* over the elevation

Plate 13
Tomb of Khan-i Jihan Tilangani (Elevation & half plan)

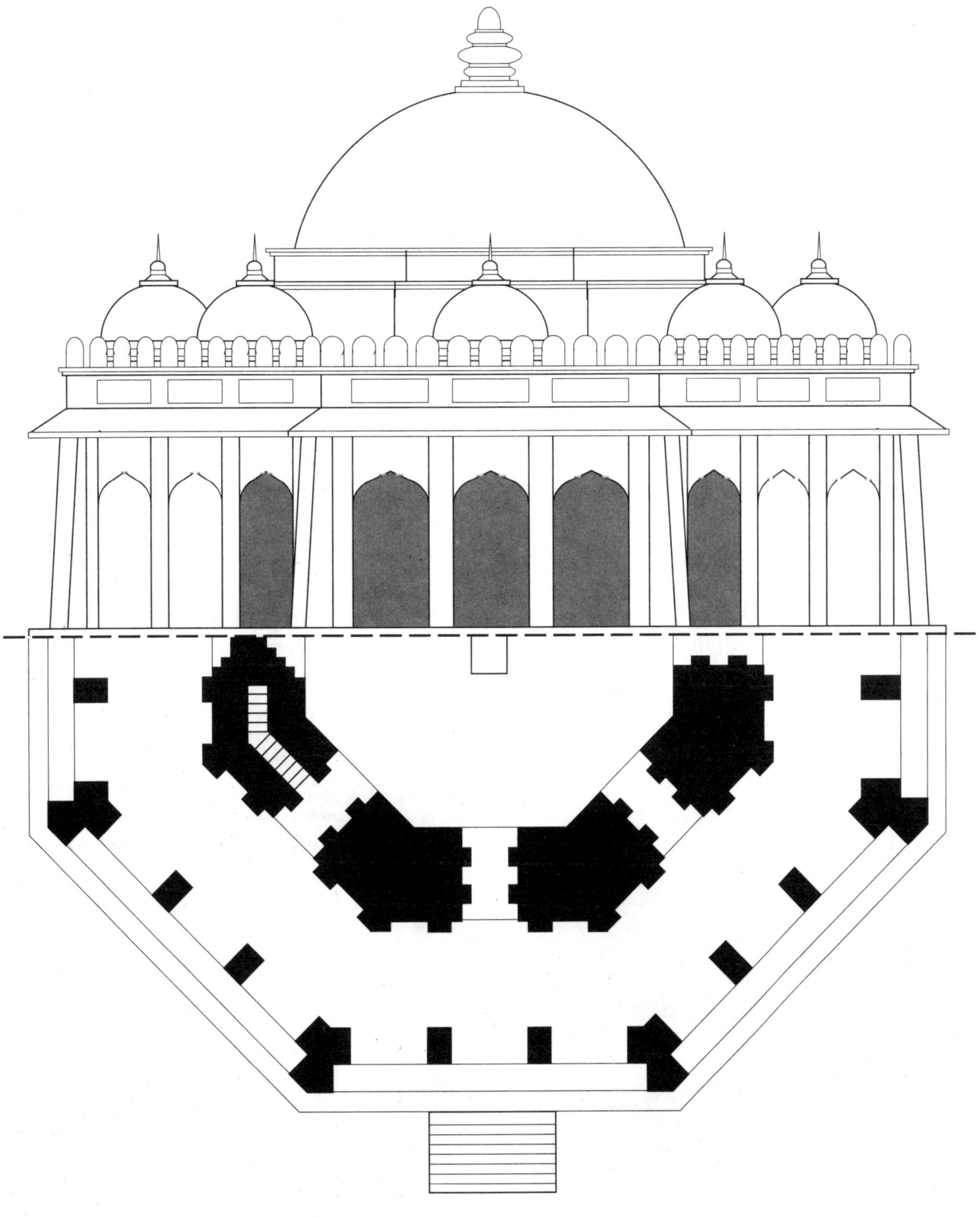

Tomb of Firuz Shah Tughluq

Delhi, c. 1389 C.E.

Firuz Shah Tughluq (1351-1388), the third ruler of the Tughluq Dynasty and successor to Muhammad Shah Tughluq, was raised to the sultanate by his army. A builder as well as a general, he was finally laid to rest in a mausolea not unlike the *Tomb of Ghiyas-ud-din Tughluq I.* This tomb was part of a *madrasa,* one of the preferred locations for a tomb as it is in association with religious discourse, a mosque and numerous students. The fortress-like form mirrors the professional predilection of the early Tughluq Dynasty --i.e., generals and warriors-- in its fortress-like appearance.

Essentially square--i.e., a **Type B-b** basic plan--with heavy, battered walls, a square chamber with a *qibla* and *mikhrab,* the plan of the *Tomb of Firuz Shah Tughluq*[31] resembles a stepped Hindu *triratha.* The major difference between this tomb and that of its predecessor, the *Tomb Ghiyas-ud-din Tughluq I,* is in the proportion of the exterior--i.e., this tomb is slightly squatter than the predecessors.

The interior chamber is square, *en plan,* and possesses three entrances. To the left of the main entrance--i.e., to the south--is the *qibla* with a *mikhrab.* The inner space is somewhat more voluminous, in proportion than that of the *Tomb of Ghiyas-ud-din Tughluq I.* Resting in the center of this space is a cenotaph which corresponds to that which is found in the crypt below--i.e., a two tiered arrangement. Above this false sarcophagus soars the dome.

Extending from the front, the south façade is a porch which mimics the width of the central block. This prominent porch is not an usual occurrence in Indian Islamic tomb architecture, but it is a feature that is more often associated with Hindu temples in India. Nonetheless, it offers a grand approach to the southern entrance of the mausoleum. The internal pace is, proportionally, more spacious than its square predecessor (See: **Figure 79**).

Either a *Manduka Mandala* or a *Paramashayika Mandala* are applicable as a design basis for the plan relatively square plan (See: **Figure 80**). However, the *Paramashayika Mandala* appears a better choice as none of the *marmas* are

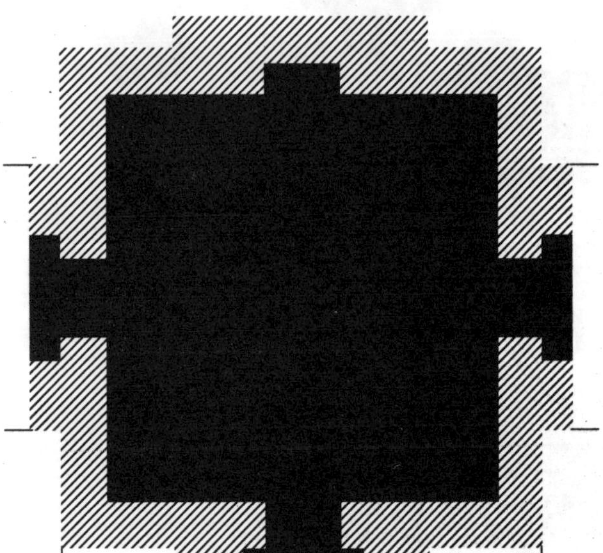

Figure 79: *Tomb of Firuz Shah Tughluq,* indication of internal space

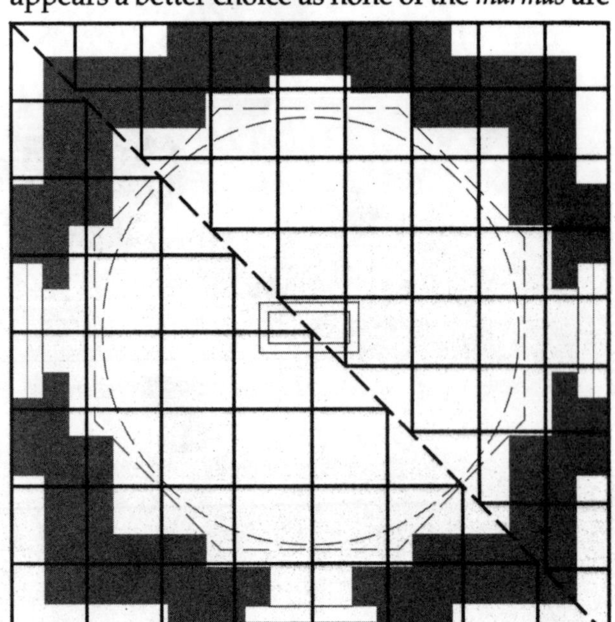

Figure 80: *Tomb of Firuz Shah Tughluq,* application of *Manduka* and *Paramashayika Mandala*

Plate 14
Tomb of Firuz Shah Tughluq (Plan)

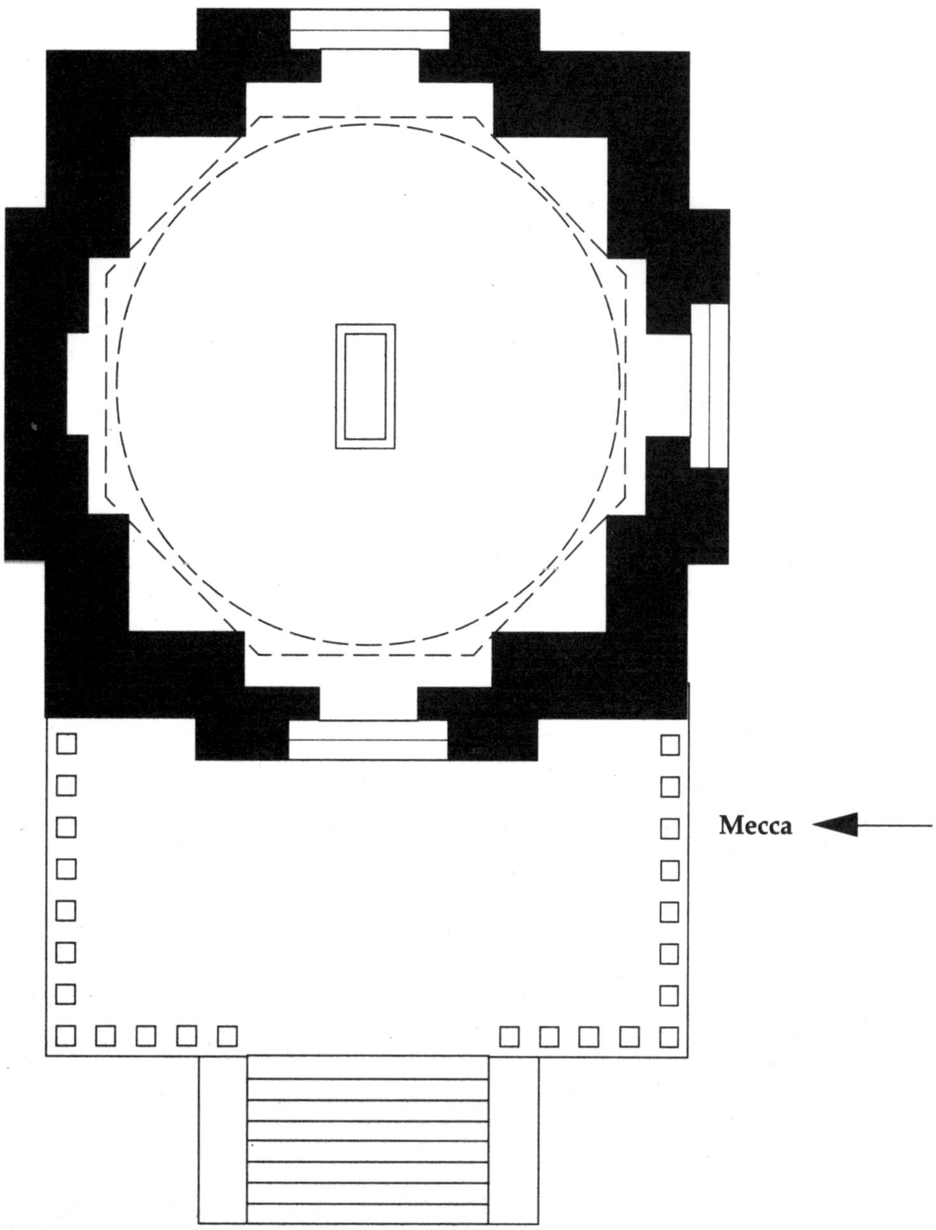

violated. On the other hand, since the design resembles a *triratha*, a circular *Manduka Mandala* is also applied (See: **Figure 80**). This *mandala*, also, possesses some merit.

As previously stated, the *Tomb of Firuz Shah Tughluq* is similar, *en plan*, to the *Tomb of Ghiyas-ud-din Tughluq I* and differs in proportion. When a *Deshiya Mandala* is superimposed over the façade, it is seen that the main block falls within the first eight ranks of *pada* and the octagon upon which the dome rests within the next two (See: **Figure 82**). Finally, the dome extends approximately one rank above the normal confines of the *mandala*.Therefore, the proportions are 12:13.

The addition of the three porches--two of a smaller dimension than the main--sets this mausoleum apart from other Islamic tombs previously and those to come in two important ways. First, it establishes a cruciform shape--i.e., a Latin cross--which, in itself, is not unusual and cannot be seen to possess any iconic value. However, in those Islamic structures which are seen to be cruciform in shape the plan tends to be cross axial and not axial as is seen here--i.e., the Greek cross. Secondly, it connects this plan to numerous Hindu temples which predate the *Tomb of Firuz Shah Tughluq*--e.g., *Shiva Temple*, Indore, and the *Shiva Temple*, Chandrehe--which possess prominent porches that extend from the main façade. This may be seen as another influence of indigenous *sthapati* upon Indian Islamic architecture.

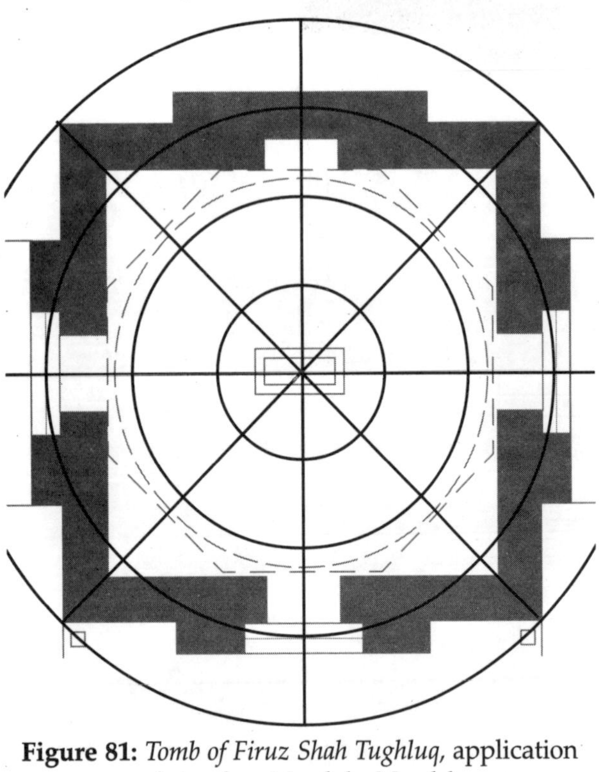

Figure 81: *Tomb of Firuz Shah Tughluq*, application of circular *Manduka Mandala*

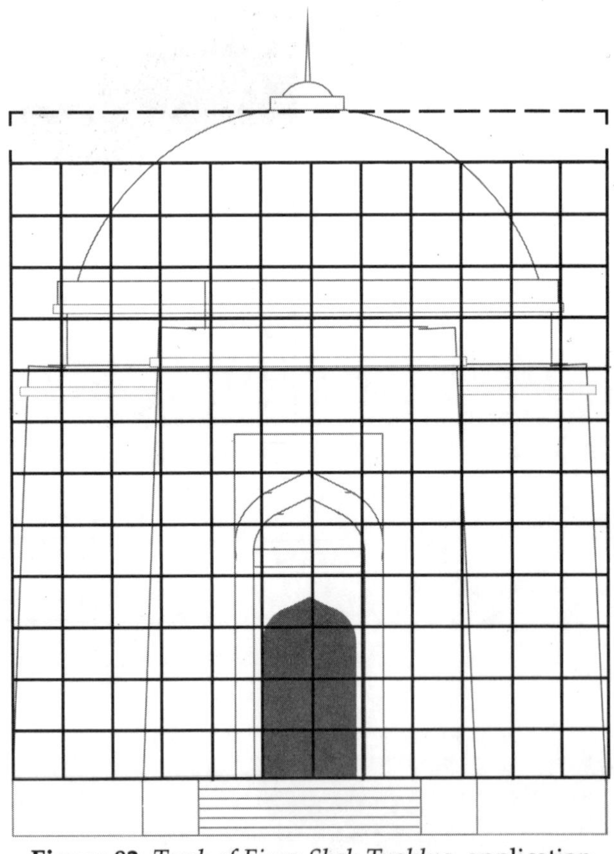

Figure 82: *Tomb of Firuz Shah Tughluq*, application of a *Deshiya Mandala* over the elevation

Plate 15
Tomb of Firuz Shah Tughluq (Elevation & half plan)

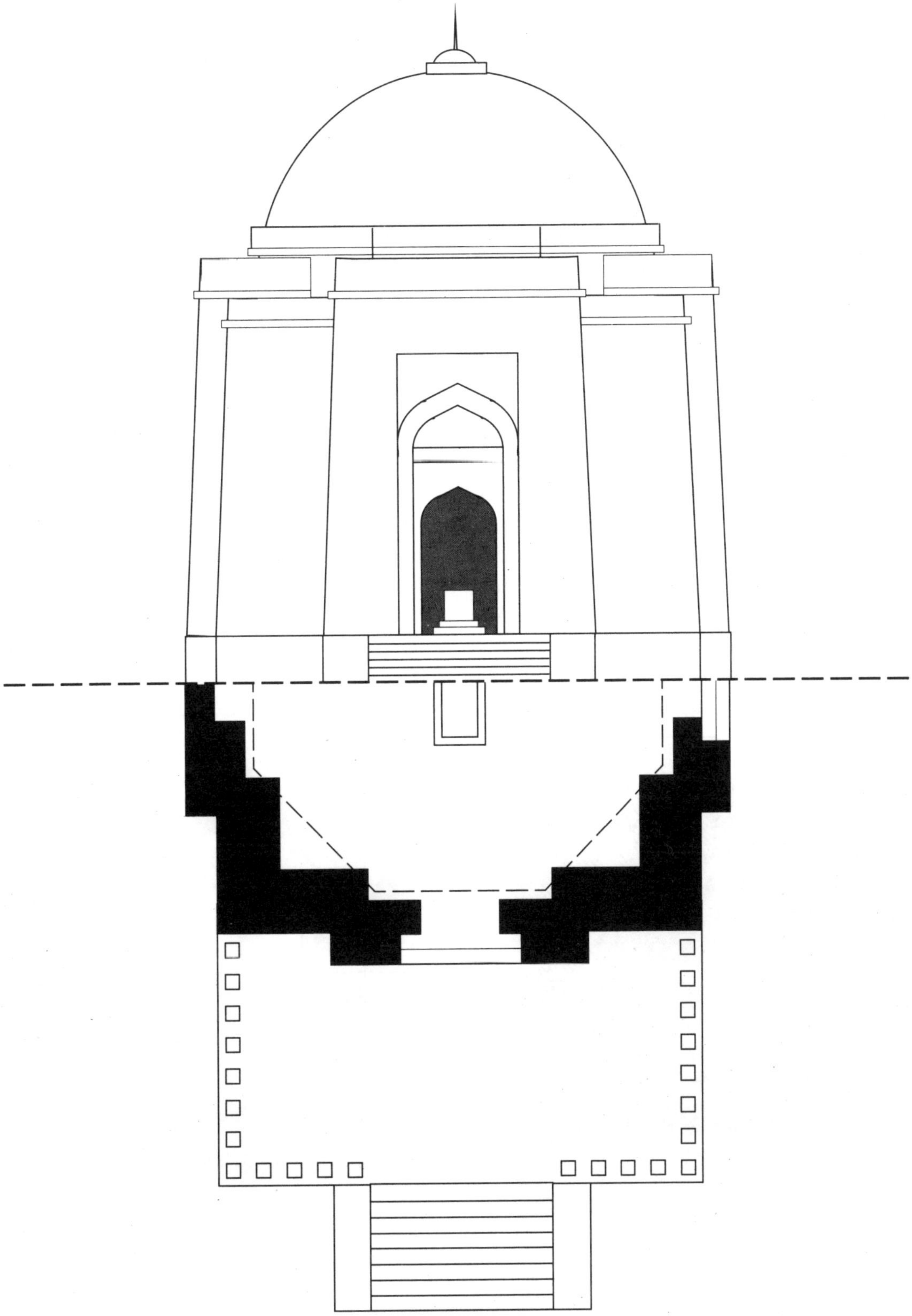

Tomb of Jalau-ud-din Mohammad Shah

Pandua, 1430 C.E.

The "one *lakh* tomb" constructed in Pandua, a one-time-capital of the Sultanate of Bengal, near the confluence of the Ganges and the Mahanadi rivers may have derived its name from the cost of the structure--i.e., one-hundred-thousand (*rupees*?). The *Eklakhi Tomb*[32] was constructed by and for Jalau-ud-din Mohammad Shah of the Ganesa-Shahi Dynasty, Sultan of Bengal (1419-1431). The *Tomb of Jalau-ud-din Mohammad Shah* (*Eklakhi*) is said to be unique in that this tomb's architects "derived their inspiration from the immediate environment and . . . [its} inimical climatic conditions."[33]

Not spectacularly grand as some of the tombs of the Timurud or the Muzaffarid Shahi, or the 'Adil Shahi or even the Qutab Shahi, the *Tomb of Jalau-ud-din Mohammad Shah* (*Eklakhi*), nonetheless, is of great interest. Several local conditions dictated the form and substance of this tomb. First, readily available stone suitable for construction was not easy to find or available in this region of Bengal. The alluvial flood plain was rich in clay, hence, the frequent utilization of brick in this area. The brick employed in the *Tomb of Jalau-ud-din Mohammad Shah* (*Eklakhi*) was sufficiently fired to withstand the frequent rains for which Bengal was and is noted.[34] Secondly, Grover asserts, and it appears rightly so, that the "bow shaped" roof-line of this tomb comes from the shape of the thatched roofs that were prevalent in this area.[35] Certainly, the slope of the roof allows for easy run off from the copious amount of rain that regularly assail this part of India.

The structure consists of a square block with octagonal towers at the four corners--i.e., a **Type C-a** basic plan. Beside being highly influenced by its provincial environs, there are a number of features which indicate its Islamic roots as well. The inner chamber of the *Tomb of Jalau-ud-din Mohammad Shah* (*Eklakhi*) is octagonal (Indo-Islamic) and four passageways lead to the exterior at the cardinal points of the compass. At the intercardinal points short, narrow passageways lead to cramped rectangular rooms.

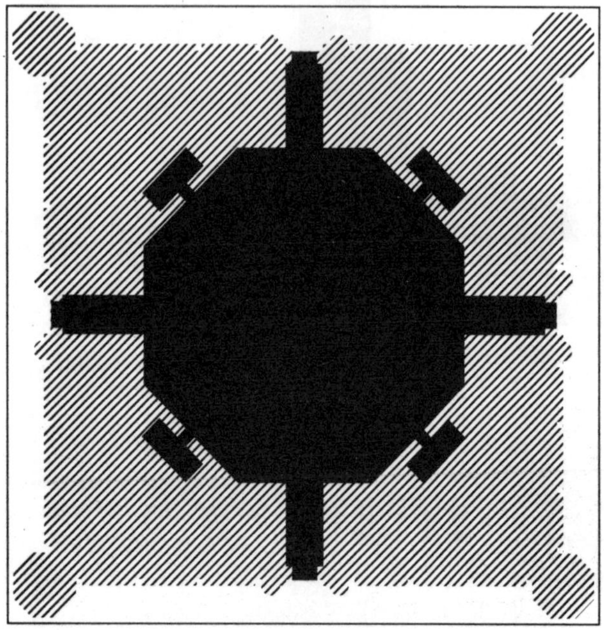

Figure 83: *Tomb of Jalau-ud-din Mohammad Shah* (*Eklakhi*), indication of internal space

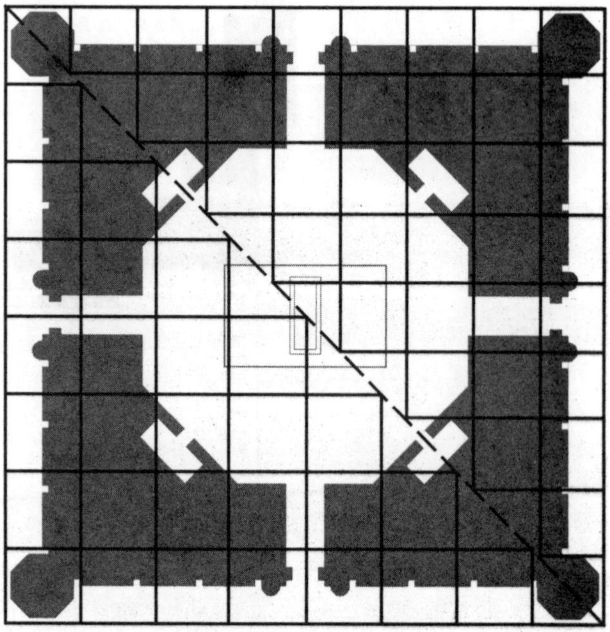

Figure 84: *Tomb of Jalau-ud-din Mohammad Shah* (*Eklakhi*), application of *Manduka Mandala* and *Paramashayika Mandala*

Plate 16

Tomb of Jalau-ud-din Mohammad Shah (Plan)

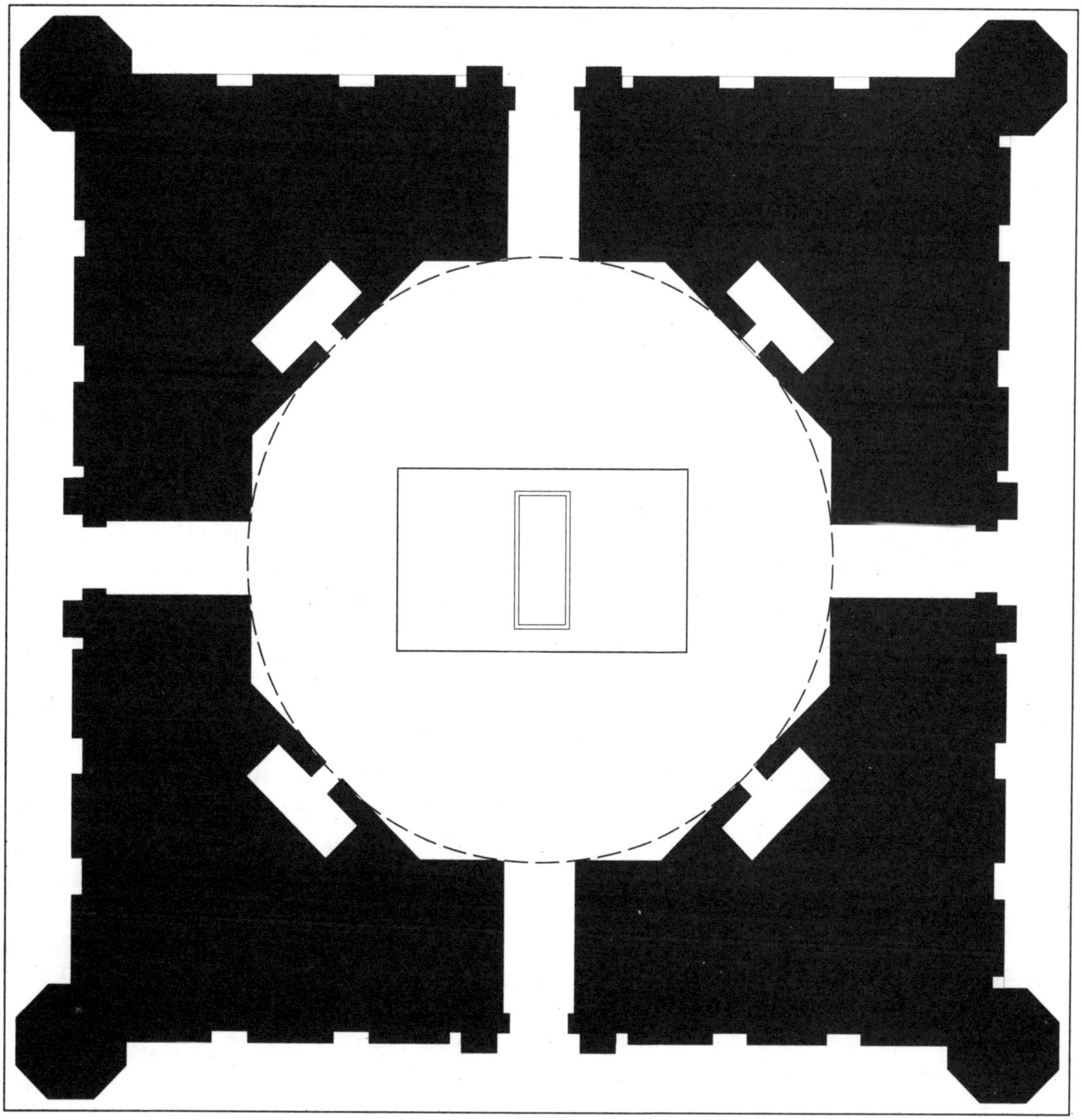

Tomb of Jalau-ud-din Mohammad Shah (Continued)

The use of these four small, constricted chambers is not known. A hemispherical dome, Indo-Islamic in nature, rises over this inner chamber but without pendentives or squinches. The unusually thick masonry block supports the dome in its entirety.

Unlike the vast majority of preceding and later Indo-Islamic tombs, the *Tomb of Jalau-ud-din Mohammad Shah* (*Eklakhi*), proportionally, possesses a restricted amount of interior space (See: **Figure 83**). The proportion of interior space to masonry is more akin to that found in the typical Hindu or Buddhist temple. Pandua was a provincial city, far from the more sophisticated Delhi. It must be assumed that here the *sthapati* exerted more influence than in the imperial capital. In addition, the thick masonry walls also aided in keeping the interior cool in the hot season, a practice long employed by the Buddhist-Hindu builders.

When a *Manduka Mandala* and *Paramashayika Mandala* are laid over the plans, the latter appears more applicable (See: **Figure 84**). It is noted that each of the small, angled, corner chambers fall within a corner *pada* of the second rank. The *Manduka Mandala* is less noteworthy.

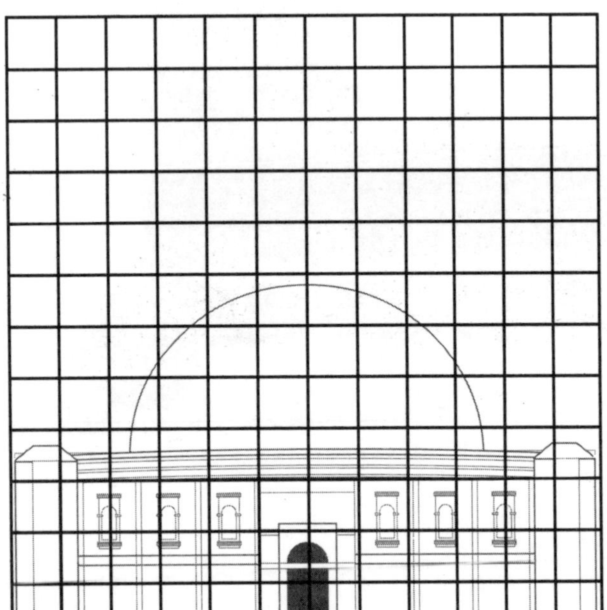

Figure 85: *Tomb of Jalau-ud-din Mohammad Shah* (*Eklakhi*), application of *Deshiya Mandala* over the elevation

As with the other mausolea in this study, the *Deshiya Mandala* is superimposed over the elevation of the *Tomb of Jalau-ud-din Mohammad Shah* (*Eklakhi*) (See: **Figure 85**). The lower three ranks of *pada* reach up to the lower edge of the bowed roof molding. The dome is seven files wide and the portal ensemble lies within the central two files of *pada*. Finally, the dome extends well into the seventh rank. Therefore, it can be said that the proportions of the 12:6.75. This proportion makes the *Tomb of Jalau-ud-din Mohammad Shah* (*Eklakhi*) as one of the exceptions for square plan Indo-Islamic tombs, which tend to be considerably taller.

The *Tomb of Jalau-ud-din Mohammad Shah* (*Eklakhi*) is unique for the reasons stated above--i.e., its thick masonry walls, its bowed roof-line and it relatively squat appearance for a square plan. The tomb does not possess a *qibla* with its corresponding *mikhrab*, but the cenotaph is oriented towards Mecca.

Nonetheless, the *Tomb of Jalau-ud-din Mohammad Shah* (*Eklakhi*) does indicate the wide variation of tomb architecture in Islamic India. The Delhi tombs during the Slave Dynasty were, generally, square, *en plan*, but were of proportionally considerable height. The tombs of the Sayyid and Lodi Dynasties tended to be octagonal, particularly for royal resting places, and were lower in height, proportionally. Finally, the *Tomb of Jalau-ud-din Mohammad Shah* (*Eklakhi*) doubtlessly may ascribe the strong indigenous influence also to the fact that Sultan Jalau-ud-din Mohammad Shah was the son of a Hindu king, the Raja Ganesa.

Plate 17

Tomb of Jalau-ud-din Mohammad Shah (Elevation & half plan)

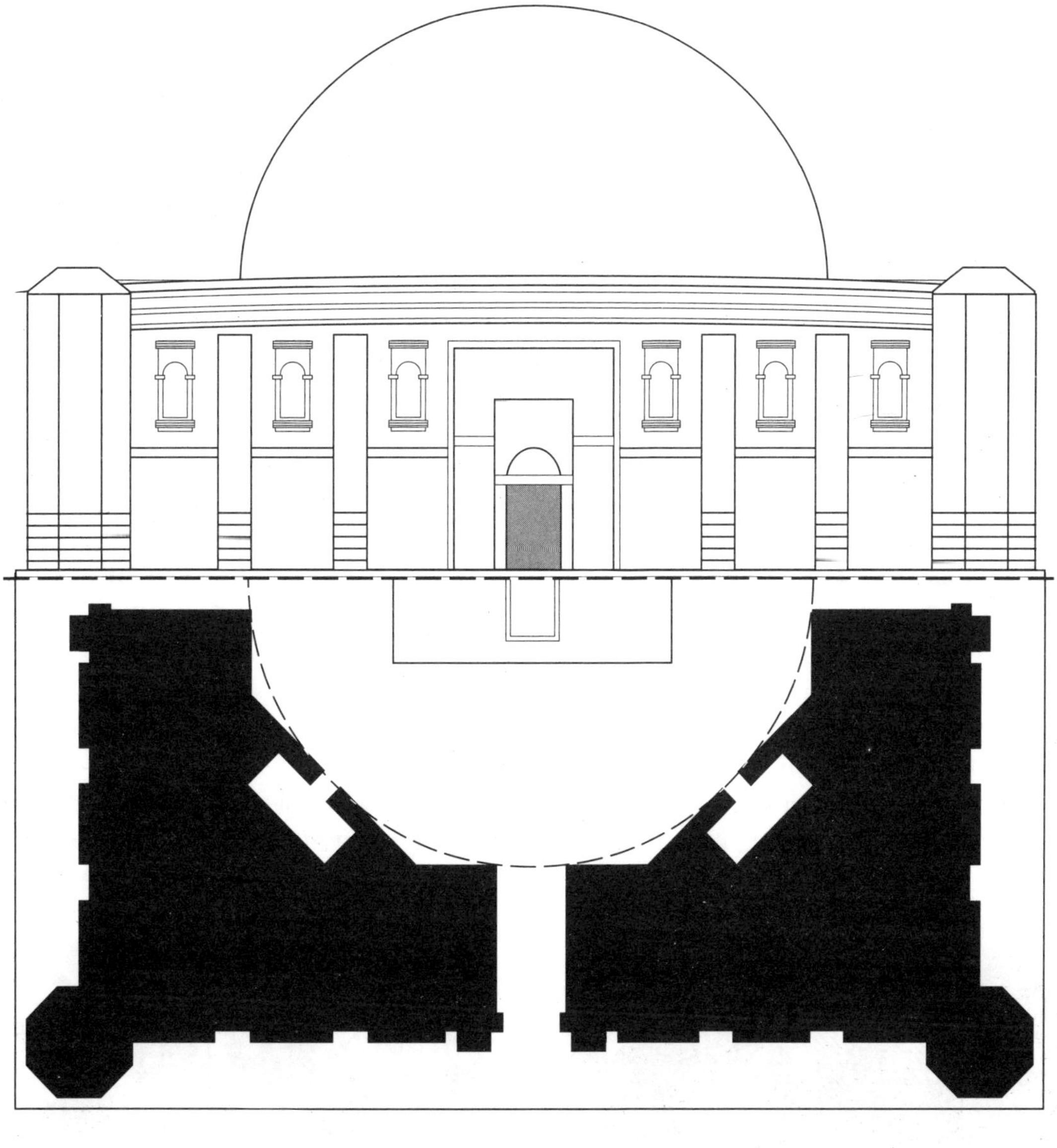

Tomb of Mubarak Shah Sayyid

Delhi, 1434 C.E.

The tomb of Mu'izz-ud-din Mubarak Shah Sayyid (1421-1434), follows the precedent established in the *Tomb of Khan-i Jihan Tilangani*. Mubarak Shah was the second sultan of the short lived Sayyid Dynasty, a dynasty that was put in place in 1414 CE, by the Mongol Timur the Lame, the feared Tamburlaine, the Scourge of God (See: *Gur-Emir*, **Plate 128**, p. 275). This dynasty's tenure was such that it is not noted for important architectural achievements. However, the *Tomb of Mubarak Shah Sayyid*[36] is of some significance.

The octagonal plan--i.e., **Type D-e** basic plan--is nearly identical to that of the standard, the *Tomb of Khan-i Jihan Tilangani*. The inner core is pierced by seven portals. The eight, on the *qibla* is formed into a *mikhrab*. As with the former the *Tomb of Mubarak Shah Sayyid* possesses a *chajja* with a modest extension and unlike the dramatic overhang that is to be seen in later tombs. The inner masonry walls are virtually as thick as found in *Tomb of Khan-i Jihan Tilangani*. However, there are a number of variations, most of which are seen in the elevation. First, the *Tomb of Mubarak Shah Sayyid* is somewhat taller in proportion to the earlier tomb and its construction indicates dressed stone rather than a rougher construction covered with stucco as is seen in the former. Over each of the central portal of the eight sided façade are found tall *chatri*, rather than the simple domes of the former. The dome of the *Tomb of Khan-i Jihan Tilangani* is hemispherical, whereas, that of the *Tomb of Mubarak Shah Sayyid* is formed in elevation, by an rather flat elliptical shape extending from a shallow drum form. The dome rests upon a sixteen sided drum, rather than the usual octagonal form seen in many tombs. Finally, both possess an ambulatory for the purpose of circumambulating; a practice also seen in both the Buddhist and Hindu traditions. Originally, the mausoleum sat within its own octagonal enclosure, but the centuries have encroached upon this space to the extent that only the tomb remains.

As with the earlier standard, the interior space is substantial (See: **Figure 86**). It is to be

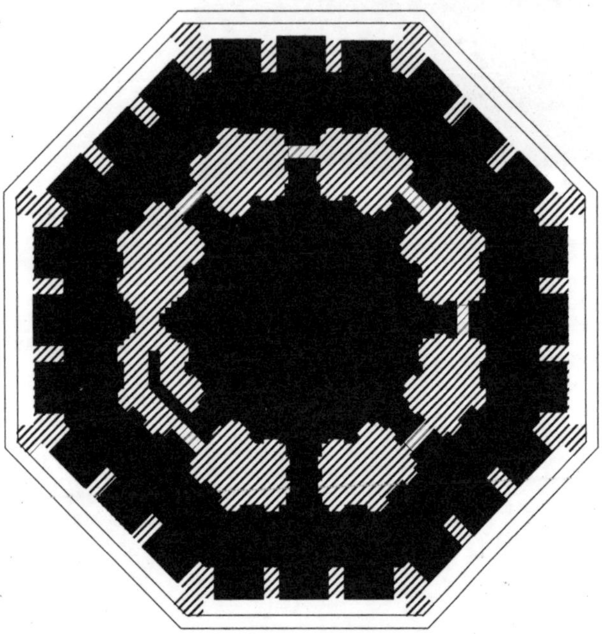

Figure 86: *Tomb of Mubarak Shah Sayyid*, indication of internal space

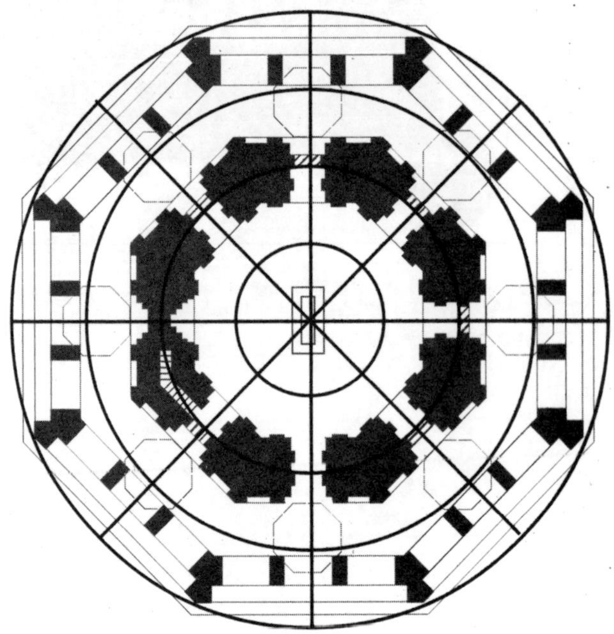

Figure 87: *Tomb of Mubarak Shah Sayyid*, application of circular *Manduka Mandala*

Plate 18

Tomb of Mubarak Shah Sayyid (Plan)

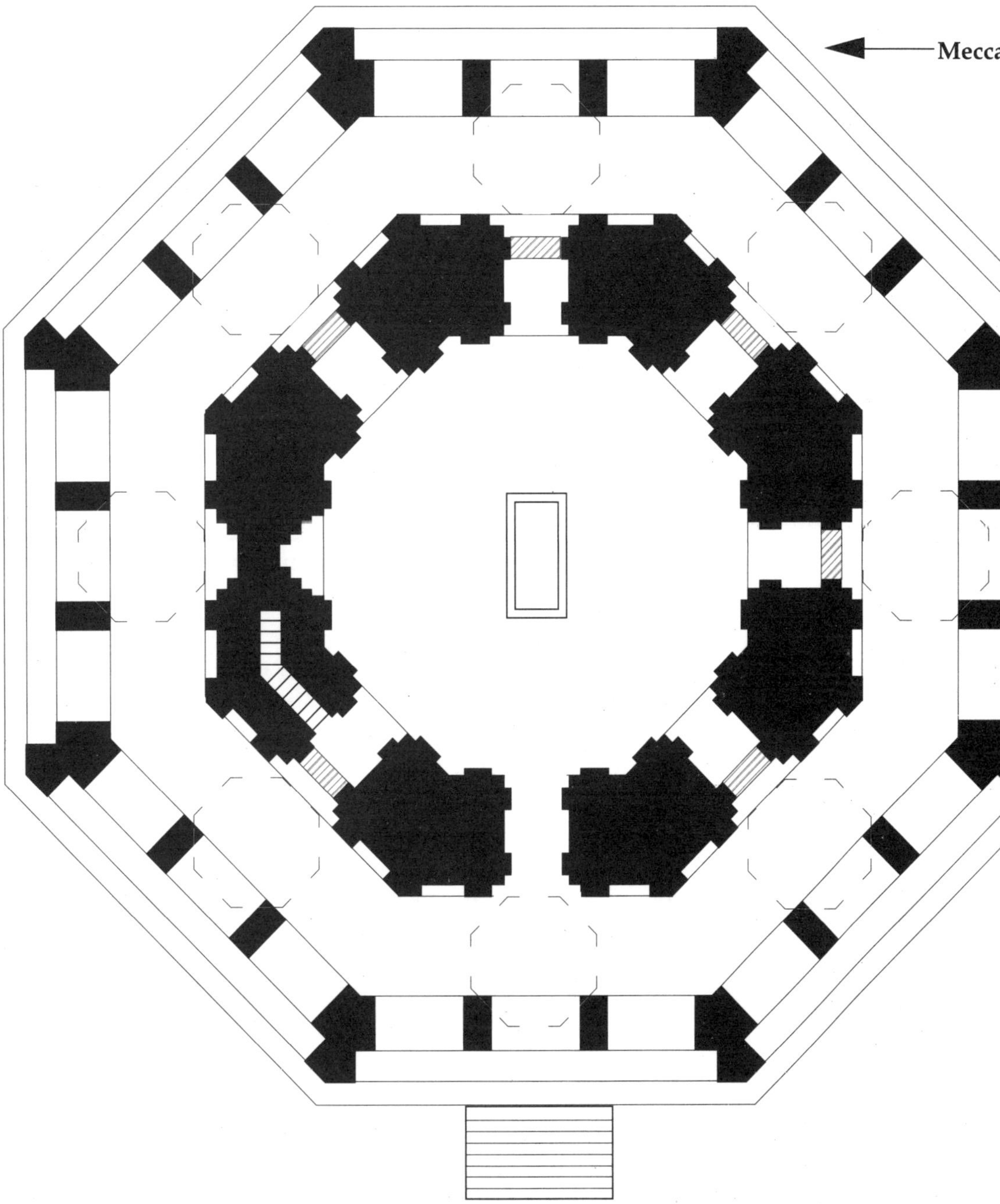

noted that later tombs of the same basic type --i.e., **Type D**--possess thinner walls allowing for more inner space than is seen here. Nonetheless, in comparison to indigenous temples, the space is considerable.

Since the basic design is composed of an octagon, a circular *Manduka Mandala* is applied (See: **Figure 87**) to the plan of the *Tomb of Mubarak Shah Sayyid* . In this application, the cenotaph is encircled by the *brahmásthana* and the domed inner area falls within the next ring. The third band runs within the ambulatory and bisects the eight small *chatri* that rest over the central portals of the eight sides, and, of course, the outer ring enfolds the whole.

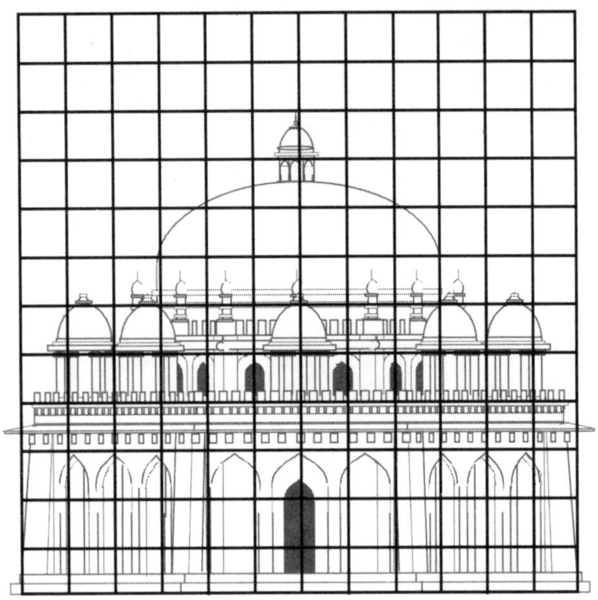

Figure 88: *Tomb of Mubarak Shah Sayyid*, application of *Deshiya Mandala* over the elevation

The application of a *Deshiya Mandala* over the elevation indicates a number of interesting proportions. The portals fall within the lower three ranks of *pada* (See: **Figure 88**). The domes of the *chatri* rest within the sixth rank Finally, the dome rises to eight and a half ranks, but, more importantly is contained within the middle six files.

Seen amongst the surrounding, lather encroaching buildings, the *Tomb of Mubarak Shah Sayyid* appears rather truncated, even squat in comparison. Indeed, the the narrowness of the ambulatory in comparison to the central space and the rather short drum, coupled with a decidedly 'squat' dome gives this impression. However, in its original form with its surrounding enclosure, it must have been imposing, indeed. Certainly, it was suitable as a depository for the last remains of a Sayyid ruler of the Delhi Sultanate.

Plate 19
Tomb of Mubarak Shah Sayyid (Elevation & half plan)

Tomb of Rani Rupmati

Ahmadabad, a. 1430-1440 C.E.

The Rani Rupmati (aka Rani Rupavati) was the queen of Nasir-ud-Din Mahmud Shah I Beghara.[37] Their relationship is said to rival that of Mumtaz Mahal and Shah Jahan. However, Sultan Mahmud Shah I Beghara had not the means to confer upon his favorite the splendor that Shah Jahan did upon his beloved Mumtaz Mahal. The Rani Rupmati is frequently described as having been an exquisitely beautiful Hindu princess, a princess of Dhar and even a beautiful shepherdess!

The *Tomb of Rani Rupmati,*[38] in Ahmadabad, is typical of the transition that is found between the indigenous Hindu style open, colonnade pavilion and the Islamic mausoleum of that period. In this it is most similar to the *Sayyid Usman Rauza* of Usmanapur, although on a much smaller scale. Square, *en plan*--i.e., **Type A-b** basic plan--it consists of six pillars across each façade and a total of thirty-two. The central four pillars are missing and this area is topped by an open dome. There are four small domes at each corner over the square bays. Over the twelve central pillars a square podium rises to support the hemispherical dome. The pillars of the east side of the mausoleum are connected by a low solid balustrade and in the center is the cenotaph.

The internal--i.e., covered--space generated by this type of design is proportionally greater than most of the other tombs in this study. The exception being the *Sayyid Usman Rauza* which, as stated above, is of similar design (See: **Figure 89**). This arrangement and this space would allow for easy access for those who wished to honor the Rani Rupmati.

In considering a *mandala* that is suitable for the *Tomb of Rani Rupmati,* both the *Manduka Mandala* and the *Paramashayika Mandala* are considered (See: **Figure 90**). It appears that the *Paramashayika Mandala* is the preferred form. It is to be noted that the inner pillars fall within the second rank of deities; the cenotaph being protected by the *brahmásthana.*

The superimposing of a *Deshiya Mandala* over the elevation of the *Tomb of Rani Rupmati,* three salient conjunctions are apparent (See:

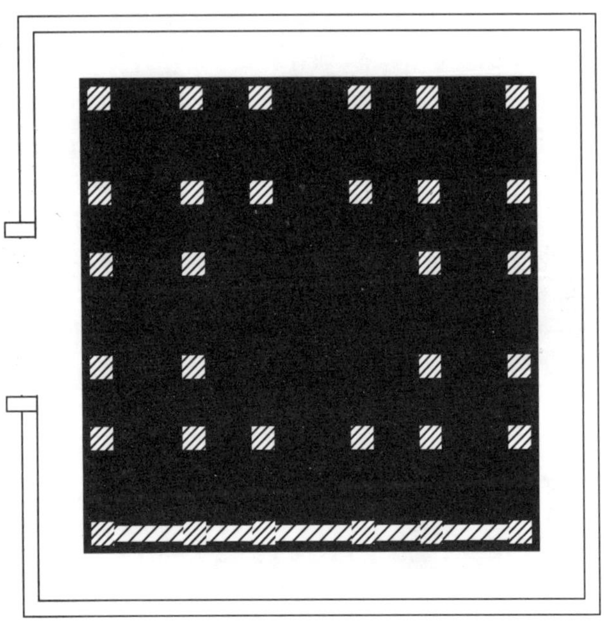

Figure 89: *Tomb of Rani Rupmati,* indication of internal space

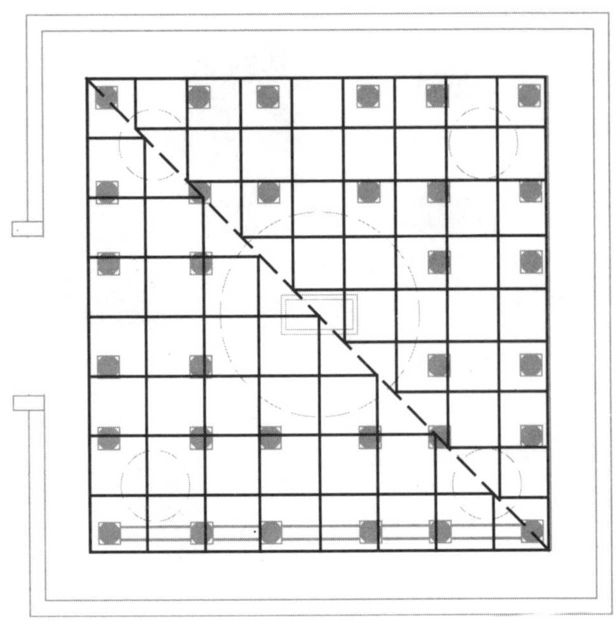

Figure 90: *Tomb of Rani Rupmati,* application of *Manduka Mandala* and *Paramashayika Mandala*

Plate 20

Tomb of Rani Rupmati (Plan)

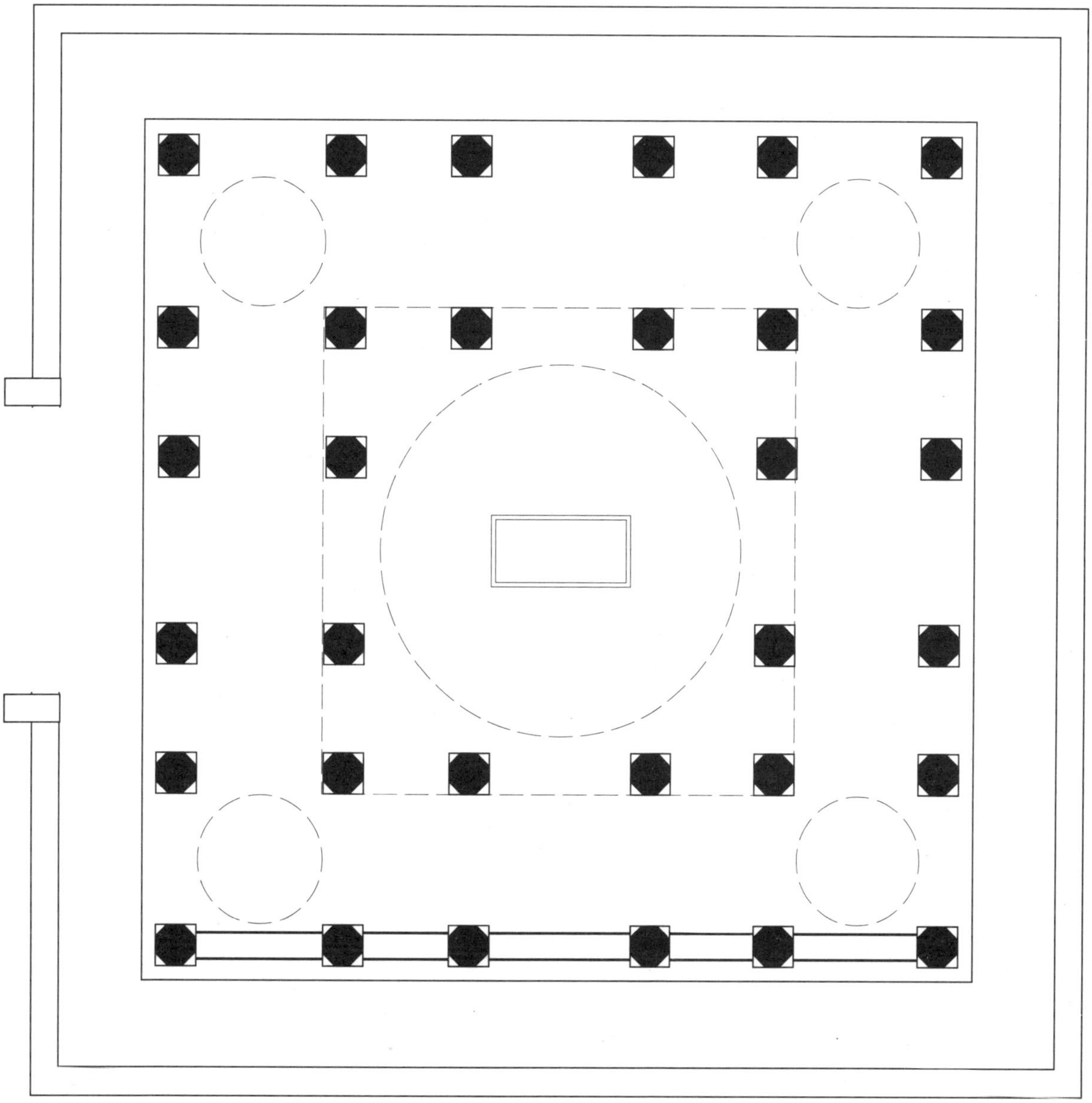

Figure 91). First, the first three ranks of *pada* fall at the lower edge of the *chajja*. Secondly, the dome is eight ranks high. Finally, the six pillars of each façade fall within the central ten files of *pada*.

It is of interest to note that *Tomb of Rani Rupmati* the and the *Mosque of Rani Rupmati* are in close proximity, but not aligned as one might find in a typical Gujarat *rauza* (See: **Figure 92**).[39] The two are not even of similar design. They were obviously built at different times. However, there is an alignment of sorts: the southwest corner of the *Tomb of Rani Rupmati* is 45^0 from the northeast corner of the *Mosque of Rani Rupmati* as indicated in **Figure 92**.

The *Tomb of Rani Rupmati* is an elegant example of the fusion of the Hindu and Islamic traditions. The relationship of the corner domes with that of the larger central dome would resurface again and again and culminate in the designs of the great Mughal tombs--i.e., the *Tomb of Humayun, Tomb of Khanan Khan* and the *Taj Mahal*. While larger tombs were being constructed in Delhi, this gem was constructed for a converted Hindu princess by a Muslim Sultan in far off Gujarat.

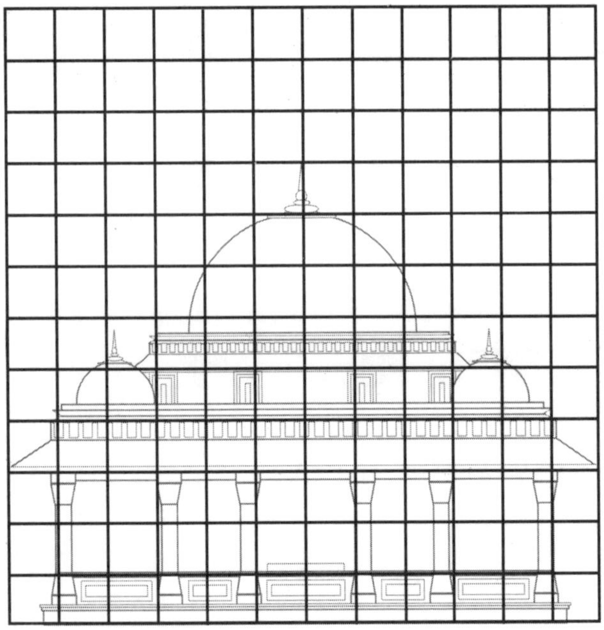

Figure 91: *Tomb of Rani Rupmati,* application of *Deshiya Mandala* over the elevation

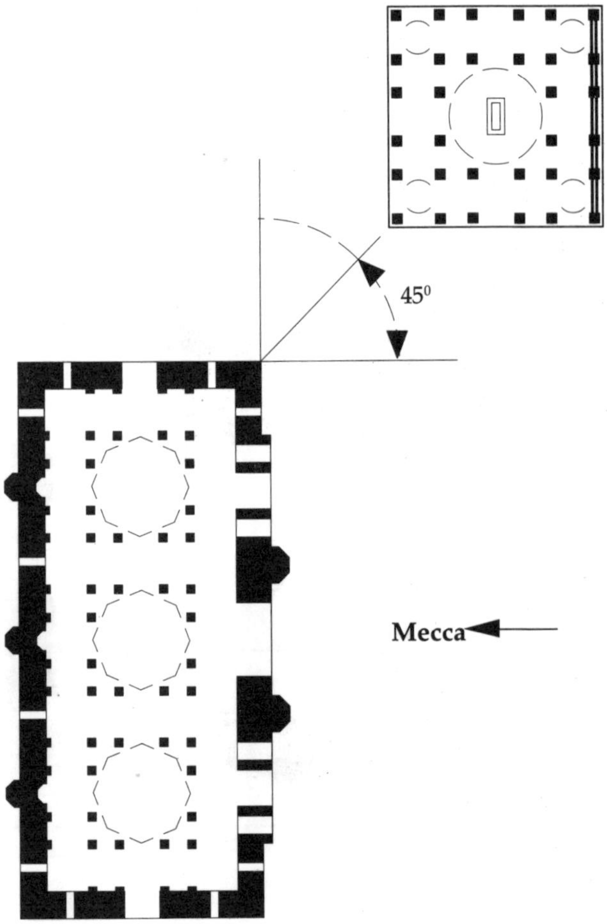

Figure 92: *Tomb of Rani Rupmati* (top) & *Masjid of Rani Rupmati* (bottom); indicating relationship

Plate 21

Tomb of Rani Rupmati (Elevation & half plan)

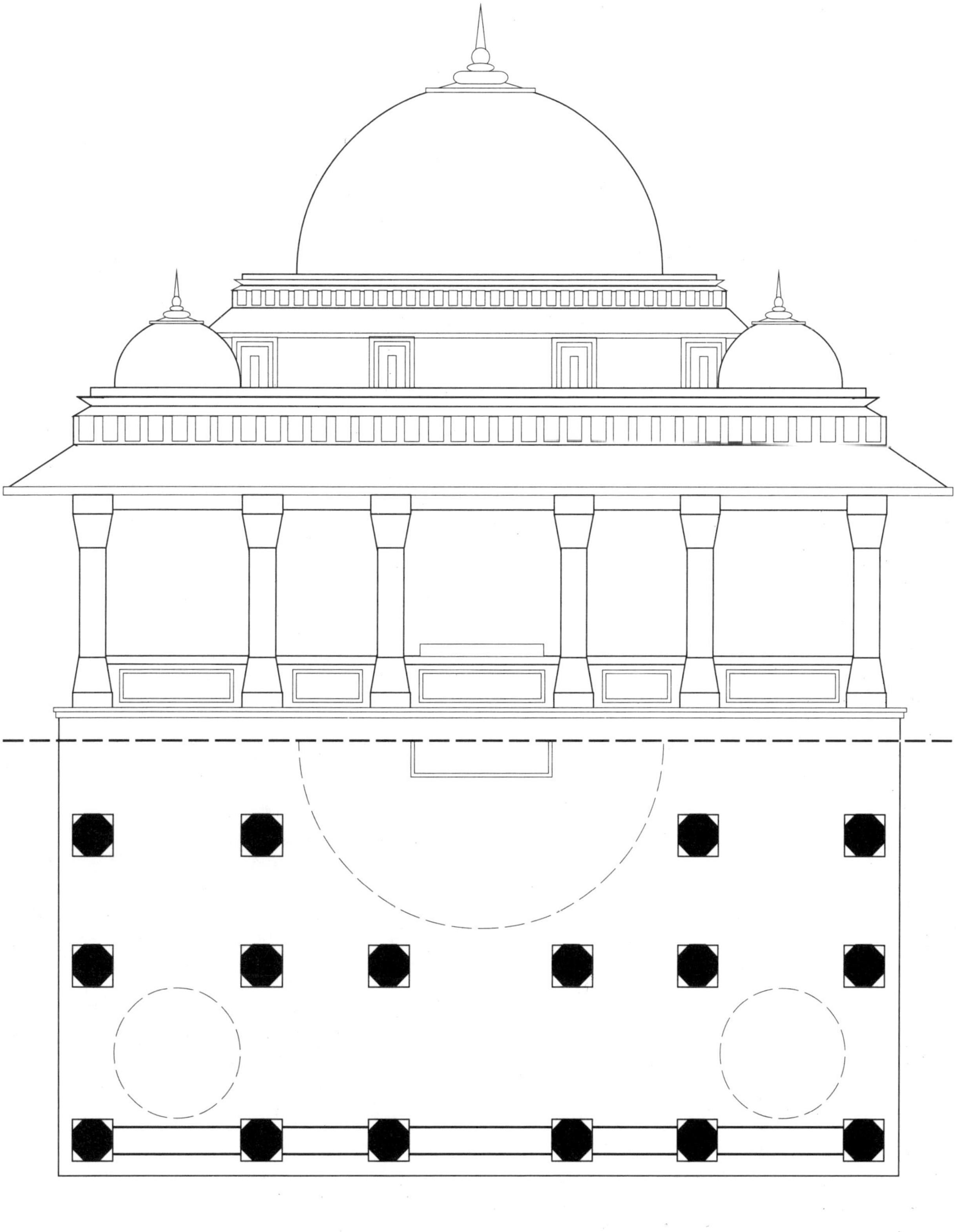

Tomb of Hushang Shah

Mandu, 1440 C.E.

To the southeast of Ahmadabad lies the provincial Malwa city of Mandu. There one finds the final resting place of the son of the Afghani noble, Dilavar Khan Ghuri, one Alp Khan. The mausoleum is known as the *Tomb of Hushang Shah.*[40] Hushang Shah or Husam al-Din Hushang Shah was the title assumed by Alp Khan when he put on the royal mantle of the Sultanate of Malwa. He was a warlike ruler, and continuously in conflict with the Gujarat Sultans, Mubarak Shah Sayyid of Delhi and the Bahmani rulers. Unfortunately his descendents also inherited this penchant and undertook fratricide and other forms of civil strife. The Ghuri Dynasty, of which Husam al-Din Hushang Shah was the second in th line, lasted but forty-four years (1392-1436).

The *Tomb of Hushang Shah* was constructed to the west of Mandu's Jami Masjid as an extension of this earlier building (See: **Figure 93**). This would seem to refer to the *rauza* ensembles so popular in neighboring Gujarat except for the fact that in the *rauza*, the mausoleum is generally to the east of the *masjid*. Here it is to the west.

Nonetheless, there are a considerable number of tombs in the Islamic world that have been appended to preexistent mosques as a matter of theological exigency. Monastic and memorial mosques frequently incorporate a tomb as the proximity of a deceased's remains to a place of prayer is most propitious.

Set within a large unencumbered open space the *Tomb of Hushang Shah* is a square block--i.e., a **Type B-d** basic plan. Indeed, the substantial tomb is the focus of the large space which mimics the massive *Jami Masjid*. Set upon a commodious podium, the tomb possesses two portals--i.e., one to the north and the main entrance to the south. Two openings with *jaali*

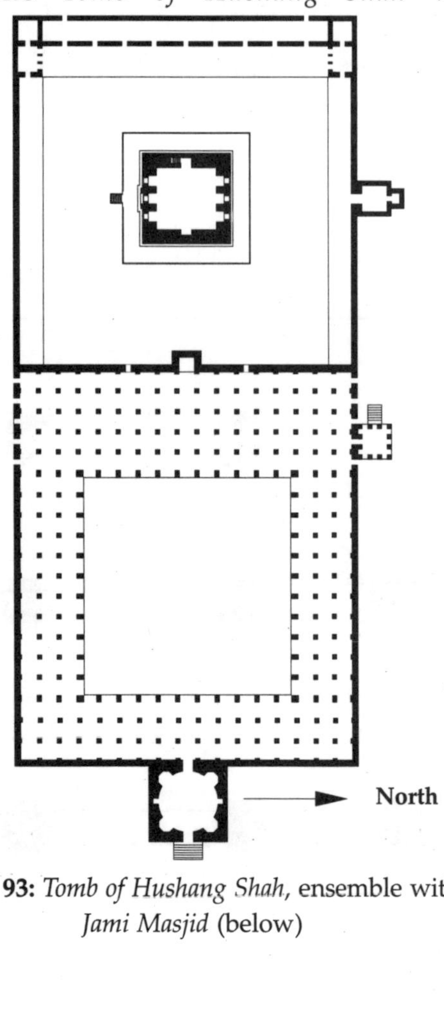

Figure 93: *Tomb of Hushang Shah,* ensemble with *Jami Masjid* (below)

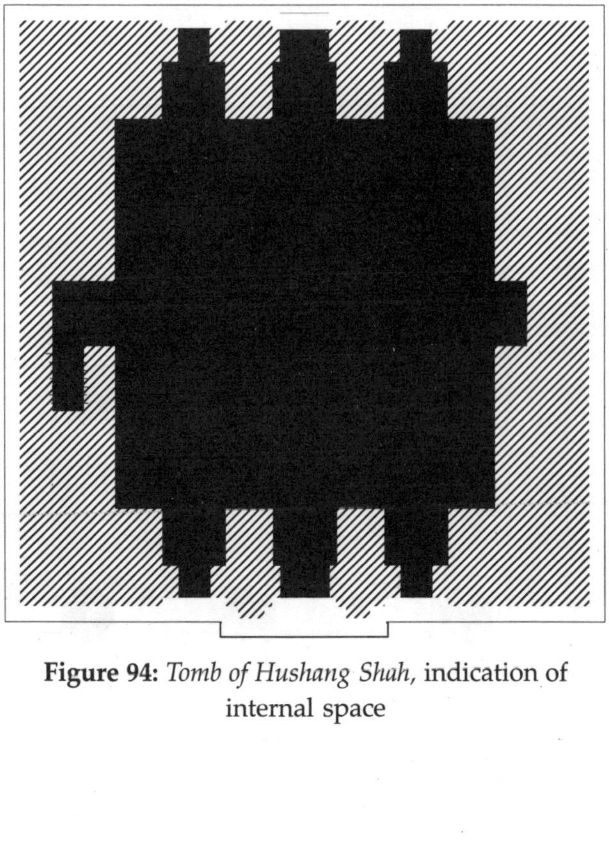

Figure 94: *Tomb of Hushang Shah,* indication of internal space

Plate 22
Tomb of Hushang Shah (Plan)

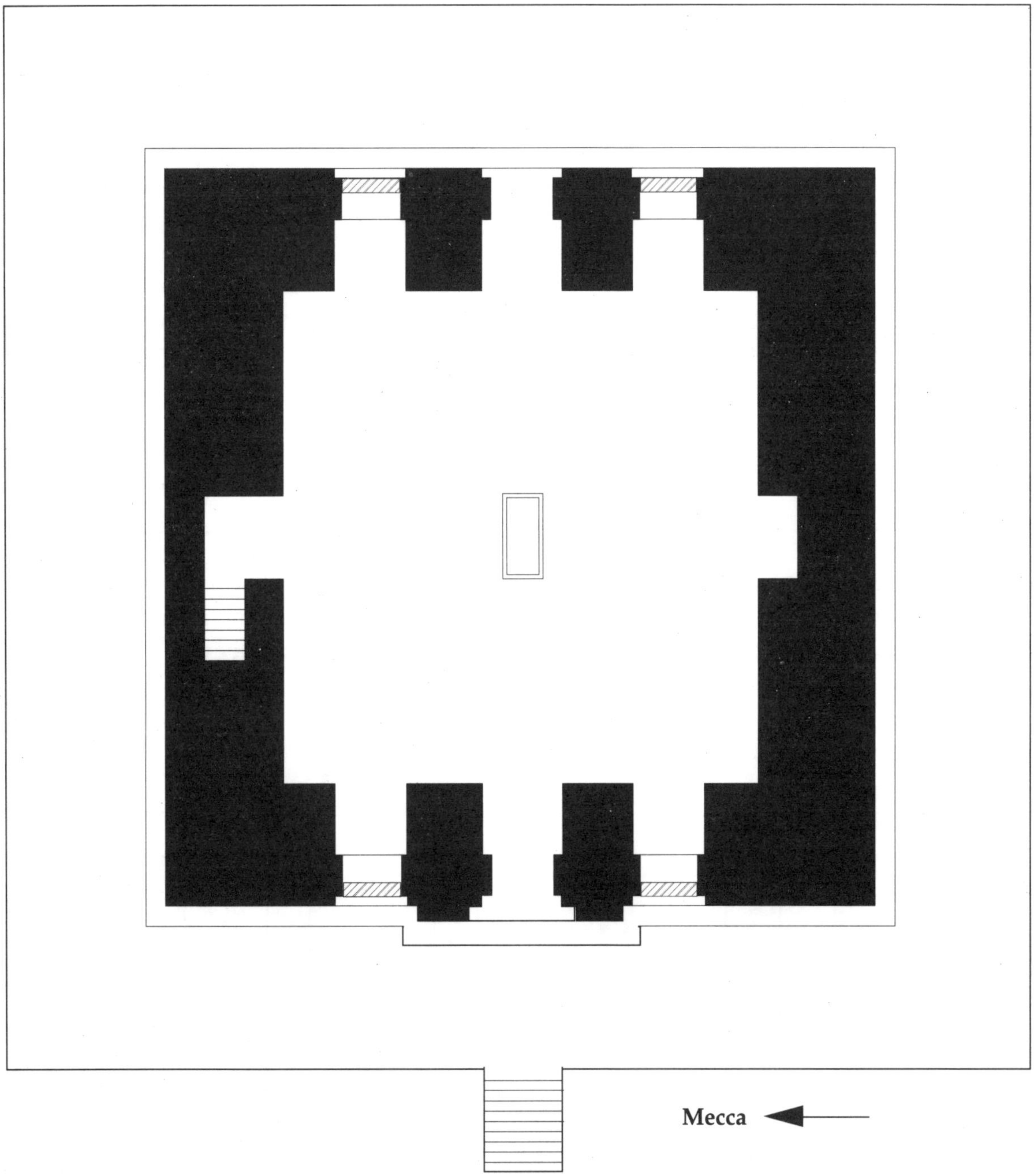

flank each of these doors. Over the square inner chamber a block extends, acting as the base for the substantial dome. At the corners of this extension are small domed structures resembling a solid or enclosed *chatri*. The whole is encased in white marble. This latter fact caused Shah Jahan to send architects to Mandu to study this mausoleum in preparation for the construction of the *Taj Mahal*.

The internal space of the *Tomb of Hushang Shah* is ample (See: **Figure 94**). Although circumambulation is possible within the tomb, it is not architecturally encouraged. However the spacious court in which the mausoleum is found more than makes up for the *Tomb of Hushang Shah's* lack of a *pradakshinapatha*.

The application of either a *Manduka Mandala* or a *Paramashayika Mandala* over the plan of the *Tomb of Hushang Shah* suggests that either could have been employed (See: **Figure 95**). In the both *mandalas* it is seen that the *brahmásthana* and the third rank enclose similar forms. The *Manduka Mandala* indicates that the two *jaali* openings are bounded by the third and sixth file of *pada*. The middle rank of the *Paramashayika Mandala* borders the eastern niche.

Finally, the application of *Deshiya Mandala* over the elevation indicates that the main block lies within the lower five ranks of pada (See: **Figure 96**). The extension of the central chamber, minus the merlons, fall within the sixth rank and the dome soars up to the ninth rank of pada. Therefore, it can be seen that the proportions of *Tomb of Hushang Shah* is 12:9.

Appended to a *masjid* of considerable size, a *masjid* which is covered by numerous domes, the square, solid *Tomb of Hushang Shah* sits within its own sizeable enclosure. Its plan is basically Buddhist-Hindu in form. The openings and domed forms of the mausoleum proclaims its Indo-Islamic genealogy.

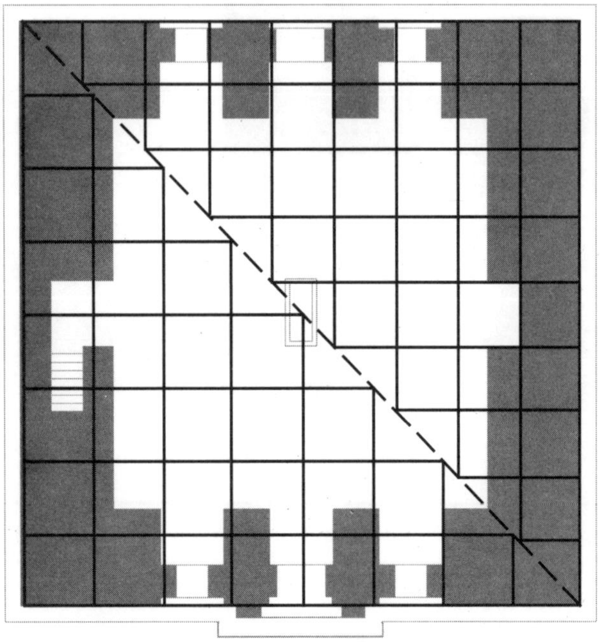

Figure 95: *Tomb of Hushang Shah,* application of *Manduka* and *Paramashayika Mandala*

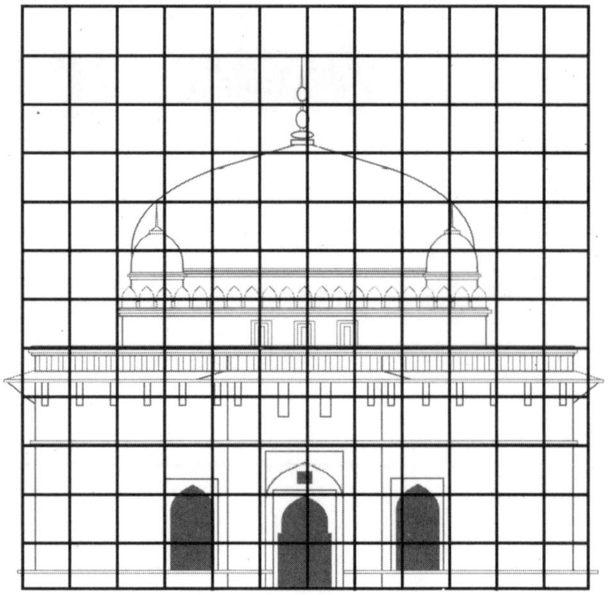

Figure 96: *Tomb of Hushang Shah,* application of *Deshiya Mandala* over the elevation

Plate 23

Tomb of Hushang Shah (Elevation & half plan)

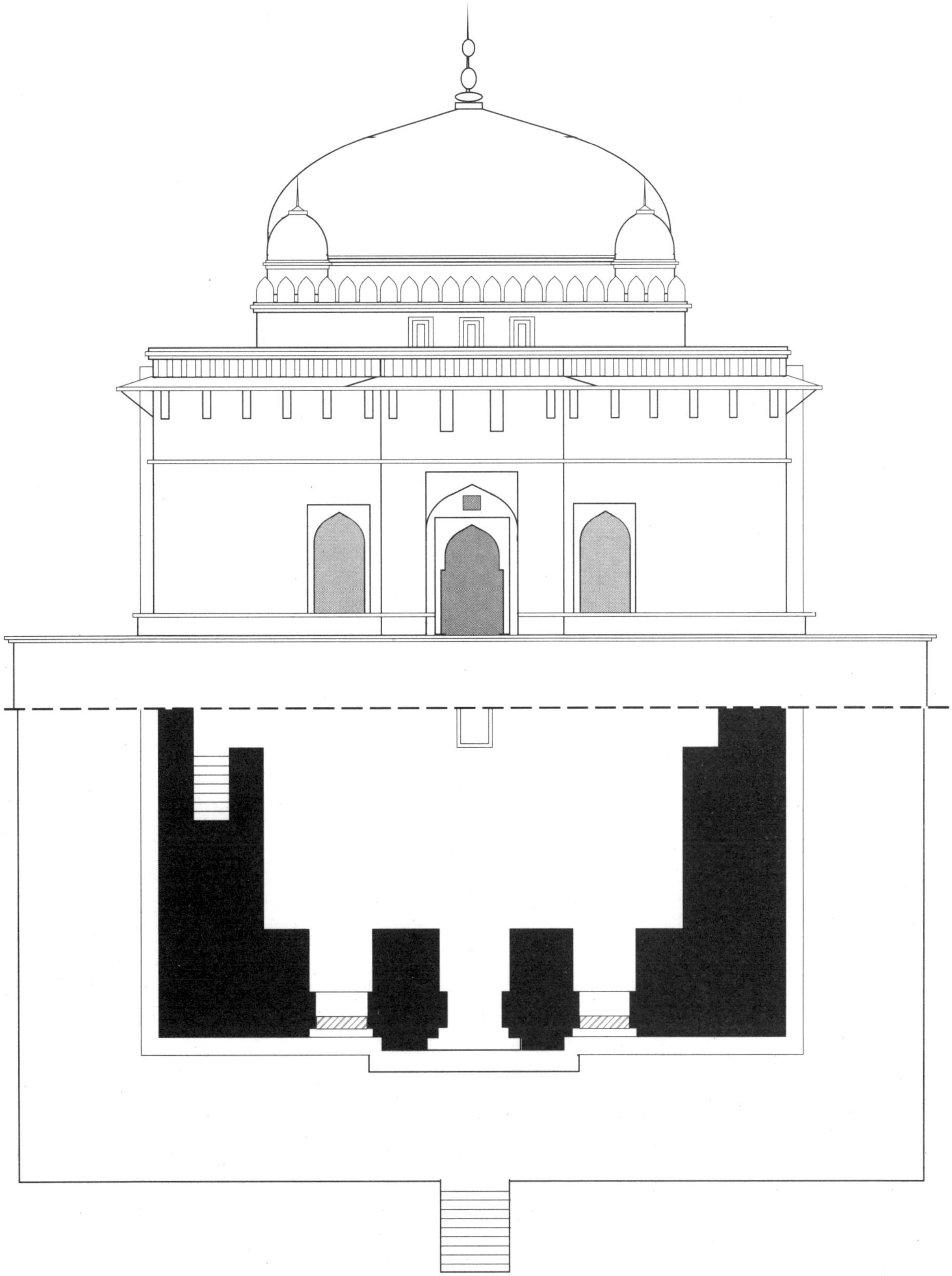

Sayyid Usman Rauza

Usmanpur, c. 1460 C.E.

The *Sayyid Usman Rauza*[41] of Usmanapur, Gujarat, is part of an ensemble of some note. It is the major element which consists of the tomb, a ablution tank and a mosque--i.e., a *rauza*. The *rauza*, an architectural motif in which a mausoleum is constructed facing or confronting a mosque of complementary design, becomes a theme with numerous variations in Indo-Islamic architecture. The *rauza* appears to be one way in which "the glory of the ruler would be duly preserved."[42] Frequently, but not exclusively, the mausoleum dominates the ensemble--e.g. the *Ibrahim Rauza*, the *Shah Navaz Khan Rauza* and the *Afzal Khan Rauza*, all of which are considered herein. The latter, the *Afzal Khan Rauza*, appears more as a unified whole than separate structures on opposition. Nonetheless, the *Rauza of Sayyid Usman* is noteworthy not because of its ensemble, but for the plan of the mausoleum--i.e., a **Type A-b** basic plan.

Heavily influenced by indigenous Hindu architectural forms, it is seen as one of the last Indo-Islamic mausoleums to utilize to such a wide extent the trabeated system favored by the Hindu *sthapati*. This is a true canopy tomb without solid walls surrounding the cenotaph. The central dome and the four, corner, subsidiary domes are vivid reminders of the *panchatayanya* temple form. More, the *Sayyid Usman Rauza* is closely related to the *Ladh Khan* in the manner of the ranks and files of columns and the predominantly cross axial composition. However, there is here interesting variations. The whole is surrounded by twelve columns on each side, amounting to forty-four encircling the perimeter of the mausoleum. This numerical configuration is utilized in both Hindu and Buddhist architecture[43] and possesses certain mystical associations. Twelve is a feminine number which denotes success completeness and perfection. In addition, it connotes immortality, a cosmic number which comprehends all numbers lower, as well as sacrifice.

Twelve is a number of major importance in this mausoleum. The central dome is supported not by eight pillars as one would expect, but by twelve. Frequently, almost exclusively, a square area (four sides or pillars) would be doubled (eight sides or pillars) and sometimes doubled again (sixteen sides or pillars) from which form or shape the dome would rise. Not so in the *Sayyid Usman Rauza*. The twelve pillars are doubled along their outer edges and two aisles (Indic: *pradakshinapatha*) are added, creating the twelve pillars per side on the outer edge of the square. Now, the doubling of

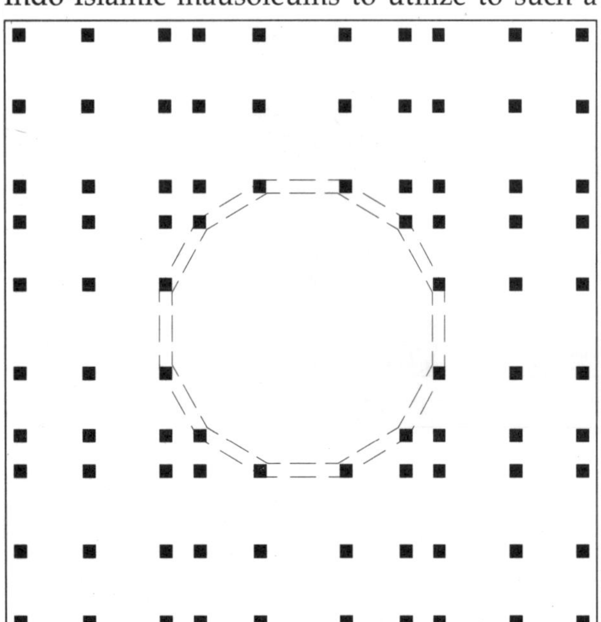

Figure 97: *Tomb of Sayyid Usman*, indicating an arrangement of ten pillars per side

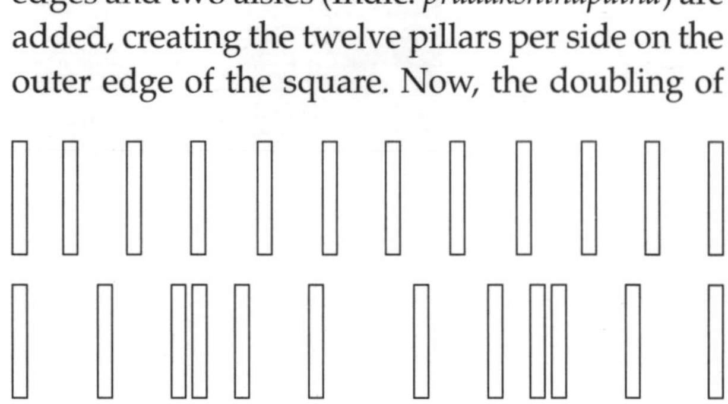

Figure 98: *Tomb of Sayyid Usman*, indicating arrangements of twelve pillars per side

Plate 24
Sayyid Usman Rauza (Plan, mausoleum)

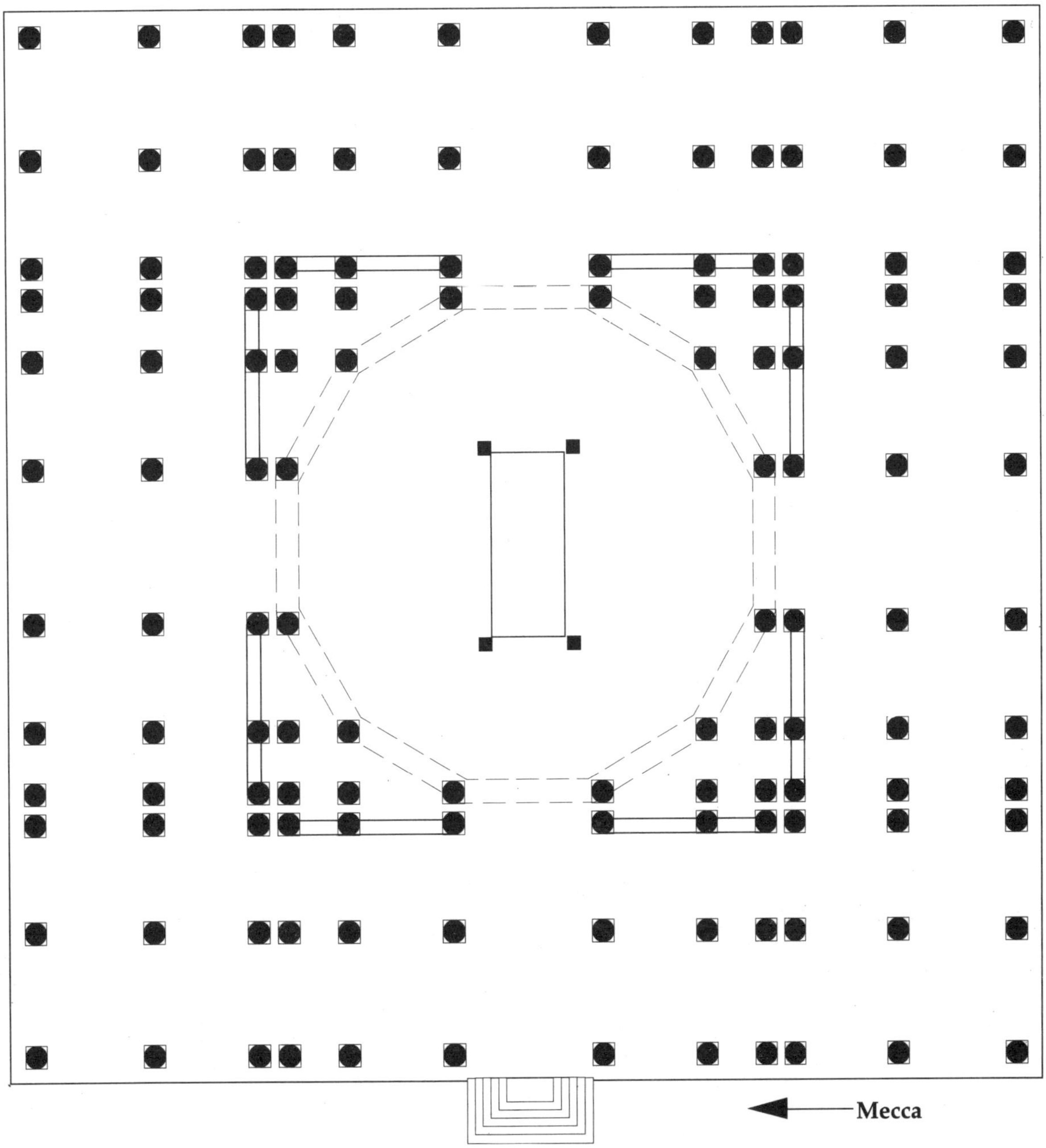

the outer pillars need not have occurred. This, however, would amounted to ten pillars per side with a total of thirty-six perimeter pillars (See: **Figure 97**). Ten, in Buddhist and Hindu iconography is a rather auspicious number--i.e., the first compound number representing unity from multiplicity, denoting completeness, success, wisdom and is associated with the sun. However, it is derived from twice five and five does possess meanings that may have been unacceptable to the Muslims--i.e., coming from the first masculine and feminine, it represents love and physical union of masculine and feminine. In addition, five is a magical number denoting the natural positive and negative elements, and therefore, may not have been acceptable.[44] On the other hand, thirty-six denotes macrocosmic completeness and is associated with the thirty-six components of Kashmiri Shaivism. In architecture it is represented by the thirty-six *chedi* which surround the central ensemble of *Wat Phra Si Rattana Mahathat* of Ayutthaya, Thailand. Numerically, thirty-six when reduced (3 + 6 = 9) is associated with the planet Mars. It is a number that is seldom seen in the architectural iconography of either Buddhism or Hinduism. Twelve was undoubtedly utilized because of its cosmic value. A numeral which was more important to the Buddhist and Hindu than to the Muslims. Its employment in this mausoleum is most interesting and may be attributed to the fact that Indian / Hindu *sthapati* were often employed in the construction of these earlier tombs.

The twelve pillars per side elevation as is represented in the *Sayyid Usman Rauza* presents a visually interesting aspect--i.e., twelve pillars evenly spaced is less interesting than twelve spaced as they are in this mausoleum (See: **Figure 98**). However, Buddhist, Hindu and Islamic design was essentially based upon balance of equals as is seen in the Islamic predilection for the nine-fold design concept as well as in the divisions of the traditional *chahar-bagh*.

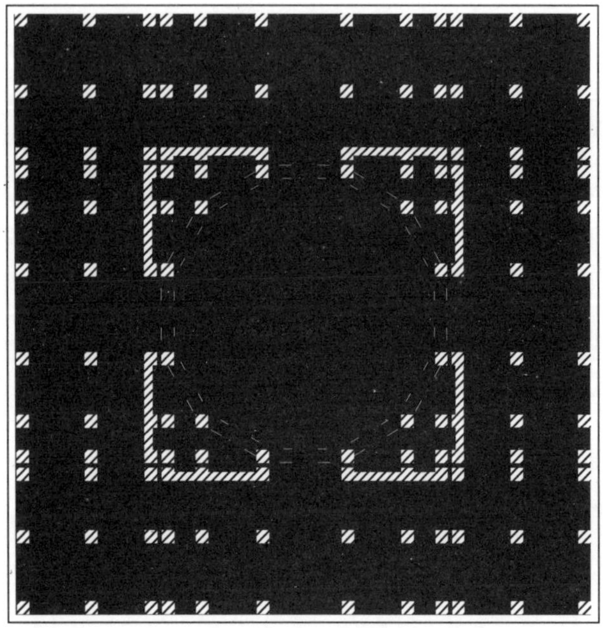

Figure 99: *Tomb of Sayyid Usman*, indication of internal space

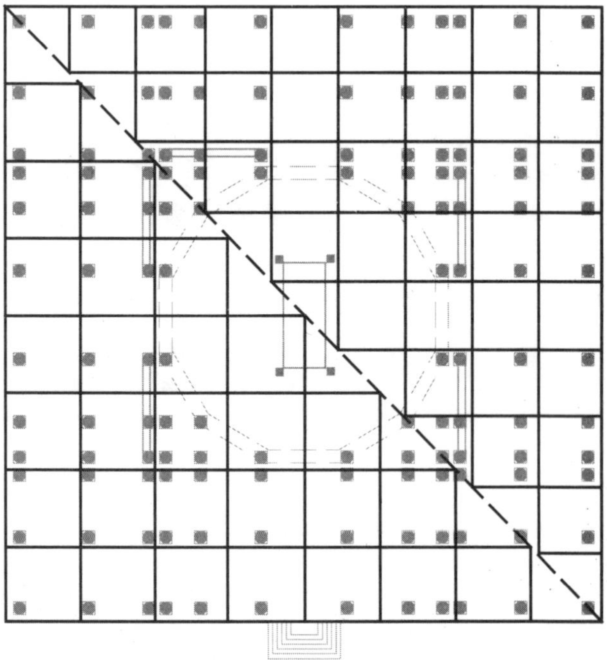

Figure 100: *Tomb of Sayyid Usman*, application of *Manduka* and *Paramashayika Mandala*

Plate 25

Sayyid Usman Rauza (Elevation & half plan)

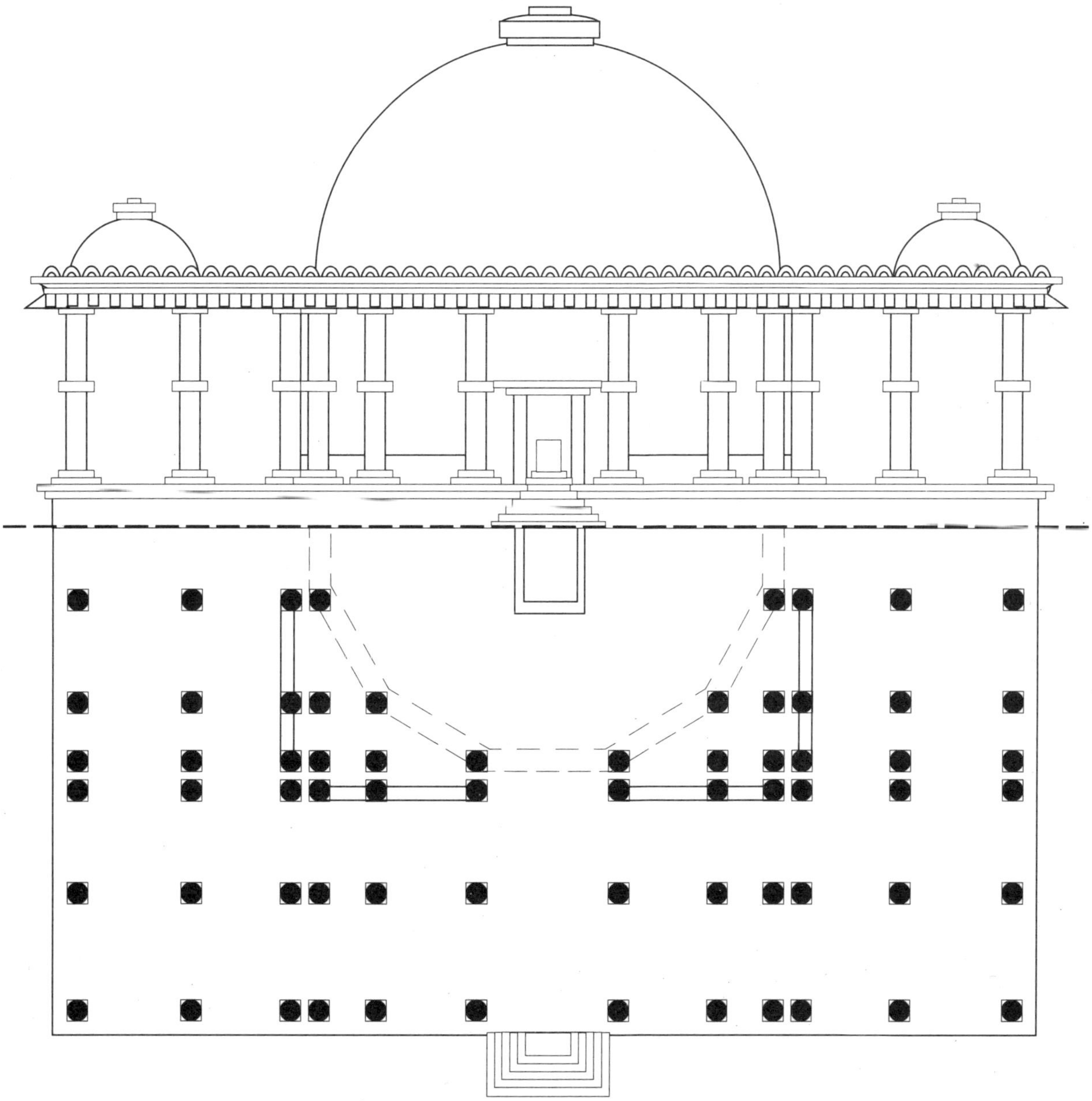

The open canopy design of the mausoleum of the *Sayyid Usman Rauza* is one that is not frequently encountered in the Indo-Islamic tombs. This is seen as a traditional influence of Islamic tombs (rain on the tomb). The area in which the sarcophagus is found, *en plan*, divided from the mausoleum's aisles (Indic: *pradakshinapatha*) by a low balustrade, square in form and enclosing the twelve dome-supporting pillars. It acts as the enclosing walls encountered in most other Islamic tombs and is here seen as representative of the **Type A-b** basic plan. The domes are hemispherical--i.e., single centered arc--in form, with a squat cupola atop each.

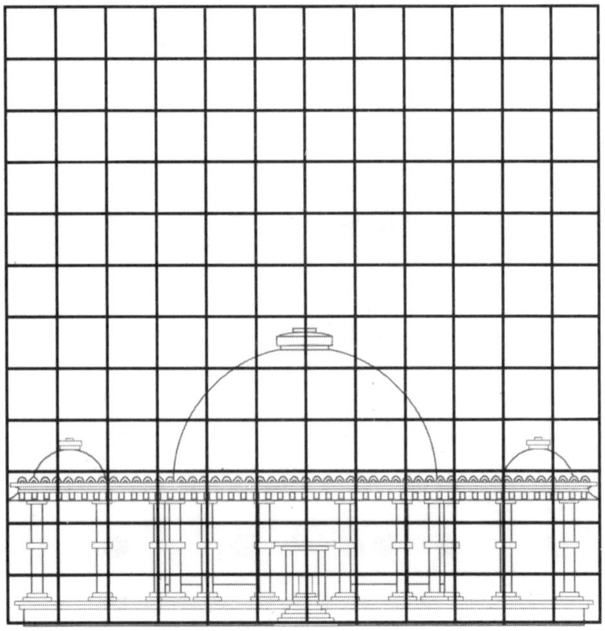

Figure 101: *Tomb of Sayyid Usman*, application of *Deshiya Mandala* over the elevation

The use of the strict canopy design without the employment solid walls allows for a considerable amount of internal space (See: **Figure 99**). When compared to previous examples as well as later examples, the *Sayyid Usman Rauza* exhibits, proportionally, more internal space than any other Indo-Islamic tomb.

When either the *Manduka Mandala* or *Paramashayika Mandala* are superimposed over the plan, the latter, the *Paramashayika Mandala* appears to offer the best solution (See: **Figure 100**). In the use of this *mandala*, the *marmas* are not compromised and the *brahmásthana* is bounded by the dodecagon of the dome's podium. The area with the low balustrade is enclosed within the ranks of the secondary mansion or rank of deities.

The elevation of the *Sayyid Usman Rauza* is considerably "squatter" than other tombs of the same or later periods. It, proportionally, is nearly half of what other square tombs exhibit (See: **Figure 101**). The area from the podium to the top of the merlons falls within the first three ranks of pada. The dome extends up to pada five-and one-half. Therefore, the proportions are 12:5.5.

The plan, rooted as it in more traditional Hindu plans, is, nonetheless, interesting in the application of the dome(s). The *Sayyid Usman Rauza* is truly a unique Indo-Islamic mausoleum.

Plate 26
Sayyid Usman Rauza (plan)

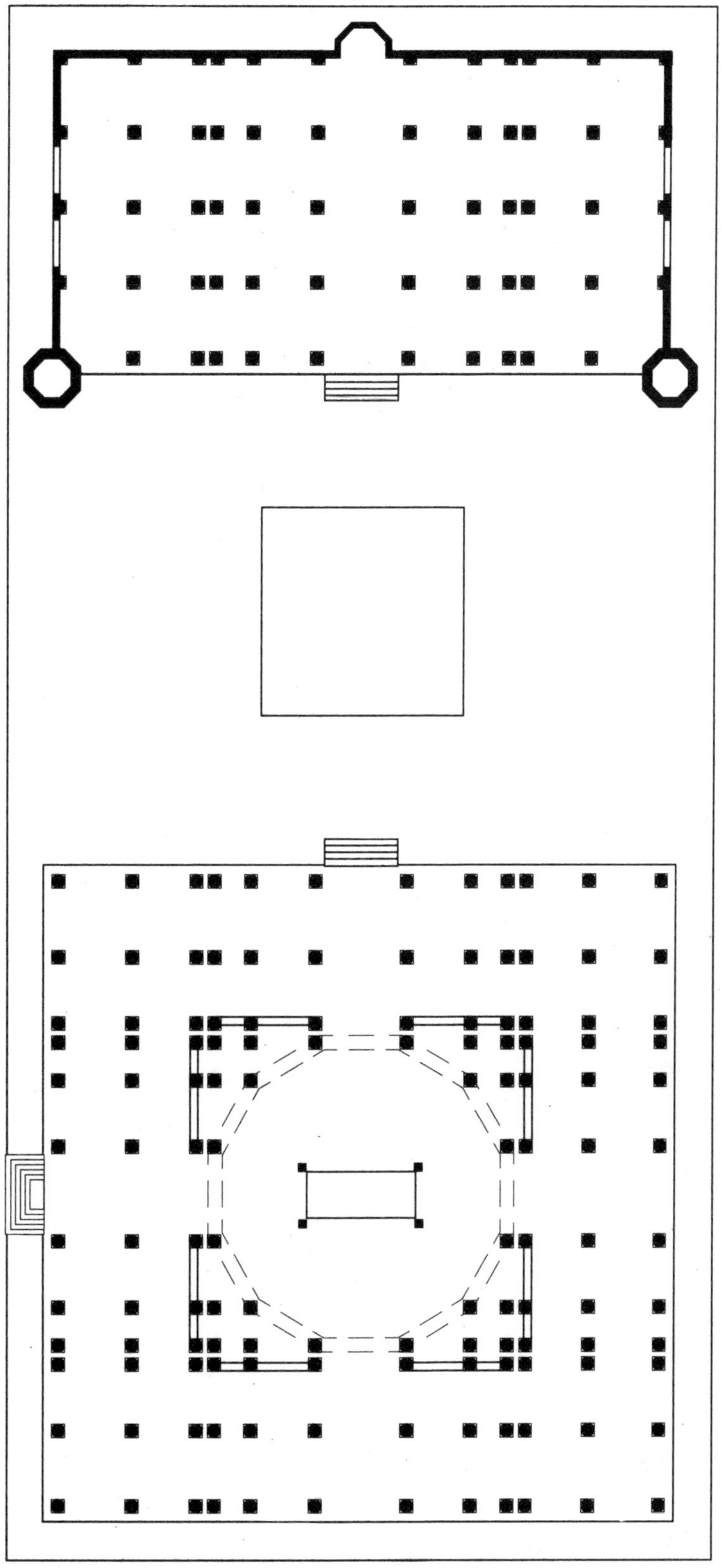

Tomb of Chotte Khan Ka Gunbad

Delhi, c. 1481 C.E.

The tomb in Delhi, locally known as the *Tomb of Chotte Khan Ka Gunbad*[45] (aka *Shish Gumbad*), is typical of the tombs of the short lived Lodi / Afgani Dynasty. It was constructed during the reign of the Lodi Sultan Buhlul Lodi, and thought to originally to have been for the Afghani noble, Mubarak Khan, the father of Darya Khan. As such it bears certain similarities to the Tughluq Dynasty--i.e., its square plan, the three entrances and the tall proportion of the façade--i.e., a **Type B-b** basic plan. On the other hand, the *Tomb of Chotte Khan Ka Gunbad* does not possess the unremitting fortress like appearance of the *Tomb of Ghiyas-ud-din Tughluq I* or the *Tomb of Firuz Shah Tughluq*. However, it appears to presage what is to come in its resemblance to the great Mughal tombs of a little over a century to come--i.e., with its basically square ninefold plan, as well as the division of the façade into a two storey arrangement.

As with the tombs of the Tughluqs, there are certain defensive manifestations that are to be seen, especially in the elevation. The corner cubes as well as the taller central façades are topped by a form of crenelations. This is also true of the plinth from which the dome rises as well as the final decorative cap-stone of the dome. The resident of this tomb, therefore, declares his connection with the warrior king and defender of the faith.

The *Tomb of Chotte Khan Ka Gunbad* is made up of four, recessed, corner blocks topped with kiosks. A taller and extending central form juts out beyond these corner blocks. On the north, south and east sides portals are pierced and give way to the central chamber. An octagonal form extends above the chamber, and upon which the dome rests. This formula is seen in later tombs--i.e., the *Tomb of Humayun*, the *Tomb of Khan Khanan* and the *Taj Mahal*.

The proportion of width to height as seen in the *Tomb of Chotte Khan Ka Gunbad* is nearly identical to that seen in the later *Tomb of Khan Khanan* (See: **Appendix C**, **Plate 116**, p. 263). The

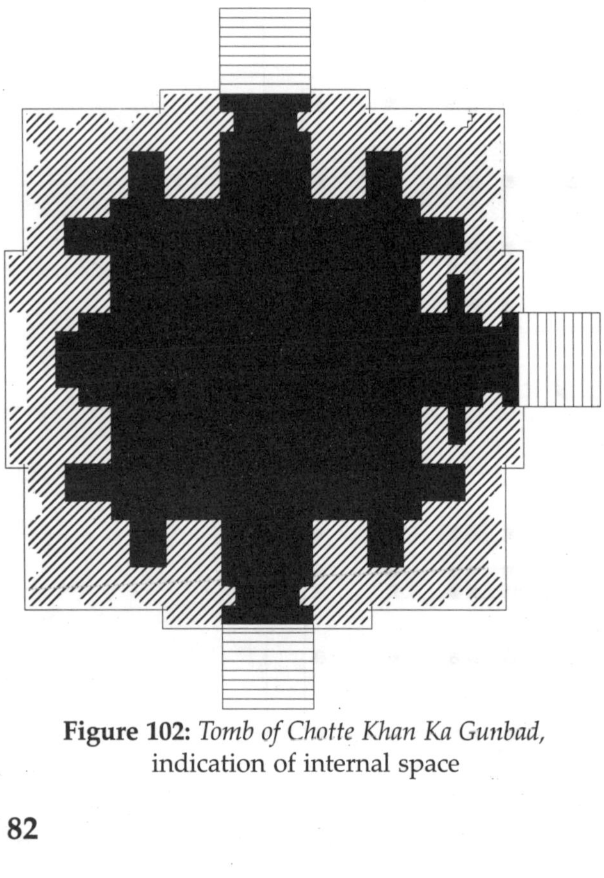

Figure 102: *Tomb of Chotte Khan Ka Gunbad*, indication of internal space

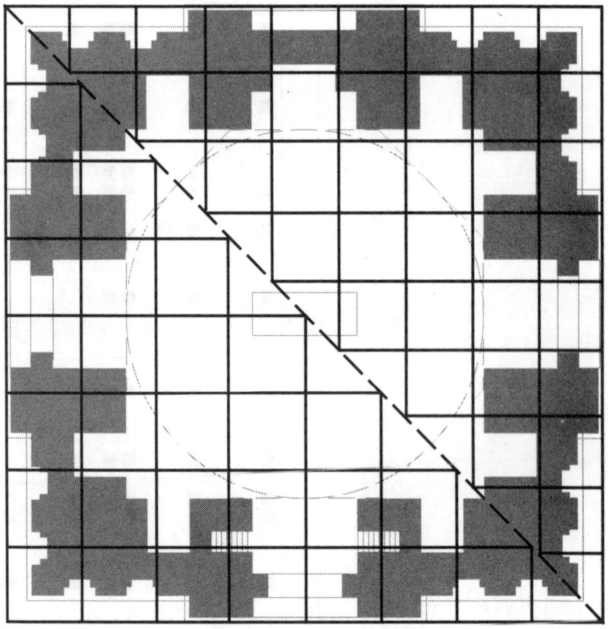

Figure 103: *Tomb of Chotte Khan Ka Gunbad*, application of *Manduka* and *Paramashayika Mandala*

Plate 27
Tomb of Chotte Khan Ka Gunbad (Plan)

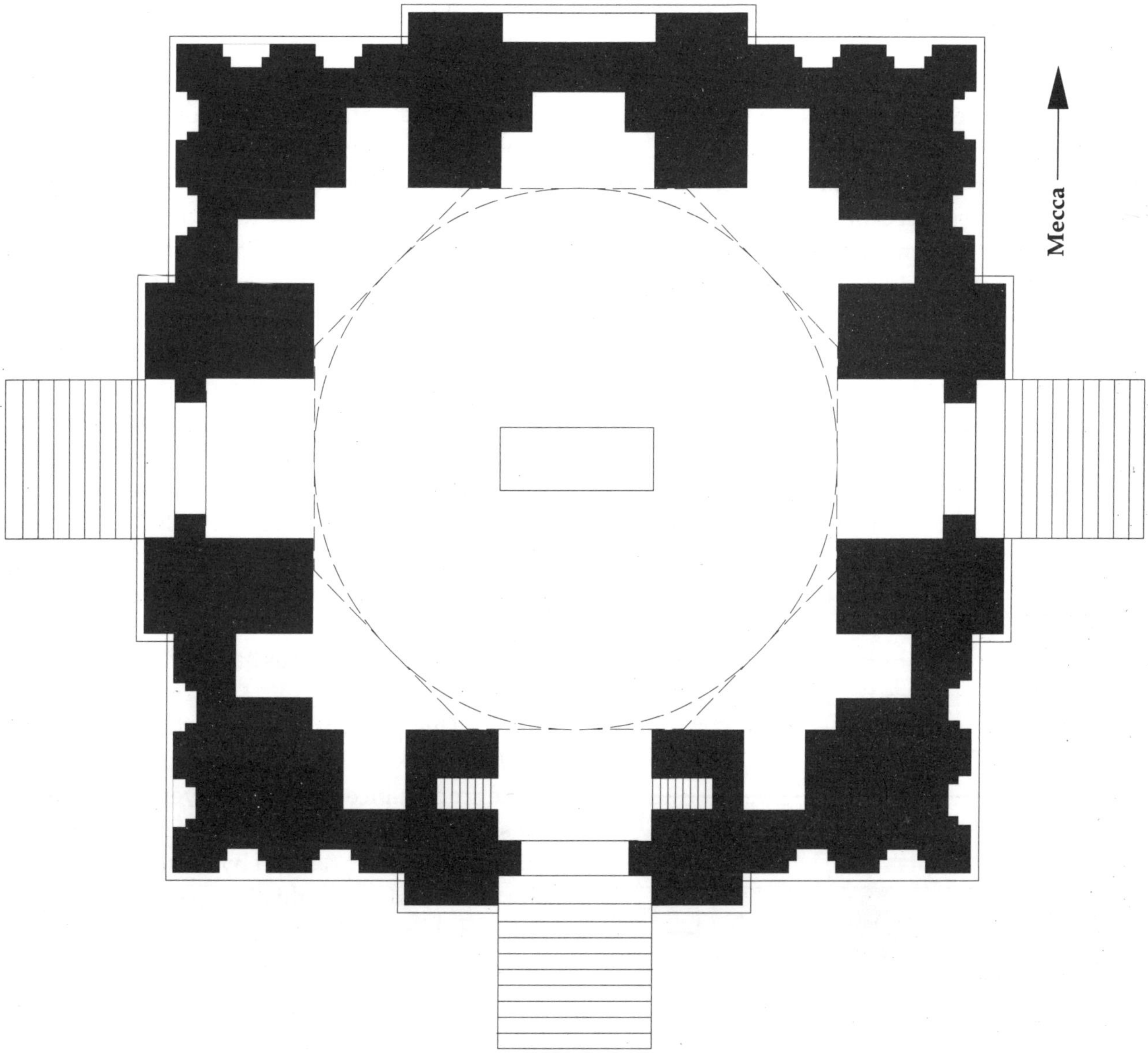

same proportion of this tomb when compared to the *Tomb of Humayun* indicates that the former is taller, in proportion than the latter. Finally, in comparing this tomb with the *Taj Mahal* it is to be seen that they are both close to the same height-width ratio. However, the main block of the *Taj Mahal* is nearly a third shorter than the *Tomb of Chotte Khan Ka Gunbad,* making the latter it appear taller in comparison.

The inner space is essentially square with wide vestibules and an equally wide *mikhrab.*

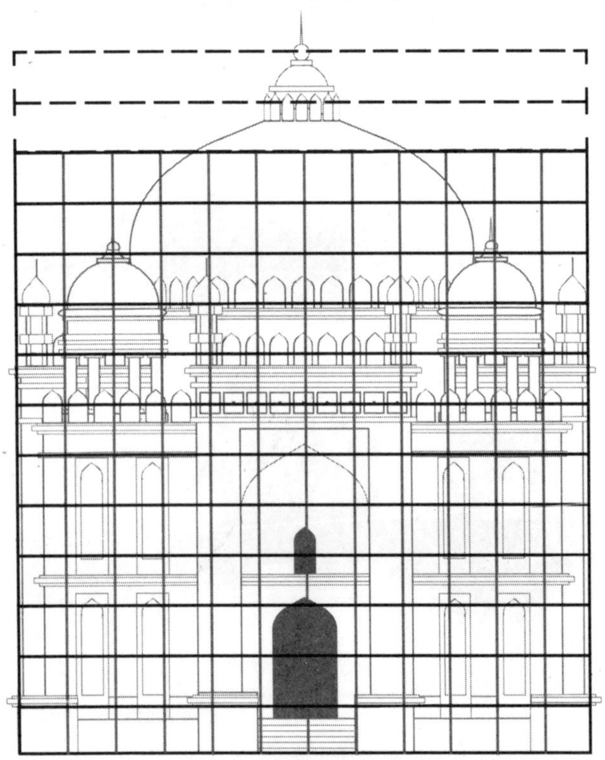

Figure 104: *Tomb of Chotte Khan Ka Gunbad,* application of *Deshiya Mandala* over the elevation

What is unique here is the fact that on each wall surface there are two rather deep niches. They add to the inner space (See: **Figure 102**) and appear to presage the addition of separate entrances that can be seen in later great Mughul tombs noted above.

In considering a possible *mandala* form to the *Tomb of Chotte Khan Ka Gunbad,* either the *Manduka Mandala* or the *Paramashayika Mandala* are applicable (See: **Figure 103**). However, the *Paramashayika Mandala* seems to possess closer conjunctions than does the *Manduka Mandala.*

Finally, in superimposing a *Deshiya Mandala* over the elevation, it is seen that the total height of the tomb exceeds the height by two ranks (See: **Figure 104**). Several tombs under consideration also possess a taller proportion (See: **Appendix C**). The plinth falls within the first rank while the dome rises above the ninth rank. Therefore, the *Tomb of Chotte Khan Ka Gunbad* may be viewed as having the proportions of 12:13.

This jewel from the Lodis, this *Tomb of Chotte Khan Ka Gunbad* would appear to possess more importance than it is given credit for in most sources. A façade which is made up of an impressive *pishtaq* flanked by blocks upon which sit substantial *chatri;* this is repeated on all four sides and from the middle rises an octagonal form surmounted by a dome. For the *Tombs of Humayun, Khan Khanan* and the *Taj Mahal,* the basic formula is constant, only the proportions of the various elements differ.

Plate 28

Tomb of Chotte Khan Ka Gunbad (Elevation & half plan)

Tomb of Mubarak Sayyid

Mahmudabad, c. 1484 C.E.

Mubarak Sayyid of Gujarat, not to be confused with Mubarak Shah Sayyid of Delhi, is known for his tomb which was one of the first in Gujarat to utilize a truly arcuated system. It was constructed during the reign of Nasir-ud-Din Mahmud Shah I Beghara (1459-1511).

Like the *Tomb of Sayyid Usman* of Usmanapur, the plan of the *Tomb of Mubarak Sayyid*[46] is essentially based on preexistent Hindu models[47]--i.e., a **Type A-b** basic plan. Specifically, there is a strong association with the *Ladh Khan* of Aihole, and the assembly halls from which that temple was based. Here is a true canopy tomb without a walled chamber for the cenotaph. What sets this tomb apart from it predecessors is the fact that rather than utilizing the trabeated system that Hindu *sthapati* had employed for millennia, the rulers insisted upon a more appropriate system of architecture for their tombs and *masjid*, a system appropriate to established Islamic practices and ideals. This system, this arcuated system had been employed by builders in the West and Near East for centuries, and although it was not originally rooted in Islamic practice, it was adapted by Islam as it best provided the large, uninterrupted space so necessary for congregational worship.[48]

The tomb consists of a façade(s) with eight pillars, totaling sixty in all. The four central pillars were not employed allowing for the surmounting dome and the space surrounding the cenotaph. As is seen in the *Tomb of Sayyid Usman* an open *jaali* surrounds this area. Two ambulating aisles (Ind.: *pradakshinapatha*) enclose

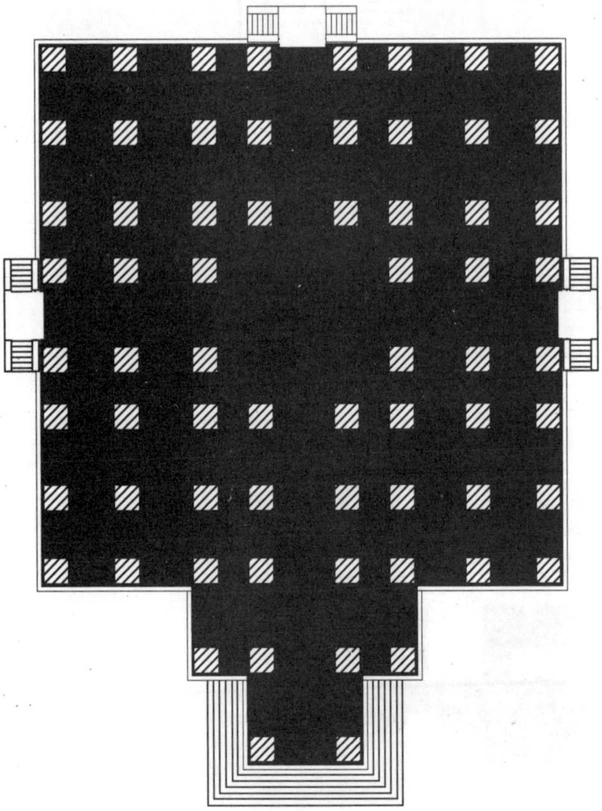

Figure 105: *Tomb of Mubarak Sayyid,* indication of internal space

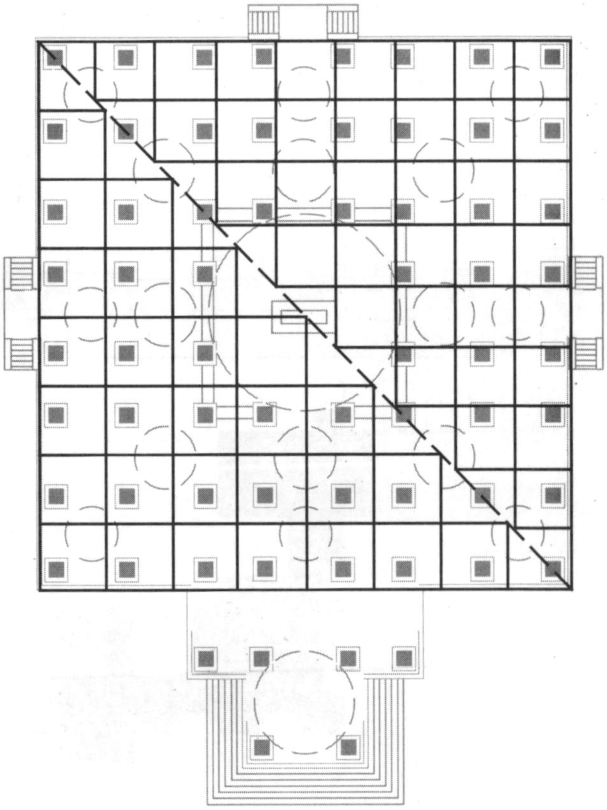

Figure 106: *Tomb of Mubarak Sayyid,* application of *Manduka* and *Paramashayika Mandala*

Plate 29

Tomb of Mubarak Sayyid (Plan)

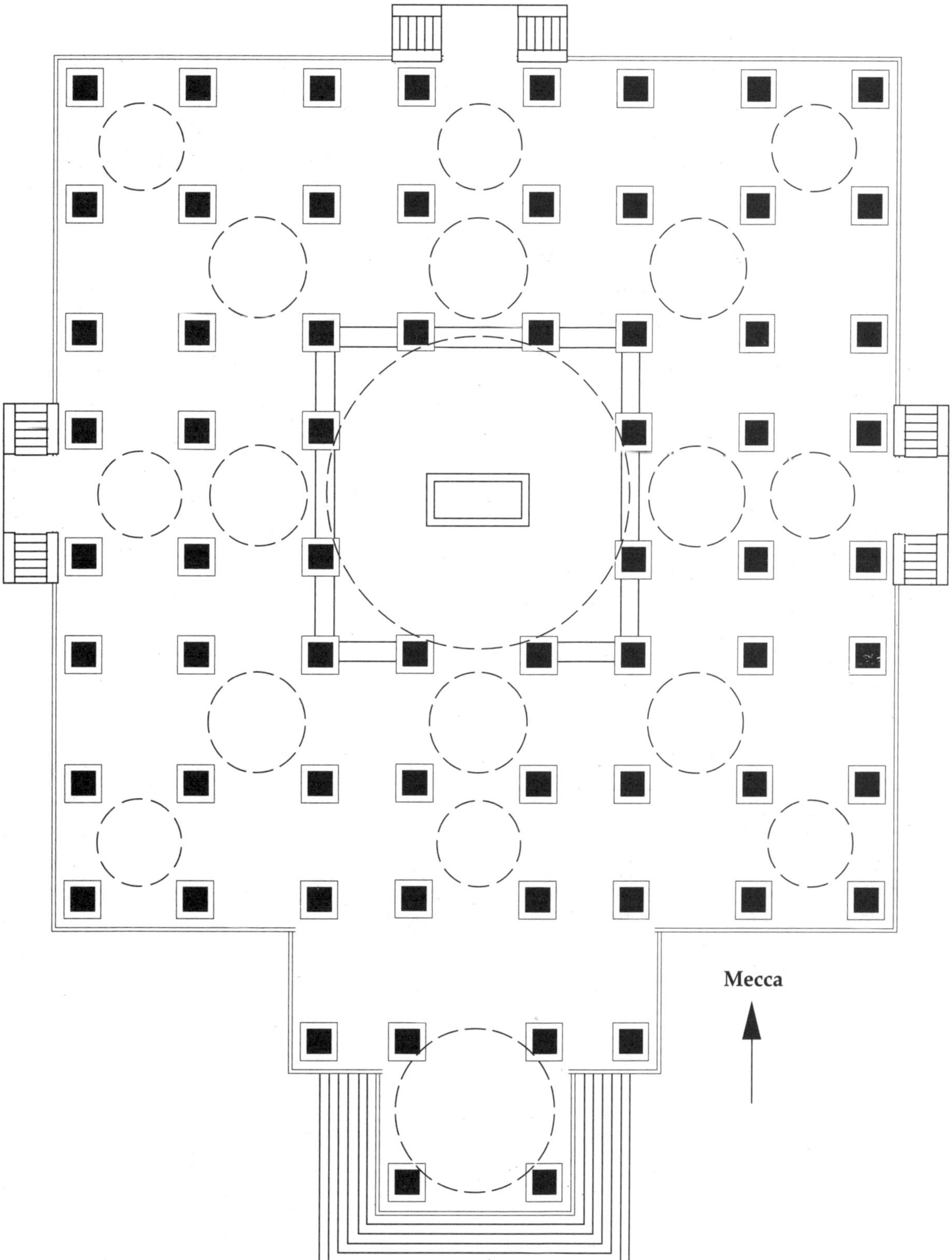

the central area. Over the square bays were placed small domes. To the east, the direction opposite the orientation towards Mecca, is an additional extension, a porch which is seen a concession to the *sthapati's* Hindu-rooted background.[49] Therefore, the east-west elevation is longer than its north-south counterpart

As with the *Tomb of Sayyid Usman*, the interior space of this tomb is considerable (See: **Figure 105**). The space is, proportionally greater than that found in the octagonal tombs and the

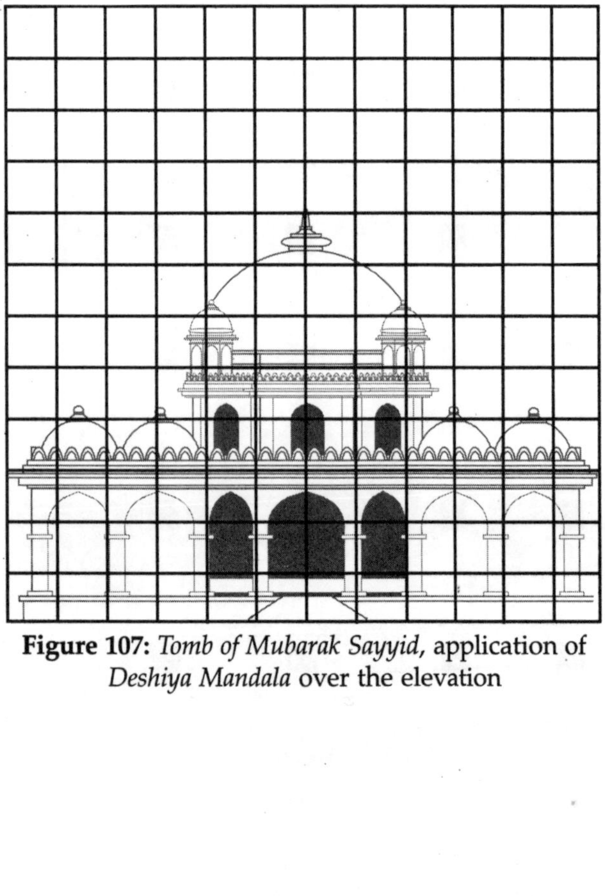

Figure 107: *Tomb of Mubarak Sayyid*, application of *Deshiya Mandala* over the elevation

later square tombs with the possible exception of Bijapur's *Gol Gumbaz*.

When applying either a *Manduka Mandala* or a *Paramashayika Mandala*, it is seen that the former is eminently suitable (See: **Figure 106**). The cenotaph and the sarcophagus below are contained within the *brahmásthana*, and each of the subsequent ranks and files of columns fall within the appropriate rank and file of *pada*.

When a *Deshiya Mandala* is superimposed over the elevation (See: **Figure 107**) it is seen that the podium, the arched openings and the *chajja*. The smaller domes over the square bays fall within the fourth rank and the total is contained within the lower eight *pada* ranks. This allots the proportion of 12:8 to the elevation of this structure.

Gujarat is known for many magnificent Indo-Islamic structures. Certainly, Ahmedabad, the capital boasts numerous examples built during the reigns of the Muzaffarid Shahi. Yet, the *Tomb of Mubarak Sayyid*, less than twenty miles outside this capital stands as a brilliant jewel in the collective crown of Gujarat. First to utilize the arcuated system as an exclusive system in the state, the square plan reflects the lesser noble status of Mubarak Sayyid. The open design, not antithetical to Islamic practice, is, nonetheless, seen as a Hindu influence. It is a suitable monument within the ranks of Indo-Islamic tombs.

Plate 30

Tomb of Mubarak Sayyid (Elevation & half plan)

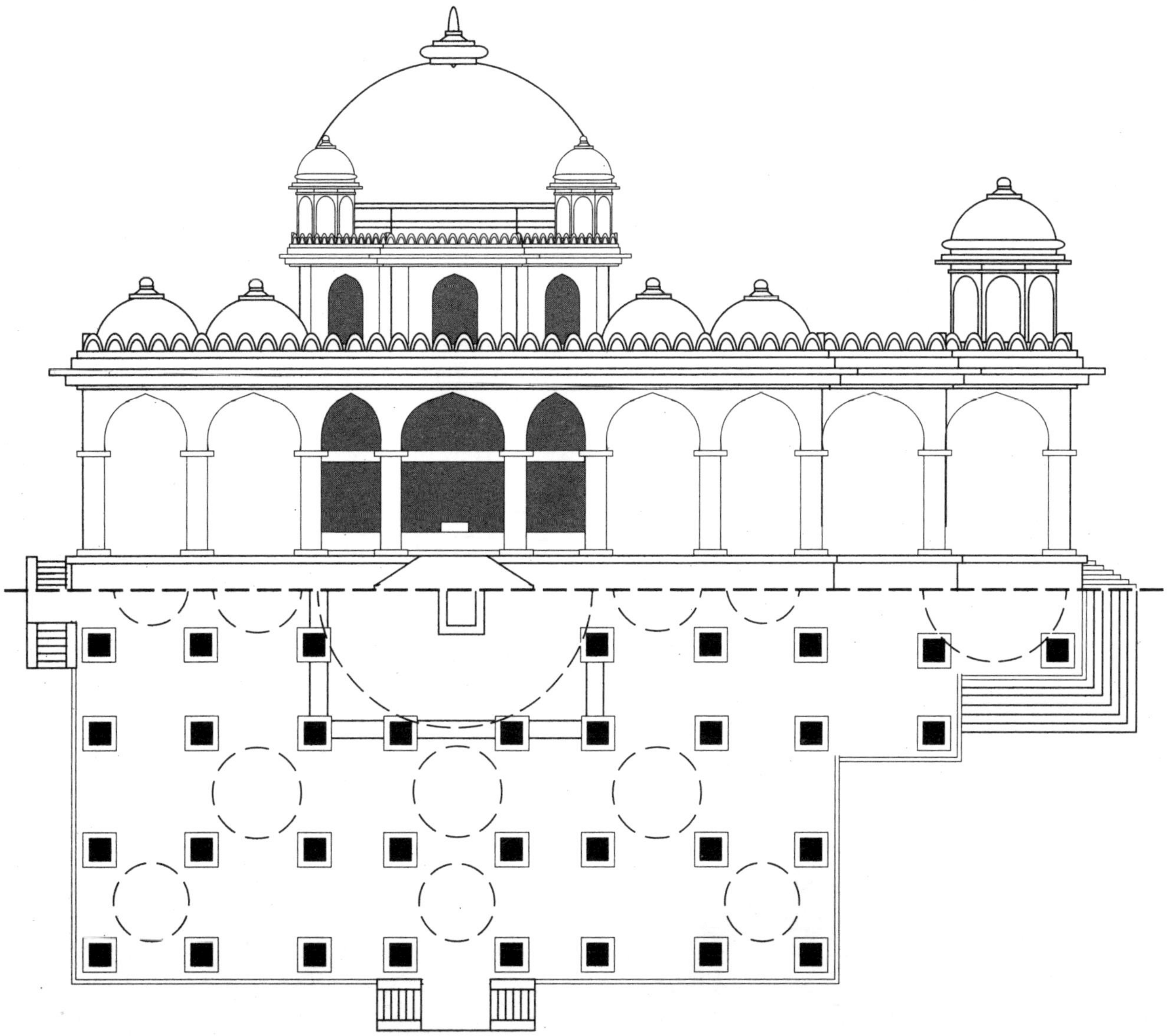

Tomb of Sikandar Lodi

Delhi, c. 1518 C.E.

The short lived Lodi Dynasty (1451-1526 C.E.) politically had neither little to recommend it nor the atmosphere to sustain it. The Delhi Sultanate had fallen from its pinnacle of power and achievement by the beginning of the Fifteenth Century, C.E. The prominent positionachieved by the Slave or Mamluk Dynasty saw an inexorable decline towards the end of the Tughluq Dynasty. By the time that the first of the Sayyids assumed power--i.e., Khizr Khan (1414-1421 C.E.)--the coffers were virtually empty and the area of the Delhi Sultanate's dominance was steadily shrinking. Through the Sayyid Dynasty and then the Lodi Dynasty, the sultanate was a mere shadow of its former glory. Even under the able leadership of Sikandar Lodi, the inexorable slide could not be effectively halted. Within nine years after his death, the Delhi Sultanate fell to the Timurud, the Great Mughal, Babur of Ferghana.

Nonetheless, the *Tomb of Sikandar Lodi*[50] stands as a monument of no mean importance. His royal tomb, a reversion to the octagonal plan--i.e., a **Type A-b** basic plan--is unique. Its singular quality is to be found in the dome which surmounts the central chamber. Unlike the single shell domes which had been constructed in the various Indo-Islamic tombs which had gone before, the dome of the *Tomb of Sikandar Lodi* is a double dome. Within the outer dome and separated by an open space is an inner dome. This particular feature becomes a hallmark of the great Mughal mausolea which were to follow--e.g., the *Tomb of Humayun, Ibrahim Rausa* and the *Taj Mahal*. In part, this is undertaken so that the soaring dome may be utilized as essential to the outer elevation without compromising the proportions of the central chamber.[51]

The employment of a double dome is neither unique to Indo-Islamic architecture nor to other cultures. Brunelleschi utilized the concept in the *Duomo* of Florence (1420-1436 C.E.) and Michaelangelo later employed this technique in the dome of *San Pietro*, Rome (1546-1564 C.E.). A number of reasons for the employment of a double dome within the Indo-Islamic tradition

Figure 108: *Tomb of Sikandar Lodi*, indication of internal space

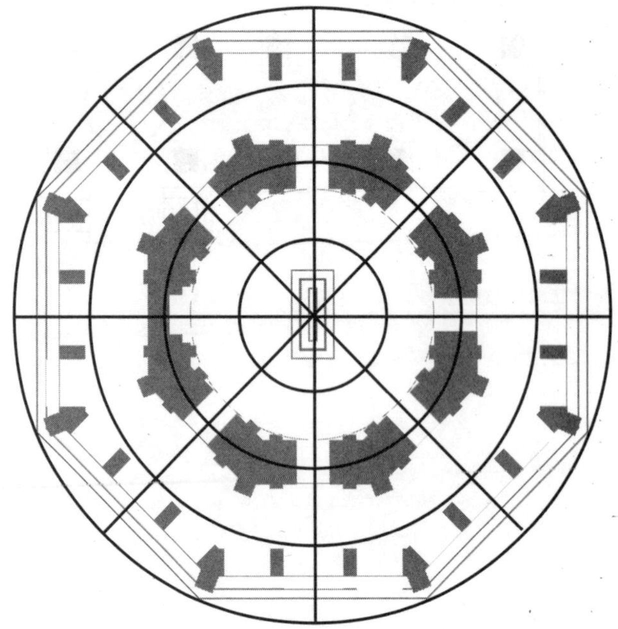

Figure 109: *Tomb of Sikandar Lodi*, application of a circular *Manduka Mandala*

Plate 31
Tomb of Sikandar Lodi (Plan)

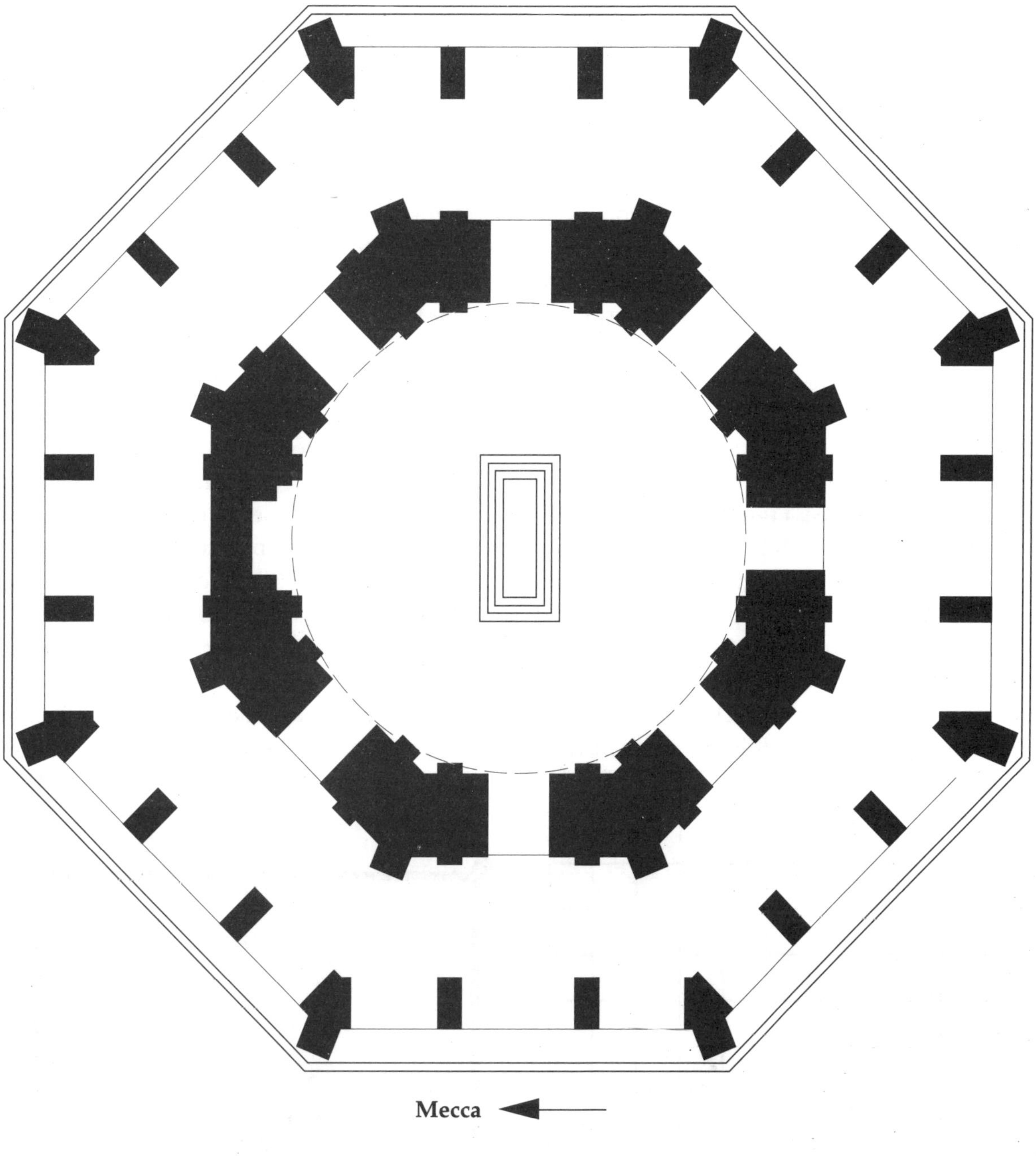

Tomb of Sikandar Lodi (Continued)

have been posited. One of the most credible explanations, at least in the early years of its employment was to create a more pleasing inner space. Certainly, the use of this form in the *Tomb of Humayun, Ibrahim Rausa* and the *Taj Mahal* have created massive problems in the minds of a number of scholars. Nonetheless, in a number of ways, Islamic architects have gone their own way, creating idioms that are unique to their needs and particular perspectives. The covering of surfaces with rich and colorful decoration in lieu of architectural sculpture is a situation that is brought to mind.

The interior space of *Tomb of Sikandar Lodi* is commensurate with the other octagonal temples of this type (See: **Figure 108**). It reflects the Indo-Islamic penchant for inner spatial areas.

As with the other octagonal tombs a circular *Manduka Mandala* is applied to this tomb with the requisite results (See: **Figure 109**). The *brahmásthana* encircles the cenotaph while the second ring lies within the thick internal wall. The third circle falls just within the piers of the verandah and the outer ring enfolds the whole. In no instance are the *marmas* compromised.

The lower level, including the arched openings and up to the base of the *chajja* are included within the lower three ranks of the *pada* of a *Deshiya Mandala* (See: **Figure 110**). The *chajja* and the surrounding balustrade are contained within the fourth rank awhile the sixteen sided drum falls within the next--i.e., the fifth rank. The dome falls between the sixth and half way into the ninth rank of *pada*. The proportions are, therefore, 12:9.5.

The *Tomb of Sikandar Lodi* is the last of the royal octagonal tombs of the Sultans of Delhi--i.e., through the Lodi Dynasty--and rests within its own enclosure (see: **Figure 111**). One more royal octagonal tomb is to be constructed--i.e., the magnificent tomb of Farid-ud-din Abul Muzaffar Shir Khan Sur, known as Sher Shah, at Sasaram. The use of a double dome sets this tomb apart from those which went before. Unfortunately, Sikandar Lodi is better known historically for moving his capital from Delhi to Agra and for his name is attached to the location of the *Tomb of Akbar* at Sikandar.

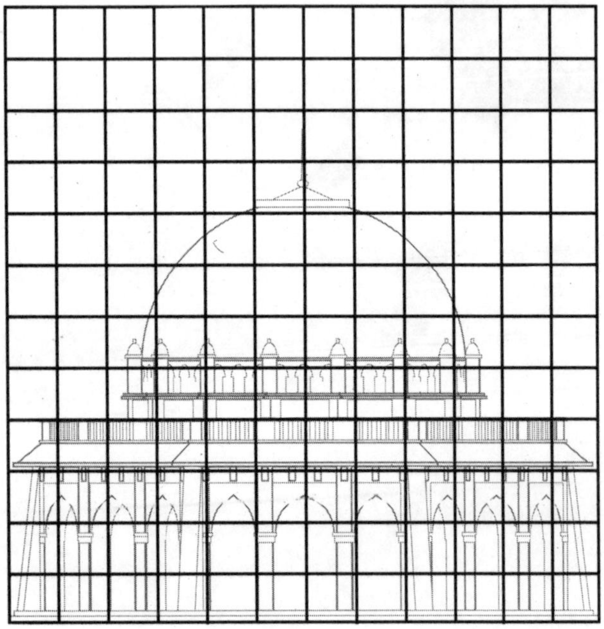

Figure 110: *Tomb of Sikandar Lodi*, application of *Deshiya Mandala* over the elevation

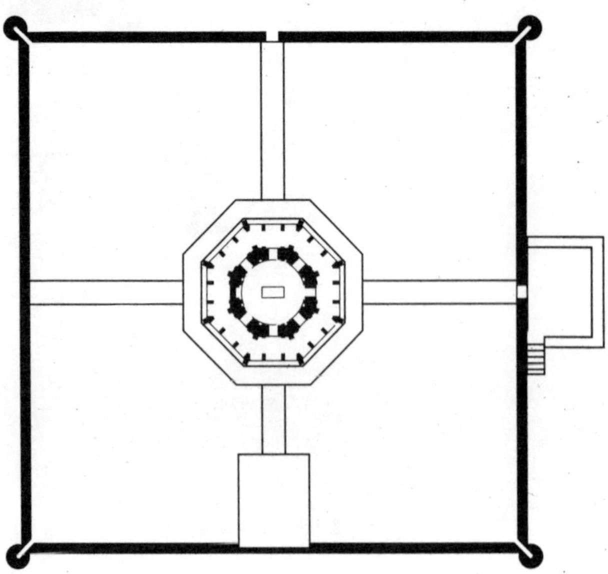

Figure 111: *Tomb of Sikandar Lodi*, ensemble

Plate 32
Tomb of Sikandar Lodi (Elevation & half plan)

Tomb of Hasan Khan Sur

Saseram, c. 1535 CE

Hasan Khan Sur is best known for his tomb which is close by that of his son. He was originally an Afghani horse breeder and nobleman in medieval India, father of eight sons, one of whom was Farid-ud-din Abul Muzaffar, known as Sher Khan Sur and later as Sher Shah. Although not a noblemen of great repute or status, his son's conquests, first as Sultan of Bengal and then as the Suri Emperor of Delhi, gave him importance far above his wildest dreams.

The *Tomb of Hasan Khan Sur*[52] was constructed in the Bihar town of Saseram, near Benares. Based upon the Lodi model, the octagonal tomb--i.e., a **Type D-e** basic plan--is placed within a square enclosure (See: **Figure 112**). This enclosure in not in the form of the traditional Mughal *chahar-bagh*; a form that was to be seen within the next thirty years in the ensemble of the *Tomb of Humayun*. To the east is the main entrance and to the north a smaller, subsidiary entrance. At the four corners of the enclosure are octagonal towers, all of which gives a distinctly fortified quality to the whole. Centered in the enclosure is the mausoleum. As with the preceding octagonal tombs it possesses three portal arches per façade. These give access to the ambulatory of this tomb. Seven openings give way to the central chamber which holds the false sarcophagus, a *qibla* and a *mikhrab*. The main entrance is in the east. It is to be noted that traditionally the main entrance is generally to the south--i.e., perpendicular to be cenotaph, Above the ambulatory (Ind.: *pradakshinapatha*) are twenty-four domes, each emphasizing the corresponding to the portals below. The octagonal chamber rises above these domes to some height and eight *chatri* mark the corners of this eight sided podium. From within the inner perimeter of these *chatri* the dome arches over the inner space, capping the whole.

As with the preceding octagonal tombs--e.g., the *Tomb of Khan-i Jihan Tilangani* and the *Tomb of Mubarak Shah Sayyid*--the internal space is abundant as befits the requirements of an Islamic tomb of this type (See: **Figure 113**). Commemorative circumambulation is fostered

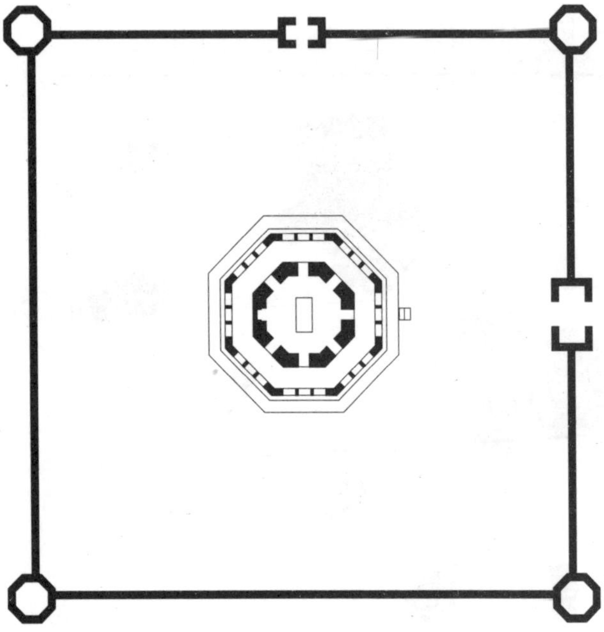

Figure 112: *Tomb of Hasan Khan Sur*, ensemble

Figure 113: *Tomb of Hasan Khan Sur*, indication of internal space

Plate 33
Tomb of Hasan Khan Sur (Plan)

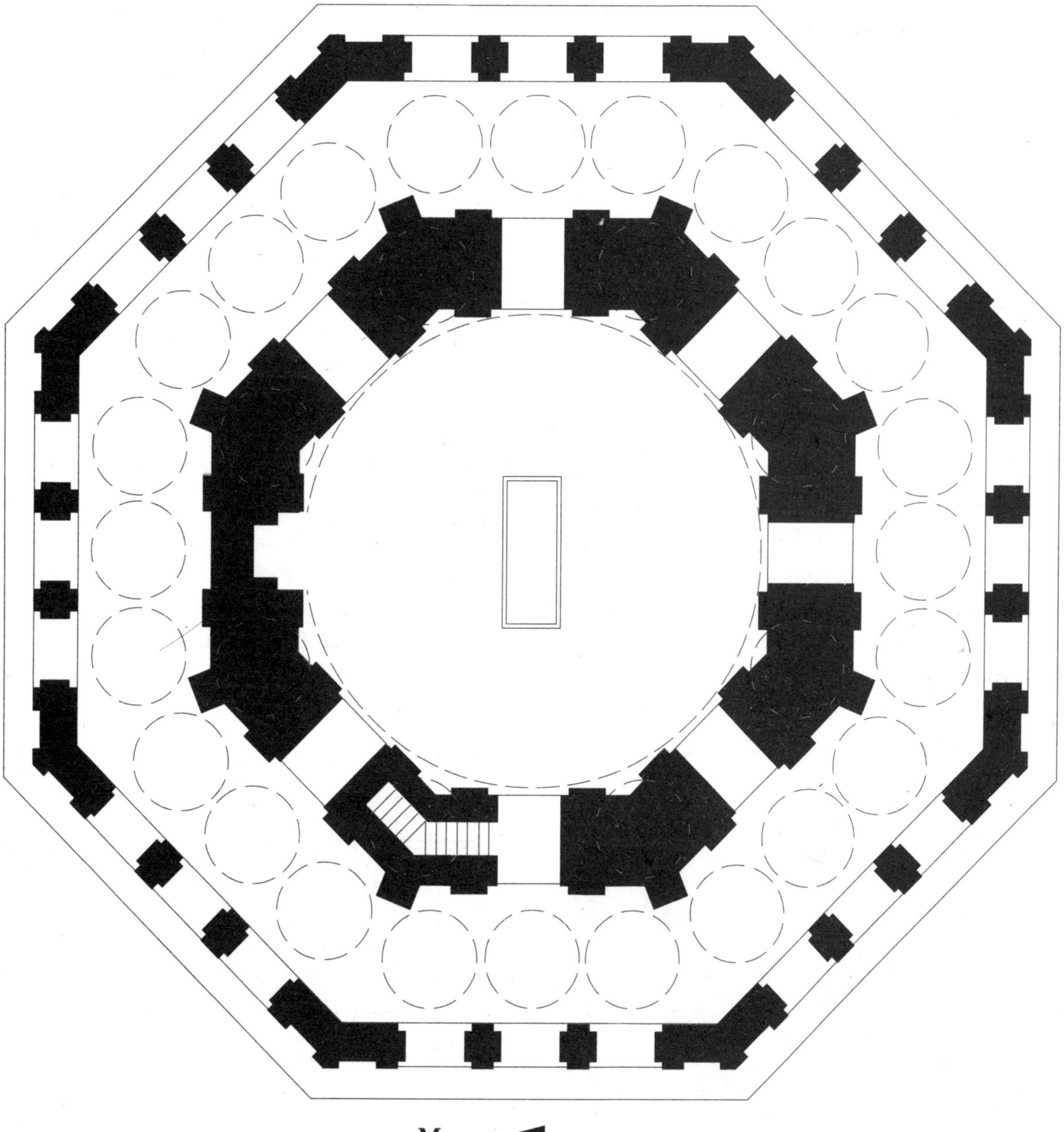

Tomb of Hasan Khan Sur (Continued)

by the wide cloister-like ambulatory.

As with the other two preceding octagonal tombs, the overlaying of a circular *Manduka Mandala* indicates a number of important conjunctions (See: **Figure 114**). First, as would be expected, the false sarcophagus and the one in the crypt below are encircled within the *brahmásthana*. The second ring enfolds the dome and is within the chamber's wall. The third circle auspiciously bisects the twenty-four small domes, And, of course, the outer ring protects the whole.

As with the preceding tombs, a *Deshiya Mandala* is superimposed over the elevation (See: **Figure 115**). The first three ranks of *pada* define the first storey. The second level, the octagonal drum extends upwards four and a half ranks of *pada*, while the dome is contained within the center six files, vertically, and extends seven and a half ranks of *pada* high. The octagonal podium for the dome falls within the eight central files of *pada*.

In addition, it is to be noted that the *Tomb of Hasan Khan Sur* is considerably shorter in proportion to its width than is the *Tomb of Mubarak Shah Sayyid* which has been characterized as 'squat.' Nonetheless, this tomb, the *Tomb of Hasan Khan Sur* gives the appearance of greater height, partially due to the height of the octagonal base above the line of the first storey. In addition, the eight kiosks (*chatri*) which punctuate the corners of this form also give the appearance of greater height. The height to width proportion is 12:7.5 (excluding the finial).

The *Tomb of Hasan Khan Sur* although not monumental in scope, is lavish in its architectural form--i.e., the twenty-four domes, the octagonal podium of considerable height (proportionally) and the eight *chatri* circling the dome. All these elements combine to form a tomb within its ensemble of no mean import.

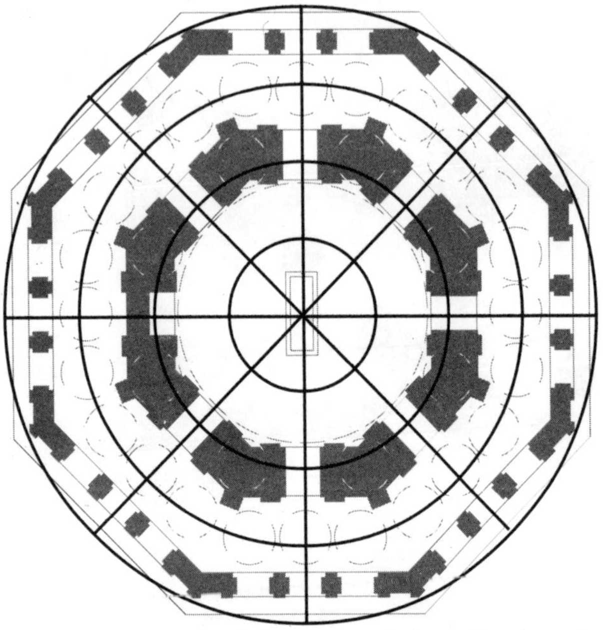

Figure 114: *Tomb of Hasan Khan Sur*, application of circular *Manduka Mandala*

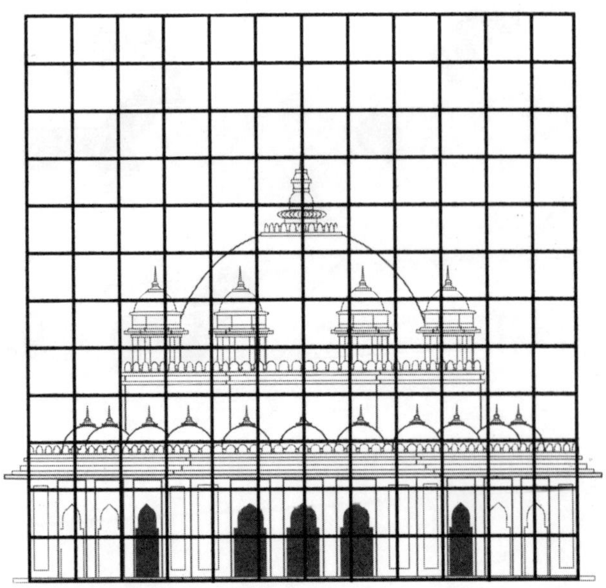

Figure 115: *Tomb of Hasan Khan Sur*, application of a *Deshiya Mandala* over the elevation

Plate 34
Tomb of Hasan Khan Sur (Elevation & half plan)

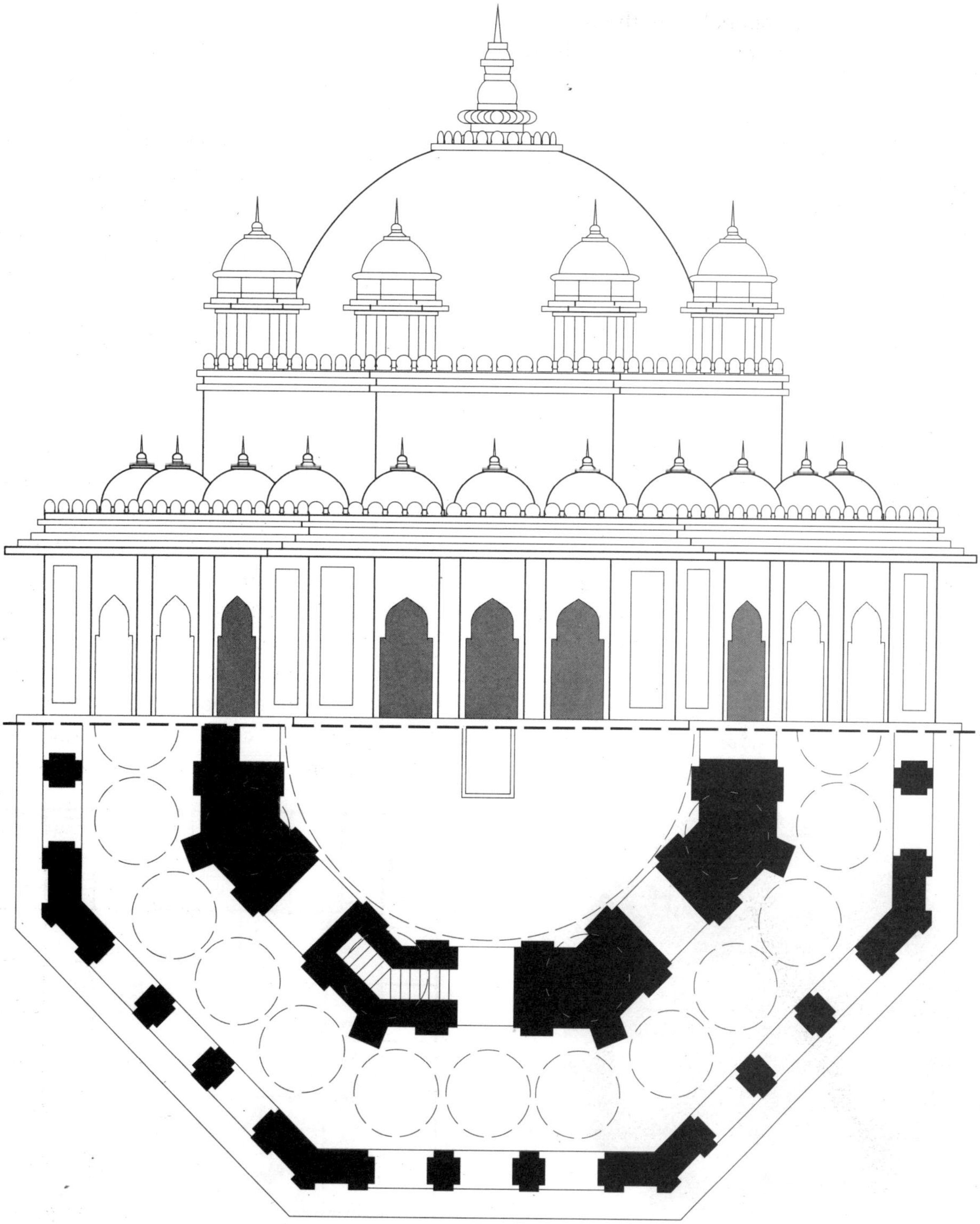

Tomb of Sher Shah

Saseram, a. 1540 C.E.

Following an octagonal plan, the *Tomb of Sher Shah*[53] (Sher Khan) at Saseram is indeed monumental. Babur's ambitious Afghani governor of Bihar, Farid-ud-din Abul Muzaffar Shir Khan Sur, known as Sher Khan, failed to recognize Humayun's ascendancy to the throne. Many nobles flocked to his banner as they appeared to feel that this third generation Afghani-Indian claim to the throne was more legitimate than the second-in-line of the recently conquering Mughals. He declared war on Humayun, defeated him in battle, and ascended to the imperial throne in 1540. Humayun fled to the west and sought refuge in the Persian court of Shah Tahnasp where he remained until he re-ascended the throne in 1555. After his victory Sher Khan assumed the imperial name of Shah (Sher Shah) in an attempt to establish his legitimacy. In truth, Sher Shah, the son of Hasan Khan Sur, was an able administrator. He accomplished much in his relatively short tenure. Besides his administrative abilities he fostered much building, not the least of which was his grand mausoleum at Sasaram.

Figure 116: *Tomb of Sher Shah*: indication of internal space

The *Tomb of Sher Shah* is related to the *Tomb of Ghiyas-ud-din Tughluq I* only as much as it, too, is situated in a small artificial lake. However, unlike the former, this mausoleum is gracious where the other is formidable, accessible where the other is forbidding, and light and airy where the other is ponderous and enclosed within fortress like walls. No two structures could be any different. Whereas Ghiyas-ud-din Tughluq was a soldier used to soldierly ways, Sher Shah had been exposed to the court of Babur, made a governor and had yearned of more.

Springing from the placid artificial lake (See: **Appendix B**) on a square, elegant, stepped platform, the square base structure, a massive terrace--some 60+ meters square--is rotated so that its corners lock into the sides of the larger square of the topmost step (See: **Plate 37**). Rotating the main terrace in this manner also aligned the mausoleum with Mecca. The terrace block serves as a substantial foundation for the octagons that mount above and culminate in a dome. At the four corners of this substantial square mass are four, rather elegant kiosk which

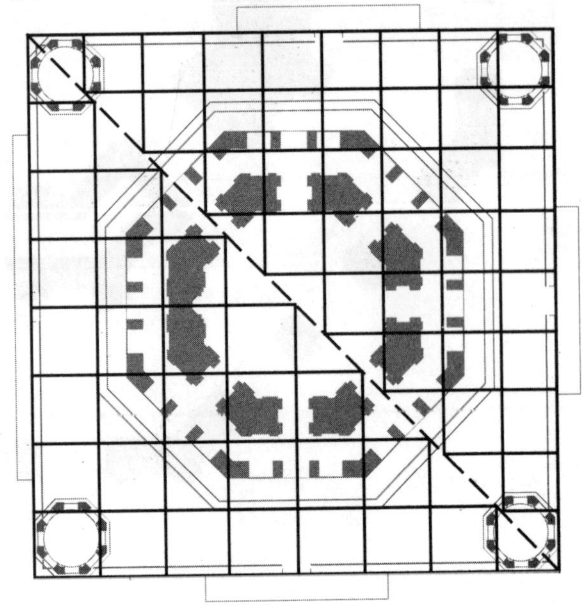

Figure 117: *Tomb Ensemble of Sher Shah* , application of *Manduka* and *Paramashyika Mandala*

Plate 35
Tomb of Sher Shah (Plan)

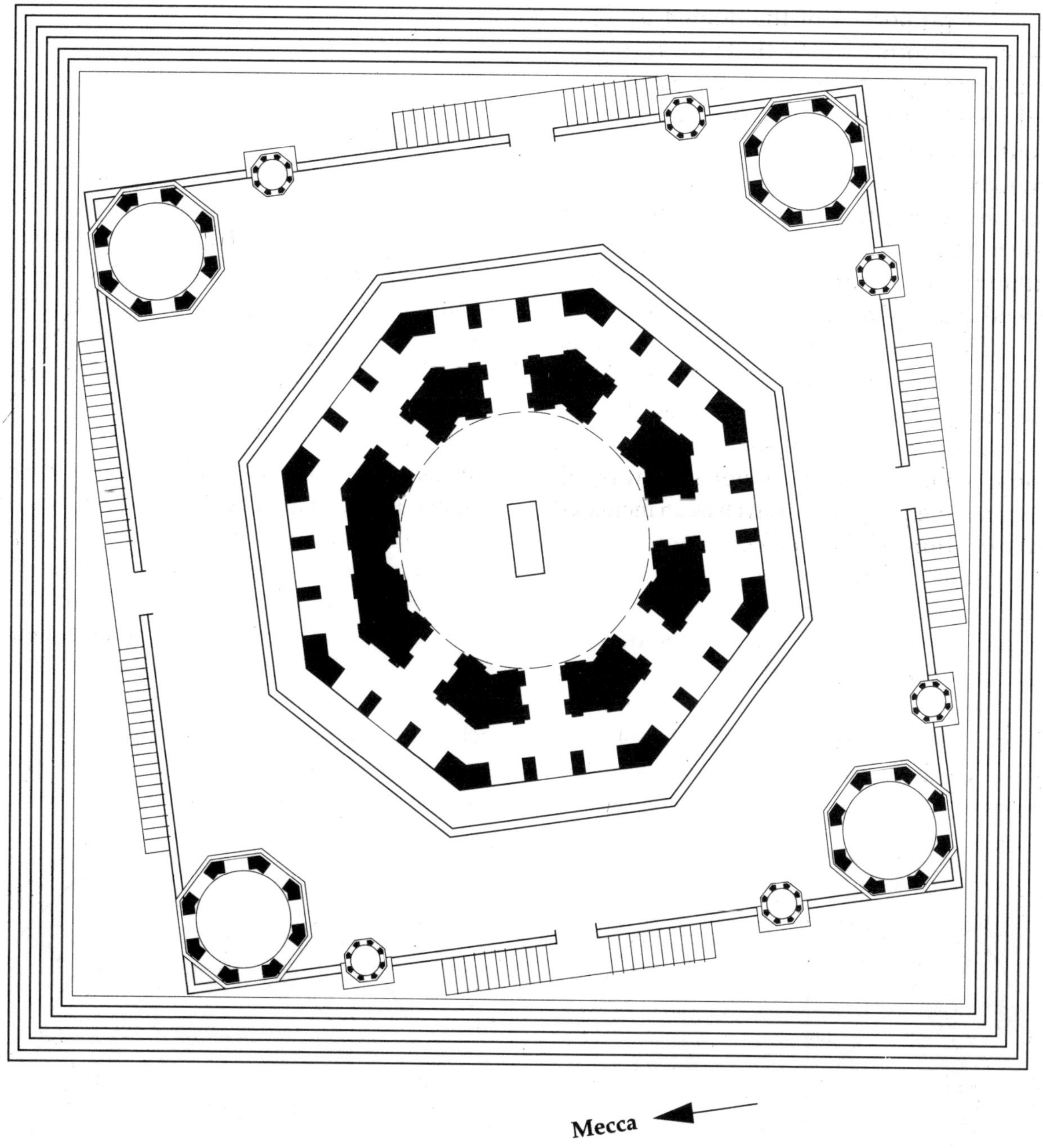

mimic the proportion of the domed octagon. Between the corner kiosks (Ind.: *chatri*) on the north, south and east aspects are smaller *chatri* cantilevered out from the main terrace. They are absent from the west side with its long, commodious, double stairway which, en plan, gives precedence to this direction. This major, western stairway differs from the preferred southern "main entrance" to the tomb--i.e., perpendicular to the cenotaph.

The mausoleum proper exhibits three arched portals on each of its eight sides, amounting to twenty-four entrances. Twenty four is a number that is of some significance in Islamic iconography. It connotes totality, all encompassing perfection, as well as an increased magnification of the perfect, macrocosmic-microcosmic number six through the doubled twelve. It is represented by: the twenty-four point star; and the number of hours in the day and night. On each of the eight corners of this first storey are eight small kiosks, abbreviated versions of the four large corner pavilions. From this point, and stepped back, a second octagonal form rises. It, too, holds eight smaller kiosks on the corners. From this point a dome is lifted--a hemisphere with as suitable and substantial finial--topping the whole.

What is most noteworthy about the *Tomb of Sher Shah* is the amount of open space. It dominates the plan. The twenty four entrances on the eight sides cover the cardinal and intercardinal points of the compass and the space flows outwards (See: **Figure 116**). With the four kiosks at the corners of the main terrace, presaging the taller, minaret-like forms that will come, the vast space relates to a congregational faith.

The application of either a *Manduka Mandala* or a *Paramashayika Mandala* appears suitable in this plan (See: **Figure 117**)--i.e., *Tomb No. 36* at Delhi, *Tomb of Sultan Iltutmish* and *Tomb of Ghiyas-ud-din Tughluq I*. The *brahmásthana* includes the sarcophagus and the realm of the inner deities falls within the inner octagonal supports. Similarly, the circular *Manduka Mandala* appears applicable when placed over the octagonal mausoleum (See: **Figure 118**). The second circle encloses the inner octagonal supports, while the third falls just inside the

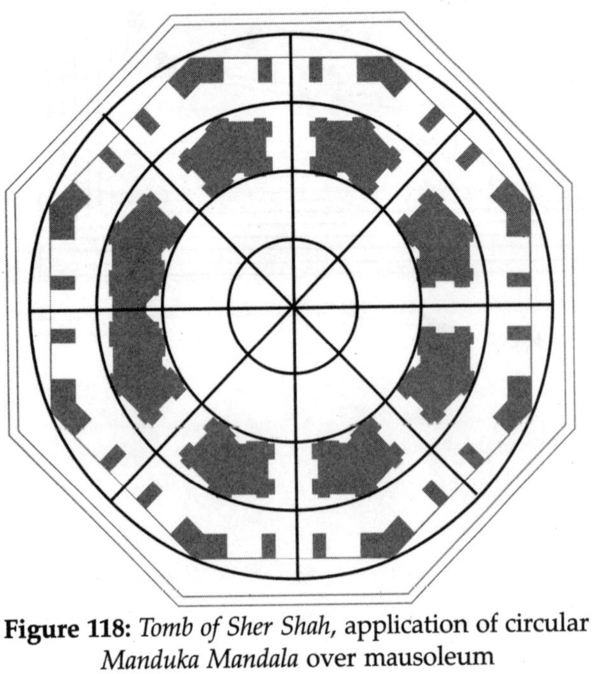

Figure 118: *Tomb of Sher Shah*, application of circular *Manduka Mandala* over mausoleum

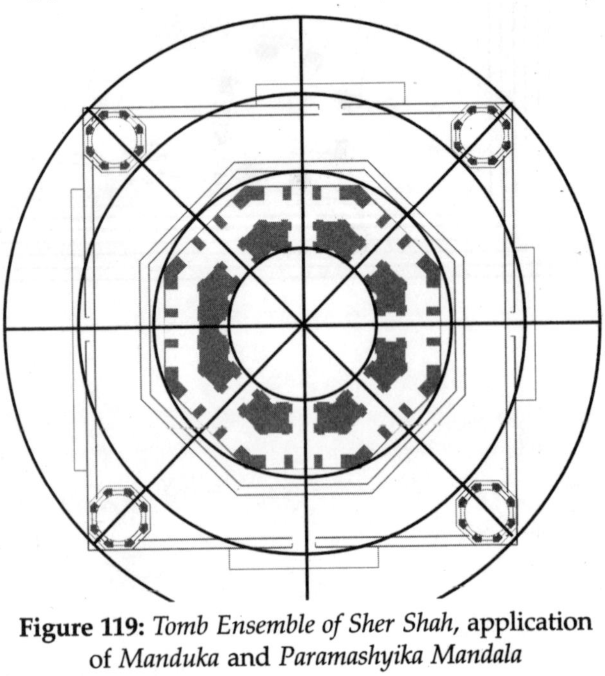

Figure 119: *Tomb Ensemble of Sher Shah*, application of *Manduka* and *Paramashyika Mandala*

Plate 36
Tomb of Sher Shah (Elevation & half plan)

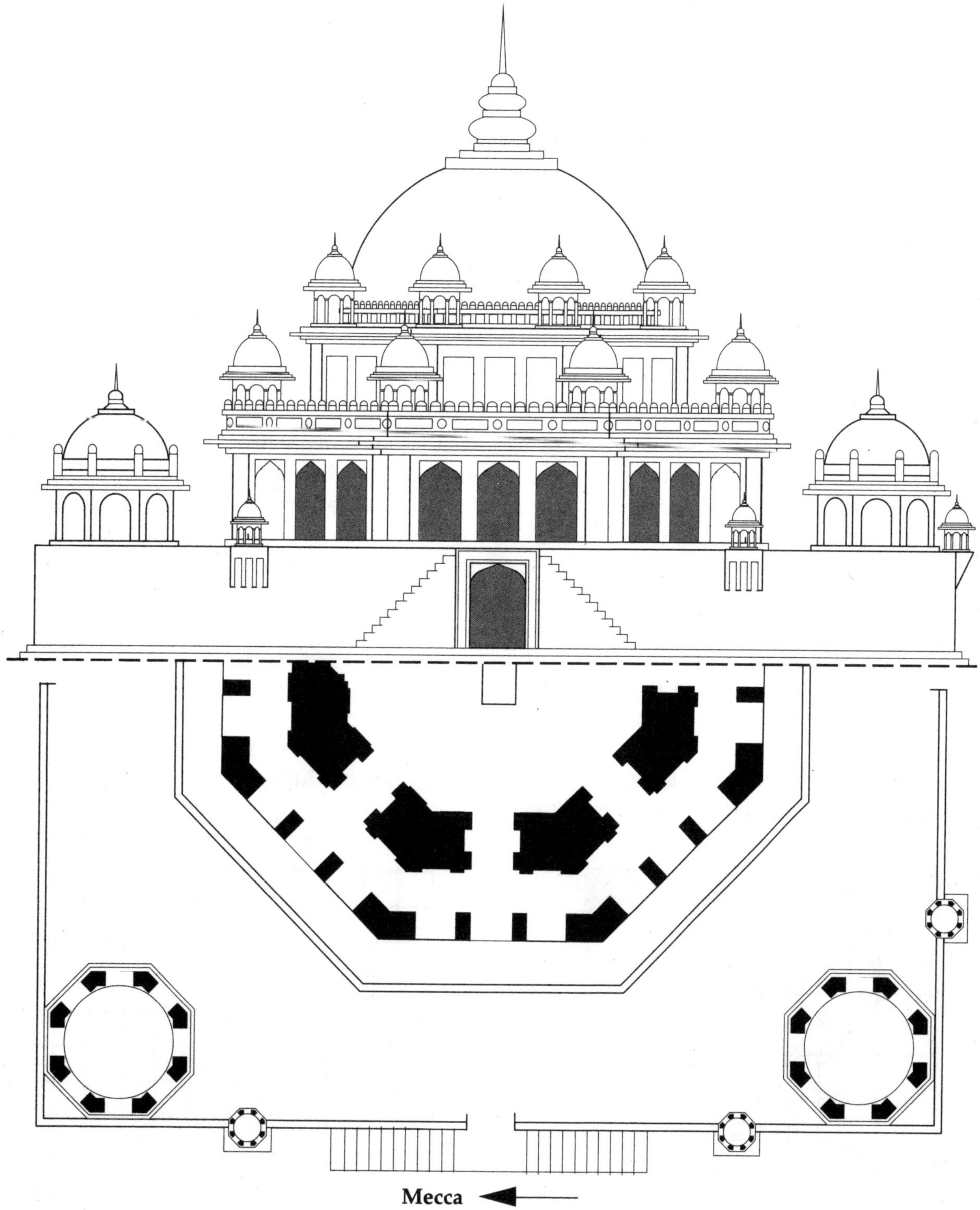

soaring dome. As with the *Manduka Mandala or* a *Paramashayika Mandala*, the inner circle, the *brahmásthana*, protects the two tiered sarcophagi. If, on the other hand, a circular *Manduka Mandala* is superimposed over the total ensemble, equally propitious results are exhibited (See: **Figure 119**). The outer circle encompasses the whole and the four kiosks at the corners, while the second circle falls just inside the kiosks. The third circle surrounds the mausoleum proper and the inner circle included the dome.

In considering geometric applications to the plan other interesting manifestations occur. If a quarter is divided into six parts certain conjunctions are noted which include both the kiosks and the mausoleum (See: **Figure 120**). This division when applied to one side, the number twelve results. Twelve, like twenty-four, is important in Islamic iconography. It is an auspicious, cosmic number which comprehends all numbers lower than itself. It relates to the signs of the zodiac, and the twelve hours of the day and the twelve of the night. In addition, if the dome's diameter is established, then this form multiplied by four establishes the width of the octagon of the mausoleum's outer limits. Then if a square encloses these four circles, the corners are the center point for four more circles of similar diameter and that establishes the outer limits of the terrace.

The external elevation of the *Tomb of Sher Shah* is impressive if not grand in its concept. From the stepped base to the finial of the dome the forms march upward and inward in silent procession. When a *Deshiya Mandala* is superimposed over the elevation, as with the previous tombs, a number of interesting conjunctions are observed (See: **Figure 94**). The lower two ranks of *pada* delineate the *chajja* The third rank encompasses the elegant mouldings and the crenellated railing which tops the first storey; the fourth rank includes the second storey's upper limit and the fifth rank enfolds that storey's decorative cap. Within ranks six, seven and eight rests the dome.

The elevation displays an elegant triangle of forms against the sky. The forms mount inexorably upwards. The varying sizes of the different masses are appealing to the eye as are the various openings. Placed on its own artificial island and turned so that the mausoleum appears askew the effect does not appear odd, rather it adds to the beauty and mystery of this tomb. The *Tomb of Sher Shah* is a fitting Mughal mausoleum to this notable Afghani.

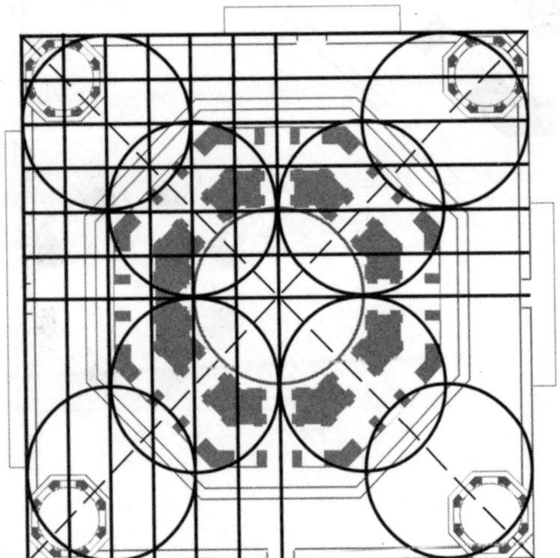

Figure 120: *Tomb of Sher Shah,* indicating geometric applications

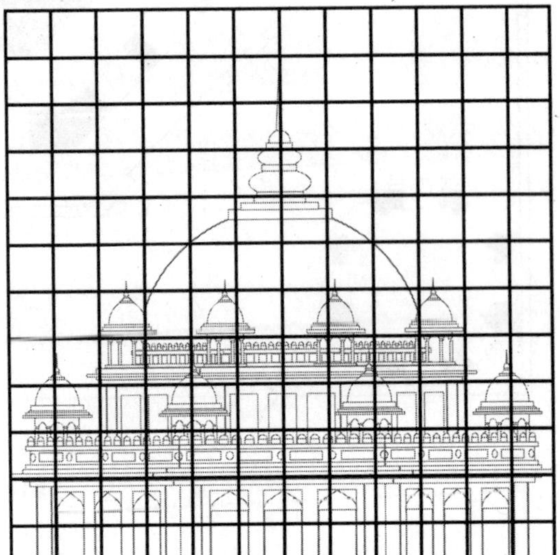

Figure 121: *Tomb of Sher Shah,* elevation with *Deshiya Mandala*

Plate 37
Tomb of Sher Shah (Ensemble)

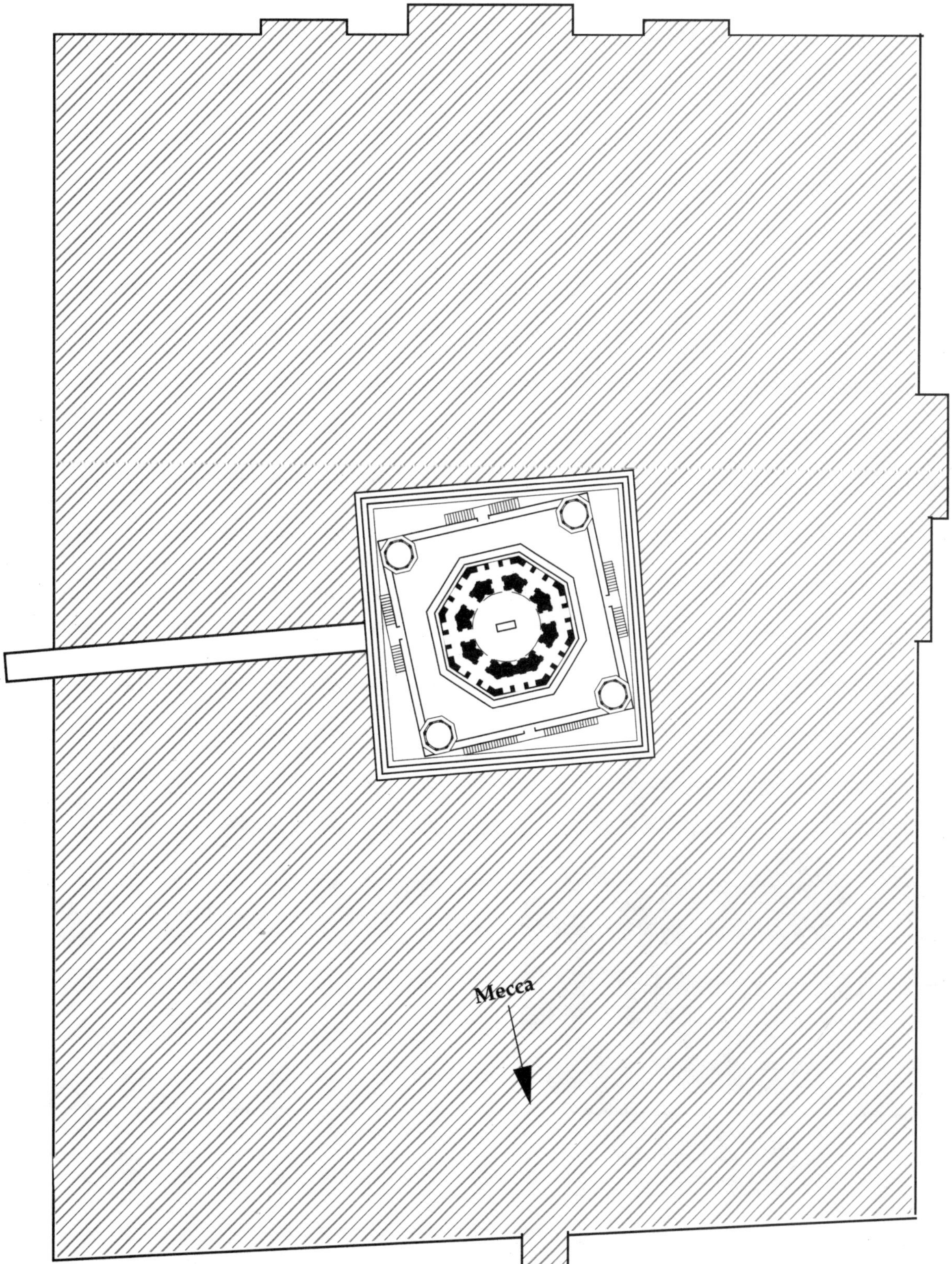

Tomb of Isa Khan Niyazi

Delhi, a. 1547 C.E.

Abutting the *Tomb of Humayun's* complex is a smaller ensemble of equal interest. The *Tomb of Isa Khan Niyazi*[54] is often overlooked in deference to the larger neighbor.

The Afghani noble, Isa Khan Niyazi, was a trusted advisor to Sher Shah Sur as well as to the emperor's eldest son, Islam Shah Sur. By the time of the construction of this tomb the formal precedents of the octagonal plan with an ambulatory had been well established--i.e., a **Type D-e** basic plan. The *Tomb of Khan-i Jihan Tilangani* (1388), *Tomb of Mubarak Shah Sayyid* (1434), *Tomb of Hasan Khan Sur* (1535), and *Tomb of Sher Shah* (1540) were apt examples for this trusted nobleman's mausoleum.

The *Tomb of Isa Khan Niyazi*, as has been stated, is well within established tradition in its octagonal form. The false sarcophagus' chamber is entered via seven doorways, the eighth being the *qibla* and reserved for the *mikhrab*. The walls of this chamber are less thick than the preceding octagonal tombs of similar design. This allows for a bit more ambient light into the interior. From this octagonal form the dome is supported upon an octagonal plinth before it springs upward. An ambulatory surrounds the cenotaph's chamber which is, doubtless, to allow for circumambulation (Ind.: *pradakshinapatha*). Each of the eight façades of the ambulatory are pierced with three arches and the whole is covered by a wide, extending *chajja*.

The mausoleum's structure allows for a substantial amount of internal space (See: **Figure 122**). The central chamber is proportionally quite spacious and the *pradakshinapatha* is, consequently, less wide in comparison. This spaciousness is underlined by the broad, octagonal terrace upon which the *Tomb of Isa Khan Niyazi* rests (See: **Plate 40**).

For an octagonal tomb, a circular *Manduka Mandala* appears most applicable to the *Tomb of Isa Khan Niyazi* (See: **Figure 123**). Here, as expected, the false sarcophagus and its counterpart in the crypt below are encircled by the inner ring (Ind.: *brahmásthana*). The second circle defines the interior of the central space,

Figure 122: *Tomb of Isa Khan Niyazi*, indication of internal space

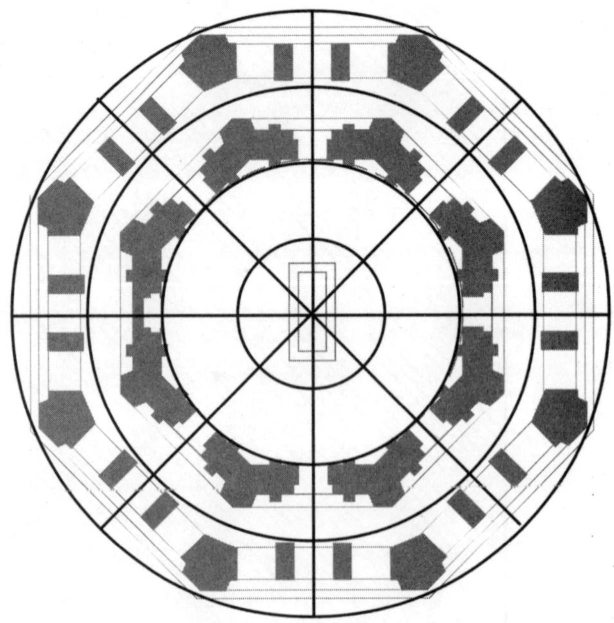

Figure 123: *Tomb of Isa Khan Niyazi*, application of circular *Manduka Mandala*

Plate 38
Tomb of Isa Khan Niyazi (Plan)

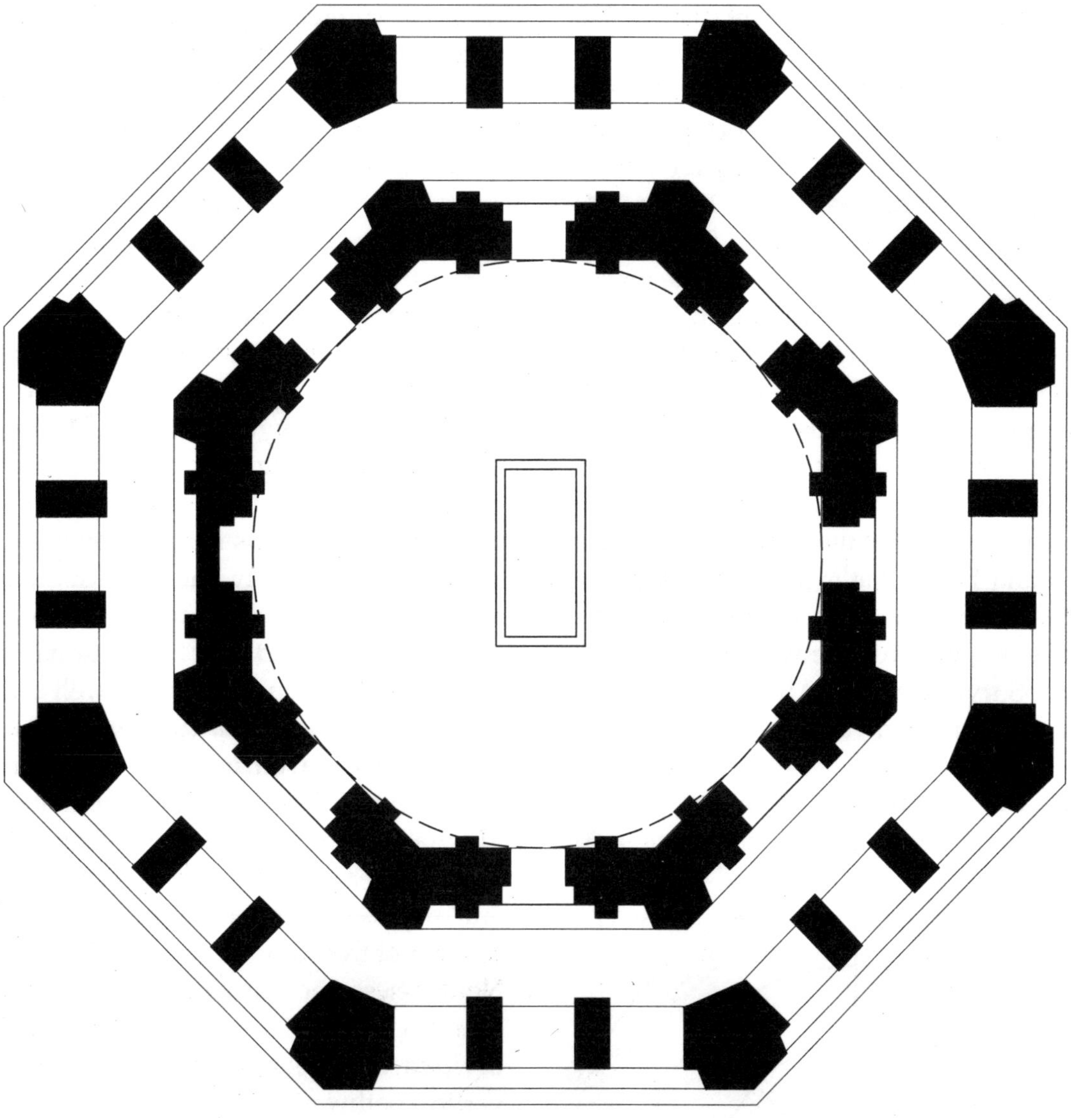

while the third falls within the ambulatory. The outer ring, of course, enfolds the whole.

If, on the other hand, a circular *Manduka Mandala* is superimposed over the octagon of the ensemble of *Tomb of Isa Khan Niyazi* certain interesting conjunctions occur (See: **Figure 124**). First, the mausoleum, as a whole, is found in the *brahmásthana*. The next ring encircles the terrace and the walk way which surrounds it. The third circle is touched by the terrace of the mosque and the outer ring included the domes of the *masjid*. Of passing interest here is the placement of the mosque. It is on the west side of the ensemble in line, as it should be, with Mecca. It is also on the westward pathway from the mausoleum. In both Buddhist and Hindu faiths and cosmology, the west is the realm of the dead. The famous *Angkor Wat* is oriented towards the west as a funerary temple for Suryavarman II. All other temples in Angkor are oriented towards the east, the preferred orientation.

As with the previous elevations, a *Deshiya Mandala* is superimposed over the *Tomb of Isa*

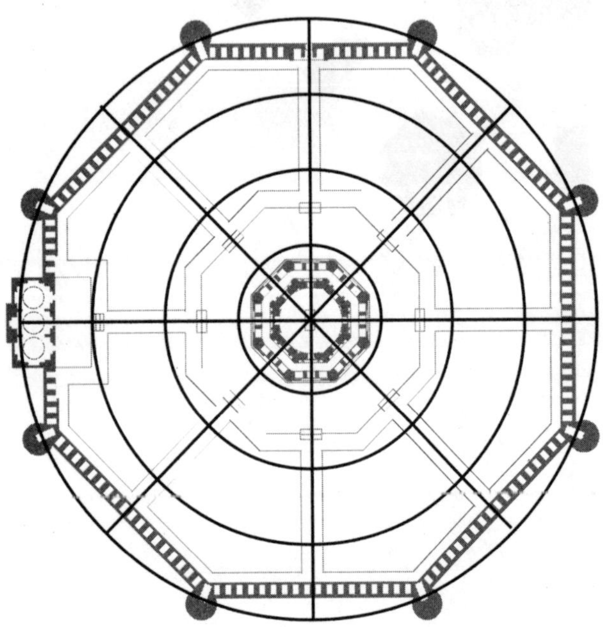

Figure 124: *Tomb of Isa Khan Niyazi*(Ensemble), application of circular *Manduka Mandala*

Khan Niyazi (See: **Figure 125**). The façades fall within the lower three ranks of pada. The fourth rank encompasses the *chajja* and the extension of the outer 'walls.' The dome falls within the sixth through eighth rank of *pada* and is approximately seven *pada* wide. The three arches of each façade fall within four files of *pada*, vertically.

By far, the most intriguing feature of the *Tomb of Isa Khan Niyazi* is the ensemble, more importantly the enclosed garden. It is octagonal. The Tughluq, Sayyid and Lodi Dynasties had utilized the octagonal plan for nearly two centuries. Their tombs were set within walled enclosures of various shapes, generally square. This does not imply the employment of the Persio-Mughal *chahar-bagh*. The Afghanis, of which Isa Khan and Sher Shah Sur had been the third generation in India, were well established and the classical *chahar-bagh* was not a normal part of their architectural repertoire (See: **Appendix B**). However, the domination of the Mughals, starting with Babur and the succeeding fourteen years to the ascendancy of Sher Shah Sur, may well have been enough to introduce the concept of the paradisal garden into their midst. Nonetheless, the 'garden' of the *Tomb of Isa Khan Niyazi* is unique. The octagon is formed. It is then divided into quarters by the imposition of a vertical pathway and a horizontal one. These are centered on the cardinal points of the octagon. Then the intercardinal points are, likewise, bisected. This establishes the eightfold division. Finally, it must be noted that the main entrance is to the north of the enclosure, rather than the normal southern side (See: **Plate 40**)

Of course the circular *Manduka Mandala* is eminently applicable to both the mausoleum as well as he total ensemble. The ancient Hindu treatise, the *Manasara*, deals with a city plan based upon this circular *mandala*--i.e., a *Manduka Mandala*. "The city plan revolves around a central

Plate 39
Tomb of Isa Khan Niyazi (Elevation & half plan)

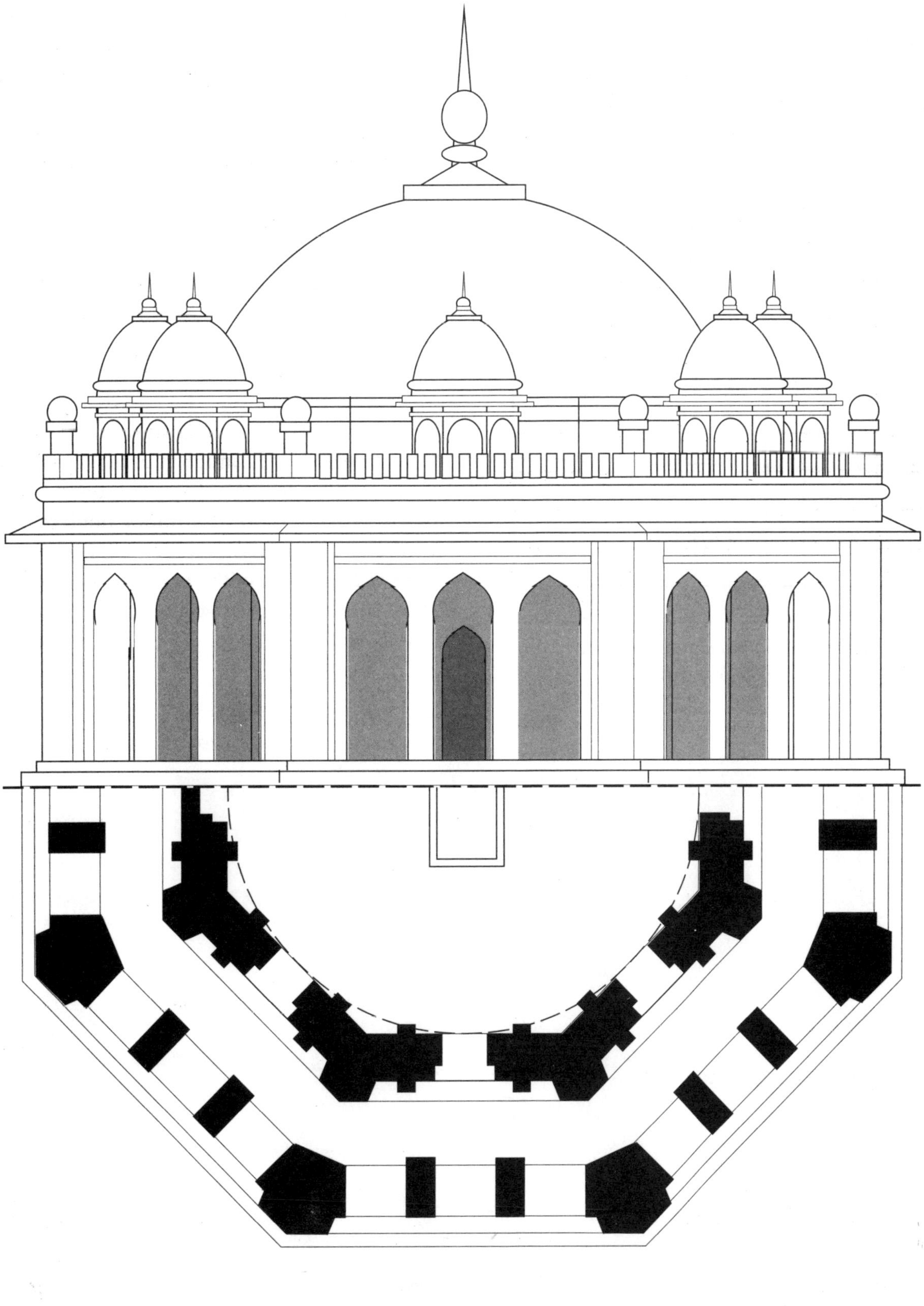

circle, the *brahmásthana,* in the center of which is to be planted a tree. This practice of a central tree or post was brought to India by the Aryans (Afghanis), and possesses not only a cosmic significance, (and . . . a place where the populous could congregate .. . to celebrate. . . . In addition, the tree or post possessed symbolically for the city what the *chattravali* iconically served to the *stupa*--i.e., the axis for the cosmic world. In that sense the . . . (mausoleum) links the real, temporal world with the cosmic, celestial world."[55] The vertical axis, the cosmic axis--i.e., the axis which passes through the finial, the dome, the false sarcophagus and the sarcophagus in the crypt of the mausoleum--from which the terrestrial axes radiate is clearly delineated in the cardinal and intercardinal pathways of the 'garden.'

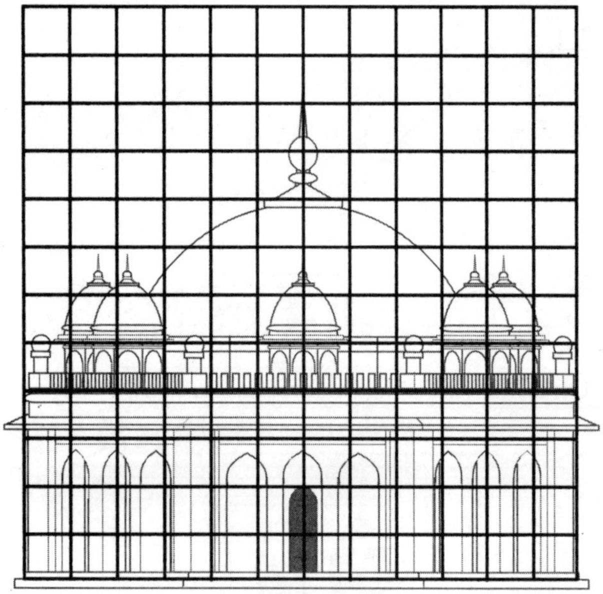

Figure 125: *Tomb of Isa Khan*, with *Deshiya Mandala*

The *Tomb of Isa Khan Niyazi* with its ensemble represents the vertical axis and horizontal axes that are cosmic components in the architecture of Islamic tombs in ways far more unique and complete than the later Mughal tombs. As the tomb of a minor nobleman, not royal, it is also unrivalled. Being adjacent to the *Tomb of Humayun* with its *chahar-bagh* offers a incomparable comparison with the *Tomb of Isa Khan Niyazi*.

Plate 40
Tomb of Isa KhanNiyazi (Ensemble)

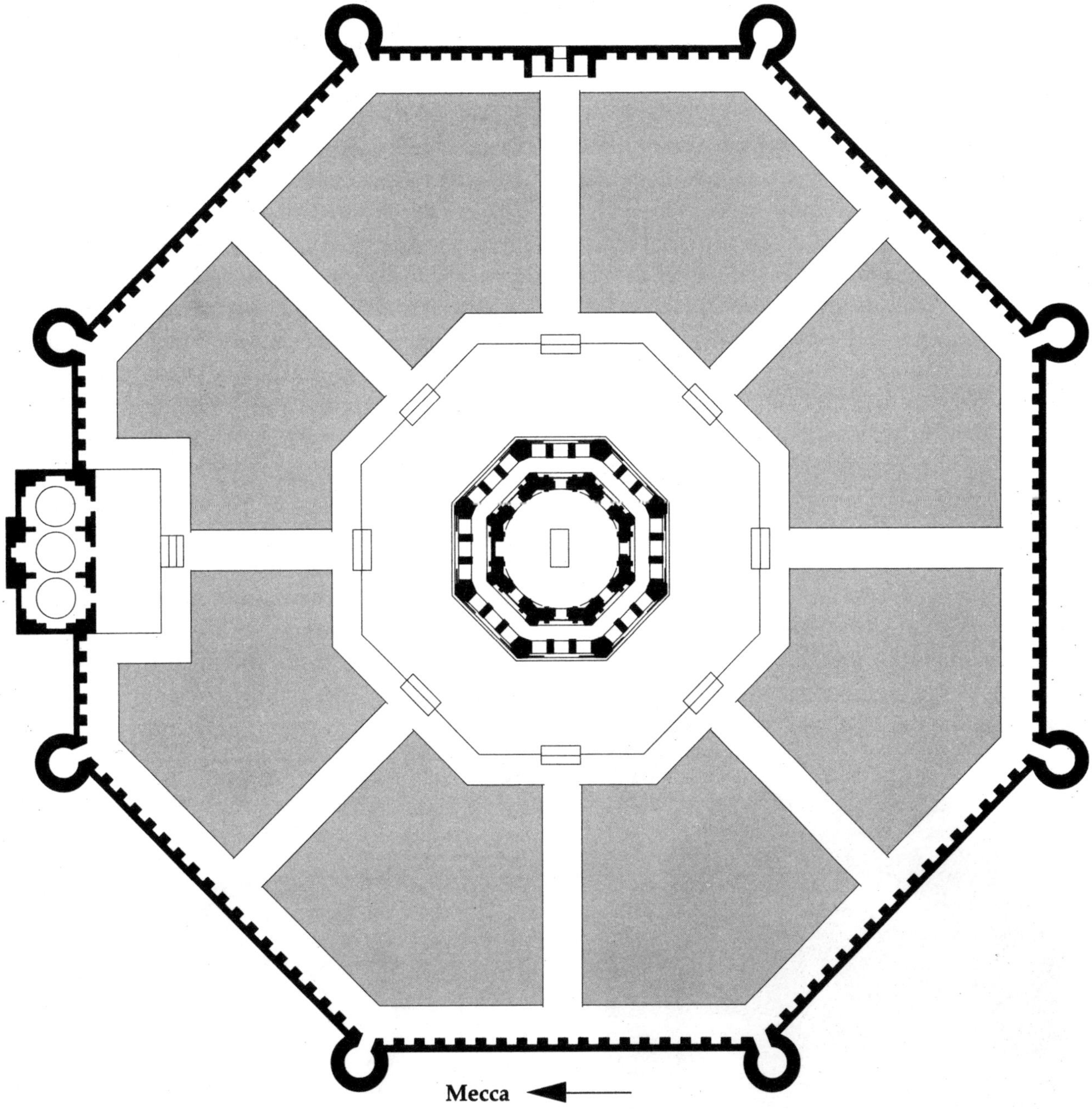

Tomb of Adham Khan

Delhi, 1562 C.E.

Adham Khan, a prominent Afghani courtier, a general and the captor of Malwa, was often referred to as Akbar's foster brother. His mother, Maham Anga (Ankah), was Akbar's wet nurse and was loved and honored by the emperor. The relationship between Adham and Akbar was apparently quite close. However, Adham Khan committed an unpardonable act when he assassinated Akbar's minister, Ataga Khan--a.k.a. 'Azam Khan--who was married to the daughter of another 'wet nurse.' For this crime and regardless of his association with the emperor, he was thrown from the ramparts of the Red Fort of Agra, not once but twice! His mother was inconsolable, therefore, Akbar constructed the tomb, in part to appease her and in part out of respect for his foster brother, Adham.

What had begun with the construction of the *Tomb of Khan-i Jihan Tilangani* in 1388 found its conclusion in the *Tomb of Adham Khan*.[56] This last of the octagonal mausoleums is somewhat aberrant midst the other tombs of Islamic India. The plan of the tomb--i.e., a **Type D-d** basic plan--was traditional for the time and is parallel to the octagonal tombs which went before. However, there are several notable differences. First, the tomb was conceived as a close representation to the *Dome of the Rock* (*Qubbat as-Sakhra*), Jerusalem (See: **Figures 20 & 21**). Second, unlike virtually all of its predecessors, the *Tomb of Adham Khan* does not possess decorative kiosks or domes over the ambulatory as is seen in the preceding octagonal canopy tombs. Third, there does not appear the ubiquitous *chatri* on the podium of the dome that were often a hallmark of Indo-Islamic tombs. The inner chamber is not in the traditional octagonal form, but is a sixteen sided form. This rises above the line of the ambulatory as a podium or base for the hemispherical dome which sits upon this form. Finally, here the ambulatory appears somewhat wider than that found in previous octagonal, canopy tombs. In truth, the *Tomb of Adham Khan* appears more Mediterranean-Islamic than Indo-Islamic.

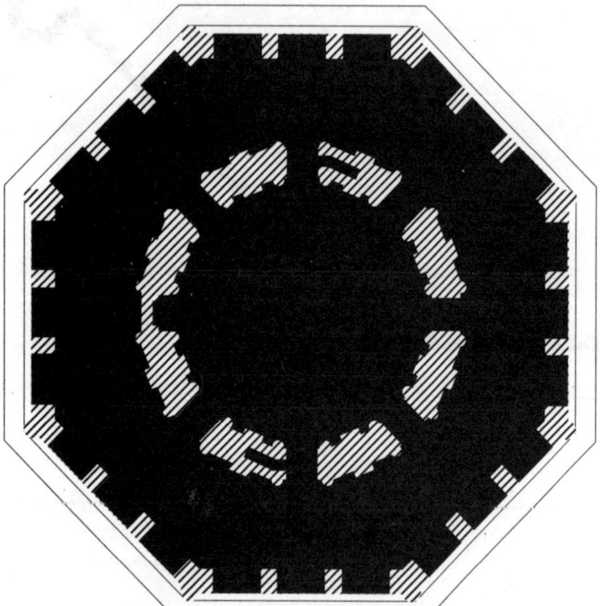

Figure 126: ***Tomb of Adham Khan,*** indication of internal space

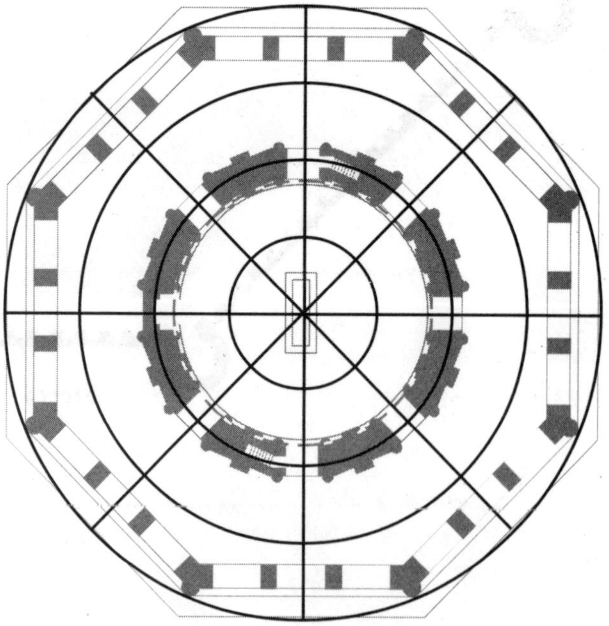

Figure 127: *Tomb of Adham Khan*, application of circular *Manduka Mandala*

Plate 41
Tomb of Adham Khan (Plan)

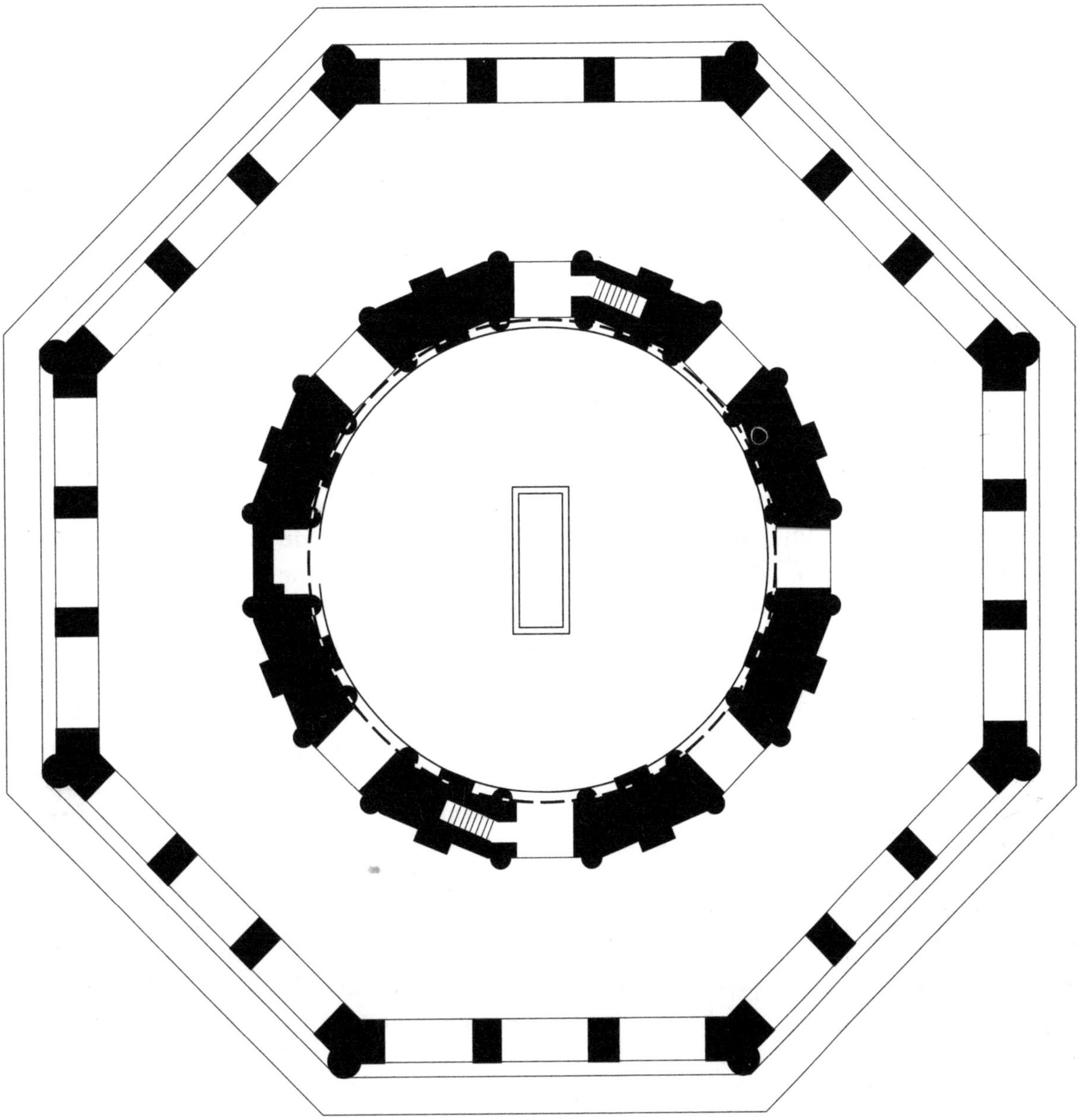

Mecca

Tomb of Adham Khan (Continued)

In comparing the internal space of the *Tomb of Adham Khan*, it is seen that it possesses approximately the same amount of space, proportionally, as the other tombs of the period of similar plan (See: **Figure 126**). The space of the ambulatory, as mentioned above, is considerably more generous and adds to the total amount of internal space.

The application of a circular *Manduka Mandala* to the octagon indicates its applicability (See: **Figure 127**). The inner circle protects the cenotaph of the central chamber as well as the sarcophagus in the crypt below. The second ring encircles the dome and is found within the thick walls of the inner chamber, while the third falls within the confines of the ambulatory.

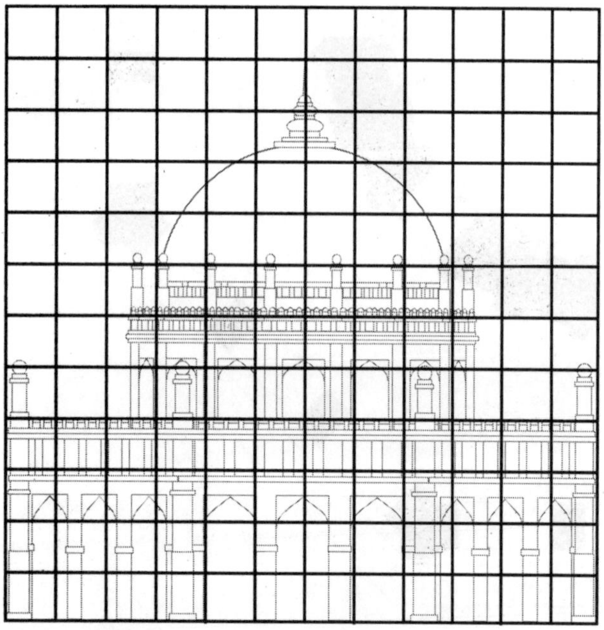

Figure 128: *Tomb of Adham Khan*, with *Deshiya Mandala* over the elevation

The superimposition of a *Deshiya Mandala* over the elevation of the *Tomb of Adham Khan* produces some interesting results. The first storey falls within the lower four ranks of *pada* (See: **Figure 101**). The second storey falls within the bottom six ranks and is seven files (vertical rows of *pada*) wide. The dome is eight *pada* wide--i.e., falling within the middle eight files--and is nearly four and a half *pada* high. Finally, the portals of each of the eight façades is one *pada* wide and two and a half high. Therefore, the proportions, width to height of the *Tomb of Adham Khan* is 12:9.5. For an octagonal tomb, the *Tomb of Adham Khan* is somewhat taller than its predecessors. Both the first storey and the sixteen-sided podium are, individually, taller than the forms of similar, preceding octagonal tombs.

The *Tomb of Adham Khan* is, indeed, unique among the *oeuvre* of Indo-Islamic tombs. True, its plan follows earlier octagonal forms--i.e., those utilized as early as the Lodi tombs. With the exception of the Mughal style arches, little recommends this monument as a typical Indo-Islamic tomb or work of architecture. It is acknowledged that the model of this tomb is the *Dome of the Rock* (*Qubbat as-Sakhra*) in Jerusalem. However, the question remains, "Why?" Akbar's other monuments seemed to follow an eclecticism that amalgamated Buddhist-Hindu-Islamic styles and forms, but not so with the *Tomb of Adham Khan*. Could it be that in his attempt to placate his foster-mother / wet-nurse, he selected a known and highly revered Islamic monument as the standard for his foster brother's tomb?

Plate 42
Tomb of Adham Khan (Elevation & half plan)

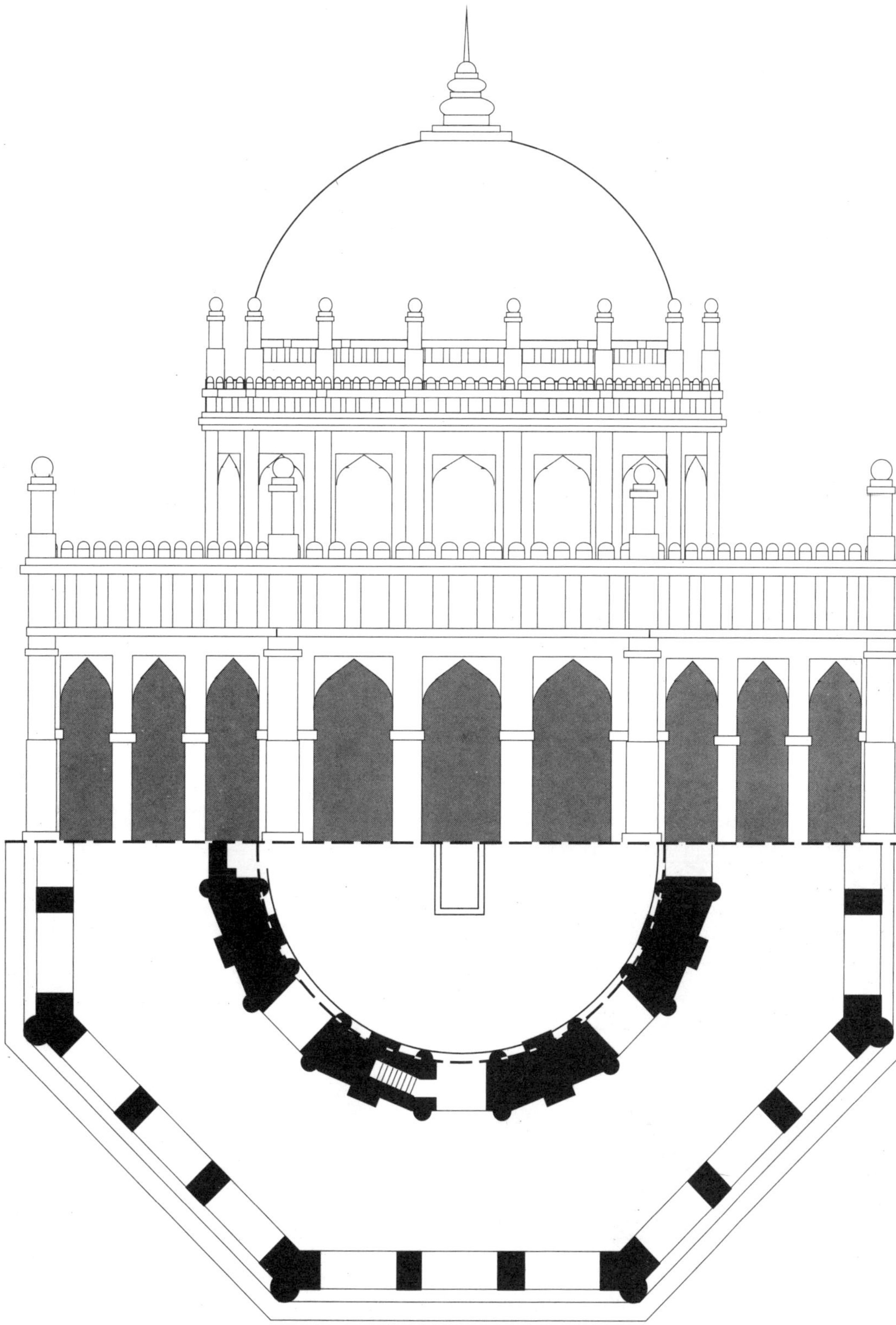

Tomb of Humayun

Delhi, 1565 C.E.

The *Tomb of Humayun*[57] is one of the more important of the Mughal tombs in India. In a sense, as the first great Mughal tomb, it is a counterpart to all that follows and finds its apogee in the *Tomb of Hazrat Mumtaz-uz-Zamani*, the renowned *Taj Mahal*. In addition Humayun's royal lineage, being the son of Babur, the founder of the Mughal (Timurud) dynasty, is underlined by the fact that the supposed *Tomb of Babur* lies within the precincts of the *chahar-bagh* that surrounds the mausoleum (See: **Plate 46**).

Having been exiled to the Persian court of Shah Tahmasp for close to fifteen years, Humayun returned with a Persian army to reclaim his throne. He died shortly after and his widow and consort, the Haji Begum, dedicated herself to raising a suitable tomb for her husband. She was aided in no small amount by Humayun's son, Akbar. The design and the building of the tomb was entrusted to the Persian Mirak Mirza Ghiyas who was assisted by a number of foreign artisans, mostly Persian as well as a small army of indigenous craftsmen.

The mausoleum and its environs are Persian in their influence. The plan is essentially based upon a square with prominent octagonal components--i.e., a **Type E** basic plan. However, here, as in many tombs of Persia, there was an eschewal of the strict outlines of the square. Essentially, the tomb consists of four blocks which are attached to a central mass that is in turn topped by a massive dome--i.e., a five part arrangement.[58] The exposed corners of these outer four blocks are trimmed off--i.e., *muthamman baghdadi*--hinting at the octagonal form of the central space under the dome. Each of these corner blocks possess five means of ingress to their central space, and from these four spaces narrow passageways lead diagonally to the central chamber. This central chamber possesses four additional passageways, oriented to the cardinal points of the compass, which lead to the central portals of each façade. In addition, there are four passageways leading, diagonally, from the deep porches of the main portals to the adjacent porch.

Figure 129: *Tomb of Humayun*, indication of internal space

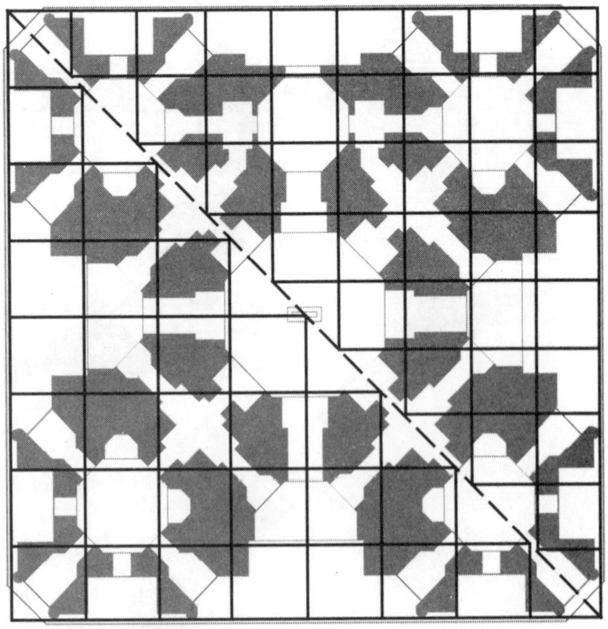

Figure 130: *Tomb of Humayun*, application of *Manduka Manduka* and *Paramashayika Mandala*

Plate 43
Tomb of Humayun (Plan)

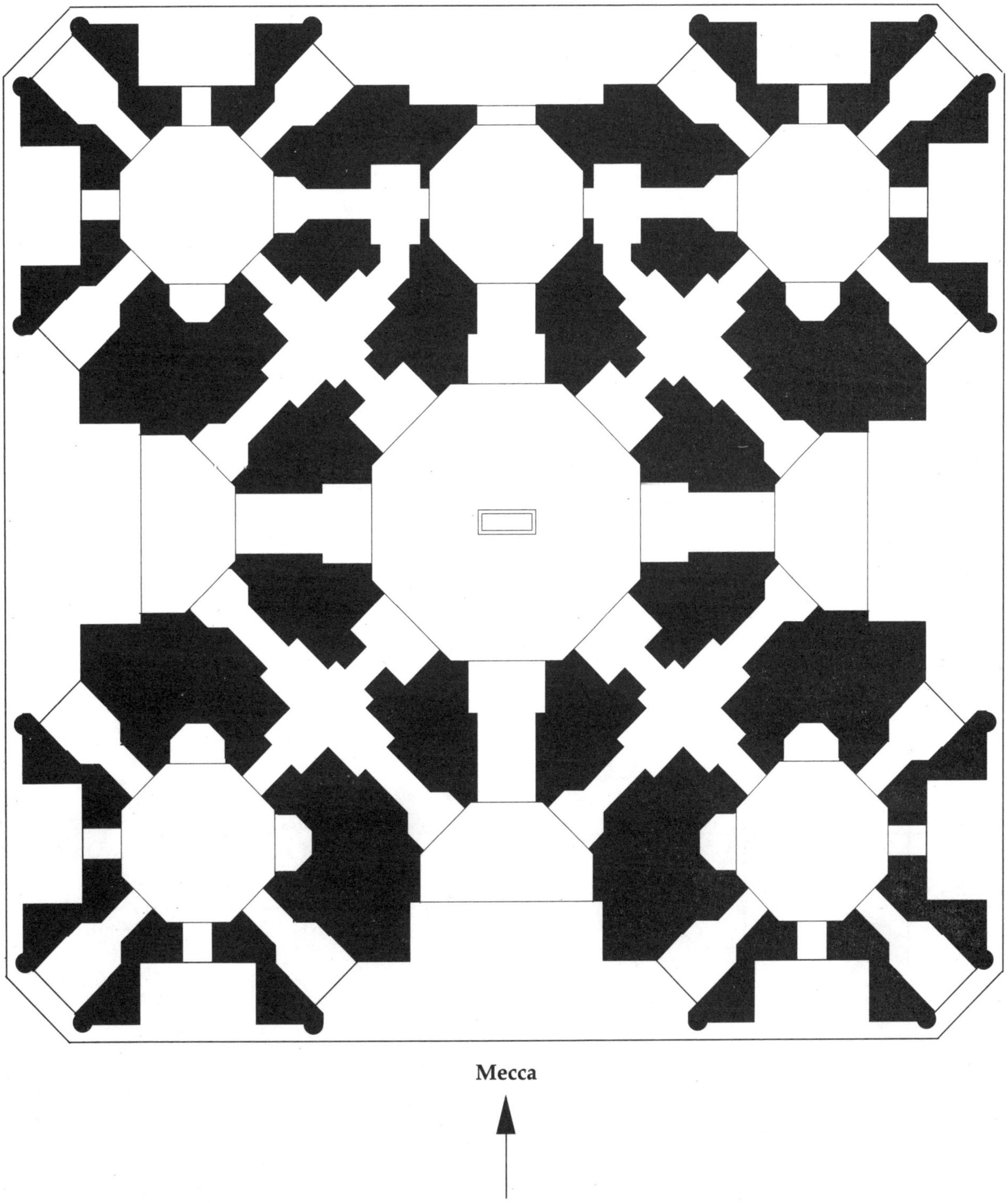

Tomb of Humayun (Continued)

The enclosed space is not as vast in proportion to the mass as one encounters in the *Tomb of Sher Shah* or the earlier canopy tombs (See: **Figure 116**). However, it is complex in the maze of passageways leading to and from the four corner chambers; to and from the main inner space; and the diagonal passageways connecting the four deep porches (See: **Figure 129**). This is not to say that the chamber holding the monarch's cenotaph is dimly lit. Quite to the contrary, there are doorways and windows on three levels which bathe the interior with sufficient light, particularly during the bright daylight hours of Delhi.

The application of either the *Manduka Mandala* or the *Paramashayika Mandala* to the mausoleum offers some solutions as well as a number of problems (See: **Figure 130**). The *Manduka Mandala's brahmásthana* encloses the cenotaph, but falls short of including the complete inner chamber. On the other hand, the *brahmásthana* of the *Paramashayika Mandala* does enfold this central space. The realms of the secondary deities includes the central block's outer confines. Finally, in both *mandalas* the deep vestibules at the cardinal points are included within the outer rank of deities.

The *Tomb of Humayun* is seen as conforming to the ninefold plan--i.e., one involving a *muthamman baghdadi* which is divided into nine sections (See: **Figure 131**). Here the central chamber is easily held in the central square, the octagonal corner chambers are to be found in the four corner squares, and the deeply recessed vestibules are held within the intervening squares at he cardinal points. All areas are linked to the central chamber by either vertical, horizontal or diagonal passageways. These link the inner chamber to the radial areas, the *hasht bihisht* ("eight paradises"). Therefore, the central chamber with its cenotaph and

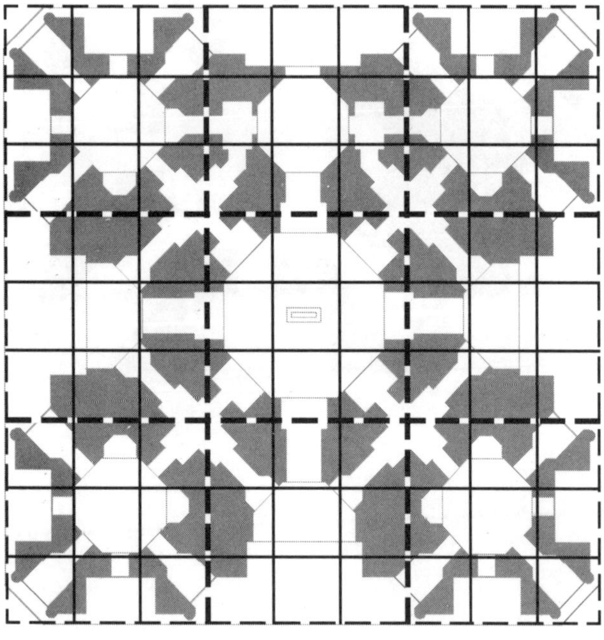

Figure 131: *Tomb of Humayun*, application of ninefold plan with *Paramashayika Mandala*

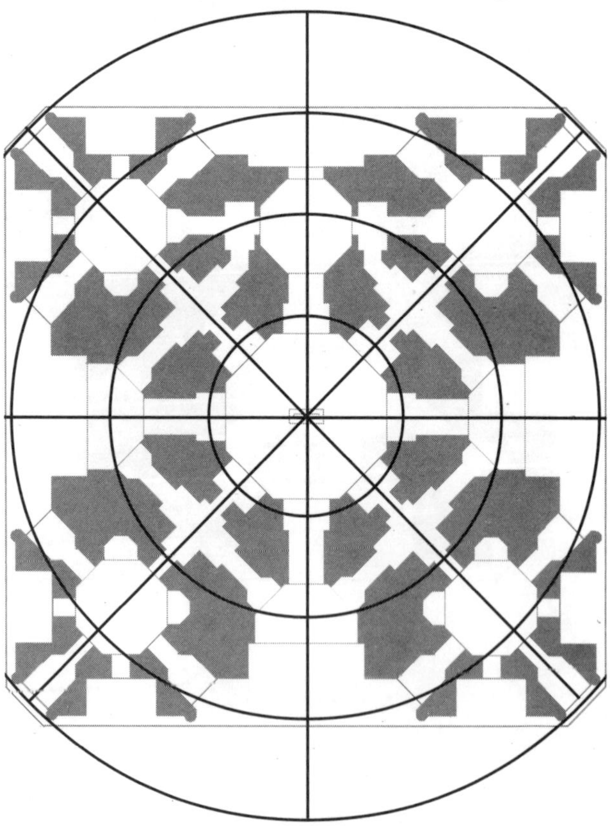

Figure 132: *Tomb of Humayun*, application of circular *Manduka Mandala*to mausoleum

Plate 44

Tomb of Humayun (Elevation & half plan)

Tomb of Humayun (Continued)

sarcophagus in the crypt below is iconographically linked to and with paradise.

On the other hand, the circular *Manduka Mandala* appears far more propitious than the *mandalas* based upon a square grid (See: **Figure 132**). The second ring falls on the outer limits of the façades deep, central porches. The third circle includes the diagonal passageways that connect the four deep porches of the façades. Finally, the inner ring embraces the central space with its cenotaph and the monarch's sarcophagus in the lower crypt.

If not only the mausoleum is considered, but also the podium and the massive coffered terrace from which the tomb ascends, then different solutions appear. In the application of the *Manduka* or the *Paramashayika Mandalas*, the inner chamber and most of the central mass is included in the *brahmásthana* (See: **Figure 133**). The whole mausoleum rests within the realm of the second tier of deities while the terrace and podium is found within the outer rank of deities.

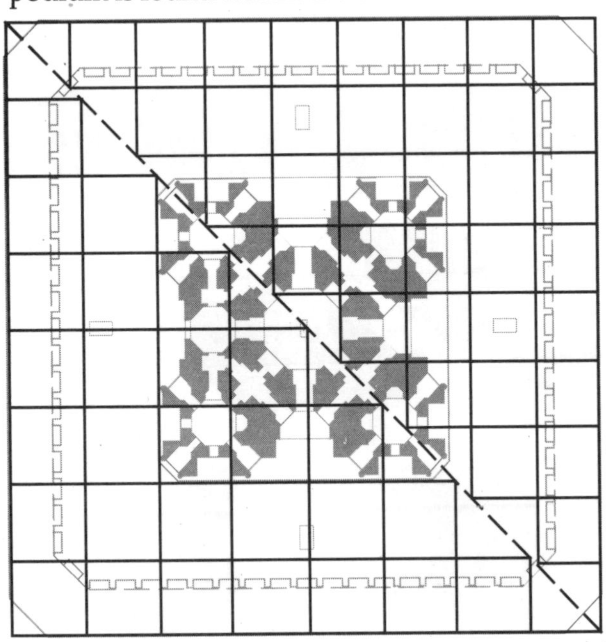

Figure 133: *Tomb of Humayun*, application of *Manduka Manduka* and *Paramashayika Mandala* to mausoleum and terrace

The circular *Manduka Mandala* seems to offer better solutions (See: **Figure 134**). The second ring touches the outer edge of the terrace while the third ring includes the whole mausoleum structure. What is even more interesting is that the *brahmásthana* enfolds virtually all of the central area.

If the whole ensemble is considered--including the mausoleum on its terrace and the *chahar-bagh*--a whole new set of relationships are encountered when a circular *Manduka Mandala* is employed (See: **Figure 135**). Here the podium and the mausoleum lies within the *brahmásthana*. Also it is to be noted that the second ring includes the main square which lies between the terrace and the entrances.

The geometric applications[59] as applied to the mausoleum of Humayun are not only interesting, but they also tend to unlock a number of doors to the understanding of the whole (See: **Plate 47** [top]). It is admitted here that these geometric applications are accomplished after the fact. Whether any or all of these applications were ever considered by the Indo-Islamic builders is purely conjectural. Nonetheless, many of these applications appear too relevant to dismiss out-of-hand.

First, it is noted that four circles, side by side and two over two, fall within a square which describes the inner mass. Where a diagonal crosses the outer circumference of the four circles this becomes the center point for a similar circle which, again sets the limit for the whole. A square that encloses this outer circle is divided into thirty-six equal squares--i.e., an *Ugrapitha Mandala*--from which various aspects of the four corner blocks are derived--the corner openings, the depth of the cardinal porches, the limits of the inner chamber, the dimension of the diagonal areas leading from the inner chamber, etc. This grid of six *pada* can be extended to the central division, creating a grid of eight *pada*,

Plate 45
Tomb of Humayun (Mausoleum, raised podium & terrace)

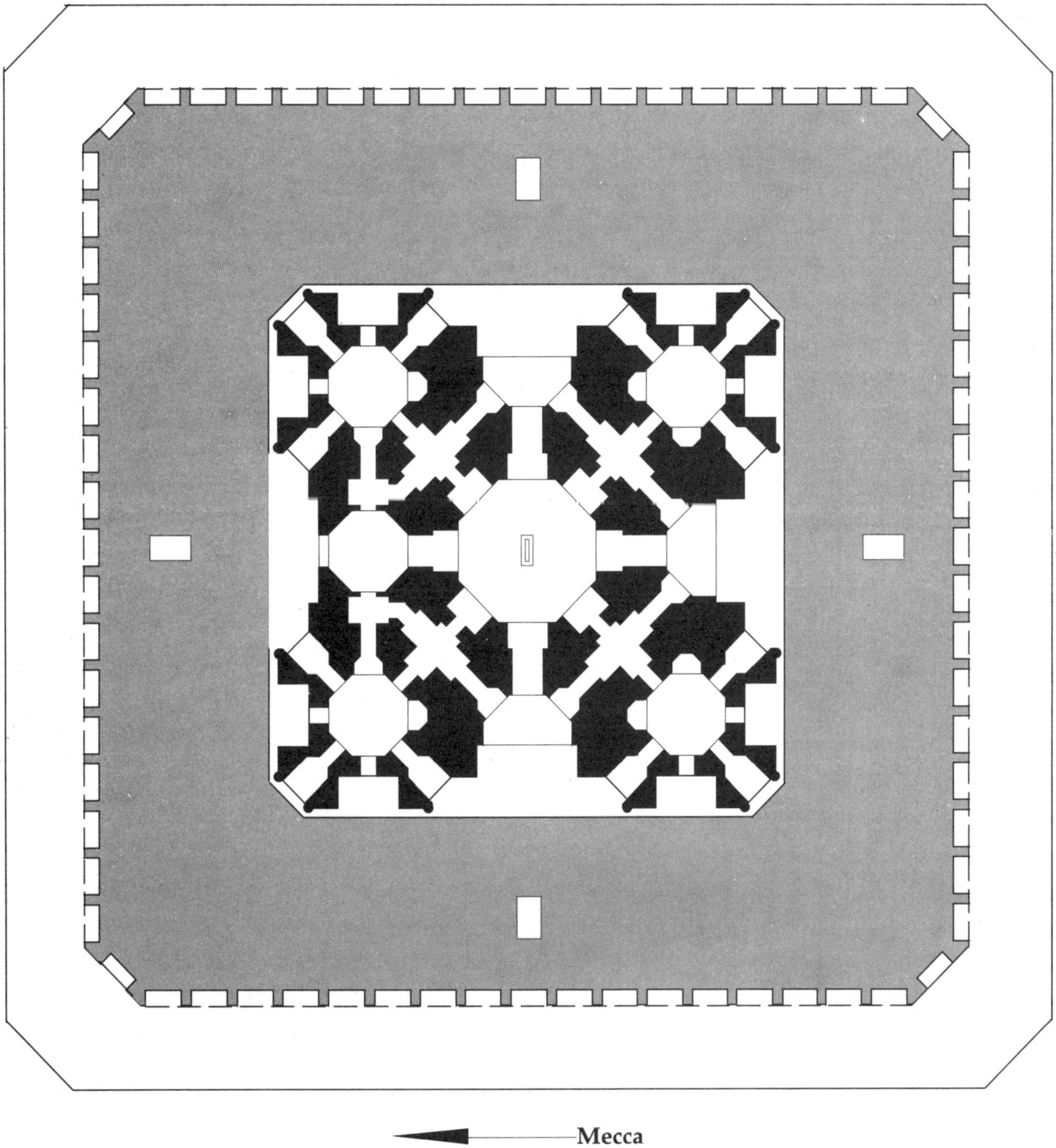

approximating a *Manduka Mandala*. It is of interest to note that the grid is oriented to the cardinal points of the compass, whereas the circles emphasize the intercardinal points. In both Islamic and Hindu architecture great importance is placed on these eight points of the compass.

As the mausoleum was the subject of this geometric application, so too, the entire ensemble is subjected to the same (See: **Plate 48** [top]). Here a circle defines the square which contains the mausoleum, podium and terrace. The extension of a line, both vertically and horizontally, from the top, bottom and sides of this central circle bisect. These bisections (four in all) become the center point for another circle(s) of similar dimensions. Again the same process is repeated with these four circles. The result, as seen in **Plate 48**, creates five circles, diagonally in either direction. It is also noted that these center points

Figure 134: *Tomb of Humayun*, application of circular *Manduka Manduka* to mausoleum & terrace

are located at the major crossings, diagonally, of the *chahar-bagh's* walkways.

Again, using the mausoleum as the starting point and overlaying it with a plan of the *chahar-bagh*, interesting, and in some cases not unexpected conjunctions occur (See: **Plate 47** [bottom]; see also: **Appendix B**). Particularly, it is seen that the central square of the *chahar-bagh* within which the terrace, podium and mausoleum are found contains the octagonal space of the central chamber. Also, the same plate location reveals another most interesting and fortuitous revelation. If the major diagonal passageways which surround the central chamber are used and a diamond is inscribed along the central axes of these passageways, it is seen that the corners of this diamond touches the inner boundary of the deep porches of the north, south and east façades (See: **Plate 47** [bottom, dotted line]). When this diamond is rotated 45^0, forming a square, the corners of this square touch the inner boundaries of the four, octagonal, corner chambers. These two forms--i.e., the diamond and square--together form an octagram, one of the most revered iconic forms within Islam. Further, it is to be noted that the eight corners touch and incorporate the eight surrounding areas--i.e., the *hasht-bihisht*--which surround the central chamber with its cenotaph.

A further interesting conjunction occurs when the circles utilized in **Plates 47 & 48** (top) are repeated vertically and horizontally over the circle which is bounded by the terrace (See: **Plate 48** [bottom]). Noteworthy is the fact that the arcs of the circles from the center point pass through the wide, cardinal point passageways and the resulting petal-like form encloses the mass of the corner cubes and the corresponding portion of the central mass.

Scholars have been known to comment on the incomprehensibility of the spatial concepts

Plate 46
Tomb of Humayun (Ensemble with ninefold division)

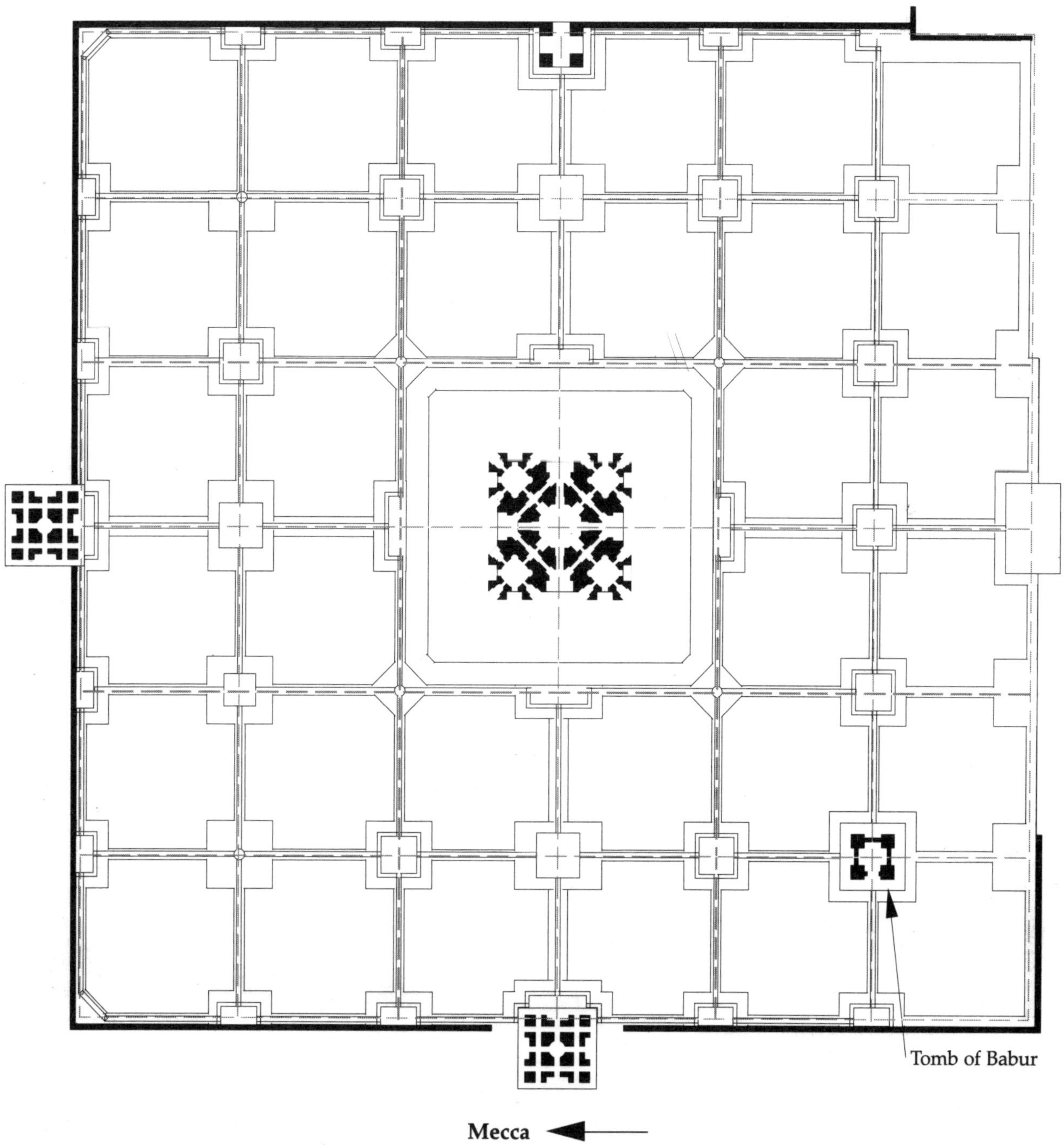

employed by the Persian architects[60] (*tuepfenscheisser*) in relation to the *Tomb of Humayun* and its ensemble. Indeed, many look upon this mausoleum as an aberration. Haji Begum had the tomb placed in the middle of a large garden of Persian design--i.e., a *chahar-bagh*. This, of course, is no aberration. The whole must be considered in any analysis--the mausoleum rising from its terrace arcade and the walled garden. Yet many comment only upon the mausoleum with its four seemingly separate, corner masses as being in competition with the central, domed mass in their apparent separateness.

Upon passing through the confines of the exterior wall from any of its approaches, one is immediately struck by the space. The grid-like garden inexorably leads to the terraced mausoleum majestically situated in the center of the park. The low, arcade terrace gives way to the five-part mass of the tomb proper--i.e., the *pancharatna* ("five jewels") or *pancharatha* ("five vehicles"). From a distance the red sandstone façade interlaced with white marble is enhanced by the effect of the shadows created by the various indentations of the elevations, the total capped by the elegant, white dome. Its reflection is multiplied in the reflecting pools like a cosmic kaleidoscope. From any of the cardinal points two of the four corner masses emerge from or dissolve into the taller central block with its dome.

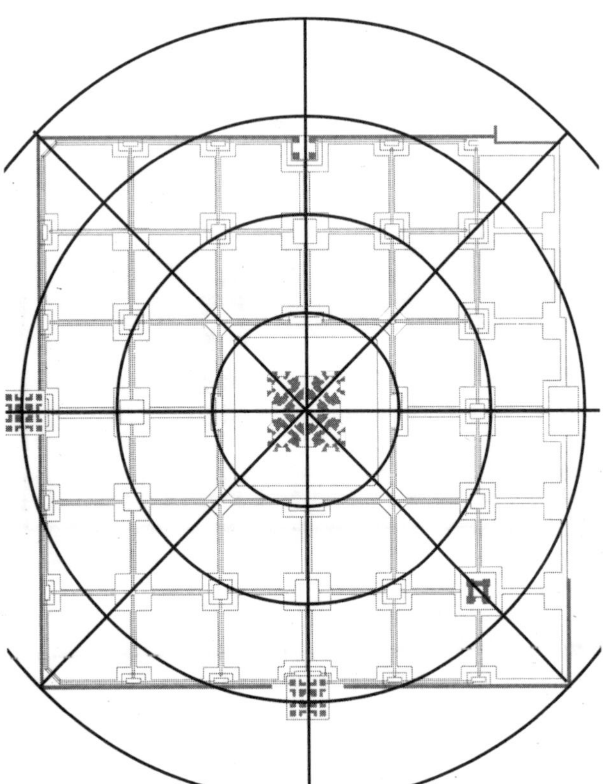

Figure 135: *Tomb of Humayun*, application of circular *Manduka Manduka* to ensemble

Much has been written about the "phase of transition" as it applies to moving from a square to an octagon, via squinches, to a dome. Can we not look upon the whole as also a "phase of transition" from the square theme of the garden to the sheared corners of the terrace and the four radiating masses of the mausoleum, to an octagon and finally the circular form of the dome? Are we to be locked into the aesthetics of a repetitious façade which may have wings or intervening forms all similarly, and repetitiously designed? When we consider, for example, the *Maha-Lingaraja Mandir* of Bhuvaneshvar, do we not marvel as the temple marches from the *Bhog Mandir*, through the *Nat Mandir*, and the *Jagamohan*, finally to the soaring *Sri Mandir*? The *Tomb of Humayun* presents us with a synthesis of five forms unlike any we have seen heretofore. It is, in a sense, to Mughal architecture what the *Bayon* is to the architecture of the Khmer Empire!

Finally, "purists" wax hot to the point of being livid when dealing with the dome. Simply, if architecture is the art of enclosing space, then nothing more can be said! Does the space have to be functional? If the architect had not constructed the shallow dome over the sepulchral chamber, then the space would have exploded into the soaring area defined by the

Plate 47
Tomb of Humayun (Mausoleum with geometric application and with *Chahar-bagh* & octagram over tomb)

Tomb of Humayun (Continued)

dome. The effect would have been awesome, and, perhaps, a bit incongruous visually (See: **Appendix C, Plate 132**). But, the fact is, he did not for whatever reason! This must be respected.

Architecture has been defined as the 'art of enclosing space.' It is a three dimensional art form akin to sculpture in its external form(s). Monumental architecture exist with parameters not necessarily the same as those applied to other forms--e.g., homes, palaces, churches, cathedrals, etc. Here, the exterior of the *Tomb of Humayun* alludes to the interior, but does not strictly define it as one sees in a French Gothic cathedral. Here the exterior is an allusion to the interior, the exterior as a whole provides an illusion of great internal space. As one enters any one of the portals, especially the portals of the corner blocks, one is thrust into a space of average dimension before following narrow corridors towards the center. Upon moving into the central chamber, the narrow confines explode into the soaring interior of substantial proportion. The effect is breathtaking.

Frankly, the fact that there is an even higher and sometimes wider space above the vault of the central chamber does not rob one of the effect of this space. In considering the whole of the *Tomb of Humayun* from afar--i.e., the four corner blocks, the central mass and the soaring dome--one is immersed in a three dimensional sculptural mass, albeit architecture, that is magnificent in its play of forms. The fact that in many instances, as here, the dome's space is cut off from normal view does not lessen the aesthetic appreciation any more than the does one experience with the *Pyramids of Gizeh,* or the great *Borobudur* of Java, or the magnificent *Bakheng* of Angkor.

The *Tomb of Humayun* is an architectural marvel of design and content, albeit off from the mainstream of accepted western architectural practices--part architecture, part sculpture as are the *Pyramids of Gizeh* and *Borobudur*. It stands, as does the *Tomb of Hazrat Mumtaz-uz-Zamani,* as a monument of a spouse for a deceased partner.

Plate 48

Tomb of Humayun (Ensemble with geometric application, and terrace, podium and tomb with geometric application)

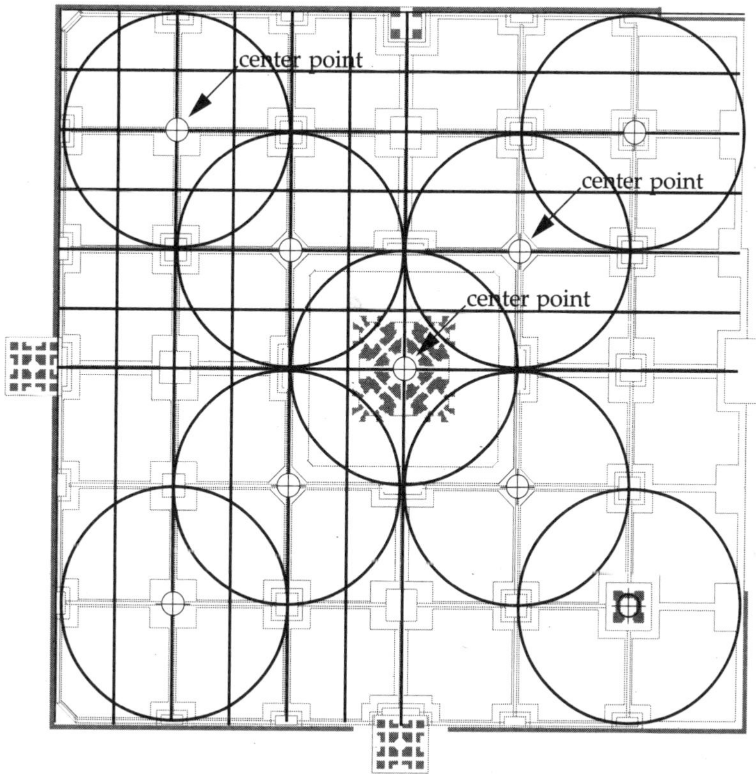

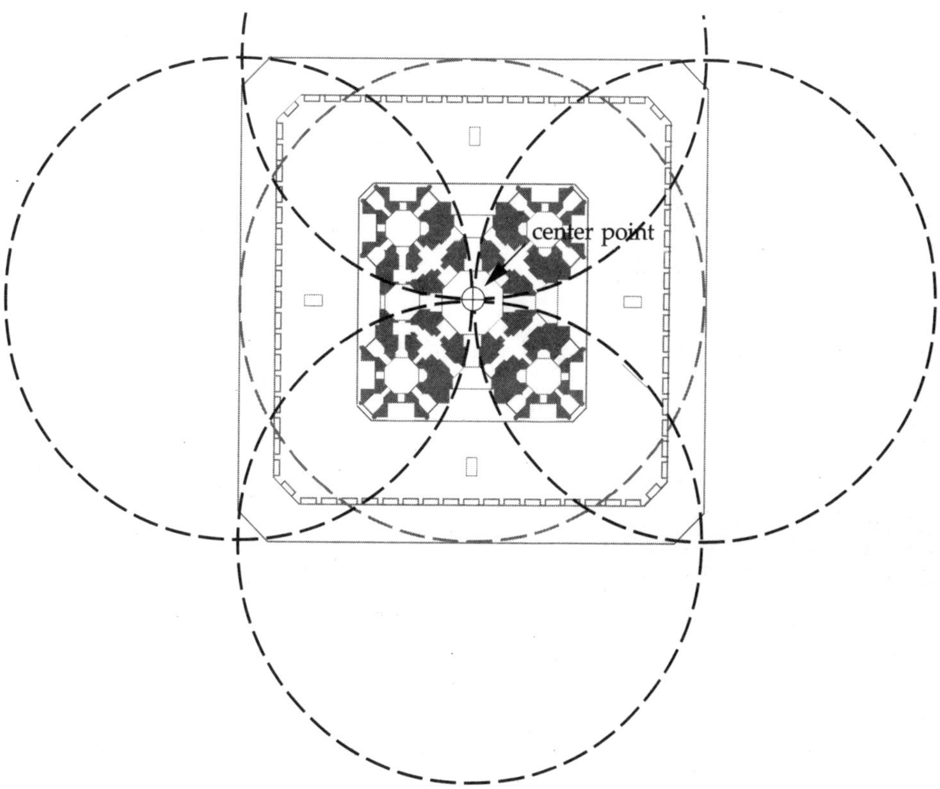

Tomb of Muhammad Ghaus

Gwalior, c. 1565 C.E.

The *Tomb of Muhammad Ghaus*[61] at Gwalior, a provincial city south of Agra, stands as an important monument in that area. A Islamic "saint" and writer who died in 1563 and his mausoleum was constructed later. The tomb has been characterized as "the most notable structure of Akbar's reign,"[62] (CA, p. 81) which is astonishing considering the twenty major monuments constructed during this Great Mughal's tenure. With its construction being contemporaneous with the *Tomb of Humayun*, it indicates a deviation from the plans of mausolea which went before. The *Tomb of Muhammad Ghaus* establishes a new model which finds variations in later mausolea--e.g., the *Tomb of Shah Daulat*[63] at Maner, and the tomb of Mirza Ghiyas, the famed *Tomb of I'timad-ud-daula*[64] at Agra.

Basically, square, *en plan*, with hexagonal towers at the four corners, the mausoleum presents the appearance of a noble residence or palace, not a tomb--i.e., a **Type C-c** basic plan. The imposing corner towers are reminiscent, *en plan*, of the towers of the *Tomb of Sultan Ghari* and find their earliest genesis in the *Tomb of the Samanids*, Bukhara, Uzbekistan (See: **Figure 26**). From the middle of each façade, a porch extends, while the space between the piers of each face is filled with pierced stone screens (Ind.: *jaali*). Although these spaces extend from ground level to the architrave, the corner towers exhibit arcuated openings on two levels, giving the whole the appearance of two stories. The corner towers and the extending porches are all crowned with *chatri*. From the enclosed, square inner chamber, a square form extends above the roof line of the square verandah. This extension possesses a *chajja* and balustrade with four smaller *chatri* at the four corners. From this square mass an octagonal form rises, a podium which supports the dome.

The spacious verandah and the central chamber holding the cenotaph allow for easy access and circumambulation, honoring the *Sufi pir Muhammad Ghaus* (See: **Figure 136**). Set within a *maqbara* with numerous smaller mausolea and cenotaphs, the *Tomb of Muhammad Ghaus* is the

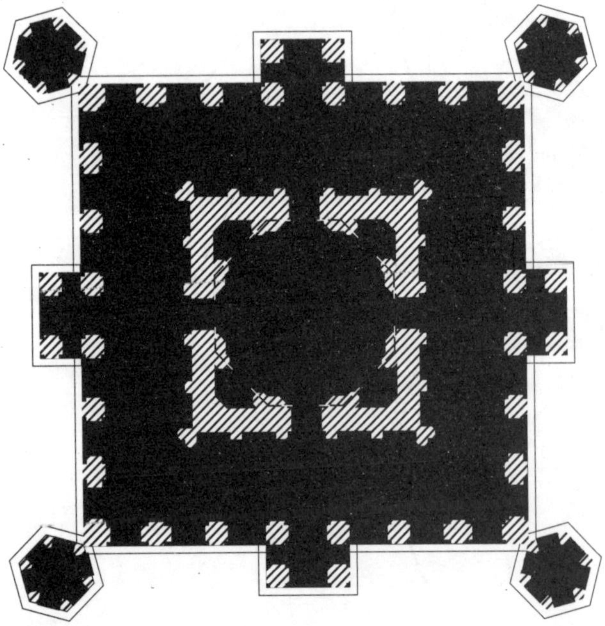

Figure 136: *Tomb of Muhammad Ghaus*, indication of internal space

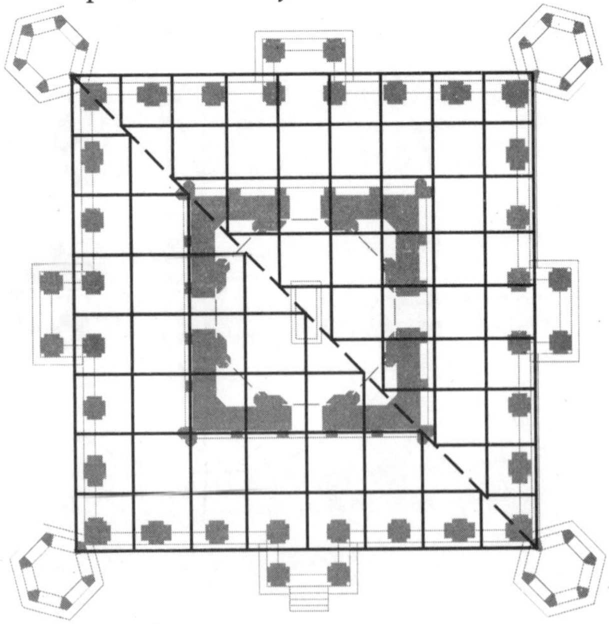

Figure 137: *Tomb of Muhammad Ghaus*, application of *Manduka Manduka* and *Paramashayika Mandala*

Plate 49
Tomb of Muhammad Ghaus (Plan)

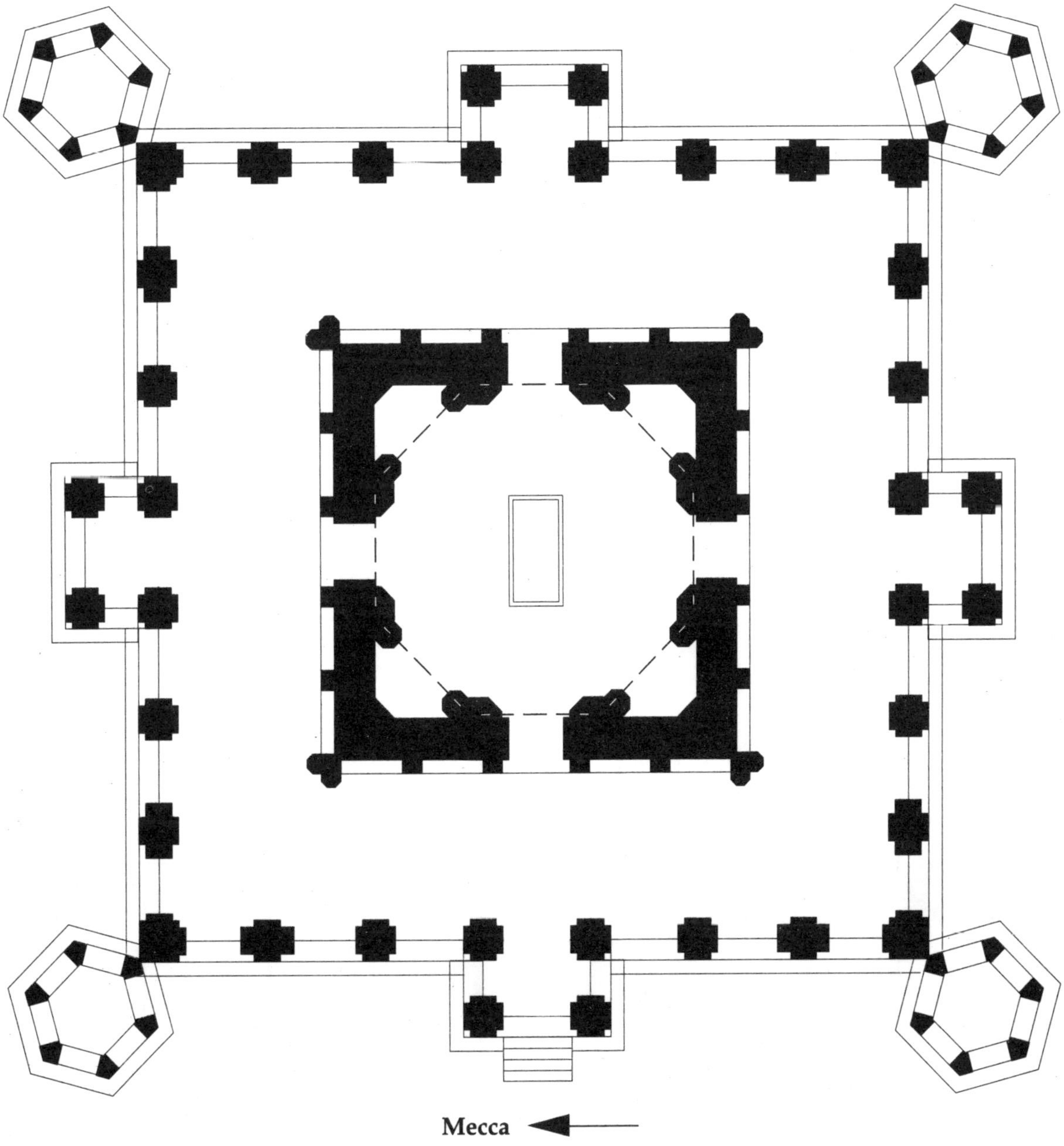

visual zenith of this cemetery.

The application of a *Manduka Mandala* or *Paramashayika Mandala* over the central block appears to offer suitable solutions (See: **Figure 137**). On the other hand, if these two *mandalas* are placed over the whole, less than suitable results occur (See: **Figure 138**). In the former the *brahmásthana* enfolds the cenotaph and the sarcophagus below. The second band includes the quare central chamber. Finally, the piers of the verandah, each are contained in one of the twenty-eight external *pada*.

Frequently, even normally, a square plan Indo-Islamic mausolea is proportionally taller than an octagonal, verandah style tomb. Not so here. As is seen the elevation of the *Tomb of Muhammad Ghaus* the first level, up to the *chajja* falls within the first three ranks (See: **Figure 139**). The square extension of the central chamber with its balustrade rests below the sixth rank. The octagonal drum and the dome fall rise to the height of the eight-and-one-half rank. Therefore the proportions are 12:8.5, similar to earlier octagonal tombs with verandahs--e.g., the *Tomb of Sikandar Lodi, Tomb of Hasan Khan Sur, Tomb of Sher Shah, Tomb of Isa Khan Niyazi* and the *Tomb of Adham Khan*.

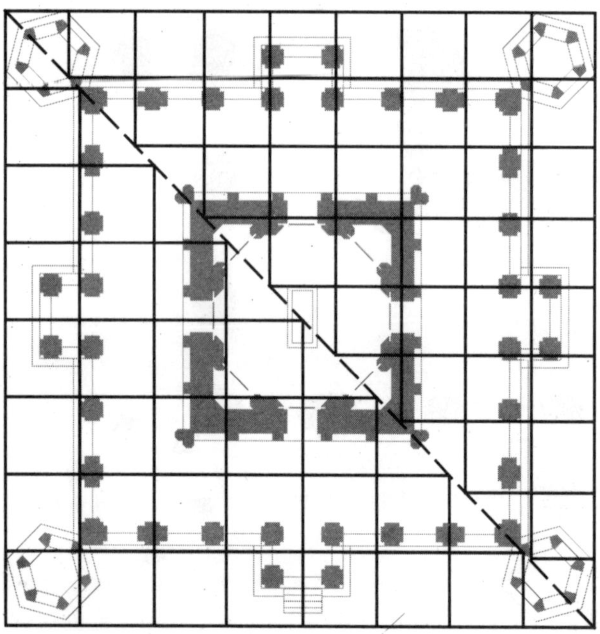

Figure 138: *Tomb of Muhammad Ghaus*, application of *Manduka Manduka* and *Paramashayika Mandala* over the whole

Nestled within the provincial city of Gwalior, far from Imperial Delhi, the *Tomb of Muhammad Ghaus* stands as another example of the many variations that can be found in Indo-Islamic tombs. It is based upon the past, but influences the future--notably: the *Tomb of Akbar, Tomb of Iftikhar Khan, Tomb of Shah Daulat, Tomb of Jahangir, Gol Gumbaz, Tomb of Jahan Begum, Tomb of I'timad-ud-daula,* and *Taj Mahal*.

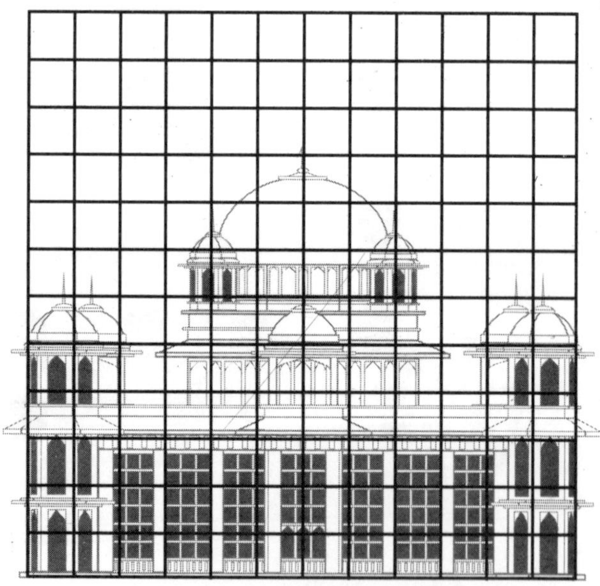

Figure 139: *Tomb of Muhammad Ghaus*, application of *Deshiya Mandala* over the elevation

Plate 50

Tomb of Muhammad Ghaus (Elevation & half plan)

Tomb of Akbar

Sikandra, 1604-1613 C.E.

At the death of Humayun, Akbar, then in Afghanistan and but thirteen years old was declared heir to the Mughal throne. In the absence of the young Abu-'l-Fath Jalal-ud-din Muhammad Akbar, the Hindu general Himu usurped the throne, assumed the title of Raja and established a brief Hindu monarchy. The young emperor returned from Kabul where he had been living and with a strong army defeated the upstart Himu and took back his throne. For a number of years he placed himself under the guardianship of Bairam Khan. Then Akbar assumed full control at eighteen years of age.

A complex man, Akbar the Great is known for his role as a builder, a mystic and a conqueror. Schooled in the orthodox Muslim tradition, he was remarkably tolerant of all faiths within his realm. To the horror of his conservative Islamic advisors, Akbar initiated and participated in theological *salons* in which all ideas were discussed, debated and analyzed openly. In these *salons* were Hindus, Jains, Jesuits, Buddhists and other representatives of the various faiths that were part of his empire and which interested him. He amassed a library, reputed to be then the largest in the Orient, which included treatises on Brahmanism, Judaism, Christianity, Jainism, and, of course Islam. Finally, he established the Din-i-

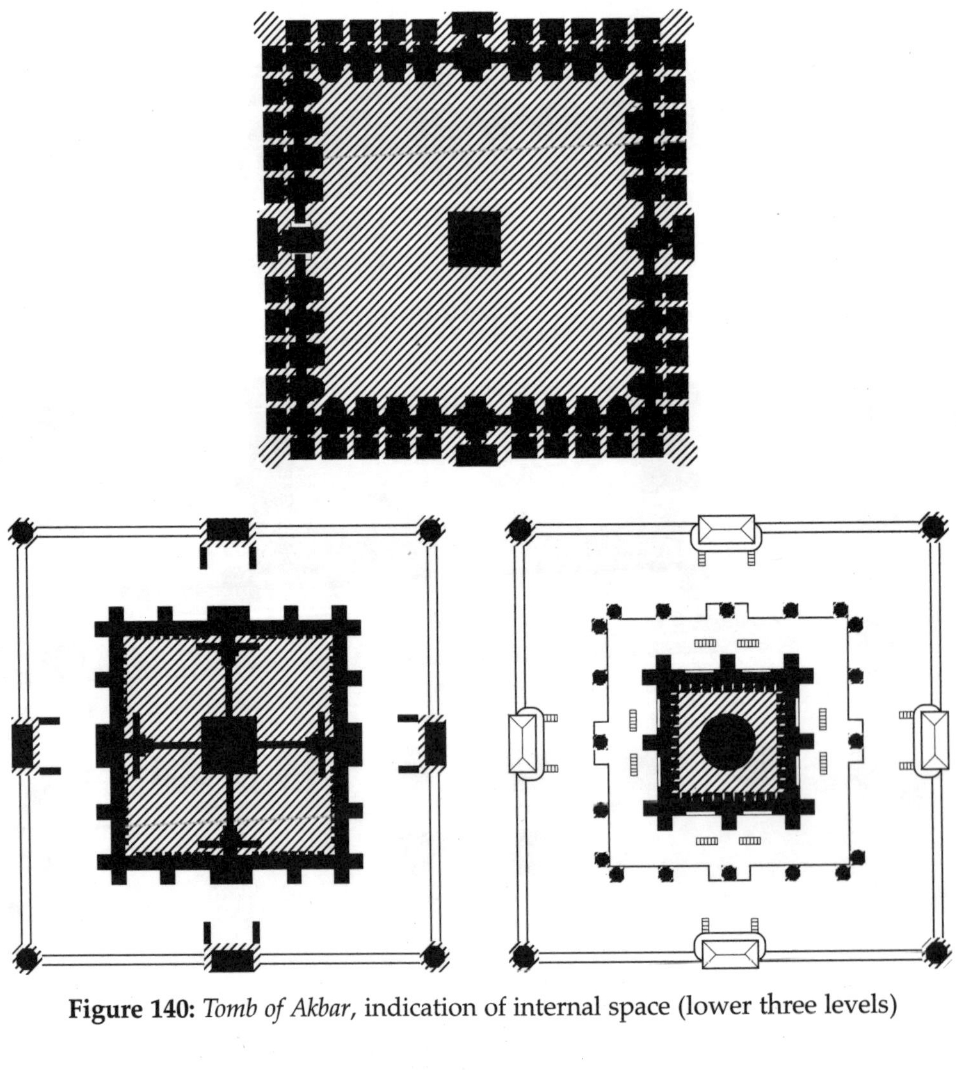

Figure 140: *Tomb of Akbar*, indication of internal space (lower three levels)

Plate 51

Tomb of Akbar (ground level plan)

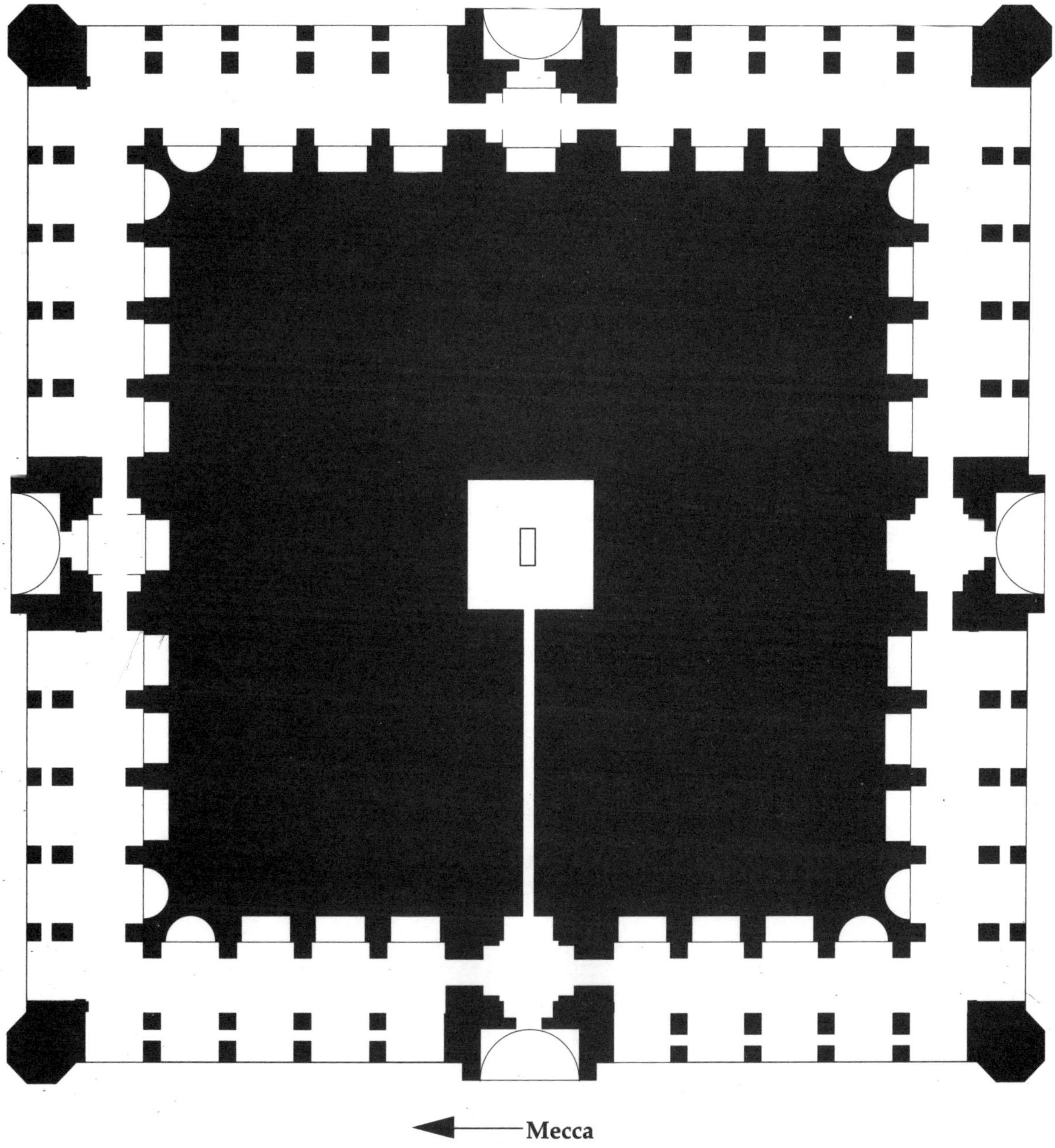

Plate 52
Tomb of Akbar (2nd storey plan with ninefold division)

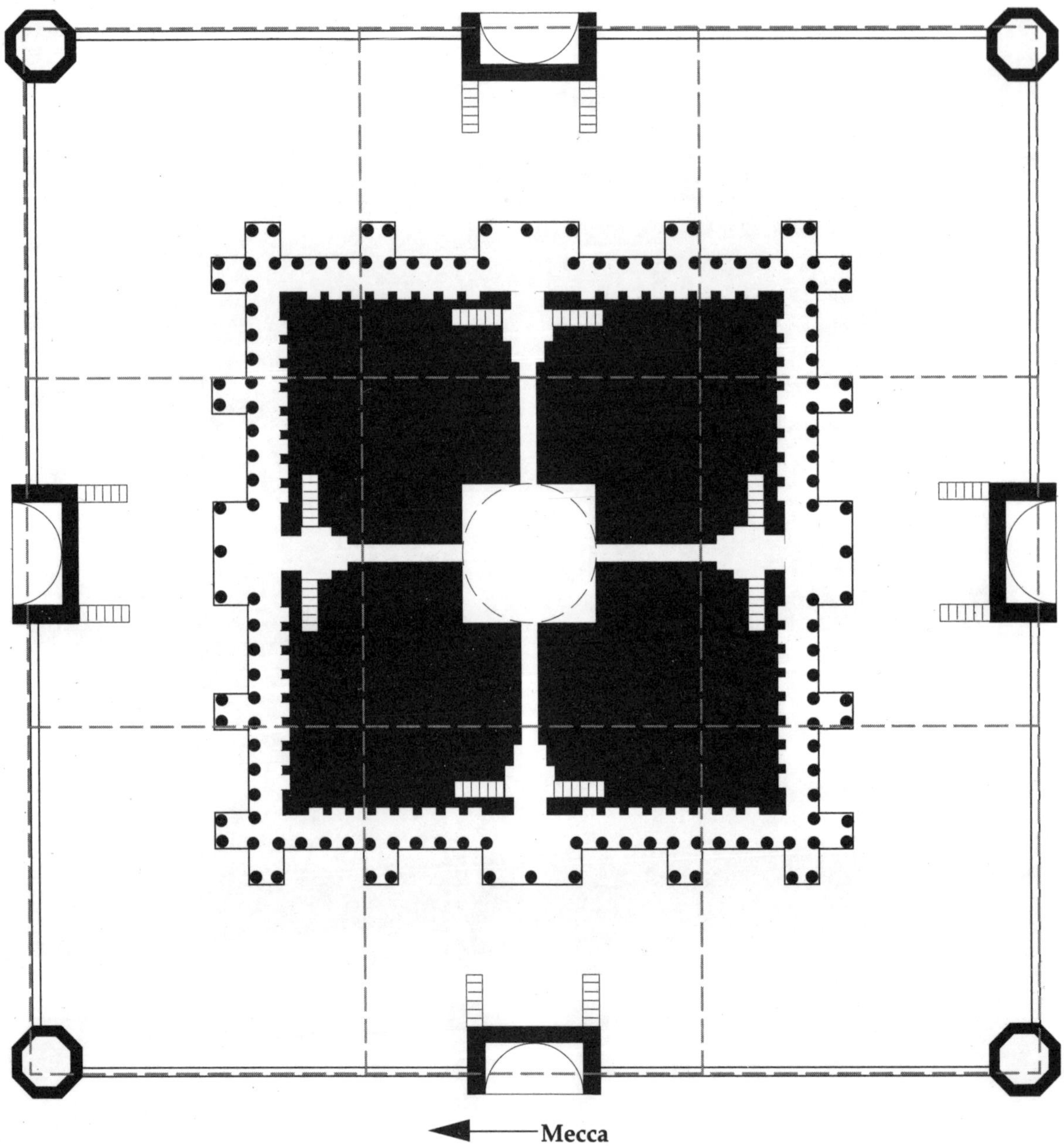

Plate 53
Tomb of Akbar (3rd storey plan)

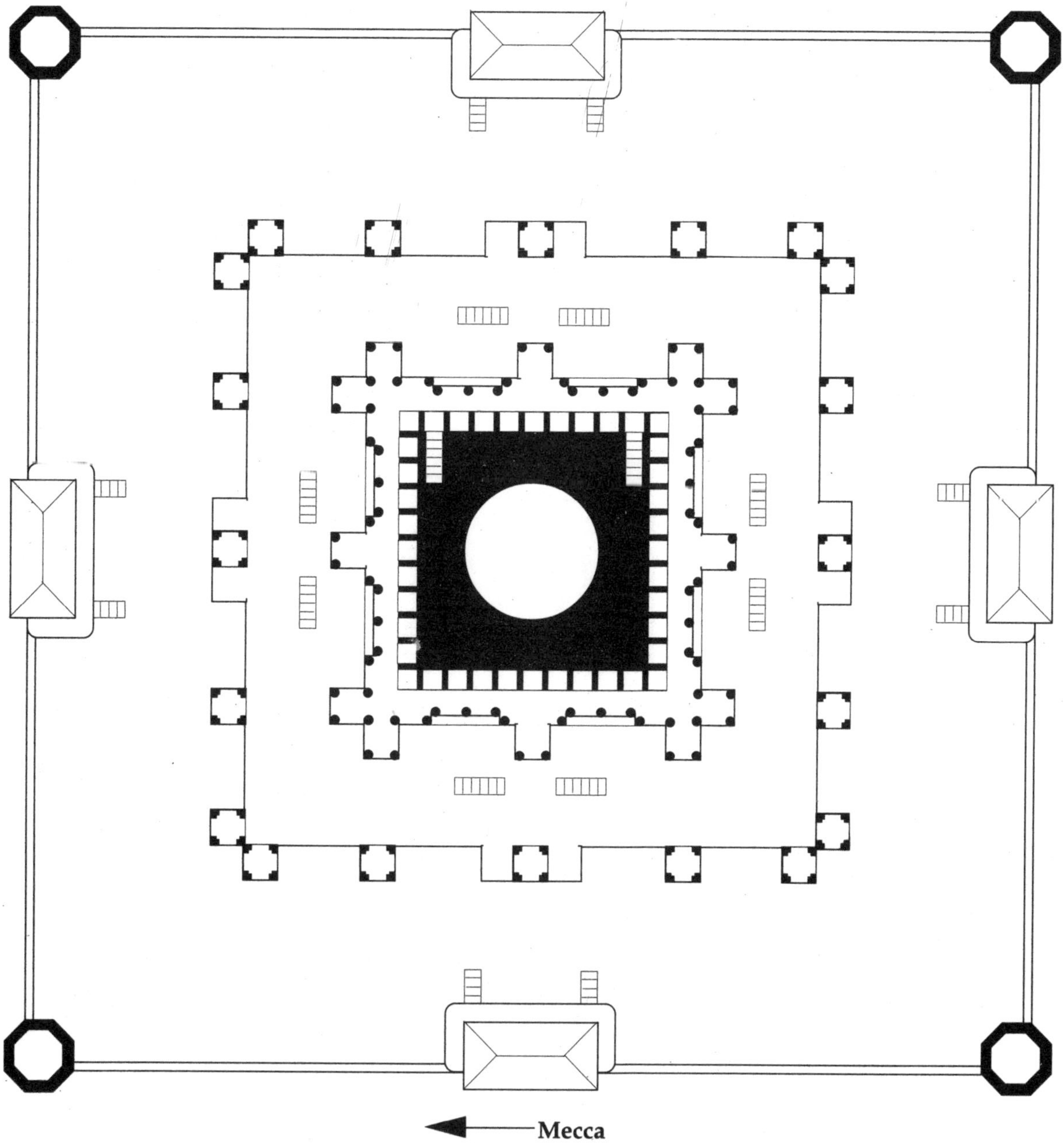

Plate 54
Tomb of Akbar (4th storey plan)

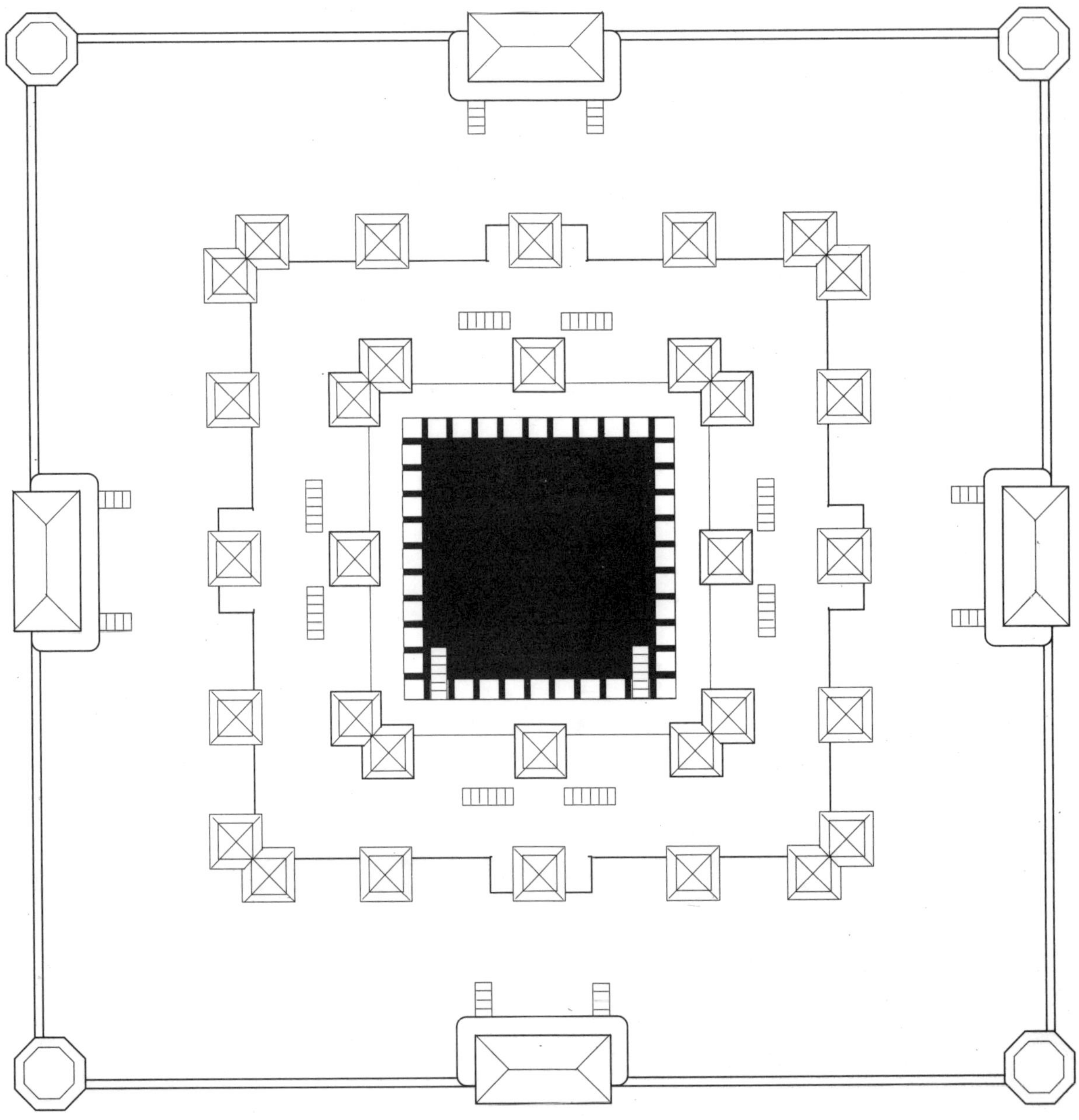

Plate 55
Tomb of Akbar (5th storey plan with ninefold division)

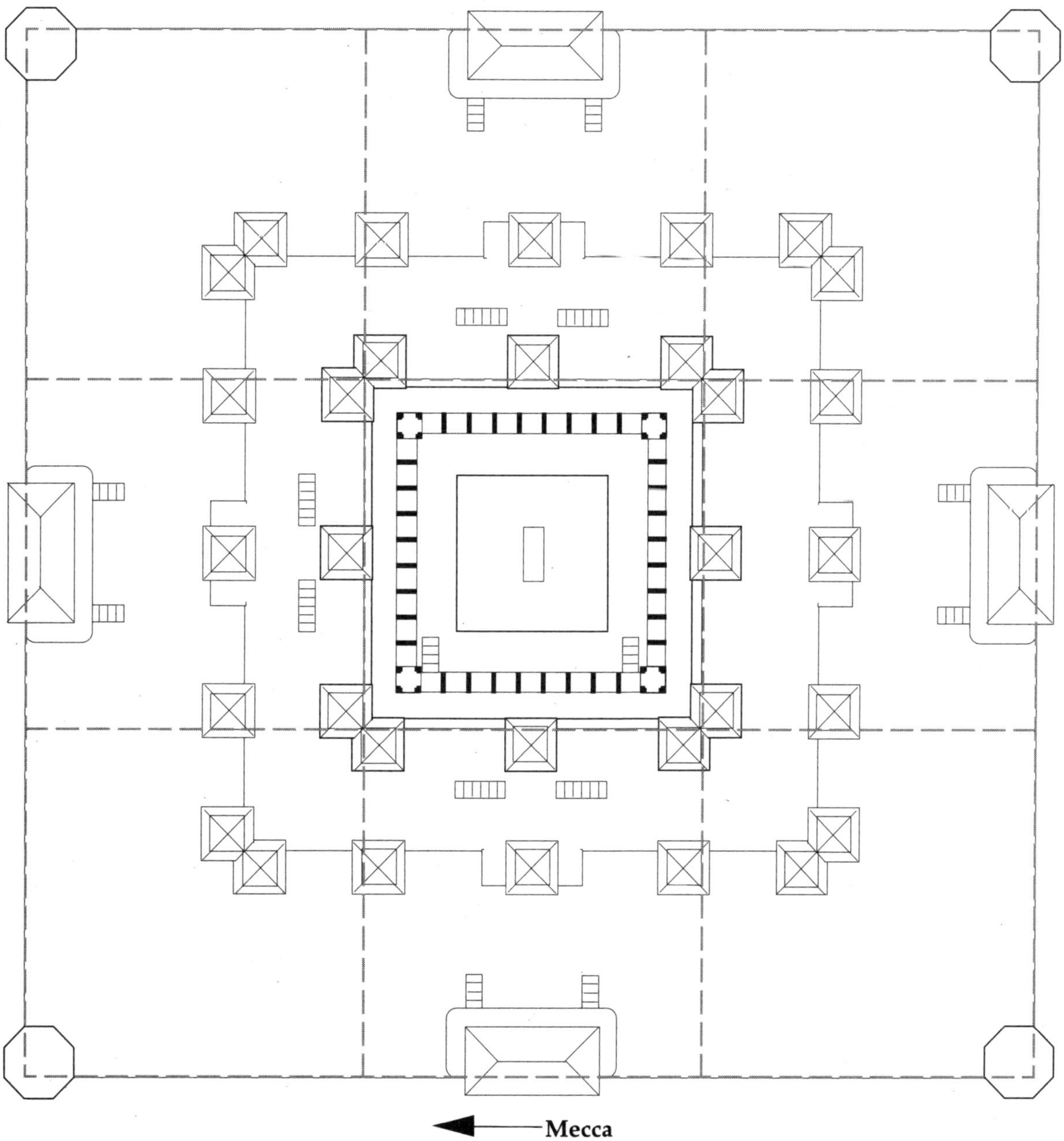

Tomb of Akbar (Continued)

Ilahi, a philosophic society of brotherhood and tolerance. Of course, "tolerance" then possessed little relationship to the term "tolerance" which is understood by today's standards.

Yet, with all his erudition and tolerance, Akbar was still a man, a king, an emperor of his time. He could be incredibly cruel in dealing with those he defeated in battle. At one point after a battle he had thousands of the vanquished slaughtered, a traditional practice of the Mongols from whom he was directly descended. Nonetheless, he was considered at his time rather enlightened and open minded.

When he ascended the throne, his empire consisted of Delhi, the Punjab region as well as the areas of the Jumna and upper Ganges. During his long years on the throne he amalgamated Rajasthan, Gujarat, Malwa, Bihar, Bengal and Orissa--in other words nearly all of present day India and Pakistan above Bombay with the exception of a large tract of the Deccan known as Gondwana. Upon the death of his brother, the King of Kabul, he annexed Afghanistan. His empire grew to the size of Europe.

His interests were varied, but paramount was architecture. Among his varied building projects was the famed *Fathepur Sikri* (See: **Appendix C, Plate 146**). It was, and still remains the most comprehensive of all his building endeavors. *Fathepur Sikri* , a few leagues from Agra, Akbar constructed his imperial city (Indic: *pura*) which in its many facets, was unrivalled--i.e., he did not follow then accepted cosmological design concepts but constructed the city along the features of the natural terrain on the top of a long ridge. The whole complex appears to be rather haphazard--i.e., Hindu or Muslim axiality does not apply except for certain individual buildings. Monarchs had heretofore constructed vast living complexes within highly fortified enclosures--e.g., the *Akharabad* (*Red Fort* of Agra) which he began, or the *Shahjahanabad* (*Red Fort* of Delhi) built by Shah Jahan. *Fathepur Sikri*, on

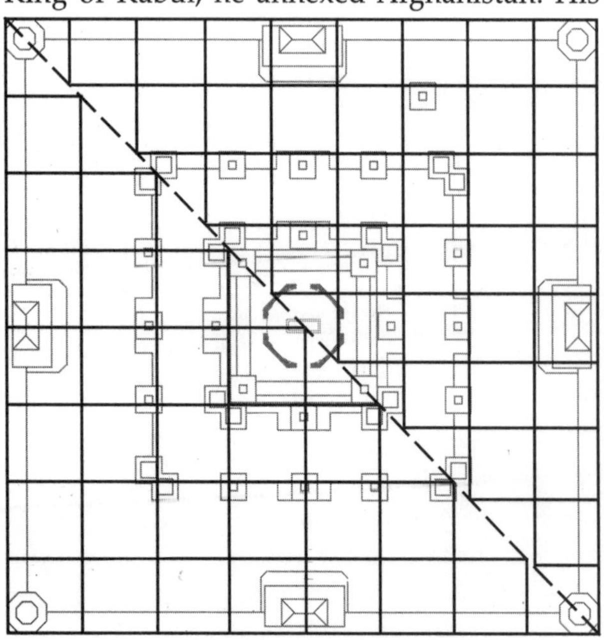

Figure 141: *Tomb of Akbar*, application of *Manduka Manduka* and *Paramashayika Mandala*

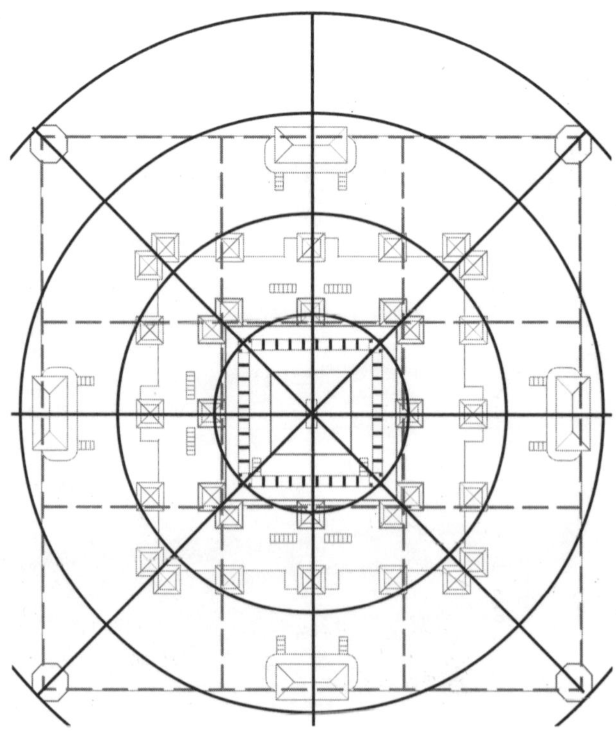

Figure 142: *Tomb of Akbar*, application of circular *Manduka Manduka*

Plate 56
Tomb of Akbar (Elevation & composite half plan)

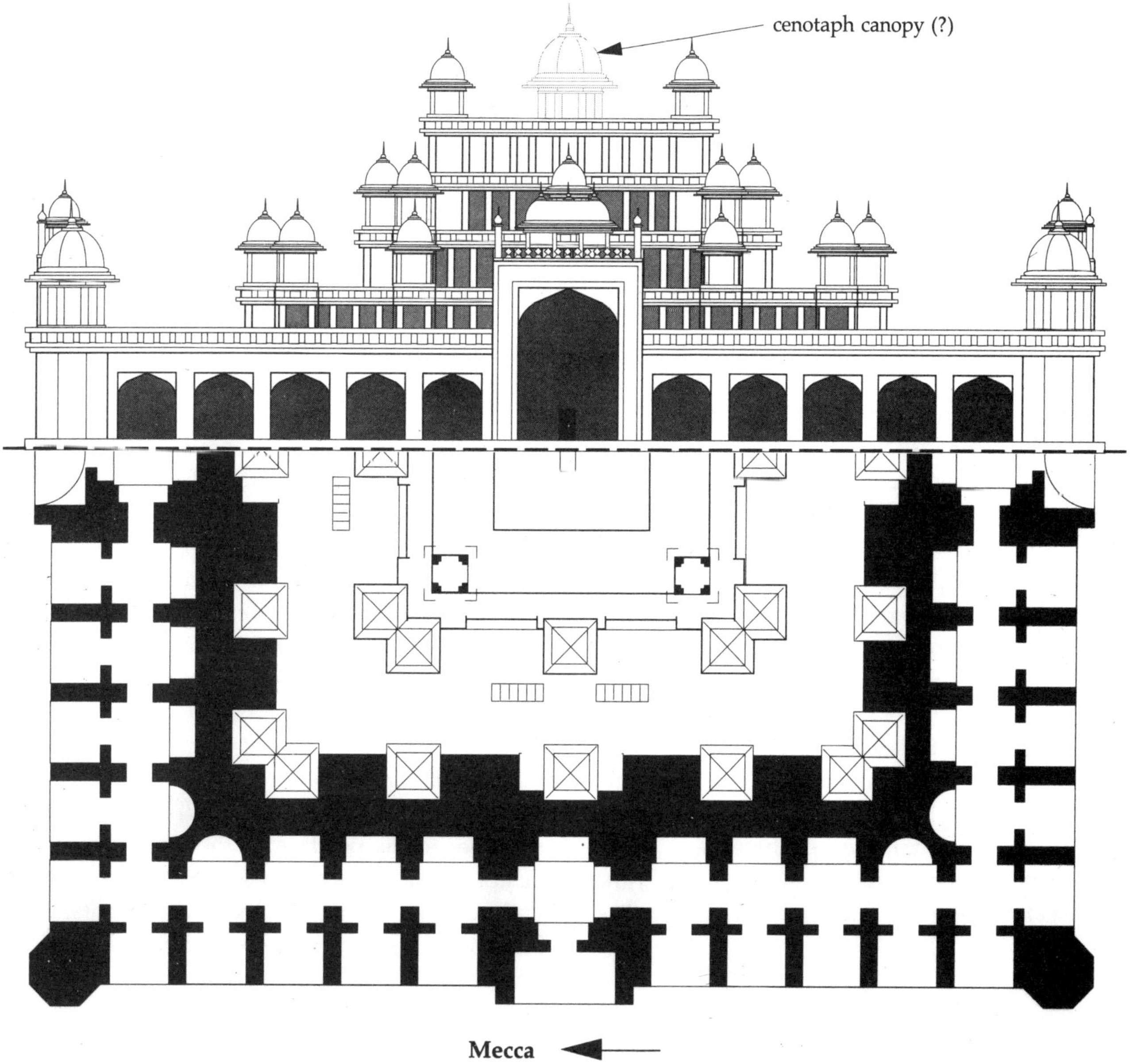

the other hand, is lightly fortified, at least by contemporary standards of that day. It was more a palace than a fort. It consists of numerous enclosures, gardens, residences, pavilions and subsidiary structures to support the needs of the emperor, his court and for the benefit of the empire.

The *Tomb of Akbar*[65] begun during the last years of his life and completed by his son, Jahangir, was the last major project that he undertook. At the time of its construction it was unique in Islamic tomb architecture. Probably due to his own mystical pantheism, his tomb is pyramidal in form. In that shape/form is appears more akin to the Buddhist *Borobudur* of Java or the Hindu *Ta Keo* of Angkor, or the Buddhist *Ananda* of Pagan--all of which he would have had some familiarity (See: **Plate 57**). The *Tomb of Akbar* consists of a large, square platform, a massive solid plinth, with deep, connected arcades on all four sides and a solid center, three-hundred-twenty feet square----i.e., cross axial and a **Type C-a** basic plan. On each corners of this raised terrace are *chatri*, which find their basis in Hindu architecture, and in the center of each façade rose a large monumental *pishtaq*. Three more solid core, arcaded terraces rise above the main plinth, each set back from the one below (See: **Plates 52-56**). A sectional view of the *Tomb of Akbar*, would show a close relationship with the pavilion of the *Kotilal* of Delhi, built over three centuries before, with its solid core and pyramidal aspect (See: **Figure 143**). The pyramidal form of this tomb is unmistakable.

Figure 143: *Garden Pavilion* (section), Kotilal, Delhi, indicating stepped terraces and rock core

In the center of the solid mass a domed crypt was inserted as if in the earth itself. Public access to the crypt area was limited to four axially arranged passageways that did not descend to the level of the sarcophagus, but to an arcaded gallery well above the stone coffin. In previous Islamic tombs entrance to the crypt could be gained by a closed and concealed entrance not normally used by the public, but only during the burial ceremony. The viewing of the sarcophagus holding the remains was not necessary. A cenotaph in the public area above the crypt served that purpose. However, not so with the stone casket holding the mortal remains of Akbar. Its placement in this crypt, out of reach from the observers above, appears to duplicate his position on life--i.e., out of reach, beyond, inaccessible, and, in a word, imperial. In addition, the placement of his remains in the crypt is opposite to his position in the *Diwan-i-Khas* at *Fathepur Sikri*, where he was physically centered and elevated above the noble supplicants. The location of the sarcophagus within this internal crypt relates to the cave-like sanctuaries of Hindu temples--i.e., the *garbha-griha*; the womb.

Unlike previous Islamic tombs in India, the *Tomb of Akbar* indicates significantly less internal space than other tombs (See: **Figure 140**). The relationship of solid mass to internal space is more akin to that found in Buddhist or Hindu temples. When viewing the pyramidal elevation, the cave-like crypt and the paucity of internal space compared to the mass, one is aware of the impact on Akbar of forces from outside the traditional Persio-Islamic influences on this heterodox, eclectic monarch. The crypt with is

Plate 57

Tomb of Akbar, Borobudur, Ta Keo & Ananda (Half-elevation comparison)

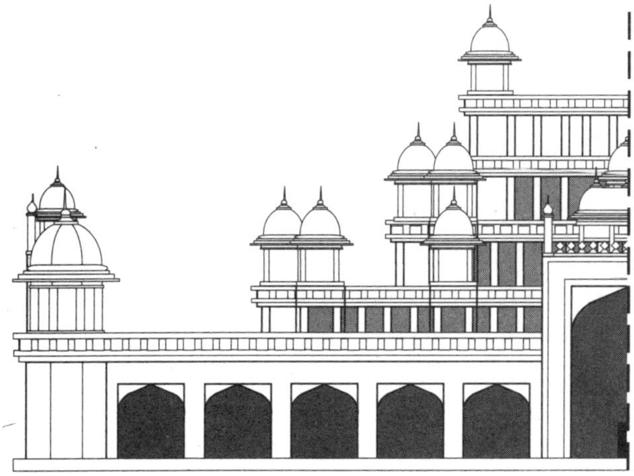

Tomb of Akbar

Borobudur (silhouette), Java, c. 760-830 C.E.

Ta Keo, Angkor (silhouette), c. 975-1050 C.E.

Ananda (silhouette), Pagan, a. 1105 C.E.

covering dome and the monumental *pishtaq* are the only elements of this tomb that are unmistakably Islamic in influence.

If either a *Manduka Mandala* or a *Paramashayika Mandala* is superimposed over the plan, it is seen that the *Manduka Mandala* posses too many problems to make it truly viable. However, the *Paramashayika Mandala* appears eminently suitable (See: **Figure 141**). The upper two levels fall within the *brahmásthana* and the dome of the surmounting pavilion is protected by the central *pada*. The square terraces above the plinth all fall within the realm of the second tier of deities. This would appear to indicate the strong influence that the Hindu *sthapatis* had upon the construction of this mausoleum, if not upon Akbar himself. In addition, the *Tomb of Akbar* indicates a further strong Hindu influence in the multiple use of the square--i.e., the sacred Hindu form--rather than the circle which denoted the celestial regions to both the Muslims and Buddhists. The great dome that was employed in the *Tomb of Humayun* with monumental effect or the domes found in the pre-Mughal Islamic tombs are not found here. The circle was, however, employed in the upper, central pavilion, but its importance to the whole is minimal. The plan is unequivocally Hindu and Buddhist in its influence.

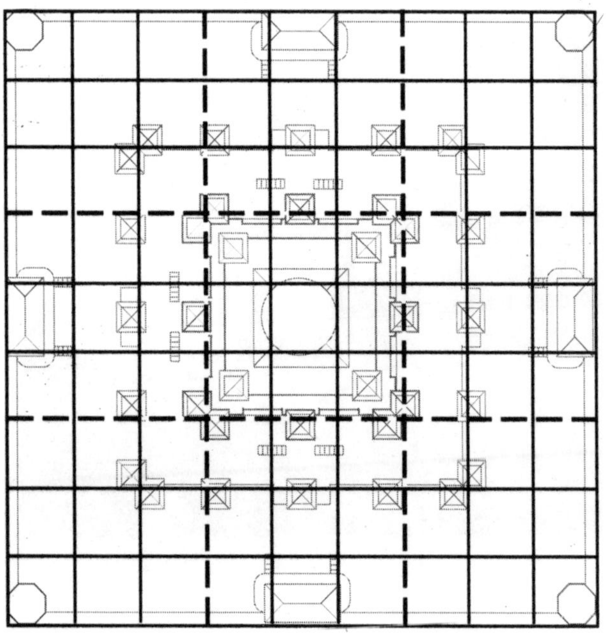

Figure 144: *Tomb of Akbar*, with *Paramashayika Mandala* indicating ninefold plan

If an circular *Manduka Mandala* is employed (See: **Figure 142**) the *brahmásthana* enfolds the upper terrace and involves the *chatri* of the third and fourth storeys, but excludes the eight corner *chatri*. The second circle enfolds all the *chatri* of the second storey, but again excludes the eight corner *chatri*. The third ring encloses the pavilions, the *pishtaq* at the cardinal points of the of the ground level and excluded the four corner *chatri*. Of course, the outer ring encloses all. It is noteworthy that all the corner *chatri* are excluded from the inclusion of the others on their particular level,

It is seen that the ninefold division has some applicability to the *Tomb of Akbar* (See: **Figure 144**). Here, the upper storeys with the cenotaph and the sarcophagus below is contained, neatly within the central square. In the application to the 2nd storey (See: **Plate 52**) the inner vestibules fall within the central, outer areas, as, of course do the four entrances. Similarly eight other prominent features of the *Tomb of Akbar* fall within the eight surrounding squares--i.e., *hasht bihisht*--the four tall *chatri* of the corners and the four gates--i.e., *dargah* or *pishtaq*--at the cardinal directions. These eight forms iconographically refer to the eight rivers which surround paradise, and the central square with the cenotaph and sarcophagus complete the icon.

As has been referred to above, the elevation of the *Tomb of Akbar* is pyramidal in form. If an equilateral triangle is superimposed over the elevation and touching the outer and upper limits--i.e., the corner *chatri*--it is seen that, of course, this form does not apply. However, if

Plate 58
Tomb of Akbar (Ensemble)

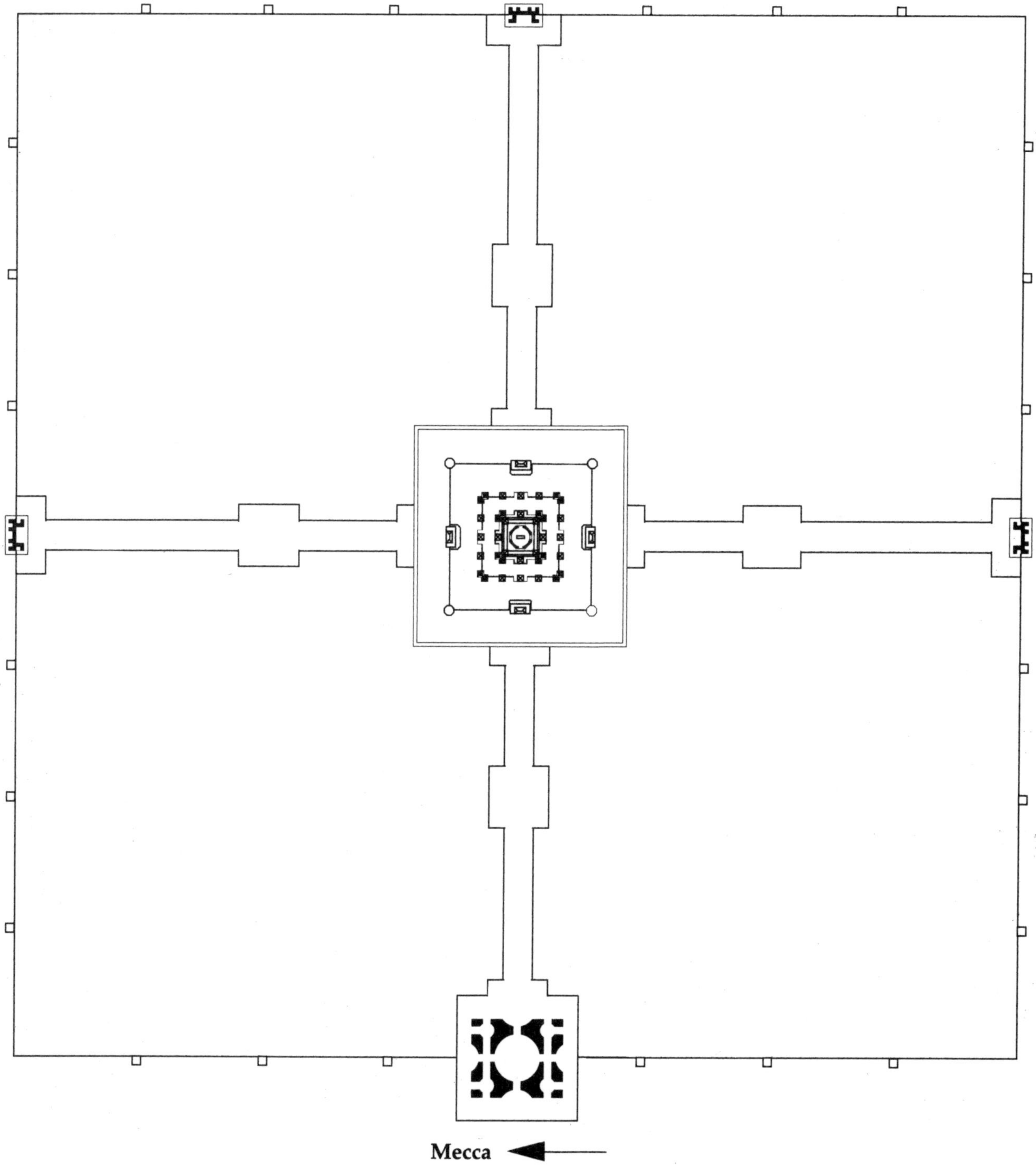

the outer points of the equilateral triangle is employed and a second triangle is drawn using the *chatri* of the second, third and fourth terraces, then a 30^0 triangle is formed (See: **Figure 145**). Within both the Buddhist and Hindu traditions, this number, this angle is most auspicious.[66]

As has been stated elsewhere in this study, the *Deshiya Mandala* possesses certain applications to a number of the plans (See: **Figure 146**). So too with the *Tomb of Akbar*. The upper two levels fall within this *mandala's brahmásthana*. What is also evident is the fact that the *brahmásthana* is used as the limits for a circle, and then the center point of each successive four *pada* square, diagonally is the center for a circle of equal dimension. This, as can be seen, amounts to five circles in any direction, including the diagonal directions. Five is an auspicious and interesting number. It is masculine but formed from the first feminine number--i.e., two--and the first masculine number--i.e., three. It represents love, the union of opposites and is revolutionary. Five is the š of twenty-five, also an auspicious number. It is the sum of the first five masculine numbers in succession--i.e., 1 + 3 + 5 + 7 + 9 = 25 (here the integer one is considered as masculine). It is a mystical and magic number which also denotes harmony.

The *Tomb of Akbar*, as with the *Tomb of Humayun*, is set within a *chahar-bagh*, although *Akbar's* funerary garden is not as developed as that of his predecessor (See: **Appendix B**). It is, nonetheless, vast (See: **Plate 58**) as befits the Great Mughal. The garden is divided into four sections--i.e., *chahar-bagh*--rather than further subdivided as is seen in the *Tomb of Humayun*. It appears deceptively simple. What does this simplified garden connote? It may be a result of Jahangir's "aesthetic" as he was in charge of finishing what his father started. On the other hand, the design may symbolize something else. The quadripartite division--i.e., *chahar-bagh*--gives emphasis to the cardinal direction walkways. More importantly, to the entrance gates, particularly the southern gate, which for the Indo-Islamic builders was the main entrance. The other three entrances were subsidiary, Nonetheless, this arrangement of four around one recalls the *pancharatna* or *pancharatha*

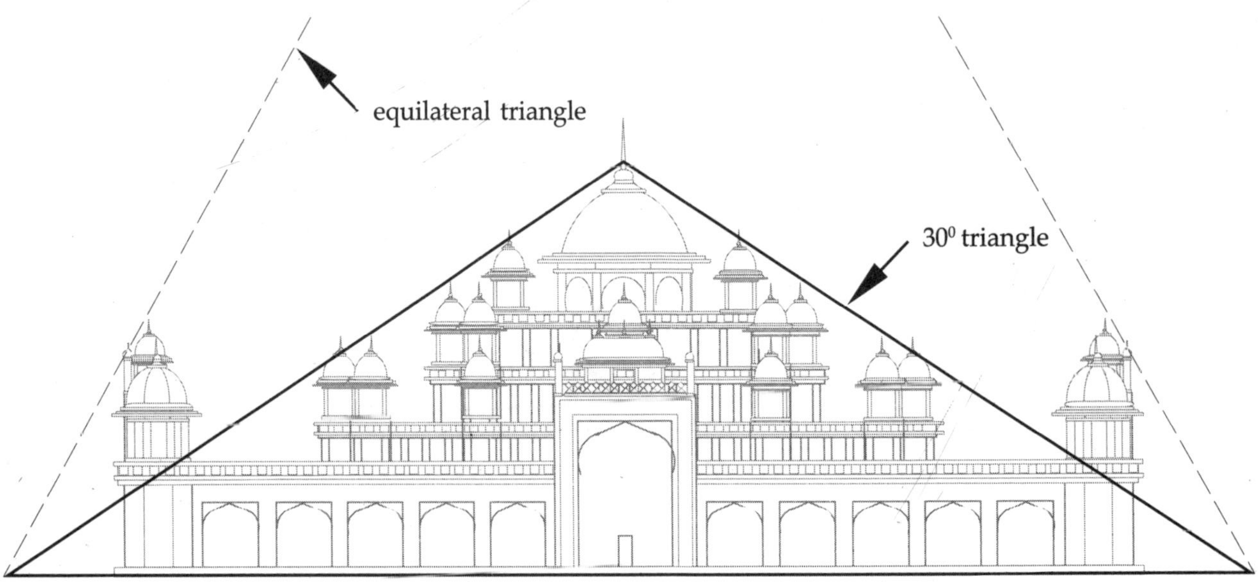

Figure 145: *Tomb of Akbar*, application of an equilateral triangle and 30^0 triangle

design sacred to Hindu *sthapati*.

Further, if one of these quadrants is divided, using a *Mahapitha Mandala*, the results are similar to that seen in the *chahar-bagh* of the *Taj Mahal* or of either the upper or lower garden of the *Shalimar Bagh*, Lahore. This division would appear most desirable, even indicated as along the outer wall of the tomb's enclosure are six large buttresses per face which correspond to the fourfold division of each quadrant (See: **Plate 58**). Do these buttresses suggest an internal division never realized?

The dimension of the enclosure is similar to that found in the *Tomb of Humayun*. However, the space occupied by the mausoleum, including its integral podium, gives the impression of something far larger. The scale is massive. This is accomplished by the horizontally based forms which mount upward as they recede in dimension of each face, much in the same way that Angkor's *Ta Keo* utilizes this visual phenomenon.

As Akbar the Great deviated from traditional, conservative Islam and into a more inclusive pantheism, so did his mausoleum blaze its way into new and, heretofore, uncharted architectural waters of Indo-Islamic architecture. Certain traditional Indo-Islamic elements remained--e.g., the *chatri*, *pishtaq* and the now traditional Indo-Islamic arches--but major forms were transmuted into a whole that parallel not only Akbar's greatness, but also is wide ranging intellectual powers.

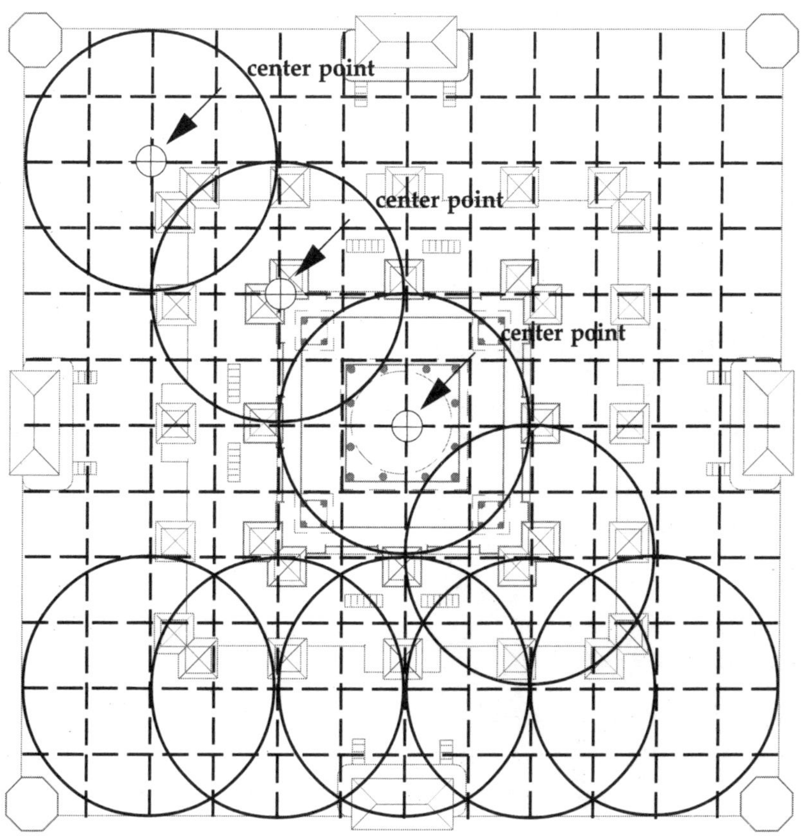

Figure 146: *Tomb of Akbar*, with *Deshiya Mandala* geometrical applications

Tomb of Mohammed Quli Qutub Shah

Golconda, a. 1612 C.E.

The Qutab Shahi poet king of Golconda, Mohammed Quli Qutub Shah (r. 1581-1612 C.E.) was laid to rest in a mausoleum of magnificence and unusual proportions. The Qutab Shahi's preferred the square plan as being appropriate for a royal tomb and freely utilized it for nobles alike. The fifth monarch's tomb was a combination of Hindu, Pathan and Moorish styles.

The *Tomb of Mohammed Quli Qutub Shah*[67] consists of a square inner chamber in which the cenotaph is found on an elevated dais. Surrounding this chamber is a deep verandah with heavy corner piers and seven arched openings on each face. The total of twenty-eight arches surrounding the verandah possesses certain cosmic implications--i.e., the number of days in the lunar calendar, a calendar assiduously relied upon by the Muslims. Atop each corner of this lower block are tall, slender minarets with bulbous, small domes similar to those found in other Qutab Shahi tombs and also apparent in the *Ibrahim Rauza* of Bijapur, a neighbor. From the perimeter of the central chamber a second storey extends upwards, approximately the same height as the ground floor block. This tall second level is one of the features peculiar to the Qutub Shahi tombs. This mass is punctuated on each of its faces with five blind arches corresponding to the middle five openings of the lower level and amounting to a total of twenty. At the corners of this block are minarets of the same design, but shorter than those of the lower block. In addition, on four, separating plinths, corresponding to the blind arcade, are miniature minaret-like forms, again these correspond in design to those of the corners. It is of interest to note that the elements above the *chajja* of this second storey are considerably higher in proportion than those found on the lower level. This, too, is peculiar to the Qutub Shahi tombs. From this second storey, a sixteen sided podium rises upwards and supports the typical, three-quarter, bulbous Qutab Shahi dome. The elevation of this and other Qutab Shahi mausoleum is one of far

Figure 147: *Tomb of Mohammed Quli Qutub Shah,* indication of internal space

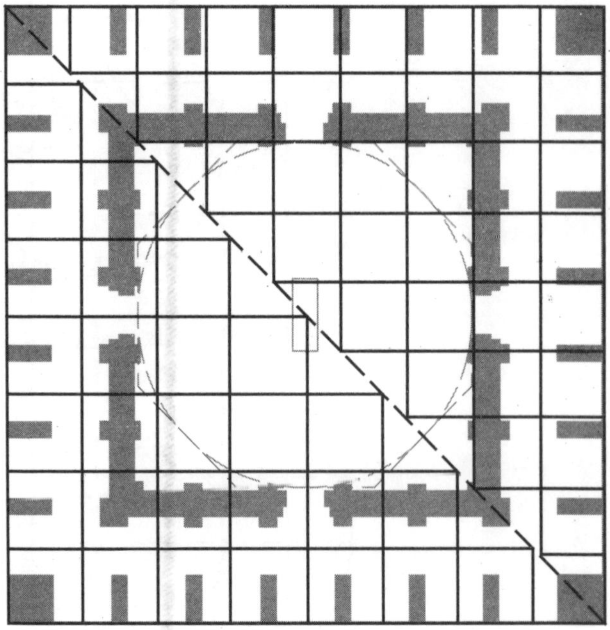

Figure 148: *Tomb of Mohammed Quli Qutub Shah,* application of *Manduka Mandala & Paramashayika Mandala*

Plate 59
Tomb of Mohammed Quli Qutub Shah (Plan)

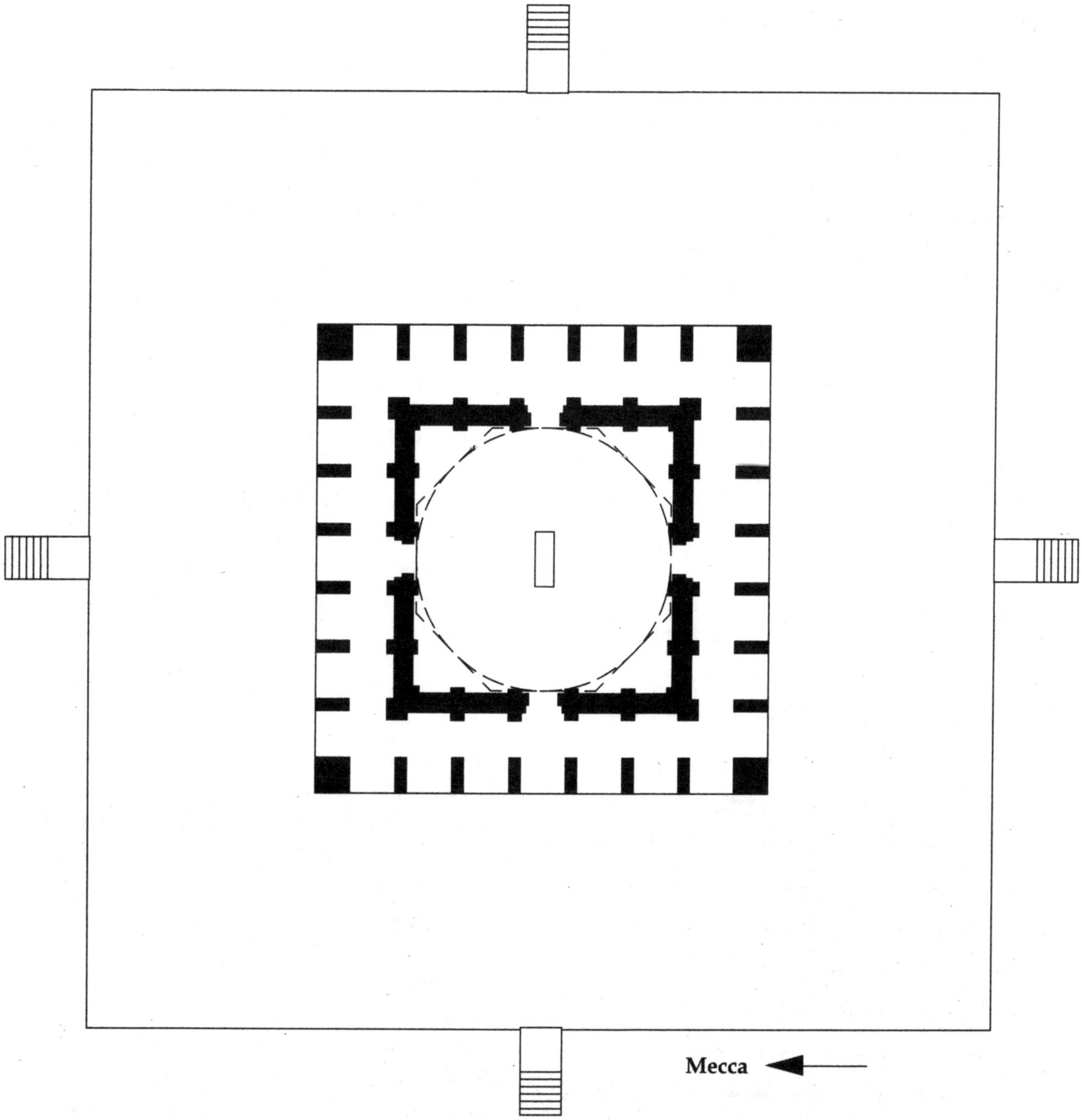

greater height than width (See: **Plate 60**; see also: **Appendix C, Plates 134, 135 & 144**). These proportions seem to mirror, or at least were influenced by the Timurud tombs of Samarqand (**Appendix C, Plate 128**).

As with the previous mausolea, the *Tomb of Mohammed Quli Qutub Shah* indicates considerable internal space (See: **Figure 147**). Not only is this great space one of considerable majesty, reflecting the status of Mohammed Quli Qutub Shah, it also provides ample room for those who wish to honor the poet king by circumambulation.

The application of either the *Manduka Mandala* or the *Paramashayika Mandala* indicates that the former is of eminent applicability (See: **Figure 148**). The *Manduka Mandala* appears to be more applicable. The cenotaph and the sarcophagus below is protected by the *brahmásthana* as , indeed, nearly the whole of the central chamber is within the second rank. The central chamber and half of the ambulatory lies within the third rank. It is to be noted that the outer piers are centered within each of the *pada* of the fourth rank.

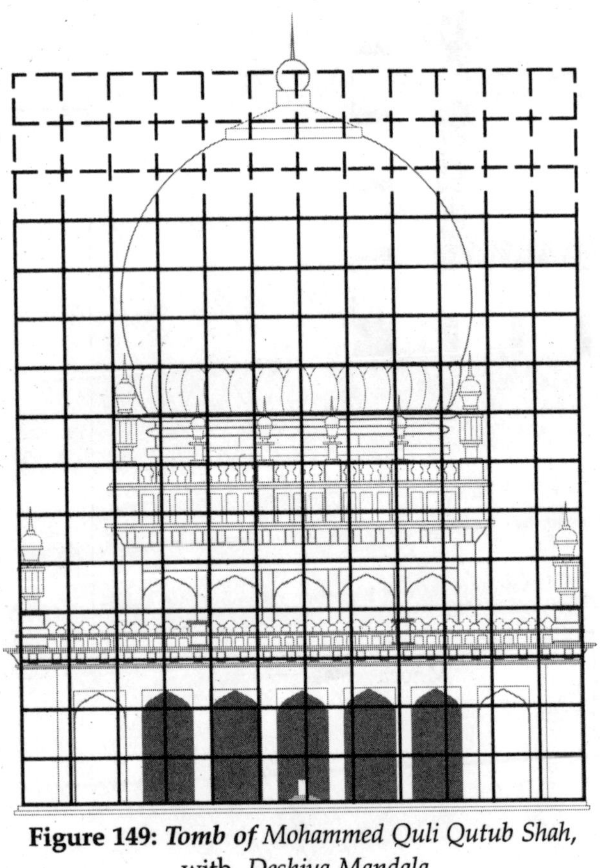

Figure 149: ***Tomb of*** *Mohammed Quli Qutub Shah,* with *Deshiya Mandala*

When the elevation is placed beneath a *Deshiya Mandala,* it is noted that the first storey is contained within the lower four ranks (See: **Figure 149**). The second storey touches the seventh rank of *pada*. The dome is contained within the eight central file of *pada* and the whole extends upwards to fourteen-and-one-half *pada*. Therefore the proportions of the *Tomb of Mohammed Quli Qutub Shah* is 12:14.5, making it, proportionally, one of the tallest of the major Indo-Islamic mausolea.

The *Tomb of Mohammed Quli Qutub Shah* is characteristic of the majority of the other Qutub Shahi mausolea. Slender minarets with three-quarter domes punctuate the corners. The height of the ground storey is virtually matched by that of the second level. Generally speaking, the architrave of the second level is wider and more developed. Finally, the whole is capped by a soaring three-quarter dome. Unlike the majority of domes which precede the Qutub Shahi, which spring from the drum and generally do not extend beyond the limits of the drum, here the dome springs from a stylized lotus and its width nearly matches the width of the second level--i.e., extends beyond the limits of the drum. These characteristics give a distinctive appearance to the Qutub Shahi tombs.

Plate 60
Tomb of Mohammed Quli Qutub Shah (Elevation & half plan)

Ibrahim Rauza

Bijapur, a. 1615 C.E.

As with many of the noble families of Islamic India, the 'Adil Shahi came to their position out of distress. Upon the death of Sultan Murad II of Turkey, his eldest son set about assassinating all his younger brothers. One of these brothers, Yusuf Adil Shah, was spirited away by his mother and sent to Persia. Later, he went to the court of the Sultan of Bidar where he proved his bravery, allegiance and was awarded the governorship of Bijapur. In 1489 he declared himself Sultan of Bijapur. Thus fathered one of the most interesting and dynamic sultanates in India, albeit Turkish in origin.

In 1580, Ibrahim 'Adil Shah II, the sixth 'Adil Shahi, ascended the throne. Known as Jagadguru Badshah, he was erudite, committed to the arts, especially literature. He died in 1626, but not before constructing his funerary complex, the famed *Ibrahim Rauza*.[68]

The term *rauza* refers to a garden, particularly the garden constructed around the tomb of Nabi Mohammed in Medina. Therefore, the name, *Ibrahim Rauza,* establishes a tenuous connection between the importance of this tomb and that of the Prophet of Islam. However, the garden of Ibrahim II's tomb is unlike that of the Medina tomb and antithetical to the traditional Indo-Islamic *chahar-bagh* (See: **Plates 63**; see also: **Appendix B**; and **Appendix C, Plates 93 & 94**).

The square mausoleum is the largest of two major constructions of the ensemble--i.e., a **Type B-c** basic plan. It sits opposite a rectangular mosque of similar style on a long, rectangular podium (See: **Plate 63**). It differs from a number of other Indo-Islamic tombs, both square and octagonal in that there is a double ambulatory (Ind.: *pradakshinapatha*). These ambulatories are of differing widths--i.e., the outer is wider than the inner--and that fact is reflected in the outer four arches of each façade--i.e., the inner two being narrower than the outer ones. Besides the spectacular dome, the four minarets at the corners of the mausoleum assume major importance.

The amount of internal space is

Figure 150: *Ibrahim Rauza, Tomb of Sultan Ibrahim II,* indication of internal space

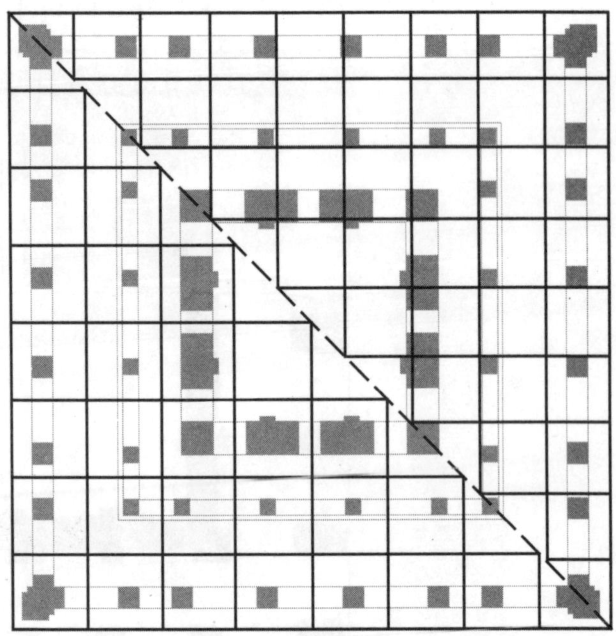

Figure 151: *Ibrahim Rauza, Tomb of Sultan Ibrahim II,* application of *Manduka Manduka* and *Paramashayika Mandala*

Plate 61
Ibrahim Rauza (Plan)

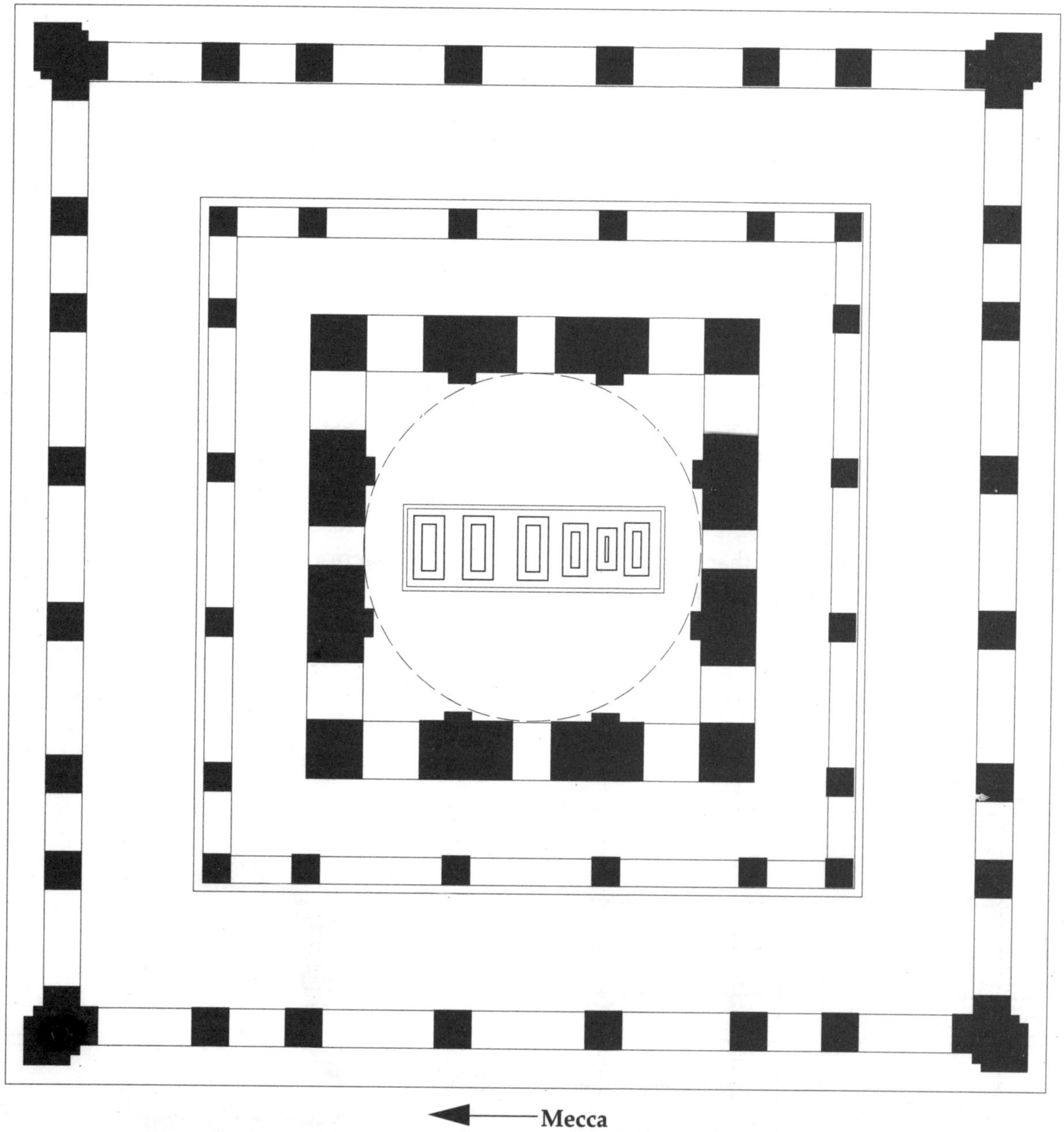

considerable and reflects the implied importance of the Bijapur sultan (See: **Figure 150**). This is, in part, due to the employment of a double ambulatory. Nonetheless, the internal space may be seen to mirror the perceived importance of this 'Adil Shahi Sultan.

Since the tomb is square, a square *mandala* is appropriate. When both the *Manduka Mandala* and the *Paramashayika Mandala* are placed over the plan of the mausoleum, important conjunctions are seen (See: **Figure 151**). If the *Manduka Mandala* is considered, the cenotaph and the sarcophagus in the crypt below fall within the *brahmásthana*, The inner chamber is included in the second rank and file; the columns delineating the inner ambulatory are within the third; and, the whole is encompassed in the fourth rank and file. On the other hand, if the *Paramashayika Mandala* is utilized, similar results occur. The whole inner chamber is included within the *brahmásthana*.

When a *Deshiya Mandala* is superimposed over the elevation of the *Ibrahim Rauza*, it is seen that the arcade and the surmounting *chajja* fall within the first three ranks of *pada* (See: **Figure 152**). The surmounting balustrade with its merlons is within the fourth rank, while the tall corner minarets extend upwards and half way into the eighth rank. The extension of the central chamber reaches the fifth rank. Finally, the dome extends to rank nine-and-one-half. Therefore the proportions of the *Ibrahim Rauza* is 12:9.5.

Much has been written about the use of the double dome. In the case of the *Ibrahim Rauza*, the double dome does not exist. Rather the central chamber ends in a deeply coved ceiling. Above this area the drum extends and the dome soars upwards (See: **Figure 153**). This great soaring space is virtually unseen, unused. However, the result of this space is clearly visible from the exterior in the bulbous, three-quarter dome which expands out over its supporting drum, a typical 'Adil Shahi penchant. The effect is spectacular! Again, we see the fact that Indo-Islamic architects, like other Islamic architects, sing to a different tune. "Islamic architecture at its best, and at its most 'Islamic', is truly a

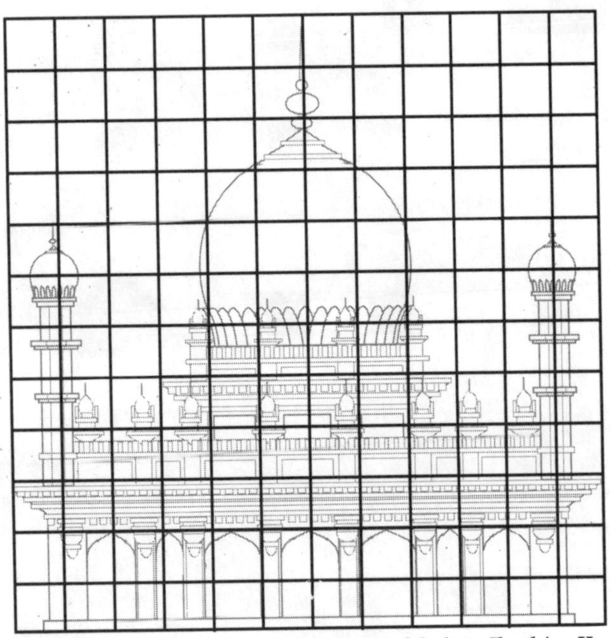

Figure 152: *Ibrahim Rauza, Tomb of Sultan Ibrahim II,* indication of *Deshiya Mandala*

Figure 153: *Ibrahim Rauza, Tomb of Sultan Ibrahim II,* section

Plate 62
Ibrahim Rauza (Elevation with half plan)

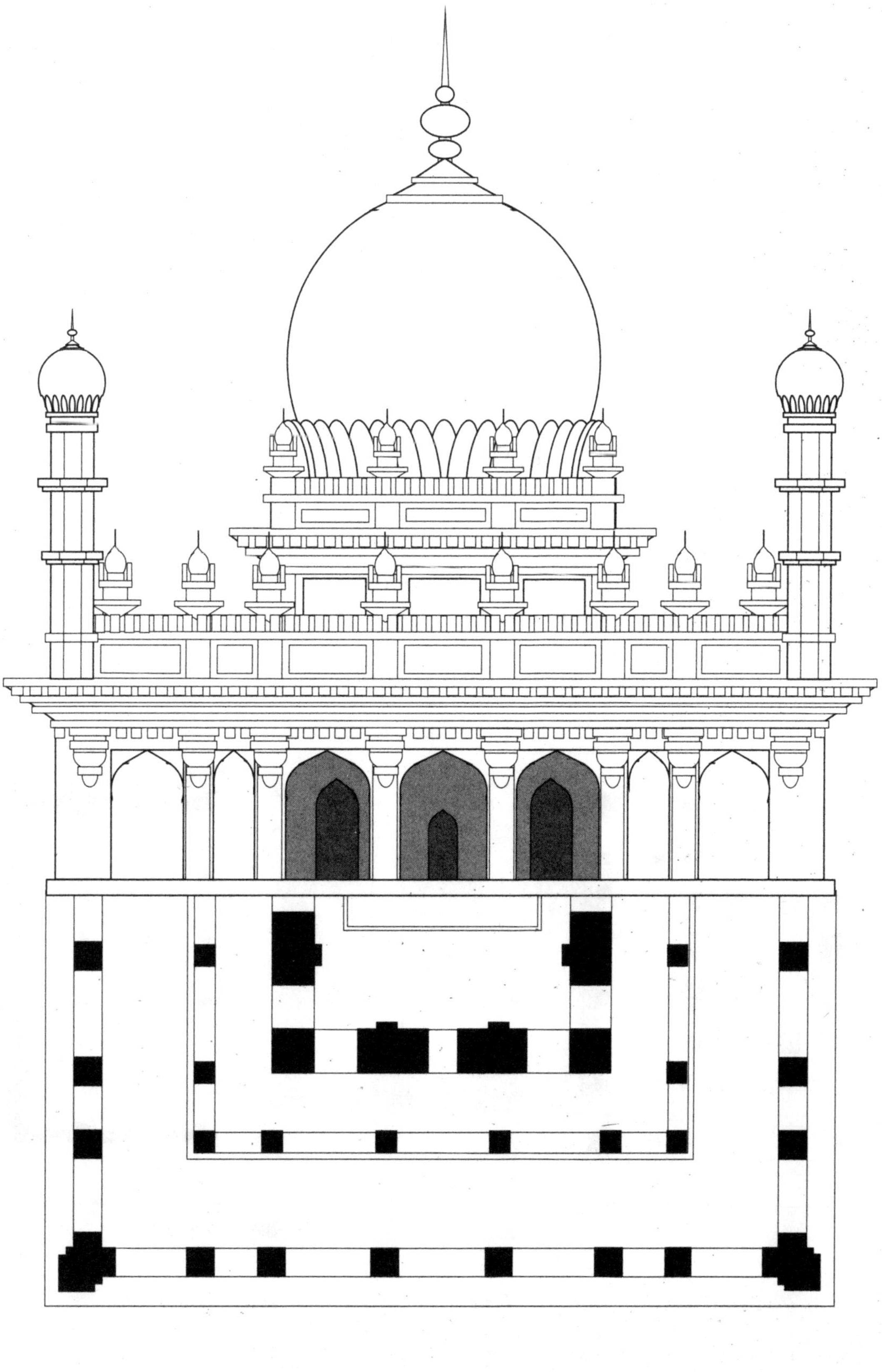

Ibrahim Rauza (Continued)

negation of architecture as conceived in Europe."[68] (EG, p. 13) This statement, indeed, finds fruition in the magnificent *Ibrahim Rausa*.

Finally, mention begs to be made of the *rauza* and its relationship to the ensemble in which it is found. As with other *rauza*, it follows tradition--i.e., a large mausoleum facing a smaller mosque with an intervening *birka* (See: **Figure 154**). Here, as normal, the mausoleum is to the east of the *masjid* which is oriented westward, towards Mecca. However, its placement within the surrounding ensemble, is truly problematical (See: **Plate 63**). Unlike the *Tomb of Humayun* (See: **Plate 46**), the *Tomb of Akbar* (See: **Plate 58**) and to some extent the *Tomb of Isa Khan* (See: **Plate 40**) all of which predate the *Ibrahim Rauza* all of which find the mausoleum centered within a *chahar-bagh*. The *Ibrahim Rauza* does not sit, symmetrically within its enclosing, but adjoins the eastern confines of the enclosure and is considerably south of the east-west axis (See: **Plate 63**; see also: **Figure 154**, "central axis"). The reason for this anomalous orientation is unclear. Certainly, not due to *feng shui*!

The *Ibrahim Rauza* stands out, stylistically, from the other Indo-Islamic tombs and finds a close relationship with the mausolea of the neighboring Qutub Shahi. Its circular domes which go beyond the mere hemisphere are a unique feature. Likewise, the tall, slender minarets with similar bulbous domes are also unparalleled. Finally, it is seen in the *Ibrahim Rauza* that the *chajja* extend out considerably farther, in proportion, than other Indo-Islamic structures. This seems to be a predilection of the 'Adil Shahi builders. The *Ibrahim Rauza* is said that it influenced the design of the *Taj Mahal*. If so, the influence is seen in the comparative height of the main dome and the podium from which it soars (See: **Appendix C, Plate 121**).

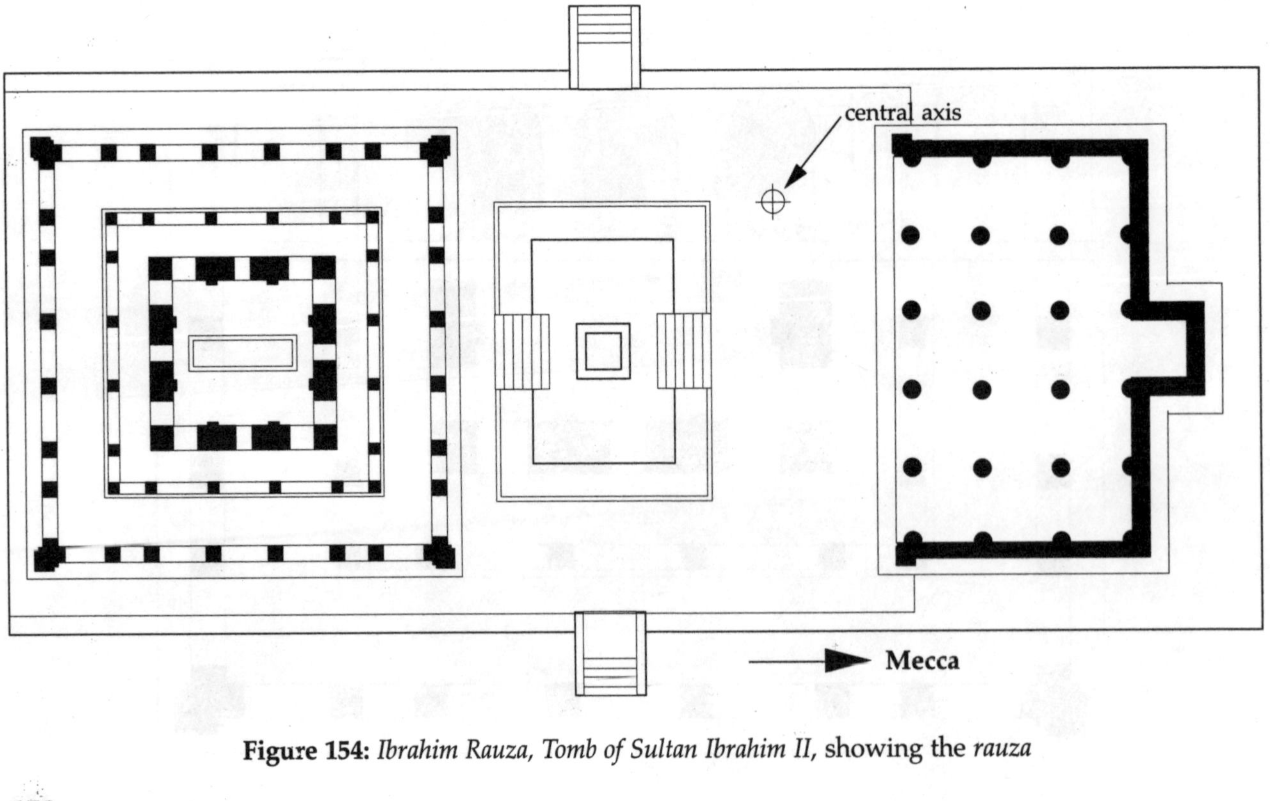

Figure 154: *Ibrahim Rauza, Tomb of Sultan Ibrahim II,* showing the *rauza*

Plate 63
Ibrahim Rauza (Ensemble)

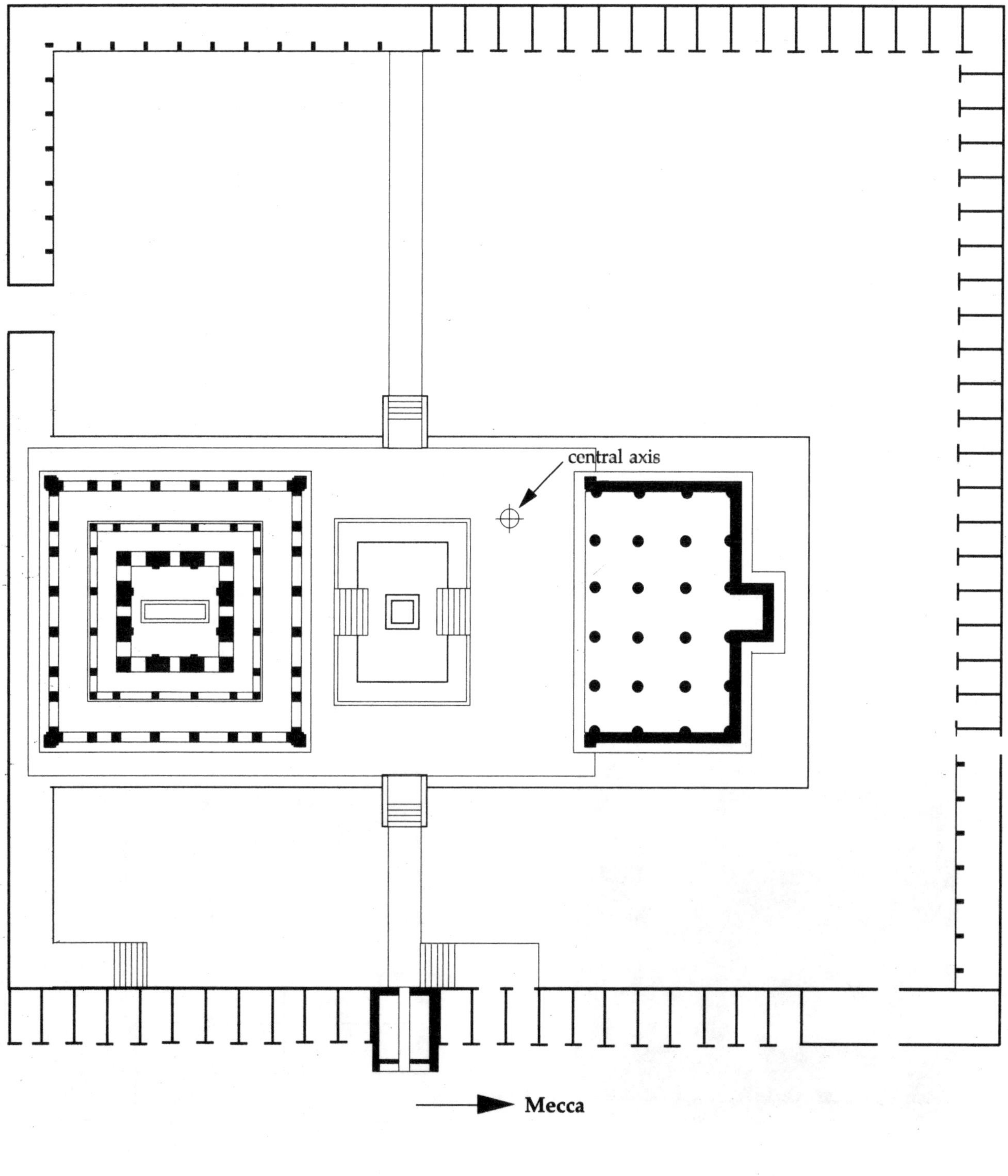

Tomb of Iftikhar Khan

Chunar, c. 1617 C.E.

Iftikhar Khan, a minor noble of Afghani descent during the reign of Jahangir, a *Nazim* of Bihar, rests in a tomb of no mean importance. The tomb, known as the old *tahsildari*, is found in the small provincial city of Chunar. The architect Ibrahim Khan Kakar is credited with the design of this mausoleum.[70] (CA, p. 152)

The *Tomb of Iftikhar Khan*,[71] like the majority of tombs constructed during the reign of the great Mughals, is square--i.e., a **Type B-c** basic plan. Placed upon a high podium, the mausoleum consists of the obligatory inner chamber in which the cenotaph rests. This space is surrounded by a verandah which, unlike many mausolea, is relatively enclosed. Five arched openings punctuate each face of the façade. The three central openings are narrower and separated from the wider, outer openings by a distance nearly equal to their individual widths. This gives the impression of solid, substantiality as opposed to the graceful elegance seen in the *Tomb of Mohammed Ghaus*, an earlier, minor tomb. Indeed, the massive quality of the tomb gives a fortress-like impression. Above each corner of the main block rise octagonal *chatri* which dominate by their size. From the square inner chamber rises a block above the level of the first storey. Upon this block an octagonal podium is further elevated from which the dome soars.

Massive as it appears, the interior space of the *Tomb of Iftikhar Khan* is commensurate with other Indo-Islamic tombs (See: **Figure 155**). Again it indicates the Islamic desire and/or need for interior space, being a congregational faith. However, it is interesting to note that *Tomb of Iftikhar Khan* does not possess a *mikhrab*, as so many other tombs do in this brief study. One may assume that even though Iftikhar Khan's status in Bihar was of some import, it was not sufficiently elevated as to warrant the inclusion of a *mikhrab*.

When a *Manduka Mandala* and/or a *Paramashayika Mandala* are superimposed over the plan, it is noted that the *Manduka Mandala* is

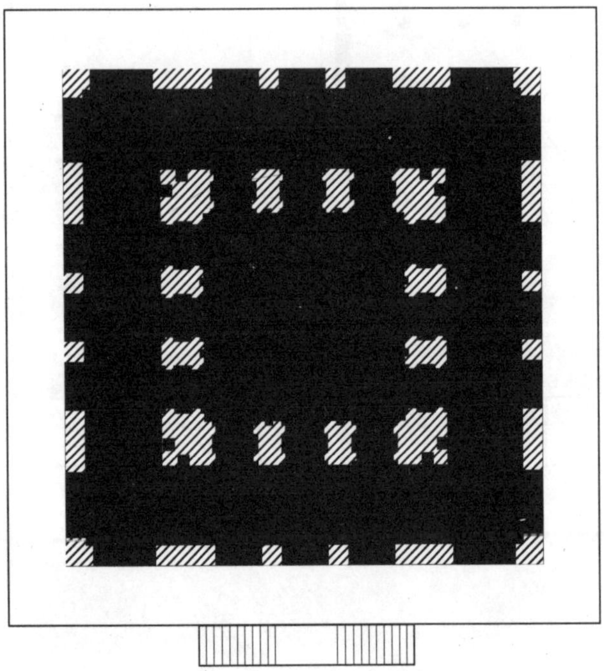

Figure 155: *Tomb of Iftikhar Khan*, indication of internal space

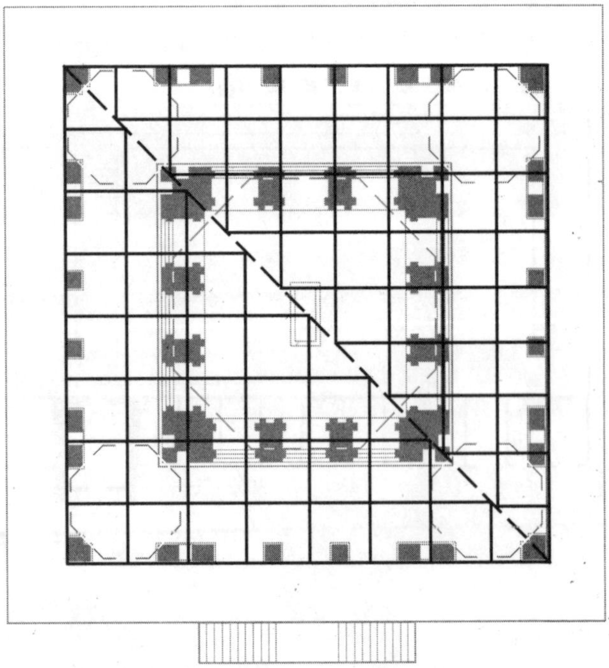

Figure 156: *Tomb of Iftikhar Khan*, application of *Manduka Mandala & Paramashayika Mandala*

Plate 64
Tomb of Iftikhar Khan (Plan)

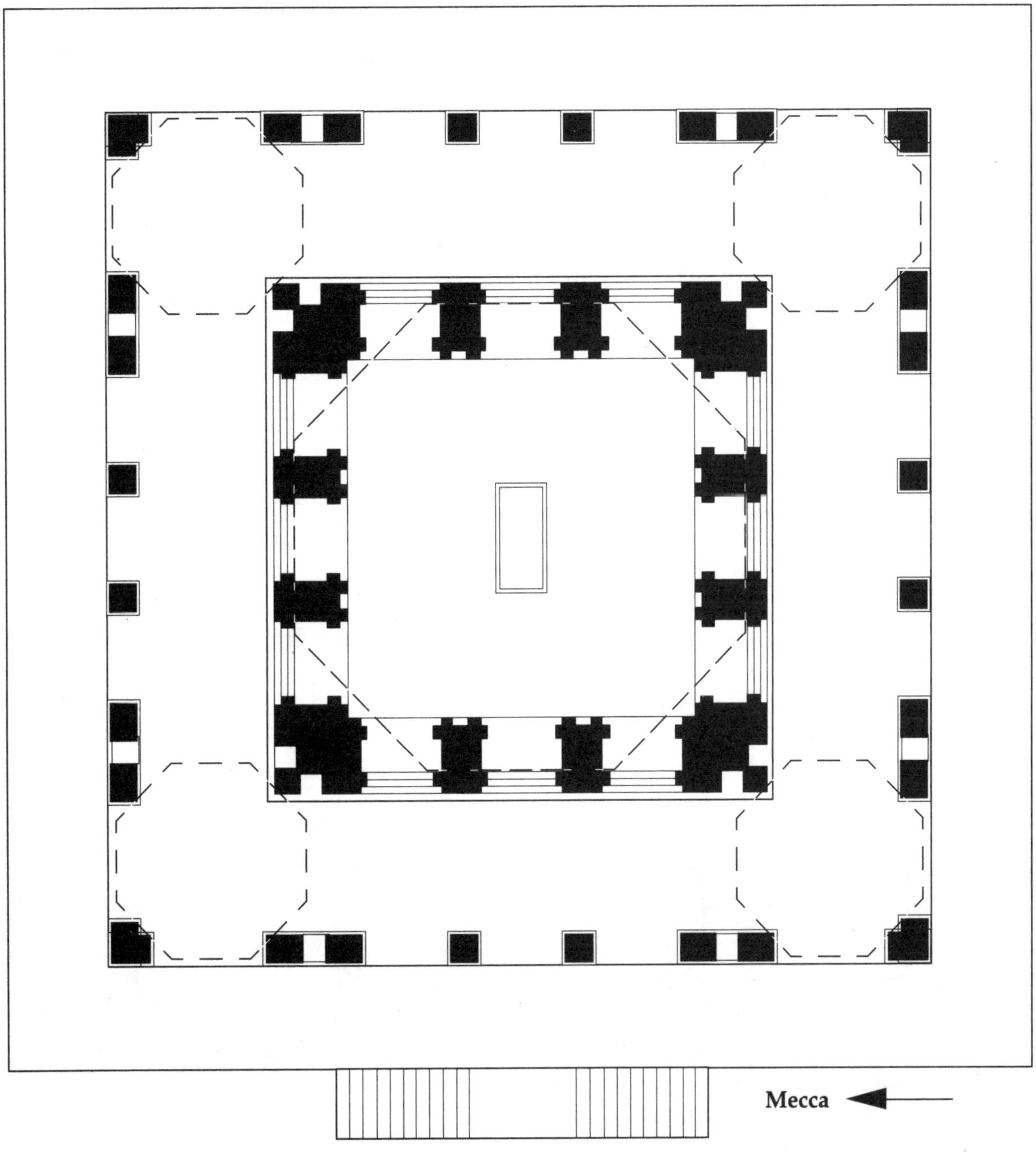

Tomb of Iftikhar Khan (Continued)

the preferred form (See: **Figure 156**). It is to be noted that in the *Manduka Mandala* the division line between the second and third rank and file bisects the small opening between the first and second opening on either side of the façades. Additionally, with the *Manduka Mandala* there is no compromise of any of the *marmas* with this *mandala*.

The proportions of the *Tomb of Iftikhar Khan* indicate, when superimposed with a *Deshiya Mandala*, that the main block, up to the *chajja*, is included within the first three ranks of *pada* (See: **Figure 157**). The second storey and the octagonal base of the dome rise to include the sixth rank, and the dome soars to embrace the ninth rank of *pada*. Therefore, the proportions of the *Tomb of Iftikhar Khan* is 12:9. It is also interesting to note that when a *Deshiya Mandala* is placed over the whole, including the podium, individual proportions may differ, but the whole remains 12:9 (See: **Figure 158**). In this configuration, the podium, the main block, up to the *chajja* is included within the lower four ranks of *pada*. The second storey and the octagonal base reach to include the sixth rank. Finally, the dome is seen to rest within the central 'five' files of *pada*.

The *Tomb of Iftikhar Khan* indicates yet another variation on a theme--i.e., a square tomb with a central chamber, a surrounding verandah, a surmounting dome, and prominent *chatri* on the four corners of the main block. Unlike a number of its close antecedents, the *Tomb of Iftikhar* appears unusually heavy in its aspect. Its appearance gives the impression of great solidity, almost fortress-like. In this aspect it recalls the *Tomb of Sultan Ghari*. Nonetheless, this tomb is noteworthy as an interesting structure raised for a minor official.

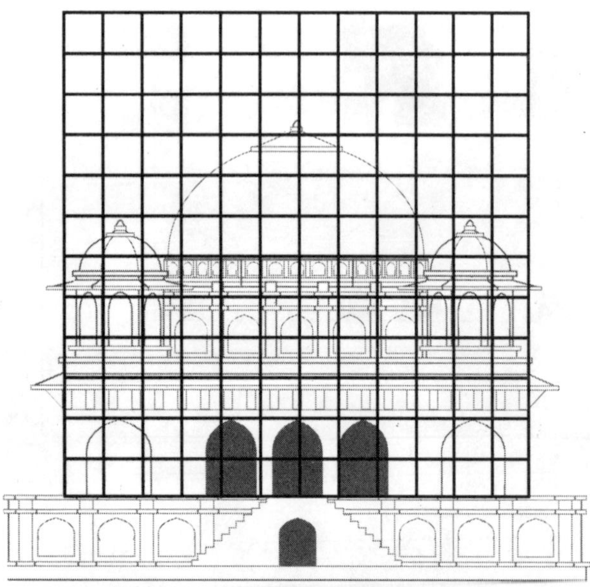

Figure 157: *Tomb of Iftikhar Khan*, indication of *Deshiya Mandala* excluding podium

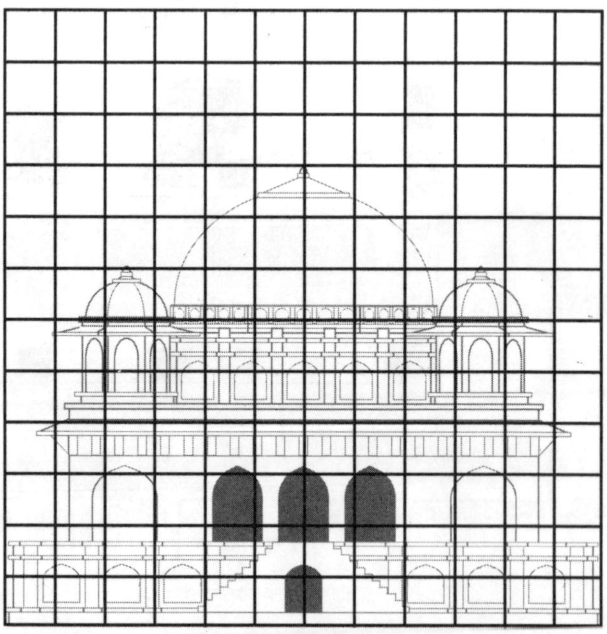

Figure 158: *Tomb of Iftikhar Khan*, indication of *Deshiya Mandala* including podium

Plate 65
Tomb of Iftikhar Khan (Elevation & half plan)

Tomb of Shah Daulat

Maner, c. 1617 C.E.

A disciple of the Sufi saint Hazrat Makhdum Yahiya Maneri, the revered Makhdum Shah Daulat was interred in a magnificent mausoleum in the provincial city of Maner, Bihar. This small city, Maner, was an early center of Sufism in Bihar and is a famous pilgrimage place. His tomb is one of the sites visited by the numerous pilgrims.

As with the *Tomb of Muhammad Ghaus*, the *Tomb of Shah Daulat* appears to be more in keeping with a noble residence than a mausoleum. Square, en plan, the mausoleum consists of a central chamber containing the cenotaph--i.e., a **Type B-c** basic plan. A wide, arcuated verandah enfolds this space. At each of the four corners, square *chatri* extend over two storied corner elements (See: Plate 67). The elevation consists of these triple-arched, two storey corner elements flanking three arches which extend upward to the brackets supporting the *chajja*. The wide *chajja* is surmounted by a balustrade, and at the corners large *chatri*, the width of the corner elements and also containing three arches per side, extend upwards. The walls of the central chamber rises above the main ground-level block and is, likewise, capped with a *chajja* and balustrade. From this extension a shallow octagonal drum supports the dome. The dome, in turn, is surmounted by a cupola.

The *Tomb of Shah Daulat* has the appearance of the type of garden pavilions that were frequently used as casual retreats for the Mughal royalty and aristocracy--e.g., the *Feria Bagh*, Ahmadnagar or the *Shahi Bagh*, Ahmadabad (See: **Appendix C; Plates 124 & 125**). Its external divisional elements recall the ninefold motif that is noted to be of importance in Indo-Islamic architecture (See: **Figure 158**).

The internal space of this mausoleum is proportionally greater than many tombs which have heretofore been considered (See: **Figure 158**). The walls of the inner chamber are,

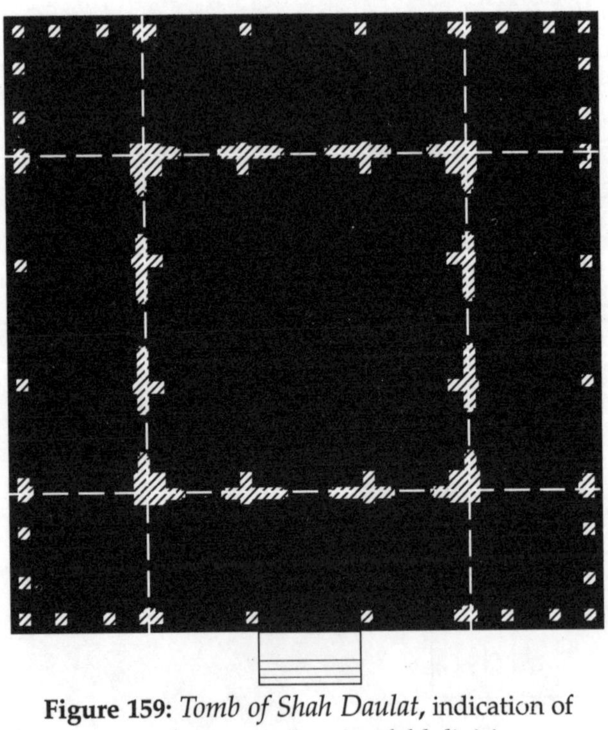

Figure 159: *Tomb of Shah Daulat*, indication of internal space and a nine-fold division

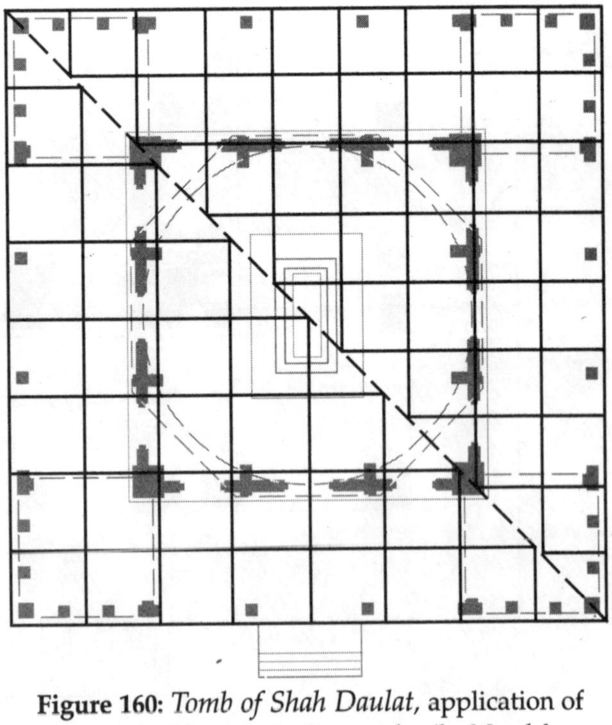

Figure 160: *Tomb of Shah Daulat*, application of *Manduka Mandala & Paramashayika Mandala*

Plate 66
Tomb of Shah Daulat (Plan)

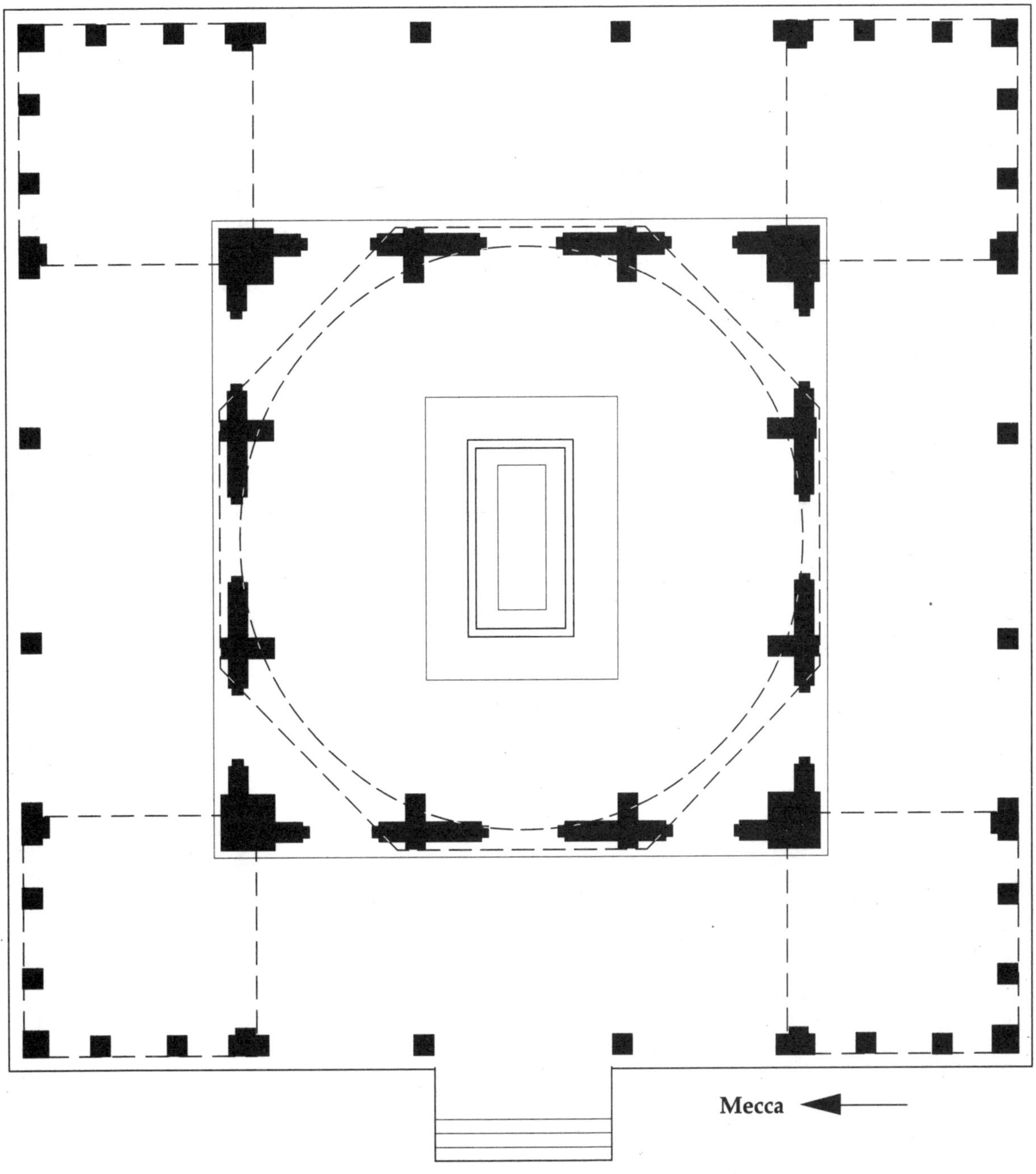

proportionally, less thick than those found in earlier tombs--e.g., the *Tomb of Muhammad Ghaus,*

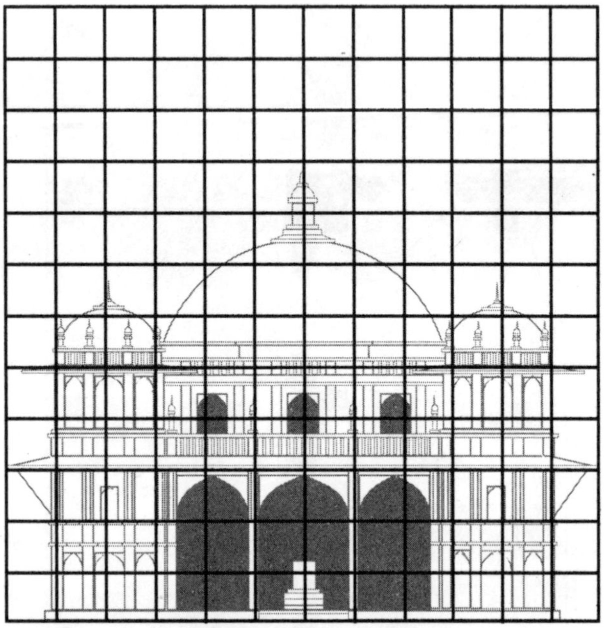

Figure 161: *Tomb of Shah Daulat,* with *Deshiya Mandala* over the elevation

which resembles this tomb. Doubtless, this is in part due to the function of this mausoleum--i.e., a site of pilgrimage.

The application of a *Deshiya Mandala* over the elevation of *Tomb of Shah Daulat* indicates that the first three ranks of *pada* come up to the edge of the *chajja* (See: Figure 160). The fifth rank touches the chajja of the corner chatri. The *Tomb of Shah Daulat's* dome is seen to be the width of six files of *pada* and the while, including the cupola is contained within the lower eight-and-one-half ranks. Therefore, the proportions of the *Tomb of Shah Daulat* is 12:8.5.

As one of the centers of pilgrimage for the Sufi Muslims, the *Tomb of Shah Daulat* appears to be sublimely suitable. The gracious façade is in contrast to thesolid *Tomb of Iftikhar Khan*. It is understandably one of the more important monuments of this part of Bihar.

Plate 67
Tomb of Shah Daulat (Elevation & half plan)

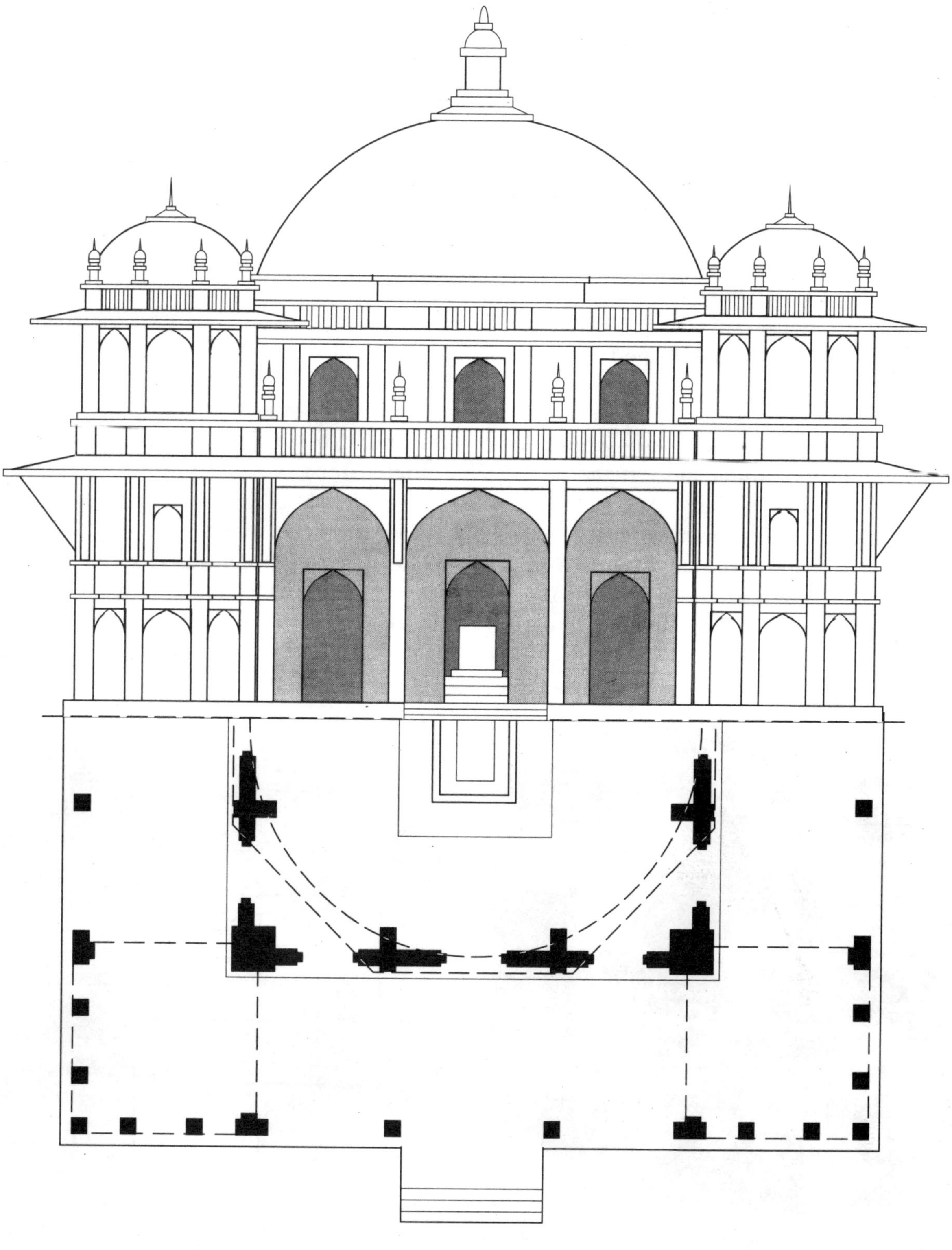

Tomb of Khan Khanan

Delhi, a. 1626 C.E.

The son of Bairam Khan--i.e., Bairam the regent for Akbar during his minority--'Abdur-rahim Khan Khanan (Khan-i-Khanan) was laid to rest in a tomb fit for a king. A poet, a patron of architecture; a companion and general to Humayun; the general-subduer of Gujarat, the Sindh and the Deccan for Akbar; and courtier during the early reign of Jahangir; 'Abdur-rahim Khan Khanan earned his lavish tomb. His live "would be a history of public affairs of the empire of Delhi during half a century."[73] Unfortunately, his tomb had been ravaged, in part to supply needed facing stone for the *Tomb of Safdar Jang*.[74]

The *Tomb of Khan Khanan*[75] owes much of its design to the tomb of his early patron and emperor, Humayun. Cubic in form and resting upon a high podium, its plan, with the extension of the central pavilion, bears resemblance to the Hindu *triratha* temple plan--i.e., a **Type B-c** basic plan. The mausoleum consists of a square central chamber which holds the cenotaph. Here, the upper reaches of the inner space is truncated with a shallow domed ceiling and above this a large chamber encased by the outer dome. This technique had been employed in a number of preceding tombs--e.g. the *Tomb of Humayun* and the *Ibrahim Rauza*, Passageways radiate towards the cardinal points and give way to four deep porches. On each façade and on either side of these wide, central recesses are smaller, shallower recesses with equally shallow passageways leading to octagonal chambers. This arrangement, this *triratha* hints at a ninefold division which many see as a hallmark of Mughal tomb architecture (See: **Figure 162**). The elegant mausoleum rests upon a podium which is made up of seventeen arched bays on each facade of this massive platform. Seventeen is a number which denotes conquest, wisdom and immortality, qualities which may be applied to 'Abdur-rahim Khan Khanan. The total number of the bays is sixty-eight--i.e., fourfold seventeen.

The masonry mass of this tomb is such that it restricts the internal space (See: **Figure 162**). Certainly it is proportionally far less than many of the preceding tombs in this brief study.

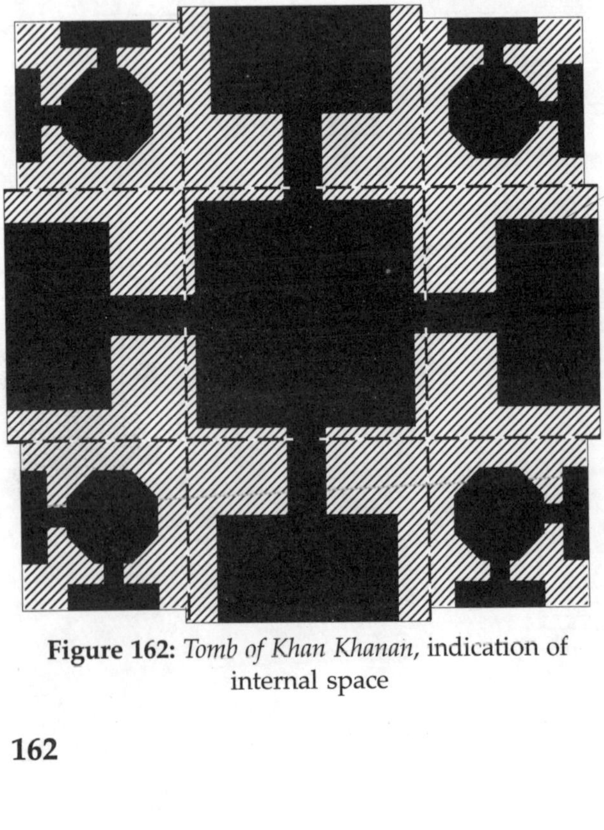

Figure 162: *Tomb of Khan Khanan*, indication of internal space

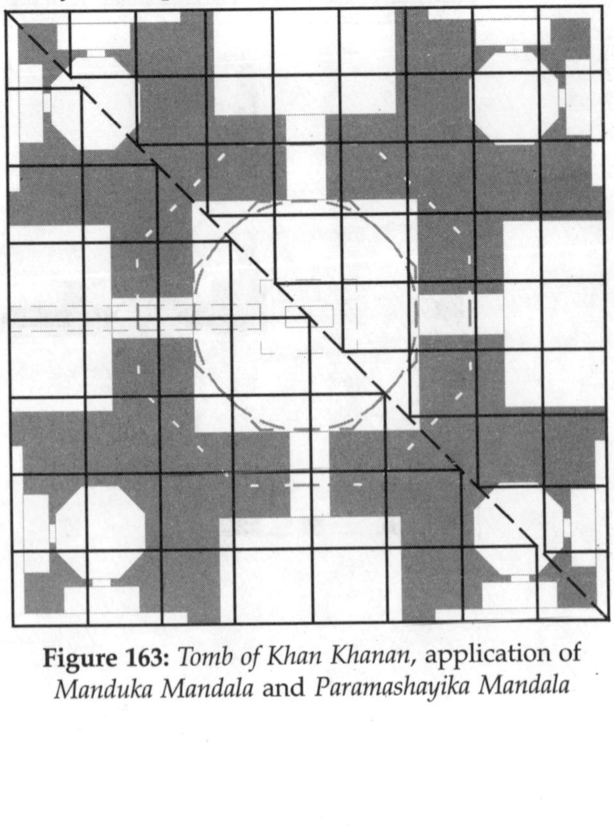

Figure 163: *Tomb of Khan Khanan*, application of *Manduka Mandala* and *Paramashayika Mandala*

Plate 68

Tomb of Khan Khanan (Plan)

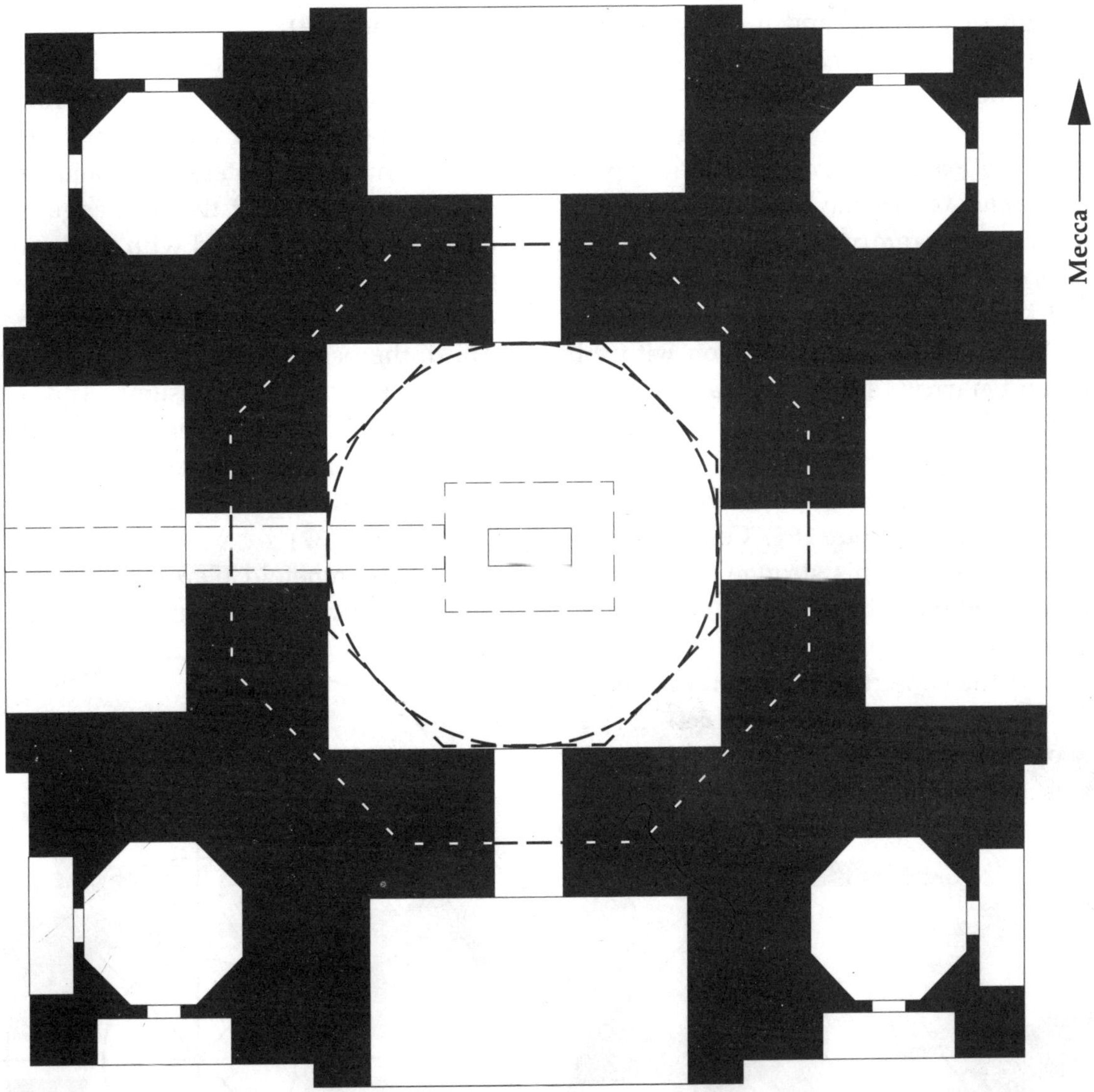

Tomb of Khan Khanan (Continued)

The height of the cube and the surmounting dome may have led the *sthapati* to give additional weight to the intervening masonry.

In the application of either a *Manduka Mandala* or a *Paramashayika Mandala,* it appears that the *Manduka Mandala* is more applicable as none of the *marmas* are compromised (See: **Figure 163**). As was stated above, the basic plan of the *Tomb of Khan Khanan* is square. However, Carr stated "the tomb itself is an octagon with four broad and narrow sides."[76] Clearly, he was describing the *triratha* quality. If an octagon is placed over the plan, it is noted that the width of the central pavilions equals the width of each side of an octagon (See: **Figure 164**). Could this have been the reason for his strange description? However, it is more interestingly noted that a circle is far more applicable for four salient reasons: 1) the corners of the central pavilions, 2) the inner corners of the smaller recesses, 3) the inner corners of the doorways of the smaller recesses, and 4) the edge of the octagon of the small rooms all touch the circumference of a circle (See: **Figure 164**).

If, then, a circular *Manduka Mandala* is placed over the plan of the *Tomb of Khan Khanan* --clearly possible as a square neatly fits within a circle--a number of interesting conjunction occur (See: **Figure 165**). First, the outer edge of the inner chamber is closely allied with the *brahmásthana.* Second, the next ring touches the inner surface of the deep recesses of the central pavilions. Third, the penultimate circle touches the outer edge of the central extensions. And, lastly, the fourth circle, naturally encompasses the whole. This application is also seen to be fortuitous in the section dealing with the *Tomb of Humayun* (See: **Figure 132**).

The ninefold plan that is viewed as an important consideration in Mughal architecture,

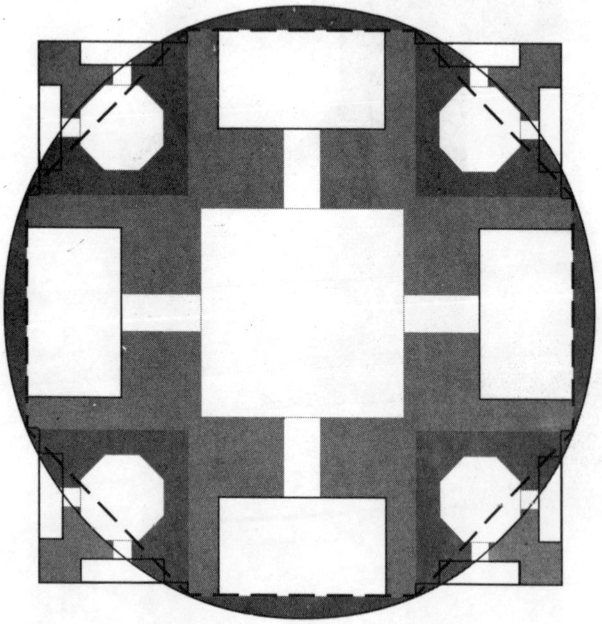

Figure 164: *Tomb of Khan Khanan,* consideration of a circular or octagonal concept

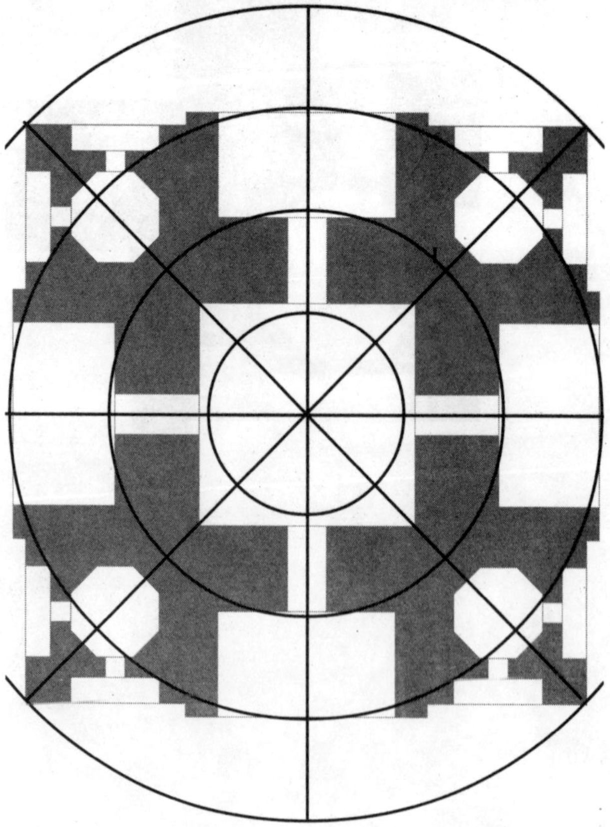

Figure 165: *Tomb of Khan Khanan,* application of a circular *Manduka Mandala*

Plate 69
Tomb of Khan Khanan (Elevation & half plan)

Tomb of Khan Khanan (Continued)

is also apparent in the plan of the *Tomb of Khan Khanan*.[77] It is seen that the major spatial elements fall within one of the areas of this plan (See: **Figure 166**). The octagonal rooms are contained within the corner elements, the deep recessed porches are contained within the middle sections and the sarcophagus chamber is centered. The implications of paradise--i.e., the central chamber with its cenotaph and sarcophagus below--and the eight rivers of paradise--i.e., symbolized by the eight surrounding areas (squares), the *hasht bihisht*--is obvious and applicable. In addition, it is interesting to note the importance placed upon those elements that occupy the cardinal points of the compass--i.e., the deep, recessed porches; and the small octagons which occupy the intercardinal points of the plan.

When a *Deshiya Mandala* is superimposed over the façade of the *Tomb of Khan Khanan* a number of conjunctions appear (See: **Figure 167**). The corner blocks rise to the five-and-one-half *pada* rank. The Central blocks are seven pada high and the width of the deep recess falls within the central four files of *pada*. The drum of the dome approximately eight-and-one-half ranks high, while the whole rises to twelve-and-one half ranks. The width of the dome is approximately six-and-one-half *pada* (file) wide. The width of the smaller recesses is one-and-one-half *pada* wide. Therefor, the proportions of the *Tomb of Khan Khanan* is seen to be 12:12.5.

Constructed six years before the beginning of the *Taj Mahal*, the *Tomb of Khan Khanan* is seen to be of no small influence to that most prestigious structure. The proportion of the main façades of the two structures are remarkably similar--i.e., the elevation of the *Taj Mahal* that is considered is the front façade that is parallel, the angle of the *muthamman baghdadi* is not included (See: **Figure 168**). The major

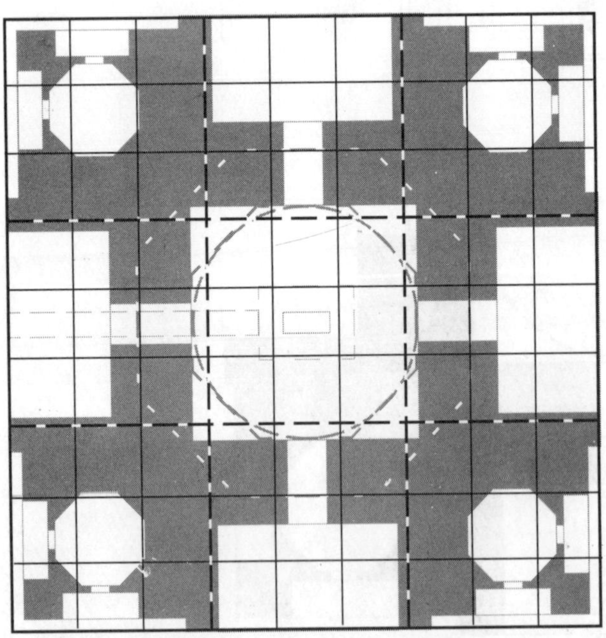

Figure 166: *Tomb of Khan Khanan*, application of ninefold plan with *Paramashayika Mandala*

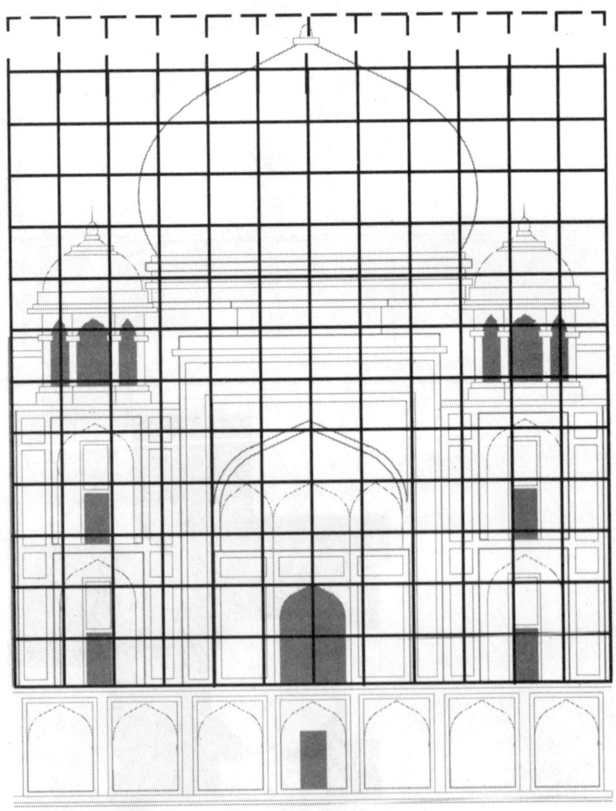

Figure 167: *Tomb of Khan Khanan*, application of *Deshiya Mandala* over the elevation

difference is seen in the height of the drum which supports the dome(s) and the shape and height of the dome(s). The proportion of the main façades to the height and width of the podiums upon which the mausolea rest is nearly identical. Both are based upon the ninefold plan, and both possess double domes.

The centuries have not been as kind to the *Tomb of Khan Khanan* as it has to the two major Mughal tombs which bracket it--i.e., the *Tomb of Humayun* and the *Taj Mahal*. Much of the finished stone which faced this tomb has been stripped as well as the stone pathways which surrounded the *Tomb of Khan Khanan*. Even the cenotaph has been reduced to a mere raised outline of what must have been a beautiful form. Nonetheless, enough has been preserved of this magnificent tomb to provide us with a hint of its former glory. The glory of a man dedicated to three Mughal emperors.

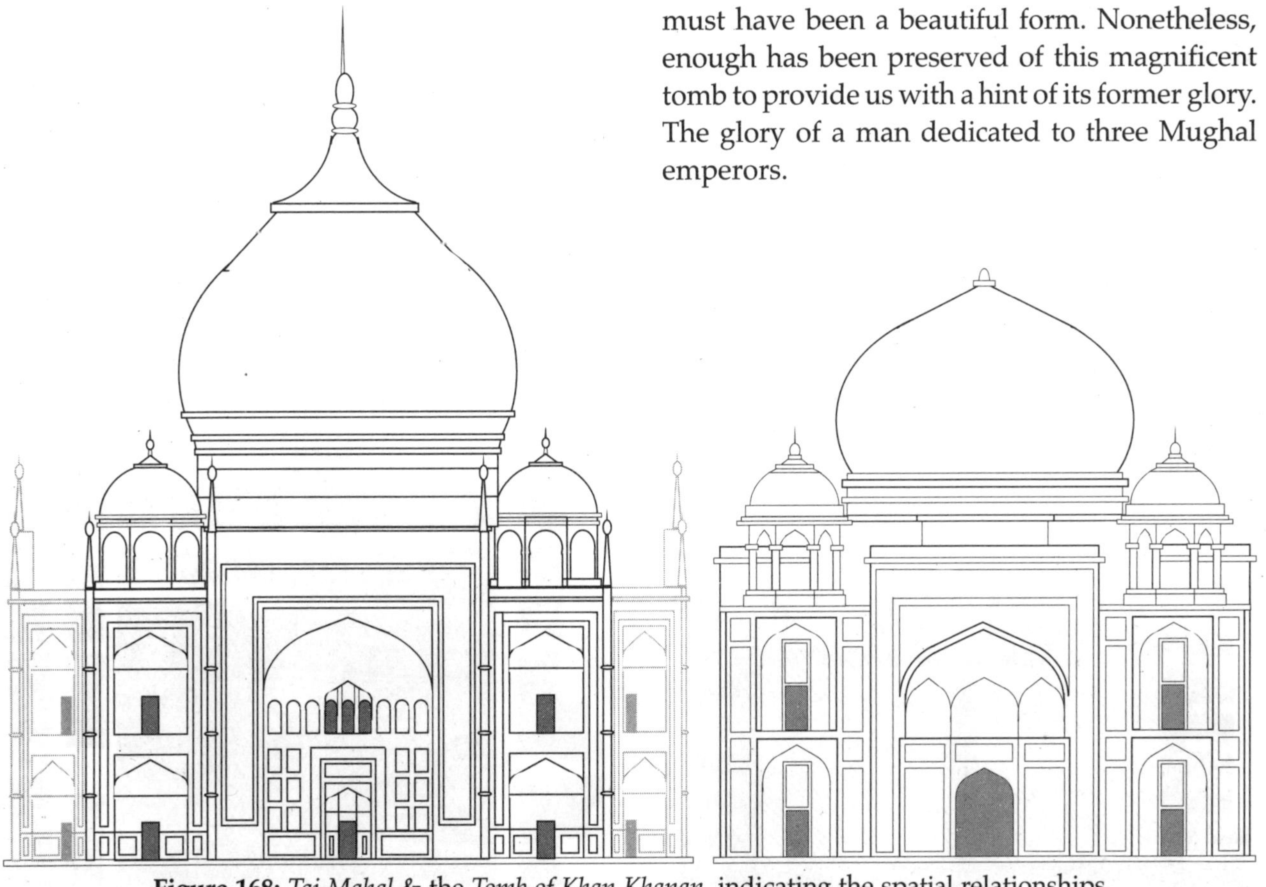

Figure 168: *Taj Mahal* & the *Tomb of Khan Khanan*, indicating the spatial relationships and proportions of main façades

Tomb of Jahangir

Lahore, 1627 C.E.

Akbar's son, Prince Salim, assumed the title of Jahangir-Nur-ud-din ("world conqueror, light of faith"). Salim had been the favored of Akbar's sons, two others had died in abject drunkenness and debauchery before the emperor's death. Jahangir, also dissolute and alcoholic, was a great disappointment to his father who had even considered one of his grandson's as his successor. Unfortunately, the Mughals had no clear laws or rules regarding succession--i.e., primogeniture did not exist. And, therefore, succession was either vested in the strongest, or the most devious, or in the opportunist, and often, the cruelest. Jahangir possessed all these qualities.

Upon ascending the throne, Jahangir (aka Jehangir) had an Afghan noble put to death so that he could take as his wife, Nur Mahal, whom he coveted while still in his father's court. Nur Mahal was a woman of talent, intelligence and incredibly ambitious. She was to be to Jahangir what Mumtaz Mahal, her niece, was to Shah Jahan. It is said that in gratitude for allowing him to marry her, Jahangir elevated her father to the position of Lord High Treasurer and *Wazir* of the Empire--i.e., I'timad-ud-daula. Mirza Ghiyas was the I'timad-ud-daula. In such an exalted position, he assumes major importance, influence and his family began to prosper in ways even he could not imagine. He and his dynasty figures prominently in the history of India.

His daughter, through the munificence of her husband, the emperor, constructed the elegant and beautiful *Tomb of I'timad-ud-daula* at Agra. His luck, or cunning did not stop there, his granddaughter, Hazrat Mumtaz-uz-Zamani (Mumtaz Mahal) became the famed wife of the Emperor Shah Jahan and was, in turn interred in the incomparable *Taj Mahal*. Following is the genealogy of this noble, but supremely influential family which is connected to two Mughal

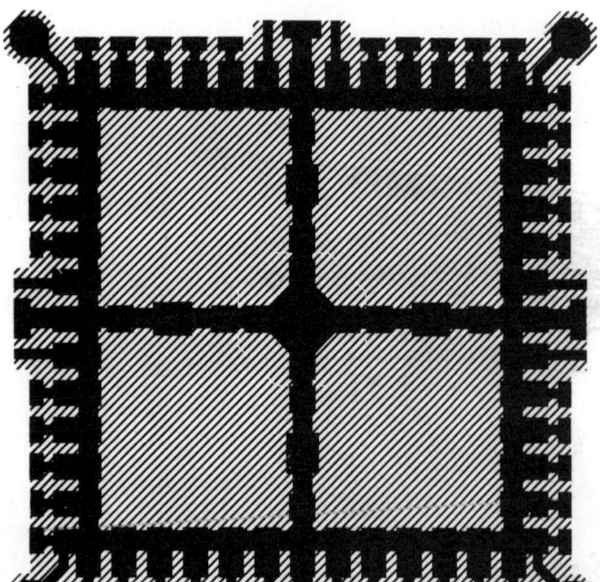

Figure 169: ***Tomb of Jihangir,*** indication of internal space

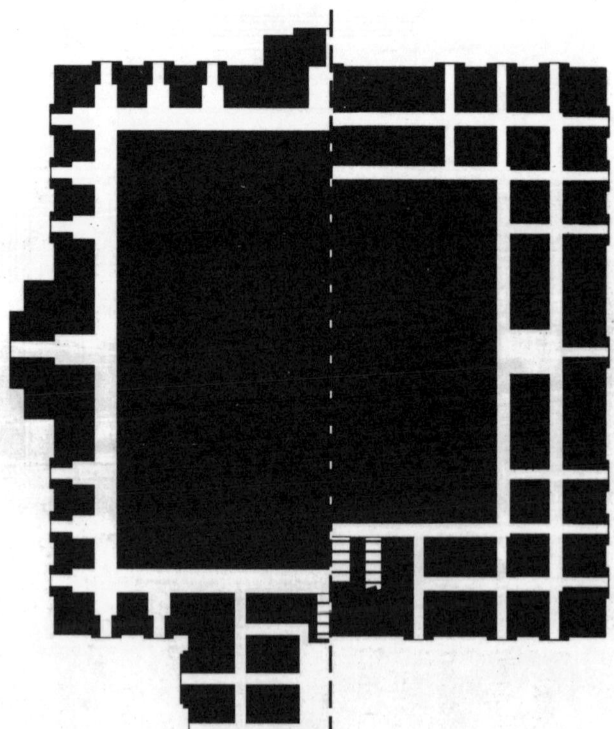

Figure 170: *That-Byin-Nyu,* b. 1165 C.E., ground floor (left) and mezzanine (right), Pagan, Burma

Plate 70
Tomb of Jahangir (Plan)

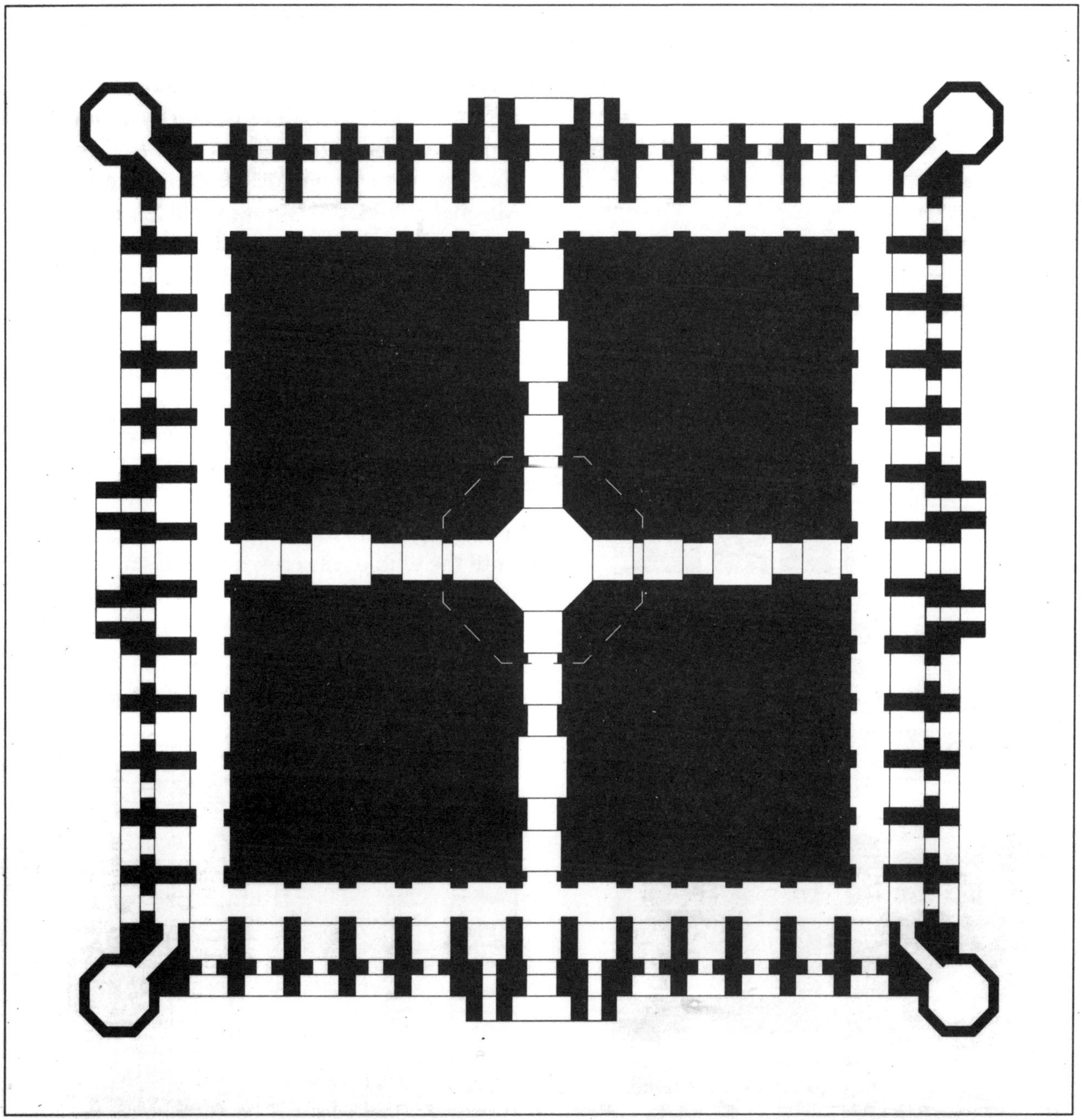

Mecca ←

Tomb of Jahangir (Continued)

emperors.

Mirza Ghiyas == Asmat Begum

Jahangir == Nur (Mahal) Jahan Asaf Khan== ?

Manmati

Shah Jahan == Mumtaz Mahal

During the twenty-one years of his reign Jahangir devoted the majority of his energies and time on the art of painting. He, however, did not stint on the completion of his father's tomb at Sikandra. His own tomb at Lahore (Shadera) commenced during his reign and was completed soon after his demise. The *Tomb of Jahangir*[78] is considered to be one of the great tombs of the Mughal dynasty. Although it does not follow established or long standing precedence, the tomb does find certain parallels with his eclectic, and some say, "heretical," father.

Its similarity to the *Tomb of Akbar* lies in its square plan, an arcade façade, four tower at the corners and a large mass of solid masonry--i.e., a **Type C-d** basic plan. However, here, the similarity stops. Whereas, the *Tomb of Akbar* was based upon a pyramid form, the elements mounting above the arcade façade, ever receding until the whole was crowned by a stately arcade with corner *chatri*, the *Tomb of Jahangir* is predominantly horizontal, punctuated, anchored by four tall towers at its corners. The plan and its implied horizontal bears resemblance to the

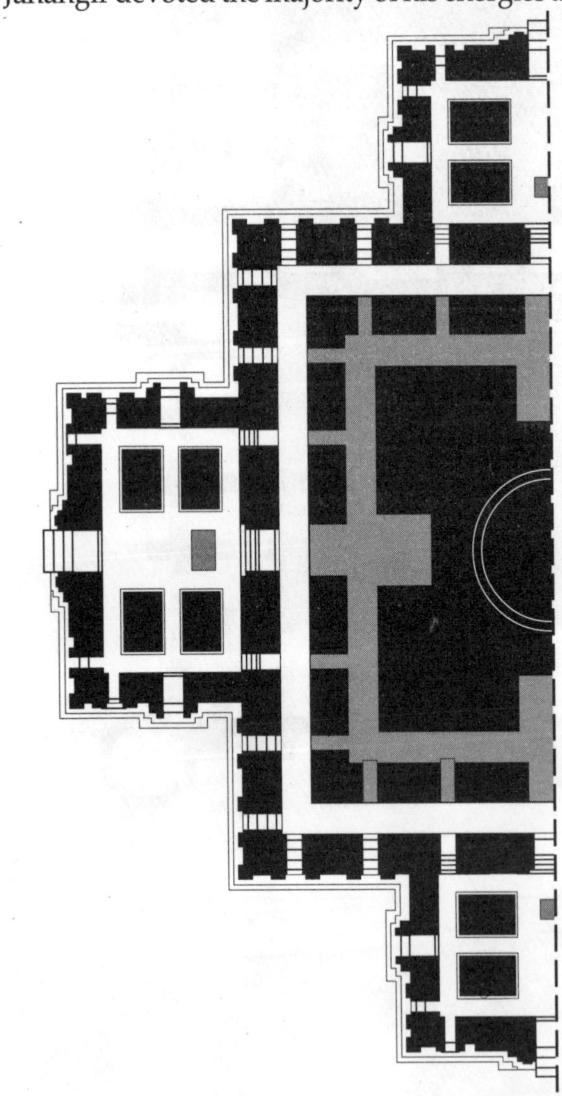

Figure 171: *Dhamma-Yan-Gyi*, b. 1165 C.E., half plan indicating bricked in areas, Pagan, Burma

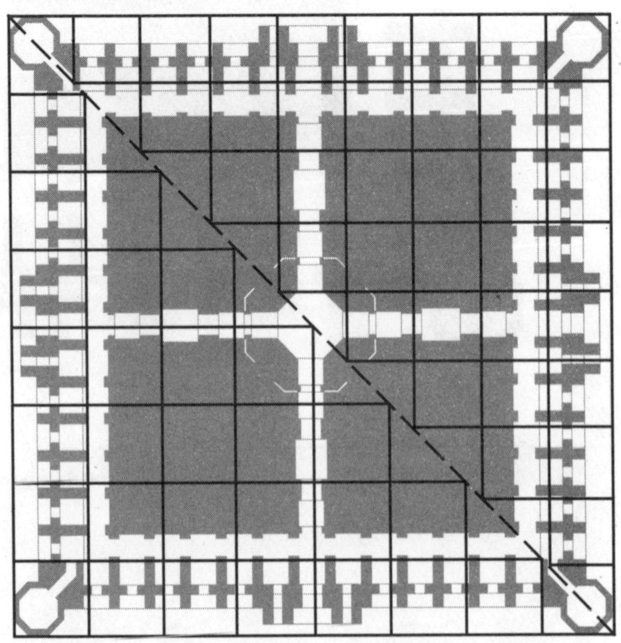

Figure 172: *Tomb of Jihangir*, application of *Manduka* and *Paramashayika Mandala* over the whole

Plate 71
Tomb of Jahangir (Elevation & half plan)

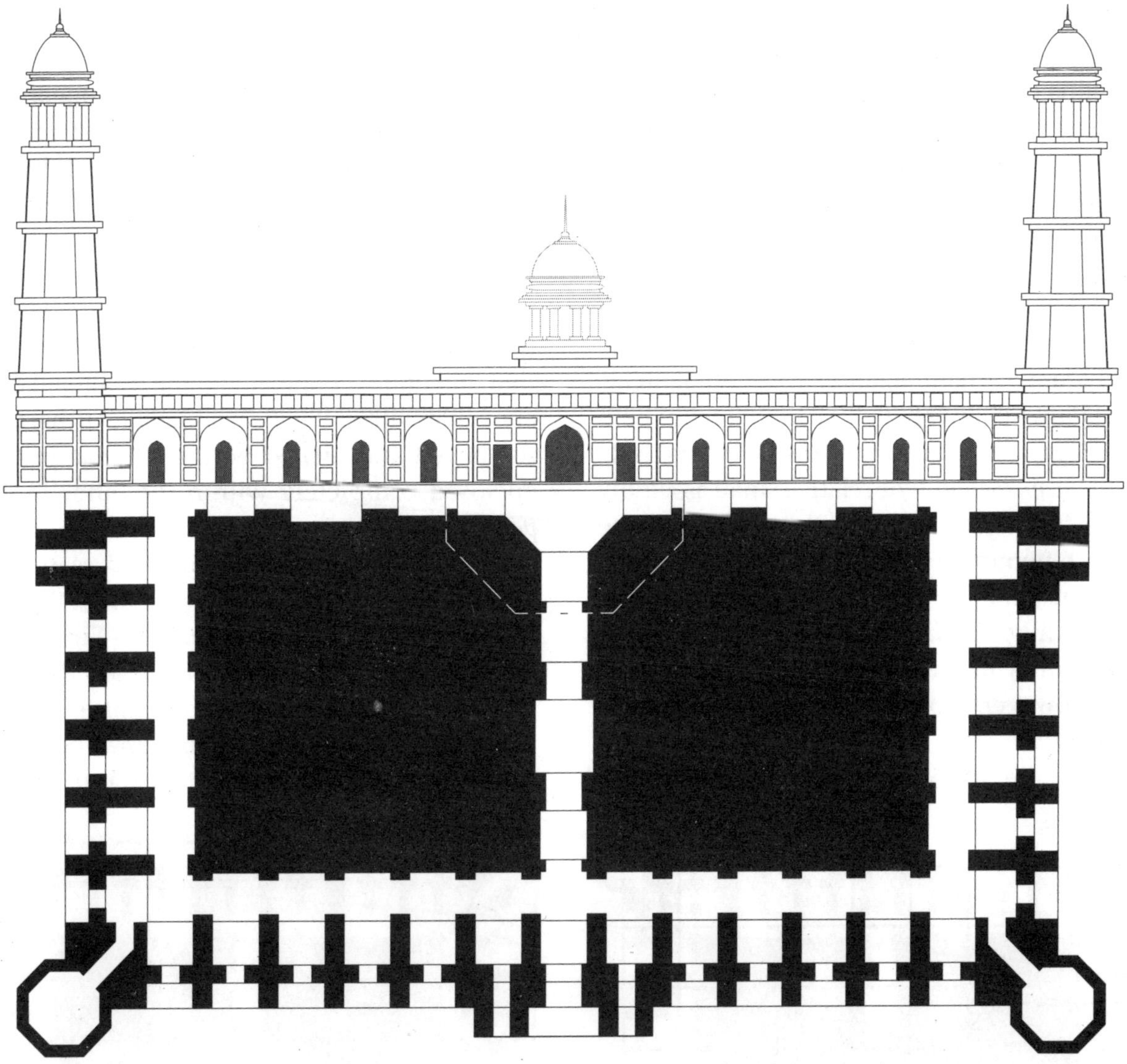

Tomb of Jahangir (Continued)

Tomb of Sultan Ghari (1231 C.E.).

The massive quality, the sheer area covered is deceptive. In proportion to the total plan, the internal space is almost minuscule (See: **Figure 169**). However, it is considerable although some what less, proportionally than that found in his father's tomb. The relationship of the mass of masonry compared to the enclosed space in the *Tomb of Jahangir* is reminiscent of the spatial relationship found in the *That-Byin-Nyu* of Pagan (See: **Figure 170**) or the fabled *Dhamma-Yan-Gyi*, also of Pagan (See: **Figure 171**). In the case of both of the Pagan temples, the narrow corridors (Ind.: *pradakshinapatha*) and the relative small assembly areas is due, in part, to the theology / architectural manifestation in which the cave, the dark place, the womb (Ind.: *garbha-griha*) is a vital concept. Theologically, spatial concepts do not apply as Buddhism is not a congregational faith as is Islam. However, *en plan*, there is a vital and viable similarity.

In the application of either a *Manduka Mandala* or a *Paramashayika Mandala* to the whole of the *Tomb of Jahangir* --i.e., including the central block and the corner towers--both appear to be applicable (See: **Figure 172**). In either *mandala*, the central chamber is protected by the *brahmásthana*. On the other hand if either a *Manduka Mandala* or a *Paramashayika Mandala* are placed solely over the main block rather than the whole, it would appear that the *Manduka Mandala* is more applicable (See: **Figure 173**). It is noted that the central chamber and the octagonal drum above lie within the *brahmásthana*, Furthermore, the bayed and arched perimeter chambers are enclosed completely within the outer rank of *pada*.

The concept of the ninefold plan is less manifest in the *Tomb of Jahangir* than in the more traditional imperial mausolea (See: **Figure 174**)--e.g., the *Tomb of Humayun*, the *Tomb of Akbar* and the *Taj Mahal*. Nonetheless, the central chamber containing the cenotaph is contained within the center area. The four entrances and the four

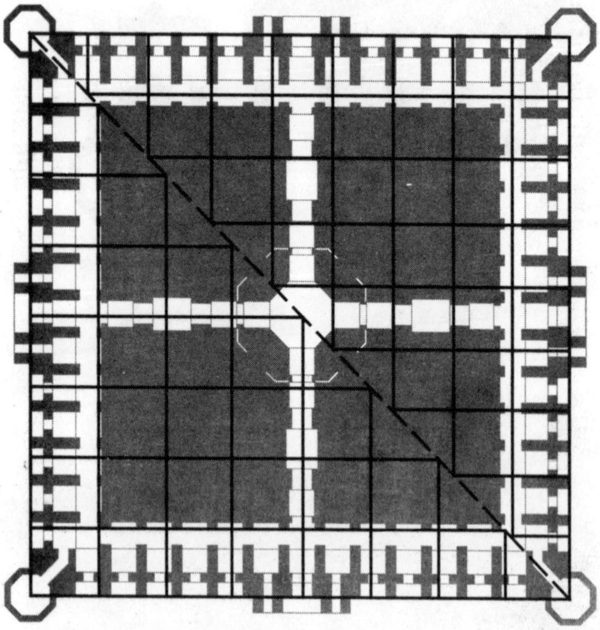

Figure 173: *Tomb of Jihangir*, application of *Manduka* and *Paramashayika Mandala* over central block

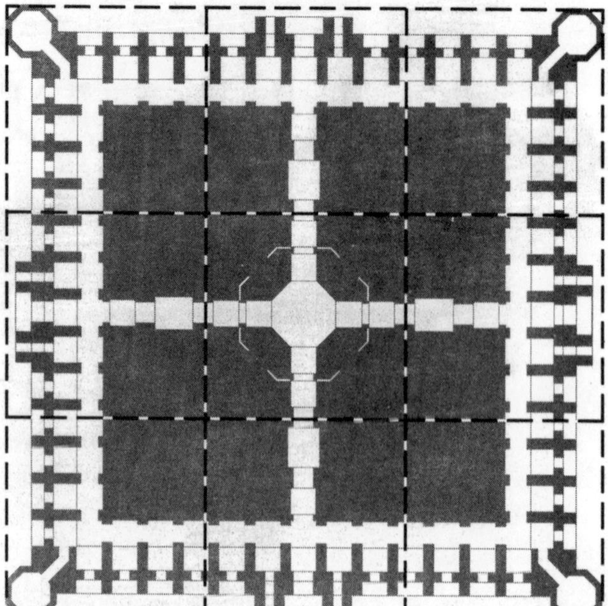

Figure 174: *Tomb of Jahangir*, application of ninefold plan

Plate 72
Tomb of Jahangir (Ensemble)

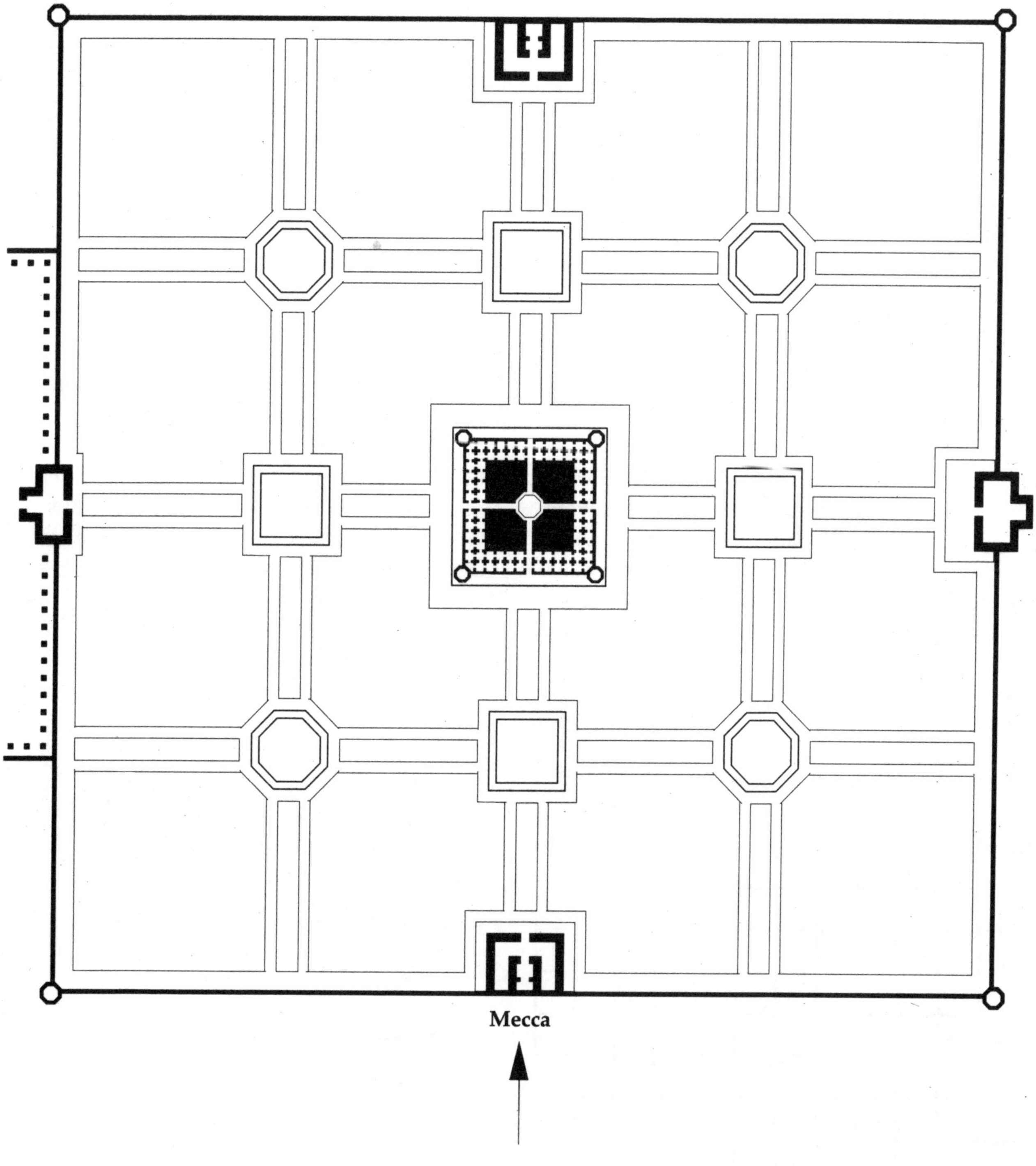

towers are contained within their own areas. This may loosely be construed as applicable to the ninefold plan.

The application of the *Deshiya Mandala* to the elevation of the *Tomb of Jahangir* produces a number of conjunctions (See: **Figure 175**). The first storey is contained within the first rank of *pada*. The corner towers, with their finials extend upwards for five ranks. The central octagonal drum is contained within the middle three files of *pada*. Therefore, the proportions of the *Tomb of Jahangir* is 12: 5. Although, this proportion is not unusual, it does, however, include the tall corner minarets. If one discounts these, the proportion is then 12:1--most unusual!

The *chahar-bagh* within which the *Tomb of Jahangir* is set is rather classical in form (See: **Plate 72**; see also: See: **Appendix B**). It is similar to the *Bakhsh Bagh* of the Red Fort, Delhi or the *Shalimar Bagh* of Lahore, forming a *Mahapitha Mandala*. If a ninefold plan is superimposed over this garden (See: **Figure 176**), it is seen that each of the eight confluence fall within one of the eight areas surrounding the central square. Again, the appropriateness of these areas being seen as iconographically parallel to one of the eight rivers of paradise--i.e., *hasht bihisht*--is underlined. It is further noted that water is an important and integral part of this *chahar-bagh*, as with the others. It is also of interest to note that each of the square areas of this *chahar-bagh* is the size of four pada as seen in **Figure 176**--i.e., a *Pechaka Mandala*. In this instance, four denotes perfection and completeness.

Secondly, if the *chahar-bagh* is placed over the plan of the *Tomb of Jahangir*, other interesting conjunctions occur (See: **Figure 177**). The chamber containing the sarcophagus is enclosed by the solid area of the tomb within the overlay. Further, and, most interesting are that the four larger, intermediary chambers which lead from the cardinal points to the central chamber fall within the influence of the square pool/ walkways of the *chahar-bagh*. Finally, the pool/ walkway divisions, both vertically and horizontally are seen to exit in the middle arcade

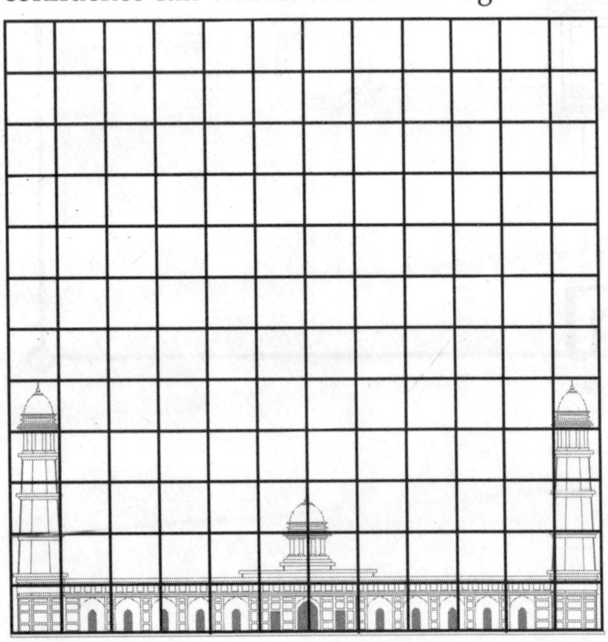

Figure 175: *Tomb of Jahangir*, application of *Deshiya Mandala* over the elevation

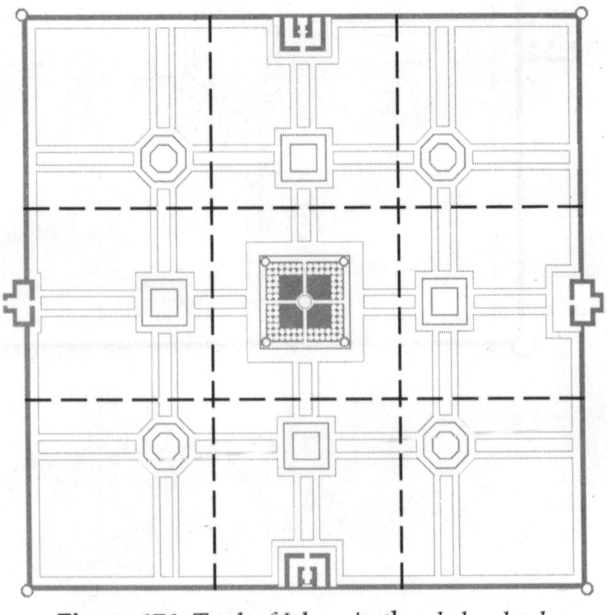

Figure 176: *Tomb of Jahangir*, the *chahar-bagh*, application of ninefold plan with *Paramashayika Mandala*

of the five on either side of the cardinal façade entrances.

Finally, the application of a simple geometric division based upon three, four and twelve is seen in **Figure 178**. This applies both vertically, horizontally and diagonally.

In considering the possibilities and implications of the various and apparently interrelated geometric design aspects of this tomb, or any Indo-Islamic tomb, is individually hazardous and conjectural. It is generally accepted that in countries in which Islam is in the vast majority, the design and construction of certain structures, especially tombs, appear to follow a rather strict and precise design procedure (See: **Figure 56**, p. 26). However, in Indo-Islamic tombs, this is far more problematical and/or futile to a point since there are two systems in operation at once--i.e., the Islamic (Persian, Pathan, Turk) and the indigenous Hindu *sthapati*.

Do tombs have anything to say about the man? From the wide ranging, liberal and open-minded character of Akbar's theology; the concern for building and conquest may find concrete manifestation in his tomb at Sikandara. On the other hand, the narrow, conservative nature of Jahangir's limited practice, may, also be manifest in the Lahore tomb. Nonetheless, we find two glorious tombs, related through form and the persons entombed. One elegant, sophisticated and soaring, the other solid, conservative and sprawling. Both are aesthetically and iconographically important and are suitable repositories for father and son, Mughal emperors.

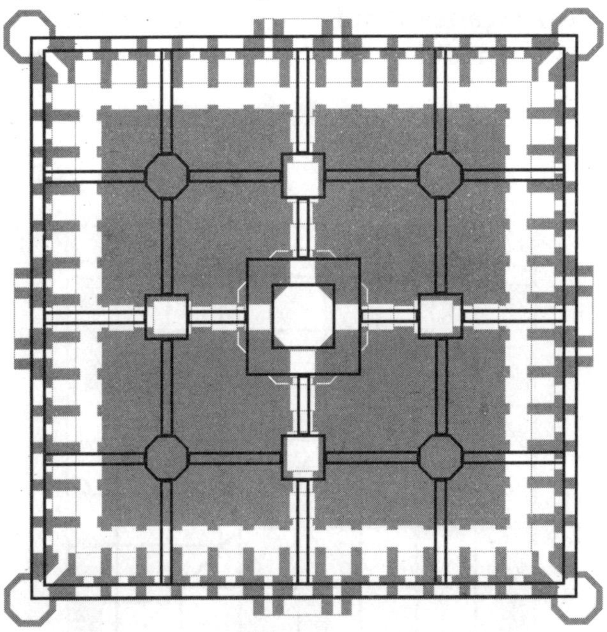

Figure 177: *Tomb of Jahangir*, with the *chahar-bagh* (simplified), superimposed

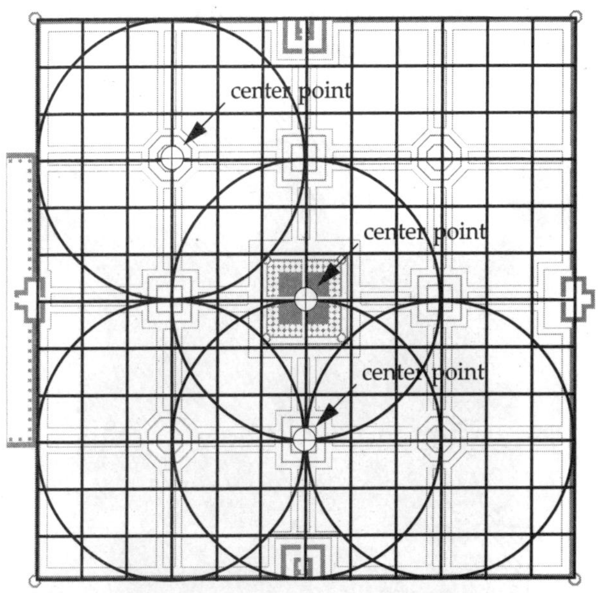

Figure 178: *Tomb of Jahangir*, the *chahar-bagh*, geometric consideration with *Deshiya Mandala*

Gol Gumbaz

Bijapur, 1626-1656 C.E.

The Sultan Muhammad 'Adil Shah of Bijapur, was a rival of the northern, the Delhi Mughal emperor, Shah Jahan. The Bijapur sultans established their domain in 1489 from the crumbling Bahmani Sultanate. Like the Qutab Shahi of Golconda, the 'Adil Shahi established a vital realm which developed a highly distinctive architectural style with strong influences from Persia, Turkey and Pathan. Foremost, is the use of bulbous domes which becomes the hallmark of these two Deccan sultanates.

Far from the Delhi-Agra centers with their spectacular, imperial architecture, Bijapur nestles in relative oblivion, protecting its equally magnificent treasures. Muhammad 'Adil Shah was the seventh of nine rulers who had built a vast power and economic base with few parallels in south-central India--i.e., the Deccan. He built a tomb that finds few rivals in India or anywhere else in the world. For sheer size the *Gol Gumbaz*[79] is without equal! Massive is the term that is often applied. But beyond this descriptive term, the *Gol Gumbaz* is also singular in that the internal space soars to a height of over one-hundred-seventy feet and is enclosed by a single dome that spans one-hundred-twenty-five feet. It is the largest dome in Asia, and the largest single-shell dome in the world.[80] This is not a double dome as many other Mughal structures--e.g., the *Tomb of Humayun, Taj Mahal* and that of his predecessor the *Ibrahim Rauza*--or even a double-shelled dome. The area under the dome is said to span the largest inclosed space in the world. The *Gol Gumbaz* dominates the Bijapur skyline, even today.

Square, *en plan*, with octagonal corner towers of seven storeys----i.e., a **Type C-a** basic plan--the *Gol Gumbaz* resembles the plan of the earlier *Tomb of Sultan Ghari*. The south, east and west façades display entrances framed in massive and developed recessed arches. Within

Figure 179: *Tomb of Muhammad 'Adil Shah (Gol Gumbaz)*, indication of internal space

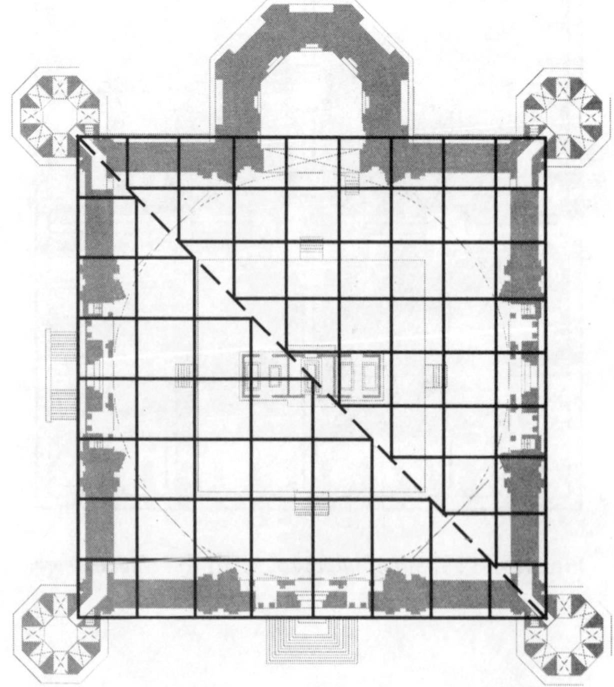

Figure 180: *Tomb of Muhammad 'Adil Shah (Gol Gumbaz)*, application of *Manduka* and *Paramashayika Mandala*

Plate 73
Gol Gumbaz (Plan)

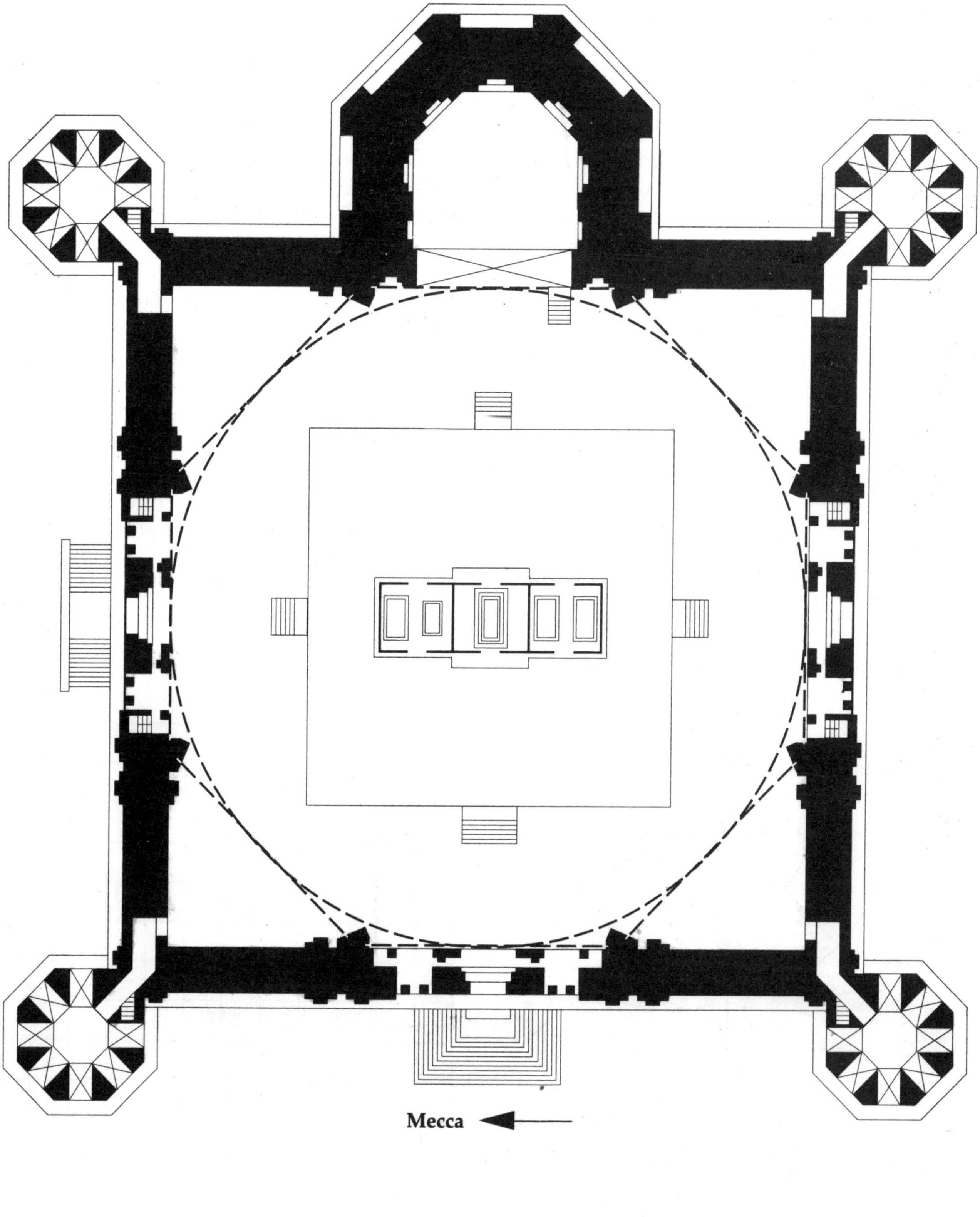

the spacious chamber is a large platform upon which is found the cenotaph of Sultan Muhammad 'Adil Shah duly oriented towards Mecca and in the crypt below his sarcophagus is found. This platform effectively separates the cenotaph(s) from those who wish to pay their respects and the floor level acts as a ambulatory (Ind.: *pradakshinapatha*).

The *Gol Gumbaz* possesses an anomalous feature. Centered in the north wall of the main block is an apse-like extension, the floor of which is elevated from the main chamber's floor level. One would normally consider this to be a highly developed *mikhrab* extending from the *qibla*. However, this apse is not a *mikhrab*, nor is the wall the *qibla*. This is the north wall. No other Indo-Islamic tomb possesses such a form. Just what this area was meant to be or used for is conjectural. However, it does appear to be a suitable locale for the various members of the royal family to stand during the internment ceremonies as well as for the traditional prayers that are offered at specific intervals after one's death. Nonetheless, it is a unique feature to an unparalleled tomb.

The interior space of the *Gol Gumbaz* is, like the mausoleum itself, massive (See: **Figure 179**). As has been stated, the floor area of the central chamber acts as an ambulatory, a feature that takes on a variant form in the double aisle of the *Ibrahim Rauza*.

If a *Manduka Mandala* and/or a *Paramashayika Mandala* are superimposed over the square block of the *Gol Gumbaz*, a number of interesting conjunctions occur (See: **Figure 180**). It is observed that in the application of the *Manduka Mandala* the realm of the second level of deities conforms, almost exactly, to the raised platform which holds the cenotaph. In the

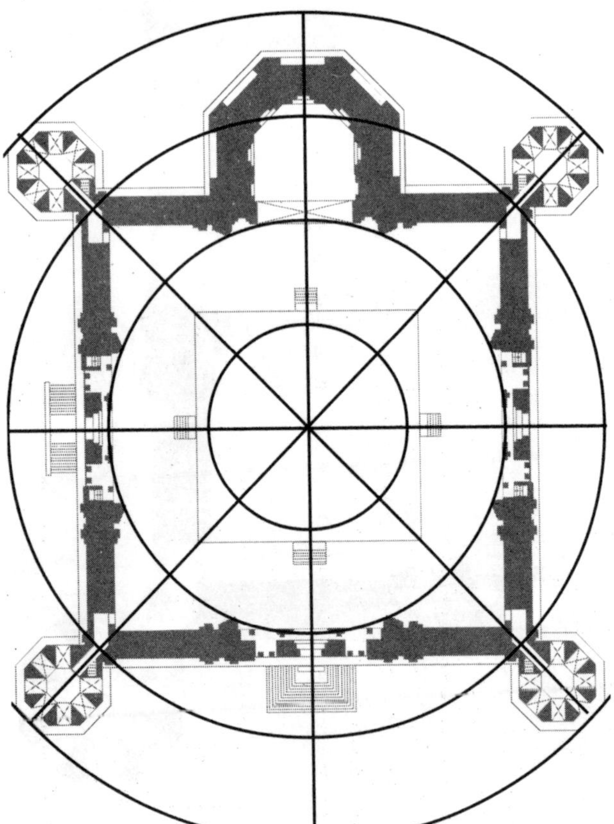

Figure 181: *Tomb of Muhammad 'Adil Shah* (*Gol Gumbaz*), application of circular *Manduka Mandala*

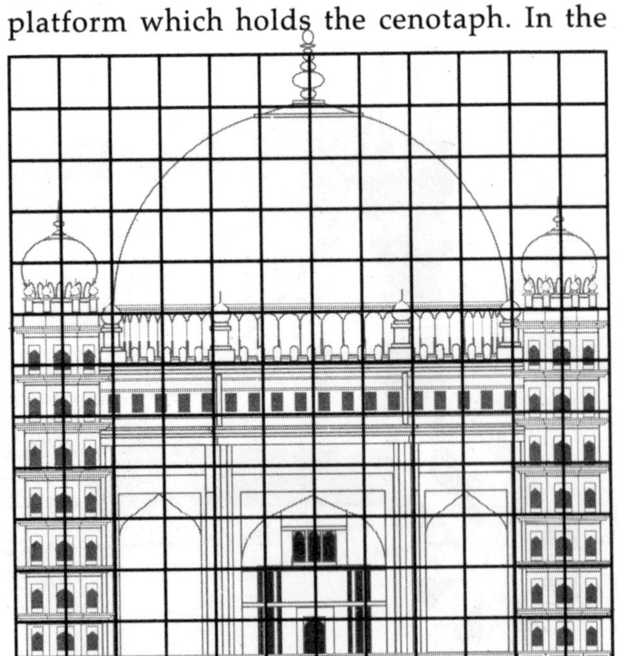

Figure 182: *Tomb of Muhammad 'Adil Shah* (*Gol Gumbaz*), application of *Deshiya Mandala* over the elevation

Plate 74
Gol Gumbaz (Elevation & half plan)

application of a *Paramashayika Mandala* the raised, rectangular dais upon which rests the sultan's cenotaph as well as those of his family is contained within the *brahmásthana.*

On the other hand, the northern apse does not fall within the square *mandala* comfortably. Therefore, a circular *Manduka Mandala* is applied over the whole (See: **Figure 181**). In this application three conjunctions are important. First, as expected, the outer ring enfolds the whole, particularly the octagonal towers in a most comfortable manner. Second, the dome's inner circumference is matched by the *mandala's* third circle. And, fourth, the inner ring, the *brahmásthana* encircles the dais with the cenotaph(s). Also, this *mandala* includes the northern apse, although, as might be expected with this eccentric addition, the inclusion does not produce any important conjunctions.

As with the other tombs within this brief study, a *Deshiya Mandala* is superimposed over the elevation. In this application, the main cube, to the balustrade falls within the first six ranks of *pada* (See: **Figure 182**). The seventh rank includes the dome's decorative moulding and the octagonal plinth upon which it rests. The dome rises to the eleventh rank of *pada*. The central form of the façade falls within the central four file of *pada*, and the dome's width is bounded by the central eight *files*. Additionally, the octagonal

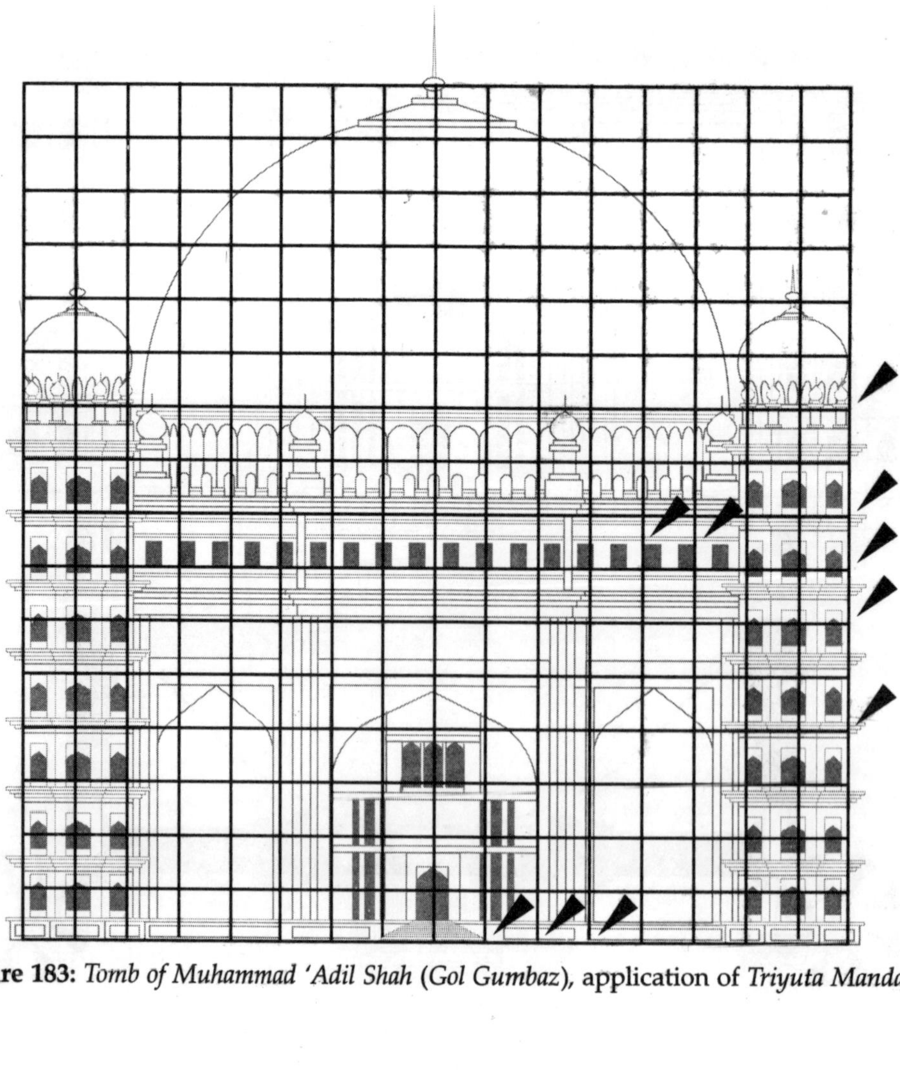

Figure 183: *Tomb of Muhammad 'Adil Shah* (*Gol Gumbaz*), application of *Triyuta Mandala*

Plate 52
Gol Gumbaz (Elevation with *Deshiya Mandala*)

corner towers are centered between the first and second files on either side. Therefore, the proportions of the *Gol Gumbaz* is 12:11.

Since the *Karnashtaka Mandala* is the basic for the application of a proportional geometric system (See: **Appendix C, Plate 141**), this writer was constrained to consider other *mandalas* as they may apply to the elevation. Since the *Manduka Mandala* appeared fortuitous, the *Triyuta Mandala* was selected to be applied (See: **Figure 183**). The *Triyuta Mandala* is double the number of *pada* per rank and/or file of the *Manduka Mandala*--i.e., sixteen, as opposed to eight--and consists of two-hundred-fifty-six *pada* as opposed to sixty-four. In this application the important ranks where conjunctions occur (noted by appropriate 'arrows' in **Figure 183**) are: four, six, seven, eight and ten. Files where conjunctions occur (numbering from the center line out in either direction) are: one, two, three, four and five.

It is accepted and acknowledged that one may find any sort of application under certain conditions. However, since geometry and architecture are stated companions in Islamic architecture, these conjectural applications were undertaken.

A mausoleum of undeniable interest, a mausoleum of eccentricities[81] which add to its appeal, a mausoleum of splendor and grandeur, *Gol Gumbaz* stands as a testament to the character of Sultan Muhammad 'Adil Shah of Bijapur. It embodies the concept of "majesty and power." *Gol Gumbaz* is doubly important as it was constructed during the reign of the great Mughal emperor Shah Jahan and stands as a counterpoint to the *Taj Mahal*.

Tomb of Jahan Begum

Ainapur, a. 1626 C.E.

There are a number of tombs of exceptional note which were constructed for the wife of an emperor or sultan. Bijapur possesses two--i.e., the *Ibrahim Rauza* originally built by Ibrahim for his consort but became his mausoleum when he predeceased her; and the *Tomb of Jahan Begam*.

Not far from the massive *Gol Gumbaz* of Muhammad 'Adil Shah at Bijapur stands the unfinished *Tomb of Jahan Begum*, at Ainapur. The mausoleum was constructed as a resting place for his consort Jahan Begum. The plan of the tomb mimics that of its massive neighbor, but in scale it was smaller, as befitted her status. Little remains today of what would have been a mausoleum of grace an delicacy.

The square plan with attached towers at its four corners--i.e., a **Type C-c** basic plan--finds precedence in earlier tombs--e.g., *Tomb of Sultan Ghari, Tomb of Muhammad Ghaus, Tomb of Jahangir* and *Gol Gumbaz*. Like the *Ibrahim Rauza* it consists of an arcuated central chamber set within a deep verandah with wide arches and punctuated by corner towers.

As with most Indo-Islamic tombs, the *Tomb of Jahan Begam* possesses, proportionally, a great amount of open space (See: **Figure 184**). This is compounded by the spacing of arched openings on its perimeter.

In the application of a *mandala*, it appears that the *Manduka Mandala* is pertinent (See: **Figure 185**). Here, the *brahmásthana* protects the central space, while the second rank encircles the inner chamber.

Unfortunately, the present condition of the *Tomb of Jahan Begam* is in such a state of ruin that it is impossible to deal with its elevation. Nonetheless, it may be assumed that its aspect may well be similar to, and/or a combination of preexistent mausolea in Bijapur. Surely, the sensibility and power of Muhammad 'Adil Shah was such as to assure such a conjecture.

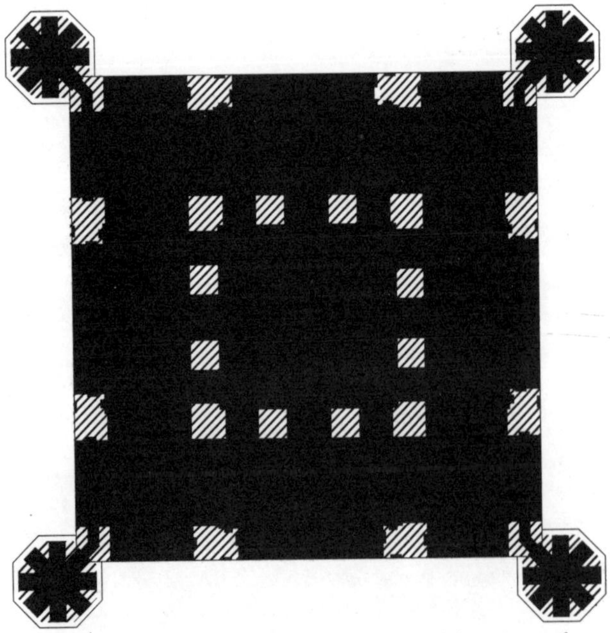

Figure 184: *Tomb of Jahan Begum*, indication of internal space

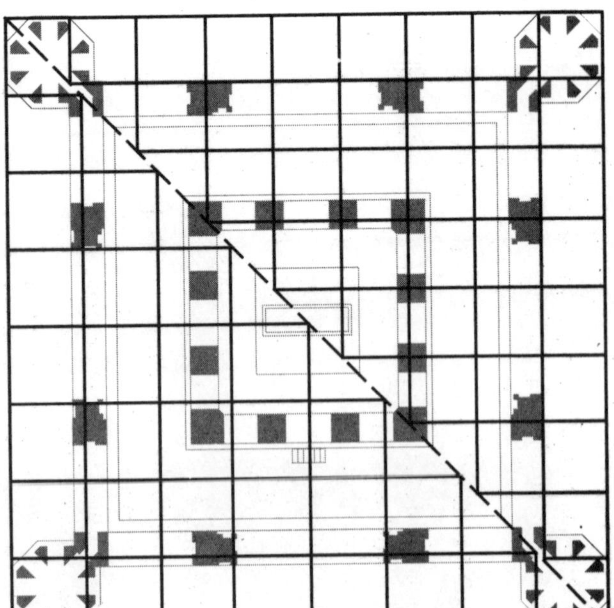

Figure 185: *Tomb of Jahan Begum*, application of *Manduka* and *Paramashayika Mandala*

Plate 75
Tomb of Jahan Begum (Plan)

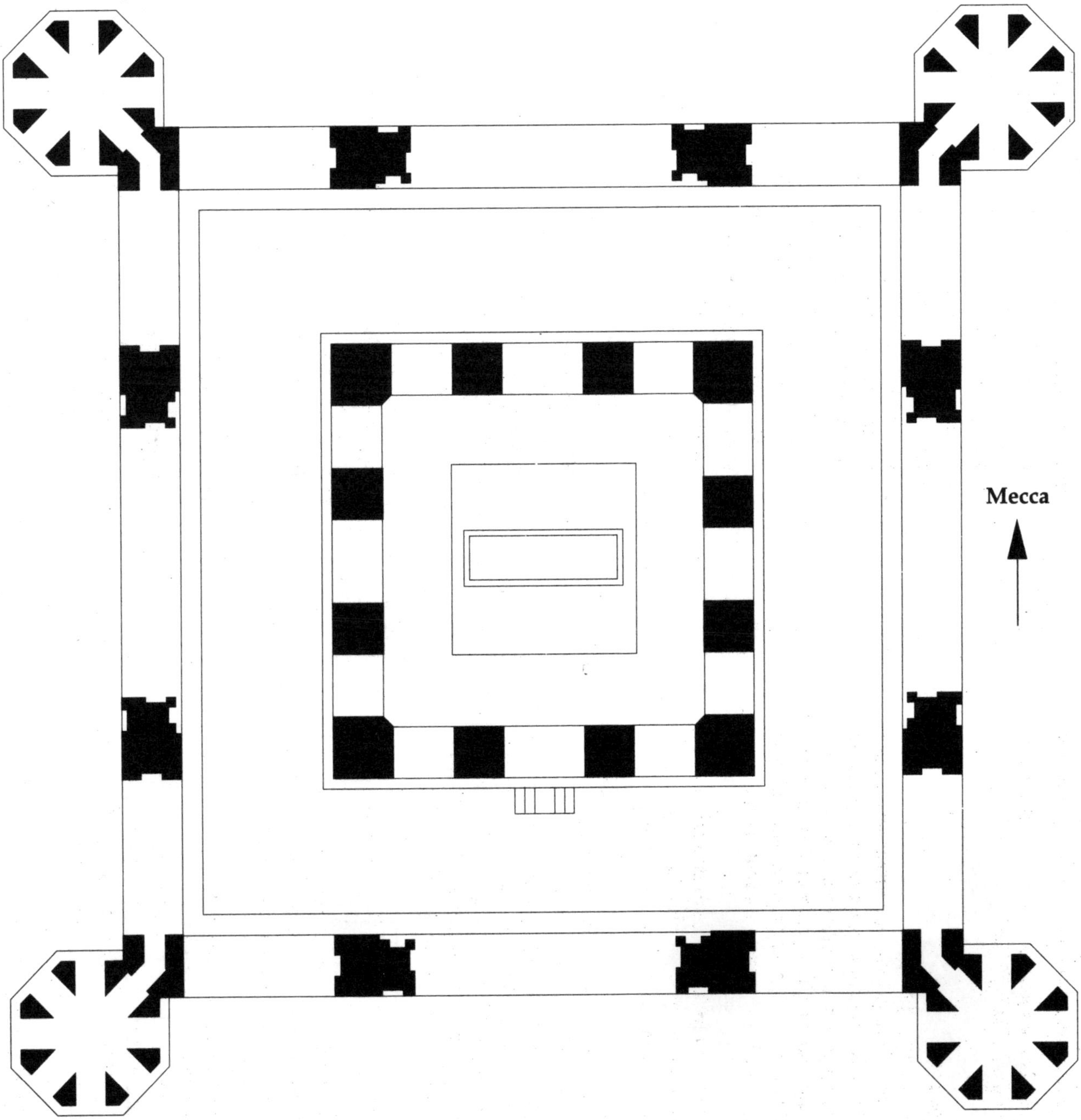

Tomb of I'timad-ud-daula

Agra, a. 1628 C.E.

Mirza Ghiyas Beg, the I'timad-ud-daula (Prime Minister), had been an impoverished Persian noble who, with his family, travelled to India in search of better times. He started in the Court of Akbar and quickly began to climb upwards. Little did he realize that he would rise to stratospheric heights within the Mughal empire.

Mirza Ghiyas Beg's influence, his connections reached into the imperial bedrooms. His daughter Mehrun-un-nisa, known later as Nur Jahan, born of Asmat Begun, became not just one of the wives of the Mughal Emperor Jahangir, but was elevated to hold the title of Empress.[83] Through her own lust for power and her incredible influence over Jahangir, Nur Jahan became the *de facto* ruler of Mughal India. Mirza Ghiyas Beg's son, Asaf Khan, served as Shah Jahan's Prime minister and also was the father of Hazrat Mumtaz-uz-Zamani, the fabled Mumtaz Mahal.

Upon his death, Nur Jahan contracted to construct his tomb. She was given free reign and unlimited capitol by her husband, the Emperor who preferred painting to architecture. Nur Jahan fell to the task with unequalled vigor. Since Mirza Ghiyas Beg was not of royal blood, there were certain constraints of scale imposed upon any tomb that would be constructed. This did not dampen the zeal of the Empress.

What the *Tomb of I'timad-ud-daula* lacks in size,[84] it more than makes up for its utter lavishness of detail and uniqueness. The *Tomb of I'timad-ud-daula* is the first of the Mughal tombs to be completely covered in white marble.[85] It is the first mausoleum in which *pietra dura* was employed so extensively. Virtually the whole surface of the *Tomb of I'timad-ud-daula* is covered with this intricate and technically demanding inlay. It is also one of the few Indo-Islamic tombs not to utilize a dome.

Square, *en plan*--i.e., a **Type C-c** basic plan--with octagonal towers at the four corners, the *Tomb of I'timad-ud-daula* mimics a number of preceding mausolea--e.g., *Tomb of Sultan Ghari,*

Figure 186: *Tomb of I'timad-ud-daula,* indication of internal space

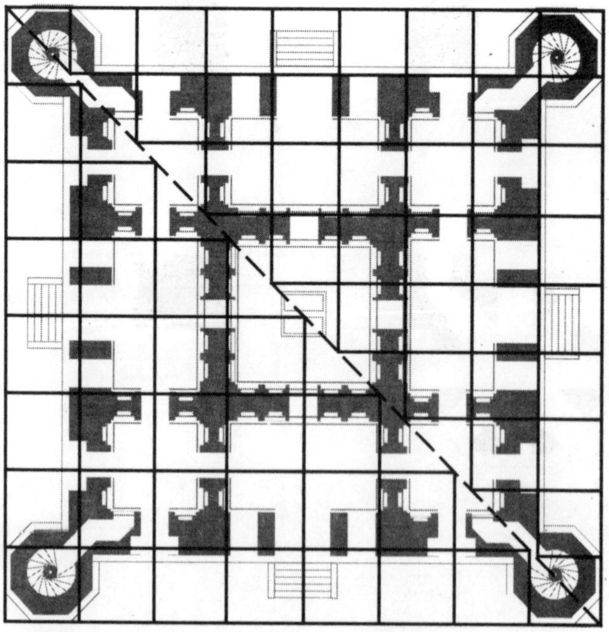

Figure 187: *Tomb of I'timad-ud-daula,* application of *Manduka Mandala* and *Paramashayika Mandala* (the whole)

Plate 76

Tomb of I'timad-ud-daula (Plan, 1st level)

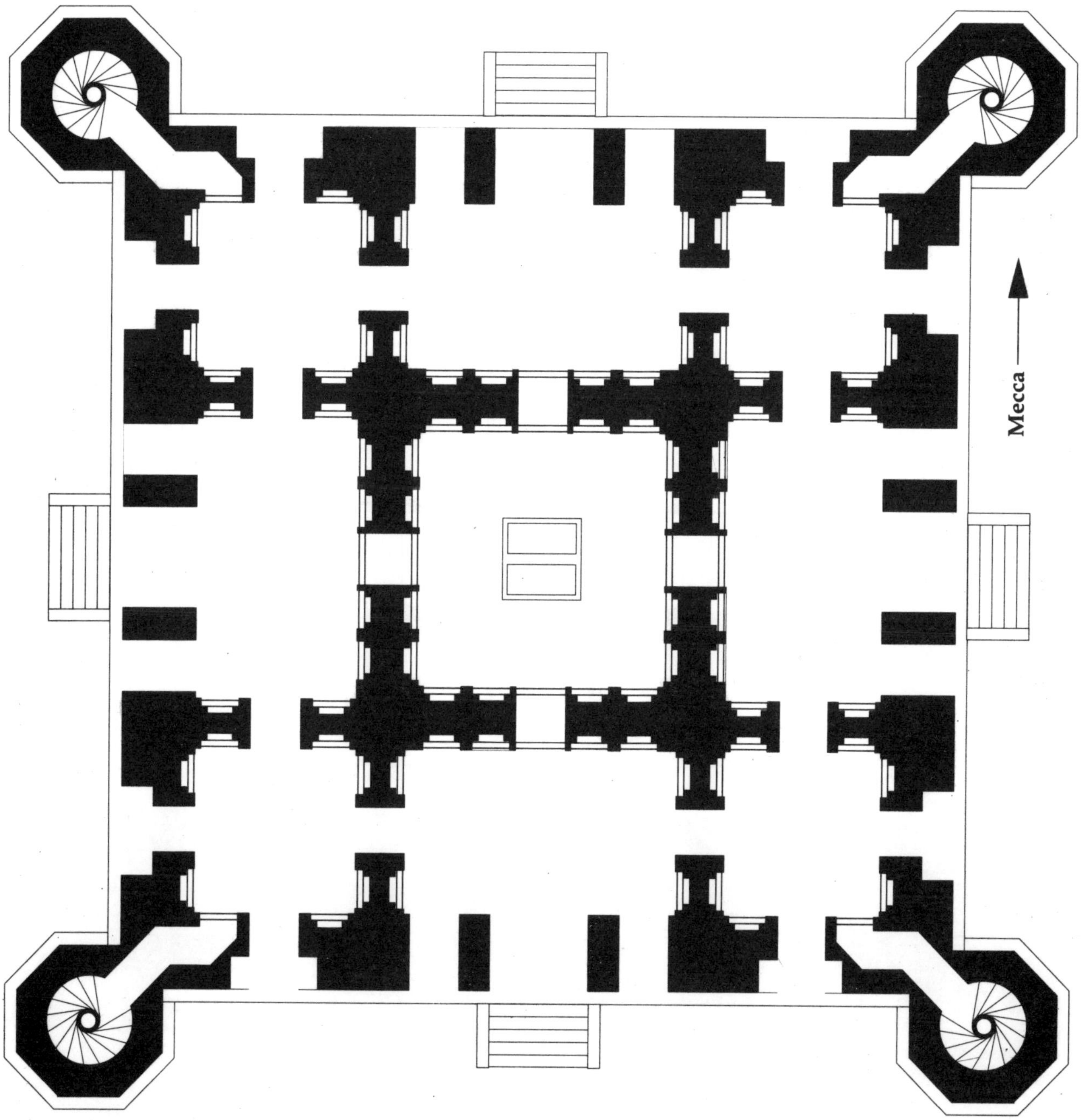

Plate 77

Tomb of I'timad-ud-daula (Plan, 2nd level)

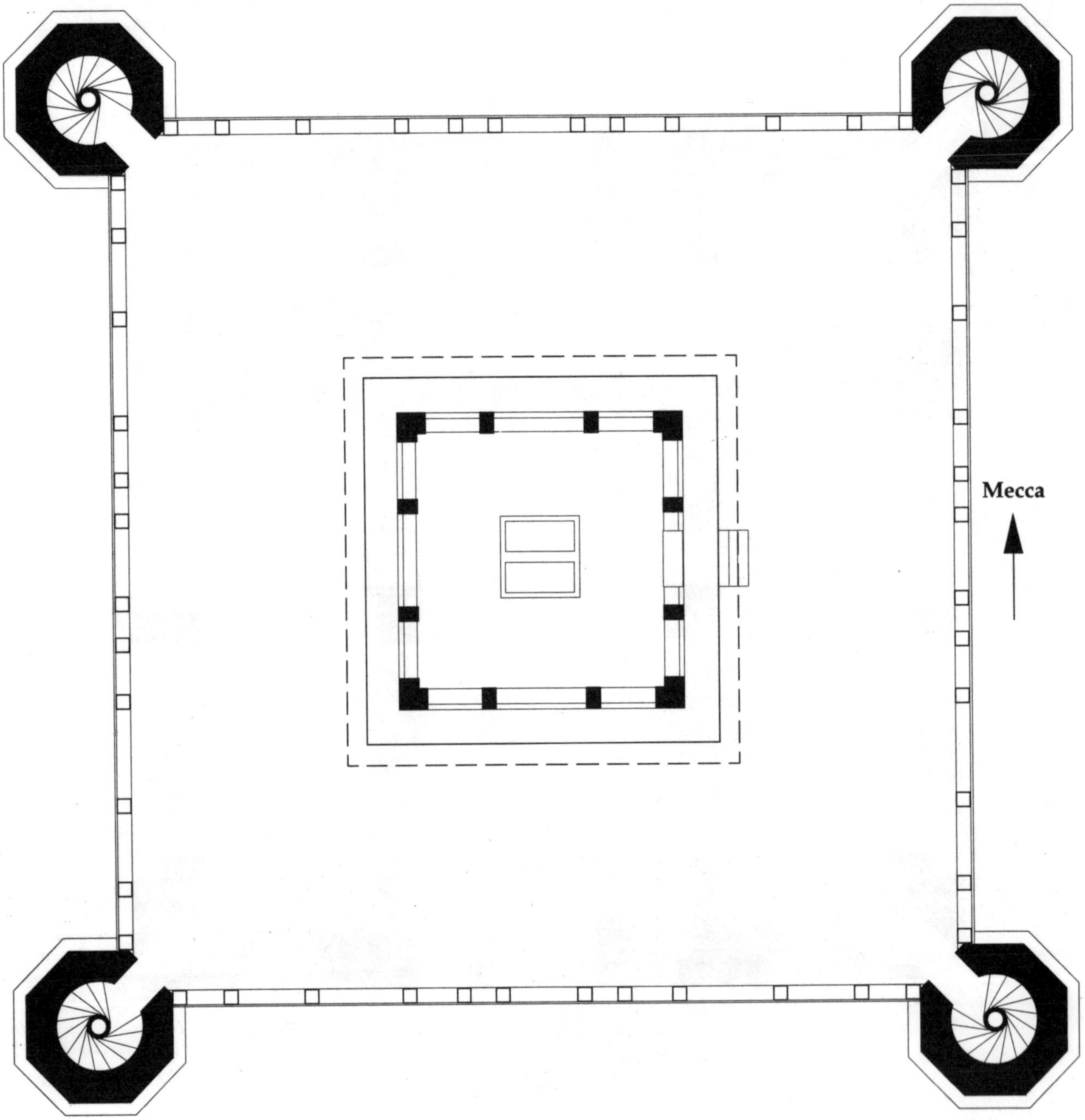

Tomb of Muhammad Ghaus, Tomb of Jahangir, Gol Gumbaz and *Jahan Begam*. The *Tomb of I'timad-ud-daula* sets upon a substantial podium, elevating it from the surrounding enclosure and, in a sense, implying that it is a valuable *objet d'art*, which, of course, it is. The mausoleum is basically an enclosed square with a raised, central chamber which hold the cenotaphs of Mirza Ghiyas Beg and Asmat Begun. Eight other spaces or rooms surround this central chamber. The mausoleum possesses four portals situated in the center of each façade by which ambient lighting bathes the interior. On either side of these doorways are two openings with intricate *jaali*. On the second level is an enclosed, square pavilion. As in the central chamber of the first level, here too another set of cenotaphs of Mirza Ghiyas Beg and Asmat Begun are to be found.

The interior space appears adequate (See: **Figure 186**). The masonry walls appear unusually thick, however, one must consider the size (scale) of this mausoleum. In proportion, the space with the intervening walls is ample. It is certainly generous enough for the *Wazir* of the Realm, the father and grandfather of two empresses.

In the application of either a *Manduka Mandala* or a *Paramashayika Mandala* to the whole of the *Tomb of I'timad-ud-daula* (See: Figure 187), it is observed that the two are nearly equal. However, the *Manduka Mandala* possesses two aspects that are important. It is to be noted that the corner spaces or rooms are bisected by the second rank and file of *pada*. Secondly, the central space is completely enclosed by the *brahmásthana*, as it also is by that of the *Paramashayika Mandala*.

On the other hand, if these two *mandalas* are applied to the square block of the *Tomb of I'timad-ud-daula* alone, other conjunctions appear which seem to shift the balance towards the *Paramashayika Mandala* (See: Figure 188). Again, the central space is enfolded by the *brahmásthana* of the *Paramashayika Mandala*. The third rank is seen to enclose all of the interior space(s). This *mandala* also suggests, yet, another fundamental iconic possibility.

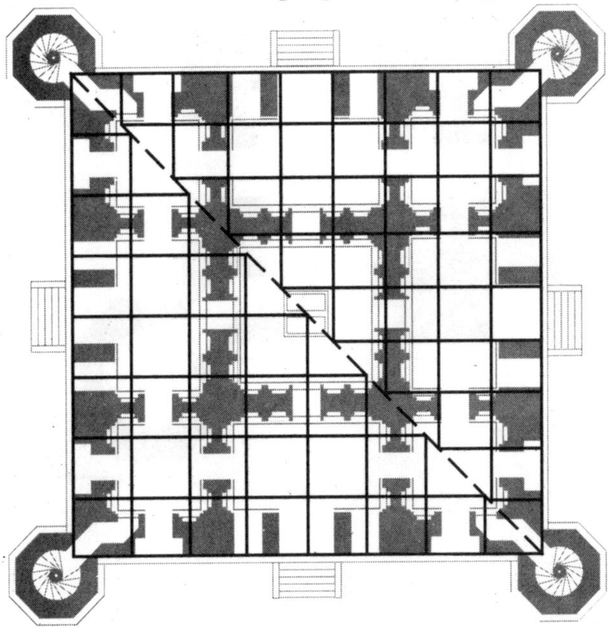

Figure 188: *Tomb of I'timad-ud-daula*, application of *Manduka* and *Paramashayika Mandala* (the central block)

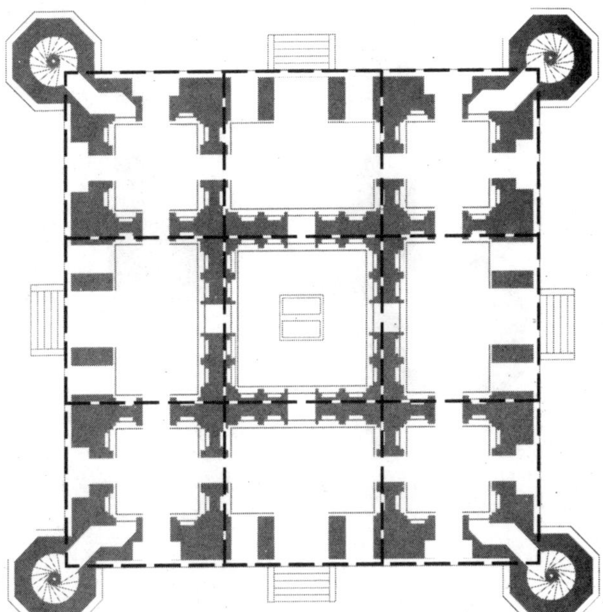

Figure 189: *Tomb of I'timad-ud-daula*, application of a ninefold plan

Plate 78

Tomb of I'timad-ud-daula (Elevation & half plan)

The plan of the *Tomb of I'timad-ud-daula* is such as to suggest the application of a ninefold plan (See: **Figure 189**). The arrangement and size of the central chamber and the surrounding eight rooms are such as to make this application obvious. Even if this plan is superimposed over the whole, the same conclusion is apparent.

One curious aspect must be considered--i.e., the appearance to two sets of cenotaphs; one on the first level and another in the pavilion of the second level. These two mirror the sarcophagi found in the crypt. The concept of the celestial axis (See: **Appendix B**) considered in Islamic tombs with the 'stacked' cenotaph over the encrypted sarcophagus coupled with the ability to circumambulate, is geometrically enhanced in the *Tomb of I'timad-ud-daula*. Certainly the sarcophagus resting in the crypt with a cenotaph of the floor above and a second cenotaph above the first appears to be an exercise in redundancy. The reason for this arrangement is unclear. Could it be a subtle means by which Nur Jahan elevated the importance of her father's scaled-down tomb? Certainly the wealth of detail which covers the tomb, inside and outside, would seem enough! Or, could these additional cenotaphs within the elegant pavilion of the second level be installed as a place of private contemplation for the empress, away from the prying eyes and bustle of the masses? There she could give due reverence to the man who was essentially responsible for her elevation to the pinnacle of power and wealth.

When a *Deshiya Mandala* is superimposed over the elevation of the *Tomb of I'timad-ud-daula several* interesting conjunctions occur (See: **Figure 190**). The lower level, including the balustrade fall within the lower three ranks of *pada*. The corner towers extend upwards six ranks of *pada* and fall within two files. Therefore, the proportions of the *Tomb of I'timad-ud-daula is* 12:6.

The *Tomb of I'timad-ud-daula*, an Indo-Islamic jewel, sets like a magnificent wedding cake of white marble, *jaali* and *pietra dura* upon its platform. It is incomparable in its delicacy and profusion of detail. Unfortunately, it is eclipsed by the mausoleum across the Yamuna, the fabled *Taj Mahal*. Nonetheless, it stands as testament to the best of Mughal architecture.

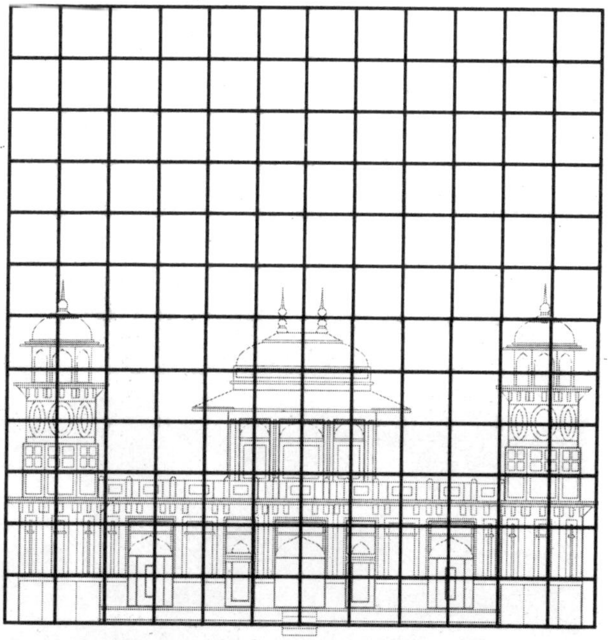

Figure 190: *Tomb of I'timad-ud-daula* (elevation), application of *Deshiya Mandala* over the elevation

Taj Mahal

Agra, 1632-1654 C.E.

Born to Asaf Khan, the brother of the Empress Nur Jahan, and given the name of Arjumand Banu, also known as Hazrat Mumtaz-uz-Zamani, but best remembered as Mumtaz Mahal--this woman of exceptional beauty and talent was taken to wife by the Mughal emperor, Shah Jahan. Mumtaz Mahal not only was a wife and mother, she was the emperor's confident and companion, companion even in battle. Shah Jahan was so enamored with Mumtaz Mahal that when she died in giving birth to their twelfth child he was devastated, absolutely grief stricken. The result of his love, affection and grief was the fabled, the incomparable *Taj Mahal*.[86]

The *Taj Mahal* has been characterized as the embodiment of architectural perfection. This may be true. Certainly volumes have been written in testament of this supposed fact. It has been stated that geometry played an abiding role in Islamic architecture. Certainly with the existence of such treatises as the *Manasara* and *Mayamata* in India, the Indo-Islamic architects and / or *sthapati* could be expected to carry on this tradition, including regional variations. Immutable as some of these laws appeared to be in Hindu architecture of India, they were not so inviolate to the Islamic world. "The application of geometric principles to the architectural production of the Islamic world shows an inclusive and flexible approach."[87]

The plan of the *Taj Mahal* presents a *muthamman baghdadi* shape--i.e., a **Type E** basic plan. Here a central, octagonal chamber becomes the axis for the whole. At the cardinal points smaller, rectangular, interior spaces give way to larger, exterior spaces (porches), while at the intercardinal directions are smaller octagonal chambers. These various chambers are connected at the cardinal and intercardinal points, creating an interconnected maze on the first level. The second level presents an even mor complex maze of corridors and internal spaces.

The amount of internal space in comparison to the whole is certainly greater than one would find in Hindu temples (See: **Figures 191 & 192**). However, it is proportionately less

Figure 191: *Taj Mahal*, indication of internal space, 1st level

Figure 192: *Taj Mahal*, indication of internal space, 2nd Level

Plate 79
Taj Mahal (Plan 1st level)

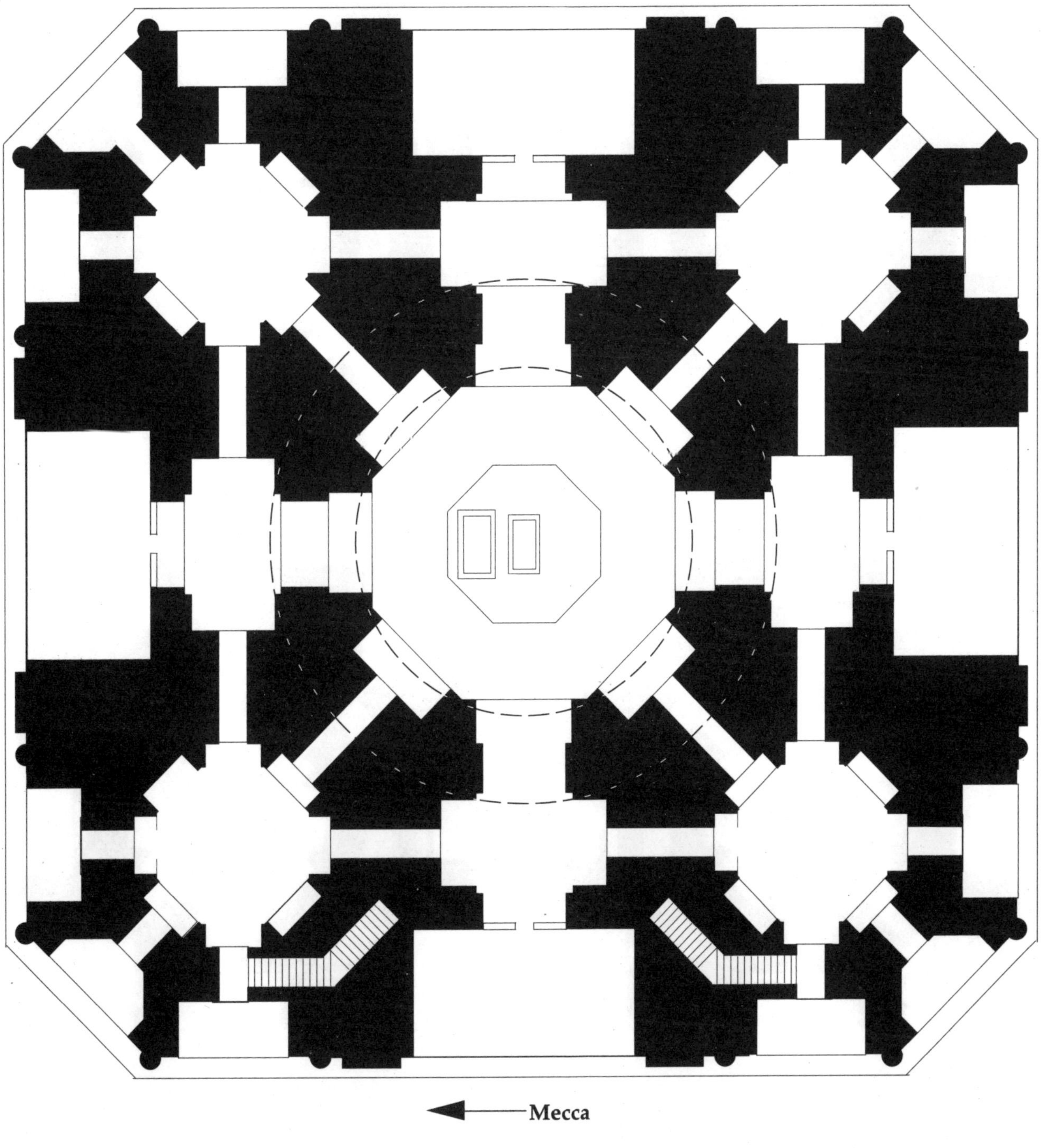

Plate 80
Taj Mahal (Plan, 2nd level)

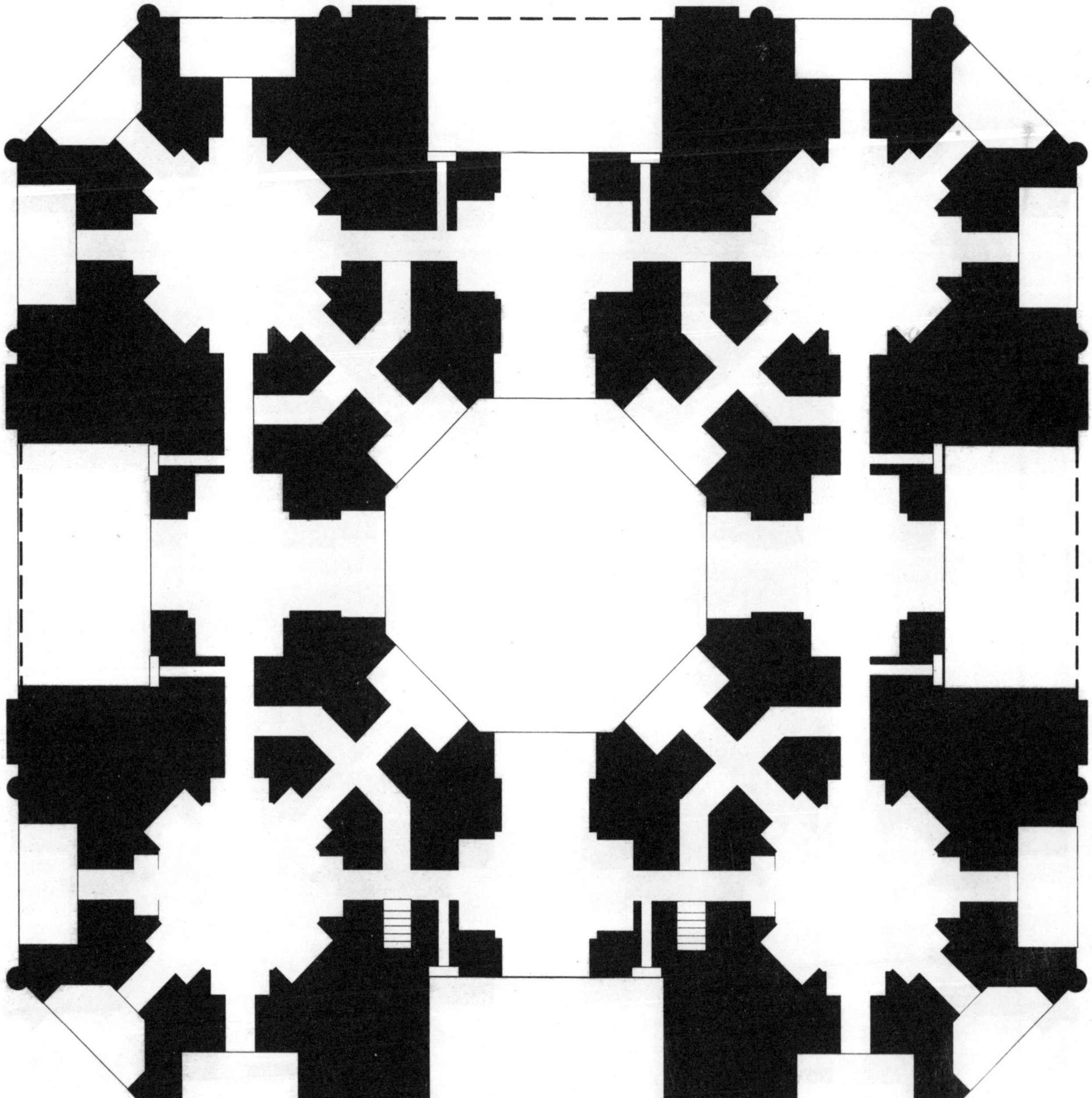

than found in preceding Indo-Islamic temples with the exception of the *Tomb of Humayun* and the *Tomb of Khan Khanan*, not to mention the *Tomb of Akbar* and the *Tomb of Jahangir*.

The application of either the *Manduka Mandala* or the *Paramashayika Mandala* indicates that the latter, the *Paramashayika Mandala* is most propitious (See: **Figure 193**). The central octagonal chamber with its cenotaphs is contained within the *brahmásthana*. The second rank finds its corners as the center point of the four, corner, octagonal chambers. The third rank encloses all the major internal spaces. If, on the other hand, a circular *Manduka Mandala* is overlaid on the plan of the *Taj Mahal* other possibilities occur (See: **Figure 194**). The central chamber is enclosed by the *brahmásthana*. The second ring touches the inner surfaces of the corner octagonal spaces, while the third encloses these four spaces. There are other applications of either the *Paramashayika Mandala* and the circular *Manduka Mandala* that will be considered later.

When considering the concept of the nine-fold design application as applied to the plan of the first level, the efficacy of this concept becomes apparent (See: **Figure 195**). It is seen that each of the major, internal spaces fall within one of the nine sections. The central square contains, of course, the central octagonal chamber with its cenotaphs.

When this design concept is enlarged to contain the podium and corner minarets other associations are apparent, although less applicable than the first consideration of **Figure 195** (See: **Figure 196**). It is noted that in this application the central square passes through the cardinal passages surrounding the central octagonal space, and that the center points of the corner octagonal spaces is in close proximity to the corners of the central square.

As with the precious mausolea, a *Deshiya*

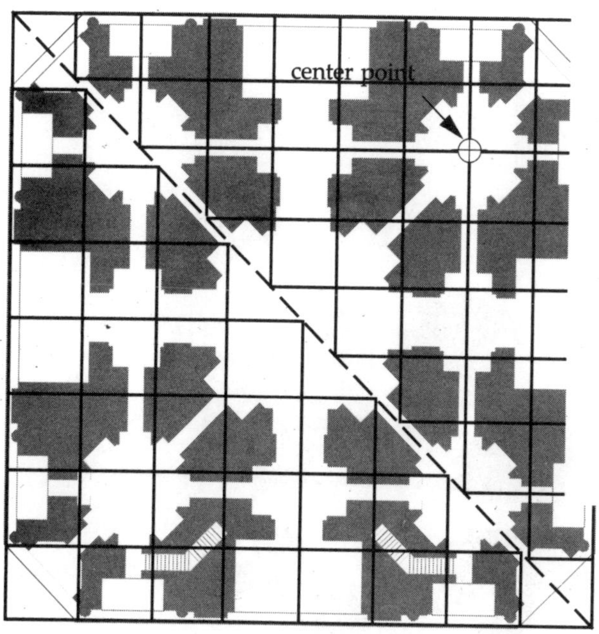

Figure 193: *Taj Mahal,*, application of *Manduka Mandala* and *Paramashayika Mandala*

Figure 194: *Taj Mahal*, application of circular *Manduka Mandala*

Plate 81
Taj Mahal (Elevation & half plan)

Mandala is laid over the elevation of the *Taj Mahal* (See: **Figure 197**). Here it is observed that the first level and the second level are contained with two ranks of *pada*, each--i.e., rising to the fourth rank. The sixth rank of *pada* is found to define the level of the *chatri* where their domes begin. The soaring dome of the *Taj Mahal* begins at the seventh rank and is contained within the middle six files of *pada*. The dome with the lower section of its elaborate finial lies within the twelfth rank of *pada*. Therefore, it can be stated that the proportions of the *Taj Mahal* are 12:12.

There appear to be other geometric considerations to take into account when dealing with the design of the *Taj Mahal*. When constructing "**Figure 192: *Taj Mahal***, indication of internal space, 2nd Level" this writer saw what appeared to be an octagon formed by the additional passageways of the second level--i.e., those not included in the first level which connected the cardinal passages. When an octagon was placed over this area, corresponding with the center of the octagonal corner chambers, and enlarged, proportionally, it was found that the outer dimension fit within the "sheared off" corner of the *muthamman baghdadi* (See: **Figure 198**). Then, when this octagon was suitably placed over the other corner octagons, it was observed that another octagon of identical dimension could be placed over the central area and the five became conjoined! Further, if the center points of these four corner octagons were considered and those center points became the corners of a square, it was observed that the sides of this square ran through the center of the cardinal passageways of the second level. Finally, this same concept is also applicable to the first level as well--i.e., the melding of the octagon and the square. If this fortuitous discovery was applicable to the *Taj Mahal*, could it, likewise, be applicable to the first, major, Mughal mausoleum of related design, the *Tomb of Humayun*? Alas! It was not to be!

The ensemble of the *Taj Mahal* is unique is among the various sepulchral Indo-Islamic monuments (See: Plate 82). The *Tomb of Isa Khan*,

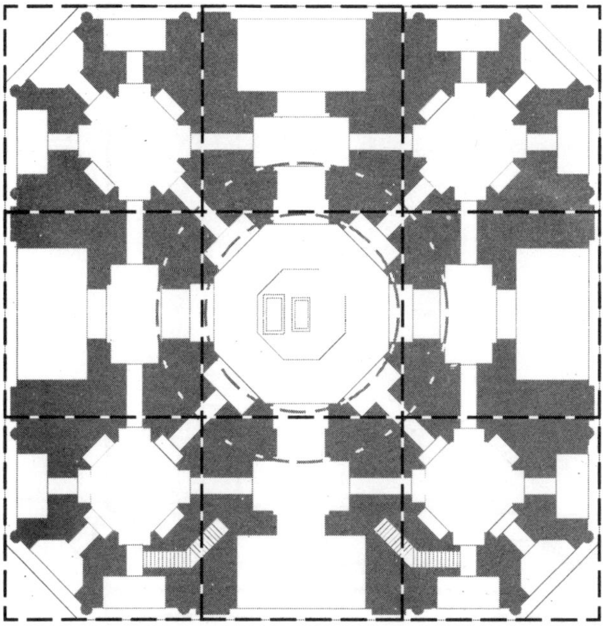

Figure 195: *Taj Mahal*, indicating ninefold division over mausoleum

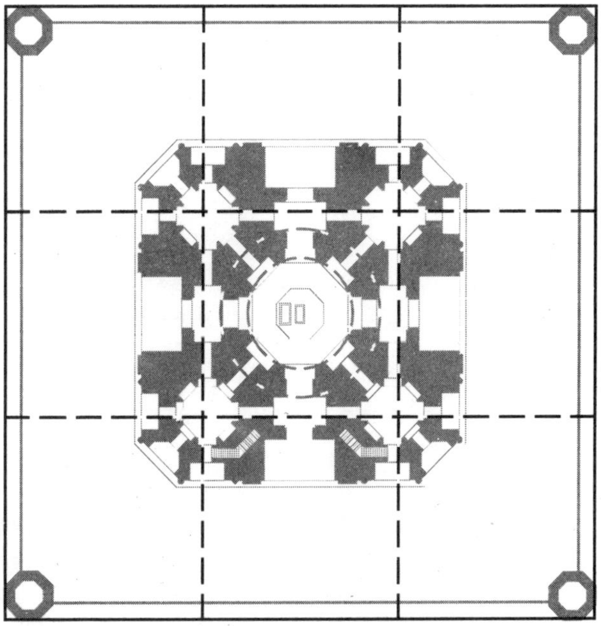

Figure 196: *Taj Mahal*, indicating ninefold division over podium

Plate 82
Taj Mahal (Ensemble)

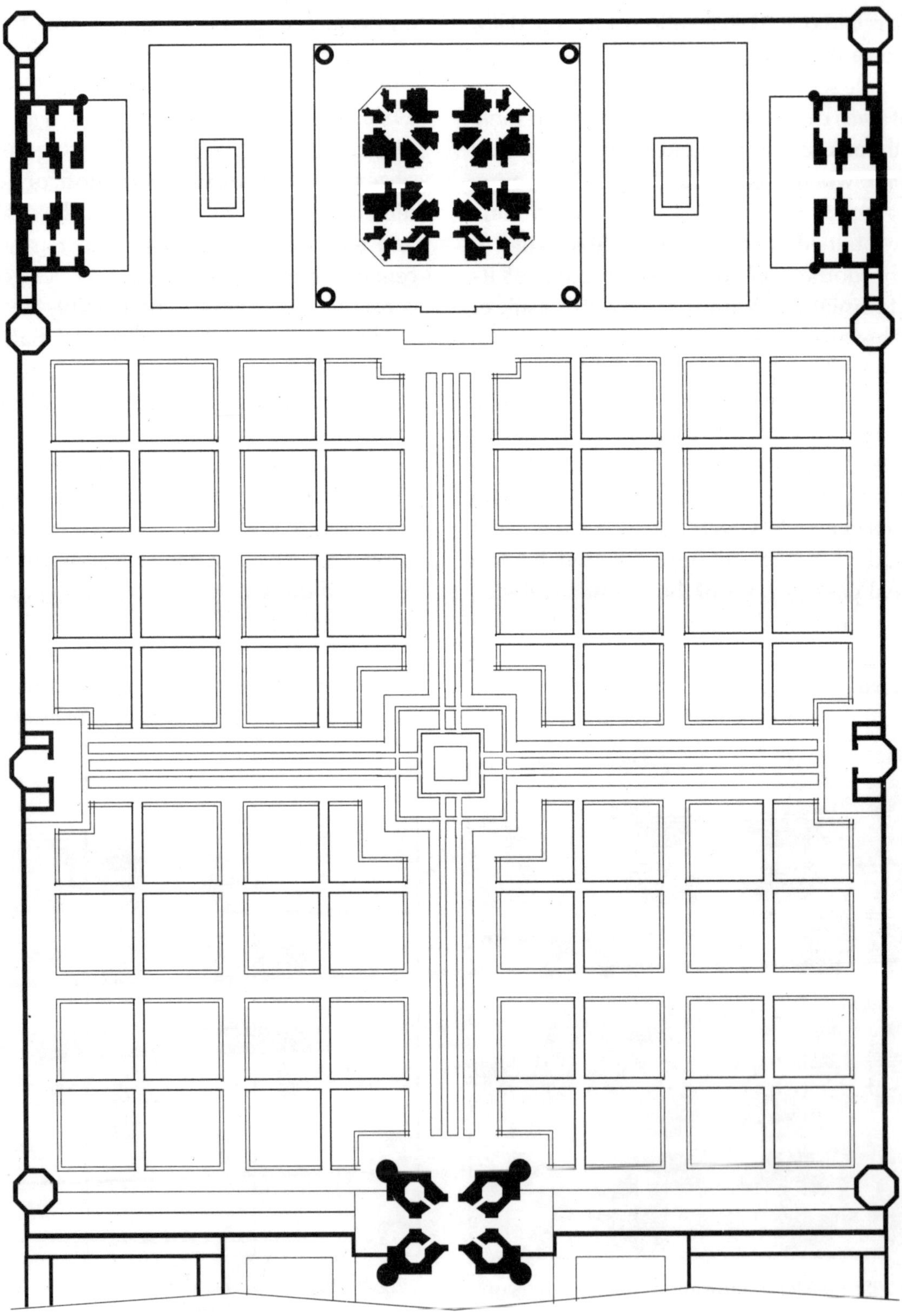

the *Tomb of Humayun*, the *Tomb of Akbar* and the *Tomb of Jahangir* all find the mausoleum in the center of a garden--i.e., a *chahar-bagh*. Not so with the *Taj Mahal*. Here the *chahar-bagh* is placed between the mausoleum and its imposing gate (See: **Appendix B**). What had, in the previously mentioned tombs, been a variation on the revolving paradisal cross axial arrangement (See: **Appendix B**) becomes horizontally axial. The mausoleum ensemble with its flanking mosque, to the left as one enters the enclosure, and resting pavilion to the right becomes the ultimate focus. Additionally, unlike the afore mentioned tombs within their gardens and each with four gates situated at the cardinal points, the *Taj Mahal* possesses but one entrance to the south. This focuses one's attention on the ensemble of tomb, mosque and resting pavilion. The other tombs did not have such an arrangement.

If the plan of *chahar-bagh*, in its simplest form, is placed over the plan of the *Taj Mahal* (See: **Plate 83**) interesting associations are noted. There is a close similarity between the walkways, both major cardinal walks and the intervening ways, with the major divisions of the interior passages. Of further note, it has been stated that there is a similarity between the arrangement of this ensemble with the *Shalimar Bagh* of Lahore (See: **Appendix B**).

The arrangement of mausoleum and masjid here is similar to the *rauza* that were common in Gujarat and Bijapur. However, traditionally a *rauza* consists of a tomb with a mosque which confront each other, and an intervening *birka* (See: *Ibrahim Rauza* and *Afzal Khan Rauza*). Additionally, the tomb and the mosque are of similar design and material, complementing each other. The *Taj Mahal* possesses a variation on this traditional *rauza* arrangement (See: Figure 199). Here the tomb confronts the *masjid* with its intervening *birka*. However, to the east of the mausoleum is another tank and a confronting pavilion. All of these elements are on a raised podium similar to that seen in the *Ibrahim Rauza*. Another variation is

Figure 197: *Taj Mahal*, with *Deshiya Mandala* over the elevation

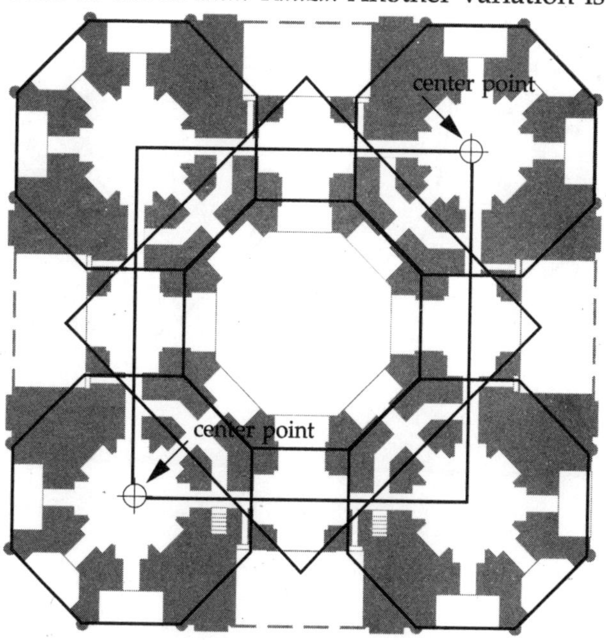

Figure 198: *Taj Mahal*, application of octagonal-square composition over tomb 2nd level plan

found in that the tomb is of gleaming white marble and the opposing *masjid* and pavilion are red sandstone. Again the focus is on the tomb, the resting place of Mumtaz Mahal. It is as if she had become the object of a cult focus. Certainly, she was such to Shah Jahan.

"Among sepulchral monuments . . . [the Taj Mahal] is without doubt the most brilliant and most successful achievement. It is here that the art capabilities of the Indian builders under the Mughals achieved the most beautiful expression."[88] Certainly, the *Taj Mahal* has engendered such superlatives as "the most brilliant and the most successful" or "the most beautiful." It is, without a doubt, one of the supreme architectural achievements in India. There are, however, others. Nonetheless, the *Taj Mahal's* beauty is compounded by its design and iconographic achievements as well.

The elements of design of the plan are not only interesting, but their interrelations are impressive. The *muthamman baghdadi* which is based upon five octagons; the *Paramashayika Mandala* as well as the circular *Manduka Mandala*; the relationship of the *chahar-bagh* to the mausoleum; and the similarity between the ensemble and the *Shalimar Bagh* all go together to weave an incredibly complex tapestry (See: **Appendix B**).

The *Taj Mahal's* ability to engender awe, aesthetic wonder and strong emotional responses, not to mention untold superlatives, is doubtless due to the fact that it has approached perfection. Not in just the particular but in the the total.

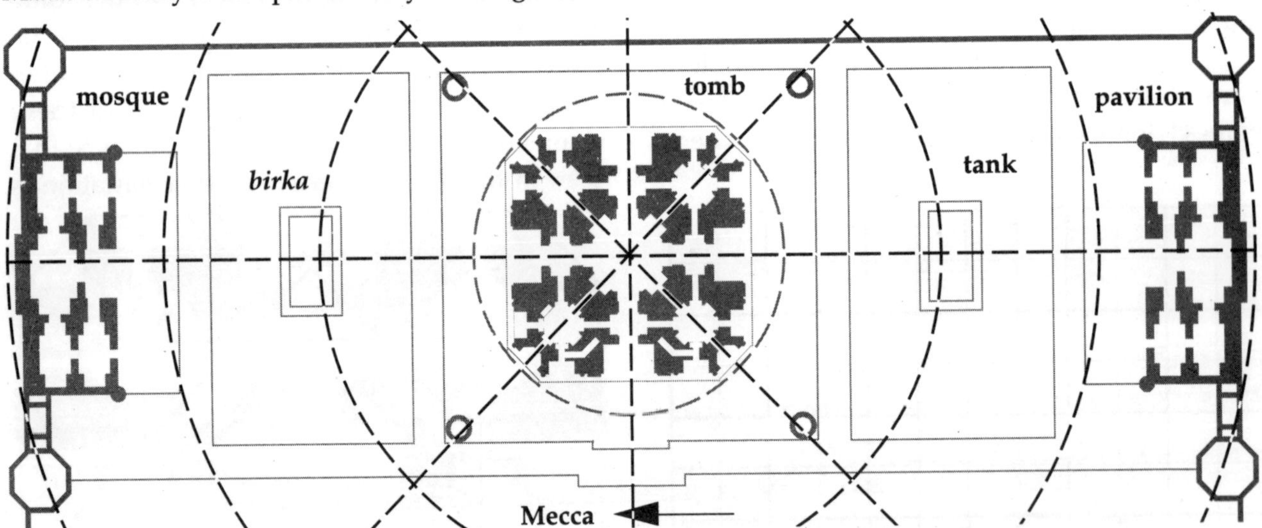

Figure 199: *Taj Mahal*, as *rauza*, and with circular *Manduka Mandala*

Plate 83

Taj Mahal (Plans of *chahar-bagh* & mausoleum)

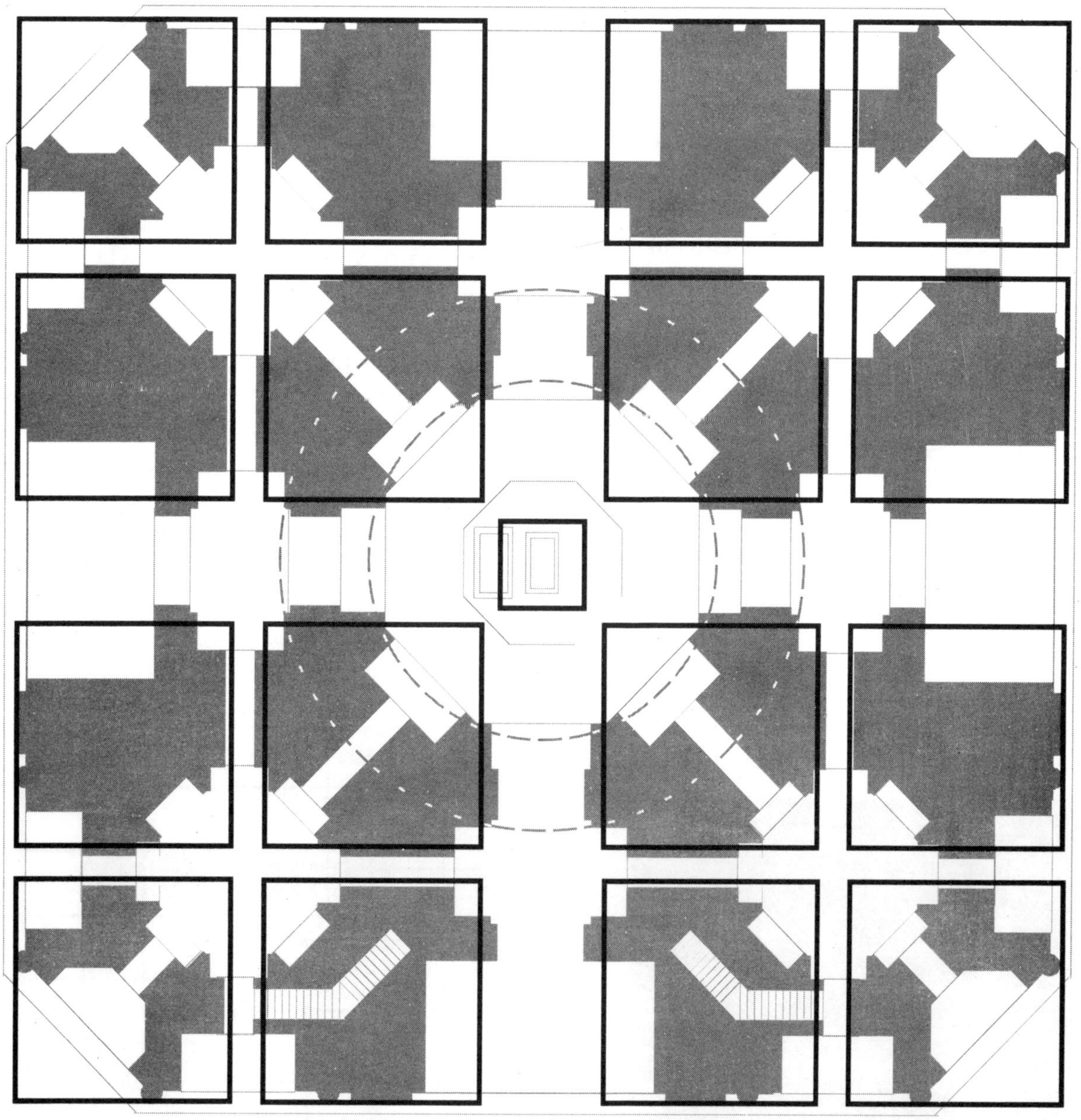

Afzal Khan Rauza

Bijapur, c. 1659 C.E.

'Abdullah Bhtari, known as Afzal Khan, was a bit of a folk legend in and around Bijapur in the seventeenth century. The *Sardar* of Bijapur, a general of Afghani descent in the armies of the Ali II, Sultan of Bijapur, and a man of immense size since he was often referred to as a "giant," Afzal Khan is best know for his defeat at the hands of the Maratha legend, Shivaji. Shivaji became a thorn in he paw of Bijapur and to the Mughal Emperor, Aurangzeb of Delhi alike. The Marathan killed Afzal Khan with a weapon fashioned like a tiger's paw--i.e., the *wagnatch*. Shivaji, then declared himself *raja* and had himself crowned shortly after Afzal Khan's defeat.

Afzal Khan, during his height, constructed his tomb at Bijapur. Unfortunately, he was not interred there, but, it is said, that his tomb lies close by the Pratapgarh Fort near Panchgani. Nonetheless this cenotaph is an apt reminder of this important general and is generally referred to as *Afzal Khan Rauza*.[89]

The *rauza* is typical of those found in Bijapur as well as Gujarat. It consists of a mausoleum and confronting *masjid* with a *birka* in the intervening space. The mausoleum is square with a central chamber and an ambulatory surrounding. Within this central space are found two cenotaphs. Neither is centered, but are found just inside the western door to this space. It must be assumed that if Afzal Khan's body had been interred below, a centralized cenotaph would have been utilized. The verandah is formed by five arches. The central arch and the two flanking arches are of the same dimension. The two arches outer arches are of a wider dimension. The confronting *masjid* is rectangular, *en plan*. What characterizes this *rauza* and sets it off from others of Bijapur is that the three elements appear as one (See: **Plates 84 & 85**). The space containing the *birka* is enclosed by an arcade on the north and south sides. Even though the mausoleum dominates, the whole is a pleasing solution.

As would be expected, the internal space of the mausoleum is of no mean amount (See: **Figure 200**). It would have allowed those who came to visit the grave of the famed general ample room to circumambulate.

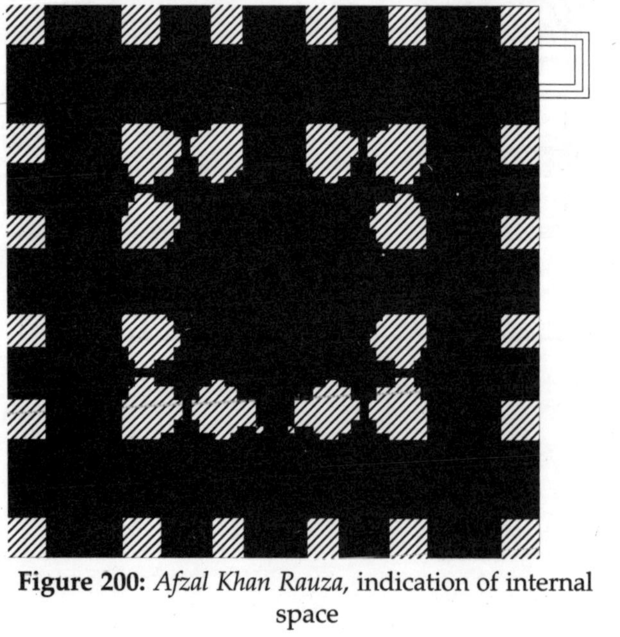

Figure 200: *Afzal Khan Rauza*, indication of internal space

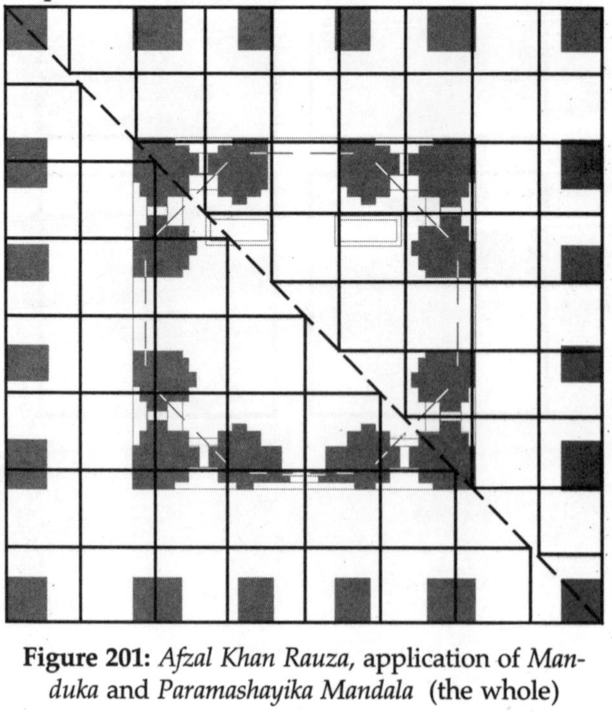

Figure 201: *Afzal Khan Rauza*, application of *Manduka* and *Paramashayika Mandala* (the whole)

Plate 84
Afzal Khan Rauza (Plan)

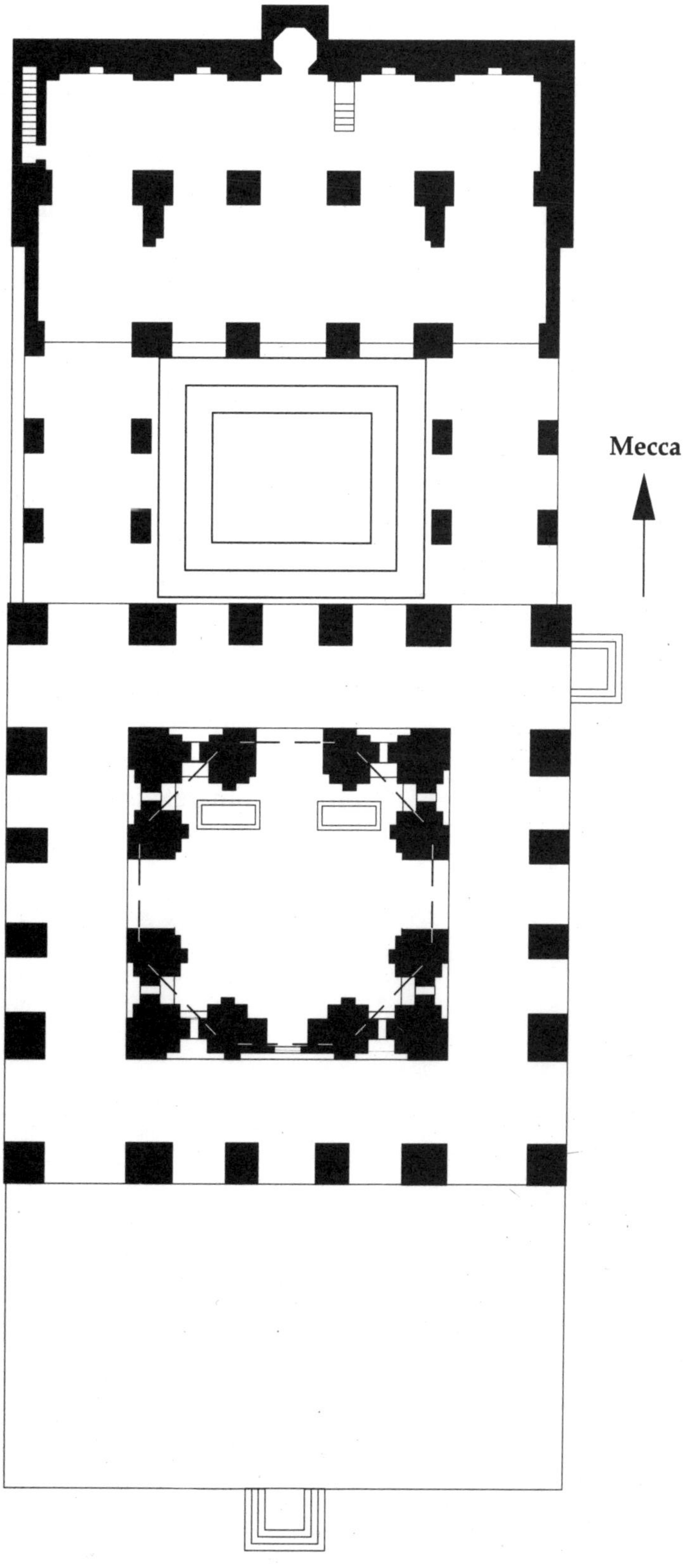

Afzal Khan Rauza (Continued)

As with the other mausolea of this study, a *Manduka Mandala* and a *Paramashayika Mandala* are superimposed over the plan of the tomb (See": **Figure 201**). In either case, there is much to recommend them. However, it appears that the *Paramashayika Mandala* is preferable.

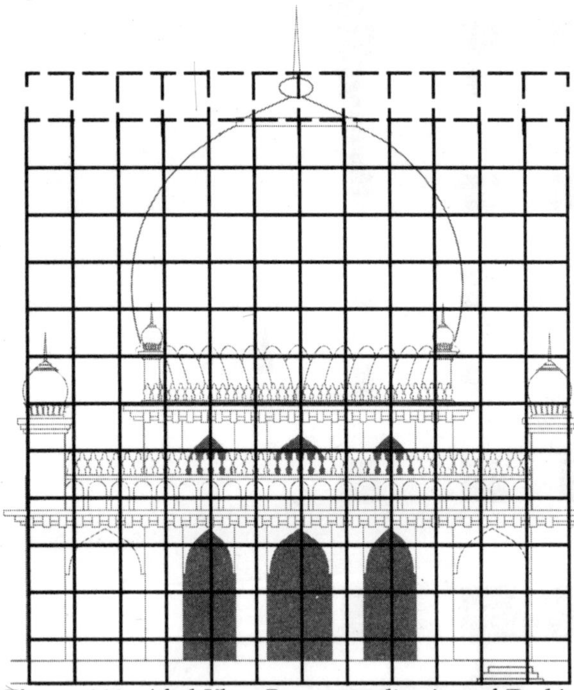

Figure 202: *Afzal Khan Rauza*, application of *Deshiya Mandala* over the elevation

Similarly, when a *Deshiya Mandala* is overlaid the elevation, a number of interesting conjunctions occur. The first level, including the merlons fall within the lower five ranks of *pada* (See: **Figure 202**). The top of the square extension from the central chamber and upon which the dome rests touches the sixth rank. The bulbous dome extends half way into the thirteen rank of *pada*. Therefore, it can be said that the proportions of the mausoleum of the *Afzal Khan Rauza* is 12:12.5.

The *Afzal Khan Rauza* is an important example of a mausoleum ensemble--i.e., *rauza*--constructed by a noble within the Bijapur Sultanate. Certainly, Afzal Khan's reputation was such as allow such a structure. What is of immense importance is the design of the *rauza* with the arcade on either side of the intervening *birka*. Its bulbous dome as well as those of the minarets is 'classical' Bijapuran. The *Afzal Khan Rauza* is a fitting cenotaph to one of Bijapur's greats.

Plate 85
Afzal Khan Rauza (Elevation & half plan)

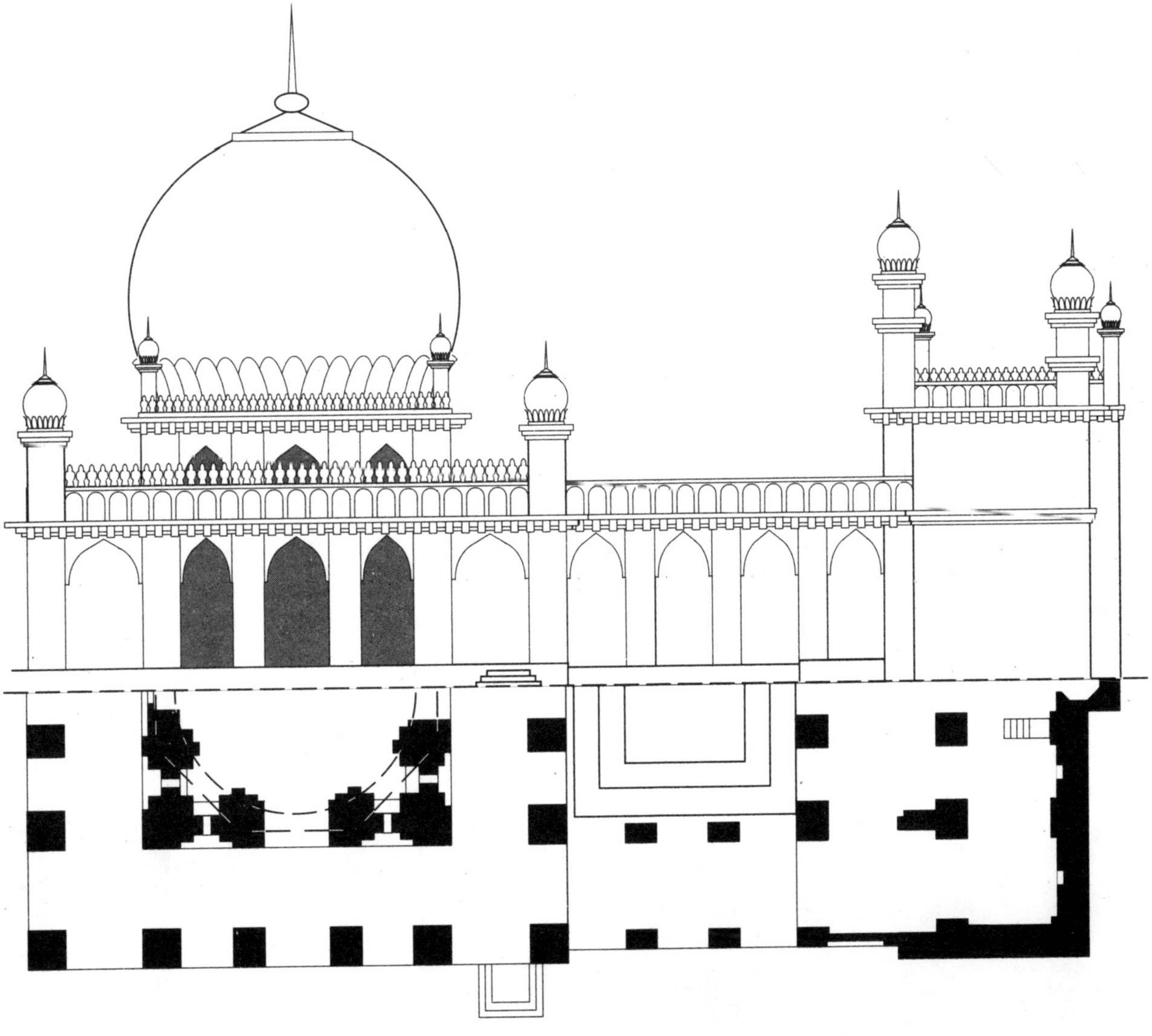

Shah Navaz Khan Rauza

Bijapur, c. 1659 C.E.

The *Shah Navaz Khan Rauza*[90] of Bijapur, is in one way typical of the Indo-Islamic tomb ensembles that were constructed outside of the major power center of imperial Delhi. Typical in that here, a square tomb--i.e., a **Type B-c** basic plan--confronts a rectangular mosque with an intervening *birka*. The 'scaled down' quality of the tomb gives evidence to the lesser status of Shah Navaz Khan, a Bijapur noble. On the other hand, the *rauza* is somewhat anomalous.

As with virtually all of the *rauza* ensembles, this group, as stated above consists of a tomb, a mosque which bracket the intervening *birka* or ablution tank, but here in three, distinct and descending widths--i.e. the mausoleum, *en plan*, is the largest element, the intervening plaza with its *birka* is next and the confronting mosque is the smallest. Whereas, the *Afzal Kkan Rauza, en plan*, provides nearly equal consideration and/or importance to the widths of these three elements (See: **Plate 84**), the *Ibrahim Rauza's* mausoleum and mosque also exhibit complementary widths with the small ablution centred within the raised podium which holds all three elements (See: **Plate 63**: & **Figure 153**) and places its emphasis squarely upon the mausoleum. Nonetheless, this unusual *rauza* is not without aesthetic or iconographic merit and interest.

As with the other Indo-Islamic tombs, the proportion of open space of the *Shah Navaz Khan Rauza* is considerable (See: **Figure 203**). Even in a tomb of obviously smaller scale, the interior space and the open arches allows for an easy flow in and out of the mausoleum.

In the application of a suitable *mandala*, it is apparent that the *Manduka Mandala* is the obvious choice (See: **Figure 204**). The supporting members (piers) fall within their respective *pada*. The cenotaph on the inner chamber and the tomb beneath fall within the *brahmásthana*, the normal two tiered arrangement. The same is true in the *Paramashayika Mandala*, but here the *marmas* are compromised.

The tomb structure of the *Shah Navaz Khan Rauza* is anomalous in its proportions. The

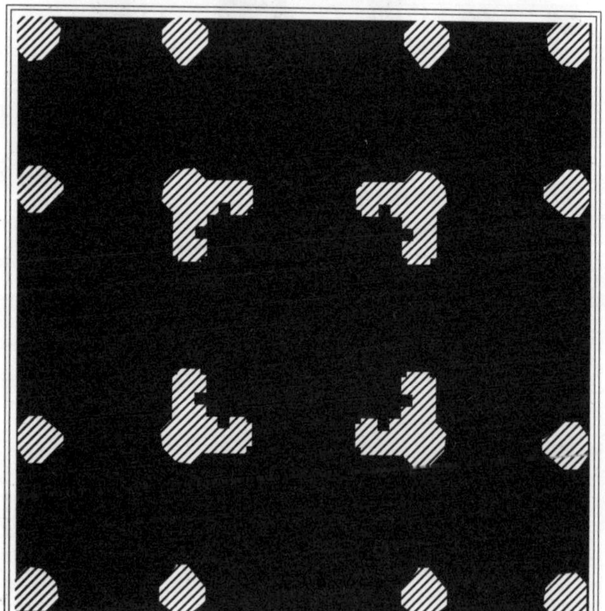

Figure 203: *Shah Navaz Khan Rauza*, indication of internal space

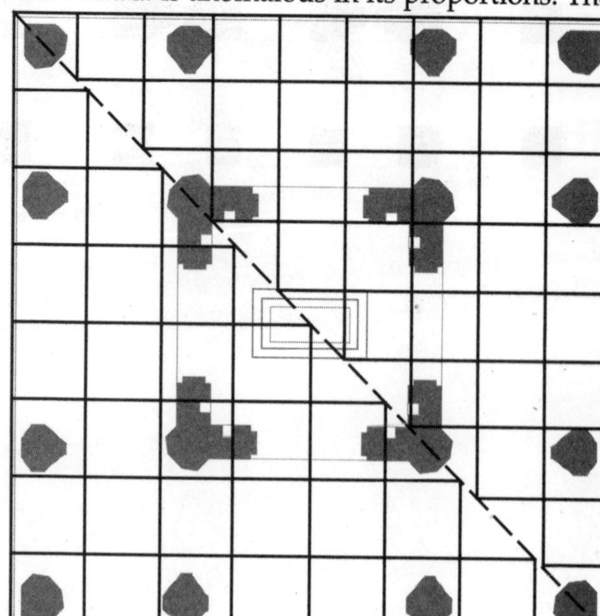

Figure 204: *Shah Navaz Khan Rauza*, application of *Manduka Mandala* and *Paramashayika Mandala*

Plate 86
Shah Navaz Khan Rauza (Plan)

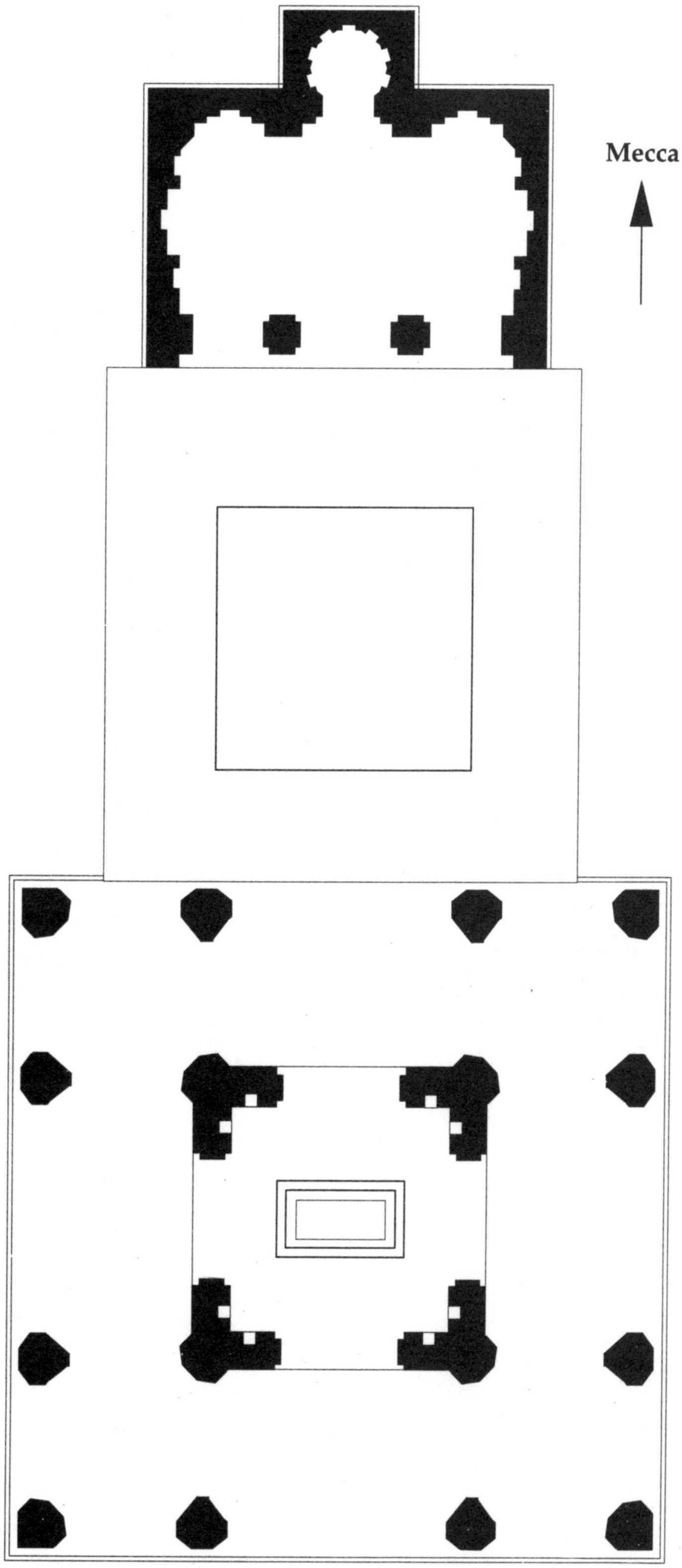

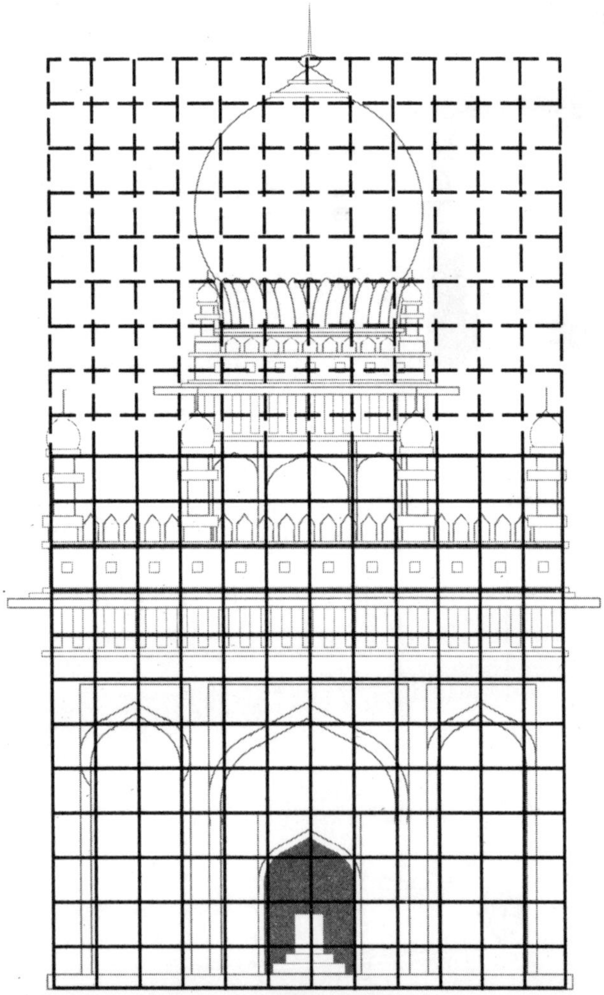

Figure 205: *Shah Navaz Rauza*, application of *Deshiya Mandala* over the elevation

lower block dominates the whole with its nearly cubic form--i.e., the height, including the parapet, is nearly equal to the width. A second, equally cubic form rising over the central space and lower mass, is set on the inner width of the verandah. This gives way to a cylindrical drum from which a typical 'Adil Shahi or Qutab Shahi-style dome juts upwards. The total visual effect is a structure in which the volumetric elements predominate vertically. The verticality of the *Shah Navaz Khan Rauza* is unremitting.

The height of the whole is approaching twice the width--i.e., 12:21 (See: **Figure 205**). Square Indo-Islamic tombs tend to be higher in proportion to their width than the octagonal tombs with their verandahs (See: **Appendix C, Plates 000** & **000**)--the exception being the *Tombs of Humayun, Akbar* and *Jahangir*. Normally, this proportion is within the 12:10 to 12:13 range (height to width). However, as in the tombs of the 'Adil Shahi and Qutab Shahi this extreme vertical proportion in comparison to other Indo-Islamic tombs is exaggerated.

Nonetheless, the *Shah Navaz Khan Rauza* is an interesting, albeit, abberant example of the tomb architecture found in Bijapur. It is the extreme in the predeliction towards the vertical and is parallel to few other mausolea in this aspect.

Plate 87

Shah Navaz Khan Rauza (Elevation & half plan)

Tomb of Ali 'Adil Shah II

Bijapur, c. 1672 C.E.

Ali 'Adil Shah II, father of Sikandar 'Adil Shah who was the last sultan-kings of Bijapur, is credited with the beginnings of his unfinished tomb. The *Tomb of Ali 'Adil Shah II*[91] built in the mold of the *Ibrahim Rauza* (c. 1615)--i.e., square, *en plan*, and with a double ambulatory: a **Type B-c** basic plan--harkens more to the Hindu temple models than to the traditional Indo-Islamic tombs which preceded it.

The square *Tomb of Ali 'Adil Shah II* rises from a high podium with a staircase to the south, fanning out dramatically as it reaches ground level. A minaret-like form punctuates the four corners of the main block. They are shorter than most of the minarets found in the 'Adil Shahi tombs, resembling an attenuated kiosk or chattri more than the soaring minarets as seen soaring at the corners of the *Ibrahim Rauza*, as well as other structures of Bijapur. Over the six central pillars on each of the four façades are shorter, thinner versions of the corner *manaras*.

As stated above, there is a double ambulatory surrounding the inner chamber. The bays of these aisles are equally paced, reflecting the spacing of the engaged columns of the central chamber. Within this central, squared space a cenotaph rests upon an elevated dais, focusing the viewers attention upon this iconic form. The original four entrances into this central area have been modified and a *mikhrab* was constructed in the opening of the western portal. This central area is surmounted by a dome. Cousens asserts through his illustration[92] that unlike the other domes normally associated with a number of the 'Adil Shahi and Qutab Shahi tombs--i.e., the exception being *Gol Gumbaz*--this dome that Cousens suggests is more traditional.[93] Like the *Gol Gumbaz*, this would see the dome as nearly hemispherical in its elevation rather than the two-thirds or three-quarter spherical dome-forms often associated with these sultanates. This does raise some concerns regarding this "restored elevation" (See: **Appendix C, Plate 144,** *Tomb of Ali 'Adil Shah II* [Cousen's elevation (top) & proposed elevation (bottom)]).

The internal space within this

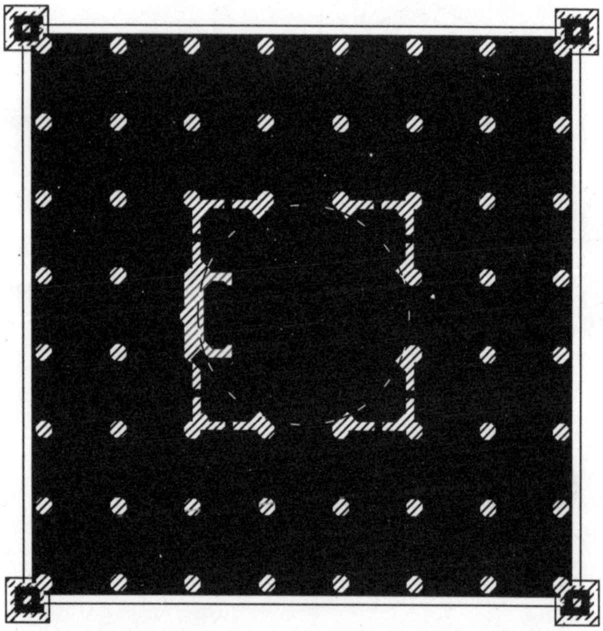

Figure 206: *Tomb of Ali II*, indication of internal space

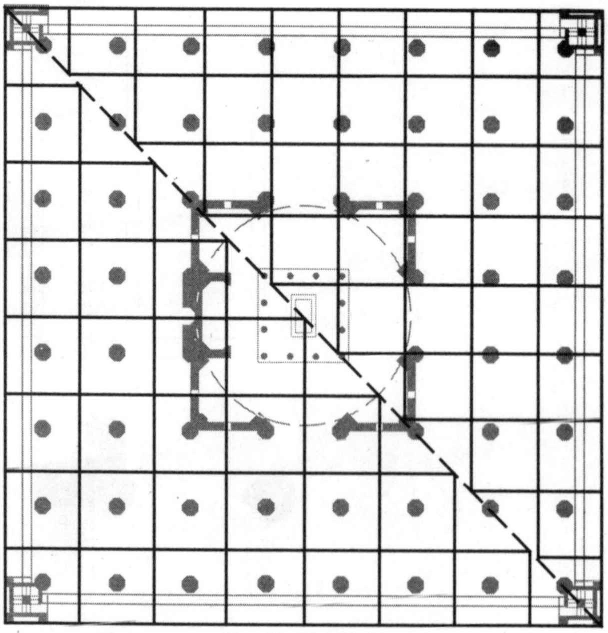

Figure 207: *Tomb of Ali II*, application of *Manduka Mandala* and *Paramashayika Mandala*

Plate 88
Tomb of Ali 'Adil Shah *II* (Plan)

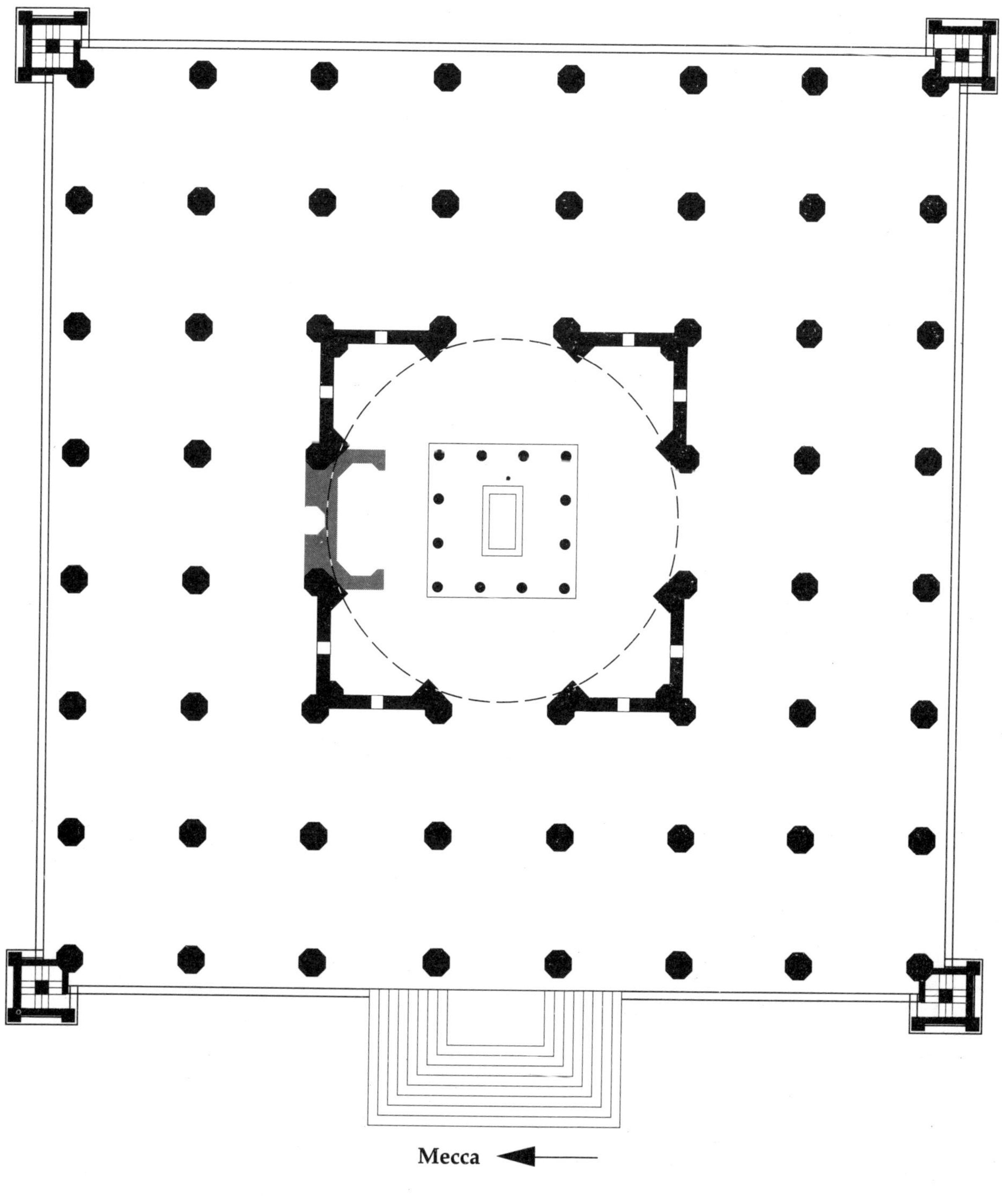

mausoleum is, proportionally, immense (See: **Figure 206**). In part, the overwhelming interior space is due to the utilization of a double aisle and is similar in that respect to the earlier *Ibrahim Rauza*.

In the application of a *Manduka Mandala* and/or a *Paramashayika Mandala*, it is apparent that the former is most applicable (See: **Figure 207**). The dais with the cenotaph rests within the *brahmásthana*. The second rank of deities holds the inner chamber while the next two ranks each hold one of the columns of the double aisle in single *padas*. Since there are eight piers per face, this is to be expected.

When superimposing a *Deshiya Mandala* over the elevation of the *Tomb of Ali 'Adil Shah II*, certain interesting conjunctions occur (See: **Figures 208 & 209**). The podium rests within the first rank of *pada*. The third rank defines the lower edge of the *chajja* and the fourth rank of *pada* lies along the bottom edge of the square extension's lower decorative band. The fifth rank defines the transition from the square extension to the springing of the dome. The dome extends, slightly into the eight rank. Therefore, this elevation possesses the proportions of 12:7.25. On the other hand, if the proposed elevation is considered, it is seen that the proportion is increased by one rank of *pada*, creating the proportion of 12:8.25.

The *Tomb of Ali 'Adil Shah II*, the last of the major tombs erected by and/or for the Sultans of Bijapur, indicates many of the stylistic traditions of the 'Adil Shahi and also of the neighboring Qutab Shahi of Golconda. It is a fitting structure to the penultimate ruler of this vital sultanate.

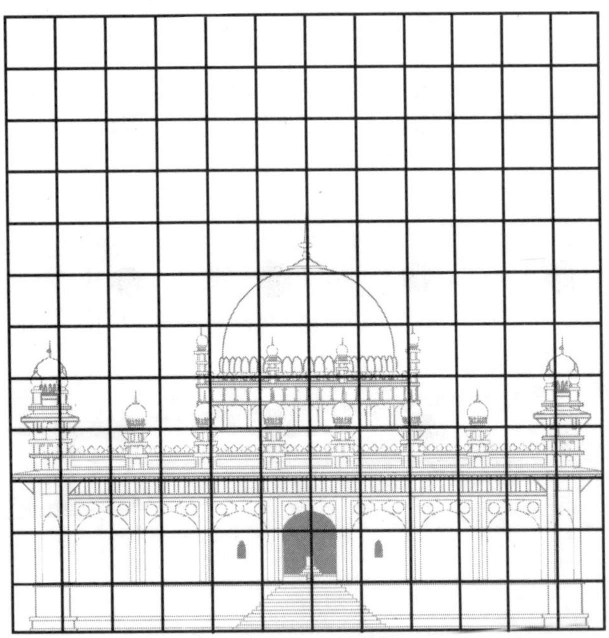

Figure 208: *Tomb of Ali II*, application of *Deshiya Mandala* over Cousen's elevation

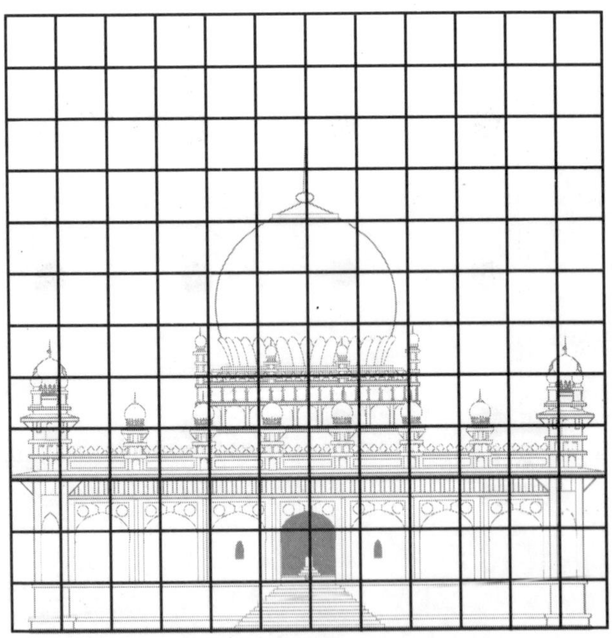

Figure 209: *Tomb of Ali II*, application of *Deshiya Mandala* over proposed elevation

Plate 89
Tomb of Ali 'Adil Shah II (Elevation [suggested] & half plan)

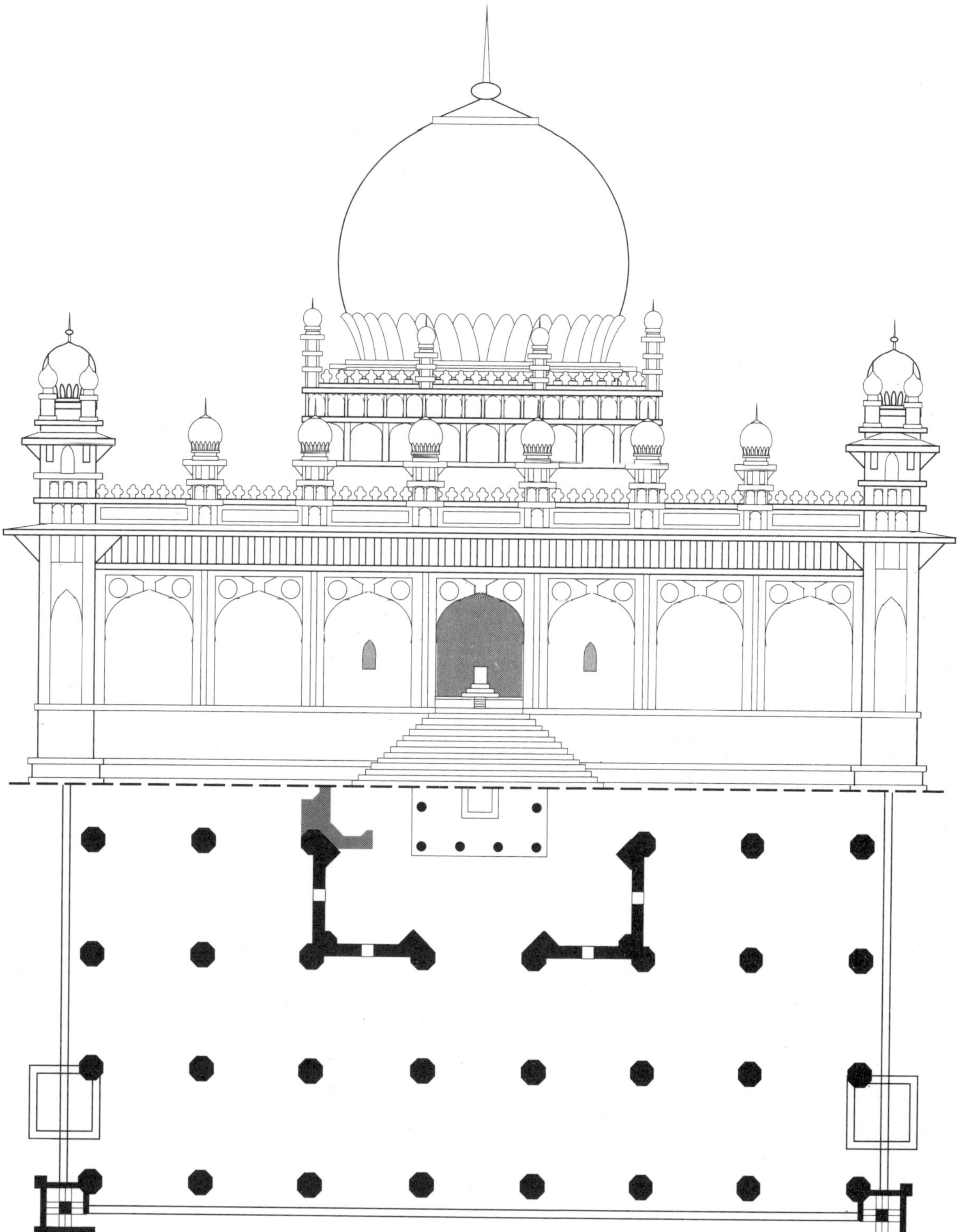

Tomb of Safdar Jang

Delhi, c. 1754 C.E.

Born in Persia, Abul Mansoor Muhammad Muqueem (aka: Mirza Muquim Abul Mansur Khan) had been given the title *Safdar Jang* by the Emperor Muhammad Shah. Upon the death of Muhammad Shah he came to Delhi, had himself appointed the Prime Minister to Mohammed Shah's son, Alam Shah, and in effect ruled the empire in his place. The *Tomb of Safdar Jang* is considered to be the last of the great Mughal mausolea, the architectural last gasp of that great dynasty.

Abul Mansoor Muhammad Muqueem was the governor or *Nawab* of Awadh as well as the Prime Minister, or *Wazir* under the reign of Nasir-ud-din Muhammad Shah. His other honors included: the *Faujdar* of Narnaul, the *Meer-e-Atash*, the governorship of Kashmir as well as the afore mentioned *Safdar Jang* and *Wazir*. Indeed he was an honored and powerful courtier. The *Safdar Jang* died in 1754, and was transported from Faizabad to Delhi where his son Shuja al-Daula, the Nawab of Awadh, had constructed this lavish tomb. The *Safdar Jang* was, apparently, more comfortable in Delhi than his provincial capital and the mausoleum his son had constructed not only mirrored the *Safdar Jang's* power and position, it also reflected the incredible wealth of Awadh.

The *Tomb of Safdar Jang*[94] is square, *en plan*--i.e., a **Type C-b** basic plan--with prominent corner towers and four entrances. The mausoleum rests upon a developed podium and within a rather eccentric *chahar-bagh* (See: **Plate 92**; see also: **Appendix B**). In this arrangement, it is seen by many as based upon the *Tomb of Humayun*. However, many of the elevational elements are such as to emphasize the vertical, one of the features that many find disconcerting in this mausoleum.

The internal space is similar but somewhat expanded in comparison to that found in the *Tomb of Humayun* and the *Taj Mahal* (See: **Figure 210**). The central space is also, proportionally, larger than the two just mentioned.

In considering a *mandala* that is suitable

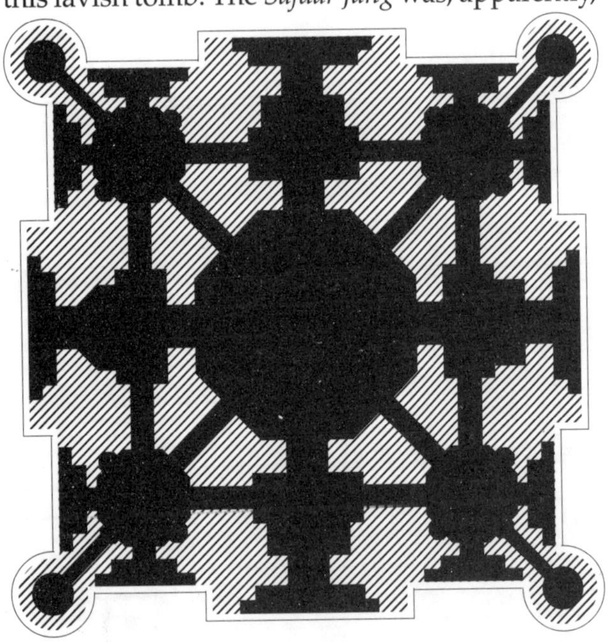

Figure 210: *Tomb of Safdar Jang*, indication of internal space

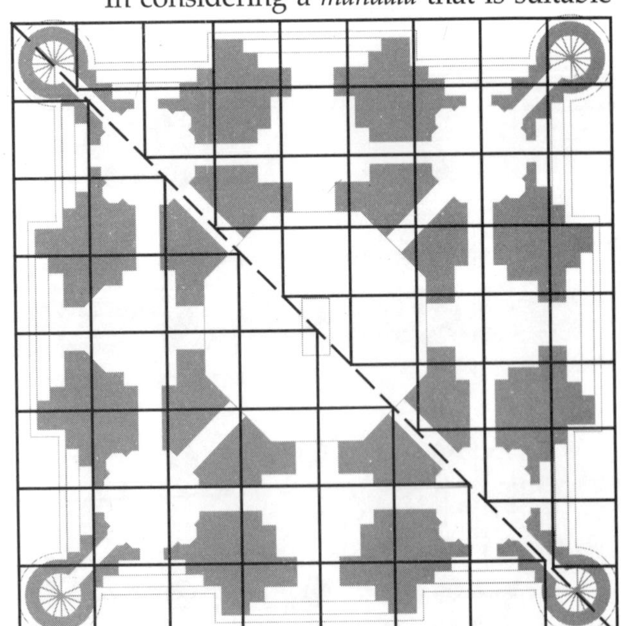

Figure 211: *Tomb of Safdar Jang*, application of *Manduka Mandala* and *Paramashayika Mandala*

Plate 90
Tomb of Safdar Jang (Plan)

for the *Tomb of Safdar Jang,* both the *Manduka Mandala* and the *Paramashayika Mandala* are considered (See: **Figure 211**). It appears that the *Paramashayika Mandala* is the preferred form. It is to be noted that the *brahmásthana* falls short of including the whole of the central space, however the.surrounding corridors (Ind.: *pradakshinapatha*) are bisected by the line between the second and third ranks and files of *pada*.

The application of a *Deshiya Mandala* over the elevation indicates the vertical nature of the *Tomb of Safdar Jang* (See: **Figure 212**). The first storey falls within the lower three ranks of *pada,* while the whole block lies within the lower six ranks. The *dargah* is to be found within the four central files. The dome, minus the finial fals within twelve ranks. Therefore, it can be said that the proportion of the *Tomb of Safdar Jang* is 12:12. This proportion places this mausoleum in the catagory of one of the taller, proportionally, mausolea.

Finally, the *chahar-bagh* surrounding the mausoleum and its podium is a bit eccentric (See: **Plate 92**). The nine-fold plan that is seen to be applicable to a number of other mausolea and their *chahar-bags*--e.g., the *Tomb of Humayun,* the *Tomb of Akbar,* the *Tomb of Jahangir* and the *Taj Mahal*--falls short of giving an acceptable result to the *Tomb of Safdar Jang* or its *chahar-bagh* (See: **Figure 212** [dashes]). On the other hand, if the nine-fold plan is applied to the traditional form of the *chahar-bagh*--i.e., excluding the outer, half-width *baghs*--the result is somewhat more acceptable (See: **Figure 213**[dots]; & **Plate 92** [bottom]).

A comparison of the *Tomb of Safdar Jang* to the main block of the *Taj Mahal* indicates that the latter is proportionally considerably taller (See solid line square: **Figure 214**). Even when the whole is considered, the *Taj Mahal* is proportionally taller. It would seem, therefore, that the criticism of "verticality" that is attached to this mausoleum must be tempered. However, it must be admitted that the vertical elements that are present in the *Tomb of Safdar Jang* are tempered by horizontal elements in the *Taj Mahal,* thereby

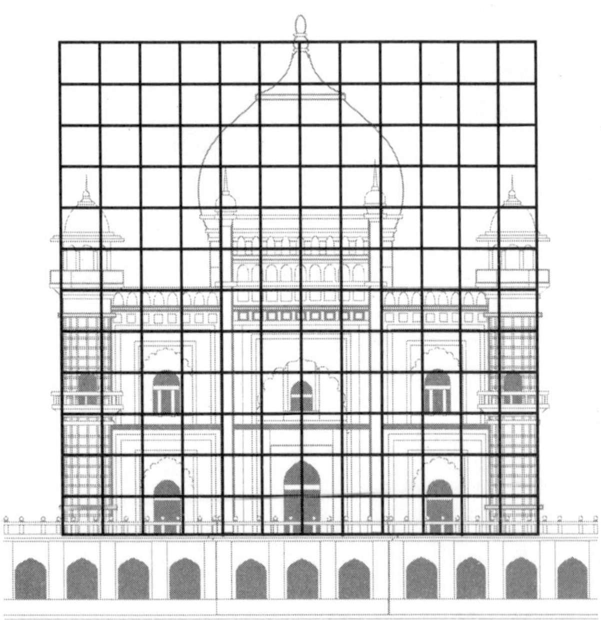

Figure 212: *Tomb of Safdar Jang,* application of *Deshiya Mandala* over the elevation

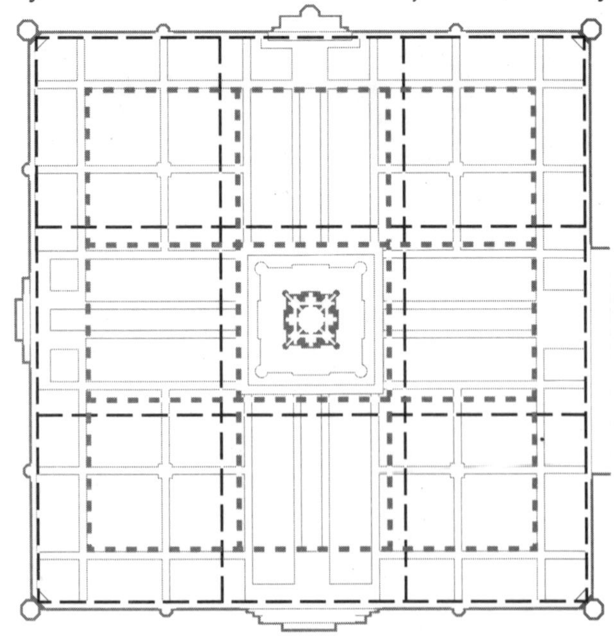

Figure 213: *Tomb of Safdar Jang,* ensemble with two applications of *nine-fold plan*

Plate 91
Tomb of Safdar Jang (Elevation with podium & half plan)

mitigating its extreme verticality. In addition, one may include the corner minarets of the *Taj Mahal's* podium as a palliation to this state.

The *Tomb of Safdar Jang* may be an anomaly when compared to the tombs of the Great Mughals, however, it is, nonetheless, an edifice of some stature and consequence in the *oeuvre* of Indo-Islamic architecture. It stands as a hallmark to the wealth and power that even lesser Mughal rulers possessed. As the last gasp it presents the depth, breadth and scope of size and concept that the ruling Islamic Indians had lavished on their abodes for the deceased.

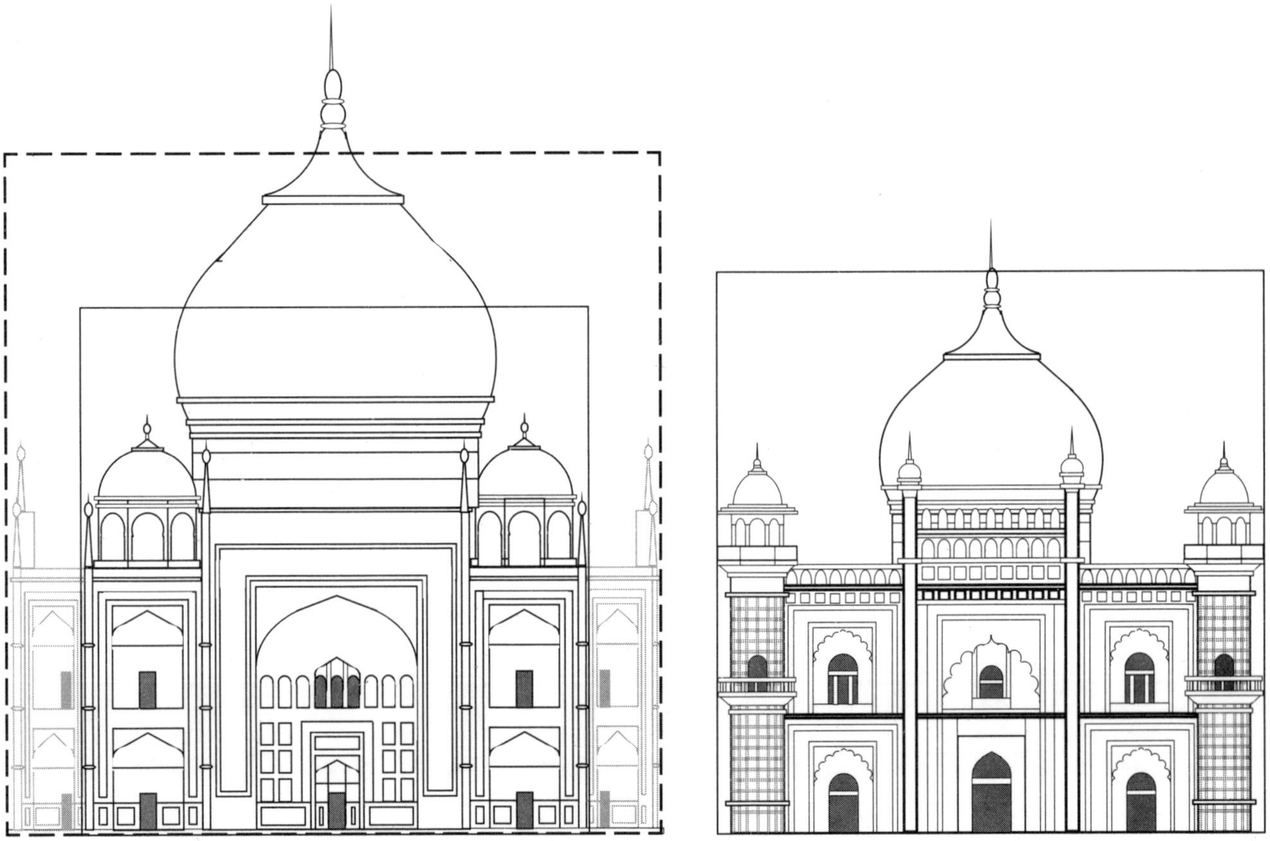

Figure 214: *Taj Mahal* & the *Tomb of Safdar Jang*, indicating the spatial relationships and proportions of main façades

Plate 92

Tomb of Safdar Jang

(Ensemble with *Pitha Mandala* [u.l.], *Ugrapitha Mandala* [u.r.] & *Deshiya Mandala* [bottom])

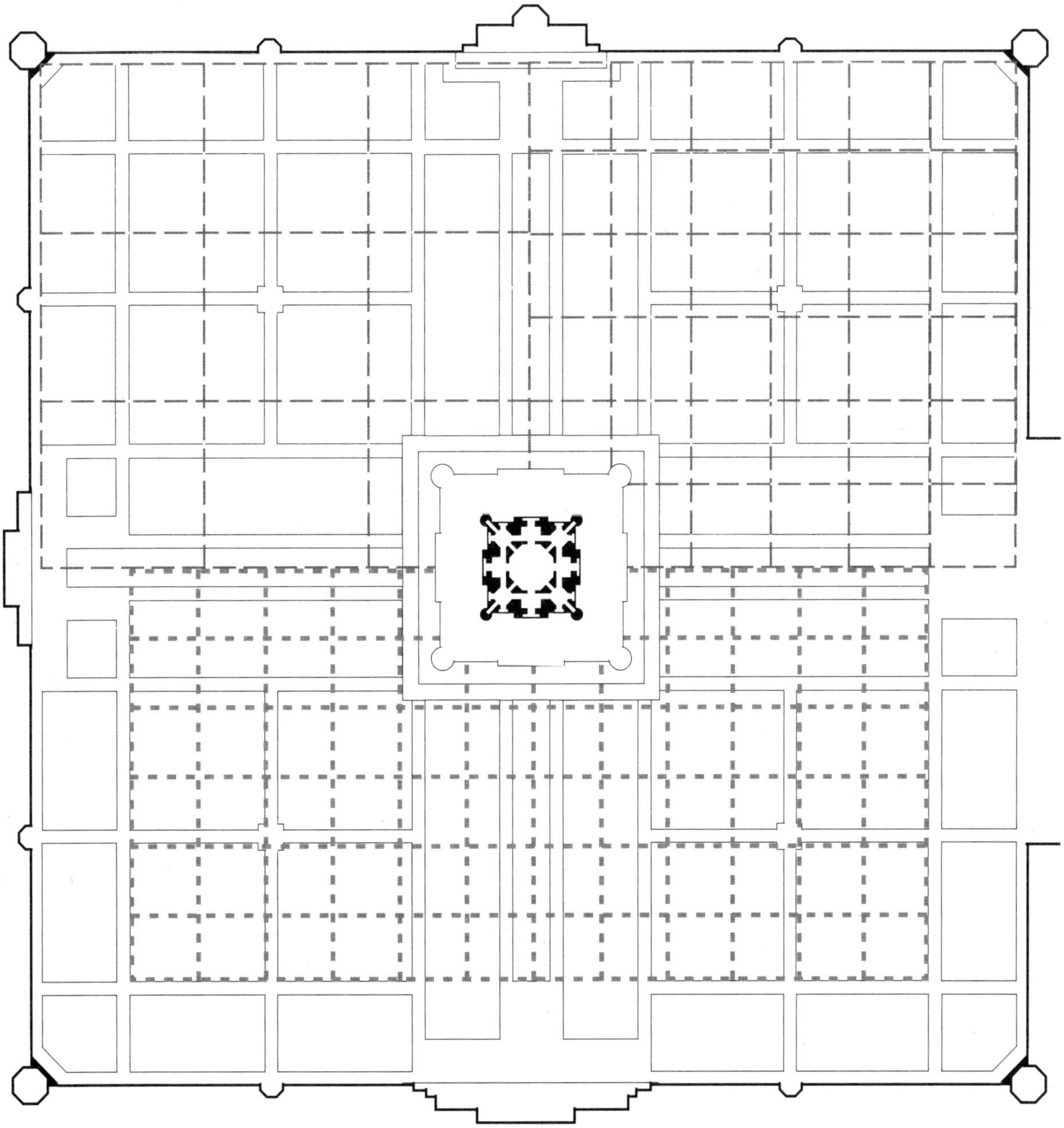

Conclusions

Islam the newest of the great worlds religions is also the least known in the west. Other than the *Taj Mahal*, or perhaps the *Great Mosque* at Cordoba, or the *Alhambra* at Granada, little has been known in the west of the glories of Islamic architecture. A Christian centered Eurocentric miasma has shrouded the great and aesthetically astounding structures of the Islamic world.

There are the great mosques--e.g., the *Great Mosque* of Samarra, the *Selimiye Cami* of Edirne, the *Umayyad Great Mosque* at Damascus, the *Mosque of Al-Hakim* at Cairo, the *Giralda* of the *Great Mosque* of Seville, the *Masjid-i-Shah* of Isfahan, or the *Masjid Badshahi* at Lahore--the important sites of learning--e.g., the *Madrasa-i Shah* at Isfahan, the *Barquqiyya* near Cairo, the *Bu-'inaniyya Madrasa* of Fez, the *Zahiriyya Madrasa* of Damascus, the *Madrasa of Sultan Ahmet* at Istanbul, or the *Madrasa of 'Abdal-Aziz Khan* at Bukhara--and the magnificent and lavish palaces--e.g., the fabulous *Topkapi Palace* of Istanbul, the *Qasr al-Jass* at Samarra, the *Palace of the Shorvan Shahs* at Baku, the *Shahjahanabad* of Delhi, or the *'Azman Palace* of Damascus--all of which suffer from lack of exposure in the West.

Few major world religions provide burial structures as magnificent or as developed as Islam. Indeed, Islamic India stands as a beacon in the Muslim world for its unparalleled brilliance in its profusion of mausolea. Truly, few other cultures can approach Islamic India in the quantity and quality of their funerary structures.

Yet with all their numbers there are two basic plans--i.e., square and octagonal--with five variations. The first basic plan is the canopy tomb--i.e., the **Type A** plan noted on p. xxii. This plan is open--i.e., a low base or podium with a series of pillars or piers in either a square or octagonal configuration and all topped by a roof, often with a dome. The last of the important canopy tombs were constructed in the late Fifteenth Century C.E., and are to be found outside of the imperial center of Delhi. Examples of the **Type A** plan are: 1) the *Tomb of Rani Rupmati*, Ahmadabad (**Plate 20**); 2) the *Sayyid Usman Rauza*, Usmanapur (**Plate 24**); and 3) the *Tomb of Mubarak Sayyid*, Mahmudabad (**Plate 29**).

By far the most prevalent plan is the square--i.e., the **Type B** plan noted on p. xxiii. This plan consists of a square block which encloses a square chamber in which the cenotaph rests that is roofed and surmounted by a dome. Often there appears a *ratha*--i.e., an extension of the four walls--giving this type of mausoleum the appearance of the Hindu *triratha* plan. A variation on this square plan is one in which the square is surrounded by an arcade of pillars or piers or, in some cases a double arcade, the latter creating two aisles. The square **Type B** plan is to be found throughout the history of Indo-Islamic India in one form or another. The simplest **Type B** plans--i.e., noted on p. xxiii as: **a-d**--are: 1) the *Tomb of Sultan Iltutmish*, Delhi (**Plate 5**); 2) *Tomb of Ghiyas-ud-din Tughluq I*, Tughluqabad (**Plate 9**); 3) the *Tomb of Firuz Shah Tughluq*, Delhi (**Plate 14**); 4) *Tomb of Hushang Shah*, Mandu (**Plate 22**); 5) the *Tomb of Chotte Khan Ka Gunbad*, Delhi (**Plate 27**); and 6) the *Tomb of Khan Khanan*, Delhi (**Plate 68**). Examples of **Type B** plan in which the square block is surrounded by one row of pillars are: 1) the *Tomb of Mohammed Quli Qutub Shah*, Golconda (**Plate 59**); 2) the *Tomb of Iftikhar Khan*, Chunar (**Plate 64**); 3) the *Afzal Khan Rauza*, Bijapur (**Plate 84**); and 4) the *Shah Navaz Khan Rauza*, Bijapur (**Plate

Conclusions (Continued)

86); followed by the **Type B** plan in which the square block is surrounded by two rows of pillars are: 5) the *Ibrahim Rausa*, Bijapur (**Plate 61**); and 6) the *Tomb of Ali 'Adil Shah II*, Bijapur (Plate 88).

The **Type C** plan--noted on p. xxiii--is essentially square in appearance, and, therefore, related to the previous. The central enclosed chamber is square or octagonal, sometimes encircled by pillars or piers, but with a significant addition--prominent corner towers. These towers are often surmounted with a chatri or a domed *kiosk* which is either extend at a 45^0 angle from the corners (**Type C-a** & **b**) or completely incorporated into a square plan (**Type C-c**). The latter is true, particularly where an arcaded verandah is found. Examples of the **Type C-a** & **b** plan are: 1) the *Tomb of Sultan Ghari*, Delhi (**Plate 3**); 2) the *Tomb of Jalau-ud-din Mohammad Shah* (*Eklakhi*), Pandua (**Plate 16**); 3) the *Tomb of Muhammad Ghaus*, Gwalior (**Plate 49**); 4) the *Tomb of Akbar*, Sikandra (**Plate 51**); 5) the *Tomb of Jahangir*, Lahore (**Plate 70**); 6) the *Gol Gumbaz*, Bijapur (**Plate 73**); 7) the *Tomb of Jahan Begum*, Ainapur (**Plate 75**); 8) the *Tomb of I'timad-ud-daula*, Agra (**Plate 76**); and 9) the *Tomb of Safdar Jang*, Delhi (**Plate 90**); while an example of **Type C-c** is to be found in the *Tomb of Shah Daulat*, Maner (**Plate 66**). Although the latter--i.e., *Tomb of Shah Daulat*--may be also considered as an example of **Type B-c**.

Types **B & C** predominate from the mid Sixteenth Century C.E. onward, particularly in the thirty-six examples considered in this study. Certainly, the square-basis tomb appears to have been the preferred form of the Mughals and those that followed. However, prior to the Timurud Dynasty, the **Type D**--i.e., the octagonal model was most popular especially for the Sayyid and Lodi Dynasties who looked upon this shape as applicable to royal burial and noted on p. xxiv. The **Type D** generally consists of an octagonal block with an octagonal chamber, although early tombs possessed a square chamber as seen in: the *Tomb No. 36*, Delhi (**Plate 1**). This simplest of octagonal mausoleum--i.e., the **Type D-a**--was supplanted by the **Type D-b** & **c** in which an arcade of pillars or piers surrounded the octagonal block. In many instances chatri or domes punctuated the roof of this ambulatory (Ind.: *pradakshinapatha*) and the bock would be covered by a dome. Examples of the **Type D-b** & **c** plan are: 1) the *Tomb of Khan-i Jihan Tilangani*, Delhi (**Plate 12**); 2) the *Tomb of Mubarak Shah Sayyid*, Delhi (**Plate 18**); 3) the *Tomb of Sikandar Lodi*, Delhi (**Plate 31**); 4) the *Tomb of Hasan Khan Sur*, Saseram (**Plate 33**); 5) the *Tomb of Sher Shah*, Saseram (**Plate 35**); 6) the *Tomb of Isa Khan Niyazi*, Delhi (**Plate 38**); 7); and the *Tomb of Adham Khan*, Delhi (**Plate 41**). The latter mausoleum--i.e., the *Tomb of Adham Khan*--built in 1562 is the last of the major mausoleums of this **Type**, and the most unusual. One other octagonal tomb has been considered herein as it is truly unique: the *Tomb of Shah Rukn-i 'Alam*, Multan (**Plate 7**). This tomb is octagonal, but with circular, battered, tapered towers at the eight corners. It is to be noted that, whereas, the Sayyid and Lodi employed the octagon for royal use, the Timurud Period saw its use exclusively for nobles--i.e, the *Tomb of Hasan Khan Sur*, the *Tomb of Isa Khan Niyazi*, and the *Tomb of Adham Khan*. The *Tomb of Sher Shah* at Saseram, is an exception. But, then the reign of the Suri was but a brief interlude in the Mughal or Timurud Period.

Finally, the tomb in which the corners have been sheared off--i.e., the *muthamman baghdadi* type--is the last to be considered. This, the **Type E**, is seen by many as the apogee of Mughal tomb architectural development and noted on p. xxiv. This **Type** consists of a combination of square and octagonal forms--i.e., a central block with four overlapping blocks at the intercardinal points--the hallmark being the "sheared off" outer corners of the outer block or blocks. The main, central block is surmounted by a large dome over the central chamber and often possesses corner blocks and/or chambers also surmounted by *chatri* or *kiosks*. Examples of the **Type E** plan are: 1) the *Tomb of Humayun*, Delhi (**Plate 43**); and 2) the *Tomb of Hazrat Mumtaz-uz-Zamani* better known as the *Taj Mahal*, Agra (**Plate 79**).

The glory of these five **Types** is not in their strict adherence to a standard, but in their variations on the standards not only en plan, but also in their elevations. The proliferation of *chatri* or *kiosks* seen on the *Tomb of Hasan Khan Sur* and his son's tomb, the *Tomb of Sher Shah*, or the total lack thereof in the *Tomb of Adham Khan* creates wondrous examples of the aesthetic variations employed. The pleasure palaces of the nobles, the palatial *kiosks* or *serai* (See: **Appendix C, Plates 124-126**) find their counterparts, their representation and funereal fulfillment in the *Tomb of Mohammad Ghaus* and the *Tomb of Shah Daulat*. If, as believed by the Muslims, that Paradise is a place of pleasure and delight, then the providing for the deceased an earthly representation of a palace of pleasure would seem quite appropriate. Certainly it offers to the pilgrims a clear representation of the rewards in the afterlife. The varieties of domes is also noteworthy. From the low domes as exemplified in the *Tomb of Sultan Iltutmish* or the *Tomb Khan-i Jihan Tilangani*, or the obviously hemispherical domes as seen in the *Tomb of Sikandar Lodi* and the *Tomb of Adham Khan*, or Moorish domes as represented in the *Tomb of Humayun* or the *Tomb of Khan Khanan*, or even the bulbous domes of the 'Adil Shahi and Qutub Shahi as seen in the *Tomb of Mohammed Quli Qutub Shahi* and the *Shah Navaz Khan Rauza*, one is aware not only of regional variations, but variations within a region. Not only the dome shapes, but also the form of the domes finds vast differences within Islamic India. The single shell early domes of India are experimented upon in shape; the dome of the *Tomb of Sikandar Lodi* introduces the first double shelled dome (See: **Appendix C, Plates 128-133**); and the non-utilitarian, sculptural domes of the *Ibrahim Rauza* and the *Taj Mahal* complete the syzygy with the domes of *Tomb of Sultan Iltutmish* or the *Tomb Khan-i Jihan Tilangani*. Then, the low, squat aspects of the *Tomb of Sultan Ghari* or the *Tomb of Khan-i Jihan Tilangani* find their opposites in the distinctly vertical character of the *Tomb of Mohammed Quli Qutub Shah* and the mausoleum of the *Shah Navaz Khan Rauza*.

A distinction found in the Indo-Islamic tombs is the two tiered arrangement of the cenotaph on the main, ground floor over the sarcophagus in the crypt below. The use of a cenotaph, a false sarcophagus is an iconic emblem of Islamic tombs. This may be because of the fact that a number of early Islamic tombs, particularly those in which important saints were buried became important pilgrimage sites. Although not *Qur'anic*, Muslims believed that one could achieve a kind of spiritual merit applicable to the afterlife by visiting the burial sites of saints and other holy personages. It was believed that the *baraka*, a potent spiritual power, that surrounded or was exuded by a saint during his lifetime, somehow was preserved in death and could effect a and influence anyone who was in close proximity to this force. Such beliefs are not exclusively Islamic. The great pilgrimage sites of Christianity--e.g., the *Cathedral* of Santiago de Compastella, the *Cathedral* of Canterbury, *San Pietro* of Rome and *Site of the Birth of Christ* in Bethlehem--were visited in order to achieve some sort of benefit or merit. Nonetheless, the cenotaph of the Islamic tomb was a visual reminder, for the simple masses, of the true sarcophagus which remained below. The cenotaph, as has been stated, becomes one of the most important iconographic devices of the Islamic tomb, and certainly required device in all Indo-Islamic mausolea. The noted variation is to be found in the *Tomb of I'timad-ud-daula* in Agra where a cenotaph is not only found in its traditional locale--i.e., the ground floor--but also a second cenotaph is located on the second level in the square, roof pavilion. This tiered arrangement obviously refers to and is an iconographical representation of the *axis mundi,* a philosophical/theological concept in which the terrestrial and celestial spheres are merged and revolve around the axis of the *Godhead*. In the Islamic mausolea, the axis passes through the buried remains, and, by implication, associates the deceased with that powerful theological concept.

A further distinction to be found in the Indo-Islamic tombs is seen in the amount of internal or enclosed space, *en plan*. Certainly, the space needed to provide for a cenotaph, plus an entrance(s) with vestibule(s) is minimal. Yet the amount of internal space seen in the tombs under consideration, herein, is over and above that which would seem necessary. One of the earlier tombs considered in this study--i.e., the *Tomb of Sultan Iltutmish* (See: **Plate 5**)--indicates that the amount of enclosed space compared to the whole is 58%±, *en plan*. By modern standards, this would appear to indicate walls that are exceedingly thick. Indeed, that is true. However, when comparing this percentage to a Hindu model--e.g., the *Brihadeshvara Temple*'**s** *garbha-griha* (See: **Figure 30**)--where the amount of enclosed space is a mere 35.8%±,[96] *en plan*, the space within the *Tomb of Sultan Iltutmish* is half again more! On the other end of the scale is the *Tomb of Shah Daulat* (See: **Plate 66**). This mausoleum gives the appearance of being squat and thick when viewing it from its exterior (See: **Plate 67**). However, the enclosed space is a surprising 95%±, *en plan.* The rest of the tombs considered fall in between these tow percentages--i.e., 58%± and 95%±. There appear to be two reasons why the Indo-Islamic tombs possess such a greater amount. First, the tombs were so constructed as to allow for pilgrims to circumambulate, to pay their respects to the deceased and to receive the baraka therein. Second, the congregational nature[97] of Islam is such that greater enclosed space required for its principle religious structures--i.e., the *masjid*--is apparently applied to the mausolea as well.

The tendency in the Indo-Islamic tombs is decidedly towards the horizontal--i.e., below 12:9 when a *Deshiya Mandala* is superimposed over the elevation. This is particularly true when applied to the octagonal tombs. Half of the square tombs, on the other hand, including the *muthamman baghdadi* tombs--i.e., **Types B, C** & **E**--under consideration tended towards verticality. The half that fell under the 12:9 proportional ratio are: the *Tomb of Sultan Ghari* (See: **Figure 64**), the *Tomb of Jalau-ud-din Mohammad Shah* (*Eklakhi*) (See: **Figure 85**), the *Tomb of Rani Rupmati* (See: **Figure 91**), the *Tomb of Hushang Shah* (See: **Figure 96**), the *Sayyid Usman Rauza* (See: **Figure 101**), the *Tomb of Humayun* (See: **Plate 112**), the *Tomb of Muhammad Ghaus* (See: **Figure 139**), the *Tomb of Akbar* (See: **Plate 113**), the *Tomb of Iftikhar Khan* (See: **Figures 157** & **158**), the *Tomb of Shah Daulat* (See: **Figure 160**), the *Tomb of Jahangir* (See: **Figure 175**), the *Tomb of I'timad-ud-daula* (See: **Figure 190**), and the *Tomb of Ali 'Adil Shah II* (See: **Figures 208** & **209**). What is the predilection towards horizontally that appears to dominate Indo-Islamic tombs? Certainly, Islamic tombs outside of India tend to be quite vertical--e.g., the Iranian *Tomb Towers*, the *Gunbad-i-Kabus*, the *Mausoleum of Oljeitu Hudabanda* (See: **Figures 36, 37** & **42**), the

Conclusions (Continued)

Turkish *Mausoleum of Huand Hatun, Doner Kumbet* (See: **Figures 38** & **40**), and the *Tomb of Timur* at Samarqand (See: **Plate 128**). Yet, of the thirty-six tombs considered in this study, only thirteen can be considered as vertically oriented--e.g., proportionally above 12:9 utilizing the *Deshiya Mandala* as the basis.

The *mandala* is a distinct iconographic form that is employed by both the Buddhist and the Hindu alike. It has been applied to the Indo-Islamic mausolea as well for one salient reason. The invading and occupying Islamic groups utilized the indigenous builders, the Hindu *sthapati,* in the construction of their various edifices. This fact has been noted by virtually every scholar writing on the subject. The use of the *mandala* had been so ingrained in the *sthapati* that it was normal for them to employ it in the raising of the various mausolea. Certainly, there were a number of Islamic requirements that were required, and these were adapted into the plan. Even in instances where Persian architects were employed, the *mandala* had become so ingrained and an important consideration that its use was utilized. After all, the *mandala* was a plan-centered concept, and apparently mattered little to the Islamic employers. Their main consideration was in three-dimensional spatial elements--i.e., domes, *dargah, pishtaq* or *iwan,* thc crypt, cenotaph, and a *mikhrab* where required. A three-dimensional element of Indian-Hindu origin--i.e., the *chatri*--was readily utilized as it did not violate or infringe upon the basic Islamic requirements. It may be surmised, therefore, that if the plan conformed to the basic square, cross axial form that had been preferred by Islam, the *sthapati's* utilization of a *mandala* was simply inconsequential. Therefore, the two basic *mandalas* that were seen as most auspicious to the Buddhist and Hindu *sthapati*--i.e., the *Manduka Mandala* and the *Paramashayika Mandala,* as well as the circular *Manduka Mandala* in cases where the structure deviated from the strict square--and have been applied in this study. In the vast majority of plans, it is seen that there appears to be a direct correlation between the plans and these *mandalas.*

The *Tomb of Sultan Ghari* utilizes a singular design feature that, for some reason, is not again employed on a regular basis until well into the Sixteenth Century--i.e., four, prominent, corner towers or conspicuous *chatri*. This practice is regularly seen from 1540 C.E. onwards in: the *Tomb of Sher Shah* (See: **Plate 36**), the *Tomb of Humayun* (See: **Plate 44**), the *Tomb of Mohammed Ghaus* (See: **Plate 51**), the *Tomb of Akbar* (See: **Plate 56**), the *Tomb of Mohammed Quli Qutub Shah* (See: **Plate 60**), the *Ibrahim Rauza* (See: **Plate 62**), the *Tomb of Iftikar Khan* (See: **Plate 65**), the *Tomb of Shah Daulat* (See: **Plate 67**), the *Tomb of Khan Khanan* (See: **Plate 69**), the *Tomb of Jahangir* (See: **Plate 71**), the *Gol Gumbaz* (See: **Plate 74**), the *Tomb of I'timad-ud-daula* (See: **Plate 78**), the *Afzal Khan Rauza* (See: **Plate 85**), the *Tomb of Ali 'Adil Shah II* (See: **Plate 85**), and the *Tomb of Safdar Jang* (See: **Plate 91**). The *Taj Mahal* also can be included (See: **Plate 81**). However it also employs four separate, soaring minarets. These corner towers, or *chatri,* or *minarets* appearing in the mausolea noted above appear to be an allusion, an intimation of a *masjid*-like character. In truth, many of the mausolea in this study possess a *mikhrab* in their *qibla,* thereby giving credence to this advertence. Therefore, these towers, or *chatri,* or *minarets* can be seen as possessing an iconographic allusion to the *minarets* which are attached to a *masjid.*

The Indo-Islamic tombs find their genesis in far earlier times and diverse locales, and, more importantly, a faith which provided these mausolea's *raison d'être.* Rising from the incredibly rich cultural loam in which they happily germinated, these tombs stand at the apogee of their genre.

Finally, the Indo-Islamic tombs reflect the wealth, the power and the need to leave a tangible legacy that many of the sultans and a number of the nobles possessed. The lavishing of such riches may seem *gauche*, but for that day and age the physical display was a necessity of rule and power. What percentage of the G.N.P. of the powers of the Twentieth Century was expended on far more transitory material--e.g., armament? The percentage is not merely *gauche*--it is obscene in comparison! We may fault those who reigned in their seemingly overzealous misuse of their resources. But, when confronted with the "incomparable" *Taj Mahal*, the "glorious" *Tomb of Humayun*, the "wondrous" *Gol Gumbaz*, the "unrivaled" *Ibrahim Rauza*, the "elegant "Tomb *of I'timad-ud-daula*, the "magnificent *Tomb of Sher Shah*," and the "stately" *Sayyid Usman Rauza*, our objections are seduced and neutralized by the beauty man has created.[97]

Bibliography

Bibliography

Acharya, P. K. *An Encyclopaedia of Hindu Architecture*. London: 1927-1946.

__________. *Architecture of Manasara, translated from the original Sanskrit*. London: 1932.

Ahmad, Mabel L. *The Secret Power of Names and Numbers: A Guide to your Destiny*. Bombay: 1991.

Alfieri, Bianca Maria. *Islamic Architecture of the Indian Subcontinent*. London: 2000.

Anuvit Charernsupkul. *The Elements of Thai Architecture*. Bangkok: 1978.

__________ and Vivat Temiyabandha. *Northern Thai Domestic Architecture and Rituals in House-Building*. Bangkok: 1978.

Asher, Catherine B. *Architectureof Mughal India*. New Delhi: 1995.

Atmadi, Parmono. *Some Architectural Design Principles of Temples in Java*. Yogyakarta: 1994.

Auboyer, Jeannine; and others. *Oriental Art: A Handbook of Styles and Forms*. Trans. Elizabeth and Richard Bartlett. New York: 1980.

Banerje, Jitendranath N. *The Development of Hindu Iconography*. 2nd ed. , Calcutta: 1956.

Banerjee, P. , et al. *Buddhist Iconography*. New Delhi: 1989.

Bary, Theodore de. *Sources of Indian Tradition*, vol. I. New York: 1958.

Batley, C. *Design Development of Indian Architecture*. Bombay: 1934

Bell, Eric T. *Numerology*. Baltimore: 1933.

Bhattacharyya, Benoytosh. *The Indian Buddhist Iconography Mainly Based on the Seadhanamealea and other Cognate Tantric Texts of Rituals*. Calcutta: 1958.

Bhattacharyya, Dipak Chandra. *Studies in Buddhist Iconography*. New Delhi: 1978.

Bhattacharya, K. "Les religions brahmaniques dan l'ancien Cambodge, d'après l'épigraphie et l'iconographie," *Cahiers de l'École Française d'Extrême-Orient*; XLIX. Hanoi: 1961.

Bhiarsri, Silpa. *Thai Buddhist Art (Architecture)*. Bangkok: 1988.

Brown, Percy. *Indian Architecture (Buddhist and Hindu Periods)*. Bombay: n. d.

__________. *Indian Architecture (Islamic Period)*. Bombay: n. d. (1965-1968).

Brunes, Tons. *The Secrets of Ancient Geomerty and Its Use*; vols. I-II. Copenhagen: 1967.

Bunce, Fredrick W. *A Dictionary of Buddhist and Hindu Iconography -- Illustrated -- Objects, Devices, Concepts, Rites and Related Terms*, New Delhi: 1996.

__________. *Numbers Found in Buddhist & Hindu Practices: an Iconographic Consideration*, New Delhi: 2002.

__________. *The Iconography of Plans: A Study of the Influence of Buddhism and Hinduism on Architectural Plans of South and Southeast Asia*, New Delhi: 2002.

Bibliography (Continued)

__________. *The Yantras of Deities and Their Numerological Foundations: an Iconographic Consideration*. New Delhi: 2000.

Burgess, J. *Muhammadan Architecture in Gujarat*. Varanasi: 1971.

Bussagli, Mario; John Shepley, trans. *Oriental Architecture/1: India, Indonesia, Indochina*. New York: 1989.

Carr, Stephen. *Archaeology and Monumental Remains of Delhi*. Allahabad: 1967.

Chandra, Lokesh. *Buddhist Iconography*. New Delhi:1991.

Chopra, P. N. , T. K. Ravindran, N. Subrahmanian. *History of South India*, 3 Vols. New Delhi: 1979.

Coedès, George. *The Indianized States of Southeast Asia*. Honolulu: 1968.

__________. "Les Etats hindouises d'Indochine et d'Indonesie," *Histoire du Monde*, Vol III. Paris: 1948.

__________. "Arte dell'Indonesia," *Civiltà dell'Oriente*, Vol. IV. Rome: 1962.

Commissariat, Manekshah Sorabshah. *A History of Gujarat: Including a Survey of its Chief Architectural Monuments and Inscriptions*. Bombay: 1938.

Coomaraswamy, Ananda Kentish. "Symbolism of the Dome," *Indian Historical Quarterly*; XIV. Calcutta: 1938, pp. 1-56.

Cousens, Henry. *Bijapur and Its Architectural Remains: With an Historical Outline of the Adil Shahi Dynasty*; (Archeological Survey of India, Vol XXXVIII, Imperial Series). reprint. Delhi: 1996.

Creswell, K.A.C. *A Short Account of Early Muslim Architecture*. Beirut: 1958.

Critchlow, Keith. *Islamic Patterns: An Analytical and Cosmological Approach*. London and New York: 1976.

Crump, Thomas. *The Anthropology of Numbers*. Cambridge: 1990.

Dagens, Bruno, ed. & trans. *Mayamata, Traite Sanskrit d'architecture, Premiere Partie*. Paris (?): 1970.

__________, ed. & trans. *Mayamata, Traite Sanskrit d'architecture, Deuxeme Partie*. Paris (?): 1970.

__________, ed. & trans. *Mayamatam, Treatise of Housing, Architecture & Iconography* (2 Vols.). New Delhi: 1994.

de Bary, Wm. Theodore (ed.) et al. *Sources of Indian Tradition*, Vol. I. New York: 1958.

Deva, Krishna. *Temples of India*, 2 Vols. New Delhi: 1995.

Dieulafoy, M. *L'art antique de la Perse*.Paris: 1884-1885.

Fergusson, James, et al. *History of Indian and Eastern Architecture*, 2 vols. Delhi: 1967.

Goodwin, Godfrey. *A History of Ottoman Architecture*. London: 1971.

Govinda, (Lama) Anagarika. *Psycho-cosmic Symbolism of the Buddhist Stupa*. Emeryville: 1976.

Bibliography (Continued)

Grover, Satish. *Islamic Architecture in India*. New Delhi: 1981.

Grube, Ernst,et al. George Mitchell, ed. *Architecture of the Islamic World: Its History and Social Meaning*. London: 1978.

Haig, Wolseley, ed. *The Cambridge History of India*. Delhi: 1958.

Hara, O. Hashnu. *Number, Name and Colour: As Applied to Character and Fate*. New Delhi: 1995.

Havell, E. B. *Encyclopaedia of Architecture in the Indian Subcontinent*. reprint. New Delhi: 2000.

Hill, D. and Grabar, O. *Islamic Architecture and Its Decoration*, A.D. 800-1500. Chicago: 1964.

Hillenbrand, Robert. *Islamic Art and Architecture*.
London: 1999.

__________. *Islamic Architecture: Form, Function & Meaning*. Edinburgh: 1994.

Hoag, John D. *Islamic Architecture*. Milan: 1975.

Husain, A. B. M. *Fathepur-sikri and its Architecture*. Dacca: 1970.

Intralib, Sonthiwan. *An Outline of the History of Religious Architecture in Thailand*. s. l. (Bangkok?): 1987.

Issam El-Said and Parman, Ayse, *Geometric Concepts in Islamic Art*. London: 1976.

Jung, C. G. *Mandala Symbolism*, trans. R. F. C. Hull. Princeton: 1973.

Koch, Ebba. *Mughal Architecture: An Outline of Its History and Development 1526-1858*. London: 1991.

Kramrisch, S. *The Hindu Temple*: Calcutta: 1946.

__________. "The Temple as Purusha," *Studies in Indian Temple Architecture*; ed. Pramod Chandra. Benares: 1975, pp. 40-47.

Kumar, Ravindra. *Secrets of Numerology: A Complete Guide for the Layman to Know the Past, Present and Future*. New Delhi: n.d.

Lalou, M. *Iconographie des etoffes peintes d'apres le Manjusrimulakalpa*. Paris: 1930.

Leksukhum, Santi. *The Redented Added-Angled Chedis and the Rabbeted-Angled Chedis of the Ayutthaya Period*. Bangkok: 1986.

Liebert, G. *Iconographic dictionary of the Indian Religions*. Leyden: 1976.

Luce, G. H. *Old Burma, Early Pagan*, 3 vols. New York: 1969.

__________. "The Greater Temples of Pagan; The Smaller Temples of Pagan; Fu-kan-tu-lu; The Tan and the Ngai;Countries Neighboring Burma; The Ancient Pyu; Economic Life of the Early Burman." *Burma Research Society*, Fiftieth Anniversary Publication, no. 2. Rangoon: 1960.

Mahapatra, Sthapaka Miranjana. *Silparärnakosa: A Glossary of Orissan Temple Architecture*. New Delhi: 1994.

Majumdar, R. C., ed.The Delhi Sultanate. Bombay: 1960.

Mani, Vettam. *Puranic Encyclopaedia*. Delhi:

1996.

March, Lionel, et al. *The Geometry of Environment*. Cambridge: 1974.

Marchal, H. *L'Architecture comparée dans l'Inde et l'Extrême-Orient*. Paris: 1944.

Mehta, Rustam. *Masterpieces of Indo-Islamic Architecture*. Bombay: 1976.

Micell, G., ed.Architcture of the Islamic World. London: 1978.

Mohammad al-Asad, et al. Martin Frishman and Hasan-Uddin Khan, eds. *The Mosque: History, Architectural Development & Regional Diversity*. London: 1994.

Morgan, W. S. *Kisah Tanah Melayu*. Singapore: 1949.

Muhammad Rabi 'ibn Muhammad Ibrahim. *The Ship of Sulaiman*. New York: 1972.

Naqoi, S. A. A. *Humanyn's Tomb and Adjacent Buildings*, Delhi: 1947.

Nath, R. *Fathepur Sikri and its Monuments*. Agra: 2000.

__________. *History of Mughal Architecture*. New Delhi: 1985.

__________. *History of Sultanate Architecture*. New Delhi: 1978.

__________. *Islamic Architecture & Style in India*. New Delhi (?): 1982.

Nayeem, M.A. *The Splendour of Hyderabad : The Last Phase of an Oriental Culture (1591-1948 A.D.)*, reprint. Hyderabad: 2002.

Nilakanta Sastri. *South India Influences in the Far East*. s. l. : 1949

Parmentier, H. *L'Art khmer primitif*. Paris: 1927.

__________. *L'Art khmer classique*. Paris: 1939.

__________. *L'Art architectural hindou dans l'inde et en Extreme-Orient*. Paris: 1948.

Pereira, Jose. *Islamic Sacred Architecture: A Stylistic History*. New delhi: 1994.

Prabhakar Apte, June. "Vastu-Purusha Mandala: Dramatic Architectural and Artistic Study of Vastu-Purusha Mandala in Vastu-Vedic, Agamic and Puranic Tradition with Special Reference to Mayamata." *1993 Seminar on Mayonic Science & Technology*, Madras (unpublished: Library of the American Institute of Indian Studies, Gurgaon, Haryana).

Prochazka, Amjad Bohumil. *Architecture of the Islamic Cultural Sphere*. Zurich: 1986.

Raja Bahrin Shah bin Raja Ahmad Shah. *The Terengganu Timber Malay House*. s. l. (Kuala Lumpur): n. d. (1981).

Rajan, K.V. Soundara. *Islam Builds in India*. Delhi: 1983.

Rapson, E. J. , et al (eds.). *The Cambridge History of India*, 6 Vols. Delhi: 1955.

Rowland, Benjamin. *The Art and Architecture of India: Hindu, Buddhist, Jain*. Baltimore: 1967.

Safrani, Shehbaz H. *Golconda and Hyderabad*.

Bibliography (Continued)

Bombay: 1992.

Santi Leksukhum. *The Redented Added-Angled Chedis and the Rabbeted-Angled Chedis of the Ayutthaya Period*. Bangkok: B. E. 2529 (1986 A. D.).

Sartono Kartodirdjo, ed. *700 Tahun Majapahit (1293-1993) Suatu Bunga Rampai*. Surabaya: 1993.

Sarkar, H. *Some Contributions of India to the Ancient Civilization of Indonesia and Malaysia*. Calcutta: 1970.

__________. *Studies in Early Buddhist Architecture of India*. Delhi: 1966.

Sevcenko, Margaret, ed. *Theories and Principles of Design in the Architecture of Islamic Societies*. Cambridge: 1988.

Sharma, P. K. *Mughal Architecture of Delhi*. New Delhi: 2000.

Sinclair, W. B. "Monasteries of Pagan," *Burma Research Society*, Fiftieth Anniversary Publication, no. 2. Rangoon: 1960.

Sivaramamurti, C. *The Art of India*. New York: 1977.

__________. *Le Stupa de Barobudur*. Paris: 1960.

Smith, Edmond W. *Akbar's Tomb*.

Snodgrass, A. *The Symbolism of the Stupa*. Ithaca: 1985.

Soucek, Pricilla P. *Content and Context of Visual Arts in the Islamic World*. University Park: 1988.

Soundara Rajan, K. V. *Ahmadabad*. New Delhi: 1980.

__________. *Islam Builds in India*. Delhi: 1983

Stierlin, Henri, ed. *Architecture of the World: India*. Lausanne: n. d.

__________. *Architecture of the World: Islamic India*. Lausanne: n. d.

Sthapaka Miranjana Mahapatra. *Silpararnakosa: A Glossary of Orissan Temple Architecture*. New Delhi: 1994.

Strachan, Paul. *Imperial Pagan: Art and Architecture of Burma*. Honolulu: 1989.

Stuart, C.M. Villiers. *Gardens of the Great Mughals*. New Delhi: 1983.

Tewari, S. P. *Hindu Iconography*. New Delhi: 1979.

Tillotson, G.H.R. *Mughal India*. London: 1990.

Vatsyayan, Kapila. *Buddhist Iconography*. New Delhi: 1989.

__________. *The Square and the Circle of the Indian Arts*. New Delhi: 1983.

Volwahsen, A. Living Architecture: Islamic-Indian. London: 1970.

Waliullah Khan, Mohammad. *Lahore and its Important Monuments*. Karachi: 1973.

Williams, C. A. S. *Outlines of Chinese Symbolism and Art Motives*. New York: 1976.

Wilson, G. et al. *Geometry for Architects*. Champaigne: 1962.

Bibliography (Continued)

Yazdani, Ghulam. *Bidar, Its History and Monuments*. London: 1947.

Appendix A

Glossaray

Glossary

A

ablaq -- (Arab.) The term refers to two-toned marble or stone decoration. Literally means 'piebald.'

amir -- (Arab.) The term refers to a commander or prince of the Islamic world.

anda -- (Indic: aka *dhatu-garbha, garbha, gaeba*) The term refers to an egg-shape, more specifically to the hemispherical form of a stupa. It is also referred to as: garbha and gaeba.

atabeg -- (Arab.) The term refers to a governor or a guardian of a prince.

axiality -- The symmetrical arrangement of the elements of a plan along a given axis. If that axis is the east-west axis, then the northern half is a duplicate of the southern half.

B

bagh -- (Arab.) The term refers to a garden, usually square or made up of square components. It may also refer to a pleasure palace.

baraka -- (Arab.) The term refers to 'blessed one' or divine grace. It may also refer to the intangible spirit emanating from a holy man, or spiritual power.

birka -- (Arab.: aka *fisqiya, haud, saqaya, sihrij*) The term refers to an ablution tank.

Brahmanic -- Here, referring to the religious practice which includes both Vedic and post-Vedic or Hindu practices.

brahmásthana -- (Indic) The term refers to the central area of a Hindu *mandala* in which the prime deity resides.

buq'a -- (Arab.) The term refers to a monastic retreat.

C

calif -- (Arab.) The term refers to a successor of the Prophet Mohammed, from the Arabic '*khalifa*.'

cami -- (Turkish: aka *masjid*) The term refers a mosque particularly one in which great numbers gather for Friday prayers.

canopy tombs -- (Eng.) The term refers to an octagonal, *en plan,* tomb which has a roofed verandah around the whole of the central chamber. The form of this central (octagonal) chamber extends above the level of the surrounding verandah as a podium for a culminating dome.

caravansari -- (Arab.; Turk.: *han*) The term refers to a resting place for travellers or caravans. Generally found on trade routs and may be fortified to protect the travellers and their goods.

cardak -- (Arab.) The term refers to a reception room generally employed during the summer months.

chahar-bagh -- (Arab.) The term refers to a plot of land, generally square, that is divided into four equal sections.

chaitya -- (Indic: aka *chetiya, stupa*) Another term for *stupa*. As in a *chaitya* hall, the *stupa* here tends to be carved from solid rock as a memorial.

chajja -- (Indic: aka *cajja*) The term refers to the overhanging eaves-stone that generally encircles a temple ot mausileum above the level of the doors.

chandi -- (Indon.: aka *candi*) The term is attached to a temple or temple complex in Indonesia--e.g., *Chandi Sewu*. It may be derived from or refer to: *chedi*, or *Candi* (goddess of death).

chatri -- (Indic) The term refers to a kiosk with a dome usually supported by four or eight pillars.

chedi -- (Thai: aka *chaitya, stupa, zeidi*) The term refers to the Thai equivalent of a *stupa*. Its form is greatly elongated into a tall thin form and may contain holy relics, ashes of monarchs, saints or other meritorious persons. In the later periods it loses its circular shape and becomes more angular.

chetiya -- (Pali: aka *chaitya*) See: *chaitya*.

cross-axiality -- The symmetrical arrangement of the elements of a plan along both axes, precisely duplicating each quadrant. This term is not applied to rectangular plans. The north-south and east-west axes divide the form. The northwest quadrant is a duplicate of the northeast, southwest and southeast quadrants. This quadrant can either be mirrored in any of the other three, or rotated 90°, 180°, and 270° to achieve the whole.

D

dagaba -- (Java.: aka *dagoba, dhatu-garbha, pagoda, stupa*) The term refers to a *stupa*, as in the *dagaba* of

Borobudur. See: *stupa*.

dagoba -- (Indic: aka *dagaba, pagoda*) A variant spelling for the term *dagaba*. See: *dagaba*.

dargah -- (Arab.) The term refers to an entrance or portal.

darih -- (Arab.) The term refers to a tomb.

dergah -- (Persia.) The term refers to a royal court.

dhatu-garbha -- (Indic: aka *anda, garbha, gaeba*) A variant term for *anda*. See: *anda*.

diwan -- (Arab.) The term refers to a royal reception chamber or enclosure. It may also refer to a ministry of the government.

F

file -- (Eng.) The term as used refers to a line *pada* in a *mandala*. Specifically, *file* refers to the vertical line of *pada*.

fisqiya -- (Arab.: aka *birka, haud, saqaya, sihrij*) The term refers to an ablution tank.

funduq -- (Arab.) The term refers to an inn or warehouse.

G

gaeba -- (Sinhalese: aka *garbha, anda*) A variant term for *anda*. See: *anda*.

garbha -- (Indic: aka *anda, gaeba*) A variant term for *anda*. See: *anda*.

garbha-griha -- (Indic) The term refers to the sanctuary, specifically of a Hindu temple. It is the place where the image of the main deity is housed and the access to it is limited to the priesthood. It is the *sanctum sanctorum* and the term refers to the womb.

ghazi -- (Arab.) The term refers to a holy warrior, one who defends the faith.

gunbad -- (Arab.: aka *qubba*) The term refers to a dome.

H

han -- (Turk.; Arab.: *caravansari*) The Turkish equivalent for *caravansari*. See: *caravansari*.

haram -- (Arab.) The term refers to private quarters in a home or mosque. Generally, it refers to women's quarters or locale.

hasht bihisht -- (Arab.) The term refers to the eight paradises. In architecture it refers to the eight rooms or areas around a central space. See also: *muthamman baghdadi*.

haud -- (Arab.: aka *birka, fisqiya, saqaya, sihrij*) The term refers to an ablution tank found in a *sahn*.

hujra -- (Arab.) The term refers to a small chamber or cell.

I

imam -- (Arab.) The term refers to a leader of prayer, a spiritual leader analogous to a minister or priest.

imam khatib -- (Arab.) The term refers to a preacher and prayer leader.

imam ratib -- (Arab.) The term refers specifically to a prayer leader.

intarsia -- (Ital.: aka *pietra dura*) See: *pietra dura* .

iwan -- (Arab.) The term refers to a roofed hall exposed at one end.

J

jabana -- (Arab.: aka *maqbara*; Persia.: *qabrstan*) The term refers to a cemetery.

jaali -- (Arab./Ind.) The term refers to a thin, stone screen with a perforated design. See also: *mashrabiya*.

jama'a -- (Arab.) The term refers to a congregation.

jami' -- (Arab.) The term refers to a large mosque where Friday prayers are held and a sermon is preached.

jihad -- (Arab.) The term refers to 'holy war,' or a war to defend the faith.

K

khan -- (Arab.) The term refers to a man of high rank, either a lord or a prince.

khanaqah -- (Arab.) The term refers to a monastic-like structure that may also contain a mausoleum.

kiosk -- (Turk.) The term refers to a summer house or a pavilion of open construction. It also refers

Glossary (Continued)

to a small, often domed architectural form supported by pillars that appears as a major ornamentsl unit, usually at the corners of larger structures. See: *chatri.*

ksar -- (Arab.) The term refers to a fortified village.

L

lahd -- (Arab.) The term refers to a burial vault. It may also refer to a niche. See also: *madfam*.

M

ma'adhdhana -- (Arab.: aka *manara, minaret, sawma'a*) The term refers to a *minaret*. See: *minaret*.

mabkhara -- (Arab.) The term refers to a censor. It also refers to any *minaret* top which resembles a censor.

madfam -- (Arab.: aka *lahd*) The term refers to a burial vault or mausoleum.

madrasa -- (Arab.) The term refers to a Muslim school or institution in which orthodox sciences are taught, generally associated with a *masjid*.

maidan -- (Arab.) The term refers to a square or plaza or ceremonial enclosure.

mamluk -- (Arab.) The term refers to a slave.

manabhat-kari -- (Indic) The term refers to stone inlay or *pietra dura*.

manara -- (Arab.: aka *ma'adhdhana, minaret, sawma'a*) The term refers to a *minaret*. See: *minaret*.

mandala -- (Indic) The term refers to a sacred Buddhist/Hindu diagram. Certain *mandalas* were employed as the basis for architectural plans. The two preferred forms for temple designs were the *Manduka Mandala* with sixty-four *pada* and the *Paramashyika Mandala* with eighty-one pada.

Manduka Mandala -- (Indic) The term refers to a *mandala* of sixty-four *pada*--i.e., eight in either direction. See: *mandala*.

maqbara -- (Arab.: aka *jabana*; Persia.: *qabrstan*) The term refers to a cemetery.

marmas -- (Indic) The term refers to the perpendicular crossing of lines within a *mandala*, created by the conjunction of four or more *pada*. In the Hindu tradition, it is considered inauspicious for any line delineating the form of the structure to fall upon a *marmas*. See: *mandala*.

maqsura -- (Arab.) The term refers to a pierced stone screen which protects an important tomb.

mashhad -- (Arab.) The term refers to a tomb or mausoleum for a martyr.

mashrabiya -- (Arab.) The term refers to a grilled window or screen usually of wood. See also: *jali*.

masjid -- (Arabic: aka *mosjid, cami*) The term refers to a mosque; literally 'a place of prostration.'

masjid-i jami' --(Arab.) The term refers to a mosque specifically for Friday prayers.

mazar -- (Arab.) The term refers to a mausoleum.

merlon -- (Fr.) The term refers to a solid element often on a battlement between two openings (crenels). Within Indo-Islamic architecture these tend to be more decorative than functional.

mihrab -- (Arabic: aka *mikhrab*) A variant of *mikhrab*. See: *mikhrab*..

mikhrab -- (Arabic: aka *mihrab*) The term refers to the "prayer niche" found in mosques in the wall facing Mecca (*qibla*). The *imam* preaches or recites the *Qur'an* from the *minbar* adjacent to the *mikhrab* during the prayers.

minaret -- (Arab.: aka *ma'adhdhana, manara,* ***sawma'a***) The term refers to a tall, slender tower(s) connected to a *masjid* from where the faithful are called to prayer.

minbar -- (Arab.) The term refers to a raised pulpit adjacent to the *mikhrab* from where the *imam* recites the *Qur'an* and delivers the sermon.

mosjid -- (Arabic: aka *masjid) The* term refers to a variation on the term *masjid*. See *masjid*.

muqarnas -- (Arab.) The term refers to small vaults, part of a larger vault that resemble honeycombs or stalactites.

musalla-- (Turkish: aka *surau*) See *surau*.

muthamman baghdadi -- (Arab/Mughal) The term refers to a square plan to which the corners have been sheared off forming an irregular octagon. See also: *hasht bihisht*

P

pada -- (Indic) The term refers to a single square found within a *mandala*. See: *mandala*.

pagoda -- (Burman: aka *dagaba, dagoba, dhatu-garbha*) A variant term for *dagaba*. See: *dagaba*.

pancharatha -- (Indic) The term refers to two separate extensions, generally in the middle portion of the surface of a wall, creating five surfaces per face. See: *ratha* & *triratha*.

Paramashayika Mandala -- (Indic) The term refers to a *mandala* of eighty-one *pada*--i.e., nine in either direction. See: *mandala*.

Pathan -- The term frequently refers to a style of Indo-Islamic architecture which finds its roots in Afghanistan (Pashtun tribe) and Iran (Persia).

pendentive -- The term refers to an inverted triangle which is the transition from a square space to a dome. See: squinch.

pietra dura -- (Ital.: aka *intarsia*) The term refers to the inlaying or fitting of small, often complexly formed, pieces of stone, both precious and semi precious, into a larger stone matrix which has been carefully carved out to receive the smaller pieces. It differs from the technique employed in a inlaid stone floor in which larger pieces of stone are fitted together in a pattern and set in concrete or other cementing agent.

pishtaq -- (Arab.) The term refers to a tall arch which frames an *iwan*. It may also refer to a large, impressive portal.

Q

qabr -- (Arab.) The term refers to a grave.

qabrstan -- (Persia.; Arab.: *jabana, maqbara*) The term refers to a cemetery.

qasaba -- (Arab.) The term refers to a citadel or capital.

qasr -- (Arab.) The term refers to a fortified residence, castle or a palace.

qibla -- (Arab.) The term refers to a wall which is perpendicular to the direction in which prayers are offered--i.e., always towards the *Ka'ba* in Mecca.

qubba -- (Arab.: aka *gunbad*) The term refers to a dome. It may also refer to a mausoleum.

Qur'an -- (Arab.) The term refers to the holy book of Islam.

R

rank -- (Eng.) The term as used refers to a line *pada* in a *mandala*. Specifically, *rank* refers to the horizontal line of *pada*.

ratha -- (Indic: aka *pushpaka*) The term refers to a extension of a wall surface, generally on all four sides. If there is a single extension, the form is called *triratha*--creating three surfaces per face. If there are two extensions, the form is called *pancharatha*--creating five surfaces per face. See: *pancharatha* & *triratha*. Also, a variant of the term *pushpaka*. See: *pushpaka*.

rauza -- (Arab./Ind.) The term refers to a an arrangement of tomb, *birka* and *masjid*. The tomb confronts the *masjid* and the *birka* is between the two.

ribat -- (Arab.) The term refers to a fortified Islamic monastery or hermitage. It may also refer to a frontier settlement.

S

sahn -- (Arab.) The term refers to a court within a *masjid*.

saqaya -- (Arab.: aka *birka, haud, fisqiya, sihrij*) The term refers to an ablution tank.

sawma'a -- (Arab.: aka *minaret, ma'adhdhana, manara*) The term refers to a *minaret*. See: *minaret*.

serai -- (Arab.) The term refers to a pavilion, often open on four sides and is used for relaxation and other pleasurable activities.

shaikh -- (Arab.: aka *sheik*) The term refers to a leader, usually a tribal chief.

shari'a -- (Arab.) The term refers to Islamic law or code.

shikhara -- (Indic) The term refers to a towerlike superstructure over the *garbha-griha* of a temple or any part thereof. It is made up of various sculptural devices and its form can vary.

sihrij -- (Arab.: aka *saqaya, birka, haud, fisqiya*) The term refers to an ablution tank.

simurgh -- (Arab.) The term refers to a phoenix, the mythical bird of countless legends.

sotoba -- (Japan: aka *stupa*) A variant term for *stupa*. See: *stupa*.

squinch -- (Arab.) The term refers to an arch-like transition from a square chamber to an octagon to the surmounting dome.

sthapati -- (Indic.) The term refers to an architect-builder, who in the Indian Hindu tradition was what the 'master builder' was to the European Medieval tradition.

stupa -- (Indic: *chedi, chaitya, chetiya, dagaba, dagoba,* *dhatu-garbha, pagoda, sotoba, zeidi*) The term refers to a Buddhist architectural form consisting of a square or circular base upon which rests a hemispherical form (*anda*). The *anda* may vary in shape from a hemisphere to bell-shape, to the form of an inverted pot or may be more angular and attenuated. Upon the *anda* rests a square or cylindrical altar-like form (*harmika*) from which a spire (*chattravali*) rises. Its origin is from a burial tumulus and was frequently employed as a vehicle for various relics.

suffa -- (Arab.) The term refers to a stone platform usually as a base for tombs.

sultan -- (Arab.) The term refers to an Islamic ruler with the rank equivalent to a king. Although, a *sultan* is referred to as 'His Highness' rather than 'His Majesty.'

surau -- (Arabic: aka *musalla*) The term refers to an area or small structure utilized by Muslims for the daily prayers. It is not a mosque, but may be equated with a chapel in the Christian world--i.e., a place of worship to which a cleric is not permanently attached.

T

triratha -- (Indic) The term refers to a single extension, generally in the middle portion of the surface of a wall, creating three surfaces per face. See: *ratha* & *pancharatha*.

turba -- (Arab.) The term refers to a mausoleum

turbe -- (Turk.) The term refers to a mausoleum.

V

visier -- (Arab.: aka *visir*) An alternate spelling for *visir*. See: *visir*.

visir -- (Arab.: aka *wazir*) See: *wazir*.

W

wazir -- (Arab.: aka *visir*) The term refers to a high governmental official, a Minister of State.

Z

zedi -- (Burman) A variant of *zeidi*. See: *zeidi*.

zeidi -- (Burman) The term refers to a *stupa* (Thai: *chedi*). See: *stupa*.

ziyara -- (Arab.) The term refers to a tomb.

Appendix B

Ensembles & the Chahar-bagh

Chahar Bagh

The garden in sacred literature has been a place of peace and beauty, an area where men and nature coexist in spiritual and physical symbiosis. To Judaism, Christianity and Islam the Garden of Eden was the first earthly garden for man and woman, a place of plenty, perfection and beauty that was denied to Adam and Eve due to their transgression. Since then man has attempted to replicate this place of repose and earthly perfection.

Paradise is also seen as a heavenly, celestial garden, the Elysium fields. The *Qur'an* says that in paradise one is surrounded by all things good and beautiful. In Paradise there is neither need nor no want. No luxury or desire is denied. Why then would not man, while on this earth, attempt to emulate this place of perfection and beauty?

Although the earthly garden is not an exclusive Islamic device, it has been utilized throughout the world as a place of refuge from the maddening crowds and the rigors of daily life. Unfortunately, until recent history, gardens had been the exclusive domain of the royal, the noble and the wealthy—e.g., the *Hanging Gardens of Babylon*, the *Gardens of the Summer Palace* outside of Beijing, the *Topkapi Gardens* of Istanbul, the *Gardens of San Souci*, the *Gardens of Versailles*, the *Rose Garden of the White House*, to mention a few. The Nineteenth Century saw the establishment of great public Gardens—e.g., the *Bois de Bologne*, Paris; the *Central Park*, New York; *Connaught Place*, New Delhi; and *Hyde Park*, London, again, to mention but a few. Here, the common folk could partake of the pleasure formerly restricted to the higher classes and meander through bowers, flower beds, shrub-lined walkways, by gurgling brooks and placid ponds.

The *chahar-bagh*, as we know it, had been employed and refined in Persia and Afghanistan before the Mughals imported it into India where it flourished and was developed even further. The garden was a device that was particularly desirable to Persia, Afghanistan and parts of northwest India. Here, there were and are areas of unyielding desert, the hot season is sweltering and unremitting, and it is an area where dust storms can inundate all. These gardens, these *baghs* offered respite from the harshness of the locale. With the exceptions of areas of northern Gujarat and much of Rajastan, India possessed one advantage over Persia and Afghanistan—i.e., the monsoons that regularly and seasonally dumped ample amounts of rain upon the parched soil.

The Mughals were practiced and efficient conquerors. However, man cannot live by war alone. The immense and incredible wealth that the Mughals had amasses found outlet in places of pleasure and relaxation from the strictures of courtly life, however brief these periods might have been for them. Gardens of beauty; gardens of pleasure; gardens that appealed to the aesthetic pleasures; gardens of sensual delights were constructed. Here the royal and the nobles could go and, for a time, throw off the mantle of their position and participate in the simple pleasures of life. These gardens, these places of beauty and peace were often devoted to sybaritic pleasures not easily attained in the palaces where protocol stiffly reigned.[94]

Conquerors they may have been, brutal they may have been, excessively ostentatious they may have been, yet, the Mughals often possessed a type of sophistication which for that day and age was matched by few. The sultans with their Turkish or Persian or Afghani backgrounds, and the Mughal Emperors could be intensely cruel, even barbaric by our standards.[95] On the other hand, they could recite and write beautiful poetry or even be competent artists. Most possessed an avid and apparently insatiable appetite for things of beauty and

Chahar Bagh (Continued)

luxury. The acquisition of rare and glorious things may have been an emblem of power and riches, however, if one can turn a phrase: 'if power corrupts, the beautiful corrupts absolutely.' Millions could be expended on conquest and war. Millions could be spent on elaborate fortifications. Millions could be lavished on a small, exquisite dwelling—e.g., the *House of Raja Birbal*, Fathepur Sikri—or a nobleman's tomb—e.g., the *Tomb of I'timad-ud-daula* at Agra—or on a bauble—e.g., the *Koh-i-noor* or the *Shah*. The seemingly limitless wealth of India fueled the incredible and often ostentatious need to display luxury in the courts of both Hindu and Islamic India. Such display was incomparable and was paralleled only by the Ming and Chi'ing of China. The Indian Courts, both Hindu and Muslim, were the envy of the upstart Courts of Europe. Even the fabulously wealthy and despotic Tsars of Russia with their vast domains could not equal the quantity found in India.

We may fault Aurangzeb for lack of filial piety and unrequited ambition in deposing his father, Shah Jahan, and imprisoning him in one of the octagonal pavilions in the *Red Fort* of Agra. But, the deposed monarch was given suitable luxuries and a magnificent view of his *Taj Mahal*. He was not denied the sight of his most glorious achievement and all that it represented.

These Garden(s) of Earthly Delights, these *chahar* (fourfold) *baghs* (gardens) were but one more way in which wealth and power were manifested in a tangible way by the Mughals. They were and are exemplified in: the *Shalimar Bagh* of Srinagar, the *Shalimar Bagh* of Lahore, the *Bakhsh Bagh* and *Mahtab Bagh* of Delhi's *Red Fort*, among many. These gardens became one of the hallmarks of the Mughals and ultimately were employed in the ensembles of many major tombs—e.g., the *Tomb of Humayun*, the *Tomb of Akbar*, the *Tomb of Jahangir* and the *Taj Mahal*.

The acknowledged paragons of the Indo-Islamic mausolea *chahar-bagh* are the *Shalimar Bagh* of Srinagar (See: **Plate 93**) and the smaller *Shalimar Bagh* of Lahore (See: **Plate 94**) built by Shah Jahan. The Lahore pleasure garden consists of three sections—i.e., two squares, one above the other on a terraced hillside, and a lower rectangular section. On the other hand, the Lahore garden, also consisting of the same three elements, but finds the rectangular section bracketed by the square elements. The Srinagar *Shalimar Bagh's* smaller, rectangular garden is at the foot of the descending terraces of the two squares, and designated as a "public garden." No such designation is attributed to any part of the Lahore *bagh*. In these gardens are to be found pavilions and *kiosks* for the delight, pleasure and privacy of the emperor and his party.

The *Shalimar Bagh* of Srinagar is the simplest in design, although it is larger than its Lahore counterpart. Each of the two square gardens are bisected, cross-axially, creating a *Pechaka Mandala* of four *pada* (*chahar*). The *Shalimar Bagh* of Lahore, on the other hand, is more complex. It, like its predecessor, consists of two square areas that are initially bisected cross-axially forming a primary *mandala* of four *pada*—i.e., a *Pechaka Mandala*. Each of these *pada* are again bisected cross-axially creating a *Mahapitha Mandala* of sixteen pada each.

The integer four plays a major role. It is a perfect number (2 + 2 = 4, and 2 x 2 = 4) which denotes completeness, perfection and worldly order. Two is the š of four, the first squared number, and is a feminine number. Not only is it an important number to Islam, it is also a sacred number to both Buddhists and Hindu alike. This division is seen in virtually every Mughal garden (*bagh*). Generally, each of the four plots of the *chahar bagh* are again divided vertically and horizontally, creating sixteen smaller plots. Sixteen, the square of four is, likewise, and auspicious number and feminine. It is formed by the addition of the first four odd numbers (1 + 3 + 5 + 7 = 16). In addition, like four it is formed by either the sum of itself or the multiple of itself (4 + 4 + 4 + 4 = 16, or 4 x 4 = 16). It assumes the qualities of four plus it also represents the balance of opposites and the visible world.

The *Bakhsh Bagh* and *Mahtab Bagh* of *Shahjahanabad* (See: **Plate 95**) in the *Red Fort* of Delhi, mimics the square and rectangular *baghs* of *Lahore's Shalimar Bagh*. The layout of the larger *Bakhsh Bagh* is identical to the Lahore model. These diminutive gardens are captive within the forts imposing ramparts which, in turn, are surrounded by the hustle and bustle of the imperial city, Delhi.

The square concept that is exemplified in the *baghs* was not solely a design concept of the Persians, or Afghani, or Mughals. The square had long been the sacred and preferred form utilized in temples, palaces and other important structures of Hindu India. Contemporaneous with the *Shalimar Baghs* of Srinagar and Lahore, the Hindu prince Raja Bir Singh Judeo (aka Bir Singh Deva) raised the massive imposing *Daitya Palace* (See: **Plate 127**) in the Bundelkhand district, south of Jhansi. This structure is square and possesses many elements akin to those found in a *chahar-bagh*. Its plan is obviously Hindu, en plan, as one room merges or opens onto another, and the whole based on a cross axial design. Hindu architectural concepts are spelled out in the *Manasara* and *Mayamata*. Here in the *Daitya Palace* the square predominates and the plan is divided often into four equal sections. To the Hindu, the square was the most sacred geometric form as it represented the celestial and its immutability. It was the Buddhists who saw this immutability not in the square but in the circle or sphere and relegated the square of the Hindu to the terrestrial sphere. This latter interpretation is similar to Islamic geometric iconography. In addition to the cross-axial character of Raja Bir Singh Judeo's palace it also can be seen to be divided into a nine-fold plan. Three and nine are most sacred Hindu numbers. Three is exemplified in: *Brahmá*, *Vishnu* and *Shiva*; *Sarasvati*, *Lakshmi* and *Parvati*; and the sacred family of father, mother and offspring. Nine is exemplified in: the *Navagraha* (the nine planets), *Navaratna* (the nine jewels) and the *Nava-Durgas*. This cross-axial square mirrors the cosmic balance, the cosmic symmetry of the Hindu. This interrelationship--i.e., one Hindu and the other Islamic--is one of the important and interesting outgrowths of Indo-Islamic cultural symbiosis.

Not only were the *chahar-baghs* of Mughal India influenced by the gardens of Persia and Afghanistan, but also the *kiosks*, the pleasure pavilions of Islamic India find their genesis in those of Persia. The *Hesht Behest* of Ishfahan (c. 1669 C.E.) is one of a long line of pavilions that were to be found in imperial Persia (See: **Plate 126**). This pavilion finds its counterpart in the *Feria Bagh* of Ahmadnagar (See: **Plate 124**) or in the *Shahi Bagh* of Ahmadabad (See: **Plate 125**). All are strictly axial, but, the *Feria Bagh* and the *Shahi Bagh* are cross-axial—an Indo-Islamic predilection.

The *chahar-bagh* possesses potent iconography. This symbolism is doubly important when a tomb is the focal point. The cosmological concept of these gardens is acknowledged. They represent both the real world—i.e., the Garden of Eden—and the paradisal garden. The tomb in the center becomes the axis of this cosmos. The square is divided into four equal parts with the tomb resting on the intersection of the axes (See: the *Tomb of Akbar* [**Plate 97**] and the *Tomb of Jahangir* [**Plate 98**]). The directional implication is unmistakable. In addition, the four extending pools that are part of these directional arms are seen to represent the four rivers of Eden. On the other hand, the

Chahar Bagh (Continued)

Tomb of Humayun's chahar-bagh is far more complex than the two ensembles of his immediate successors noted above—i.e., *Tomb of Akbar* uses the Srinagar *Shalimar Bagh* as its model or the *Tomb of Jahangir* which utilizes the *Shalimar Bagh* of Lahore as its design genesis. The *bagh* of the *Tomb of Humayun* (See: **Plate 96**) is basically an *Urgapitha Mandala* with thirty-six *pada*, or, more simply a *Pitha Mandala* of nine larger *pada*. Each of these larger *pada* are bisected cross-axially, except the central *pada* creating the thirty-six *pada*—i.e., an *Ugrapitha Mandala* noted above. Here the nine-fold design establishes the eight regions surrounding the central area—i.e., the mausoleum on its podium. As has been stated earlier, the eight sections are seen as icons of the eight rivers if paradise. The eight paradisal rivers are contrasted to the four rivers of the earthly Eden.

"If the garden was conceived as a microcosm of the physical world axially organized in accordance with basic cosmological ideals, the tomb in the center epitomized those ideals: the square plinth stood for the material universe, the dome for the circle of eternity, while the octagon could symbolize the transition from the one to the other. . . ."[96] The horizontal division of the *chahar-bagh* with the tomb as axis can be represented graphically (See: **Figure 215**).

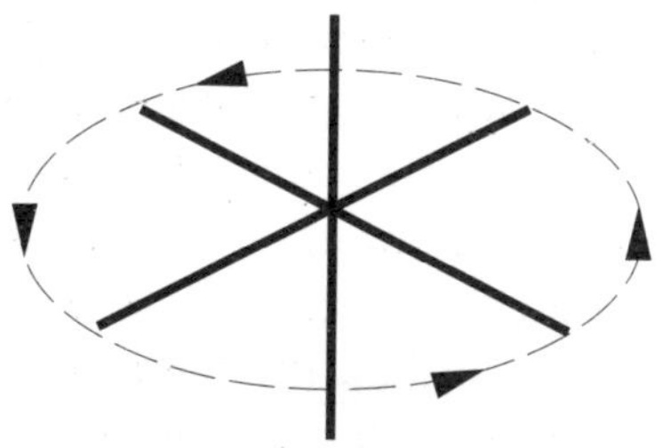

Figure 215-- a revolving axis

The concept of the tomb as axis is further underlined by the fact that virtually every Islamic tomb or mausoleum is basically cross-axial, en plan, whether square or octagonal. By extension this cosmic axis is focused, or revolves around the remains of the deceased. He then becomes, by pride of place, the center. To take this concept one step further, it may then be implied that where wives and family are buried with the deceased—e.g., Muhammad 'Adil Shah, Sultan of Bijapur in the *Gol Gumbaz*—the male is centered and the wives and other members of the family are tangential, thereby gaining their luster from the *pater familia*; a patristic state of affairs. There are few exceptions.

The central cenotaph of the *Taj Mahal* and the sarcophagus in the crypt below refer and hold the Mumtaz Mahal, while that of Shah Jahan rests to the side. However, this was not the original concept. It is said that Shah Jahan had planned his tomb to mirror the *Taj Mahal* across the Jumna, mirror it in every way. It was to be axially in line with the ensemble of his favorite, Mumtaz Mahal.[97] Such a concept is indeed grand, imperial. The totals effect would have been unbelievable in its scope. When the Emperor Aurangzib buried his father, Shah Jahan, who had been deposed four years earlier, he may have acceded to his father's wishes by placing his body in this subsidiary position—i.e., next to the centered and adored Mumtaz Mahal—or, he may have done so to honor the Mumtaz Mahal, or, it may have been a final mark of the low esteem that this ambitious Mughal had for his father. Who is to know?

Nonetheless, the tomb centered in a *chahar-bagh* is a potent reminder of the here and now. The mausoleum in the center refers to the hereafter and becomes an iconic axis, particularly with the often dominating dome, and the two-tiered arrangement of the cenotaph and the sarcophagus.[98] Four notable exceptions are apparent within the major ensembles under consideration in this study—i.e., the *Tomb of Sher Shah*, the *Tomb of Isa Khan*, the *Ibrahim Rausa* and the *Taj Mahal*.

Chahar Bagh (Continued)

The *Tomb of Sher Shah* at Saseram, built in 1540 before the Mughals commenced their grand mausoleum complexes, may be seen as a transitional ensemble (See: **Plate 37**). It is set in the near center of an artificial lake rather than a Persian inspired garden. However, its placement with the surrounding body of water may be viewed as possessing a certain iconographic concept. As has been stated, water has been a symbol of cleansing, both physical and spiritual for many of the world religions. Ablution is one of the required activities for all Muslims prior to prayer. Not only is it sacred to Muslims, more importantly it is sacred to both Buddhists and Hindus alike. Therefore, this water centered tomb would have appealed to the Buddhists and Hindu of India as well as the Muslims. It signifies cleansing, more importantly, the cleansing of the spirit, especially of the one for whom the mausoleum was raised.

The *chahar bagh* was normally conceived of as a square form. Yet, the *Tomb of Isa Khan* at Delhi, of 1547, is found in the center of an ensemble that is octagonal (See: **Plate 40**). Constructed eighteen years before the *Tomb of Humayun* to which it is adjacent, it appears to be antithetical to its massive neighbor. Centered and placed upon a large, low terrace, the tomb is the focal point, much in the same way that the *Tombs of Humayun, Akbar* and *Jahangir* are. The enclosure is bisected at the cardinal points as well as the intercardinal points, creating eight equal wedge shapes. Not only four and sixteen are auspicious numbers, as has been noted above, but also eight is a favorable integer. Eight, as four and sixteen is a feminine number. It symbolizes perfection, divine justice and the balance between opposites--e.g., attraction and repulsion, positive and negative. Eight is an evenly even number and the first cube number--i.e., 2^3 (2 x 2 x 2 = 8). Next to the square, the octagon and octagram appear time and again in Islamic art and design and appear to be a favored shape. The Qur'an does not set guidelines for the garden, the *Paradisal Garden*. It is not relegated to the square. This garden, this octagonal garden must also be seen as a variation on the *chahar bagh*. In addition, as with the other gardens and funerary ensembles, the ensemble of *Tomb of Isa Khan* lies within a fortified enclosure. Within Christian iconography, the walled garden signifies purity and chastity. This interpretation is not seen to be applicable to Islamic iconography, although both purity and chastity have their place within this faith. The walled garden, when applied to a tomb ensemble must be viewed as a sacred precinct that is related to the *Paradisal Garden*.

The *Ibrahim Rauza* built in 1615 in Bijapur is the third anomalous ensemble (See: **Plate 63**). Set within an enclosure that is square is the only similarity that this tomb has to those major *chahar baghs* that went before--i.e., the *Tomb of Humayun* (1565) and the *Tomb of Akbar* (1604-1613). This is doubtlessly due to the fact that the sultans of Bijapur were independent and separate from the Mughal Empire until 1686 C.E. Bijapur had always been its own master, going its own way until the were subdued. The great *Gol Gumbaz* is testament of this fact. Nonetheless the *Ibrahim Rauza* is eclectic in a number of ways. The Tomb with its facing mosque rest upon a raised rectangular terrace. The proportion of this terrace is close to the same proportion as that of Shah Jahan's *Shalimar Bagh*. The tomb is square while the mosque is rectangular. The terrace is not centered within the larger square enclosure on the vertical axis, rather, the mausoleum end of the terrace is abutted to the external wall of the enclosure and, again not centered but below the central, horizontal axis as shown in **Plate 63**. The reason for this arrangement is, indeed, a conundrum.

Finally, the incomparable *Taj Mahal*, the tomb built by Shah Jahan for his beloved consort

Chahar Bagh (Continued)

Hazrat Mumtaz-uz-Zamani, is universally considered to be one of the world's most beautiful structures (See: **Plate 99**). Its perfection is lauded far and wide. Yet, as a tomb within a *chahar bagh,* it presents a deviation from what had gone before. The magnificent, preceding tombs--i.e., the *Tomb of Humayun*, the *Tomb of Akbar*, the *Tomb of Jahangir*--found their mausolea placed within the center of their *chahar bagh*. Not so with the *Taj Mahal*! Here he tomb rises from the end of its *chahar bagh*. It is to be noted, as many have done before, the proportions of the *Taj Mahal's chahar bagh* is nearly identical to the lower *bagh* and the intervening rectangle of Shah Jahan's *Shalimar Bagh* (See: **Plates 94& 99**). Within the rectangle sits the mausoleum on a substantial plinth, flanked by a *kiosk* and an identical *masjid*. This arrangement differs dramatically from preexisting standards. Nonetheless, the effect of the whole, particularly when entering the confines of the *chahar bagh* from the central portal of the imposing gate is breathtaking, incomparable, unparalleled in its impact. Our eye is immediately drawn down the waterways to the tomb. If the *chahar bagh* of a tomb ensemble is the *Paradisal Garden*, then surely this is as close to Paradise mortal man can approach. Its beauty and perfection is to be found in the deviation from the standard.

If, as has been stated, that the proposed tomb of Shah Jahan was to mirror the *Taj Mahal* on the opposite bank of the Jumna and connected by a bridge, then an additional iconographic consideration must be made. The two mausolea could be superimposed forming a symbolic single ensemble (See: **Plate 100**). In such an imposition, the two would have been closely related to the plan of the *Shalimar Bagh* of Lahore as **Plate 100** indicates. The two mausolea, connected by a cosmic bridge would symbolically be not only connected, but become one. This would solve the "problem" of the seemingly eccentric layout of the Taj Mahal's ensemble, creating a unity. Unfornately, we have only to dream, to surmise, not only the total effect in actuality, but also in concept.

Finally, the ensemble of the *Tomb of Safdar Jang* (See: **Plates 92 & 101**) presents an interesting conundrum. It simply does not conform to andy of the *chahar-bagh* designs heretofore considered. It is divided into four mirrored cross-axial sections. In that it conforms to the rudimentary definition of a *chahar-bagh*. However, there are numerous deviations. Neither the *Pitha Mandala*, nor the *Ugrapitha Mandala* is easily applicable to this *chahar-bagh* as is indicated in **Plate 92**. each quarter consists of a typically square, cross-axially bisected element. These elements are then surrounded with sections approximately half the width of the smaller square plots (See: **Plate 101**). The four tanks exist outside of the four *baghs*. Two mandalas are seen to have possible applications to this chahar-bagh--i.e., an *Ubhayachandita Mandala* of one-hundred-sixty-nine *pada* applied to the whole and an *Ugrapitha Mandala* applied only to one of the quarters. The *Ubhayachandita Mandala* presents numerous problems in that a number of elements fit rather uncomfortably within this *mandala*. On the other hand, a *Ugrapitha Mandala* contains the quarter elements rather comfortably, however it does not ccontain the four tanks which radiate out in the cardinal directions from the mausoleum on its podium. One may conjecture that in this application the four tanks relate to the four rivers of the earthly Garden of Eden and, therefore, are outside of the celestial sphere. As has been stated, an application of the nine-fold plan over the ensemble does not produce a happy solution.

The *Tomb of Safdar Jang* is admittedly somewhat outside the pale of the traditional Indo-Islamic tomb as far as its proportions are concerned. It is characerized as "a pretentious, ungainly structure"[99] of which "its proportions and the arrangement of its formal elements highlight the disintegration . . . (of Mughal architecture and in which) . . . the vertical proportions are emphasized . . . ."[100] Nonetheless, the *Tomb of Safdar Jang* remains the least breath of what was great.

Plate 93

Shalimar Bagh, Srinagar (Ensemble with ninefold division)

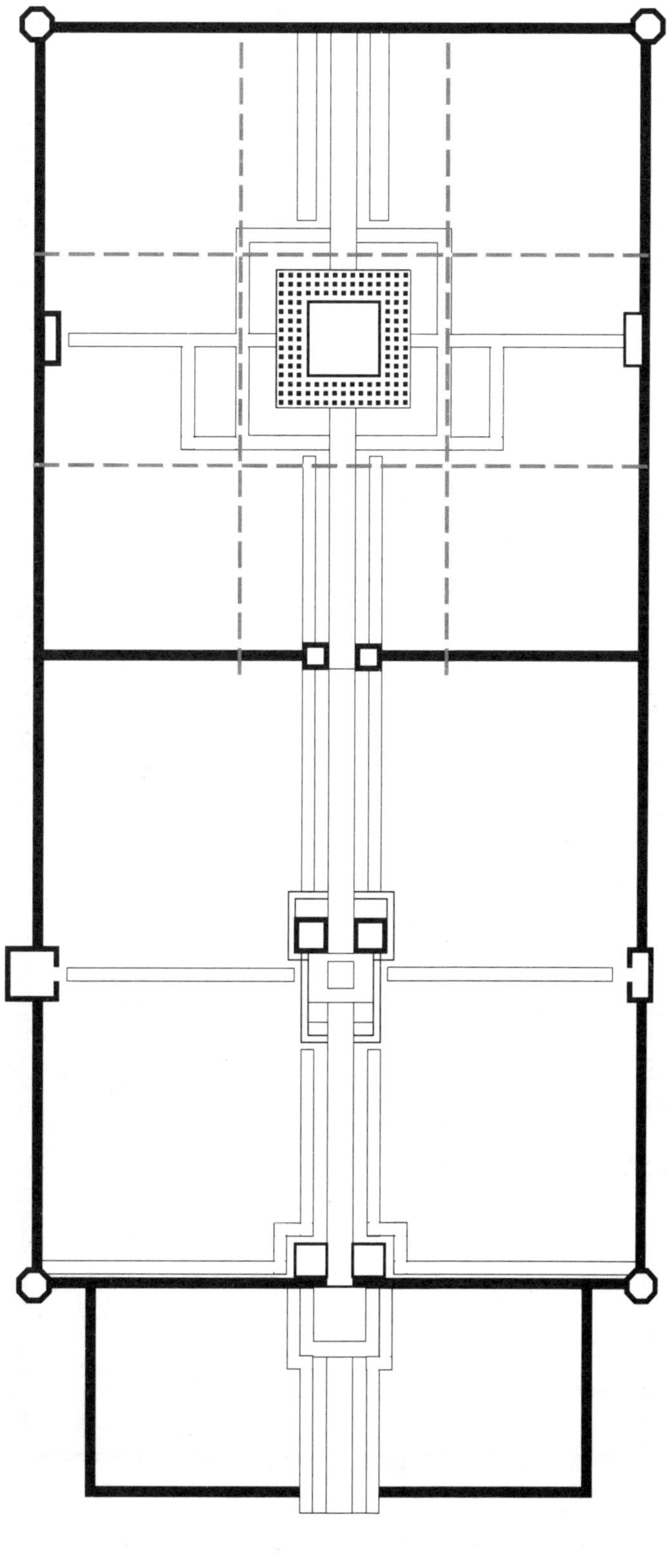

Plate 94

Shalimar Bagh, Lahore, 1634 CE

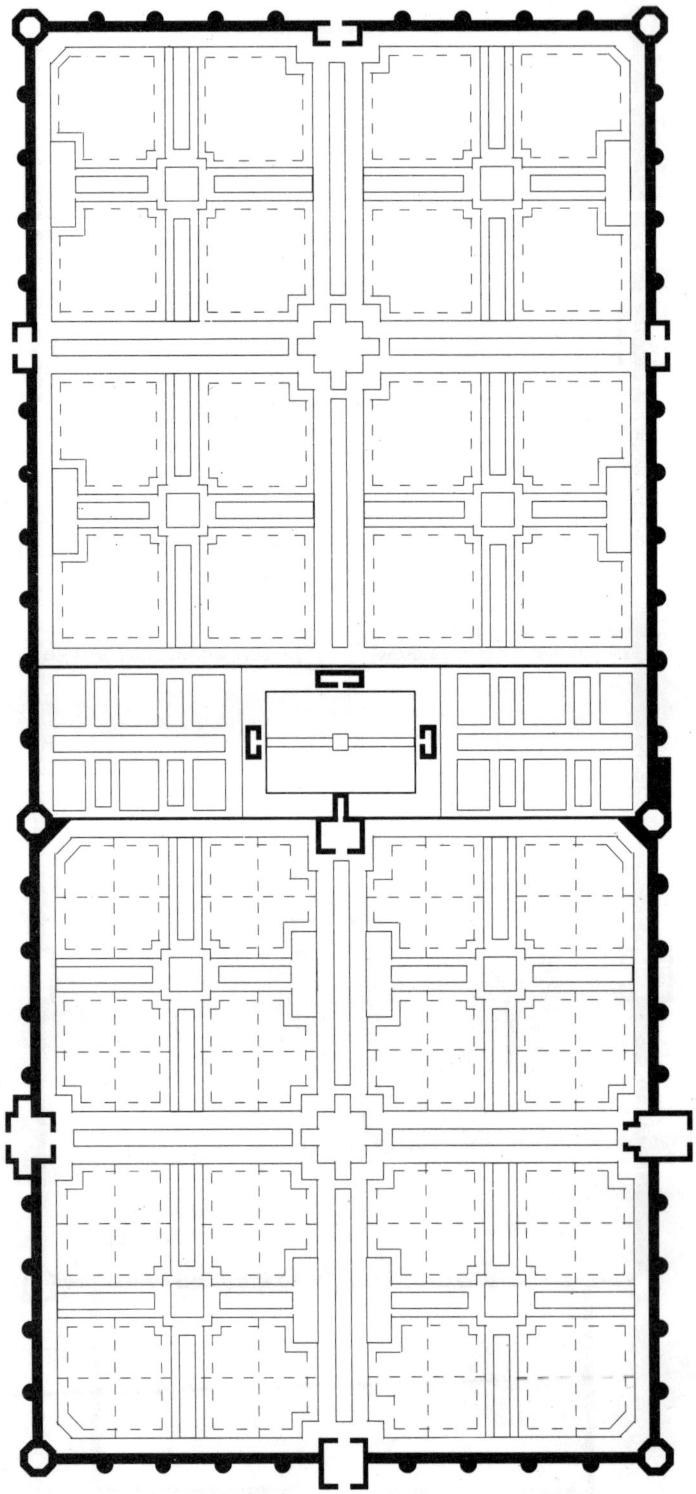

Plate 95

Shahjanahanabad (Red Fort, Delhi) (*Bakhsh Bagh & Mahtab Bagh*)

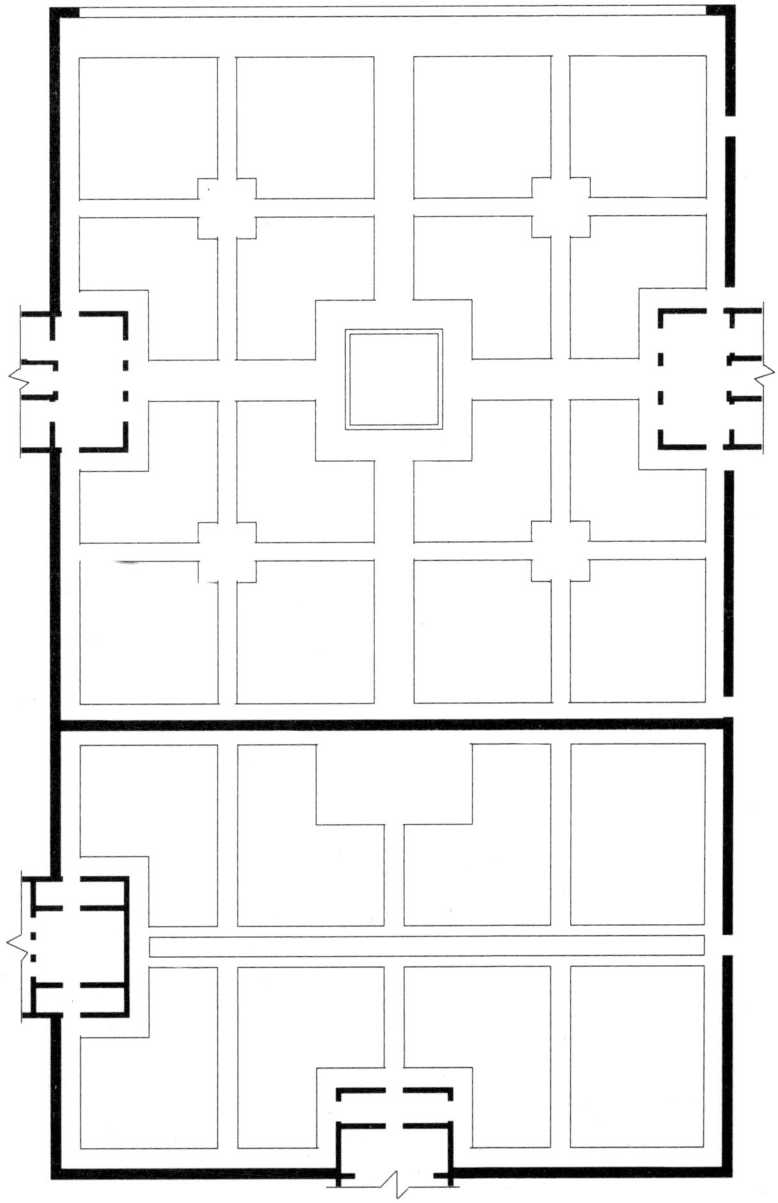

Plate 96
Tomb of Humayun (Ensemble with ninefold division)

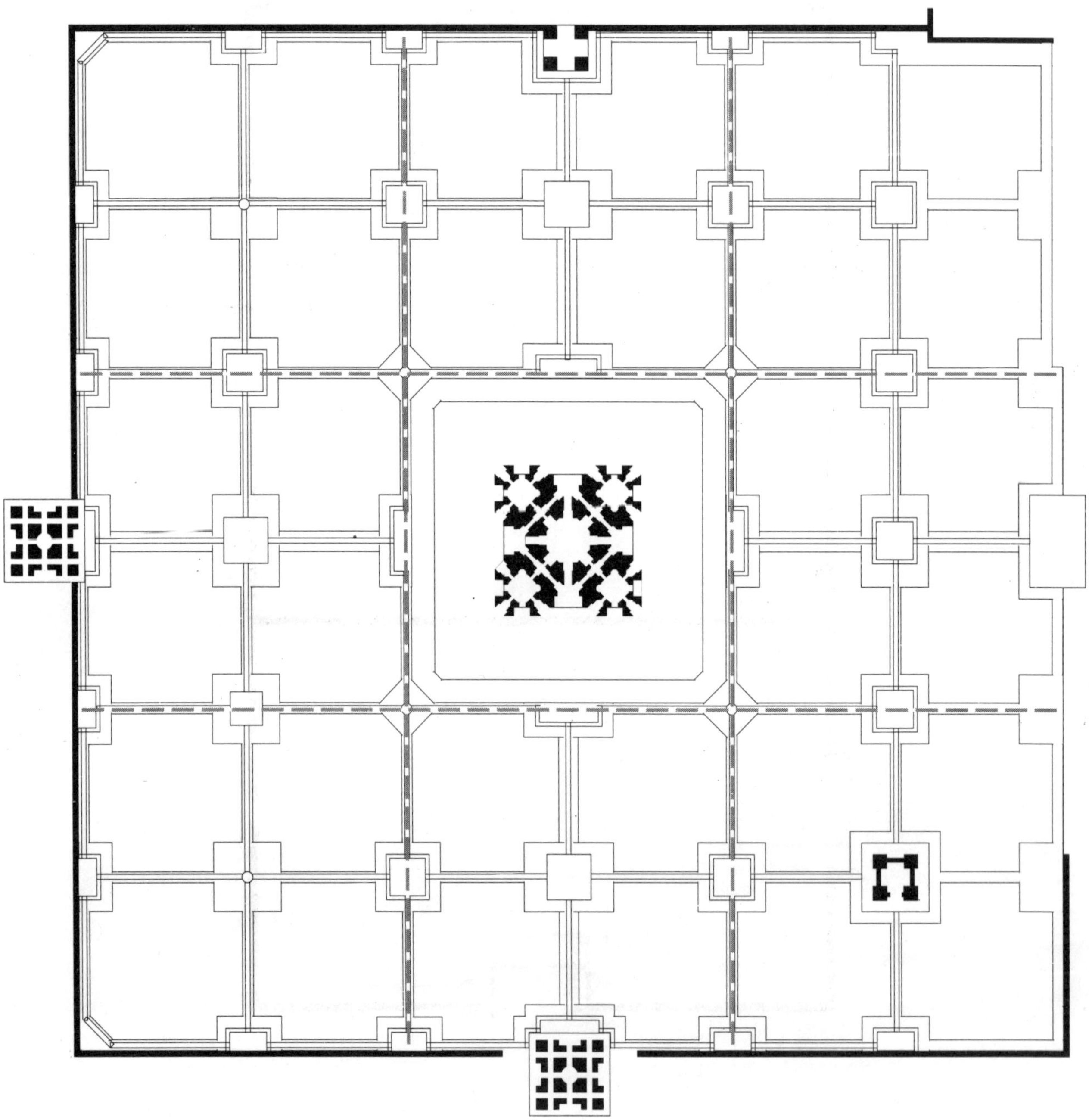

Plate 97
Tomb of Akbar (Ensemble with *Shalimar Bagh* [right])

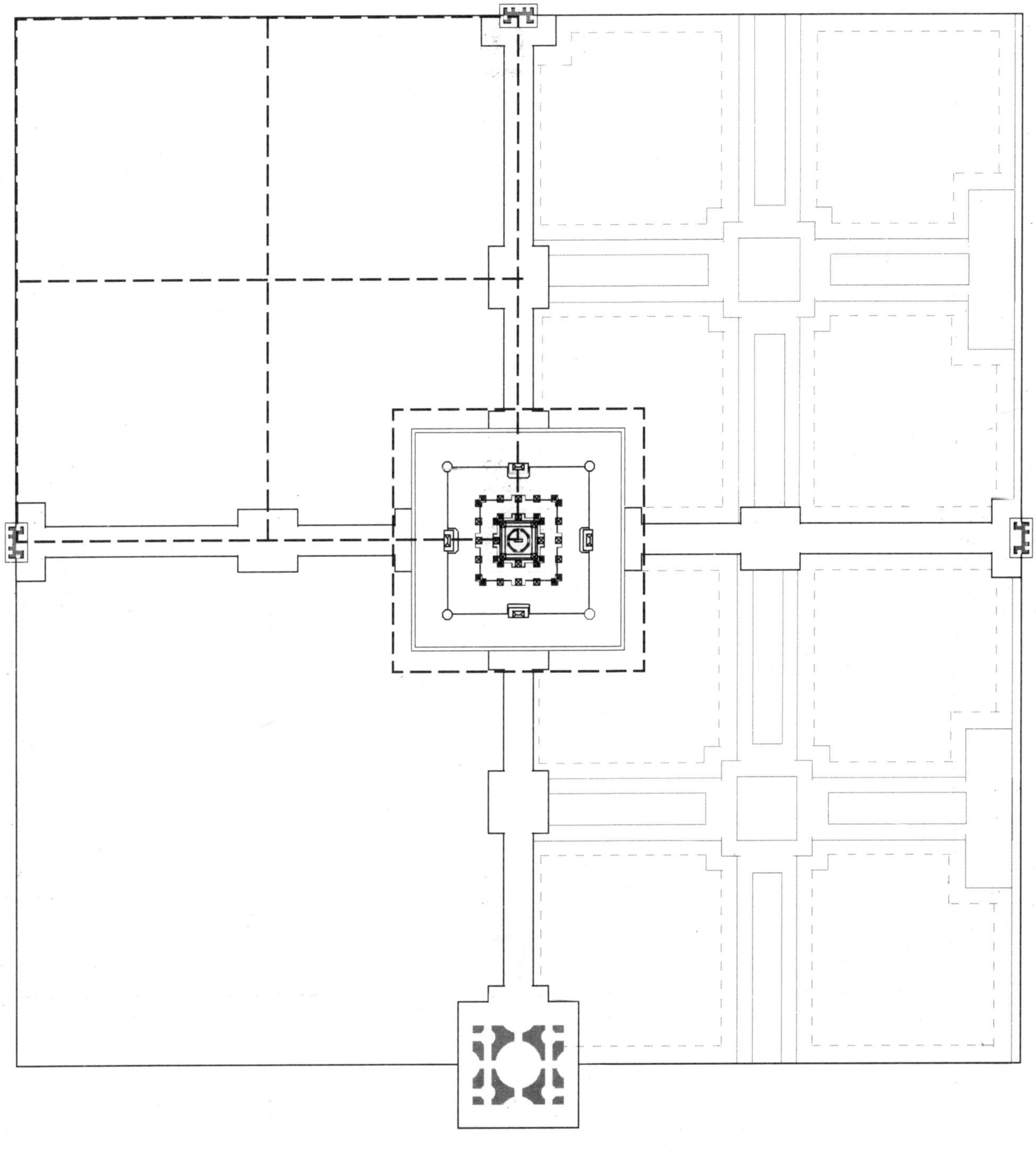

Plate 98
Tomb of Jihangir (Ensemble with *Shalimar Bagh*)

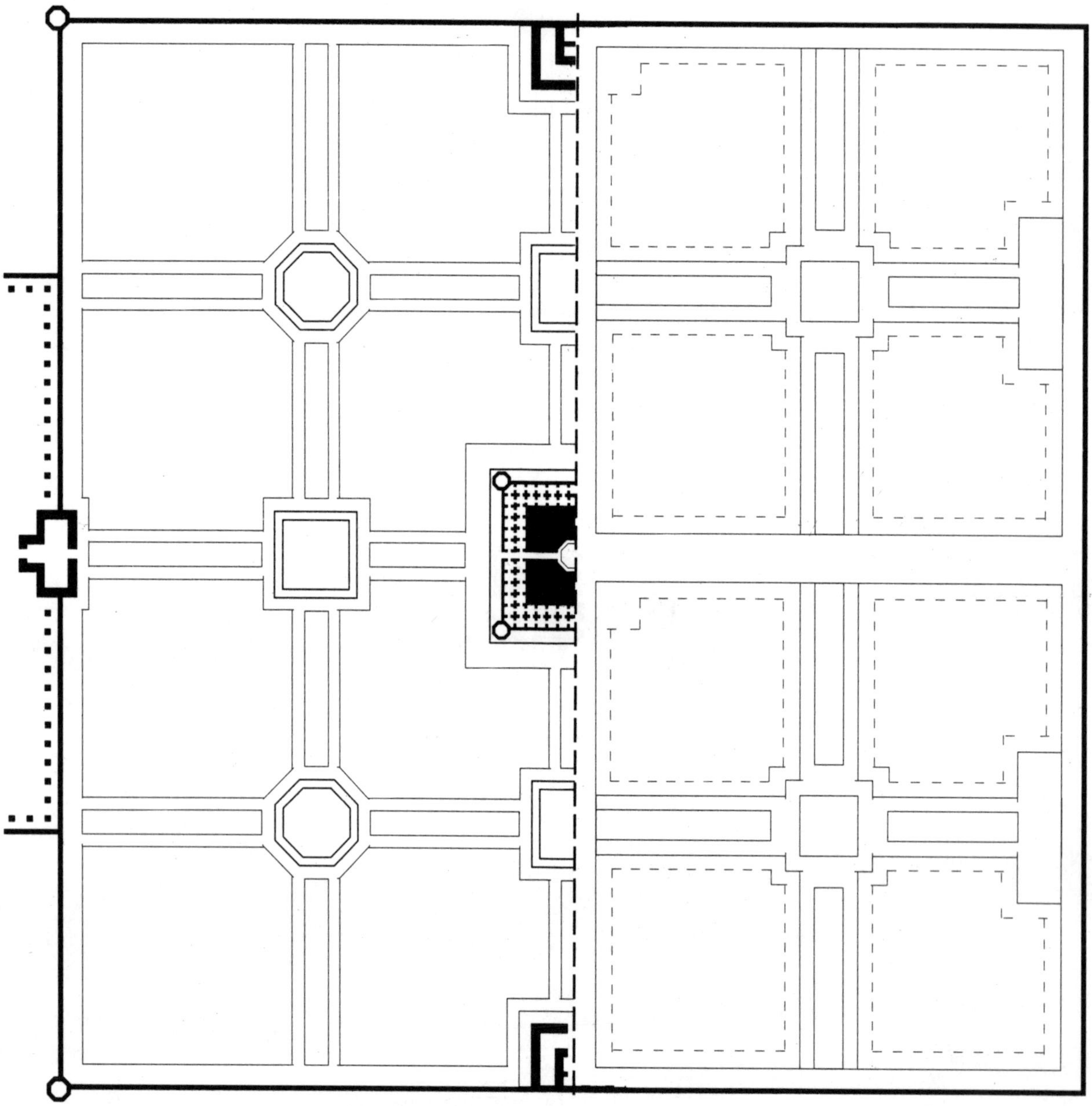

Plate 99
Shah Jahan's *Shalimar Bagh* & *Taj Mahal* Ensemble (Details)

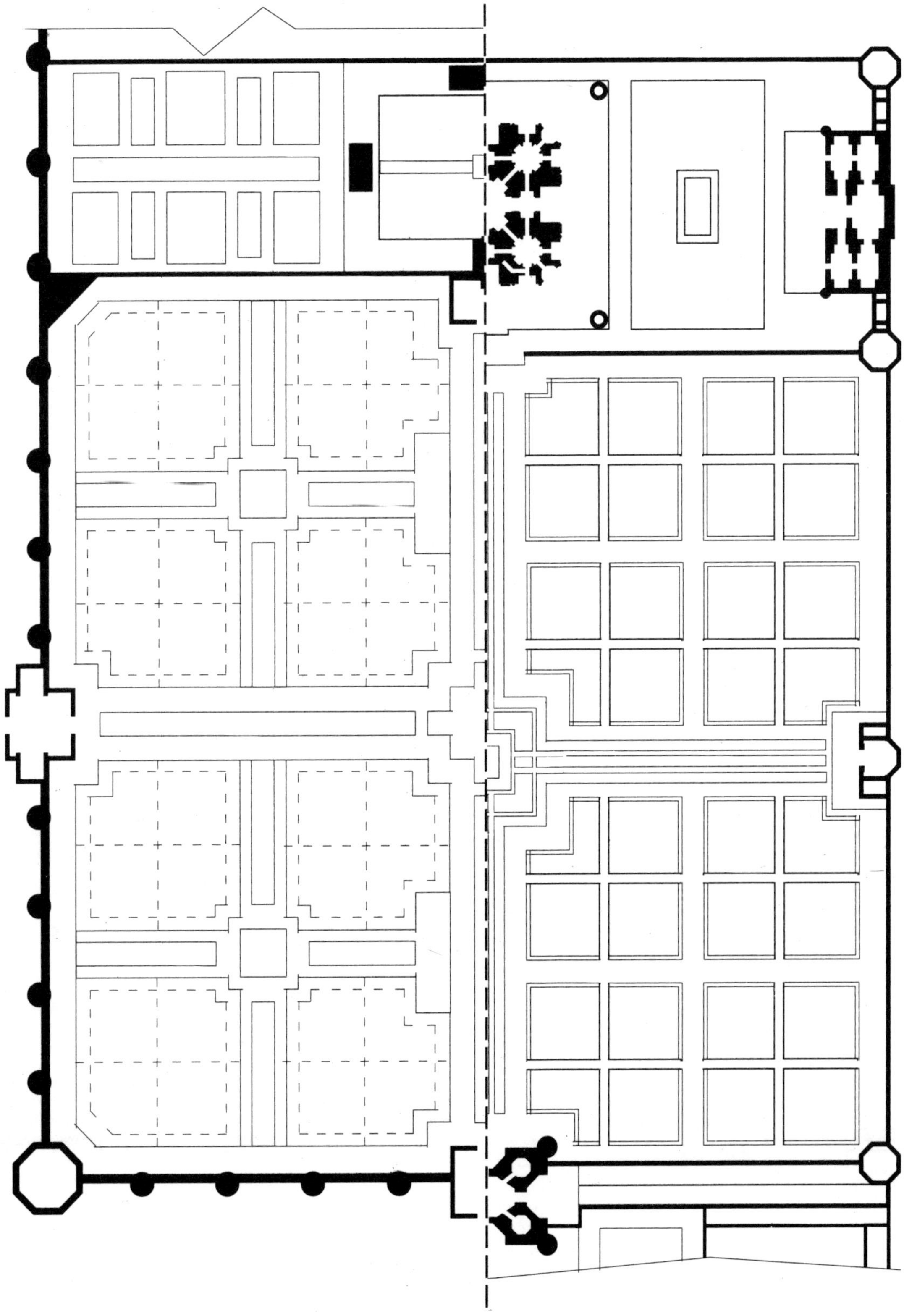

Plate 100

Taj Mahal (mirrored [l.]) & *Shalimar Bagh,* Lahore (r.)

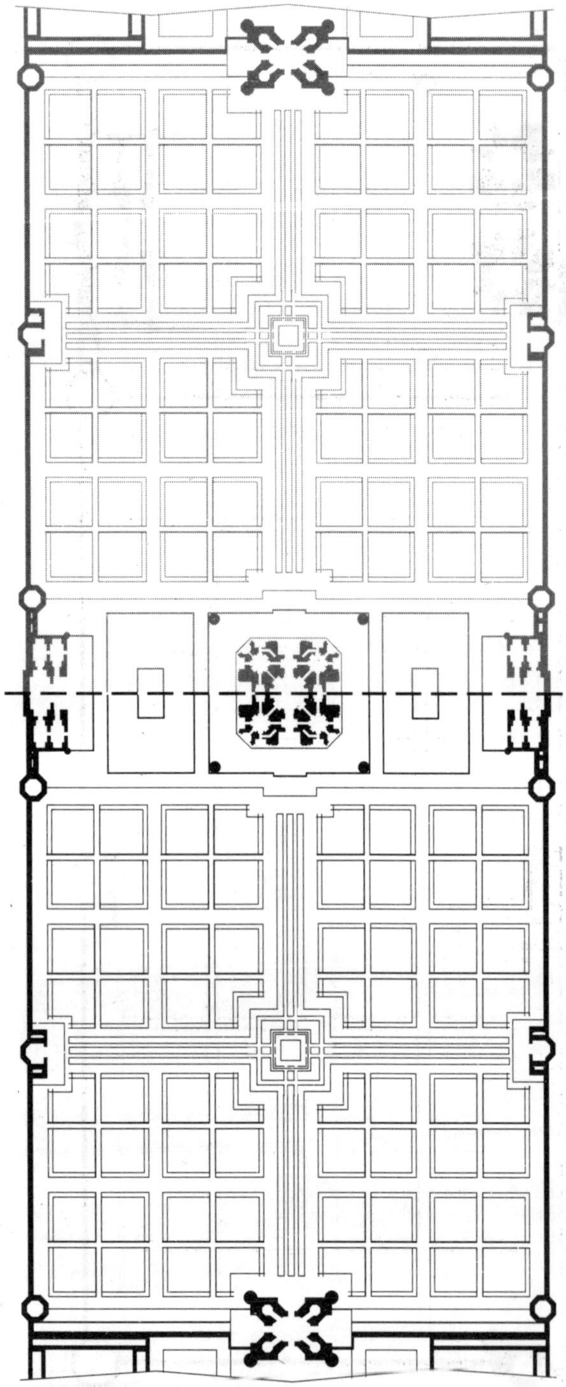

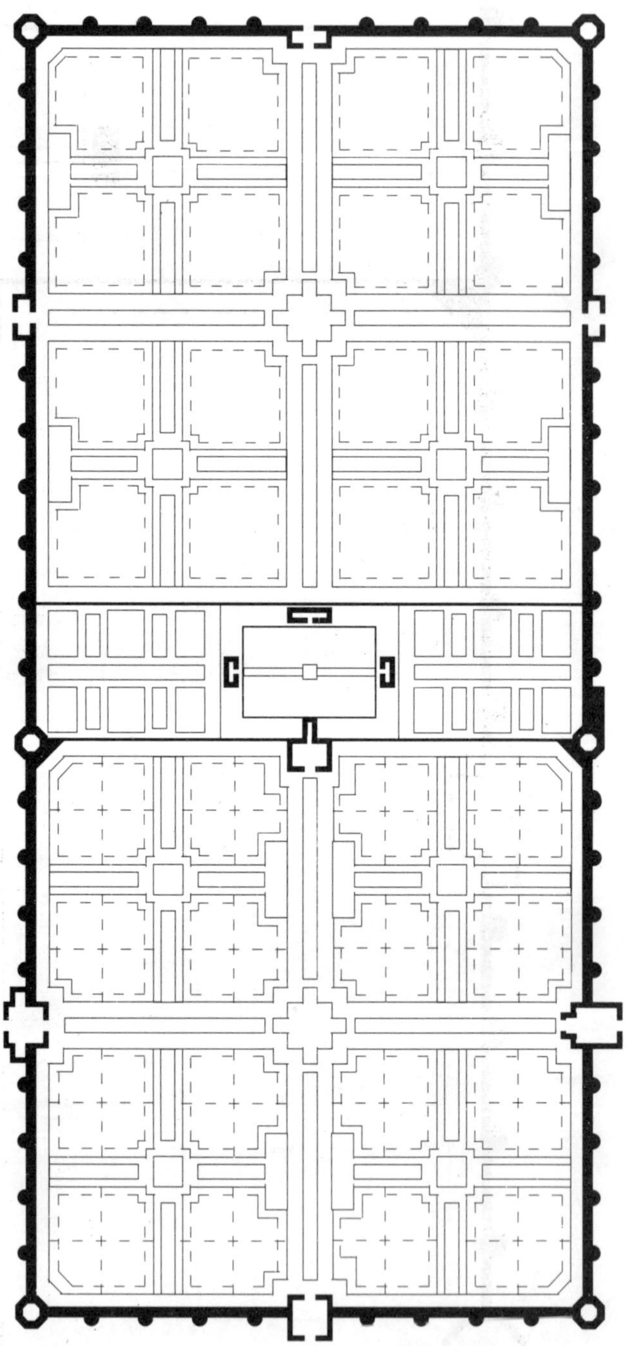

Plate 101

Tomb of Safdar Jang (Ensemble with *Ubhayachandita Mandala* [l.] & *Ugrapitha Mandala* [u.r.])

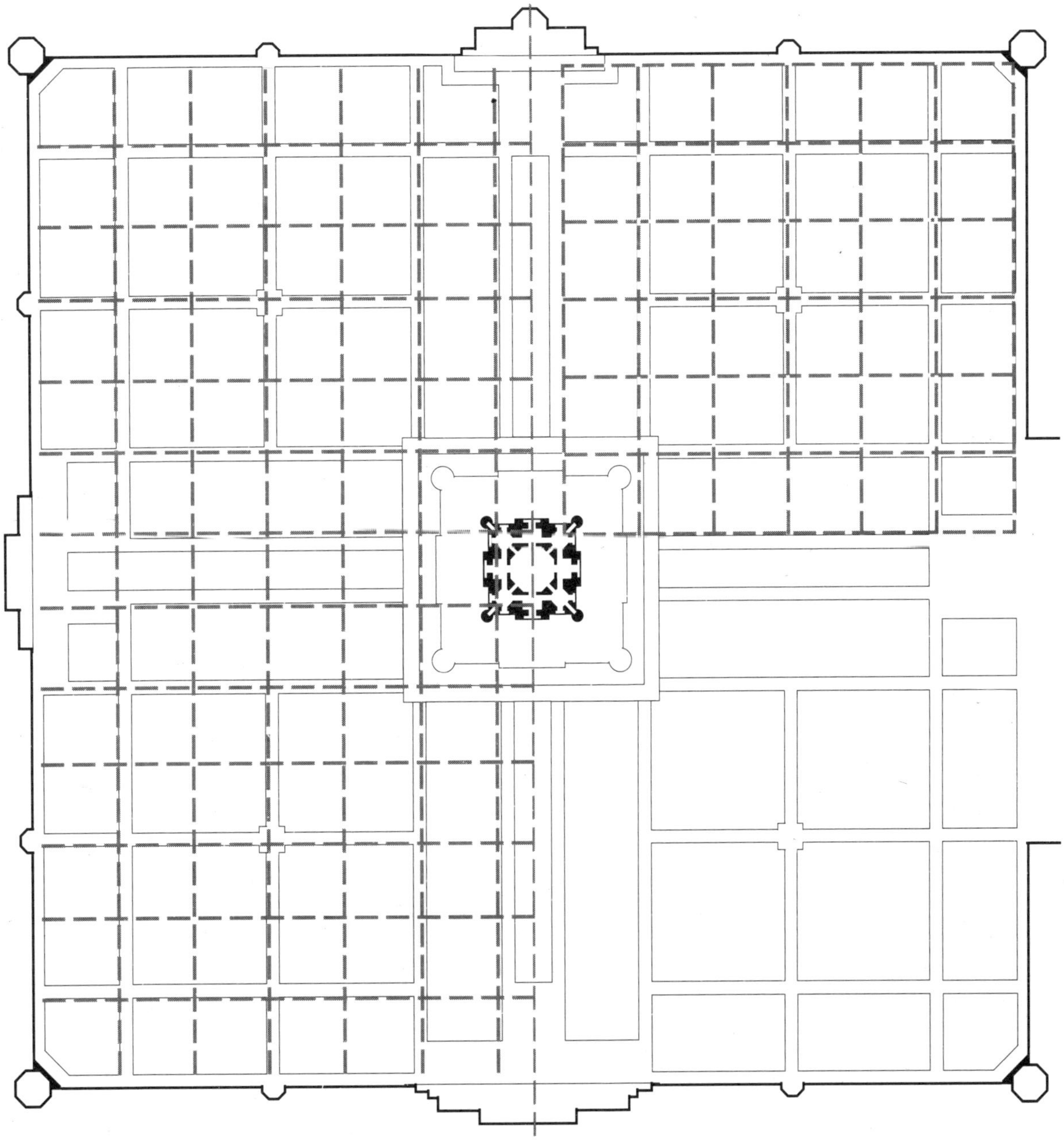

Appendix C

Proportional Comparisons and Miscellaneous Plans

Plate 102
Proportional Comparison with *Deshiya Mandala*

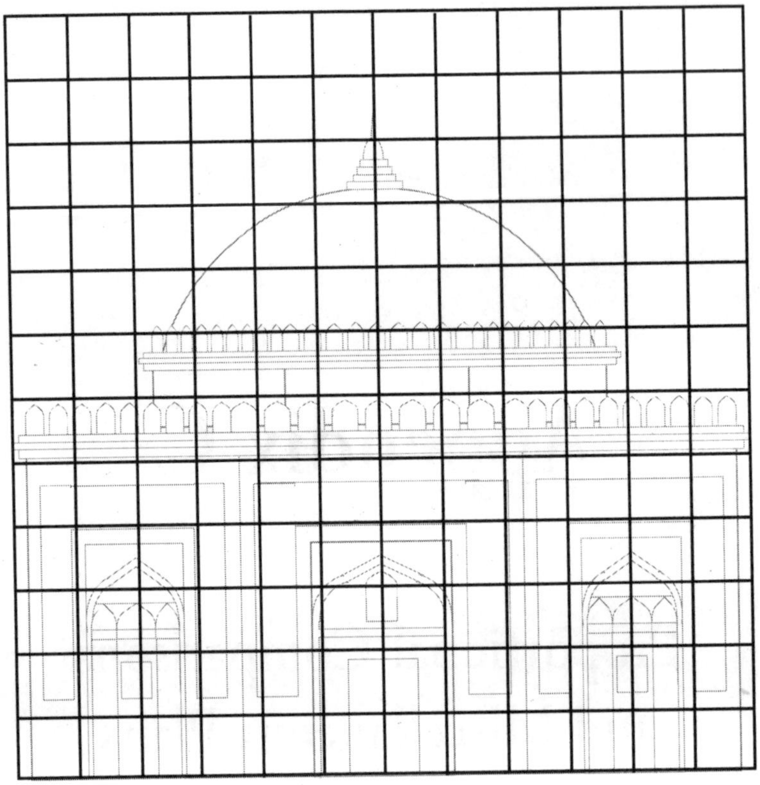

Tomb No. 36 (12:9.5)

Tomb of Sultan Ghari (12:6)

Plate 103
Proportional Comparison with *Deshiya Mandala* (Continued)

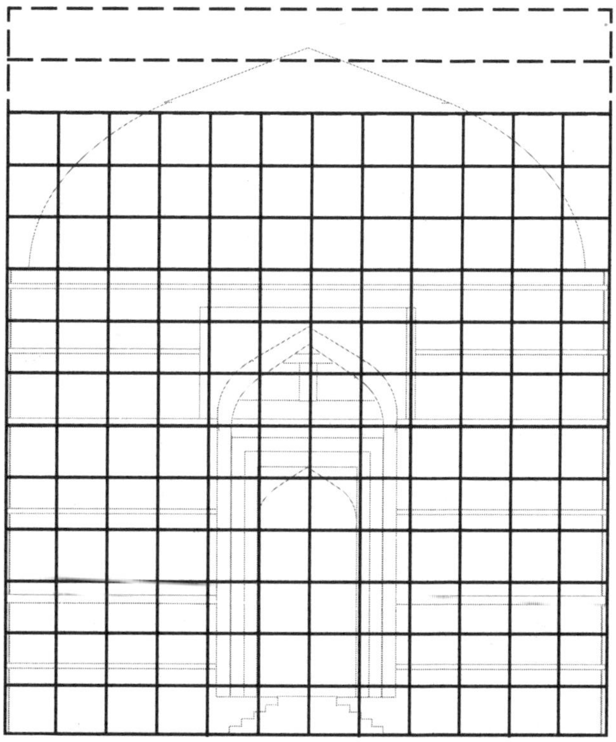

Tomb of Sultan Iltutmish (12:13.5)

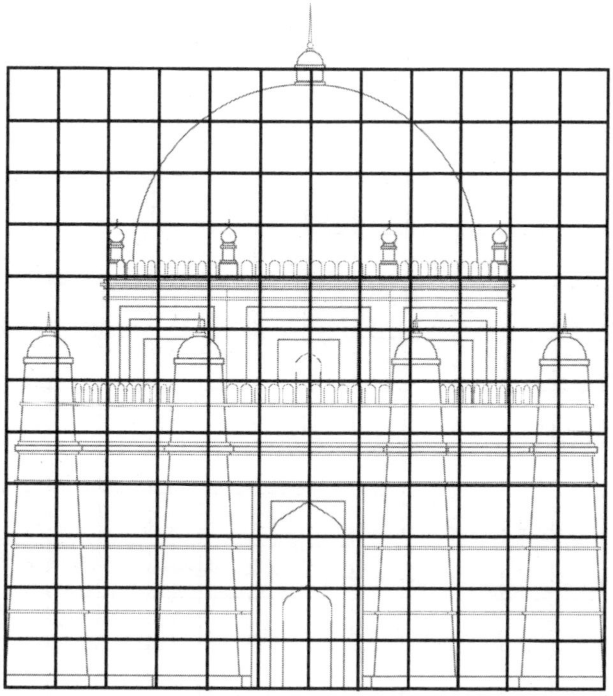

Tomb of Shah Rukn-i 'Alam (12:12)

Plate 104
Proportional Comparison with *Deshiya Mandala* (Continued)

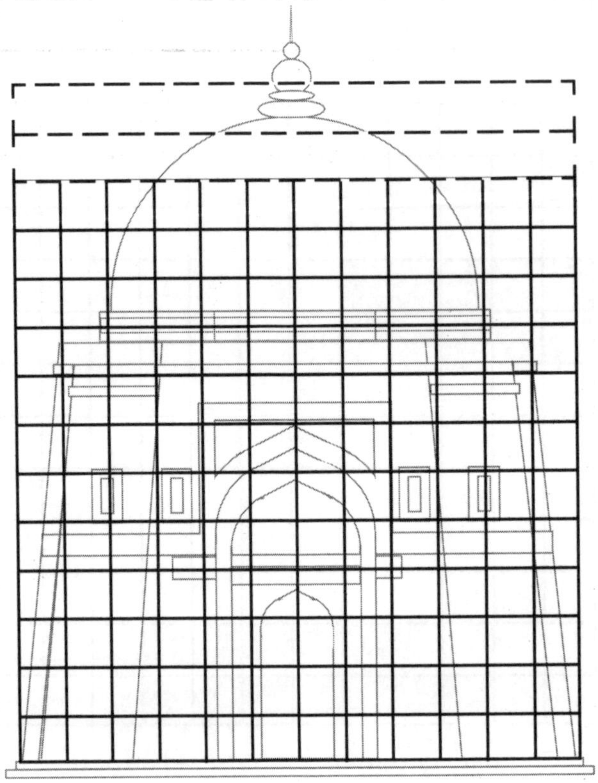

Ghiyas-ud-din Tughluq I (12:13.5)

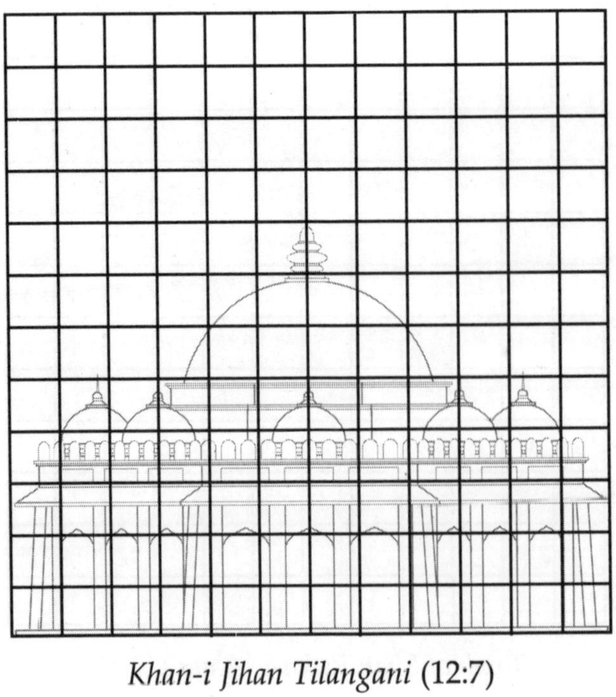

Khan-i Jihan Tilangani (12:7)

Plate 105
Proportional Comparison with *Deshiya Mandala* (Continued)

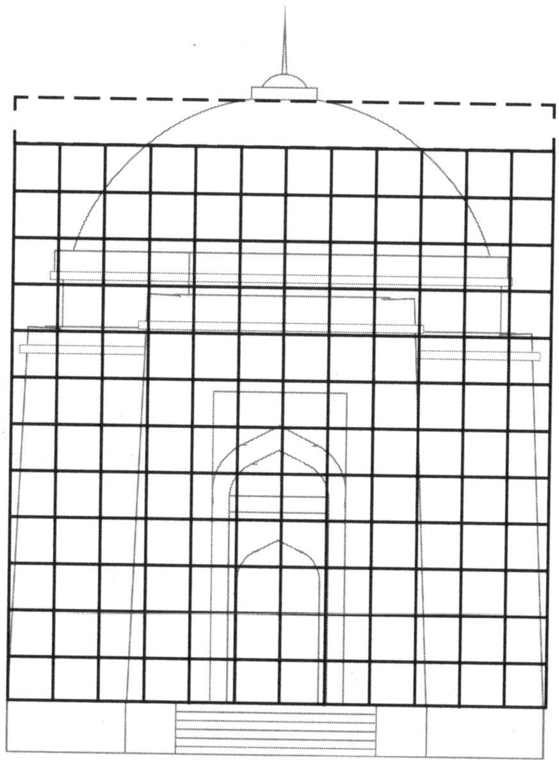

Tomb of Firuz Shah Tughluq (12:13)

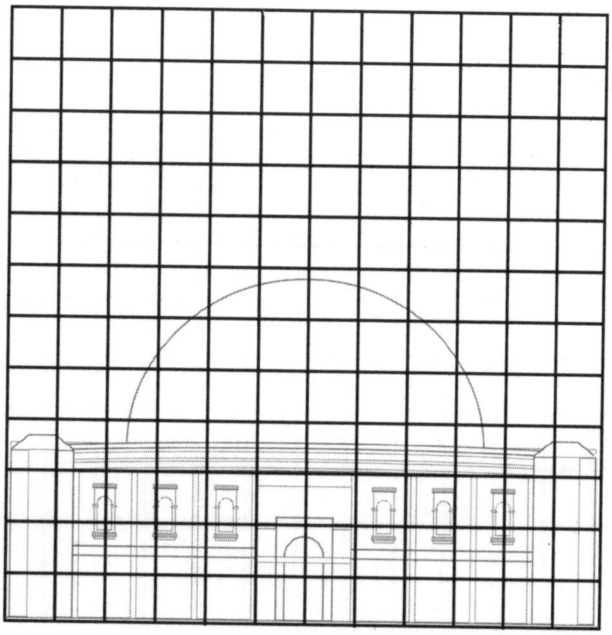

Eklakhi Tomb (12:6.75)

Plate 106
Proportional Comparison with *Deshiya Mandala* (Continued)

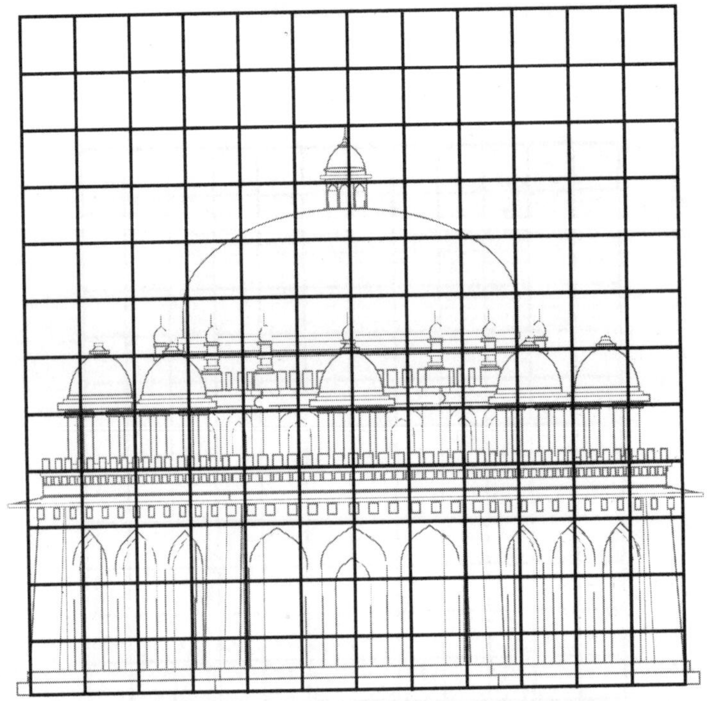

Tombs of Mubarak Shah Sayyid (12:9.5)

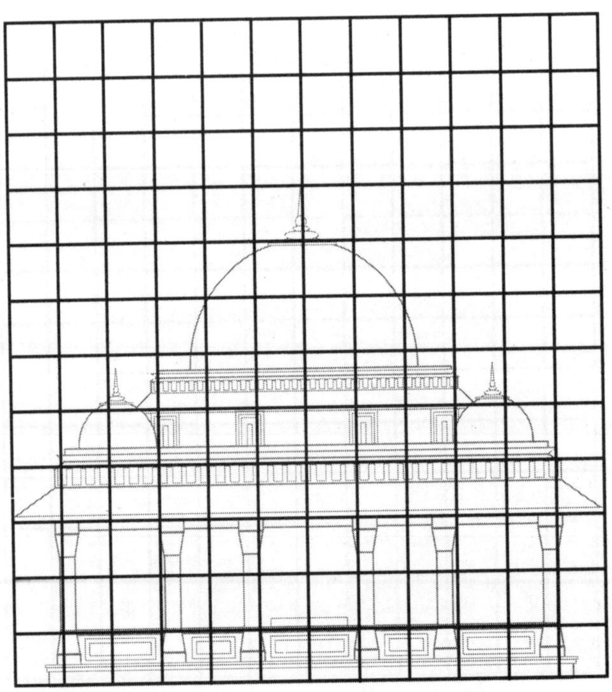

Tombs of Rani Rupmati (12:8)

Plate 107
Proportional Comparison with *Deshiya Mandala* (Continued)

Tomb of Hushang Shah (12:9.5)

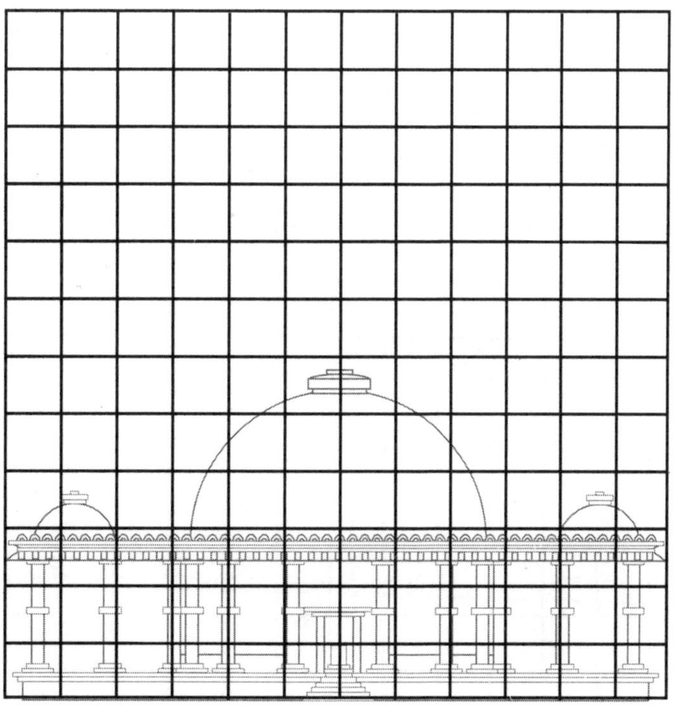

Tomb of Sayyid Usman (12:5.5)

Plate 108

Proportional Comparison with *Deshiya Mandala* (Continued)

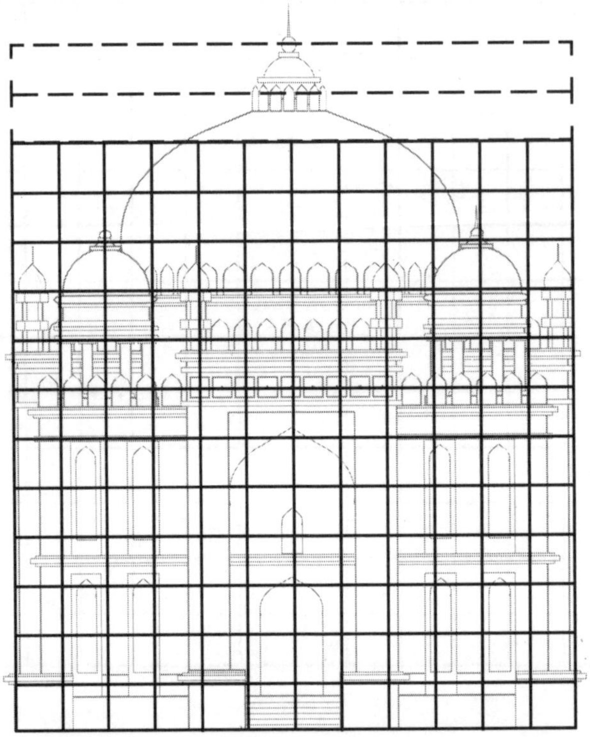

Tomb of Chotte Khan Ka Gunbad (12:13.5)

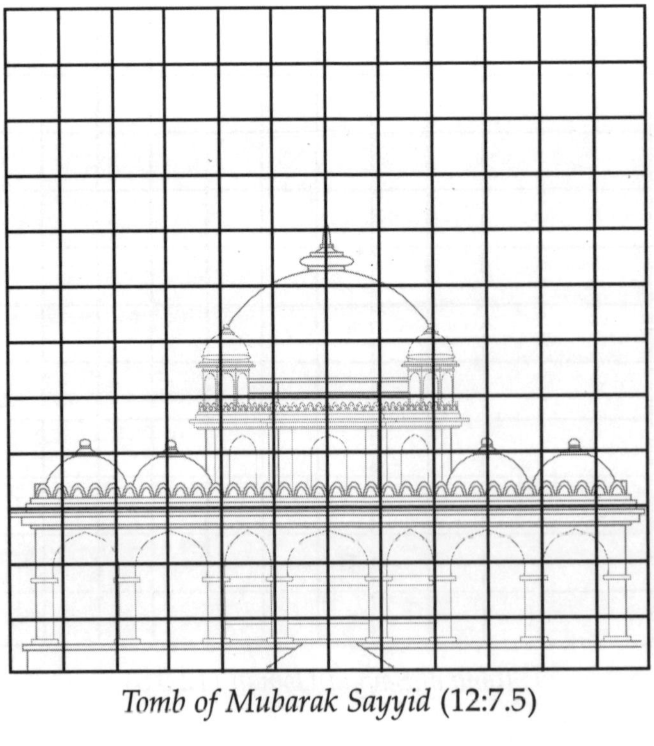

Tomb of Mubarak Sayyid (12:7.5)

Plate 109
Proportional Comparison with *Deshiya Mandala* (Continued)

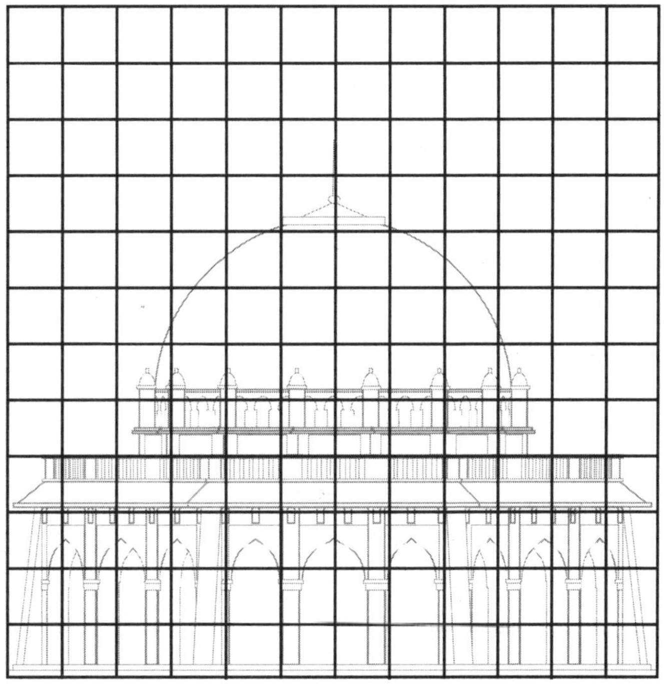

Tomb of Sitandar Lodi (12:8.25)

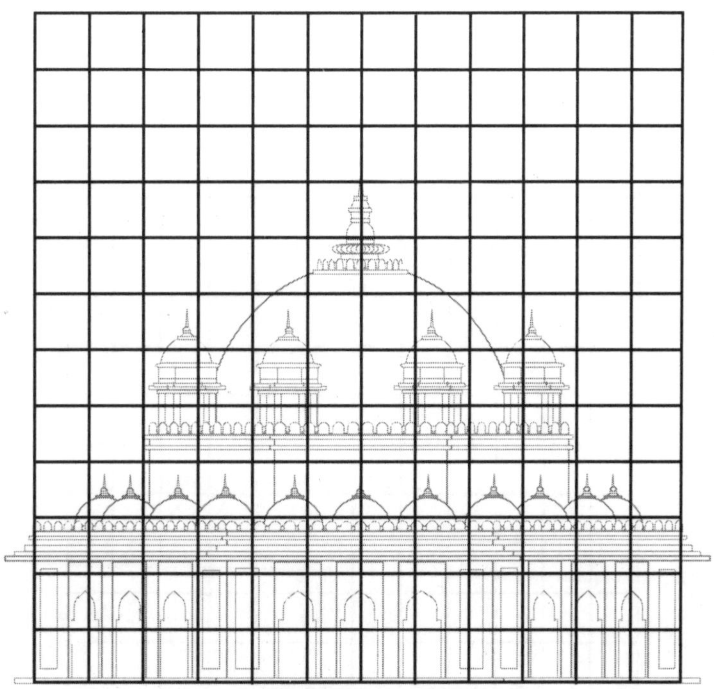

Tomb of Hasan Khan Sur (12:8)

Plate 110
Proportional Comparison with *Deshiya Mandala* (Continued)

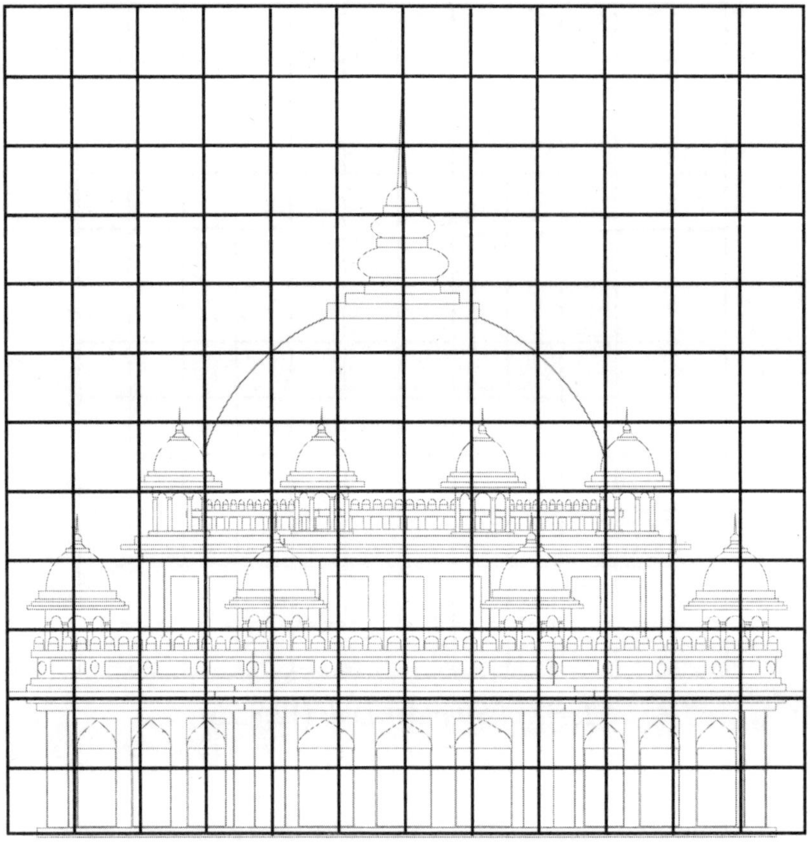

Tomb of Sher Shah (12:9.5)

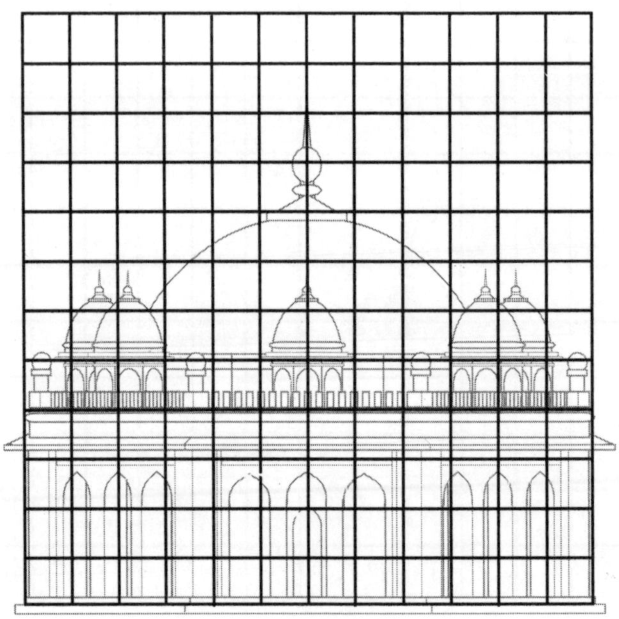

Tomb of Isa Khan Niyazi (12:8)

Plate 111
Proportional Comparison with *Deshiya Mandala* (Continued)

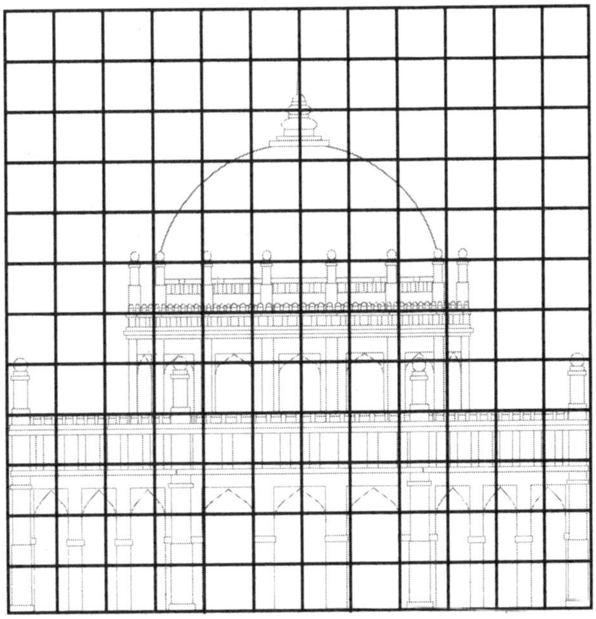

Tomb of Adham Khan (12:9.5)

Tomb of Humayun (12:8.5)

Plate 112
Proportional Comparison with *Deshiya Mandala* (Continued)

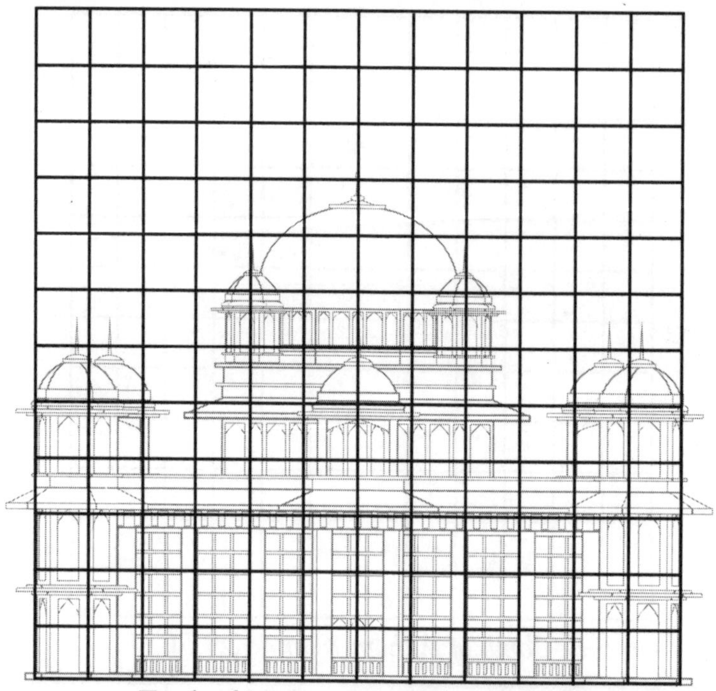

Tomb of Muhammad Ghuas (12:8.5)

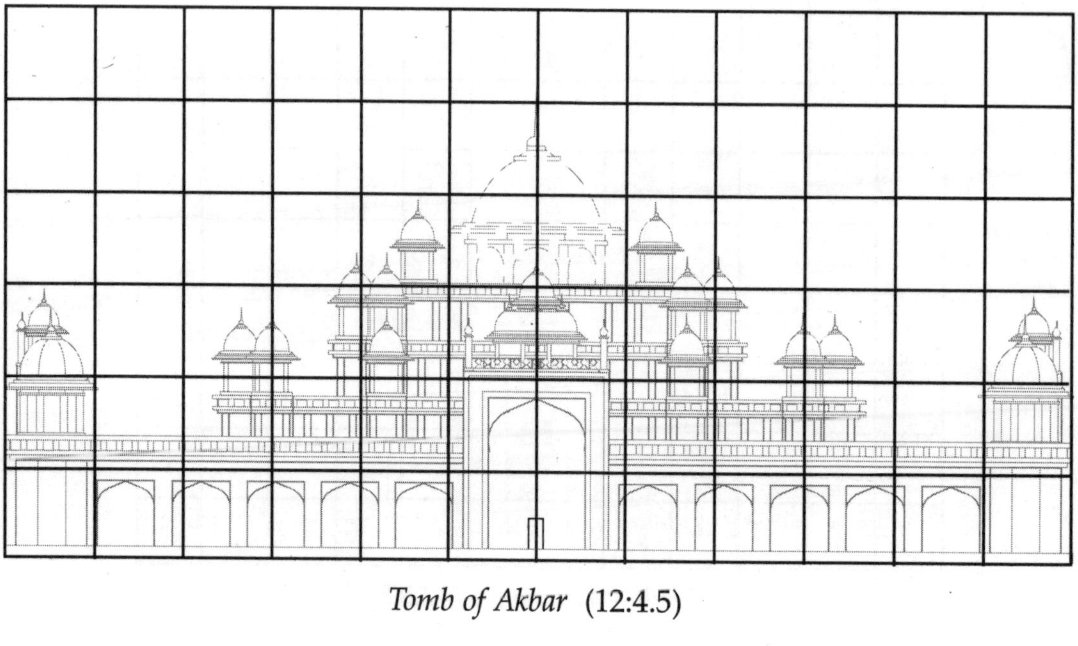

Tomb of Akbar (12:4.5)

Plate 113
Proportional Comparison with *Deshiya Mandala* (Continued)

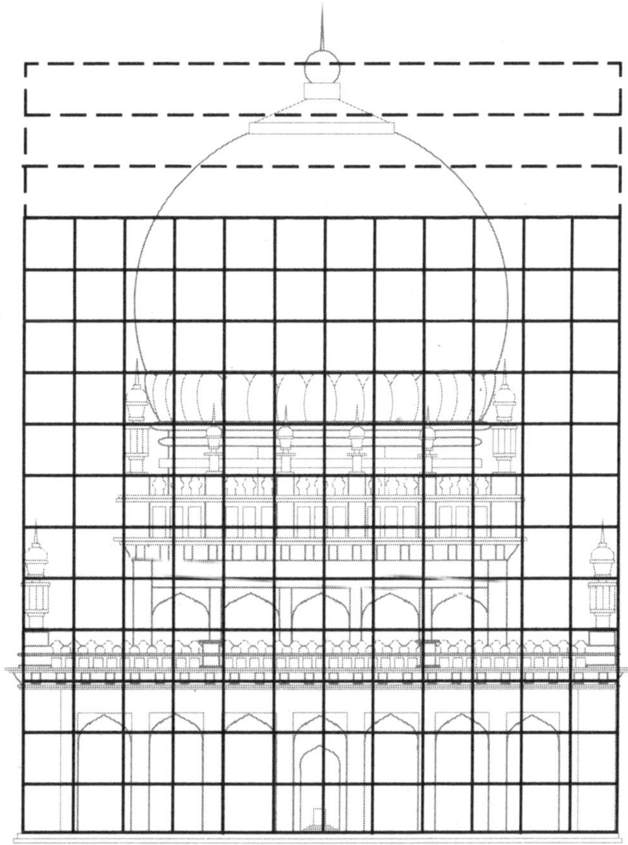

Tomb of Mohammed Quli Qutub Shah (12:14.5)

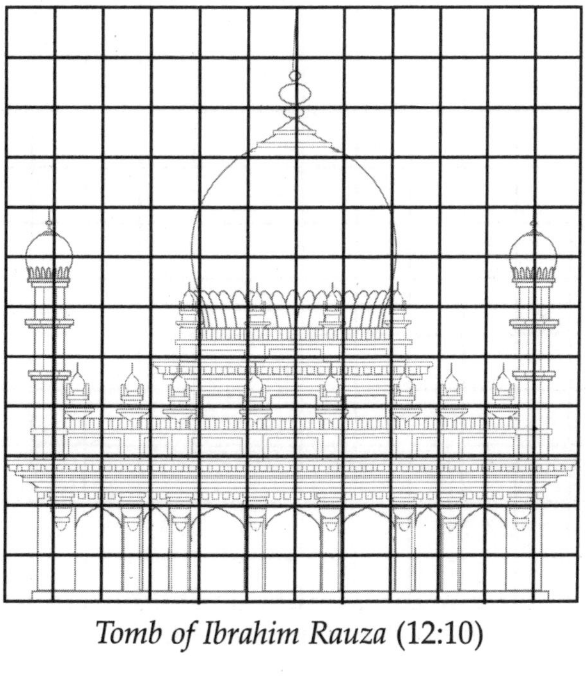

Tomb of Ibrahim Rauza (12:10)

Plate 114
Proportional Comparison with *Deshiya Mandala* (Continued)

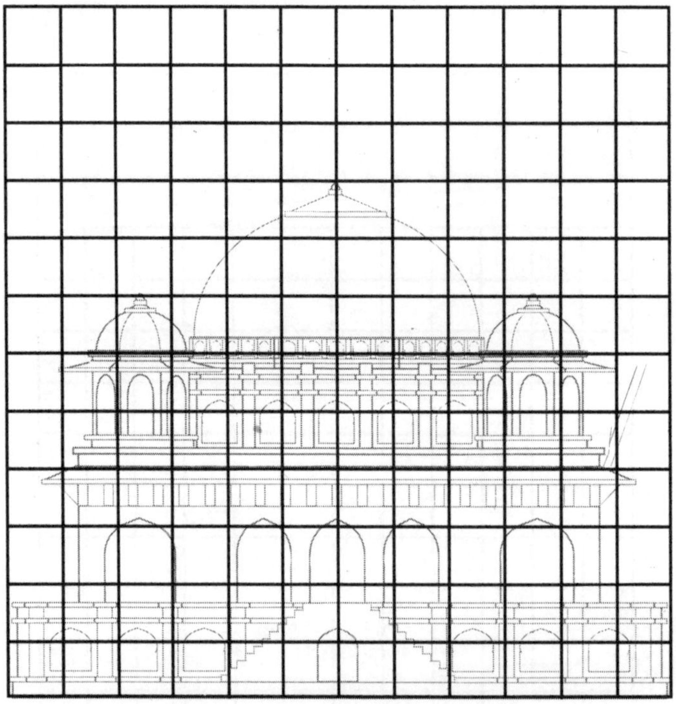

Tomb of Iftikhar Khan (12:9)

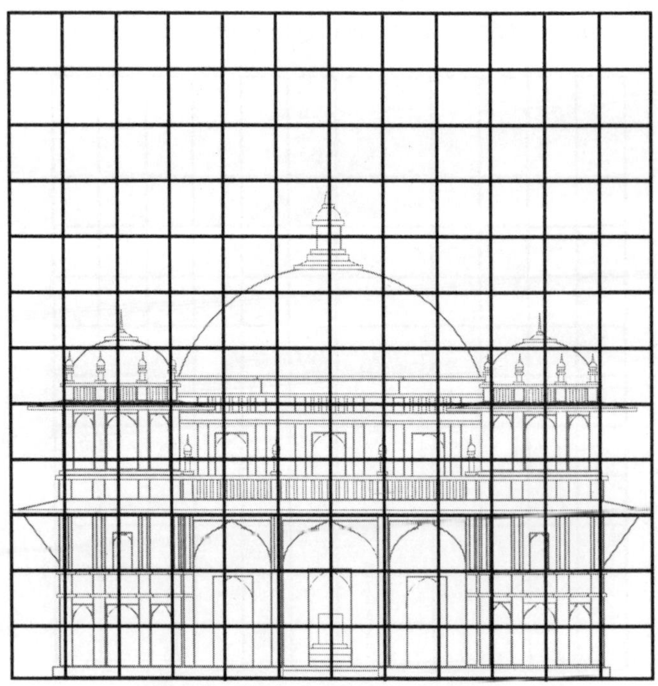

Tomb of Shah Daulat (12:8.5)

Plate 115
Proportional Comparison with *Deshiya Mandala* (Continued)

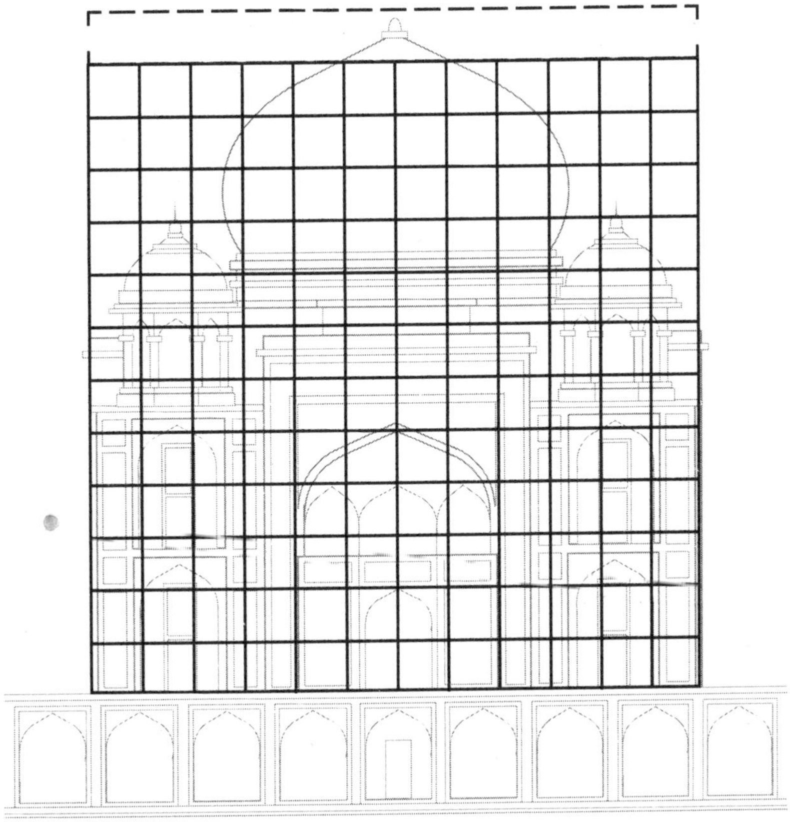

Tomb of Khan Khanan (12:12.5)

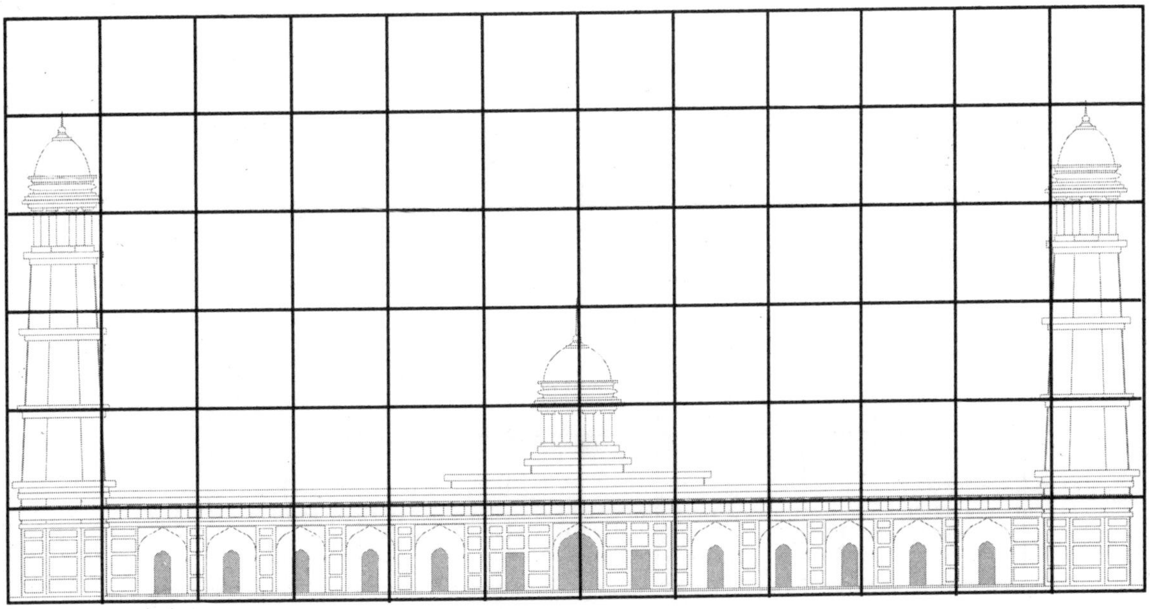

Tomb of Jihangir (12:5)

Plate 116
Proportional Comparison with *Deshiya Mandala* (Continued)

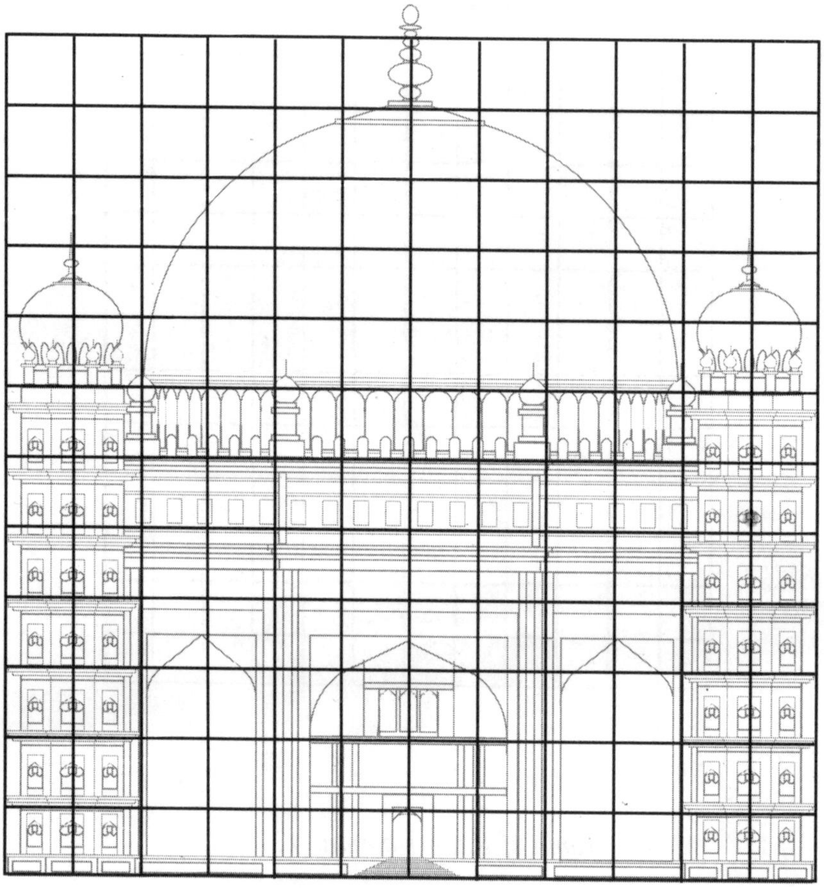

Tomb of Gol Gumbaz (12:11)

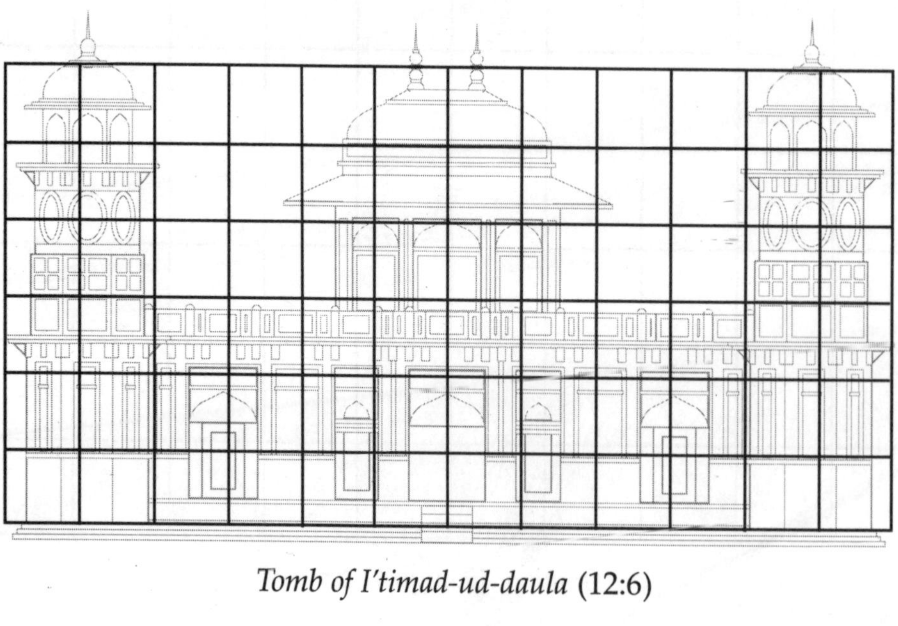

Tomb of I'timad-ud-daula (12:6)

Plate 117
Proportional Comparison with Deshiya Mandala (Continued)

Taj Mahal (12:12)

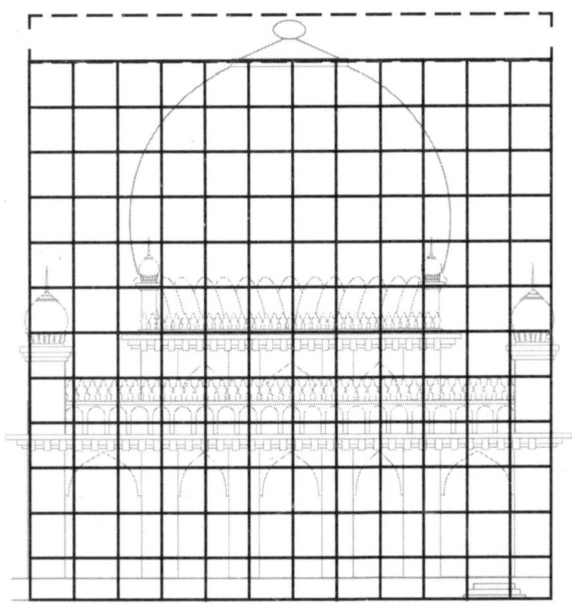

Afzal Khan Rauza (12:12.5)

Plate 118
Proportional Comparison with *Deshiya Mandala* (Continued)

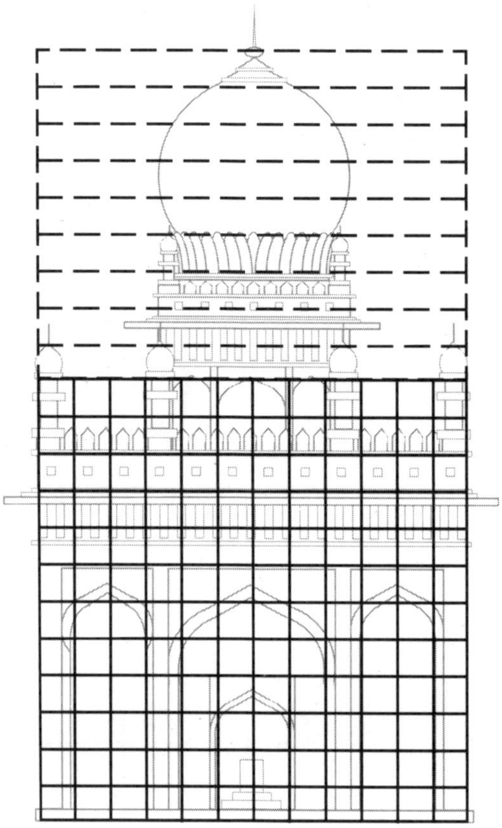

Shah Navaz Rauza (12:20,5)

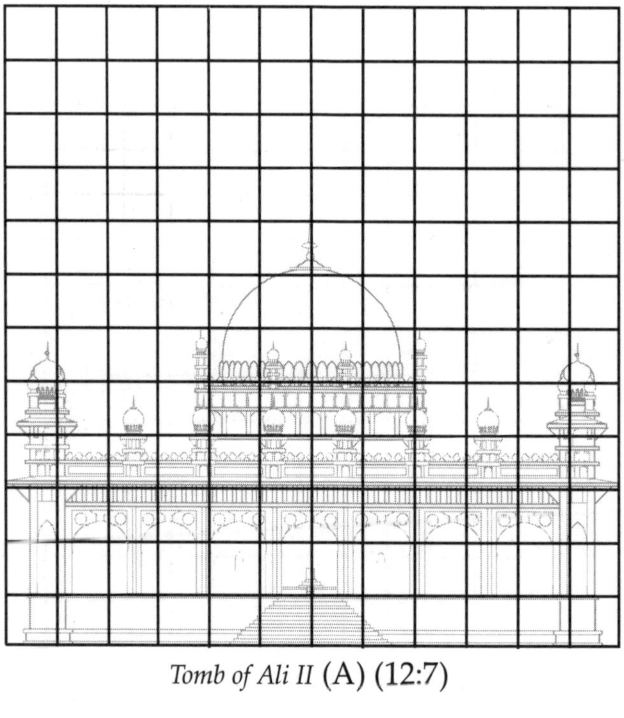

Tomb of Ali II (A) (12:7)

Plate 119
Proportional Comparison with *Deshiya Mandala* (Continued)

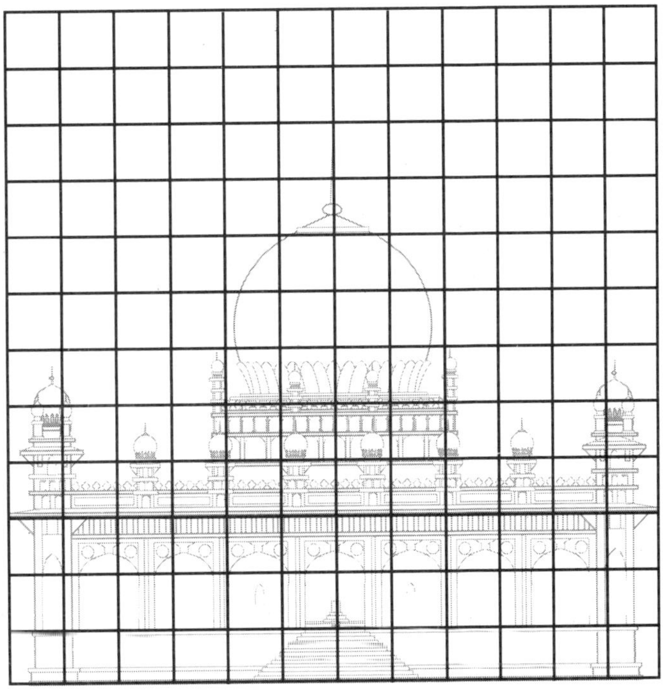

Tomb of Ali II (B) (12:7)

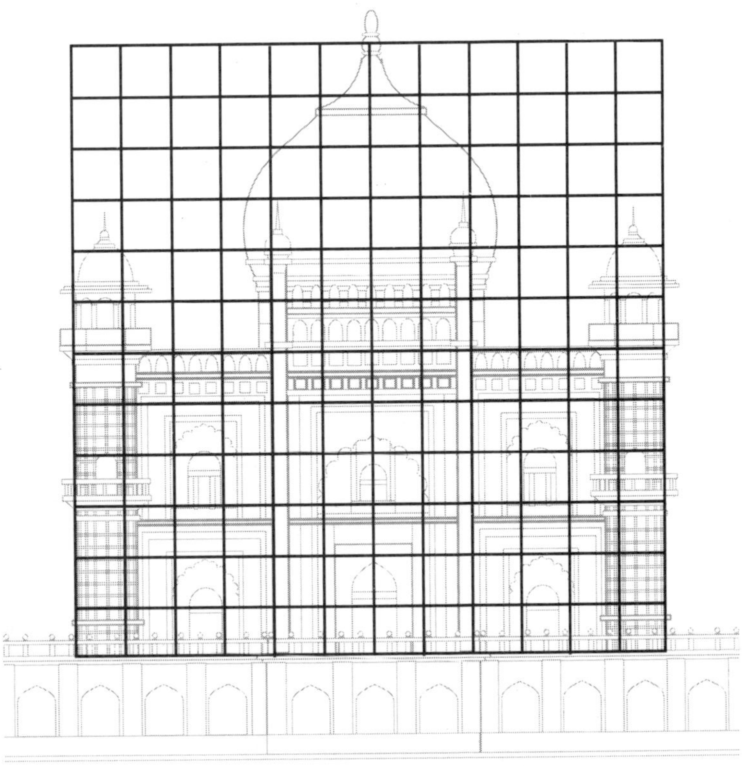

Tomb of Safdar Jang (12:12)

Plate 120 -- Proportional Comparison, Elevations

Dome and drum to ground of *Gur-Emir* (a), *Ibrahim Rauza* (b), *Mohammed Quli Qutb Shah* (c) & *Taj Mahal* (d)

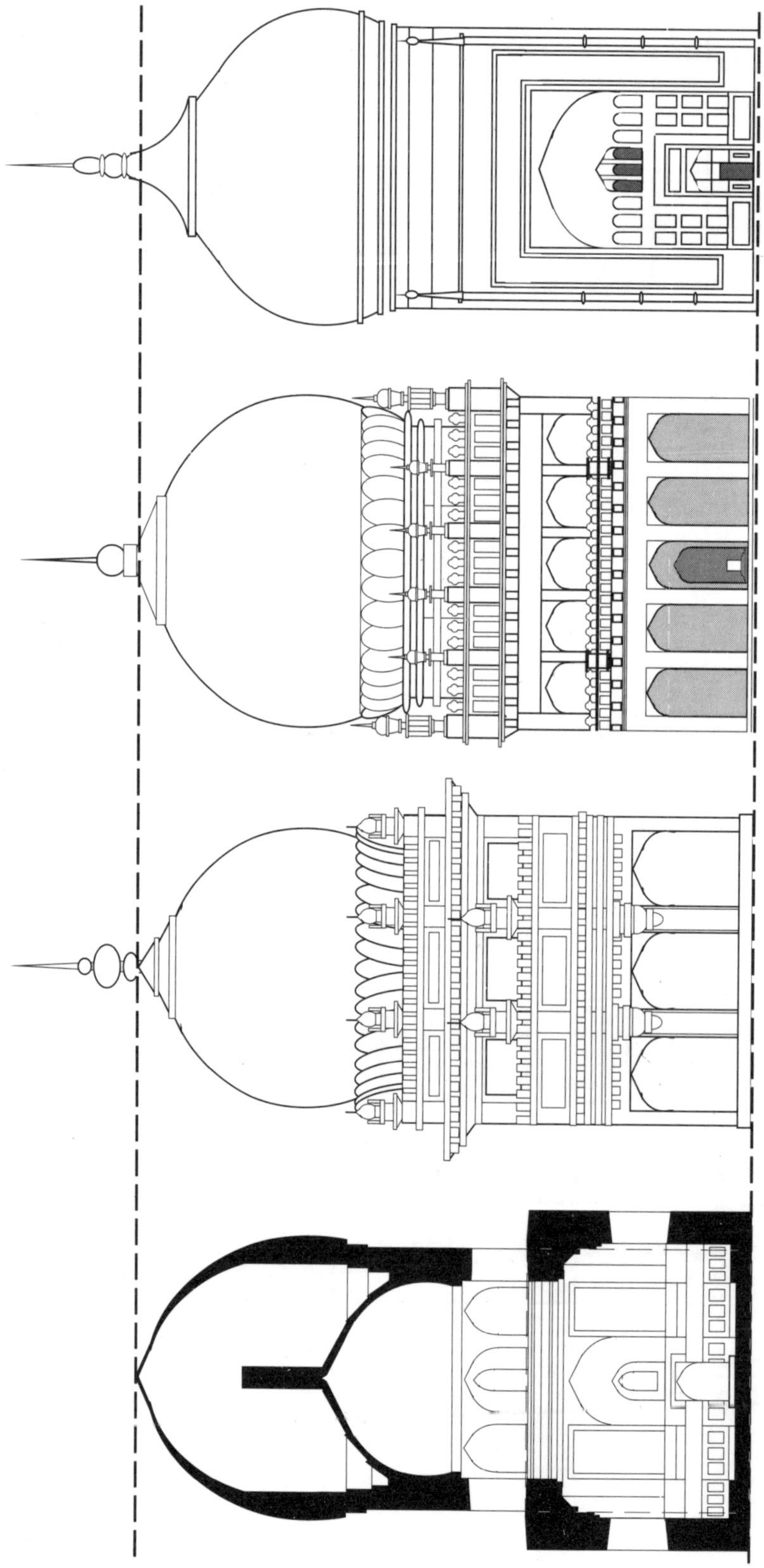

(d) (c) (b) (a)

Plate 121 -- Proportional Comparison, Elevations

Width to height of Tombs of Chotte Khan Ka Gunbad (a), Khan Khanan (b) & Taj Mahal (c)

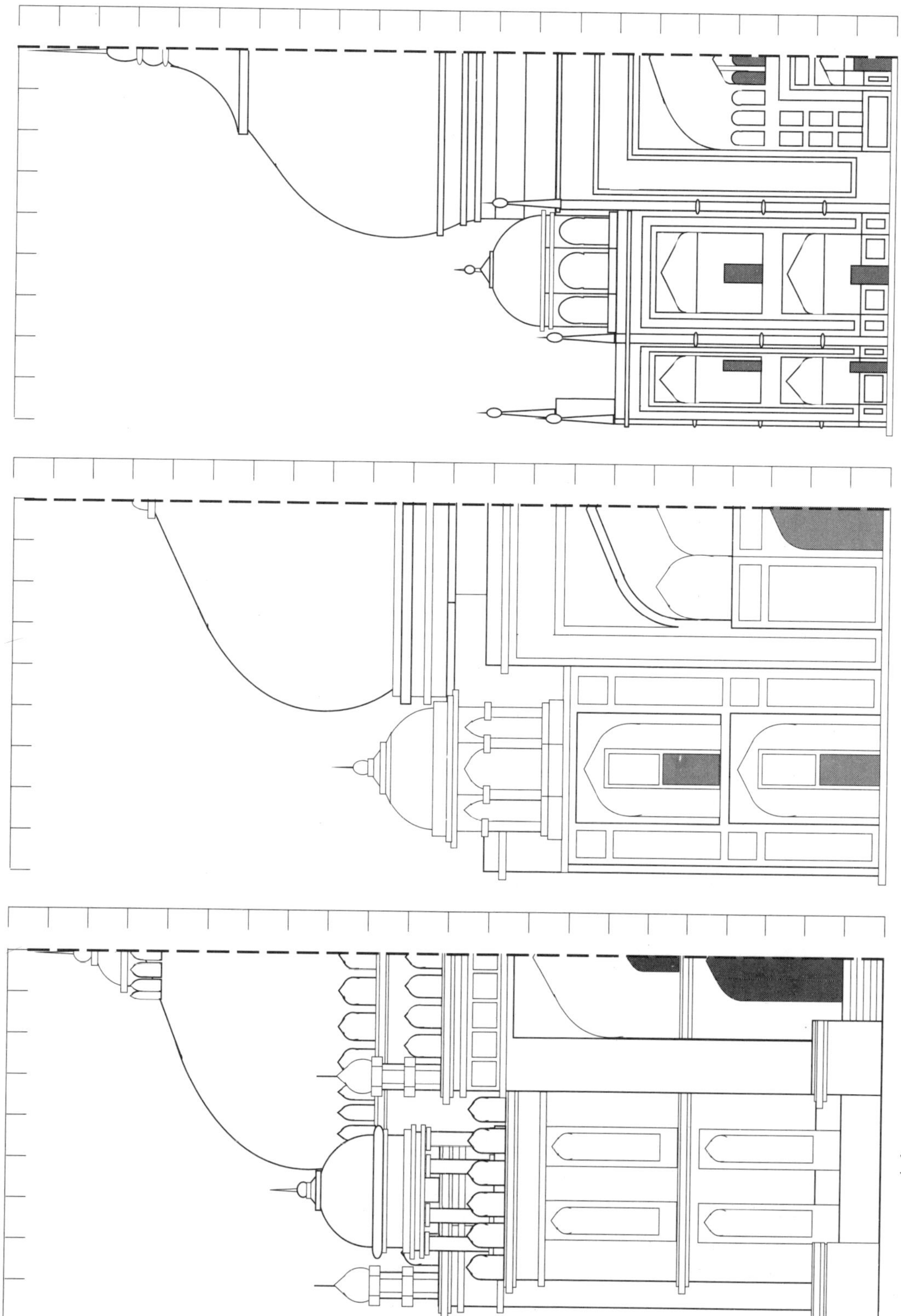

(c)

(b)

(a)

Plate 122 -- Proportional Comparison, Elevations

Half elevation of the Tomb of Humayun & the Taj Mahal

Plate 123

Nine-fold example; *Feria Bagh*, Ahmadnagar, 17th C. CE

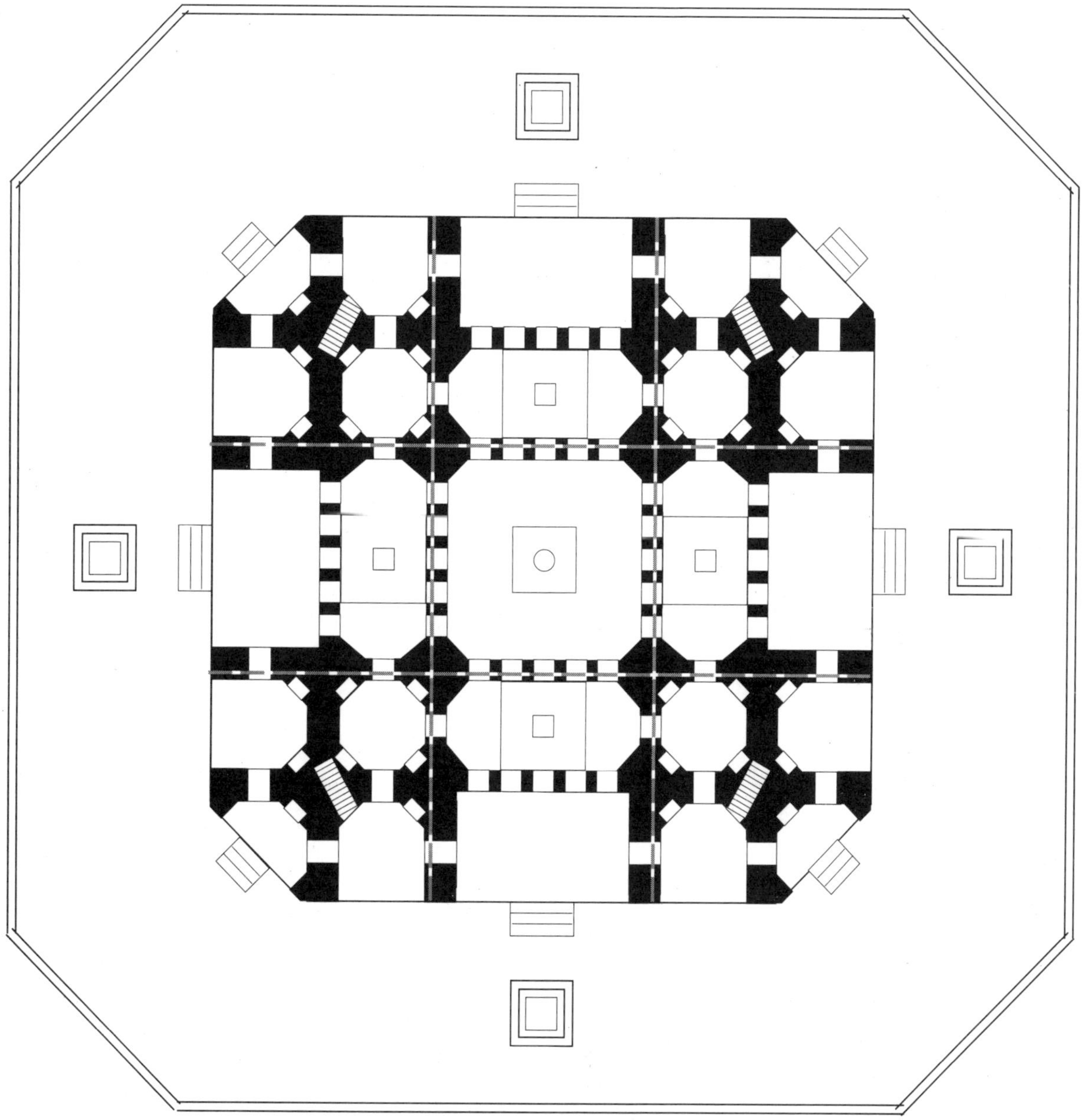

Plate 124
Nine-fold example; *Shahi Bagh*, Ahmadabad, c. 1623

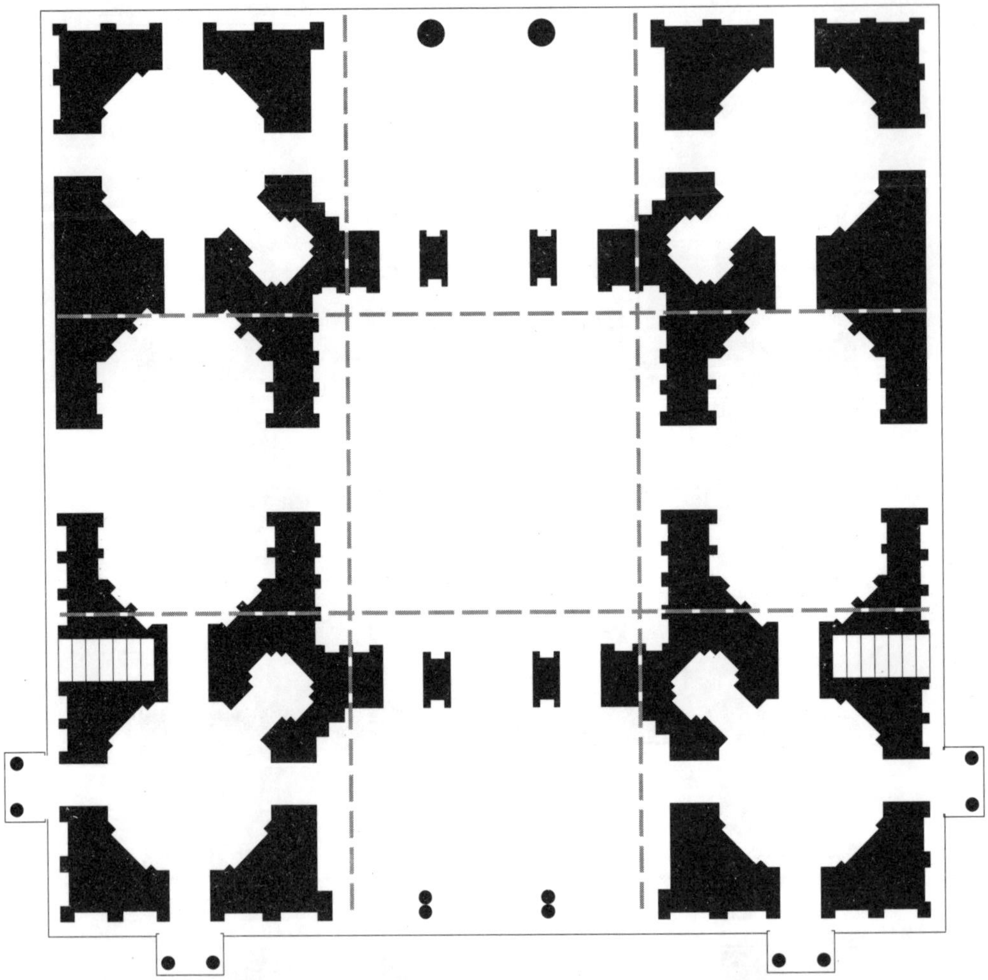

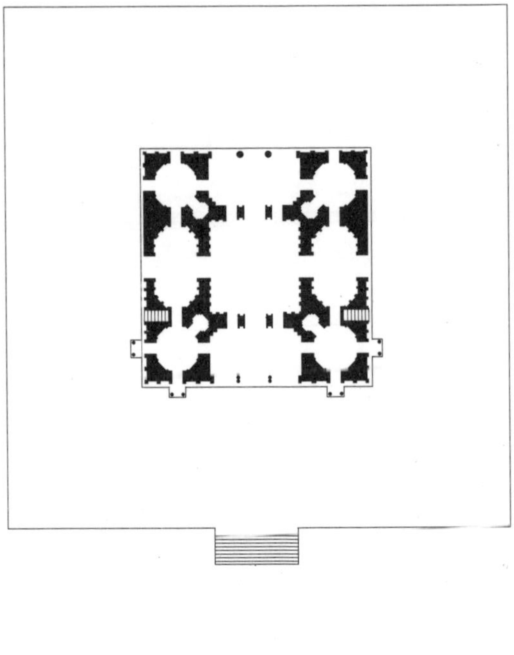

Plate 125

Nine-fold example; *Hesht Behest*, Isfahan, c.1669

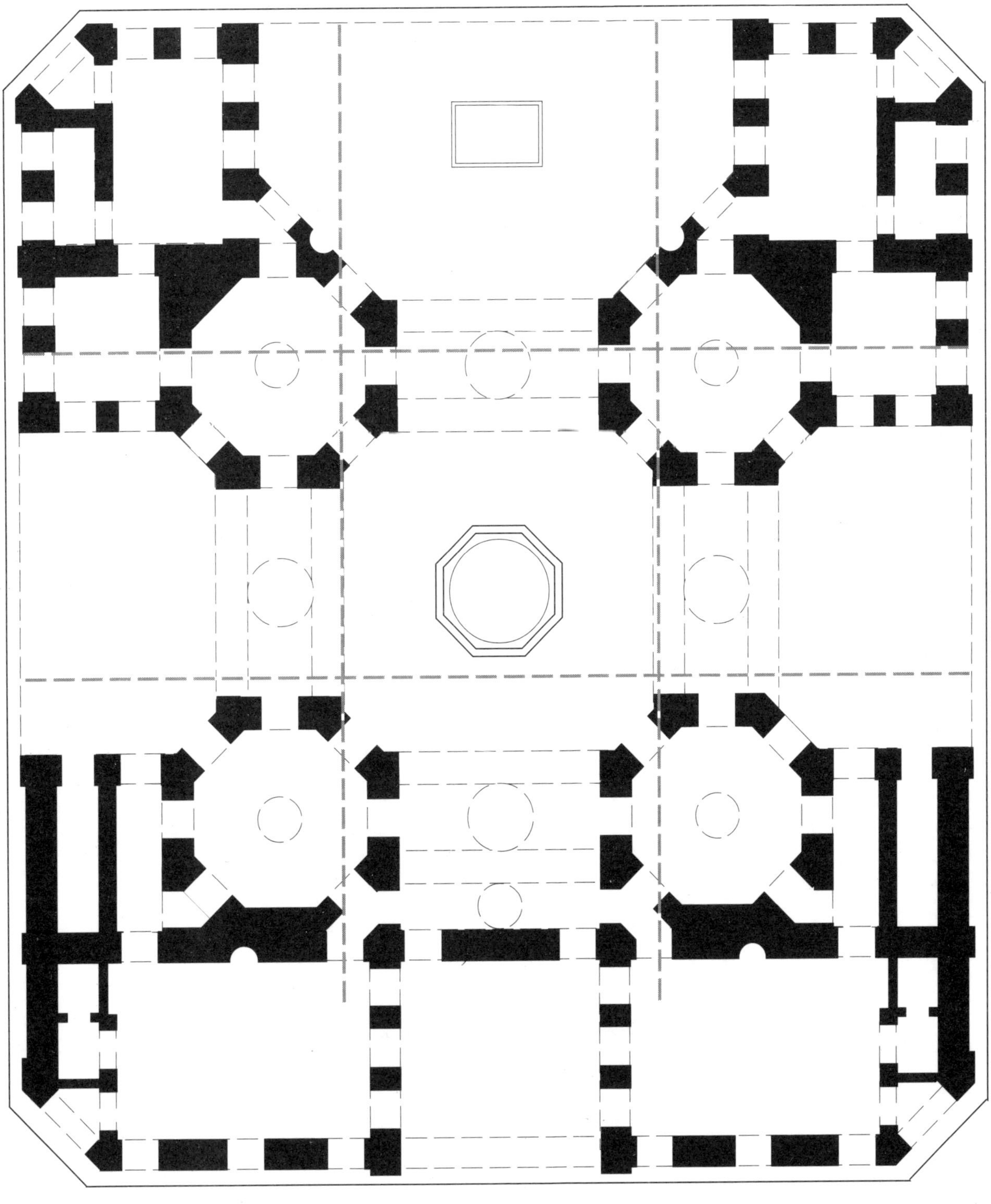

Plate 126

Nine-fold example; Palace of Bir Singh Judeo, Bundelkhand, (1605-1627)

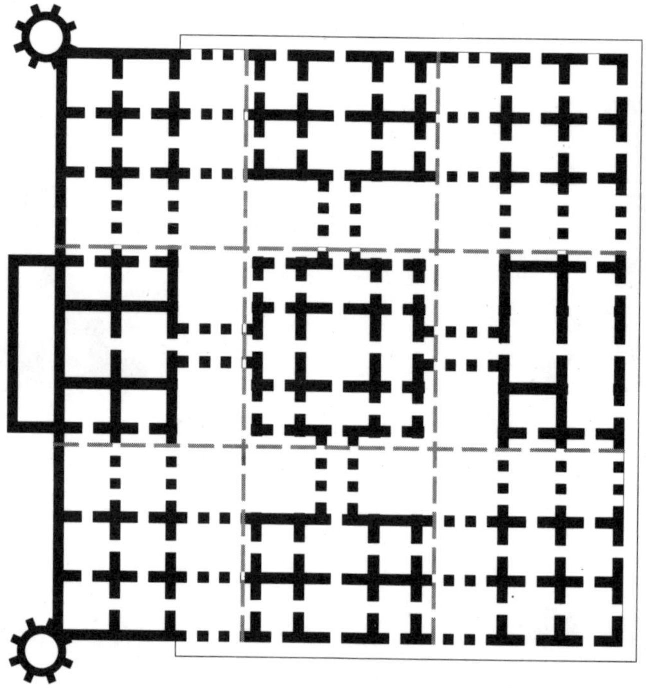

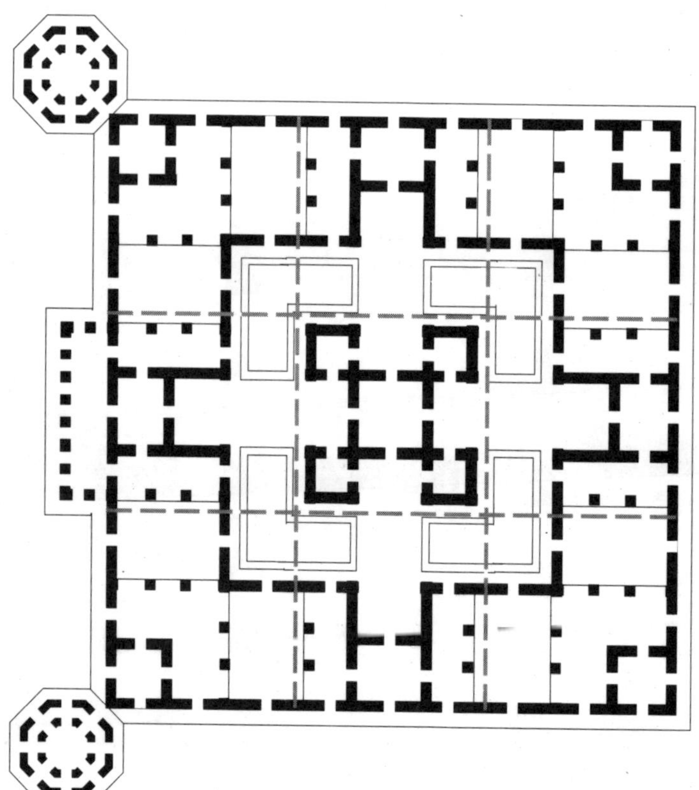

Plate 127

Tomb of Timur Section, Samarqand (16th C. CE)

Plate 128
Ibrahim Rauza Section

Plate 129
Gol Gumbaz Section

Plate 130
Taj Mahal Section

Plate 131

Taj Mahal Section Comparison ([a] with double dome; [b] without double dome)

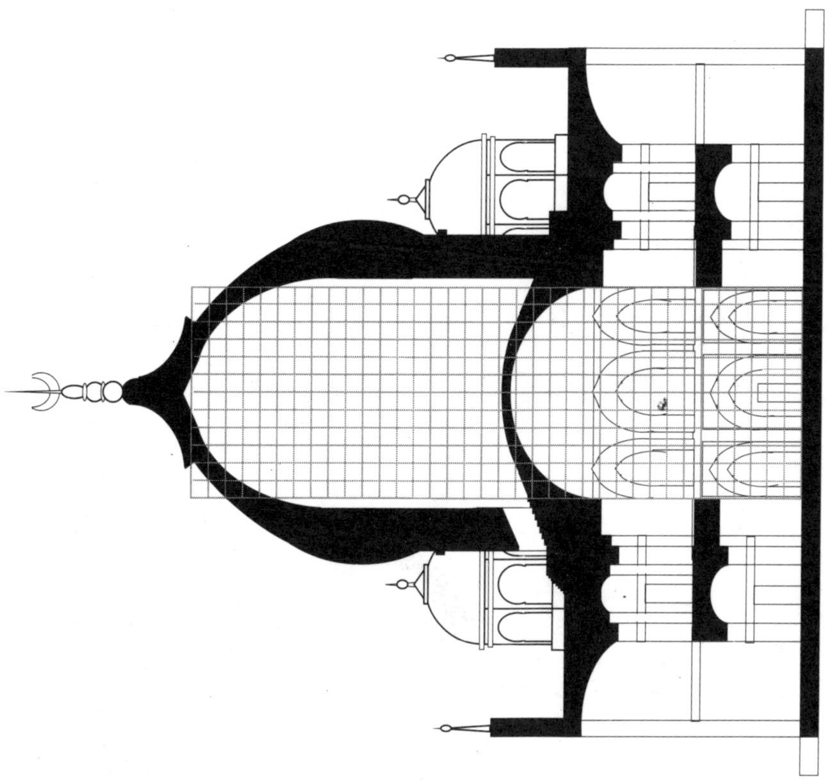

[a] *Taj Mahal*, indicating threefold *Deshiya Mandala* over the central chamber with double dome. Proportion is 12:17.25

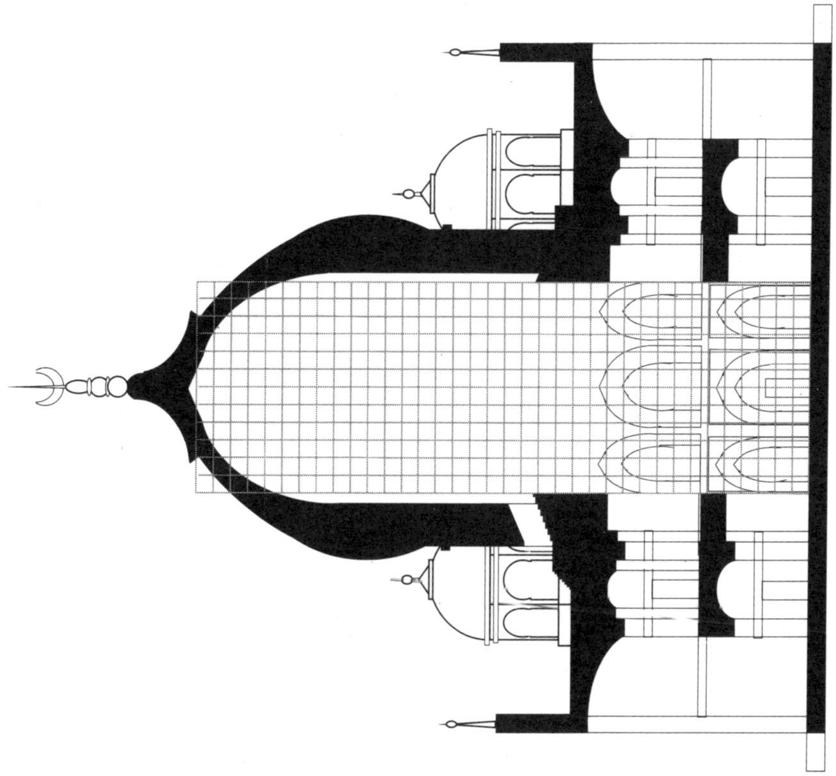

[b] *Taj Mahal*, indicating threefold *Deshiya Mandala* over the central chamber without double dome. Proportion is 12:36.25

Plate 132
Tomb of Mubarak Sayyid Section

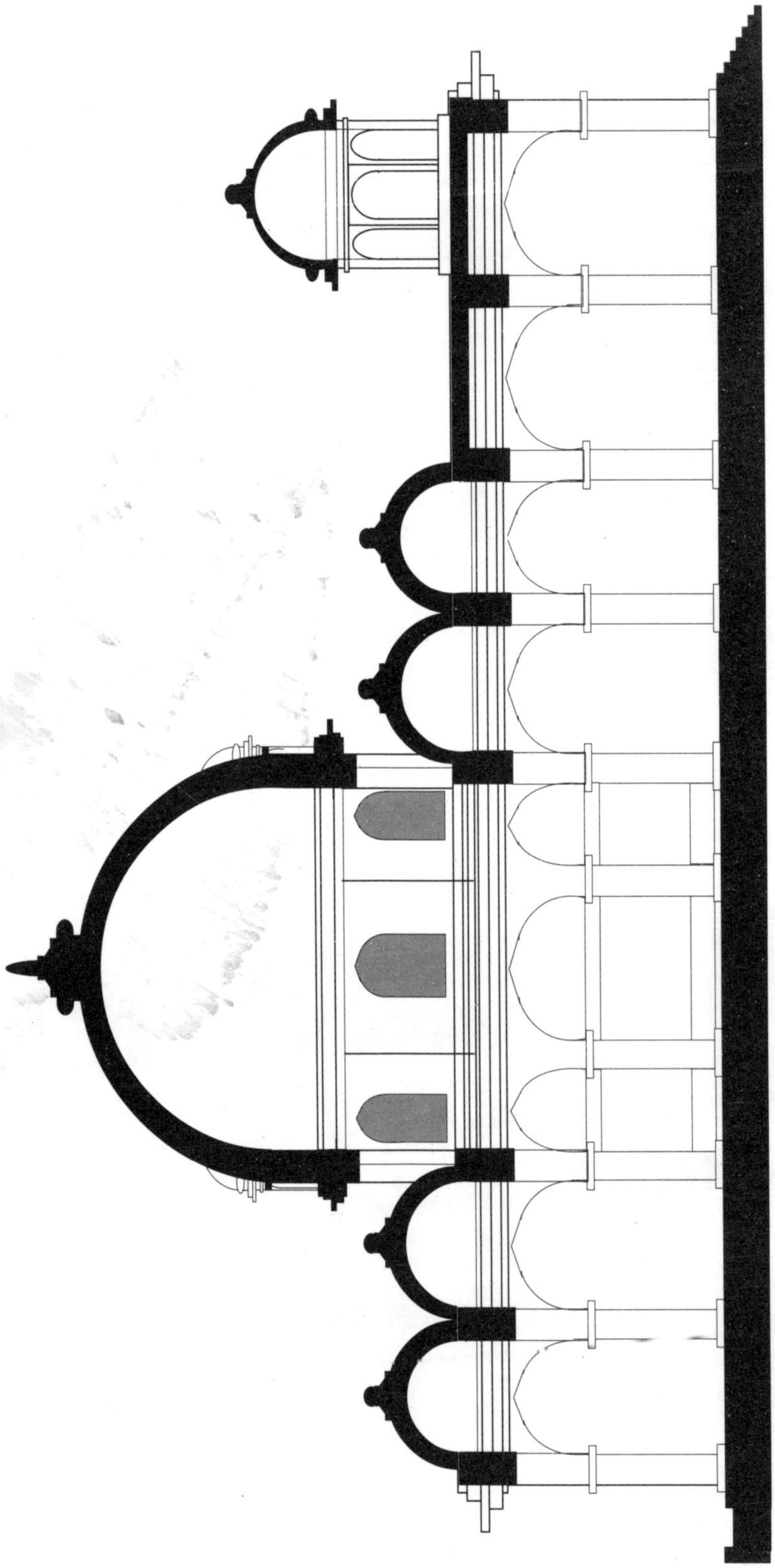

Plate 133

Tomb of Mohammed Quli Qutub Shah Elevation & half plan

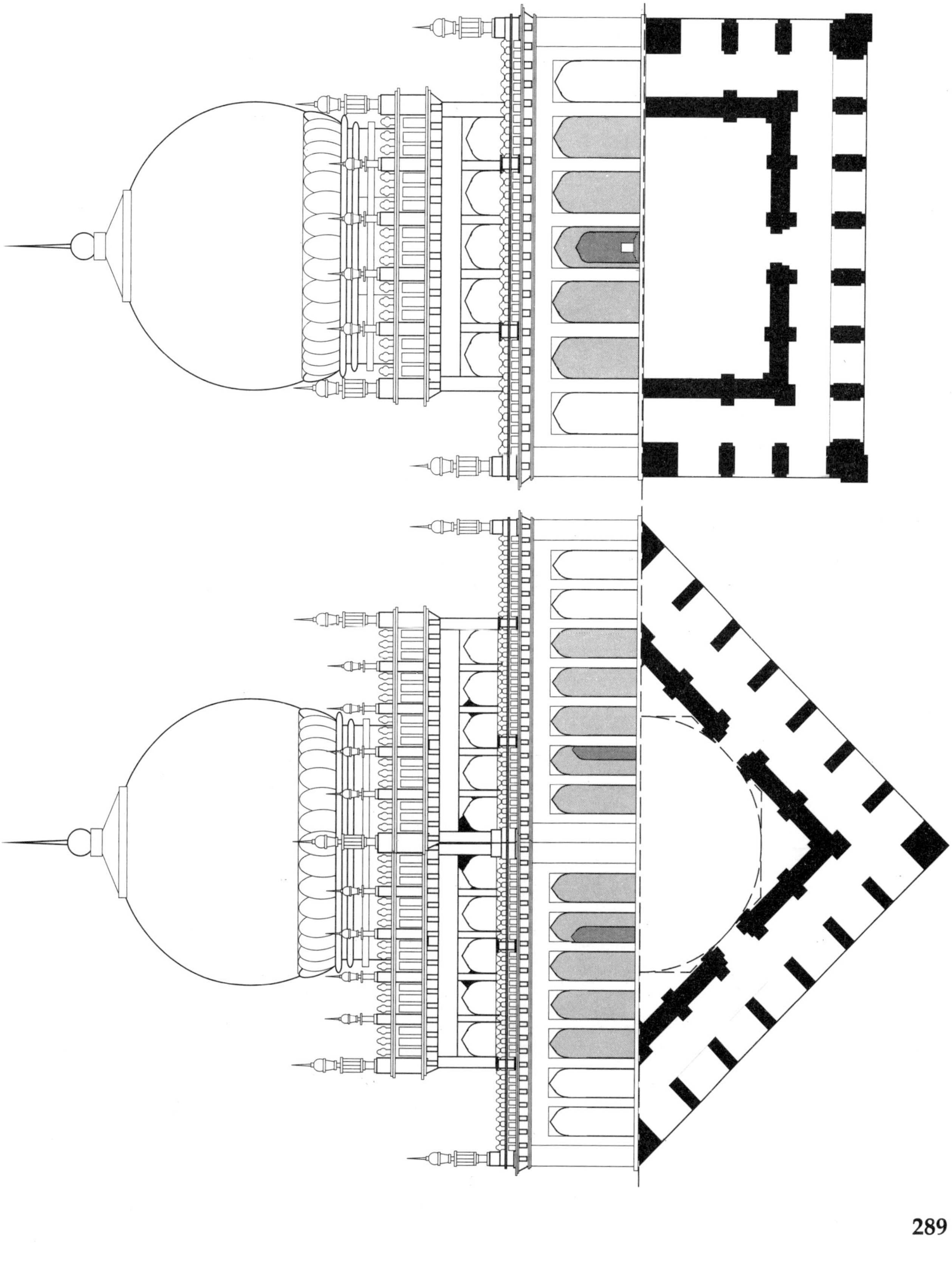

Plate 134
Tomb of Shah Navaz Khan Elevation & half plan

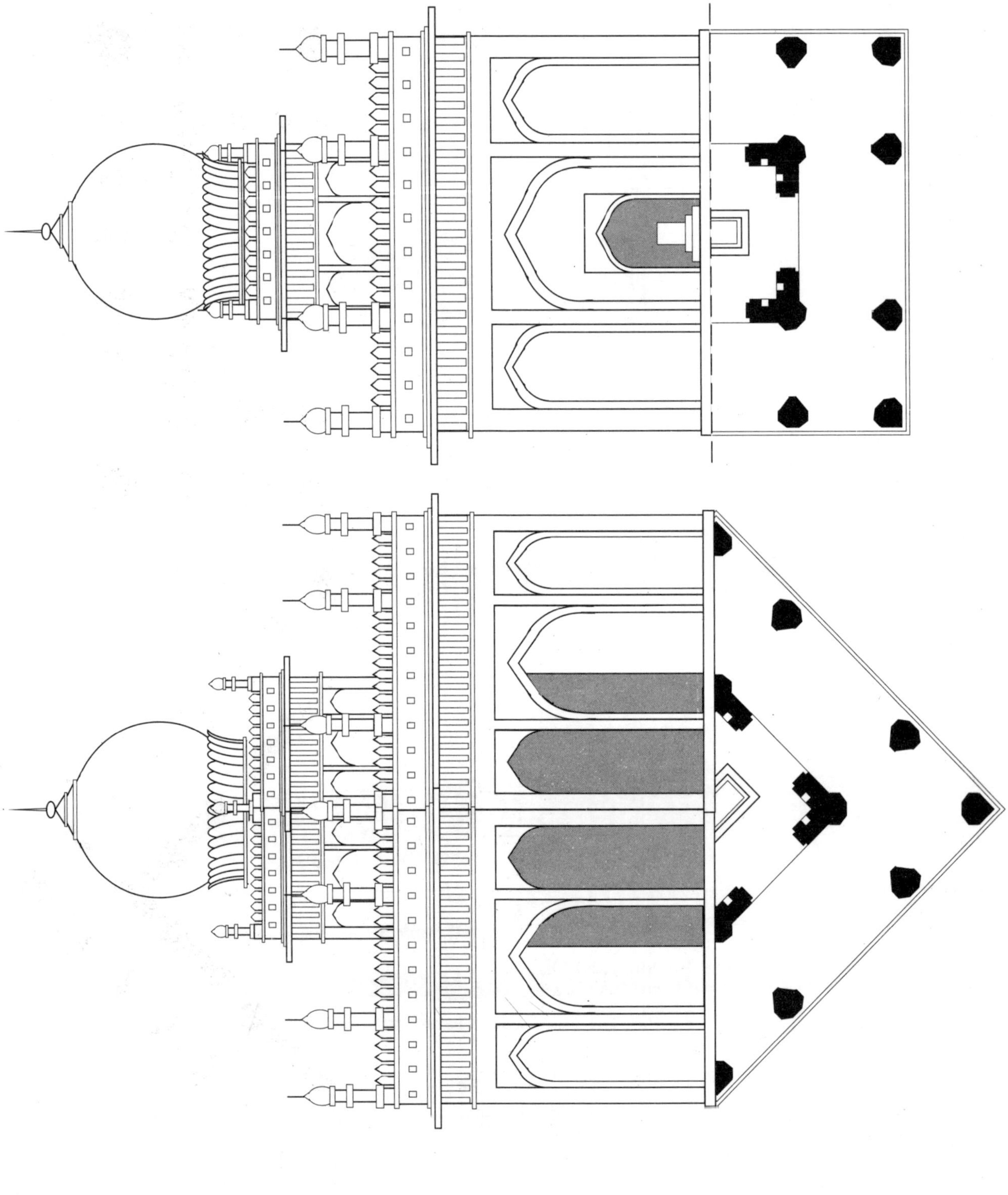

Plate 135
Tomb of Humayun Elevation with podium

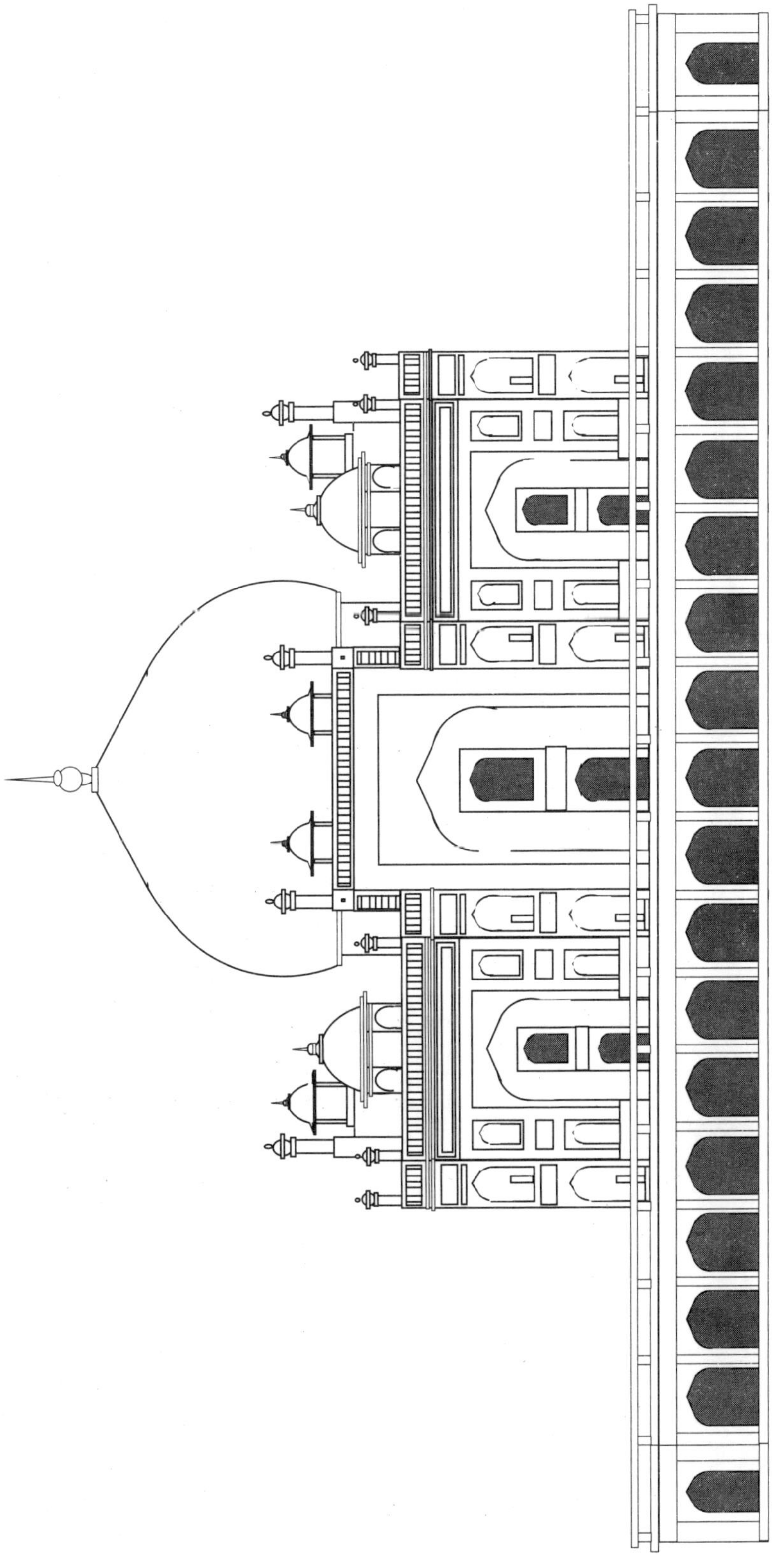

Plate 136

Tomb of Khan Khanan Elevation with podium

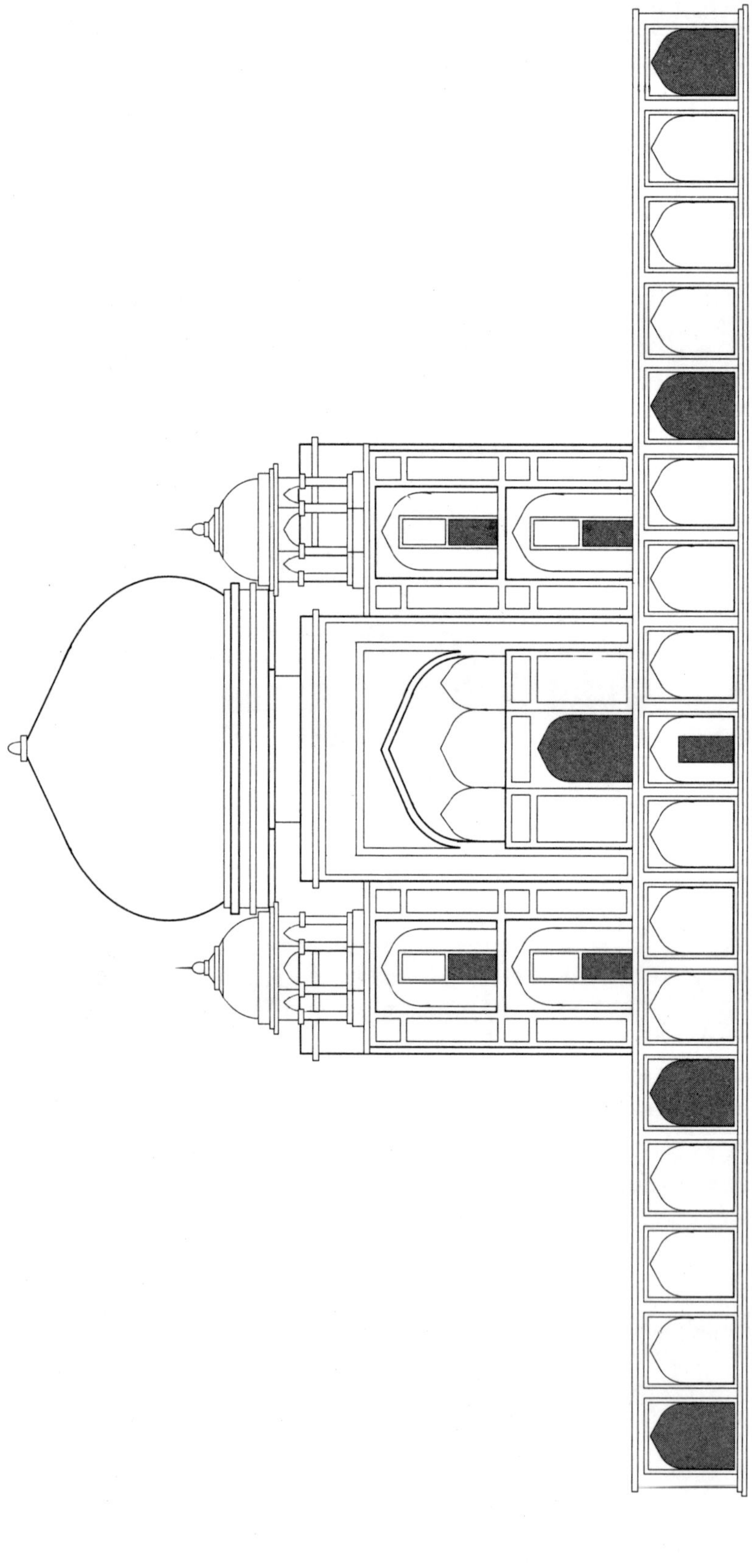

Plate 137

Taj Mahal Elevation with podium

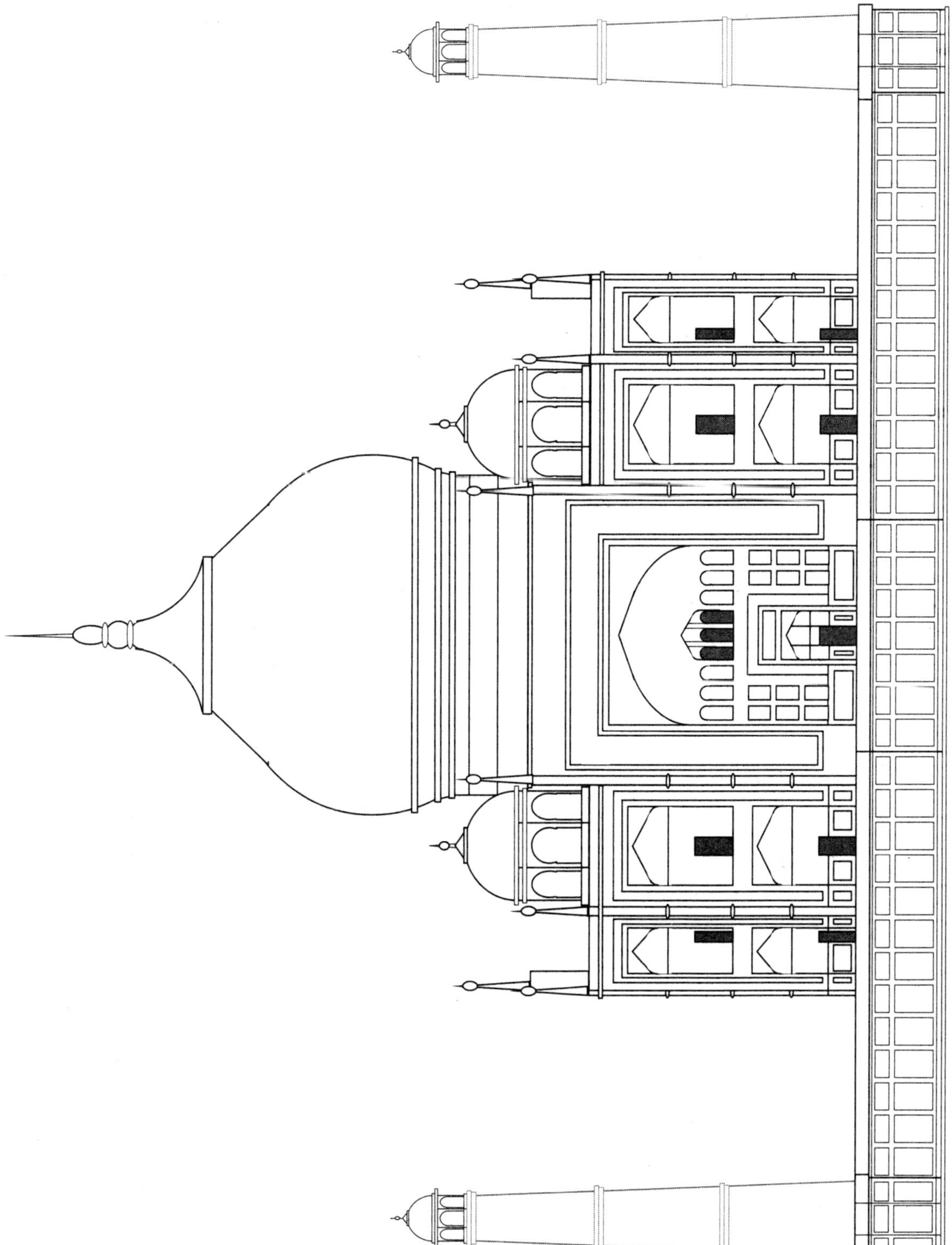

Plate 138

Tomb of Safdar Jang Elevation with podium

Proportional Geometric System

In a section labelled "Architectural drawings and design techniques," Lewcock[101] illustrates a "system of proportion," This has been used above (See: **Figure 56**; See also: **Figures 120, 146** & **178**). It must be noted that the *Samanid Tomb* is a product of a thoroughly Muslim area (country), unlike India where the Muslims, though ruler, were a distinct minority and often deferred to the indigenous *sthapati*. However, there appears some value in considering this system further and apply it to a number of Indo-Islamic tombs.

In this 'system' a *Karnashtaka Mandala* (with eighteen *pada* in a rank) is the basis for his consideration. This is an important and auspicious *mandala* as it is based on the numeral three, nine (3^3) and eighteen (3 x 6), and is related to the *Paramashayika Mandala* (with nine *pada* per rank). There may be other *mandalas* that would be appropriate--e.g., the *Triyuta Mandala* (with sixteen *pada* per rank) as it is based upon the *Manduka Mandala* (with eight *pada* per rank). Four tombs are considered: the *Tomb of Sultan Iltutmish, Tomb of Firuz Shah Tughluq. Tomb of Khan-i Jihan Tilangani* and *Gol Gumbaz.* There are a number of conjunctions, but whether or not they were associated with the design process or merely fortuitous happenings is conjectural. Nonetheless, through Islamic design process, ephemeral as it may now appear to be, and the Hindu process based upon know treatises--e.g., *Manasara* and *Mayamata*--the Indo-Islamic tombs came into being.

Plate 139
Tomb of Sultan Iltutmish, Proportional Geometric System

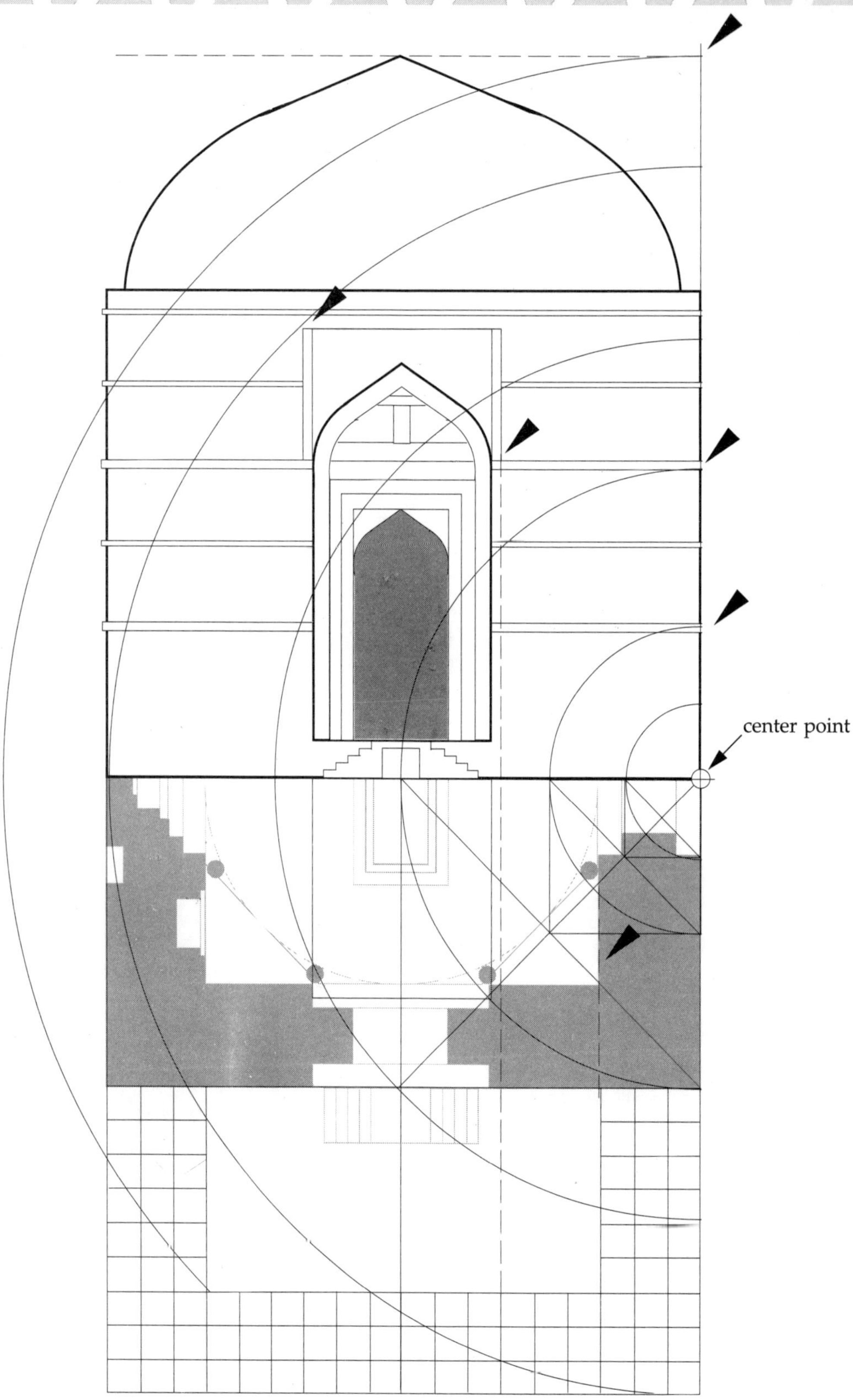

Plate 140

Tomb of Firuz Shah Tughlaq, Proportional Geometric System

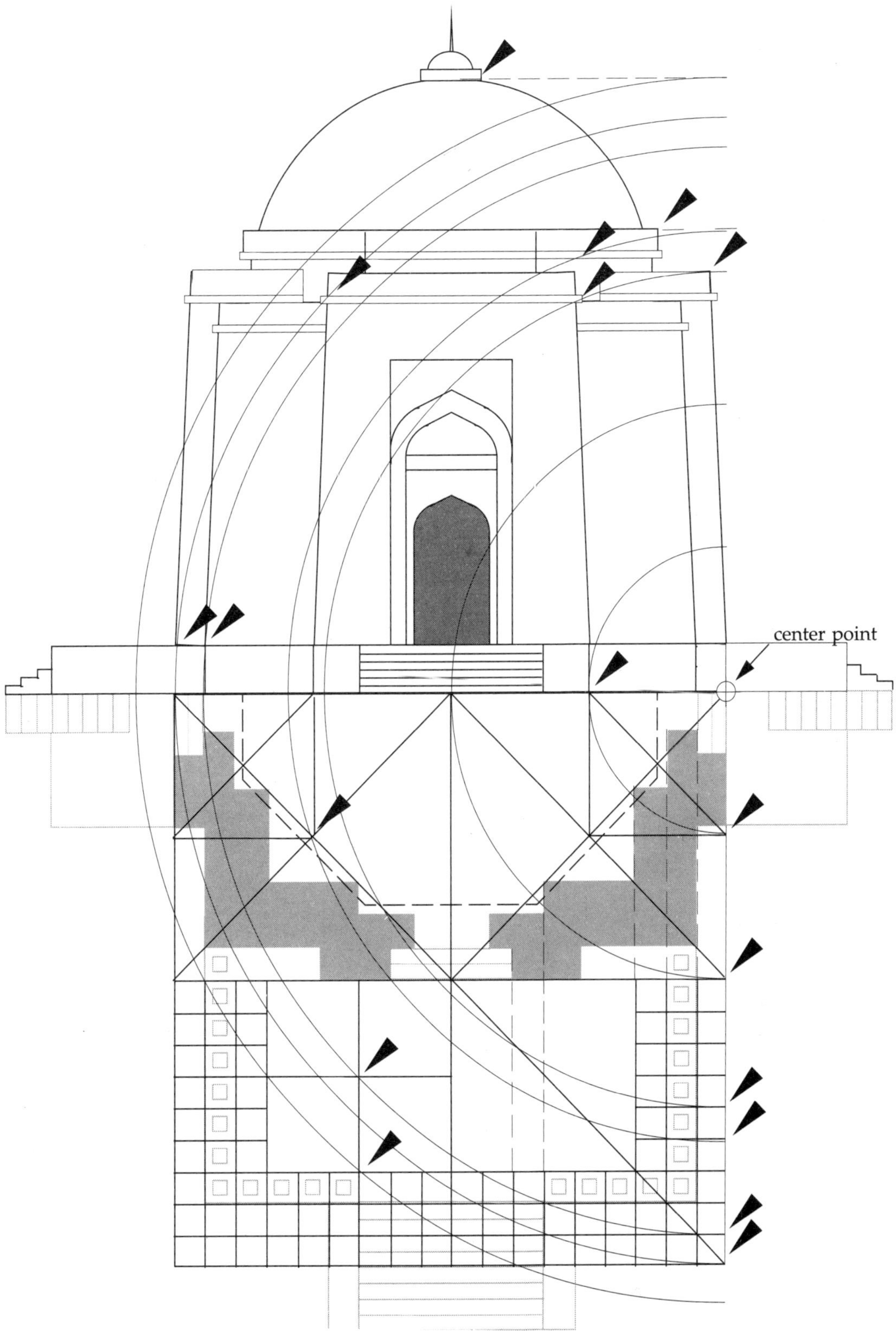

Plate 141

Tomb of Khan-i Jihan Tilangani, Proportional Geometric System

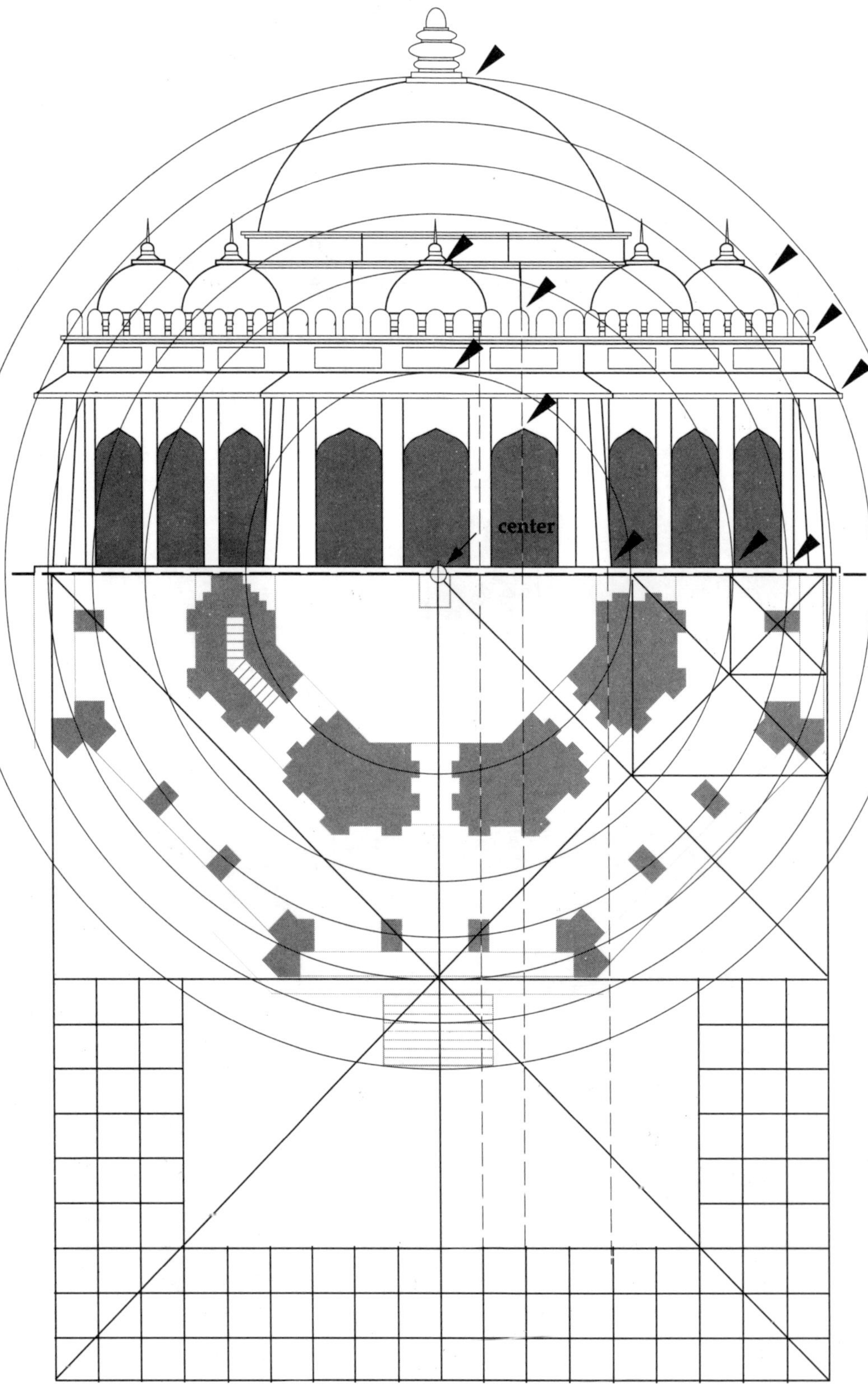

Plate 142

Gol Gumbaz, Proportional Geometric System

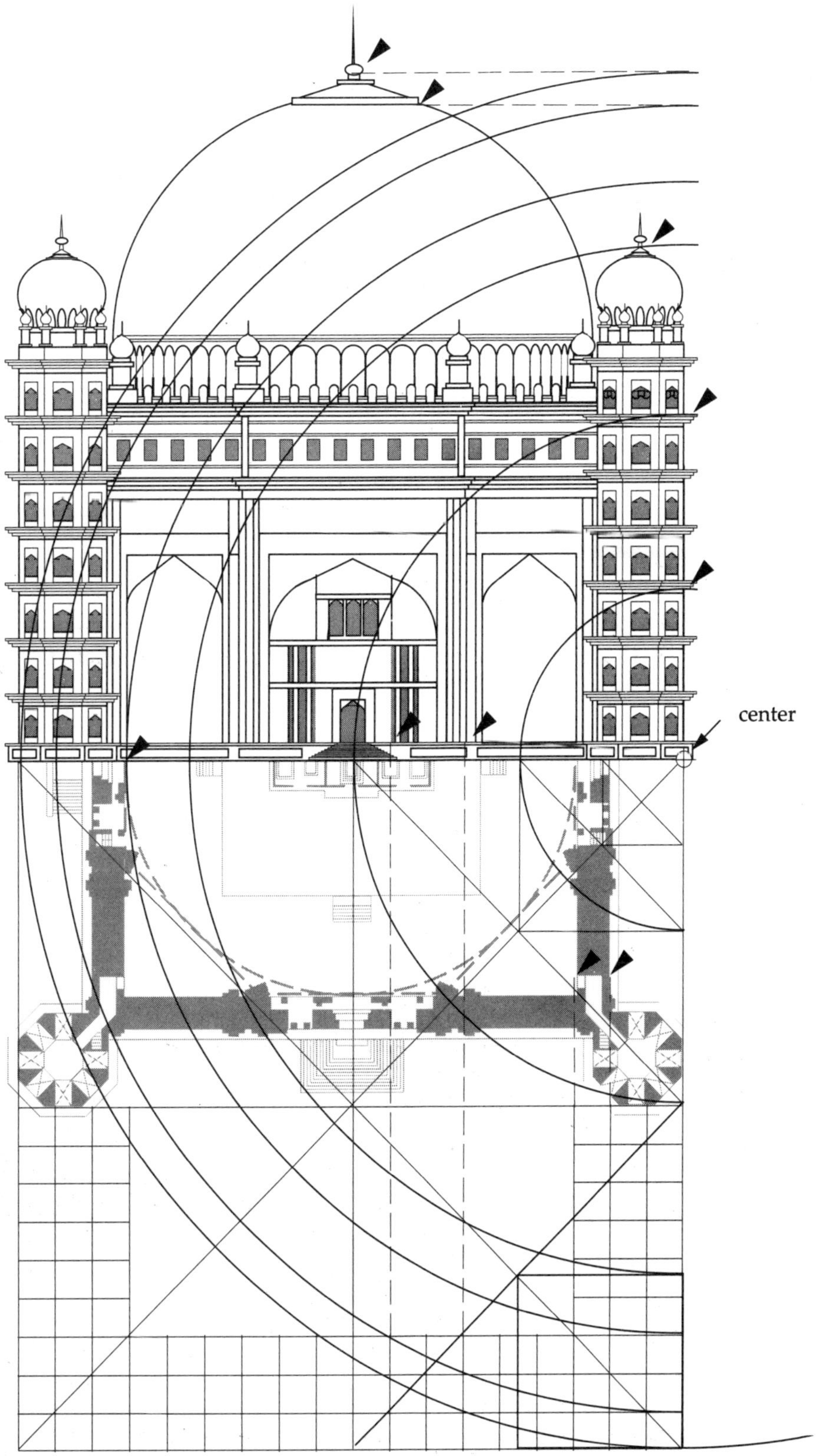

Plate 143

Miscellaneous Plans: *Tomb of Ali II* (Cousen's elevation & proposed elevation)

"Restored Elevation of Tomb of Ali II" as seen in HC, **Plate C**

Proposed Elevation of Tomb of Ali II, utilizing 'Adil Shahi-style dome

Plate 144

Miscellaneous Plans: *Masjid-i Jami*, Delhi, 1650-1656 CE

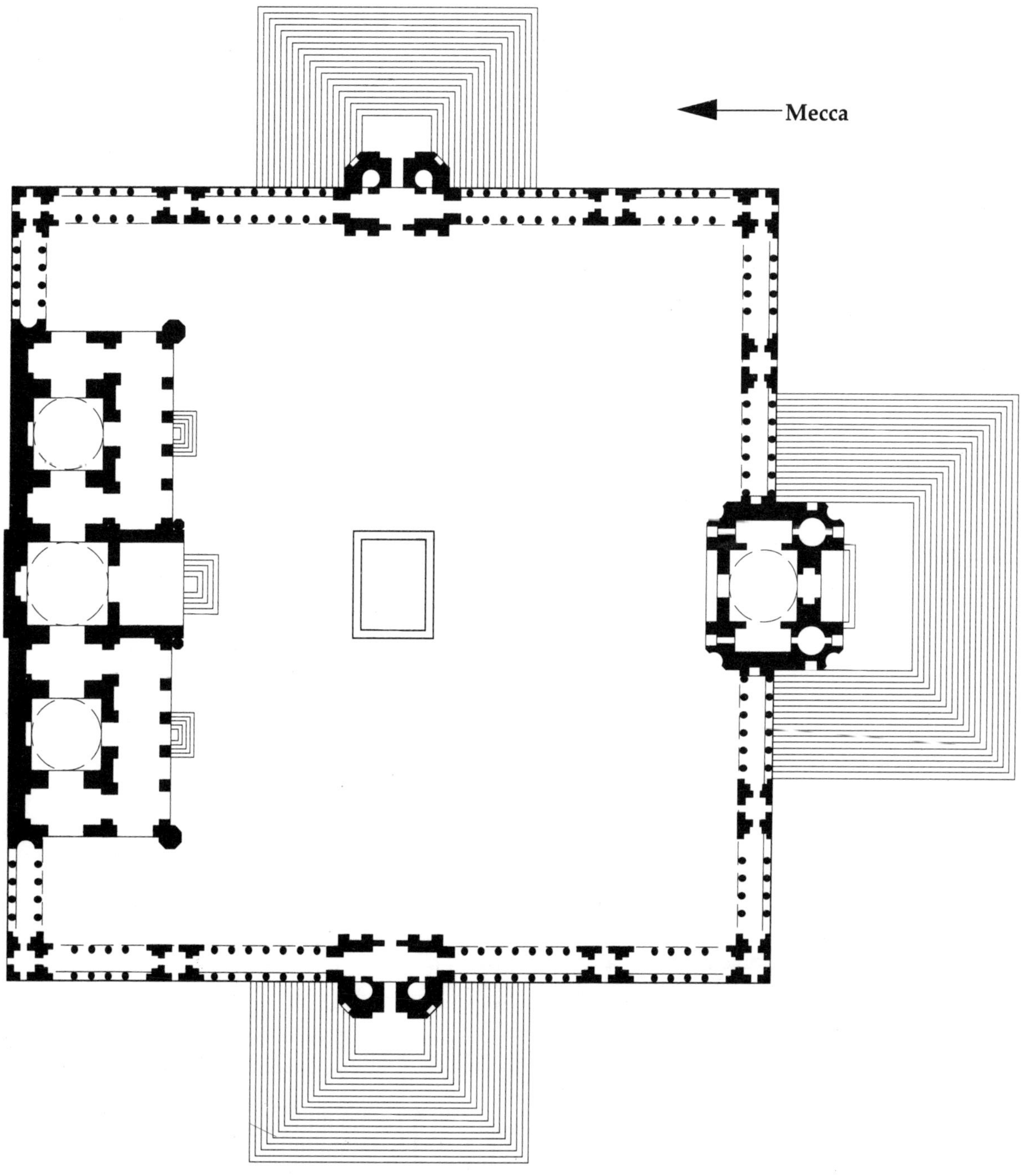

Plate 145

Miscellaneous Plans: *Fathepur Sikri* (1569 -1574 CE)

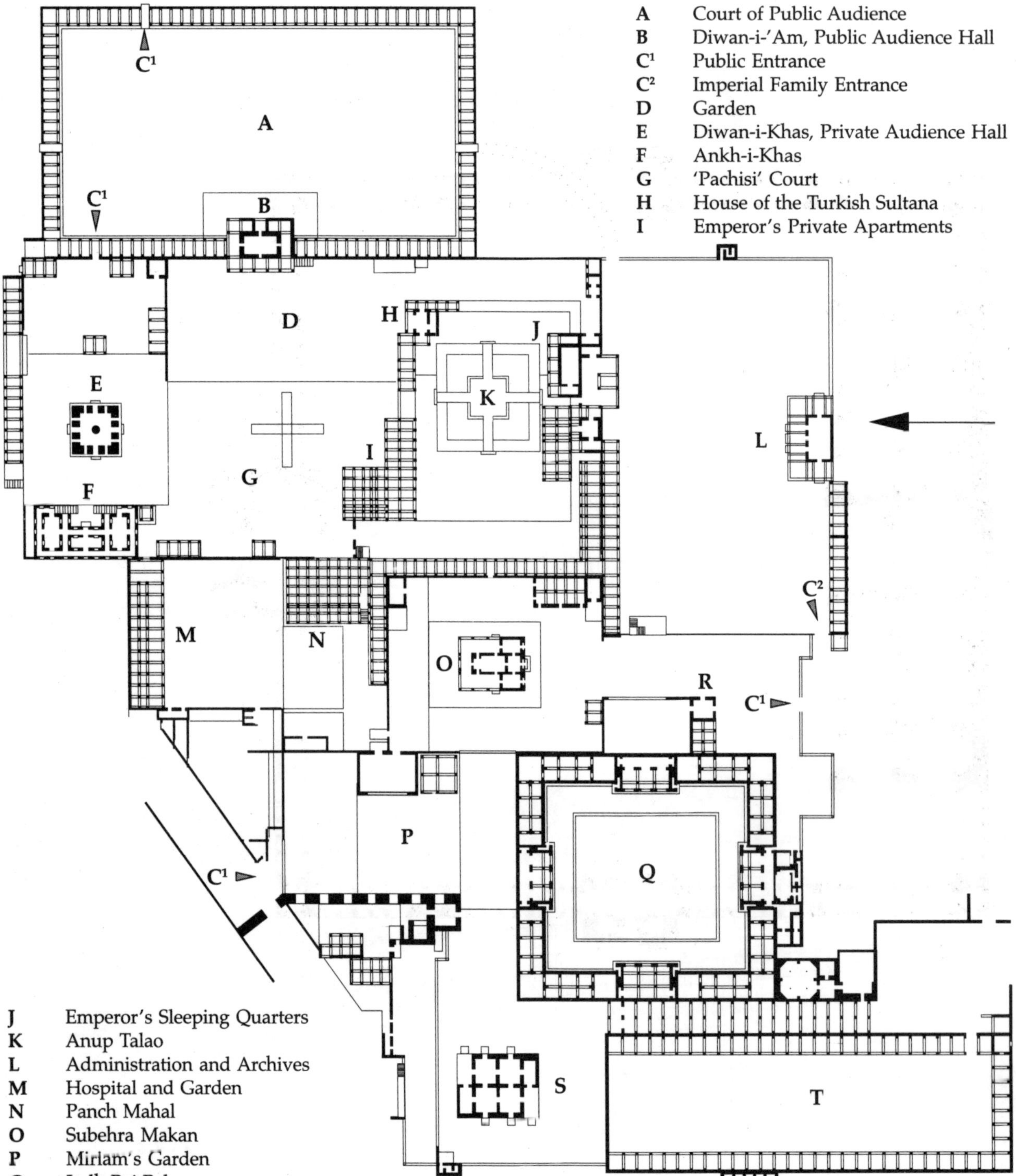

- A Court of Public Audience
- B Diwan-i-'Am, Public Audience Hall
- C[1] Public Entrance
- C[2] Imperial Family Entrance
- D Garden
- E Diwan-i-Khas, Private Audience Hall
- F Ankh-i-Khas
- G 'Pachisi' Court
- H House of the Turkish Sultana
- I Emperor's Private Apartments
- J Emperor's Sleeping Quarters
- K Anup Talao
- L Administration and Archives
- M Hospital and Garden
- N Panch Mahal
- O Subehra Makan
- P Miriam's Garden
- Q Jodh Bai Palace
- R Hawa Mahal
- S House of Raja Birbal
- T Stables for Camels and Horses

Plate 146

Miscellaneous Plans: *Qutub Shahi Tombs,* Golconda

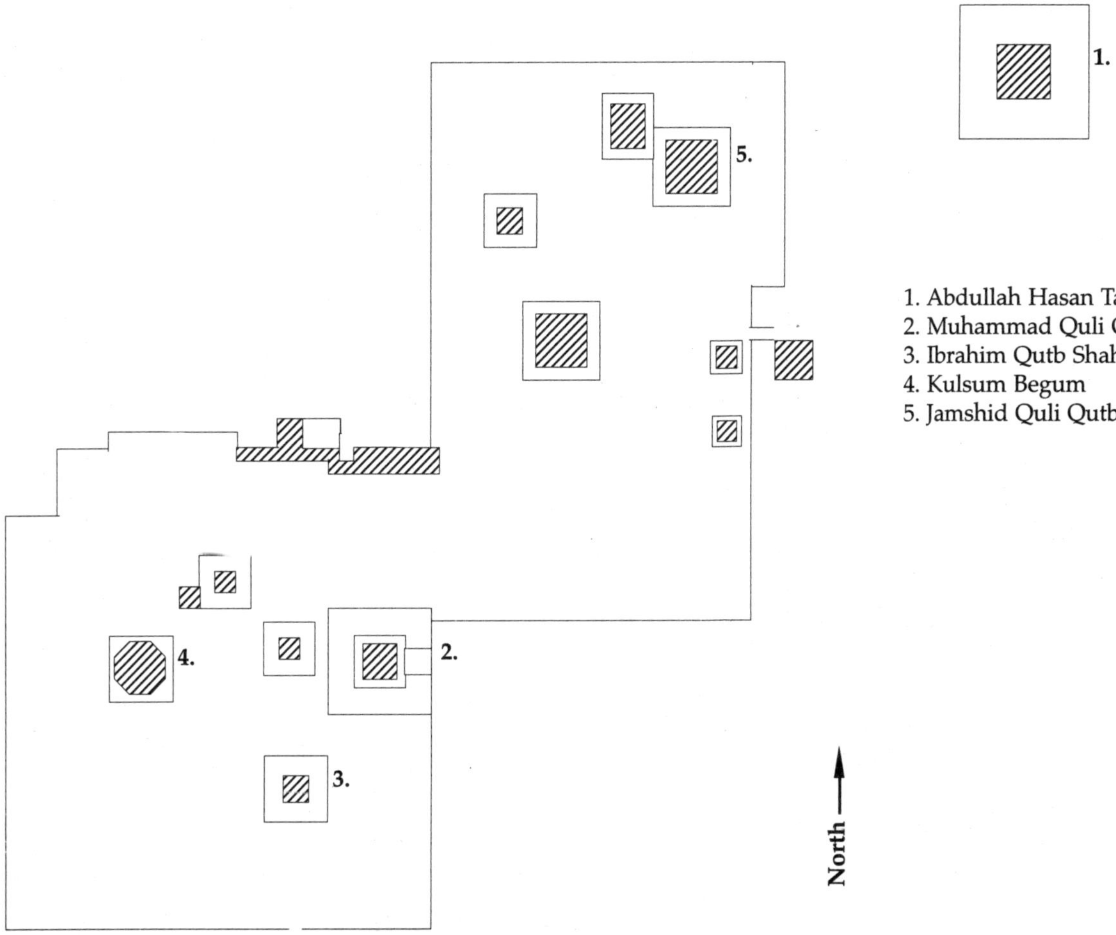

1. Abdullah Hasan Tana Shah
2. Muhammad Quli Qutb Shah
3. Ibrahim Qutb Shah
4. Kulsum Begum
5. Jamshid Quli Qutb Shah

Plate 147

Miscellaneous Plans: *Taj Mahal* (9-fold plan, 5-fold octagon & *chahar-bagh* plan)

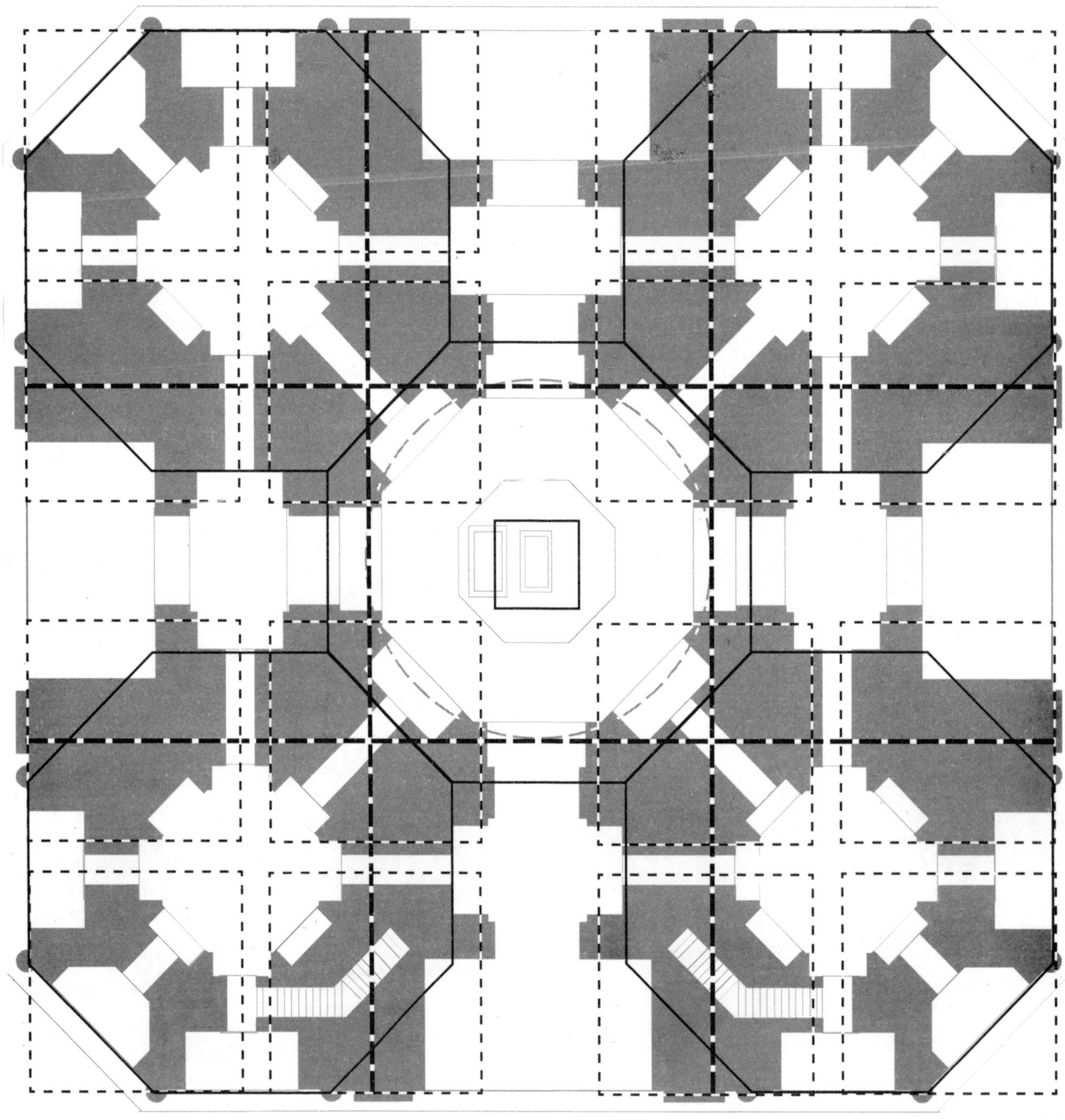

Nine-fold plan
Five fold octagon
Chahar-bagh plan

Appendix D

Major Muslim Rulers of India

Major Muslim Rulers of India

Ghaznavid Dynasty
(977-1186)

Sabuktigin of Ghazni	977-997
Ismail	997-998
Yamin-ud-Dawlah Mahmud .	998- 1030
Jalal-ud-Dawlah Mohammad	1030-1031
Shihab-ud-Dawlah Masud I	1031-1041
Shihab-ud-Dawlah Mawdud	1041-1050
Masud II	1050
Baha-ud-Dalwah Ali	1050
Izz-ud-Dawlah Abdul al-Rashid	1050-1053
Qiwam-ud-Dawlah Tughril	1053
Jamal-ud-Dawlah Farrukhzad	1053-1059
Zahir-ud-Dawlah Ibrahim	1059-1099
'Ala-ud-Dawlah Masud III	1099-1115
Kamal-ud-Dawlah Shirzad	1115
Sultan-ud-Dawlah Arslan Shah	1115-1118
Yamin-ud-Dawlah Bahram Shah	1118-1152
Muizz-ud-Dawlah Khusrta Shah	1152-1160
Taj-ud-Dawlah Khusraw Malik	1160-1186

Ghurid Sultanate
(1163-1215)

Ghiyath-ud-Din Mohammed II of Ghur	1163-1203
Shihab-ud-Din Mohammed III	1173-1206
Ghiyath-ud-Din Mahmud	1206-1212
Baha-ud-Din Sam II	1212-1213
'Ala-ud-Din Atsiz	1213-1214
'Ala-ud-Din Mohammed IV	1214-1215

Delhi Sultanates
(1206-1526)

Slave or Mamluk Dynasty 1206-1320

Qutb-ud-din Aibak, 1st Sultan of Delhi	1206 -1210
Aram Shah	1210-1211
Shams-ud-din Iltutmish	1211-1236
Rukn-ud-din Firuz	1236
Raziyya (Radiyya Begum)	1236-1240
Mu"izz-ud-din Bahram	1240-1242
'Al-ud-din Mas'ud	1242-1246
Nasir-ud-din Mahmud	1246-1266

House of Balban

Ghiyas-ud-din Balban	1266-1287
Mu'izz-ud-din Kaiqubad	1287-1290
Kaiumarth	1290

The Khaljiz

Jalal-ud-din Firuz Khaljiz	1290-1296
Rukn-ud-din Ibrahim (II)	1296
'Ala-ud-din Muhammad Khaljiz	1296-1316
Shihab-ud-din 'Umar	1316
Qutb-ud-din Mubarak	1316-1326
Nasir-ud-din Khusrav	1320

Tughluq Dynasty 1320-1414

Ghiyas-ud-din Tughluq Shah I	1320-1325
Muhammad Shah Tughluq Shah (II)	1325-1351
Mahmud Ibn Mohammed	1351
Firuz Shah Tughluq	1351-1388
Ghiyas-ud-din Tughluq Shah II	1388-1389
Abu Bakr Tughluq	1389-1390
Mohammed Tughluq Shah (III)	1390-1393
Sikandar Tughluq Shah I	1393
Mahmud Tughluq Shah II	1394-1396
interregnum	

Mahmud Tughluq	1399-1413
Daulat Khan Lodi	1413-1414

Sayyid Dynasty 1414-1450

Khizir Khan Sayyid	1414-1421
Mu'izz-ud-din Mubarak Shah II Sayyid	1421-1434
Muhammed Shah Sayyid (IV)	1434-1444
'Ala-ud-din Alam Shah Sayyid	1444-1451

Lodi Dynasty 1451-1526

Buhlul Lodi	1451-1489
Nizam Khan, Sikandar Lodi	1489-1517
Ibrahim Shah Lodi (II)	1517-1526

Bengal Sultanate (1282-1576)

Iliyas Shahi Dynasty 1342-1415

Nasir-ud-din Bughra	1282-1291
Rukn-ud-din Kaukaus	1291-1301
Shams-ud-din Firuz Shah	1301-1322
Shihab-ud-din Bughra Shah	1322-1324
Ghiyas-ud-din Bahadur Shah	1324-1336
Fakhr-ud-Din Mubarak Shah	1336-1350
Ali Mubarak , 'Ala-ud-din Ali Shah	1341-1342
Malik Iliyas Haji, Shams-ud-din Iliyas Shah	1342-1358
Ikhtiyar-ud-din Gaji Shah	1349-1352
Sikandar Shah	1358-1390
Ghiyas-ud-din Azam Shah	1390-1410 or 1396?
Sultan-ud-Salatin Saif-ud-din Hamza Shah	1142 or 1396-1405?
Shihab-ud-din Bayazid Shah	1412-1414 or 1405-1415?
Ala-ud-din Firoz Shah	1414?-15

Major Muslim Rulers of India (Continued)

Ganesa-Shahi Dynasty 1493-1538

Raja Ganesh	1415-1418
Jalal-ud-din Muhammed Shah	1419-1431 or 1432?
Shams-ud-Din Ahmad Shah	1431 or 1433? - 1435? 1437?

Ilyas-Shahi Dynasty 1435-1487

Nasir-ud-din Mahmud Shah	1435 or 1437?-1459
Rukn-ud-din Barbak Shah	1455-1476
Shams-ud-din Yusuf Shah	1474-1481 or 1483?
Sultan Sikandar Shah II	1482
Jalal-ud-Din Fateh Shah	1482 - 1484 or 1487

Hussain-Shahi Dynasty 1493-1538

Alauddin Hussain Shah	1493-1519
Nasib Shah, Nasir-ud-Din Nusrat Shah	1519 -1533
'Ala-ud-Din Firuz Shah II	1533
Ghiyas-ud-din Mahmud Shah	1533-1538

Shir Shah Sur Dynasty 1538-1563

Farid-ud-din Abul Muzaffar Shir Shah Sur	1538-1545
Islâm Shâh	1545-1553
Firuz Shah	1553
Muhammad Mubariz Khan, Muhammad Shah Adil	1553-1555
Ghiyas-ud-din Bahadur Shah	1555-1560
Jalal-ud-din, Ghiasuddin II Abul Muzaffar Jalal Shah	1560-1563
Ghiasuddin III	1563

Taj Karrani Dynasty 1563-1576

Taj Khan Karrani	1563-1565
Sulaiman (II) Khan Karrani	1565 -1572
Bayazid Karrani	1572
Daud Khan	1572-1576

Kashmir Sultanate
(1346-1589)

Shah Mirza, Shams-ud-Din I	1346-1349
Jamshid	1349-1350
'Ali Sher, 'Ala-ud-Din	1350-1359
Shirashamak Shihab-ud-din	1359-1378
Hindal Qutb-ud-Din	1378-1393
Sikandari	1393-1413
'Ali Shah	1413-1420
Zainal-'Abidin	1420-1470
Haidar Shah	1470-1472
Hasan Shah	1472-1484
Muhammad Shah	1484-1487
Fath Shah	1487-1499
Muhammad Shah (2nd reign)	1499-1505
Fath Shah (2nd reign)	1505-1514
Muhammad Shah (3rd reign)	1514-1515
Fath Shah (3rd reign)	1515-1517
Muhammad Shah (4th reign)	1517-1528
Ibrahim Shah I	1528-1529
Nazuk Shah, Nadir	1529-1530
Muhammad Shah (5th reign)	1530-1537
Shams-ud-Din II	1537-1538
Isma'il Shah I	1538-1540
Ibrahim Shah II	1540
Nazuk Shah, Nadir (2nd reign)	1540-1546
Haidar Dughlat	1546-1550
Nazuk Shah, Nadir (3rd reign)	1550-1551
Ibrahim Shah II (2nd reign)	1552-1334
Isma'il Shah II	1554
Habib Shah, Mahmud	1555

Chakk Dynasty

Muhammad Ghazi Shah	1555-1562

Nasir-ud-DinHusain Shah	1562-1570
Muhammad 'Ali Shah	1570-1579
Muhammad Yusuf Shah	1579
Mubarak Shah	1579
Lohar Shah	1580
Muhammad Yusuf Shah (2nd reign)	1580-1586
Muhammaad Ya'qub Shah	1586-1589

Bahmani Sultanate
(1347-1527)

Ismail Mukh (Afghani)	1347
Hasan Bahman Shah ('Ala-ud-din I)	1347-1358
Muhammad Shah I	1358-1377
Mujahid Shah	1377
Daub Khan	1377
Muhammad Shah II	1377-1397
Yaj-ud-din Firoz Shah	1397-1422
Ahmad Shah	1422-1435
'Ala-ud-din II	1436-1458
Humayun	1458-1461
Nizam Shah	1461-1463
Muhammad Shah III Lashkari	1463-1482
Mahmud Shah	1482-1518
Ahmad Shah III	1518-1521
'Ala-ud-Din	1521-1522
Wali-Allah Shah	1522-1525
Kalim-Allah Shah	1525-1527

(See: 'Adil Shah of Bijapur, Qutab Shahi of Golconda, 'Imad Shahi of Berar, Nizam Shahi of Ahmednagar and Barid Shahi of Bidar

'Adil Shah of Bijapur Sultanate
(1489-1686)

Yusuf 'Adil Shah	1489-1512
Ismail 'Adil Shah	1512-1534
Mallu 'Adil Shah	1534-1535
Ibrahim 'Adil Shah I	1536-1557
Ali 'Adil Shah I	1557-1580
Ibrahim 'Adil Shah II	1580-1626
Muhammad 'Adil Shah	1626-1656
Ali 'Adil Shah II	1656-1672
Sikandar 'Adil Shah	1672-1686

Qutab Shahi of Golconda Sultanate
(1512-1687)

Quli Qutub Qutbul-mulk Shah	1512-1543
Jamsheed Quli Qutub Shah	1543-1550
Subhan Quli Qutub Shah	1550
Ibrahim Quli Qutub Shah	1550-1580
Muhammad Quli Qutub Shah	1580-1612
Muhammad Qutub Shah	1612-1626
'Abdullah Qutub Shah	1626-1672
Abdul Hasan (Qutub) Tana Shah	1672-1687

'Imad Shahi of Berar Sultanate
(1490-1574)

Fath-Allah 'Imad ul-Mulk Shah	1490-1504
'Ala-ud-Din 'Imad Shah	1504-1529
Darya 'Imad Shah	1529-1562
Burhan 'Imad Shah	1562-1568
Tufal Khan Dakhni	1568-1572

Nizam Shahi of Ahmednagar Sultanate (1490-1680)

Nizam-ul-Mulk Bahri.	1490
Malik Ahmad, Ahmad Nizam Shah I	1490-1509
Burhan Nizam Shah I	1509-1553
Hussain Nizam Shah I	1553-1565
Murtaza Nizam Shah I	1565-1586
Hussain Nizam Shah II	1586-1589
Isma'il Nizam Shah	1589-1591
Burhan Nizam Shah II	1591-1595
Ibrahim Nizam Shah	1595-1596
Bahadur Nizam Shah	1596-1603
Murtaza Nizam Shah II	1603-1610
Burhan Shah III	1610-1631
Hussain Nizam Shah III	1631-1633

Barid Shahi of Bidar Sultanate (1492-1687)

Amir Qasim Barid Shah I	1492-1504
Amir Barid Shah I	1504-1542
'Ali Barid Shah I	1542-1579
Ibrahim Barid Shah	1579-1587
Qasim Braid Shah II	1587-1591
'Ali Braid Shah II	1591
Amir Barid Shah II	1591-1600
Mirza 'Ali Barid Shah	1600-1609
Amir Barid Shah III ('Ali Shah II)	1609-1618

Muzaffarid Shahi of Gujarat Sultanate (1391-1583)

Muzaffar (Khan) Shah I	1391-1411
Shams-ud-Din Muzaffar Shah I	1411-1442
Mohammed KArim Shah	1442-1451
Nasir-ud-Din Ahmad Shah I	1442-1451
Qutb-ud-Din Ahmad Shah II	1451-1458
Da'ud Shah	1458-1459
Nasir-ud-Din Mahmud Shah I Beghara	1459-1511
Shams-ud-Din Muzaffar Shah II	1511-1526
Nasir-ud-Din Sikandar Shah	1526
Nasir-ud-Din Mahmud Shah II	1526
Qutb-ud-Din Bahadur Shah	1526-1535
Humayun occupies Gujarat	(1535-1536)
Qutb-ud-Din Bahadur Shah	1536-1537
Miran Muhammad Shah III	1537
Nasir-ud-Din Mahmud Shah III	1537-1554
Ghiyath-ud-Din Ahmad Shah III	1554-1561
Shams-ud-Din Muzaffar Shah III	1561-1573
Akbar occupies Gujarat	(1573-1583)
Shams-ud-Din Muzaffar Shah III	1573-1583

Jaunpur Sultanate (1394-1476)

Malik Sarvar (Sharqi)	1394-1399
Malik Qaranful, Mubarak Shah	1399-1402
Shams-ud-Din Ibrahim Shah	1402-1440
Nasir-ud-Din Mahmud Shah	1440-1457
Muhammad Shah	1457-1458
Husen (Husain) Shah	1458-1476

Malwar Sultanate
(1392-1531)

Ghuri Dynasty 1392-1436

Dilvar Khan Ghuri	1392-1405
Husam-ud-Din Hushang Shah	1405-1435
Ghazni Khan, Muhammad Shah I	1435-1436
Masud Khan, Masud Shah	1436

Khalji Dynasty 1436-1531

Mahmud I, Khalji	1436-1469
Ghiyath Shah	1469-1500
Nasir Shah	1500-1510
Mahmud II	1510-1531

Mughul Dynasty (Timurud)
(1526-1876)

Zahir-ud-din Muhammad Babur, King of Ferghana, "the Great Mughul"	1526-1530
Nasir-ud-din Humayun	1530-1540
Suri Period	1540-1555
Sher Khan (Sur Sher Shah)	1540-1545
Islam Sur Shah	1545-1553
Firuz	1553
Mohammed Adil	1553-1555
Sikandar	(opposition) 1554-1555
Ibrahim	(opposition) 1554-1555
Timurud reassertion	1555
Nasir-ud-din Humayun	1555-1556
"Raja" (General) Himu	1556
Jalal-ud-din Akbar the Great,	1556-1605
Nur-ud-din Jahangir	1606-1627

Major Muslim Rulers of India (Continued)

Dawar Bakhsh	16271628
Shihab-ud-din Shah Jahan	1628-1666
Murab Bakhsh	(1657)
Shah Shuja'	(1657-1658)
Muhiy-ud-din Aurangzib	1658-1707
A'zam Shah	1707
Kam Bakhsh	1707
Qutb-ud-din Shah Alam Bahadur	1707-1712
'Azim-ush-Shan	1712
Mu'izz-ud-din Jahandar Shah	1712-1713
Muhiy-ud-din Farrukh-siyar	1713-1719
Rafi'-ud-Darajat	1719
Rafi'-ud-Daula Shah Jahan II	1719
Nasir-ud-din Muhammad Shah	1719-1748
Mujahid-ud-din Ahmad Shah Bahadur	1748-1754
'Aziz-ud-din 'Alamgir II	1754-1759
Jhah Jahan III	1759
Jalal-ud-din Shah 'Alam II	1759-1788
Bidar Bakht	1788-1806
Mu'in-ud-din Muhamad Akbar II	1806-1857
Siraz-ud-din Bahadur Shah II	1857-1876
Victoria, Empress of India	1878

Appendix E

Chronology of Islamic Monuments in India

	INDIA	ISLAMIC WORLD	EUROPE
600			*San Vitale*, Ravenna, (526-547 CE)
	Mahayana Caves (450-642), Ajunta (Hindu)	*Mosque of the Prophet*, Medina *Masjid al Haram*, Mecca	
650	*Dharmmaraja-ratha*, Mahaballipuram (Hindu)		
700	*Shore Temples*, Mahaballipuram (Hindu)	*Dome of the Rock* (*Qubbat as-Sakhra*), Jerusalem *Omayyad Mosque*, Damascus	
	Shore Temples, Mahaballipuram (Hindu)		
750			
	Kailasha Temple, Elura (Hindu)	*Great Mosque*, Cordoba	*Palatine Chapel*, Aachen
800			
		Mosqueof 'Amr ibn al-'As, Cairo *Great Mosque*, Samarra	
850			
		Mosqueof Ahmad ibn Tulun, Cairo *Qubbat as-Sulaybiyya*, Samarra	
900			

	INDIA		ISLAMIC WORLD	EUROPE
900				
			Madinat al-Zahra' Palace, Cordoba	
950				
		Shiva Temple, Chandrehe (Hindu)		
	Ghaznavid Dynasty 977-1173: Sabuktigin of Ghazni 977-997			
1000	Mahmud of Ghazni 997- 1030	***Brihadeshvara Temple***, Tanjore (Hindu)	**Al-Hakim Mosque**, Cairo **Gunbad-i-Kabus**, Gurgan	
				Speyer Cathedral, Speyer
				Katholikon, Phocis
1050			**Masjid-i-Jami**, Isfahan	
				San Marco, Venice
			Tomb Tower, Demavand	
1100				***St. Etienne***, Caen ***Ananda Temple***, Pagan
1150				
				That-Byin-Nyu, Pagan
	Muhammad of Ghur 1173-1206			
1200		***Qutb Minar***, Delhi		***Amiens Cathedral***, Amiens
				St. Dimitri, Vladimir

Date	Dynasty	INDIA		ISLAMIC WORLD	EUROPE
1200	**Slave Dynasty** 1206-1320	Qutb-ud-din Aibak 1206 -1210	***Quwwat-ul-Islam***, Delhi		
		Sultan Iltutmish 1210-1236	***Tomb No. 36***, Delhi		
			Sultan Ghari Tomb, Delhi		
			Iltutmish Tomb, Delhi		
			Surya Temple (Hindu), Konarak	***Haund Hatun Tomb***, Kayseri	***Cologne Cathedral***, Cologne
1250					
		Jalal-ud-din 1290- ?		***Doner Kumbet*** (*mausoleum*), Kayseri	***Palazzo Pubblico***, Florence
1300			***'Ala'i Darwaza***, Delhi	***Oljeitu Tomb***, Sultaniya	
		Ala-ud-din ? - -1320			
	Tughluq Dynasty 1320-1414	Ghiyas-ud-din Tughluq I 1320-1325	***Shah Rukn-i 'Alam Tomb***, Multan	***Friday Mosque***, Timbuktu	
		Muhammad bin Tughluq 1325-1351	***Ghiyas-ud-din Tomb***, Delhi	***Alhambra***, Granada	***Doge's Palace***, Venice
1350		Firus Shah 1351-1388		***Tomb of Sultan Hasan***, Cairo	
			Jami' Masjid, Srinagar	***Tughtabeg Khatun Tomb***, Urgench	
1400			***Khan-i Jihan Tilangani Tomb***, Delhi	***Great Mosque***, Hangchou	***Cathedral Dome***, Florence
			Firuz Shah Tughluq Tomb, Delhi		
	Sayyid Dynasty 1414-1450		***Mubarak Shah Sayyid Tomb***, Delhi	***Tomb of Mehmet I***, Bursa	
1450	**Lodi Dynasty** 1451-1526		***Sayyod Usman Tomb***, Usmanpur	***Masjid-i-Kabud (Blue Mosque)***, Tabriz	
			Chotte Khan Ka Gunbad Tomb, Delhi		
			Mubarak Sayyid Tomb, Mahmudabad		
1500					***Cathedral of the Annunciation***, Kremlin

	Dynasty	INDIA		ISLAMIC WORLD	EUROPE
1500	**Lodi Dynasty** 1451-1526				*Tempietto*, Rome
	Mughul Dunasty 1526-1858	Babur, King of Ferghana 1526-1530	***Hasan Khan SurTomb***, Sasaram(1535)		
		Humayun 1530-1540	***Sher Shah Tomb***, Sasaram (1540)		
1550		Sher Khan (Sher Shah) 1540-1555	***Isa Khan Tomb***, Delhi (1547)	***Mihrimah Mosque***, Istanbul	***St. Peter's Dome***, Rome
		Suri Dynasty 1540-1555	***Adham Khan Tomb***, Delhi (a562)	***Suleymaniye Cami***, Istanbul	
		Humayun 1555-1556	***Humayun Tomb***, Delhi (1565)		
		Akbar the Great 1556-1605	***Muhammad Ghuas Tomb***, Delhi (1565)	***Selim II Mosque***, Edirne	***Villa Rotonda***, Vicenza
1600		Jahangir 1606-1627	***Akbar Tomb***, Sikandra (1604-13)	***Sultan Ahmet Mosque***, Istanbul	
			Iftikhar Khan Tomb, Churar (1614)	***Masjid-i-Shah***, Isfahan	
		Shah Jahan 1628-1666	***Ibrahim Rauza***, Bijapur (1615)		
			Muhammed Quli Qutub Shah Tomb, Golconda(1615)		
			Shah Daulat Tomb, *Maner (1617)*		***Versailles***
1650			***Khan Khanan Tomb***, Delhi (1626)		
			Gol Gumbaz, Bijapur (1626)		
		Aurangzib 1658-1707	***Jahan Begum Tomb***, Delhi (1626)		
		Bahadur Shah 1707- ?	***Jihangir Tomb***, Lahore (1627)		***St. Paul's***, London
			I'timad-ud-daula Tomb, Agra (1628)		
		Jahandar Shah	***Taj Mahal***, Agra (1632)	***Hesht Behest***, Isfahan	
1700		Farrukhsiyar ? -1719	***Wazir Khan Mosque***, Lahore (1634)		
		Muhammad Shah 1719-1748	***Jami' Masjid***, Delhi (1644)	***Masjid-i-Jami***, Isfahan (extensively rennovated)	
			Afzal Khan Tomb, Bijapur (1659)		
			'Pearl Mosque,' *Red Fort*, Delhi (1662)		
			Ali II Tomb, Bijapur (1672)		
			Badshahi Mosque, Lahore (1673)		
1750			***Safdar Jang Tomb***, Delhi		
1800					

	INDIA	ISLAMIC WORLD	EUROPE
1800		*Mosqueof Muhammad 'Ali,* Cairo	
1850			
1900			

Notes

Introduction

[1] Ernst Grube, et al. George Mitchell, ed., *Architecture of the Islamic World: Its History and Social Meaning*. London: 1978, p. 44.

[2] Robert Hillenbrand, *Islamic Art and Architecture*. London: 1999; p. 76.

[3] *Ibid.*

The Genesis of Form

[4] EG, *op. cit.,* p. 14.

[5] Fredrick W. Bunce, *The Iconography of Plans: A Study of the Influence of Buddhism and Hinduism on Architectural Plans of South and Southeast Asia,* New Delhi: 2002, p. 6.

[6] Mohammad al-Asad, et al., Martin Frishman and Hasan-Uddin Khan, eds., *The Mosque: History, Architectural Development & Regional Diversity,* London: 1994; pp. 56-57.

[7] *Ibid.,* p. 16. EG, Helen Philon, p. 250.

[8] MA, *op. cit.,* pp. 55-70. EG, pp. 112-143.

[9] EG, *op. cit.,* p. 132. Henri Sterlin, *Islamic India,* Lausanne: n.d.; pp. 53-85.

[10] FWB, *op. cit.,* pp. 16-17.

[11] For example: Latin cross, Greek cross, Tau cross, the cross of St. Andrew, the Cyrillic cross, etc.

[12] Henri Sterlin, *Architecture of the World: Islamic India*. Lausanne: n. d., pp. 43-44. Vettam Mani, *Puranic Encyclopaedia*. Delhi: 1996; p. 837, describes *Vastupurusha* as a ghost of large proportion and is considered a primordial being (man). It is also a name that is associated with *Vishnu*.

[13] FWB, *op. cit.,* pp. 36-38.

[14] *Ibid.,* p. 38.

[15] EG, *op. cit.,* p. 46.

The Tombs

[16] HS, *op. cit.,* p. 52.

[17] *Ibid.* Sterlin's reference to "a square with sloping corners" is most unusual, to say the least. An octagon is an octagon and a square is inner chamber does make a "a square with sloping corners" any less octagonal.

[18] Satish Grover, *Islamic Architecture in India*. New Delhi: 1981, p. 12.

[19] SG, p. 30. This mosque presents an entrance gate of some height as well as circular towers at the corners. All appear to be more defensive in nature than those forms which are later associated with mosques in India.

[20] *Ibid.,* p. 15.

[21] Steven Carr, *Archaeology and Monumental Remains of Delhi*. Allahabad: 1967; p. 73. The attachment of a tomb to an existing mosque is a practice that had been utilized throughout Islam for centuries before this. Its employment is thrologically akin to the encorporation of royal and noble tombs within the various churches, bascilicas, cathedrals and monasteries of Christendom.

[22] EG, *op. cit.,* p. 274.

[23] One must also place in this category the *Tomb No. 36,* of Delhi. Certainly, the Tomb of *Tomb of Khan-i Jihan Tilangani* is the first octagonal tomb which a surrounding verandah, a type which was to become most popular in India, prior to the Mughals. The octagon and octagram were highly auspicious forms within the Islamic world.

[24] The fortress-like quality of these early tombs may be based on the need for the new, foreign conquerors to establish their presence in a solid, visual manner. It may also be an architectural expression of *jihad*.

[25] EG, *op. cit.,* p. 268.

[26] *Ibid.,* p. 47.

[27] It is to be noted in the application of the *Deshiya Mandala* over the various elevations of the tombs in this study that the square tombs, before the Mughal invasion, tend to be taller than their octagonal counterparts. These proportions tended to be 12:12, or 1:1. Of course there are one or two notable exceptions.

[28] EG, *op. cit.,* as cited by Gary Martin, p. 268. SG, p. 34..

[29] FWB, *op. cit.,* p. 9. India, particularly the central plateau can be unremittingly hot during the dry months. Early on, the builders found that if they

constructed thick masonry walls, the interior tended to be cooler as one would find in a natural cave. The thick walls give up their heat during the dark, night hours when the temperature is generally cooler, thereby heating the inner areas. When the outside begins to heat up during the day the interior tends to be somewhat cooler than the outside, therefore creating a natural temperature control. This is known as the "fly wheel" effect. Not only were the thick walls of the Hindu temples, in part, for temperature control, they also represented the sacred cave. The Mughals devised far more efficient cooling systems for their palaces. Noteworthy, is the system used in the *Red Fort* of Agra. Thin, double masonry walls were constructed. This in itself acted as an insulating barrier. However, angled slits were placed near the floor on the interior and near the top on the exterior and water was allowed to flow down these inner areas, evaporating and cooling the interior as the breeze moved naturally from the hot exterior to the interior (See: drawing following).

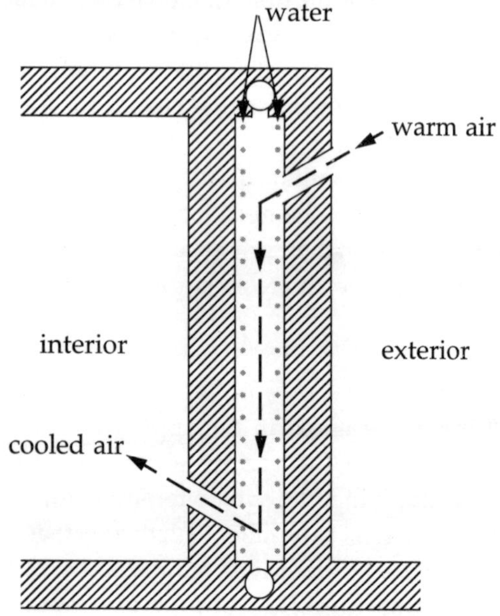

[30] The proportions of the octagonal "canopy tombs" are generally wider than they are tall, a marked contrast to the earlier and to the later square type tombs. They emphasize the horizontal by the wide surrounding *chajja,* the triple portals of each of the eight faces, the often elborate entablature, their decorative merlons, and the repeat horizontal elements of the dome's podium. The horizontal is often capped by the *chattris* or domes around the roofline of the ambulatory.

[31] SC, *op. cit.*, p. 157.

[32] SG, *op. cit.*, pp. 55-56.

[33] *Ibid.*, p. 55.

[34] Low fired brick, though frequently used in south and southeast Asia, are inherently unstable over time. Constant and profuse rain coupled with the warm temperature tends to foster microscopic life-forms--i.e., mould, etc.--which over a period of time degrade the low fired, porous brick. The same type of brick was employed in Pagan, but here, the climate is relatively arid and the bricks are not subjected to the continuous damp weather. Also, in Demavand, Iran, the climate is extremely arid, hence the relatively good state of those low fired brick structures.

[35] This is not the only structure which finds its form/genesis in preexistent structures. The monolithic *Chaitya Hall* (I C. B.C.E.) of Karli is seen as representing earlier bamboo structures which formed a tunnel vault, covered with thatch.

[36] SC, *op. cit.*, pp. 159-161.

[37] There is some confusion with regards this queen and the mosque and tomb which are ascribed to her. E. B. Havell: pp. 137-139; Plates LIV & LV; and Figures 36 & 37; refers to and illustrates both the tomb of Rani Rupavati and the Mosque of Rani Rupavati. However, in his text he fails to mention or cite either the Plates or the Figures. Further, he assigns no date(s) to these structures. Satish Grover, pp. 78-79 considers the Mosque of Rani Rupavati, and dates the mosque as "(AD 1515)." In Fig. 4.24 he illustrates "Rani Rupavati's mosque," but is not the same as EH illustrates and describes. The Internet site: www.ioc-tokyo.ac.jp/-islamarc in dealing with Ahmadabad illustrates the "Mosque of Rani Rupmati/ Ahmadabad" and illustrates both the plan and elevation that SG illustrates. This site assigns no date. The Internet site: www.ahmedabad.com/incity/ history displays the same elevation as seen in EH and in the site www.ioc-tokyo.ac.jp. The date given is "1430-1440 A. D." Numerous other sources ascribe a similar date. However, if Rani Rupmati (Rupavati)

Notes (Continued)

was, indeed the queen of Mahmud (Mohmed) Shah I Beghara (1458-1511) then she would have had to have both the mosque and the tomb constructed at least eighteen years before the reign of Mahmud Shah I Beghara and during the reign of Nasir-ud-Din Ahmad Shah I (1411-1442). Unlikely!

[38] SG, *op. cit.*, p. 78. E. B. Havell, *Encyclopaedia of Architecture in the Indian Subcontinent*. reprint. New Delhi: 2000., p. 136-139.

[39] Internet site: www.ioc-tokyo.ac.jp/islamarc/WebPage1/htm_eng/ahmadabad/rani_rupmati1_e.htm.

[40] SG, *op. cit.*, pp. 47-50.

[41] EH, *op. cit.*, pp. 75-76.

[42] SG, *op. cit.*, p. 99.

[43] The forty-four *chandi perwara* in the third rank surrounding the central ensemble of the *Chandi Sewu*, and the forty-four *chandi perwara* in the fourth rank surrounding the central ensemble of the *Loro Jonggrang*, both of Prambanan, Java; as well as the forty-four ground level shrines surrounding the *Bakheng* of Angkor, Kamboja, are salient examples.

[44] In addition it represents the *Pancha-Buddhas* as is seen architecturally in the five-sided *Dhamma-Yazika* of Pagan.

[45] EG, *op. cit.*, p. 269.

[46] SG, *op. cit.*, pp. 72-74. EH, pp. 76-77

[47] This forest of pillars as already seen in the *Sayyid Usman Rauza* (1460 C.E.) and the *Tomb of Rani Rupmati* (a. 1430 C.E.) is a technique frequently utilized by Hindu builders when covering large spaces--e.g., the *mahamandapa* of the *Brihadeshvara Temple*, Tanjore, or the "Hall of One Thousand Pillars" in the Madurai complex of *Sundareshvara and Minakshi*. One may even make comparison with the *Great Hypostyle Hall* of Karnak, or the "Throne Hall of Xerxes" at the *Palace of Persepolis*, or even the *Great Mosque* of Samara. However, when employing a trabeated system, the imposition of numerous supporting pillars is a necessity. It would have been a conclusion reached by any number of independent, isolated builders.

[48] This was, as has been stated, not an Islamic much less an Indo-Islamic invention. The arcuated system had long been a tradition in the area known as the Middle east. The fact that it heretofore had not been employed by the Hindu in India may, in part, be attributed to the fact that the Hindu faith is not a congregational faith. The Islamic builders had utilized the arcuated system early in its development, particularly in the *Mosque of Cordoba*. There, an arcuated system is employed, but with a forest of columns.

[49] SG, *op. cit.*, p. 101. This orientation is typical of Hindu temples which are oriented towards the east. Also, what may be observed is that the southern entrance which is normally the "main entrance" in Indo-Islamic tombs--e.g., *Tomb of Mubarak Shah Sayyid, Tomb of Firuz Shah Tughluq, Tomb of Khan-i Jihan Tilangani*, etc.--is treated the same as the north entrance.

[50] *Ibid*, pp. 107-108. Internet site:http://archnet.org/library/sites/one-site.tcl?site_id=2208, pp. 1 +4.

[51] Visual impressions being paramount to the Indo-Islamic builders, there is often a discrepancy between what is seen outside and what is actualized inside. The double dome as first used in the *Tomb of Sikander Lodi* (c. 1518 C.E.) is seen to be so constructed as not to compromise the spatial relationship of the central chamber, and one may add, to focus one's eyes on the cenotaph. A comparison has been made utilizing the *Taj Mahal*. If the inner dome was removed, the resulting space would become incongruous. Nonetheless the soaring dome is essential to the spatial relationship as seen in the *Taj Mahal's* elevation (See: **Appendix C, Plate 132**, p. 279).

[52] Percy Brown, *Indian Architecture (Islamic Period)*. Bombay: n. d. (1965-1968), Plate LX. The Internet site: www.ioc-tokyo.ac.jp/-islamarc/WebPage1/htm/sasaram/hasan_ks1.htm. pp. 1-4.

[53] HS, *op. cit.*, pp. 51-52. SG, *op. cit.*, pp. 117-118. EH, *op. cit.*, 154-157. EG, 272

[54] HS, *op. cit.*, p. 78.

[55] FWB, *op. cit.*, p. 46.

[56] SC, *op. cit.*, pp. 200-202. SG, *op. cit.*, pp. 119-120.

[57] HS, *op. cit.*, p. 53. EG, p. 269. SG, *op. cit.*, pp. 12-124. EH, 1*op. cit.*, 57-159.

[58] EH, *op. cit.*, p. 158: and SG, *op. cit.*, p. 123,

Notes (Continued)

both see this arrangement as indicative of the Hindu *pancharatna* ("five jewels") or, more appropriately, the *pancharatha* temple plan--i.e., that in which the main temple is surrounded by four subsidiary temples at the intercardinal points.

[59] HS, *op. cit.*, pp. 53-54. Sterlin notes that the plans of "Persian monumental architecture is determined by geometric relationships." He then illustrates on p. 53, the "Geometric analysis of Humayun's tomb. . . ." **Figure 136** is an interpolation of his analysis.

[60] *Ibid*, p. 54. EH, p. 159.

[61] R, Nath, *Islamic Architecture & Style in India*. New Delhi (?): 1982.

[62] Catherine B. Asher, *Architecture of Mughal India*. New Delhi: 1995, p. 81.

[63] See: pp. 156-159, herein.

[64] See: pp. 182-187, herein.

[65] SG, *op. cit.*, p. 149. EH, p. 176. HS, *op. cit.*, pp. 54-55. EG, *op. cit.*, pp. 272-273.

[66] FWB *op. cit.*, pp. 156-59, 402, 432-35

[67] SG, *op. cit.*, pp. 118-121.

[68] Henry Cousens, *Bijapur and Its Architectural Remains: With an Historical Outline of the Adil Shahi Dynasty*, Delhi: 1996, p. 13.

[69] EG, *op. cit.*, p. 13. The Eurocentric stance that architectural units or elements had to possess some utilityarian raison d'être is not just negated by Islamic architecture, but in much of Asian architecture, particularly as seen in India. If architecture is "the art of enclosing space"--i.e., a western definition--how then does one approace the pyramids of Egypt, or *Borabudur* of Java, or the massive gopura of southern Indian temples, or the temple mounts of the Khmers?

[70] CA, *op. cit.*, p. 152.

[71] *Ibid.*

[72] *Ibid.* pp. 154-155.

[73] SC, *op. cit.*, p. 214, quoting Erskine.

[74] G.H.R. Tillotson, *Mughal India*. London: 1990, p. 50.

[75] HS, *op. cit.*, p. 84. SC, *op. cit.*, pp. 214-215.

[76] SC, *Ibid.*

[77] Ebba Koch, *Mughal Architecture: An Outline of Its History and Development 1526-1858.* London: 1991, p. 45.

[78] EH, *op. cit.*, 207. EG, *op. cit.*, 273.

[79] HC, *op. cit.*, Plates LXXXV-LXXXVI, LXXXVIII-LC. EG, *op. cit.*, 267. SG, *op. cit.*, 99-103.

[80] Michaelangelo's dome of *St. Peter's* is larger, but it is a double-shelled dome, but does cover as large a space as does that of *Gol Gumbaz.*

[81] The basic plan of the *Gol Gumbaz* finds its Indo-Islamic genesis as early as the *Tomb of Sultan Ghari*, the prominent corner towers are also not revolutionary or eccentric. However, The huge, unencumbered central space plus the fact that it is covered by a single shell dome is most unusual in the annals of Indo-Islamic tombs and may be viewed as an eccentricity. Moreover, the apsidal extension towards the north is most unusual. First, it destroys the cross axial symmetry that so many of the tombs exhibit. Second, its placement towards the north is a conundrum. If it had been towards the west, then one could consider it a *mikhrab*. Finally, its scale is problematical as it does not fit within either a square *mandala* or a circular *mandala*..

[82] HC, *op. cit.*, **Plates XCVI & XCVII.**

[83] EH, *op. cit.*, p. 200. Nur Jahan was neither the first, nor the last royal wife or mistress to wield such influence and / or immense power in the history of the world. Sabina Poppae of Rome, Catherine II of Russia; Agnes Sorel Diane de Poitiers and Mme. de Pompadour of France are five notable examples. The first wife of a Mughal emperor was frequently elevated to the position of empress, although, this was often merely an honorary title, the empress held little or no power. However, Nur Jahan was not only elevated to the level of an empress, her position and power over her husband allowed her unparallelled power. Her position was equal to the power that Diane de Poitiers held over Henri II of France, in the Sixteenth Century French Court. Jihangir cared more for painting and drinking and frequently allowed his wife to exercise the duties normally reserved for the emperor.

[84] The Tomb of I'timad-ud-daula has been likened to a jewel, a bijou, a wedding cake; small in scale, elegant in design and lavish in detail.

[85] The *Tomb of Humayun* employs white marble on the surface of the dome and as a foil for the

red sandstone on the façades.

[86] SG, *op. cit.*, pp. 155-157; EH, *op. cit.*, pp. 206-207; HS, *op. cit.*, pp. 55-56.

[87] MA, *op. cit.*, p. 56.

[88] Internet: ignca.nic.in/agra, p. 1.

[89] HC, *op. cit.*, pp. 97-98; **Plates LXXXII & LXXXIII.**

[90] HC, *Ibid.*, p. 111, & **Plates CIII-CIV**.

[91] HC, *Ibid.*, pp. 107-109.

[92] HC, *Ibid.*, **Plate C**.

[93] HC, **Plate C**, indicates in the "RESTORED ELEVATION OF TOMB OF ALI II" a hemispherical dome. It seems a bit ludicrous to assume that an 'Adil Shahi would construct a tomb which all but the dome follows eastablished tradition for the Bijapur Sultanate. **Appendix C, Plate 000** indicates the elevation found in HC, Plate C and a proposed elevation using a typical 'Adil Shahi dome.

[94] EH, *op. cit.*, p. 215; EG, *op. cit.*, p. 270; CA, *op. cit.*, pp. 305-306

Conclusions

[95] An exception to this predeliction is seen in the tombs which employ the *muthamman baghdadi* form. The amount of enclosed space of the *Taj Mahal* with its *muthamman baghdadi* form is 40%±, *en plan.* The amount of enclosed space found in the *Tomb of Humayun* is similar.

[96] FWB, *op.cit.*, pp 16-17.

[97] The adjectives used here are taken from a number of different sources as they were applied to the particular monuments.

Appendix B

[94] The *Mill* at Versailles is a prime example of these gardens, albeit in Europe. Here the King and Queen could "play" at being simple peasants. Here the could garden, milk cows, and cavort without the suffocating protocol, the corsets, wigs, and restricting garb required in the *Hall of Mirrors*.

[95] Patricide, fratricide and even filicide were not unheard of and too often practiced on a fairly regular basis.

[96] EG. *op. cit.*, p. 47.

[97] It has been said that Shah Jahan planned his tomb ensemble to mirror not only the layout of the *Taj Mahal*, but also to mirror the value of the white marble in a considerably darker stone.

[98] This symbol, additionally, finds a parallel in the Buddhist stupa--e.g., the *Ruvanveliseya Dagoba* (See: **Figure 11**)--in which the square posium symbolizes the terestrial sphere (which can be related to the *chahar-bagh*), the hemispherical *anda* with its implied lowerhalf represents the celestial sphere (which may see a parallel in the dome or covering *kiosk*), and the chattravali (which sees its Buddhist parallel in the dome's or coveroing *kiosk*'s finials) is the cosmic axis to which all is related and around which all revolves in a cosmological dance.

[99] EH, *op. cit.*, p. 215.

[100] EG, *op. cit.*, Garry Martin, p. 270.

Appendix C

[101] EG, *op. cit.*, pp. 131-132.

Index

Index (Continued)

Index (Continued)

Index (Continued)

Index (Continued)

Acknowledgements

I wish first to acknowledge the various sources used and consulted in the preparation of the computer generated plates and figures included in this work. The program which is used in the presentation of the Plates and Figures is Adobe PageMaker 6.0. The source of each image (Plate) is noted in the sections of the various monuments within this study and in Appendices. Nonetheless, I considered it important to acknowledge my debt to them and their works again. They, and the works are: Bianca Maria Alfieri, *Islamic Architecture of the Indian Subcontinent*; Catherine B. Asher, *Architecture of Mughal India*; Jeannine Auboyer and others, *Oriental Art: A Handbook of Styles and Forms*; Percy Brown, *Indian Architecture (Buddhist and Hindu Periods)*; and *Indian Architecture (Islamic Period)*; Parmono Atmadi, *Some Architectural Design Principles of Temples in Java*; C. Batley, *Design Development of Indian Architecture*; J. Burgess, *Muhammadan Architecture in Gujarat*; Mario Bussagli; John Shepley, trans. *Oriental Architecture/ 1: India, Indonesia, Indochina*; Stephen Carr, *Archaeology and Monumental Remains of Delhi*; P. N. Chopra, T. K. Ravindran, N. Subrahmanian, *History of South India*; Henry Cousens, *Bijapur and Its Architectural Remains: With an Historical Outline of the Adil Shahi Dynasty*; K.A.C. Creswell, *A Short Account of Early Muslim Architecture*; Keith Critchlow, *Islamic Patterns: An Analytical and Cosmological Approach*; Krishna Deva, *Temples of India*; Godfrey Goodwin, *A History of Ottoman Architecture*; E. B. Havell, *Encyclopaedia of Architecture in the Indian Subcontinent*; Robert Hillenbrand, *Islamic Art and Architecture*; John D. Hoag, *Islamic Architecture*; Ebba Koch, *Mughal Architecture: An Outline of Its History and Development 1526-1858*; Rustam Mehta, *Masterpieces of Indo-Islamic Architecture*; S. A. A. Naqoi, *Humanyn's Tomb and Adjacent Buildings*; R. Nath, *Fathepur Sikri and its Monuments*, and *History of Mughal Architecture*; Jose Pereira, *Islamic Sacred Architecture: A Stylistic History*; Amjad Bohumil Prochazka, *Architecture of the Islamic Cultural Sphere*; K.V. Soundara Rajan, *Islam Builds in India*; Benjamin Rowland, *The Art and Architecture of India: Hindu, Buddhist, Jain*; Margaret Sevcenko, (ed.) *Theories and Principles of Design in the Architecture of Islamic Societies*; P. K. Sharma, *Mughal Architecture of Delhi*; Edmond W. Smith, *Akbar's Tomb*; Henri Stierlin, (ed.) *Architecture of the World: India*, and *Architecture of the World: Islamic India*; C.M. Villiers Stuart, *Gardens of the Great Mughals*; G.H.R. Tillotson, *Mughal India*; G. Wilson, *et al*, *Geometry for Architects*; and GhulamYazdani, *Bidar, Its History and Monuments*.

There are others who I wish to acknowledge: K. Srinivasan, First Secretary, and Peter Loo, Education Officer, High Commission of India, Kuala Lumpur, for their assistance and time; Vipula Wanigasekera, Counsellor, High Commission of Sri Lanka, Kuala Lumpur, for his assistance and information proffered; the American Institute of Indian Studies, Gurgaon, for their unstinting assistance; Professor Madya H. M. Bukhari Lubis, Universiti Kebangsaan Malaysia, Bangi, for his information regarding Islamic practices; and Susheel Mittal, New Delhi, for supplying me with various information and making much needed contacts.

Finally, I dedicate this work to Christiaan Karl Covell Bunce and Jules Gim.